CONSUMER BEHAVIOR

IMPLICATIONS FOR MARKETING STRATEGY

The Irwin Series in Marketing

Gilbert A. Churchill, Jr., Consulting Editor
University of Wisconsin, Madison

Alreck and Settle
The Survey Research Handbook
2nd edition

Arens and Bovée
Contemporary Advertising
5th edition

Bearden, Ingram and LaForge
Marketing: Principles and Perspectives

Belch and Belch
Introduction to Advertising and Promotion: An Integrated Marketing Communications Approach, *3rd edition*

Berkowitz, Kerin, Hartley, and Rudelius
Marketing, *4th edition*

Bernhardt and Kinnear
Cases in Marketing Management
6th edition

Bonoma and Kosnik
Marketing Management: Text and Cases

Boyd, Walker, and Larreche
Marketing Management: A Strategic Approach with a Global Orientation
2nd edition

Burstiner
Basic Retailing, *2nd edition*

Cadotte
The Market Place: A Strategic Marketing Simulation

Cateora
International Marketing, *8th edition*

Churchill, Ford, and Walker
Sales Force Management, *4th edition*

Cole and Mishler
Consumer Business Credit Management, *10th edition*

Cravens
Strategic Marketing, *4th edition*

Cravens and Lamb
Strategic Marketing Management Cases, *4th edition*

Crawford
New Products Management, *4th edition*

Dillon, Madden, and Firtle
Essentials of Marketing Research

Dillon, Madden, Firtle
Marketing Research in a Marketing Environment, *3rd edition*

Engel, Warshaw, and Kinnear
Promotional Strategy, *8th edition*

Faria, Nulsen, and Roussos
Compete, *4th edition*

Futrell
ABC's of Selling, *4th edition*

Hawkins, Best, and Coney
Consumer Behavior, *6th edition*

Lambert and Stock
Strategic Logistics Management
3rd edition

Lehmann and Winer
Analysis for Marketing Planning
3rd edition

Lehmann and Winer
Product Management

Levy and Weitz
Retailing Management, *2nd edition*

Mason, Mayer, and Ezell
Retailing, *5th edition*

Mason, Mayer, and Wilkinson
Modern Retailing, *6th edition*

Mason and Perreault
The Marketing Game!, *2nd edition*

McCarthy and Perreault
Basic Marketing: A Global-Managerial Approach, *11th edition*

McCarthy and Perreault
Essentials of Marketing: A Global-Managerial Approach, *6th edition*

Meloan and Graham
International and Global Marketing: Concepts and Cases

Patton
Sales Force: A Sales Management Simulation Game

Peter and Donnelly
A Preface to Marketing Management
6th edition

Peter and Donnelly
Marketing Management: Knowledge and Skills, *4th edition*

Peter and Olson
Consumer Behavior and Marketing Strategy, *3rd edition*

Peter and Olson
Understanding Consumer Behavior

Quelch
Cases in Product Management

Quelch, Dolan, and Kosnik
Marketing Management: Text and Cases

Quelch and Farris
Cases in Advertising and Promotion Management, *4th edition*

Quelch, Kashani, and Vandermerwe
European Cases in Marketing Management

Rangan
Industrial Marketing Strategy: Cases and Readings

Rangan
Readings in Industrial Marketing Strategy

Smith and Quelch
Ethics in Marketing

Stanton, Buskirk, and Spiro
Management of a Sales Force
9th edition

Thompson and Stappenbeck
The Marketing Strategy Game

Walker, Boyd, and Larreche
Marketing Strategy: Planning and Implementation

Weitz, Castleberry, and Tanner
Selling: Building Partnerships
2nd edition

CONSUMER BEHAVIOR

IMPLICATIONS FOR MARKETING STRATEGY

DEL I. HAWKINS
University of Oregon

ROGER J. BEST
University of Oregon

KENNETH A. CONEY
Late of Arizona State University

SIXTH EDITION

IRWIN

Chicago • Bogotá • Boston • Buenos Aires • Caracas
London • Madrid • Mexico City • Sydney • Toronto

Sponsoring editor: Nina McGuffin
Senior developmental editor: Andy Winston
Marketing manager: Jim Lewis
Project editor: Waivah Clement
Production supervisor: Laurie Kersch
Designer: Larry J. Cope
Interior and cover designer: Stuart Paterson, Image House, Inc.
Cover image: Oskar Fischinger *Circles, Triangles, and Squares.* © National Museum of American Art, Washington, D.C.
Interior illustration: Electronic Publishing Services, Inc.
Art coordinator: Heather Burbridge
Compositor: CRWaldman Graphic Communications, Inc.
Typeface: 10/12 Times Roman
Printer: Von Hoffmann Press, Inc.

Library of Congress Cataloging-in-Publication Data

Hawkins, Del I.
Consumer behavior : implications for marketing strategy / Del I. Hawkins, Roger J. Best, Kenneth A. Coney.—6th ed.
p. cm.—(The Irwin series in marketing)
Includes bibliographical references and index.
ISBN 0-256-13972-5 ISBN 0-256-16547-5 International Student Edition
1. Consumer behavior—United States. 2. Market surveys—United States. 3. Consumer behavior—United States—Case studies. 4. Market surveys—United States—Case studies. I. Best, Roger J. II. Coney, Kenneth A. III. Title. IV. Series.
HF5415.33.U6H38 1995
658.8′342′0973—dc20 94–30028

Printed in the United States of America
1 2 3 4 5 6 7 8 9 0 VH 1 0 9 8 7 6 5 4

PREFACE TO THE FIRST EDITION

The purpose of this text is to provide the student with a usable, managerial understanding of consumer behavior. Most students in consumer behavior courses aspire to careers in marketing management. They hope to acquire knowledge and skills that will be useful to them in these careers. Unfortunately, some may be seeking the type of knowledge gained in introductory accounting classes; that is, a set of relatively invariant rules that can be applied across a variety of situations to achieve a fixed solution that is known to be correct. For these students, the uncertainty and lack of closure involved in dealing with living, breathing, changing, stubborn consumers can be very frustrating. However, if they can accept dealing with endless uncertainty, utilizing an understanding of consumer behavior in developing marketing strategy will become tremendously exciting.

The rules governing human behavior, although they do not operate like the rules developed for accounting systems, can be applied in a marketing context. Having students recognize this is a major challenge. It is our view that the utilization of a knowledge of consumer behavior in the development of marketing strategy is an art. This is not to suggest that scientific principles and procedures are not applicable. Rather, it means that the successful application of these principles to particular situations requires human judgment that we are not able to reduce to a fixed set of rules.

Let us consider the analogy with art in some detail. Suppose you want to become an expert artist. You would study known principles of the visual effects of blending various colors, of perspective, and so forth. Then you would practice applying these principles until you developed the ability to produce acceptable paintings. If you had certain ''natural'' talents, the right teacher, and the right topic, you might even produce a ''masterpiece.'' The same approach should be taken by one wishing to become a marketing manager. The various factors or principles that influence consumer behavior should be thoroughly studied. Then, one should practice applying these principles until acceptable marketing strategies result. However, while knowledge and practice can in general produce acceptable strategies, ''great'' marketing strategies, like ''masterpieces,'' require special talents, effort, timing, and some degree of ''luck'' (what if Mona Lisa had not wanted her portrait painted?).

The art analogy is useful for another reason. All of us, professors and students alike, tend to ask: ''How can I use this concept of, say, social class to develop a successful marketing strategy?'' This makes as much sense as an artist asking: ''How can I use blue to create a great picture?'' Obviously, blue alone will seldom be sufficient for a great work of art. Instead, to be successful, the artist must understand when and how to use blue in conjunction with other elements in the picture. Likewise, the marketing manager must understand when and how to use a knowledge of social class in conjunction with a knowledge of other factors in designing a successful marketing strategy.

This book is based on the premise described above. That is, it is based on the belief that a knowledge of the factors that influence consumer behavior can, with practice, be used to develop sound marketing strategy. With this in mind, we have attempted to do three things. First, we present a reasonably comprehensive description of the various behavioral concepts and theories that have been found useful for understanding consumer behavior. This is generally done at the beginning of each chapter or at the beginning of major subsections in each chapter. We believe that a person must have a thorough understanding of a concept in order to successfully apply that concept across different situations.

Second, we present examples of how these concepts have been and can be utilized in the development of marketing strategy. We have tried to make clear that these examples are *not* "how you use this concept." Rather, they are presented as "how one organization facing a particular marketing situation used this concept." The difference, while subtle, is important.

Finally, at the end of each chapter, we present new marketing situations and ask the student to apply the concepts to these situations. We view this as an important part of the learning process. To provide continuity to the class and text, we describe in some detail in the first chapter a firm that must develop a marketing strategy for an addition to its product line. We do not refer back to this firm in the content part of the text; instead, several of the discussion and project situations presented at the end of each chapter relate to this firm. By discussing these questions, the student can develop a feel for how the many concepts we discuss relate to each other in the context of a single product category.

We have attempted to write a useful and enjoyable text. The degree to which we have accomplished this goal was greatly increased by the assistance of numerous individuals and organizations. To all of them we express our gratitude. To our students, colleagues, friends, and families who suffered with us as we wrote, we express our love.

Del I Hawkins
Roger J. Best
Kenneth A. Coney

PREFACE TO THE SIXTH EDITION

The boundaries of knowledge regarding consumer behavior have continued to expand since we wrote the first edition. We have tried to reflect this expansion in this edition. Otherwise, our philosophy and objective as expressed in the preface to the first edition remain intact. We hope you will take a few minutes to read that statement.

While our philosophy as expressed in the preface to the first edition has not changed in the 15 years since we wrote it, a number of other features of the text have. First, and most noticeably, the text is now in full color. We are convinced that this makes the book easier and more enjoyable to read. This in turn provides value to our customers—the students and faculty who use the text.

In addition to adding color, we have made ads and pictures of products, point-of-purchase displays, and other visible marketing actions more a part of the text's pedagogy. We highlight many of these as Managerial Applications. The reason for this label is to remind students, instructors, and ourselves that managers, regulators, and others are constantly applying their knowledge of consumer behavior. In our book, these ads and other pictures are more than just decoration; they enhance the reality and practicality of the material.

In the first edition, we used one case (detailed example) that we carried through every chapter. Based on customer feedback, we now use a series of cases at the end of each section. This provides students with exposure to the application of consumer behavior principles across a wide range of situations. Coupled with this has been a dramatic increase in the number of in-chapter examples of applications of the materials.

With every edition, we have tried to improve our instructions on how to apply the material. However, as we stated in the original preface, this is not accounting and there are no invariant rules that apply across groups, products, and situations. Therefore, we provide processes and procedures that will help the students apply the material across environments.

We provide four types of learning aids at the end of each chapter. First, there is a brief summary that repeats the primary points of the chapter. Next is a set of review questions that the students or instructor can use to test the *acquisition of the facts* contained in the chapter. These questions can all be answered by repeating the material in the chapter. They require memorization which we believe is an important part of learning.

The third learning aid is an extensive set of discussion questions. These questions can be used to help develop or test the students' *understanding of the material* in the chapter. Answering the questions requires the student to utilize the material in the chapter to reach a recommendation or solution. However, they can be answered without external activities such as customer interviews (they can be assigned as in-class activities).

The final learning aid at the end of each chapter is a set of application exercises. These require the students to utilize the material in the chapter in conjunction with external activities such as visiting stores to observe point-of-purchase displays, interviewing customers or managers, or evaluating television ads. They range in complexity from short evening assignments to term projects.

In the first three editions of the text, we incorporated coverage of organizational buying behavior and social issues throughout the text but did not provide separate chapters. In the fourth edition, we concentrated our coverage of organizational buying behavior in a separate chapter. In this edition, we developed a separate chapter covering consumerism, the regulation of marketing practices, and cause marketing. While we still provide examples of these activities throughout the text, we believe that they are important enough topics to justify their own chapter.

More important changes are happening outside of the book. This edition is accompanied by an expanded instructor's manual, including a new "Teacher's Kit" of ideas on course structure and teaching techniques. The test bank has also been fully revised and greatly expanded to over 2,500 questions. A set of video cases is available, as are 70 four-color acetates and a computerized test bank.

Finally, we enjoy studying consumer behavior. Most of the faculty we know enjoy teaching consumer behavior. With every edition, we have tried to make this a book that students would enjoy reading and that would get them excited about an exciting topic.

Numerous individuals and organizations helped us in the task of writing this edition. We are grateful for this assistance. Particular thanks are due our reviewers:

Linda Alwitt
DePaul University

Eric J. Arnold
California State University–Long Beach

Raj Arora
University of Missouri–Kansas City

Don Bacon
University of Denver

Kenneth W. Day
Jacksonville State University

Gerald A. Ford
Metropolitan State University

Jon Freiden
Florida State University

Peggy S. Gilbert
Southwest Missouri State University

Clark Leavitt
Ohio State University

Tom Marpe
Winona State University

Lois Mohr
Georgia State University

Vernon Murray
DePaul University

Suzanne O'Curry
DePaul University

Robert O'Keefe
DePaul University

Susan Petroshius
Bowling Green State University

Jackie Snell
San José State University

Shirley M. Stretch
California State University–Los Angeles

David Szymanski
Texas A&M University

Philip Titus
Bowling Green State University

Alexandra Uhlmann–Maier
Babson College

Professor Richard Pomazal of Wheeling Jesuit College provided particularly valuable assistance. Likewise, our colleagues at Oregon—David Boush, Marian Friestad, and Lynn Kahle—generously responded to our requests for assistance. All should be held blameless for our inability to fully incorporate their ideas.

The text would have had higher quality, been more fun to read, and been much more fun to write had Ken Coney been able to write it with us. Once again, this edition is dedicated to his memory. By his life he said to us:

Cherish your dreams
Guard your ideals
Enjoy life
Seek the best
Climb your mountains

Del I. Hawkins
Roger J. Best

CONTENTS IN BRIEF

CONTENTS

CONSUMER BEHAVIOR

IMPLICATIONS

FOR MARKETING

STRATEGY

SECTION ONE

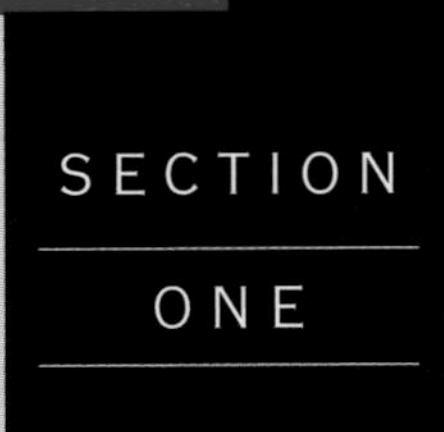

INTRODUCTION

Attitudes/Needs
Marketing activities
Culture
Subcultures
Values
Demographics
Social status
Reference groups
Households
Emotions
Personality
Motives
Perception
Learning (memory)
CONSUMER LIFESTYLE
Situations
Problem recognition
Information search
Evaluation and selection
Store choice and purchase
Postpurchase processes
Situations
Experiences

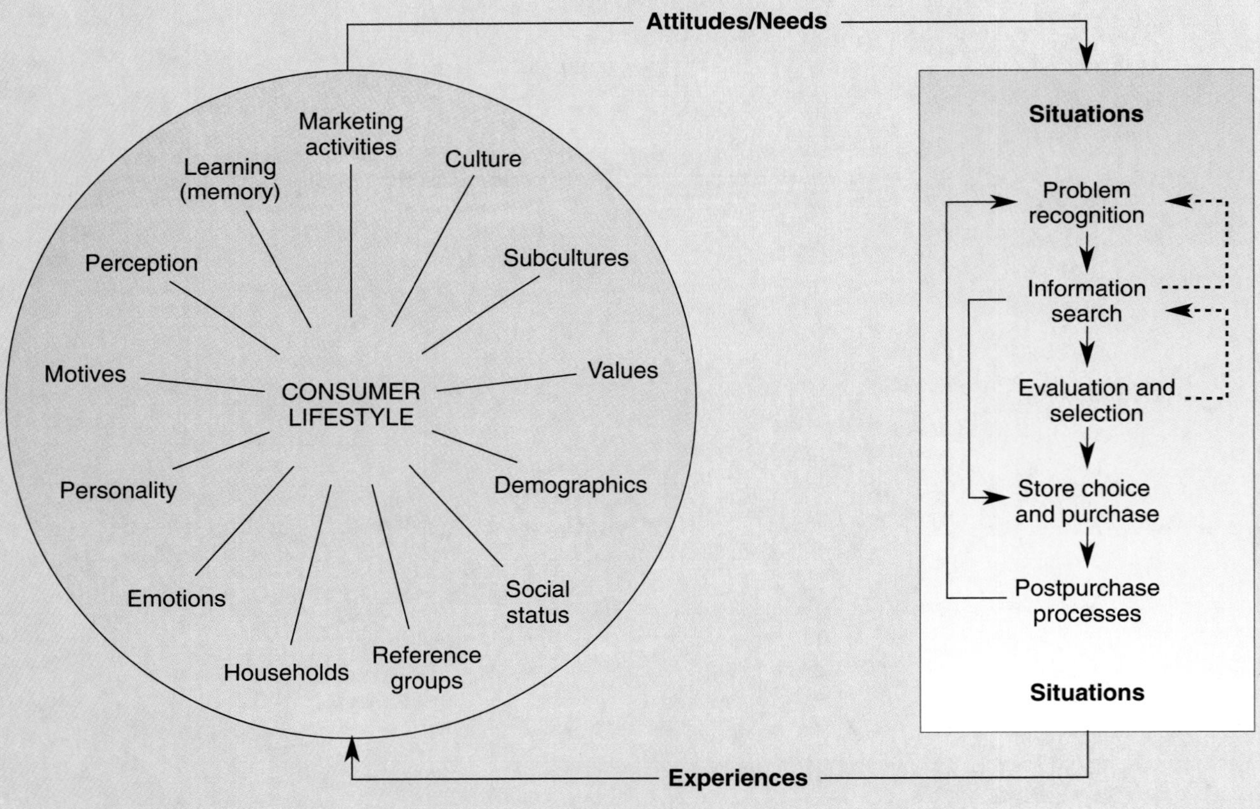

What is consumer behavior? Why should we study it? Do marketing managers actually utilize knowledge about consumer behavior in developing market strategy? How can we organize our knowledge of consumer behavior in order to apply it more effectively? These and a number of other interesting questions are addressed in the first chapter of the text. This chapter seeks to indicate the importance and usefulness of the material to be covered in the remainder of the text as well as provide an overview of this material. In addition, the logic underlying the model of consumer behavior shown on the facing page is presented.

CONSUMER BEHAVIOR AND MARKETING STRATEGY

- Procter & Gamble created the disposable diaper market in Japan when it introduced Pampers. The product was an unmodified version of the American product and was marketed using the same rational approach used in the United States. However, Japanese competitors soon reduced P&G's share to less than 10 percent. ''We really didn't understand the consumer,'' says Ed Artzt, P&G's CEO.

  Based on consumer research, P&G redesigned the diapers to be much thinner. It also introduced pink diapers for girls and blue for boys. Advertising was changed from a rational approach (a diaper is shown absorbing a cup of water) to a more indirect, emotional approach (a talking diaper promises toddlers that it won't leak or cause diaper rash). Finally, the Procter & Gamble corporate name was made prominent in both packaging and design. Unlike Americans, Japanese consider corporate identity and reputation to be critical. P&G is now in second place in Japan with more than a 20 percent share.

- For four years, Coca-Cola conducted ''blind'' (unbranded) taste tests comparing the formula that is now new Coke with what is now Classic Coke as well as with competitive brands. Almost 200,000 consumers took part in these tests. The results indicated significant preference for the taste of the new formula. Based on this research, new Coke was introduced and the old version was discontinued. Shortly thereafter, consumer pressure caused the firm to reintroduce the original formula as Coca-Cola Classic. Now, Coca-Cola Classic is the leading soft-drink brand (19.8 percent), followed by Pepsi (18.8 percent). New Coke, with the taste most consumers appear to prefer, is tied for 10th place (1.6 percent).

- Owens-Corning has spent over $600 million advertising its Fiberglas insulation with the Pink Panther as a ''spokesperson,'' using such slogans as ''Think pink,'' ''Think more pink,'' and ''Beat the cold with pink.'' Pink has no functional association with Fiberglas. The color was added years ago by Owens-Corning to differentiate a new, less itchy version from their then current version.

A new competitor recently made plans to enter the market with a pink insulation. Owens-Corning had not registered the color as a trademark because all previous attempts to register colors had failed. In response to the new competitor, Owens-Corning requested registration from the U.S. Trademark Trial & Appeal Board but was denied. However, a U.S. circuit-court of appeals overturned the board's decision and gave Owens-Corning exclusive rights to market pink insulation. A major factor in the decision was research showing over 50 percent consumer recognition of pink insulation as Owens-Corning's brand.

The preceding examples summarize several attempts to apply an understanding of consumer behavior in order to develop an effective marketing strategy or to regulate a marketing practice. The examples cited reveal three main facts about the nature of our knowledge of consumer behavior. First, successful marketing decisions by commercial firms, nonprofit organizations, and regulatory agencies require extensive information on consumer behavior. It should be obvious from these examples that *organizations are applying theories and information about consumer behavior on a daily basis.*

Each of the examples also involved the collection of information about the specific consumers involved in the marketing decision at hand. Thus, at its current state of development, *consumer behavior theory provides the manager with the proper questions to ask.* However, given the importance of the specific situation and product category in consumer behavior, it will often be necessary to conduct research to answer these questions. Appendix A at the end of the text provides an overview of the consumer behavior research process. Thomas S. Carroll, chief executive officer of the marketing-oriented Lever Brothers Company, explains the importance of consumer behavior research this way:

> Understanding and properly interpreting consumer wants is a whole lot easier said than done. Every week our marketing researchers talk to more than 4,000 consumers to find out:
>
> - What they think of our products and those of our competitors.
> - What they think of possible improvements in our products.

> - How they use our products.
> - What attitudes they have about our products and our advertising.
> - What they feel about their ''roles'' in the family and society.
> - What their hopes and dreams are for themselves and their families.
>
> Today, as never before, we cannot take our business for granted. That's why understanding—and therefore learning to anticipate—consumer behavior is our key to planning and managing in this ever-changing environment.[1]

Finally, the examples indicate that *consumer behavior is a complex, multidimensional process.* Coca-Cola has substantial evidence that consumers prefer the *taste* of new Coke to the *taste* of Classic Coke. Yet Classic Coke outsells new Coke 10 to 1. Obviously, the soft-drink purchase decision involves more than just taste.

Our primary goal is to help you obtain a usable managerial understanding of consumer behavior. The key aspect of this objective is found in the phrase, *usable managerial understanding.* We want to increase your understanding of consumer behavior in order to help you become a more effective marketing manager. Our secondary goal in developing your knowledge of consumer behavior is to enhance your understanding of a major aspect of human behavior. Most developed societies are legitimately referred to as consumption societies. Therefore, a knowledge of consumer behavior can enhance our understanding of ourselves and our environment. Figure 1–1 illustrates the various ways a knowledge of consumer behavior can be used.

Sufficient knowledge of consumer behavior currently exists to provide a usable guide to marketing practice, but the state of the art is not sufficient for us to write a cookbook with surefire recipes for success. We will illustrate how some firms were able to combine certain ingredients for success under specific conditions. However, as conditions change, the quantities and even the ingredients required for success may change. It is up to you as a student and future marketing manager to develop the ability to apply this knowledge to specific situations. To assist you, we have included example situations and questions at the end of each chapter and a series of short cases at the end of each section which can be used to develop your application skills. Also, Appendix B at the end of the text provides a list of key questions for a consumer behavior audit for developing marketing strategy.

It is important to note that *all marketing decisions are based on assumptions about consumer behavior.* It is impossible to think of a marketing decision for which this is not the case. For example, a decision to match a competitor's price reduction must be based

FIGURE 1–1 Understanding Consumer Behavior

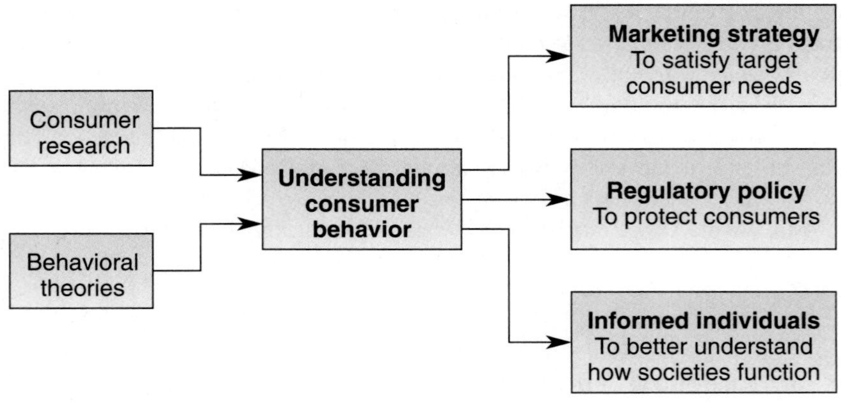

on some assumption about how consumers evaluate prices and would respond to a price differential between the two brands. Therefore, *all marketing strategy and tactics are based on explicit or implicit beliefs about consumer behavior.* Decisions based on explicit assumptions and sound theory and research are more likely to be successful than are decisions based solely on implicit intuition. Thus, a knowledge of consumer behavior can be an important competitive advantage. It can greatly reduce the odds of bad decisions such as the following:

> BIC Corp. introduced a small $5 bottle of perfume to be sold in supermarkets and drugstore chains where it had tremendous distribution strength. The perfume was to be easy and convenient to buy and use. However, as one expert said in examining the $11 million dollar loss project: ''Fragrance is an emotional sell, not convenience or utility. The BIC package wasn't feminine. It looked like a cigarette lighter.''[2]

MARKETING STRATEGY AND CONSUMER BEHAVIOR

To survive in a competitive environment, an organization must provide target customers more value than is provided by its competitors. **Customer value** *is the difference between all the benefits derived from a total product and all the costs of acquiring those benefits.* For example, owning a car can provide a number of benefits (depending on the person and the type of car), including flexible transportation, image, status, pleasure, comfort, and even companionship. However, securing these benefits requires paying for the car, gasoline, insurance, maintenance, and parking fees, as well as risking injury from an accident, adding to environmental pollution, and dealing with traffic jams and other frustrations. It is the difference between the total benefits and the total costs that constitutes customer value.

The importance of understanding value *from the customer's perspective* can be seen in a recent product introduction by La Choy (a Hunt-Wesson Inc. brand). La Choy was a well-known brand. Frozen food sales had been growing rapidly, as had ethnic food sales. La Choy management decided to launch a line of large, meaty, frozen egg rolls to be used as a main course rather than as appetizers as the smaller egg rolls then available were used. The logic seemed sound. Unfortunately, the large egg rolls could not be microwaved (the shells became soggy) and they took 30 minutes to heat in a regular oven. Consumers considered value in frozen foods of this type to include quick preparation. The egg rolls were a market failure and were withdrawn within two years.[3]

Providing superior customer value requires the organization to do a better job of anticipating and reacting to customer needs than the competition does. As Figure 1–2 indicates, an understanding of consumer behavior is the basis for marketing strategy formulation, and the consumer's reaction to this marketing strategy determines the firm's success or failure. Before we examine consumer behavior theories, concepts, and applications, it will be worthwhile to review the key marketing decisions which are based on an understanding of consumer behavior.

Marketing strategy as described in Figure 1–2 is conceptually very simple. It begins with an analysis of the market the organization is considering. This requires a detailed analysis of the organization's capabilities, the strengths and weaknesses of competitors, the economic and technological forces affecting the market, and the current and potential customers in the market. Based on the consumer analysis portion of this step, the organization identifies groups of individuals, households, or firms with similar needs. These

FIGURE 1-2 Marketing Strategy and Consumer Behavior

market segments are described in terms of demographics, media preferences, geographic location, and so forth. One or more of these segments are then selected as target markets based on the firm's capabilities relative to those of the competition (given current and forecast economic and technological conditions).

Next, marketing strategy is formulated. Marketing strategy seeks to provide the customer with more value than the competition does while still producing a profit for the firm. Marketing strategy is formulated in terms of the marketing mix. That is, it involves determining the product features, price, communications, distribution, and services that will provide customers with superior value. This entire set of characteristics is often referred to as the **total product**. The total product is presented to the target market which is consistently engaged in processing information and making decisions designed to maintain or enhance its lifestyle (individuals and households) or performance (businesses and other organizations).

The reaction of the target market to the total product produces an image of the product/brand, sales (or lack thereof), and some level of customer satisfaction among those who did purchase. Sophisticated marketers seek to produce satisfied customers rather than mere sales—because satisfied customers are more profitable in the long run.

Note again that an *analysis of consumers* is a key part of the foundation of marketing strategy, and *consumer reaction* to the total product determines the success or failure of the strategy. Before providing an overview of consumer behavior, we will examine marketing strategy formulation in more detail.

Examine Managerial Application 1–1. Both these ads appeared in the same issue of *Outside* magazine and therefore are targeted at the same consumers. What assumptions about consumer behavior underlie each ad? Which approach is best? Why?

MARKET ANALYSIS COMPONENTS

Market analysis requires a thorough understanding of the organization's own capabilities, the capabilities of current and future competitors, the consumption patterns of potential customers, and the economic, physical, and technological environment in which these elements will interact. Remember that the organization's objective is to provide superior customer value. To provide superior value, the firm *must* know (1) how consumers determine value, (2) its own and (3) its competitor's capabilities with respect to customer value creation, and (4) the relevant economic, physical, regulatory, and technological environments.

The Consumers

It is not possible to anticipate and react to customers' needs and desires without a complete understanding of consumer behavior. Knowing customers' current needs is reasonably complex but can generally be determined by direct marketing research. Companies expend considerable effort on such research as the following example indicates:

> USAA, a financial services company, sends questionnaires to 500,000 customers every year. Customers are asked about their satisfaction with the firm, future needs, and ideas for new products. Based on this research, USAA launched a growth and income fund that quickly attracted $77 million in assets.[4]

However, anticipating evolving consumer needs requires *understanding* the consumer, which in turn requires understanding the behavioral principles which guide consumption behaviors. These principles are covered in depth in the balance of this text. The following example indicates how subtle these needs can be:

> Canola oil has the smallest amount of saturated fat of any cooking oil and is therefore relatively healthy. Research for InterMountain Canola recommended that advertising for a potato chip made with canola oil stress how good the chips are for the consumer. However, the marketing manager's theory of consumer behavior was that the image that consumers had of potato chips could not be altered to include ''healthy'' (this would be based on learning and attitude-change theory). Motivation research designed to uncover emotions, feelings, and hidden attitudes was therefore conducted. This research revealed that canola oil reduced consumers' guilt feelings about consuming junk food. The manager changed the advertising slogan from ''Choose to be healthy'' to ''A taste you can feel good about.'' The chips are a success.[5]

The Company

A firm must fully understand its own ability to meet customer needs. This involves evaluating all aspects of the firm, including its financial condition, general managerial skills, production capabilities, research and development capabilities, technological

MANAGERIAL APPLICATION

1–1

Two Different Approaches to the Same Consumers

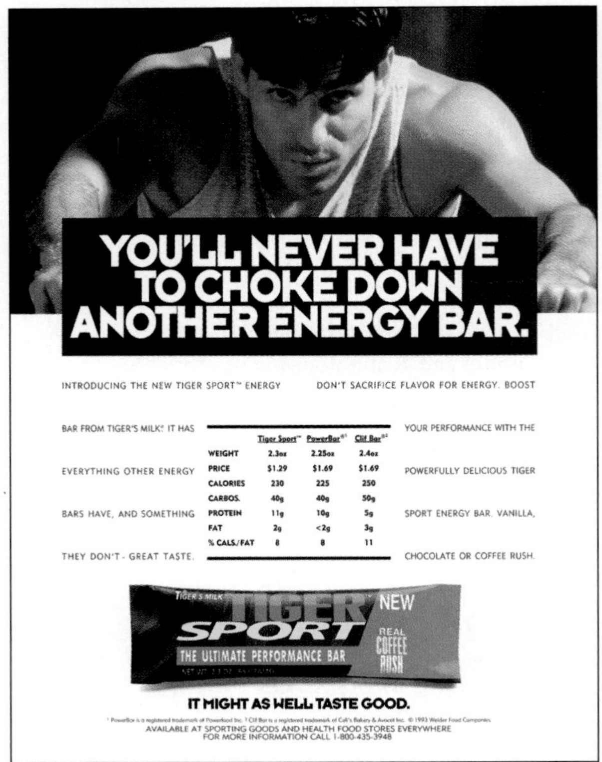

sophistication, reputation, and marketing skills. Marketing skills would include new-product development capabilities, channel strength, advertising abilities, service capabilities, marketing research abilities, market and consumer knowledge, and so forth.

Many of these are internal, while others (such as credit ratings and reputation) are based on the reaction of those outside the firm to current or past firm activities. Failure to adequately understand one's own strength can cause serious problems. IBM's first attempt to enter the home computer market with the PC Jr. was a failure largely for this reason. While IBM had an excellent reputation with large business customers and a very strong direct sales force for serving them, these strengths were not relevant to the household consumer market.

Determining one's own capabilities involves:

1. An internal assessment of such factors as the firm's financial condition.
2. An external assessment of such factors as its reputation or sales force quality.

The external assessments can range from informal input from industry analysts to sophisticated marketing research.

The Competitors

It is not possible to consistently do a better job of meeting customer needs than the competition does without a thorough understanding of the competition's capabilities and strategies. This requires the same level of knowledge of a firm's key competitors that is required of one's own firm. In addition, for any significant marketing action, the following questions must be answered:

1. If we are successful, which firms will be hurt (lose sales or sales opportunities)?
2. Of those firms that are injured, which have the capability (financial resources, marketing strengths) to respond?
3. How are they likely to respond (reduce prices, increase advertising, introduce a new product)?
4. Is our strategy (planned action) robust enough to withstand the likely actions of our competitors or do we need additional contingency plans?

The Conditions

The state of the economy, the physical environment, government regulations, and technological developments affect consumer needs and expectations as well as company and competitor capabilities. The deterioration of the physical environment has produced not only consumer demand for environmentally sound products but also government regulations affecting product design and manufacturing. Managerial Application 1–2 illustrates a product developed in response to increased environmental concerns.

International agreements such as the GATT agreement (General Agreement on Tariffs and Trade) have greatly reduced international trade barriers and thus increased the level of both competition and consumer expectations for many products. The development of computers has changed the way many people work and has created new industries. The recession in most of the world during the late 1980s and early 1990s made lasting changes in the way that individuals and organizations evaluate products. This in turn altered the nature of retailing as well as the market positions of manufacturing firms.

Clearly, a firm cannot develop a sound marketing strategy without anticipating the conditions under which that strategy will be implemented.

TARGET-MARKET SELECTION

Perhaps the most important marketing decision a firm makes is the selection of one or more market segments on which to focus. A **market segment** *is a portion of a larger market whose needs differ somewhat from the larger market.* Selecting a target market involves four steps:

1. Identifying product-related need sets.
2. Grouping customers having similar need sets.
3. Describing each group.
4. Selecting an attractive segment(s) to serve.

Product-Related Need Sets

Organizations approach market segmentation with a set of current and potential capabilities. These capabilities may be a reputation, an existing product, a technology, or some other skill set. The first task of the firm is to identify need sets that the organization is capable (or could become capable) of meeting. The term *need set* is used to reflect the fact that most products in developed economies satisfy more than one need. Thus, as we saw earlier, an automobile can meet more needs than just basic transportation. Some customers

MANAGERIAL APPLICATION

1–2

A Product Developed in Response to Increased Environmental Concerns

purchase automobiles to meet transportation and status needs. Others purchase cars to meet transportation and fun needs. Still others purchase cars to meet transportation, status, and fun needs. Managerial Application 1–3 shows two ads for automobiles. What needs does the Hyundai ad appeal to? The Oldsmobile ad?

Customer needs are not restricted to product features. Their needs also include types and sources of information about the product, outlets where the product is available, the price of the product, services associated with the product, the image of the product or firm, and even where and how the product is produced (Is it made in America? Is it made in an environmentally sound manner?). For example, many Hispanics desire the same product features as non-Hispanics do but want communications about the product to be in the Spanish language and carried in Spanish language media. Since their need set is unique, they constitute a market segment.

The first step is to identify the various need sets that the firm's current or potential product might satisfy. This will typically involve consumer research (particularly focus groups and depth interviews) as well as logic and intuition.

Customers Having Similar Need Sets

The next step is to determine who has the need sets that have been identified. For example, the need for moderately priced, fun, sporty transportation appears to exist in many young single individuals, young couples with no children, and middle-aged couples whose children have left home.

This step may involve consumer research—including focus group interviews, surveys, and product concept tests (see Appendix A). It could also involve (1) an analysis of current consumption patterns and (2) deductions based on an understanding of consumer behavior.

MANAGERIAL APPLICATION

Oldsmobile and Hyundai Appeal to Different Need Sets

Description of Each Group

Once consumers with similar need sets are identified, they should be described in terms of their demographics, lifestyles, and media usage. In order to design an effective marketing program, it is necessary to have a complete understanding of the potential customers. It is only with such a complete understanding that we can be sure that we have correctly identified the need set. In addition, we cannot communicate effectively with our customers if we do not understand the context in which our product is purchased and consumed, how it is thought about by our customers, and the language they use to describe it. Managerial Application 1–4 shows how Radio Shack positions its cordless phone in the context of the lifestyle of one of its target markets.

Attractive Segment(s) to Serve

Once we are sure we have a thorough understanding of each segment, we must select those segments we wish to target. This decision is based on our ability to provide each segment with superior customer value at a profit. Thus, the size and growth of the segment, the intensity of the current and anticipated competition, the cost of providing the superior value, and so forth are important considerations. Exhibit 1–1 provides a simple worksheet for use in evaluating the attractiveness of various market segments.

It is important to remember that each market segment requires its own marketing strategy. Each element of the marketing mix should be examined to determine if changes are required from one segment to another. Sometimes each segment will require a completely different marketing mix, including the product. At other times, only the advertising message or retail outlets may need to differ. Mazda targets its *929* automobile at "baby boomers," using ads with conservative cues (women in pearls and classical music in the background) and copy that focuses on luxury and safety. It targets its *MX-3* at "Generation X," using bright colors and loud music with copy that declares that Mazda had taken the "plain old apple pie car and replaced it with a jalapeno."[6]

MANAGERIAL APPLICATION

1-4

Radio Shack Positions Its Cordless Phone in the Context of a Target Market's Lifestyle

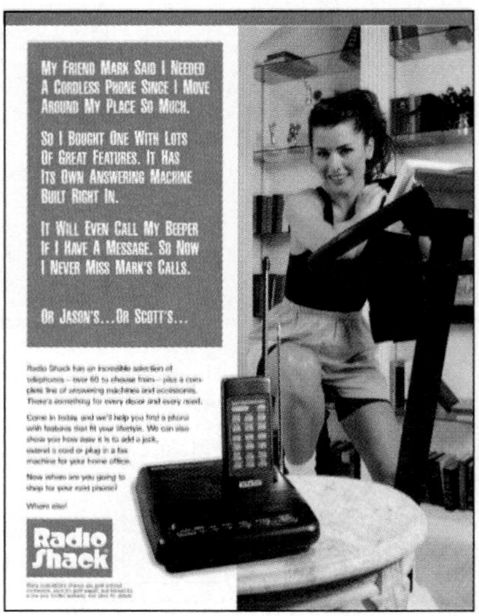

EXHIBIT 1-1 Market Segment Attractiveness Worksheet

Criterion	**Score***
Segment size	________
Segment growth rate	________
Competitor strength	________
Customer satisfaction with existing products	________
Fit with company image	________
Fit with company objectives	________
Fit with company resources	________
Fit with other segments	________
Investment required	________
Stability/predictability	________
Cost to serve	________
Sustainable advantage available	________
Leverage to other segments/markets	________
Risk	________
Other (________)	________

*Score on a 1 to 10 scale, with 10 being most favorable.

MARKETING STRATEGY

It is not possible to select target markets without simultaneously formulating a general marketing strategy for each segment. A decisive criterion in selecting target markets is the ability to provide superior value to those market segments. Since customer value is delivered by the marketing strategy, the firm must develop its general marketing strategy as it evaluates potential target markets.

Marketing strategy is basically the answer to the question: *How will we provide superior customer value to our target market?* The answer to this question requires the formulation of a consistent marketing mix. The **marketing mix** is the product, price, communications, distribution, and services provided to the target market. It is the combination of these elements that meets customer needs and provides customer value. In Managerial Application 1–1, the Tiger Sport Energy Bar promised value by offering better taste and a lower price than its competitors.

The Product

A **product** *is anything a consumer acquires or might acquire to meet a perceived need.* We use the term *product* to refer to physical products and primary services. Thus, an automobile is a product as is a transmission overhaul or a ride in a taxi. Over 15,000 new products and new versions of existing products are introduced to supermarkets alone each year. Obviously, many of these will not succeed. To be successful, products must meet the needs of the target market better than the competition does. Managerial Application 1–5 presents a new product that stresses its performance superiority.

Meeting the needs of the customer better than the competition does is not a simple task. Making specialized products for a few customers will provide them with product features very close to their needs. However, it is generally less expensive to manufacture only one version of a product. Thus, marketers must balance the benefits that target consumers derive from customization of product features against the cost of providing multiple versions of the product. This is a particularly important consideration in international marketing.

Until fairly recently, American-made automobiles could be ordered with any combination of accessories desired. This resulted in hundreds of versions of each car model and, therefore, high costs. In contrast, Japanese manufacturers provided only a few combinations of accessories for each model. This helped make possible their cost and quality advantages. It soon became clear that many customers would forgo some choice in accessory combinations to obtain higher quality at a lower price. Now, American manufacturers also use the accessory package approach. Understanding the customers' desires and the customers' willingness to trade high levels of one attribute (choice in accessory combinations) for improvements in other attributes (price and quality) gave the Japanese manufacturers an initial competitive advantage in this market.

Price

The **price** *is the amount of money one must pay to obtain the right to use the product.* One can buy ownership of a product or, for many products, limited usage rights (i.e., one can rent or lease the product). Economists often assume that lower prices for the same product will result in more sales than higher prices. However, price sometimes serves as a signal of quality. A product priced "too low" might be perceived as having low quality. Owning expensive items also provides information about the owner. If nothing else, it indicates that the owner can afford the expensive item. This is a desirable feature to some

MANAGERIAL APPLICATION

1–5

Philips DCC Stresses Performance Superiority

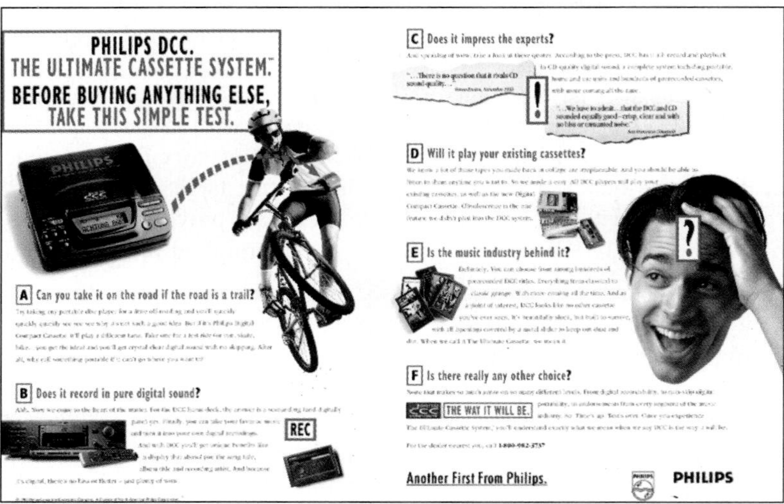

consumers. Therefore, setting a price requires a thorough understanding of the symbolic role that price plays for the product and target market in question.

It is important to note that the price of a product is not the same as the cost of the product to the customer. As described earlier, the **cost** of owning and using an automobile includes insurance, gasoline, maintenance, finance charges, license fees, and parking fees, in addition to the purchase price. One of the ways that firms seek to provide customer value is to reduce the nonprice costs of owning or operating a product. If successful, the total cost to the customer decreases while the revenue to the marketer stays the same or even increases.

Distribution

Having the product available where target customers can buy it is essential to success. Only in rare cases will customers go to much trouble to secure a particular brand. Since customers differ in where and how they shop, products aimed at multiple market segments often require multiple distribution channels. This can lead to difficult channel management issues. For example, many appliances and items such as luggage are sold to many market segments. To effectively cover all the attractive segments, a marketer may want to distribute through full-service department stores, discount outlets, and catalog showroom merchants. However, full-service department stores don't like to see items they carry advertised at discounted prices that they cannot match. Thus marketers sometimes must limit their channels, or develop strategies such as channel-specific product models. Obviously, sound channel decisions require a sound knowledge of where target customers shop for the product in question, as the following example shows:

> Huffy Corp., a $700 million bicycle manufacturer, did careful research before launching a new bicycle called Cross Sport. The new bike was a cross between a mountain bike and the traditional thin-framed 10-speed bicycle. Focus groups

and product concept tests revealed strong consumer acceptance. Huffy quickly launched the $159 Cross Sport through its strong mass distribution channels such as Kmart and Toys "R" Us. Unfortunately, the fairly serious adult rider that these bikes targeted demands individual sales attention by knowledgeable salespeople. Such salespeople are found at specialty bike shops, not at mass retailers. As Huffy's president said: "It was a $5 million dollar mistake."[7]

Communications

Marketing communications include: advertising, the sales force, public relations, the packaging, and any other signal that the firm provides about itself and its products. An effective communications strategy requires answers to the following questions:

1. *Whom, exactly, do we want to communicate with?* While most messages are aimed at the target-market members, others are focused on channel members or those who influence the target-market members. For example, pediatric nurses are often asked for advice concerning diapers and other nonmedical infant care items. A firm marketing such items would be wise to communicate directly with these individuals.

Often it is necessary to determine who within the target market should receive the marketing message. For a children's breakfast cereal, should the communications be aimed at the children or the parents or both? (The answer depends on the target market and varies by country.)

2. *What effect do we want our communication to have on the target audience?* Often a manager will state that the purpose of advertising and other marketing communications is to increase sales. While this may be the ultimate objective, the behavioral objective for most marketing communications is often much more immediate. That is, it may seek to have the audience learn something about the product, seek more information about the product, like the product, recommend the product to others, feel good about having bought the product, or a host of other communications effects. It is only by having precise communications objectives that we can determine if advertising is accomplishing the task we want it to.

3. *What message will achieve the desired effect on our audience?* What words, pictures, and symbols should we use to capture attention and produce the desired effect? Marketing messages can range from purely factual statements to pure symbolism. The best approach depends on the situation at hand. Managerial Application 1–6 shows how Philip Morris used the cowboy symbol in its marketing communications to change the image of Marlboro cigarettes from a feminine to a masculine image. Developing an effective message requires a thorough understanding of the meanings the target audience attaches to words and symbols as well as a knowledge of the perception process.

4. *What means and media should we use to reach the target audience?* Should we use personal sales to provide information? Can we rely on the package to provide needed information? Should we advertise in mass media or use direct mail? If we advertise in mass media, which media (television, radio, magazines, newspapers) and which specific vehicles (television programs, specific magazines, and so forth) should we use? Answering these questions requires an understanding both of the media that the target audiences use and of the effect that advertising in those media would have on the product's image.

5. *When should we communicate with the target audience?* Should we concentrate our communications near the time that purchases tend to be made or evenly throughout the week, month, or year? Do consumers seek information shortly before purchasing our product? If so, where? Answering these questions requires a knowledge of the decision process used by the target market for this product.

MANAGERIAL APPLICATION

1–6

Marketing Communications Alter Product Perceptions

Used with permission from Philip Morris

Close your eyes and think of Marlboro cigarettes. What comes to mind? Is it an effeminate, sissy cigarette with an ivory tip or a red beauty tip? Certainly not when one thinks of the Marlboro man!

Philip Morris began marketing Marlboro in 1924 as an extremely mild filter cigarette with either an ivory tip or a red beauty tip! It was advertised in a very plush atmosphere and was widely used by women. By the 1950s, the image described above was firmly established. In addition, all filter cigarettes were viewed as somewhat effeminate.

By the mid-1950s, it was becoming increasingly apparent that filter cigarettes would eventually take over the market. Philip Morris decided to make Marlboro acceptable to the heavy user market segment—males. To accomplish this, everything but the name was changed. A more flavorful blend of tobaccos was selected along with a new filter. The package design was changed to red and white with an angular design (more masculine than a curved or circular design). One version of the package was the crushproof box—again, a very rugged, masculine option.

The advertising used "regular guys," not professional models, who typified masculine confidence. The Marlboro cowboy (a real cowboy) was introduced as "the most generally accepted symbol of masculinity in America." To lend credence to the new brand it was tied to the well-known Philip Morris name with "new from Philip Morris" in the introductory advertising.

How successful was it? What did you think of a few minutes ago when asked to think about Marlboro? Think how drastically attitudes had to be changed to bring about such a dramatic product image shift.

Service

Earlier we defined *product* to include primary services such as haircuts, car repairs, and medical treatments. Here, **service** *refers to auxiliary services that are performed to enhance the primary product or service.* Thus, we would consider car repair to be a product (primary service) while free pickup and delivery of the car would be an auxiliary service. While many texts do not treat service as a separate component of the marketing mix, we do—because of the critical role it plays in determining market share and relative price in competitive markets. A firm that does not explicitly manage its auxiliary services is at a competitive disadvantage. Note the importance that Hyundai placed on services in its ad in Managerial Application 1–3.

Auxiliary services cost money to provide. Therefore, it is essential that the firm furnish only those services that provide value to the target customers. Providing services that customers do not value can result in high costs and high prices without a corresponding increase in customer value. This in turn will lead to lower sales and an ultimate inability to compete. This is what happened to many full-service department stores as consumers' desires for personal service declined relative to their desire for quality products at lower prices.

CONSUMER DECISION PROCESS

As Figure 1–2 illustrated, the consumer decision process intervenes between the market strategy (as implemented in the marketing mix) and the outcomes. That is, the outcomes of the firm's marketing strategy are determined by its interaction with the consumer decision process. The firm can succeed only if consumers see a need which your product can solve, become aware of your product and its capabilities, decide that it is the best available solution, proceed to buy it, and become satisfied with the results of the purchase. A significant part of this entire text is devoted to developing an understanding of the consumer decision process.

OUTCOMES

Product/Brand Image

The most basic outcome of a marketing strategy is an image of the product or brand in the consumer's mind. This image consists of a set of beliefs, pictorial representations, and feelings about the product or brand. It does not require purchase or use for it to develop. It is determined by communications about the brand as well as by direct experience with it. Most marketing firms specify the image they want their brands to have and measure these images on an ongoing basis. This is because a brand whose image matches the desired brand image of a target market is likely to be purchased when a need for that product arises.

Sales

Sales are a critical outcome as they produce the revenue necessary for the firm to continue in business. Therefore virtually all firms evaluate the success of their marketing programs in terms of sales. As we have seen, sales are likely to occur only if the initial consumer analysis was correct and if the marketing mix matches the consumer decision process.

Customer Satisfaction

Marketers have discovered that it is more profitable to maintain existing customers than to replace them with new customers. Retaining current customers requires that they be satisfied with their purchase and use of the product.

FIGURE 1–3 Creating Satisfied Customers

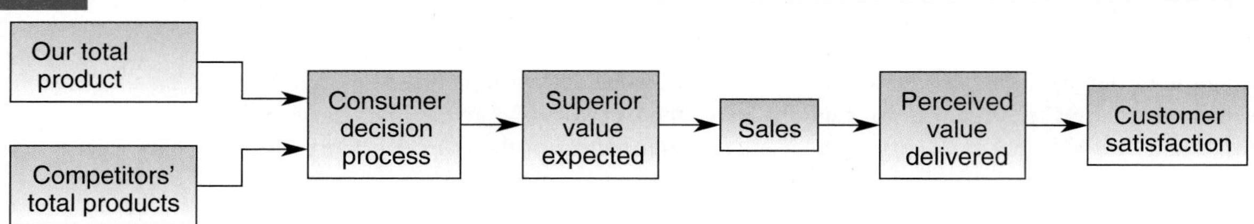

In Figure 1–3 you see that convincing consumers your brand offers superior value (relative to the competition) is necessary in order to make the initial sale. Obviously, one must have a thorough understanding of the potential consumers' needs and of their information acquisition processes to succeed at this task. However, *creating satisfied customers*, and thus future sales, requires that customers continue to believe that your brand offers superior value after they have used it. That is, you must deliver as much or more value than your customers initially expected. This requires an even greater understanding of consumer behavior. Honda's recent efforts in this area are described below:

> Honda's "E.T. Phone Home" project had the factory workers who actually assemble the cars as well as marketing managers conduct telephone interviews with over 47,000 Accord owners. The interviews sought to determine customer satisfaction levels with all aspects of the Accord as well as ideas for improvements. The interviews were conducted by those who would have to make any necessary changes. The results of the three months of interviews will be incorporated into the 1995 and 1996 Accords.[8]

THE NATURE OF CONSUMER BEHAVIOR

Figure 1–4 emphasizes the fact that consumer behavior is a function of the individual involved, the product category, and the current situation. A moment's reflection will make this clear. You undoubtedly prefer different television shows, foods, clothes, and beverages than do your parents and even some of your closest friends. You also spend more or less time evaluating a product before purchasing it than do some of your acquaintances. Each person is, to some extent, unique as a consumer. Marketers attempt to group consumers who are similar, though seldom identical, into market segments as described earlier.

While you differ from other consumers, your own purchasing behavior will also differ from one product category to another. The amount of effort and time you would spend deciding which, if any, stereo system to purchase would probably be much greater than what you would expend deciding on buying a new compact disk. Both of these purchase processes would probably differ from the one you would use to purchase a soft drink from a vending machine.

Finally, your purchasing and consumption behavior for the same product will often change depending on the situation you are in. For example, many college students will consume different types and quantities of beverages at a graduation celebration with their parents and grandparents than they would at a similar celebration with their classmates.

Since consumer behavior is influenced by individual characteristics, product characteristics, and situational characteristics, our understanding of consumer behavior must incorporate all three of these influences. All three of these influences are described in the chapters that follow.

FIGURE 1–4 Consumer Behavior Is Product–Person-Situation Specific

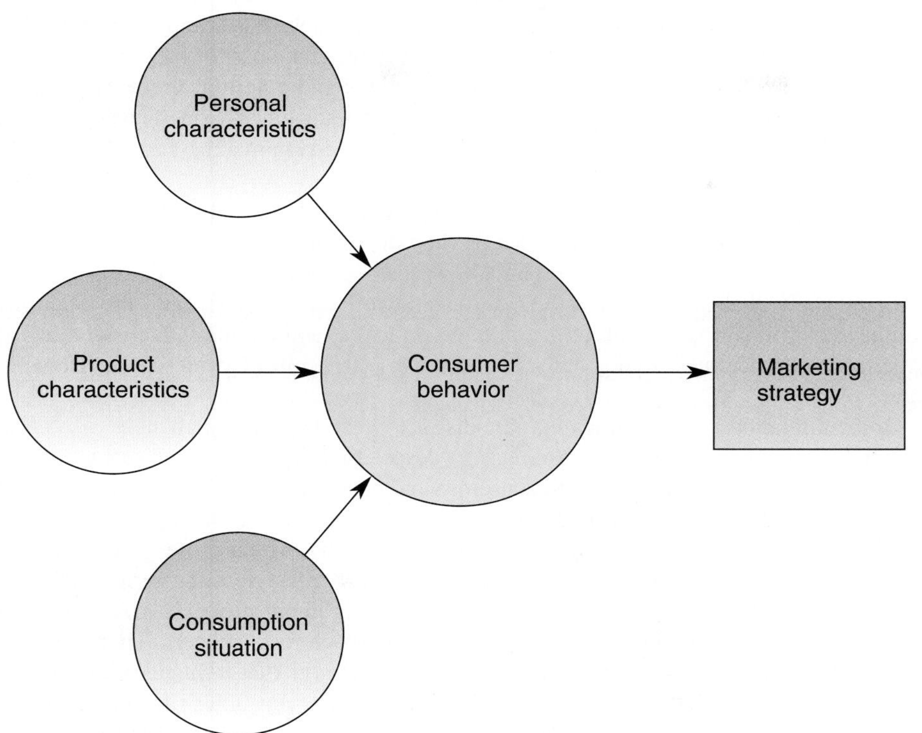

FIGURE 1–5 Consumer Lifestyle and Consumer Decisions

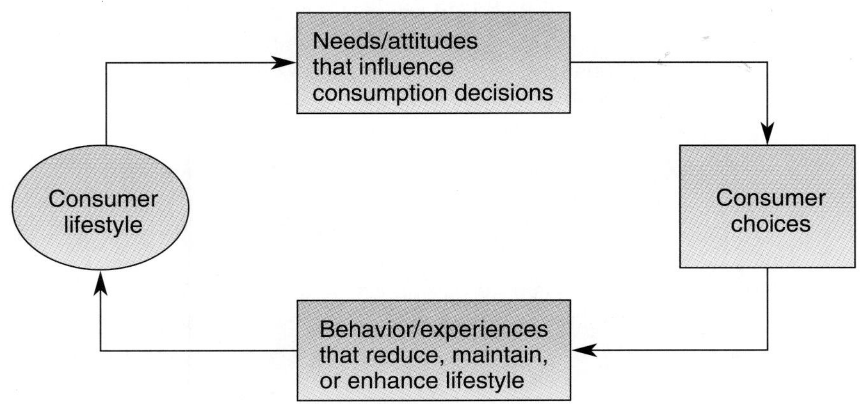

The Nature of Consumption

Consumers purchase and consume products to maintain or enhance their lifestyles. This process is shown in Figure 1–5. Past decisions, time-related events such as aging, external events such as job changes, and internal decisions such as trying a new hobby, lead to lifestyle changes that require the purchase and/or consumption of products to maintain and enhance.

We do not mean to imply that consumers think in terms of lifestyle. None of us consciously thinks: *I'll have a Diet Coke in order to enhance my lifestyle.* Rather we make decisions consistent with our lifestyles without deliberately considering lifestyle. Most consumer decisions involve very little effort or thought on the part of the consumer. They are what we call **low involvement** decisions. Feelings and emotions are as important in many consumer decisions as facts and physical product attributes. Nonetheless, most consumer purchases involve at least a modest amount of decision making and most are influenced by the purchaser's current and desired lifestyle.

What do we mean by the term *consumer lifestyle*, and why is it so vital to an understanding of how and why consumers act as they do? Quite simply, your **lifestyle** is *how* you live. It includes the products you buy, how you use them, what you think about them, and how you feel about them. It is the manifestation of your self-concept—the total image you have of yourself as a result of the culture you live in and the individual situations and experiences that comprise your daily existence. It is the sum of your past decisions and future plans.

Both individuals and families exhibit distinct lifestyles. We often hear of "career-oriented individuals," "outdoor families," "devoted mothers," or "swinging singles." One's lifestyle is determined by both conscious and unconscious decisions. Often we make choices with full awareness of their impact on our lifestyle, but generally we are unaware of the extent to which our decisions are influenced by our current or desired lifestyle.

Maintaining or changing an individual or household lifestyle often requires the consumption of products. It is our contention that thinking about products in terms of their relationship to consumer lifestyle is a very useful approach for managers. Therefore, managers need to understand consumer lifestyles and the factors that influence them.

As illustrated in Figure 1–6, 13 basic factors influence consumer lifestyle: marketing activities, culture, subcultures, values, demographics, social status, reference groups,

FIGURE 1–6 Factors that Determine and Influence Consumer Lifestyle

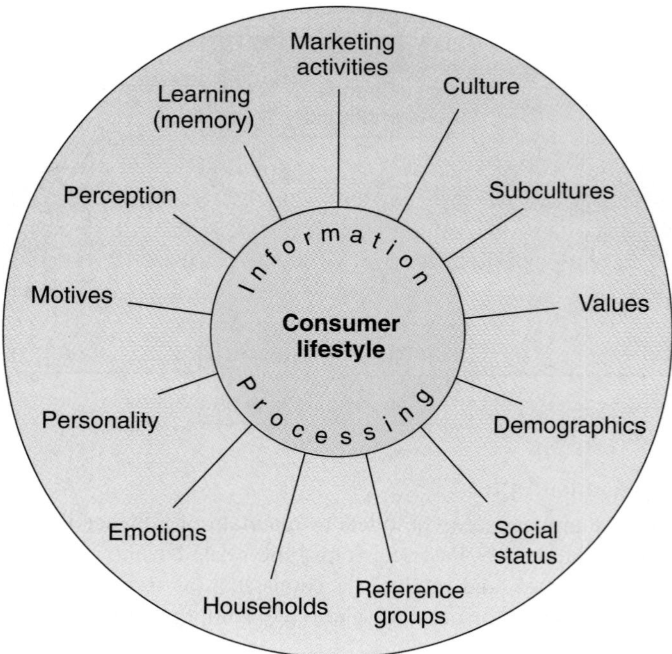

Consumer Decision-Making Process

FIGURE 1–7

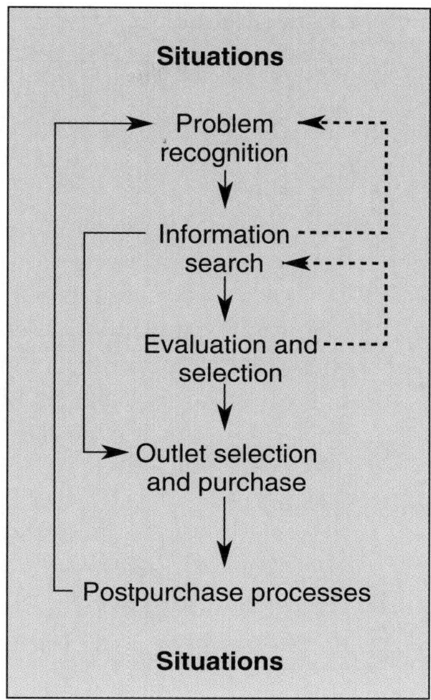

households, emotions, personality, motives, perception, and learning. Information processing links the influences to consumers.

Consumer decisions result from perceived problems (*I'm thirsty.*) and opportunities (*That looks like it would be fun to try.*). We will use the term *problem* to refer both to problems and to opportunities. Consumer problems arise in specific situations and may trigger one or more levels of the consumer decision process as shown in Figure 1–7. It is important to note that for most purchases, consumers devote very little effort to this process, and emotions and feelings often have as much or more influence on the outcome as do facts and product features.

Since the consumer decision process interacts with the firm's marketing strategy to determine the firm's success, we have devoted a complete section of the text to this process. The results of the consumer decision process are experiences which change or maintain the consumer's current or desired lifestyle. Figure 1–8 shows our overall model of consumer behavior.

STUDYING CONSUMER BEHAVIOR

This should be a fascinating course for you. The fact that you are enrolled in this class suggests that you are considering marketing or advertising as a possible career. If that is the case, you should be immensely curious about why people behave as they do. Such a curiosity is virtually essential for success in a marketing-related career. That is what marketing is all about—understanding and anticipating consumer needs and developing solutions for those needs. Exhibit 1–2 shows how Black & Decker gains and uses such an understanding.

Even if you do not pursue a career in marketing, analyzing the purpose behind advertisements, package designs, prices, and other marketing activities is an enjoyable activity.

FIGURE 1–8 Overall Model of Consumer Behavior

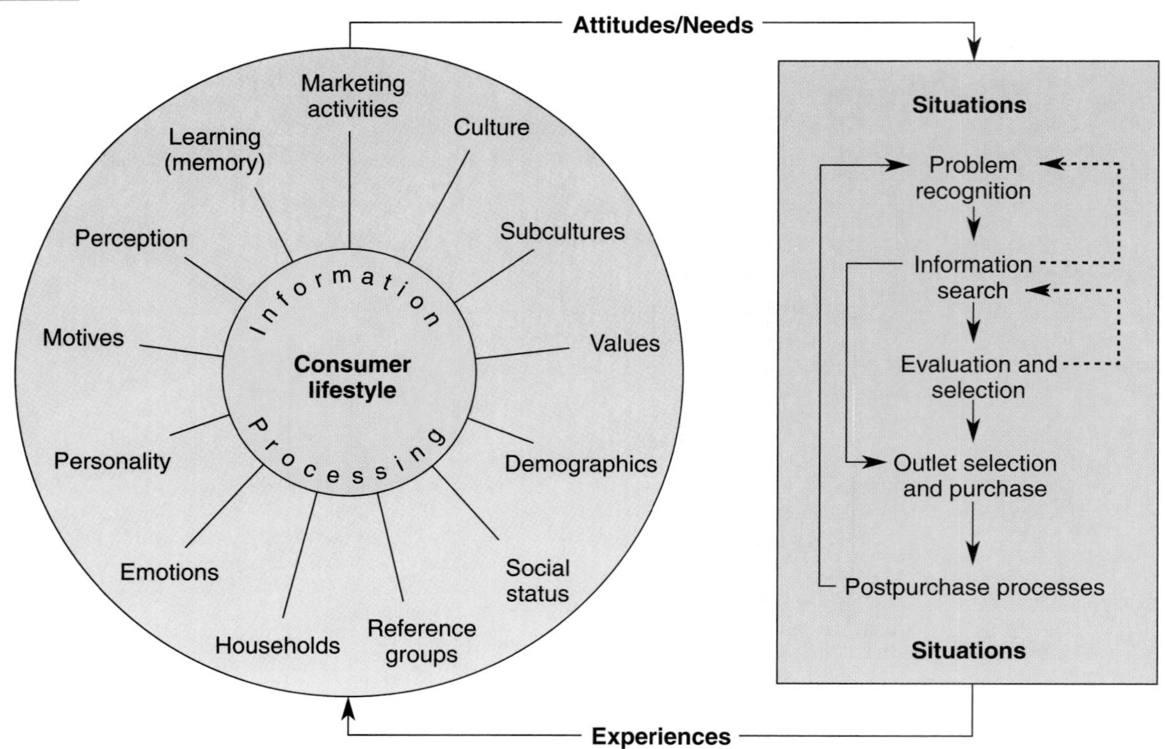

In addition, it will make you a better consumer and a more informed citizen. A knowledge of consumer behavior will enable you to evaluate social and regulatory issues such as the following:

> Consumer groups have pressed for regulation against R.J. Reynolds' use of "Old Joe" the Camel ads as surveys have consistently shown widespread brand recognition of Camel cigarettes among young children and a strong liking of Old Joe among individuals under 18.[9]
>
> The Food and Drug Administration recently ordered three manufacturers of vegetable oil to remove claims on their labels that state that the products contain no cholesterol. The FDA believes that the claims of No Cholesterol are misleading *even though they are true.*[10]

Finally, much of the material is simply interesting. For example, it is fun to read about China's attempt to market *Pansy* brand men's underwear in America, or Ford having to change the name of its *Pinto* automobile in Brazil after it learned that *pinto* was slang for a "small male sex organ." So have fun, study hard, and expand your managerial skills as well as your understanding of the environment in which you live.

REVIEW QUESTIONS

1. What conclusions can be drawn from the examples at the beginning of this chapter?
2. What are the three major uses or applications of an understanding of consumer behavior?
3. What is *customer value* and why is it important to marketers?
4. What is required to provide superior customer value?

EXHIBIT 1–2

Black & Decker Develops *Quantum* Based on Consumer Knowledge

Black & Decker (B&D) had a moderately successful line of relatively inexpensive power tools with the Black & Decker brand. In the early 1990s, B&D developed an expensive, high-quality line called *DeWalt* for the professional market. Initial research with consumers revealed that the serious Do-It-Yourselfer (DIYer) wanted higher quality tools than the inexpensive line but few were willing to pay for the level of quality in the *DeWalt* line.

Therefore, B&D identified 50 homeowners who owned more than six power tools. B&D managers questioned these DIYers about the tools they used and why they had picked particular brands. They went with them on shopping trips and watched as they purchased tools and other items for projects. They observed them in their shops and questioned them as they used the tools. The B&D executives (and an industrial psychologist who accompanied them) tried to determine what these DIYers liked and disliked about particular brands and tools, how the tools felt when they used them, what problems they had while doing projects or cleaning up afterward, and so forth. They also tried to understand the emotional side of DIY projects by asking questions such as: *What was your project? How did you feel when you completed it?*

B&D learned that these consumers were frustrated when cordless tools ran out of power during a job. They were concerned with saws whose blades kept spinning after being switched off and they hated cleaning up sawdust after completing a project. While confident in their own abilities, they would also like access to expert advice on how to use their tools or deal with problem projects. These and other findings were verified with larger sample research. B&D developed more powerful battery-driven tools and saws with name *Quantum* with better safety switches and built-in vacuums to control sawdust. They also developed PowerSource, which provides free maintenance checks on Quantum tools and a toll-free hotline staffed by DIY experts.

B&D's consumer research did not stop with product features. The color of the tools was carefully researched as well. Black was ruled out as this was the color of the lower-priced line. Consumer research found that the deep green used on B&D's garden products was associated with quality and reliability. The name *Quantum* was also based on consumer research. It beat out such names as *Excell, Caliber*, and *Excaliber*. Consumers said it implied a product that was a step ahead of others and they could pronounce it easily. The Black & Decker name does not appear on the *DeWalt* products or packages because the professional contractors did not think B&D could make sophisticated tools. However, the serious DIYers had high regard for B&D and its name appears prominently on *Quantum* products and packages.

The *Quantum* line was launched in August. At the end of October, B&D had 200 employees—from assembly-line workers to marketing executives—telephone 2,500 purchasers of *Quantum* tools to ascertain customer satisfaction and gather ideas for improvements.

As one analyst says: "Black & Decker has become very good at taking market share away from rival companies. They just know their customer."

Source: S. Caminiti, "A Star Is Born," *Fortune*, Autumn/Winter 1993, pp. 44–47

5. What role does an understanding of consumer behavior play in the development of marketing strategy and tactics?
6. What is involved in the *consumer* analysis phase of market analysis in Figure 1–2?
7. What is involved in the *company* analysis phase of market analysis in Figure 1–2?
8. What is involved in the *competitor* analysis phase of market analysis in Figure 1–2?
9. What is involved in the *conditions* analysis phase of market analysis in Figure 1–2?
10. Describe the process of *market segmentation.*
11. How does one choose an attractive target market?
12. What is *marketing strategy*?
13. What is a *marketing mix*?
14. What is a *product*?
15. What is a *price*? How does the price of a product differ from the cost of the product to the consumer?
16. Is a lower price always preferred to a higher price?
17. What does an effective communications strategy require?
18. How is *service* defined in the text?
19. What is involved in creating satisfied customers?
20. What three factors determine consumer behavior?
21. Describe the nature of consumption.
22. What is meant by *consumer lifestyle*?
23. What factors affect consumer lifestyle?
24. Describe the consumer decision process.

DISCUSSION QUESTIONS

25. a. Why would someone buy a pair of inline skates? An aquarium? An expensive restaurant meal? Bottled water?
    b. Why would someone else not make those purchases?
    c. How would you choose one brand and/or model over the others? Would others make the same choice in the same way?
26. Of what use, if any, are models such as the one in Figure 1–8 to managers?
27. What changes would you suggest in the model? Why?
28. Describe your lifestyle. How does it differ from your parents' lifestyle?
29. Do you anticipate any changes in your lifestyle in the next five years? What will cause these changes? What new products or brands will you consume because of these changes?
30. Describe a recent ________ purchase you made. To what extent did you follow the consumer decision-making process described in this chapter? How would you explain any differences?
    a. Major
    b. Minor
31. Describe a purchase that you have been satisfied with and one which resulted in dissatisfaction. What caused the satisfaction and dissatisfaction?
32. Evaluate the model of marketing strategy shown in Figure 1–2.
33. Describe several ''total products'' that are more than their direct physical features?
34. Describe the needs that a ________ might satisfy and the total cost to the consumer of obtaining the benefits of the total product.
    a. Stereo system.
    b. Large motorcycle.
    c. Home-brew beer kit.
    d. Dress suit.
    e. Dog.
    f. Personal computer.
35. Describe how the situation would affect your choice of product versions or brands of the following:
    a. Restaurant meal.
    b. Beverage.
    c. Movie.
    d. Shirt.
    e. Cologne.
    f. Compact disk.
36. The FDA recently ordered three manufacturers of vegetable oil to remove claims on their labels that state the products contain no cholesterol. The FDA believes that the claims of no cholesterol are misleading *even though they are true.*[11] How would you explain this?

APPLICATION ACTIVITIES

37. Interview the manager or marketing manager of a firm that sells to households or individuals. Determine how this individual develops marketing strategy. Compare this person's process with the approach described in the text.
38. Interview the manager or marketing manager of a firm that sells to households or individuals. Determine this person's level of concern with customer satisfaction. Also determine what this person believes causes customers to be satisfied or dissatisfied.
39. Interview five students and have them describe their last unsatisfactory purchase. What seems to cause customer dissatisfaction among students?
40. Interview five students. Have them describe the last three beverages they consumed and the situations in which they were consumed. What can you conclude about the impact of the situation on consumer behavior? What can you conclude about the impact of the individual on consumer behavior?
41. Posing as a customer, visit one or more stores that sell ______. Report on the sales techniques used (point-of-purchase displays, store design, salesperson comments, and so forth). What beliefs concerning consumer behavior appear to underlie these strategies? It is often worthwhile for a male and a female student to visit the same store and talk to the same salesperson at different times. The variation in sales appeal is sometimes quite revealing.
    a. Expensive furniture.
    b. Inexpensive furniture.
    c. Expensive jewelry.
    d. Seafood.
    e. Power tools.
    f. Indoor plants.
    g. Pets.
    h. Personal computers.
42. Look through recent copies of a magazine such as *Advertising Age* or *Business Week*, and report on three applications of consumer behavior knowledge (or questions) to marketing decisions.
43. Interview individuals who sell ______. Try to discover their personal ''models'' of consumer behavior for their products.
    a. Expensive furniture.
    b. Inexpensive furniture.
    c. Expensive jewelry.
    d. Seafood.
    e. Power tools.
    f. Indoor plants.
    g. Pets.
    h. Personal computers.
44. Interview three individuals who recently made a major purchase and three others who made a minor purchase. In what ways were their decision processes similar? How were they different?

REFERENCES

[1]''Marketing-Oriented Lever Uses Research,'' *Marketing News*, February 10, 1978, p. 9.

[2]C. Power, ''Flops,'' *Business Week*, August 16, 1993, pp. 79–80.

[3]Ibid.

[4]T. P. Pare, ''How to Find Out What They Want,'' *Fortune*, Autumn/Winter 1993, pp. 39–41.

[5]Ibid.

[6]C. Miller, ''Xers Know They're a Target Market,'' *Marketing News*, December 6, 1993, p. 2.

[7]See footnote 2.

[8]See footnote 4.

[9]G. Levin, ''Poll Shows Camel Ads Are Effective with Kids,'' *Advertising Age*, April 27, 1993, p. 7.

[10]''FDA Orders Vegetable Oil Makers to Drop No-Cholesterol Claim,'' *Marketing News*, June 10, 1991, p. 8.

[11]Ibid.

SECTION TWO

EXTERNAL INFLUENCES

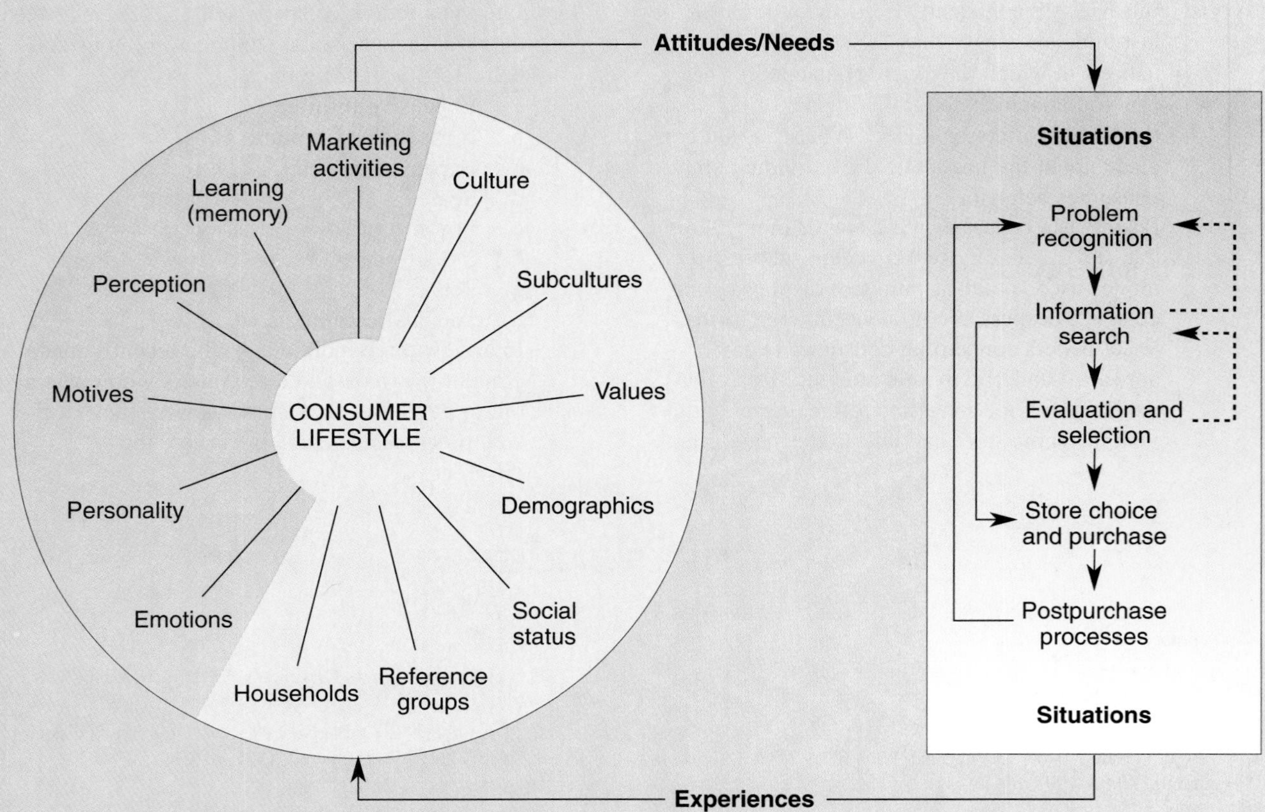

The shaded area of our model shown at the left is the focal point of this section of the text. Any division of the factors that influence behavior into separate and distinct categories is somewhat arbitrary. For example, we have chosen to consider learning in the next section of the text, which focuses on internal influences. However, a substantial amount of human learning involves interaction with, or imitation of, other individuals. Thus, learning also could be considered a group process. Section Two examines groups as they operate to influence consumer behavior. Our emphasis is on the functioning of the group itself and *not* the process by which the individual reacts to the group.

This section starts with large-scale, macrogroup influences and progresses to smaller, more microgroup influences. As we progress, the nature of the influence exerted by the group changes from general guidelines to explicit expectations for certain behaviors. The pattern of influence is illustrated in Figure II-1.

Nature of Group Influences

FIGURE II–1

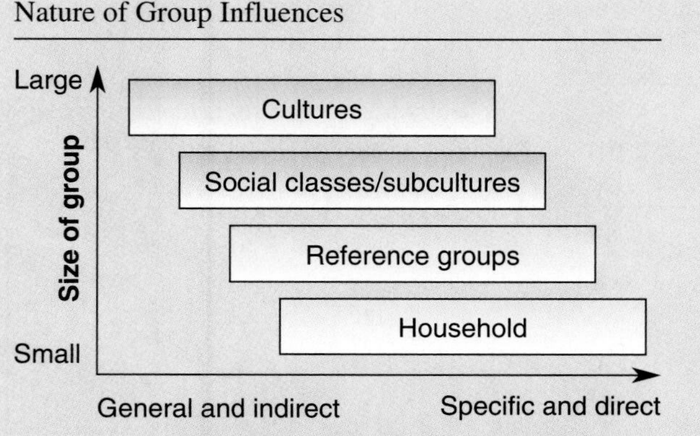

CHAPTER 2

CROSS-CULTURAL VARIATIONS IN CONSUMER BEHAVIOR

According to U.S. standards, Brazil should represent a major market opportunity for cereals and other breakfast foods. Brazil has a population of approximately 165 million. Further, the age distribution favors cereal consumption—48 percent of the population is under 20 years of age. In addition, per capita income is high enough to allow the purchase of ready-to-eat cereals. In examining the market, Kellogg Company noticed one additional positive feature—there was no direct competition!

Unfortunately, the absence of competition was due to the fact that Brazilians do not eat an American-style breakfast. Thus, the marketing task facing Kellogg and its ad agency, J. Walter Thompson, was to change the nature of breakfast in Brazil.

Novelas, soap operas, are very popular and influential in Brazil. Therefore, Kellogg began advertising on the novelas. The first campaign showed a boy eating the cereal out of the package. While demonstrating the good taste of the product, it also positioned it as a snack rather than as a part of a breakfast meal. The campaign was soon withdrawn.

An analysis of the Brazilian culture revealed a very high value placed on the family with the male the dominant authority. Therefore, the next campaign focused on family breakfast scenes with the father pouring the cereal into bowls and adding milk.

The second campaign was more successful than the first. Cereal sales increased, and Kellogg has a 99.5 percent market share. However, annual ready-to-eat cereal consumption remains below one ounce per capita.[1]

Marketing across cultural boundaries is a difficult and challenging task. As Figure 2–1 indicates, cultures may differ in demographics, languages, nonverbal communications, and values. This chapter focuses on cultural variations in *values* and *nonverbal communications*. First, however, we briefly indicate the important role that demographics play in differentiating countries and cultures.[2]

Before we begin our discussion, we need to point out that while marketing strategy is heavily influenced by such variables as values, demographics, and languages, it also influences these variables. For example, television advertising in China is extensive and reflects many Western values. Over time, such advertising will influence not only how many Chinese choose to live (lifestyle) but also what they value and how they think and feel.

DEMOGRAPHICS

Demographics describe a population in terms of its size, structure, and distribution. While cultures and countries frequently are not synonymous, demographic data are generally available only for countries or other political units.

A critical aspect of demographics for marketers is income. However, the average income in a country is not as important as the distribution of income. One country with a relatively low average income can have a sizable middle-income segment while another country with the same average income may have most of the wealth in the hands of a few individuals (compare Brazil and Israel in Table 2–1).

The economic, climatic, and social structures of a country influence how consumers allocate their income. Table 2–2 shows large differences across countries in the manner in which households allocate their resources. For example, Mexican households spend

FIGURE 2–1 Cultural Factors Affect Consumer Behavior and Marketing Strategy

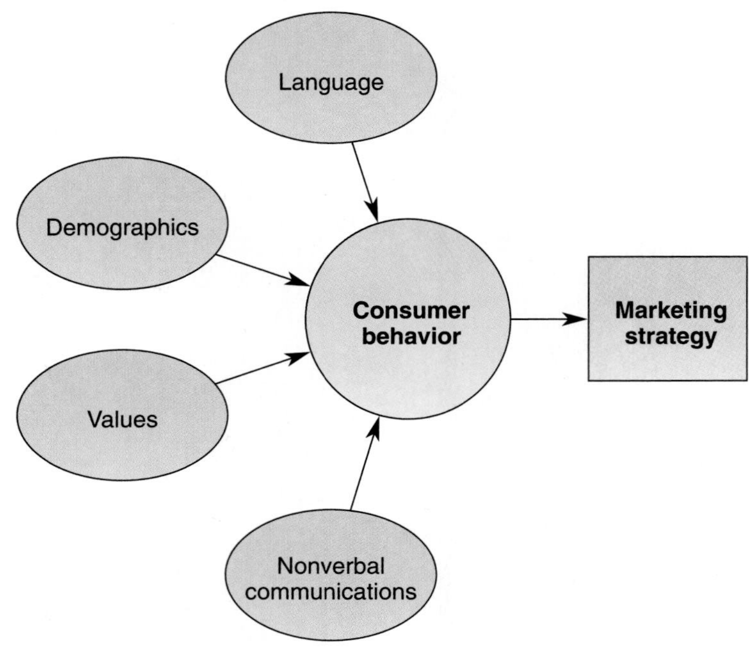

TABLE 2–1 Income Distribution across Countries

Percent of Population	Percent of Country's Income Received by Population Segments[a]								
	U.S.	Brazil	France	Poland	Israel	Kenya	Indonesia	Thailand	Japan
Top 10%	25.0%*	51.3%	25.5%	21.6%	23.5%	45.4%	27.9%	35.3%	22.4%
Next 10%	16.9	16.2	15.3	14.5	16.1	15.5	14.4	15.4	15.1
Next 20%	25.0	16.8	23.5	23.0	24.5	18.9	21.1	20.3	23.1
Next 20%	17.4	8.8	17.2	17.9	17.8	11.1	15.8	13.5	17.5
Next 20%	11.0	4.8	12.1	13.8	12.1	6.4	12.1	9.4	13.2
Lowest 20%	4.7	2.1	6.3	9.2	6.0	2.7	8.7	6.1	8.7
Per capita income (000)[b]	22.5	2.3	18.3	4.3	12.0	.4	.6	1.6	19.0

*Read as the top 10 percent receive 25% of the country's income.

[a]Source: R. Sookdeo, "The New Global Consumer," *Fortune*, Autumn–Winter 1993, pp. 68–76.

[b]In 1992 U.S. dollars. Source: *World Fact Book 1992* (Washington, D.C., Central Intelligence Agency, 1992).

twice as much of their income on appliances and other nonessential consumer goods as do Indian households.

Figure 2–2 shows the age distribution of the United States and the Philippines. What product opportunities does this figure suggest for each country? Even if all other aspects of the two countries were identical, the demographic variable *age* would dictate different product and communications mixes.

TABLE 2–2

How Households Allocate Their Income

Category	U.S.	Mexico	West Germany	Poland	Iran	Kenya	Singapore	Thailand	India
	Country								
Food	10%	35%	12%	29%	37%	38%	19%	30%	52%
Clothing	6	10	7	9	9	7	8	16	11
Housing, utilities	18	8	18	6	23	12	11	7	10
Medical care	14	5	13	6	6	3	7	5	3
Education	8	5	6	7	5	10	12	5	4
Transportation	14	12	13	8	6	8	13	13	7
Other*	30	25	31	35	14	22	30	24	13
Per capita income (000)[b]	22.5	3.2	19.2	4.3	1.5	.4	13.9	1.6	.4

*Includes appliances and other consumer durables.

[a]Source: R. Sookdeo, ''The New Global Consumer,'' *Fortune*, Autumn–Winter 1993, pp. 68–76.

[b]In 1992 U.S. dollars. Source: *World Fact Book 1992* (Washington, D.C., Central Intelligence Agency, 1992).

FIGURE 2–2

Age Distribution: United States and Philippines

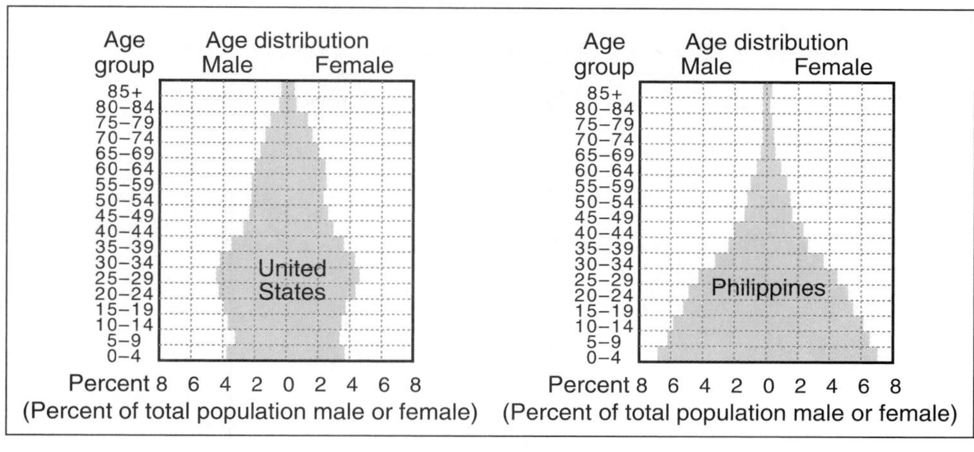

Even countries within the European Community (EC) have dramatically different demographics. These demographic differences continue to hinder the EC's movement toward a unified social system. For example, less than 5 percent of the British workforce is in agriculture, compared with 30 percent in Greece. Table 2–3 illustrates numerous other demographic and related differences between EC counties. Which of these differences do you feel will have the most impact on marketing strategy for a consumer product?

While demographic differences between countries are important, they are relatively obvious despite the frequent absence of accurate or comparable data.[3] We will now focus our attention on the equally important though more subtle influences exerted by culture.

TABLE 2-3 Differences across European Community (EC) Countries

Category	Country												
	All EC	W. Germany	Italy	G. Britain	France	Spain	Netherlands	Belgium	Portugal	Greece	Denmark		
Age (%)													
Age 18–24	15	13	15	15	15	16	15	14	16	15	13	18	13
Age 65+	19	21	18	20	19	17	17	18	17	17	17	15	20
Marital Status (%)													
Single	24	25	29	19	22	29	20	18	24	24	16	30	21
Married	59	55	60	61	55	60	60	68	66	67	56	62	63
Living as married	3	2	1	5	7	0	8	4	0	1	14	1	1
Divorced/widowed	13	17	10	15	13	10	11	9	10	9	14	7	14
Occupation (%)													
Management	14	22	6	15	19	4	20	10	16	7	18	10	12
White collar	25	28	23	32	23	14	28	34	19	24	29	23	25
Skilled blue collar	16	16	15	20	9	17	18	15	12	30	18	17	17
Unskilled blue collar	20	14	30	26	10	21	15	16	32	10	23	25	18
Never worked	25	19	26	7	39	44	20	24	21	29	12	25	29
Income[a]		19.2	16.7	15.9	18.3	12.4	16.6	17.3	8.4	7.7	17.7	11.2	20.2
Age Leaving School (%)													
15 or less	38	9	58	43	33	63	20	29	53	49	17	36	36
16/17	18	19	8	32	19	10	23	16	10	5	5	29	21
18 or more	40	59	34	24	41	28	53	54	29	46	71	34	43

[a]In 1992 U.S. dollars. Source: *World Fact Book 1992* (Washington, D.C., Central Intelligence Agency, 1992).

THE CONCEPT OF CULTURE

Culture is that complex whole which includes knowledge, belief, art, law, morals, customs, and any other capabilities and habits acquired by humans as a members of society.[4]

Several aspects of culture require elaboration. First, culture is a *comprehensive* concept. It includes almost everything that influences an individual's thought processes and behaviors. While culture does not determine the nature or frequency of biological drives, such as hunger or sex, it does influence if, when, and how these drives will be gratified. Second, culture is *acquired*. It does not include inherited responses and predispositions. However, since most human behavior is learned rather than innate, culture does affect a wide array of behaviors.

Differences across European Community (EC) Countries (*Continued*)

TABLE 2–3

Category	Country												
	All EC	W. Germany	Italy	G. Britain	France	Spain	Netherlands	Belgium	Portugal	Greece	Denmark	Ireland	Luxembourg
Media and Language													
Speak English (%)	44	44	16	100	31	12	72	34	25	28	61	100	44
Magazines read	2.3	3.7	2.0	1.7	3.0	1.3	2.6	2.6	1.2	1.3	1.9	1.6	2.3
No magazines read (%)	16	4	24	7	20	31	6	18	32	20	2	3	8
No newspapers read (%)	27	10	30	33	19	43	15	22	49	50	23	42	24
Household Features (%)													
Apartment	44	62	58	18	41	55	27	10	38	53	39	4	23
House	56	38	42	82	59	45	73	90	62	47	61	96	77
Owned	59	40	68	67	54	80	46	72	59	72	60	82	77
Urban location	68	80	73	78	66	48	87	43	47	59	77	55	55
3+ bedrooms	51	42	40	59	54	73	55	61	50	18	26	87	48
Telephone	83	89	88	85	85	65	95	78	51	74	86	52	73
Computer	15	16	12	22	14	8	20	15	7	6	14	12	12
Any freezer space	76	73	89	81	77	55	82	86	91	27	92	58	91
Microwave oven	25	36	6	48	25	9	19	21	4	2	14	20	16
Washing machine	86	88	96	78	88	87	91	88	66	74	76	81	93
Cable TV	19	29	0	3	9	22	87	88	4	0	34	40	89
CD player	19	24	9	20	23	11	43	26	9	5	20	14	30
Private garden	52	49	36	84	54	9	72	80	17	30	68	85	71
Automobile	69	69	80	63	75	62	69	77	45	48	64	70	71

Source: Reproduced from *Reader's Digest Eurodata—a Consumer Survey of 17 European Countries* (Pleasantville, N.Y.: The Reader's Digest Association, Inc., 1991).

Third, the complexity of modern societies is such that culture seldom provides detailed prescriptions for appropriate behavior. Instead, in most industrial societies, culture supplies *boundaries* within which most individuals think and act.

Finally, the nature of cultural influences is such that we are *seldom aware* of them. One behaves, thinks, and feels in a manner consistent with other members of the same culture because it seems "natural" or "right" to do so. The influence of culture is similar to the air we breathe; it is everywhere and is generally taken for granted unless there is a fairly rapid change in its nature.

The Functioning of Culture

Culture operates primarily by setting rather loose boundaries for individual behavior and by influencing the functioning of such institutions as the family structure and mass media. Thus, *culture provides the framework within which individual and household lifestyles evolve.*

The boundaries that culture sets on behavior are called **norms**. Norms are simply rules that specify or prohibit certain behaviors in specific situations. Norms are derived from cultural values. **Cultural values** are widely held beliefs that affirm what is desirable. It is not necessary for a culture's values to be logically consistent. In fact, some tension or strain between conflicting cultural values is characteristic of most advanced societies. This array of abstract, and sometimes conflicting, cultural values that characterize industrialized societies leaves room for a variety of distinct lifestyles to evolve within each society.

Violation of cultural norms results in **sanctions** or penalties ranging from mild social disapproval to banishment from the group. Conformity to norms is usually given explicit and obvious rewards only when a child is learning the culture (socialization) or an individual is learning a new culture (acculturation). In other situations, conformity is expected without reward. For example, in America we expect people to arrive on time for business and social appointments. We do not compliment them when they do arrive on time, but we tend to become angry when they arrive late. Thus, as Figure 2–3 indicates, cultural values give rise to norms and associated sanctions which in turn influence consumption patterns.

The preceding discussion may leave the impression that people are aware of cultural values and norms and that violating any given norm carries a precise and known sanction. This usually is not the case. We tend to ''obey'' cultural norms without thinking because to do otherwise would seem unnatural. For example, we are seldom aware of how close we stand to other individuals while conducting business. Yet, this distance is well defined and adhered to, even though it varies from culture to culture.

Cultures are not static. They typically evolve and change slowly over time.[5] However, there can be major changes during relatively short time periods due to rapid technological advances, conflicts between existing values, exposure to another culture's values, or dramatic events such as a war. Marketing managers must understand both the existing cultural

FIGURE 2–3 Values, Norms, Sanctions, and Consumption Patterns

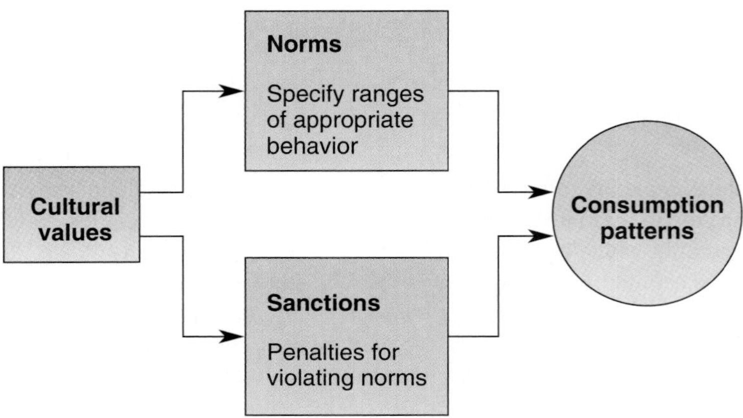

EXHIBIT 2–1

Cross-Cultural Marketing Mistakes

- A U.S. electronics firm landed a major contract with a Japanese buyer. The U.S. firm's president flew to Tokyo for the contract signing ceremony. Then the head of the Japanese firm began reading the contract intently. The scrutiny continued for an extraordinary length of time. At last, the U.S. executive offered an additional price discount.

  The Japanese executive, though surprised, did not object. The U.S. executive's mistake was assuming that the Japanese executive was attempting to reopen negotiations. Instead, he was demonstrating his personal concern and authority in the situation by closely and slowly examining the document.
- Another electronics company sent a conservative American couple from the Midwest to represent the firm in Sweden. They were invited for a weekend in the country where, at an isolated beach, their Swedish hosts disrobed. The Americans misinterpreted this not uncommon Swedish behavior and their resulting attitudes destroyed a promising business relationship.[7]
- Crest initially failed in Mexico when it used its U.S. approach of providing scientific proof of its decay prevention capabilities. Most Mexicans assign little value to the decay prevention benefit of toothpaste.
- Coca-Cola had to withdraw its 2-liter bottle from the Spanish market after discovering that it did not fit local refrigerators.[8]
- Procter & Gamble's commercials for Camay, in which men directly complimented women on their appearance, were successful in many countries. However, they were a failure in Japan, where men and women don't interact in that manner.[9]

values and the emerging cultural values of the societies they serve.[6] The examples in Exhibit 2–1 illustrate the negative consequences of a failure to understand cultural differences.

Numerous American companies have awakened to the need for general cultural sensitivity. General Motors, Procter & Gamble, and Exxon committed $500,000 each for cross-cultural training for their employees. Red Wing Shoe Company put 21 executives through a three-day training program on the Middle East. As Red Wing's president explained: "We always give the customer what he wants. If we're playing in his ballpark, we'd better know his rules."[10] As Managerial Application 2–1 indicates, sophisticated firms such as Coca-Cola Company can succeed in numerous cultures.

VARIATIONS IN CULTURAL VALUES

Cultural values are widely held beliefs that affirm what is desirable. These values affect behavior through norms, which specify an acceptable range of responses to specific situations. A useful approach to understanding cultural variations in behavior is to understand the values embraced by different cultures.

MANAGERIAL APPLICATION

2–1

Coca-Cola's Marketing Strategy Is Effective in Many Cultures

There are a multitude of values that vary across cultures and affect consumption. Figure 2–4 offers a classification scheme consisting of three broad forms of cultural values—*other-oriented*, *environment-oriented*, and *self-oriented*. The cultural values that have the most impact on consumer behavior can be classified in one of these three general categories. Individual values can affect more than one area, but their primary impact is generally in one of the three categories.

Other-oriented values reflect a society's view of the appropriate relationships *between individuals and groups* within that society. These relationships have a major impact on marketing practice. For example, if the society values collective activity, consumers will look toward others for guidance in purchase decisions and will not respond favorably to "be an individual" promotion appeals.

Environment-oriented values prescribe a society's relationship to *its economic and technical as well as its physical environment.* As a manager, you would develop a very different marketing program for a society that stressed a problem-solving, risk-taking, performance-oriented approach to its environment than you would for a fatalistic, security, and status-oriented society.

Self-oriented values reflect the objectives and approaches to life *that the individual members of society find desirable.* Again, these values have strong implications for marketing management. For instance, the acceptance and use of credit is very much determined by a society's position on the value of postponed versus immediate gratification.

Exhibit 2–2 provides a list of 18 values that are important in most cultures. The list is not meant to be exhaustive but does include the major values that are relevant to consumer behavior in industrialized societies. Most of the values are shown as dichotomies (e.g., materialistic versus nonmaterialistic). However, this is not meant to represent an either/or

Value Orientations Influence Behavior

FIGURE 2–4

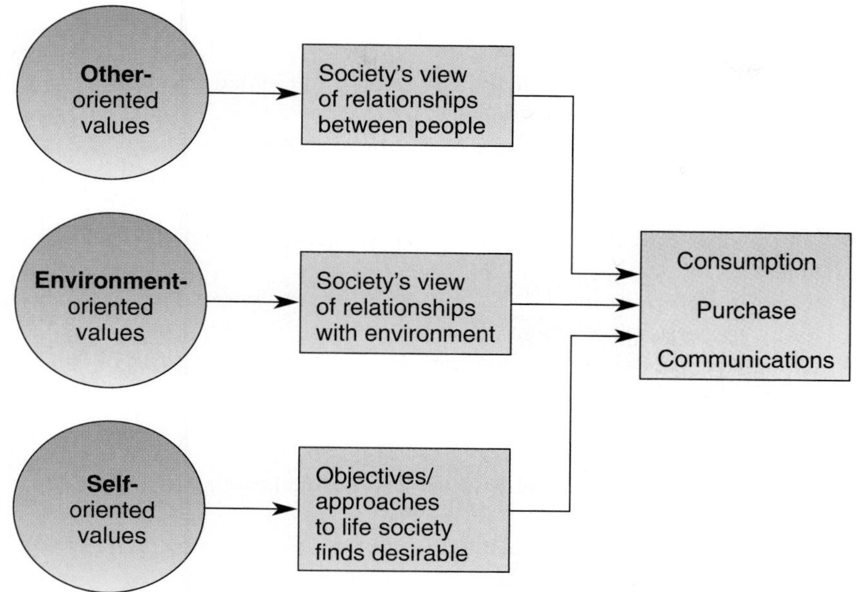

situation. Instead, a continuum exists between the two extremes. For example, two societies can each value tradition, but one may value it more than the other and, therefore, be closer to the tradition end of the scale. For several of the values, a natural dichotomy does not seem to exist. For a society to place a very low value on cleanliness does not necessarily imply that it places a high value on ''dirtiness.'' These 18 values are described in the following paragraphs.

Other-Oriented Values

Individual/Collective Does the culture emphasize and reward individual initiative, or are cooperation with and conformity to a group more highly valued? Are individual differences appreciated or condemned? Are rewards and status given to individuals or to groups? Answers to these questions reveal the individual or collective orientation of a culture.

In Japan, compared with the United States, there is a weaker sense of individualism and a stronger pressure to conform to and associate with one's reference groups. Therefore, motivating and compensating Japanese sales personnel using individual-based incentive systems and promotions would be inappropriate. Likewise, such themes as ''be yourself,'' ''stand out,'' and ''don't be one of the crowd'' are effective in the United States but not in Japan. However, these generalizations are less accurate today than in the recent past. Evidence indicates that the Japanese, particularly the younger generation, are becoming more individualistic:

> Mizuho Arai knows what she likes. A 20-year-old uniformed office worker by day, at night she wears loafers, a sweater, Levi's 501s, and a black parka. Shopping with an L.L. Bean bag over her shoulder, she prefers bargain outlets to traditional department stores and designer boutiques. ''I don't like to be told what's trendy. I can make up my own mind.''[12]

EXHIBIT 2–2 Cultural Values of Relevance to Consumer Behavior

Other-Oriented Values
- *Individual/Collective.* Are individual activity and initiative valued more highly than collective activity and conformity?
- *Romantic Orientation.* Does the culture believe that ''love conquers all''?
- *Adult/Child.* Is family life organized to meet the needs of the children or the adults?
- *Masculine/Feminine.* To what extent does social power automatically go to males?
- *Competitive/Cooperative.* Does one obtain success by excelling over others or by cooperating with them?
- *Youth/Age.* Are wisdom and prestige assigned to the younger or older members of a culture?

Environment-Oriented Values
- *Cleanliness.* To what extent is cleanliness pursued beyond the minimum needed for health?
- *Performance/Status.* Is the culture's reward system based on performance or on inherited factors such as family or class?
- *Tradition/Change.* Are existing patterns of behavior considered to be inherently superior to new patterns of behavior?
- *Risk Taking/Security.* Are those who risk their established positions to overcome obstacles or achieve high goals admired more than those who do not?
- *Problem Solving/Fatalistic.* Are people encouraged to overcome all problems, or do they take a ''what will be, will be'' attitude?
- *Nature.* Is nature regarded as something to be admired or overcome?

Self-Oriented Values
- *Active/Passive.* Is a physically active approach to life valued more highly than a less active orientation?
- *Material/Nonmaterial.* How much importance is attached to the acquisition of material wealth?
- *Hard Work/Leisure.* Is a person who works harder than economically necessary admired more than one who does not?
- *Postponed Gratification/Immediate Gratification.* Are people encouraged to ''save for a rainy day'' or to ''live for today''?
- *Sensual Gratification/Abstinence.* To what extent is it acceptable to enjoy sensual pleasures such as food, drink, and sex?
- *Humor/Serious.* Is life to be regarded as a strictly serious affair, or is it to be treated lightly?

Ms. Arai is typical of the younger generation of Japanese consumers. ''They don't listen to us,'' complains Kenichi Mizorogi, the cosmetics manager for Shiseido Co. In the late 1980s, Shiseido launched its very successful *Perky Jean* makeup line with the theme: ''Everyone is buying it.'' ''That would never work now,'' says Mizorogi. Indeed, recent research has found that the 18–21 age group (a $33 billion market) places major emphasis on individuality.

The different values held by younger and older Japanese illustrate the fact that few cultures are completely homogeneous. Marketers must be aware of differences between cultures and within cultures.

Romantic Orientation Is the "boy meets girl, overcomes obstacles, marries, and lives happily ever after" theme common in popular literature? Is there freedom of choice in the selection of mates? A Listerine ad in Thailand showing a boy and girl, obviously fond of each other, failed. It was changed to two girls discussing Listerine and was successful.[13] Advertisements portraying courtship activities are not effective in India, where most marriages are arranged by their parents. In contrast, Unilever's female body spray, Impulse, is successfully marketed in 31 countries, using a straightforward romantic theme.[14]

Adult/Child To what extent do the primary family activities focus on the needs of the children instead of those of the adults? What role, if any, do children play in family decisions? What role do they play in decisions that primarily affect the child?

Variation in attitudes toward children can be seen in the percent of the respondents from various countries who agree with the statement: "Marriage without children is not complete."[15]

Austria	62%	Luxembourg	45%
Belgium	46	Netherlands	31
Denmark	21	Norway	31
Finland	44	Portugal	74
France	69	Spain	44
Great Britain	28	Sweden	30
Greece	72	Switzerland	41
Ireland	49	West Germany	53
Italy	63		

China's policy of limiting families to one child has produced a strong focus on the child. In fact, many of these children receive so much attention that they are known in Asia as "little emperors." H. J. Heinz is successfully marketing a rice cereal for Chinese babies. Its premium price (75 cents a box where average workers earn only $40 a month) and American origin give it a quality image. The convenience of the instant cereal is also an advantage in a country where 70 percent of the women work outside the home. Nestlé is in the process of entering this market with a competing product line.[16]

Masculine/Feminine Are rank, prestige, and important social roles assigned primarily to men? Can a female's life pattern be predicted at birth with a high degree of accuracy? Does the husband or wife, or both, make important family decisions? Basically, we live in a masculine-oriented world, yet the degree of masculine orientation varies widely, even across the relatively homogeneous countries of Western Europe. This variance can be seen in the percent from each country who agree with the statement: "Women should have more freedom to do what they want."[17]

Austria	63%	France	51%
Belgium	47	Great Britain	79
Denmark	58	Greece	52
Finland	63	Ireland	78

Italy	48	Spain	57
Luxembourg	49	Sweden	60
Netherlands	59	Switzerland	58
Norway	49	West Germany	69
Portugal	38		

Both obvious and subtle aspects of marketing are influenced by this dimension (see Chapter 3). Obviously, you would not portray women executives in advertisements in Muslim countries. However, suppose you were going to portray a furniture or household appliance purchase decision for a Dutch market. Would you show the decision to be made by the husband, the wife, or made jointly? A joint decision process would probably be used. Or suppose you had an office in a Muslim country. Would you follow the common American practice of hiring a female secretary? To do so would be an affront to many of your Muslim clients.

Competitive/Cooperative Is the path to success found by outdoing other individuals or groups, or is success achieved by forming alliances with other individuals and groups? Does everyone admire a winner? Variation on this value can be seen in the way different cultures react to comparative advertisements. For example, Mexico and Spain ban such ads while the United States encourages them.

As one would expect in a cooperative culture, the Japanese have historically found comparative ads to be distasteful. However, focus group research for Pepsi-Cola Japan found that younger consumers would appreciate advertising that mocked a rival in a frank and funny way. Based on this research, PepsiCo launched a TV spot in which rap singer Hammer depicted market leader Coke as the beverage that turns you into a nerd. Pepsi's cola sales jumped 19 percent.[18]

Youth/Age Are prestige, rank, and important social roles assigned to younger or older members of society? Are the behavior, dress, and mannerisms of the younger or older members of a society imitated by the rest of the society? While American society is clearly youth-oriented, the Confucian concept practiced in Korea emphasizes age. Thus, mature spokespersons would tend to be more successful in Korean advertisements than would younger ones.

Environment-Oriented Values

Cleanliness Is cleanliness "next to godliness," or is it a rather minor matter? Is one expected to be clean beyond reasonable health requirements? In the United States, a high value is placed on cleanliness. In fact, many Europeans consider Americans to be paranoid on the subject of personal hygiene. For example, over 90 percent of all adult Americans use deodorant. In contrast, the percentage of adult males and females using deodorants from various European countries are:[19]

	Male	*Female*		*Male*	*Female*
Austria	30%	53%	Luxembourg	44%	65%
Belgium	46	61	Netherlands	60	76
Denmark	80	89	Norway	83	85
Finland	75	81	Portugal	63	52
France	47	66	Spain	53	66
Great Britain	69	81	Sweden	80	86
Greece	28	35	Switzerland	71	74
Ireland	56	72	West Germany	60	70
Italy	52	60			

Performance/Status Are opportunities, rewards, and prestige based on an individual's performance or on the status associated with the person's family, position, or class? Do all people have an equal opportunity economically, socially, and politically at the start of life, or are certain groups given special privileges? A status-oriented society is more likely to prefer "quality" or established brand names and high-priced items over functionally equivalent items with unknown brand names or lower prices. This is the case in Japan, Hong Kong, Singapore, the Philippines, Malaysia, Indonesia, Thailand, and most Arabic countries, where consumers are attracted by prestigious, known brands.

A recent study found that almost 80 percent of the respondents in the United Kingdom agreed that a well-known brand name would have a moderate or strong influence on their purchase decisions. In contrast, less than 30 percent of the German respondents assigned that level of importance to the brand name.[20] The marketing implications in terms of advertising strategies, branding, and new-product development are significant. (How would your strategy change if you were exporting an established American product to Germany versus to the United Kingdom? What if it were a new product from Mexico?)

Tradition/Change Is tradition valued simply for the sake of tradition? Is change or "progress" an acceptable reason for altering established patterns? Societies that place a relatively high value on tradition tend to resist product changes. "All innovation is the work of the devil" is a quote attributed to Muhammad. Little wonder that economic development and modern business and marketing practices often are unwelcome in Muslim cultures? The marketing impact of England's tradition-oriented culture can be seen in the fact that three-fourths of its population claim to be generally brand loyal (compared to half in France and Germany).[21]

Risk Taking/Security Do the "heroes" of the culture meet and overcome obstacles? Is the person who risks established position or wealth on a new venture admired or considered foolhardy? This value has a strong influence on entrepreneurship and economic development. The society that does not admire risk taking is unlikely to develop enough entrepreneurs to achieve economic change and growth. New-product introductions, new channels of distribution, and advertising themes are affected by this value.

Problem Solving/Fatalistic Do people react to obstacles and disasters as challenges to be overcome, or do they take a "what will be, will be" attitude? Is there an optimistic, "we can do it" orientation? In the Caribbean, difficult or unmanageable problems are often dismissed with the expression "no problem." This actually means: "There is a problem, but we don't know what to do about it—so don't worry!"[22]

Mexico also falls toward the fatalistic end of this continuum. As a result, Mexican customers are less likely to express formal complaints when confronted with an unsatisfactory purchase.

This attitude affects advertising themes and the nature of products that are acceptable. For example, Japanese advertising does not stress control over the environment to the same extent that American ads do.

Nature Is nature assigned a positive value, or is it viewed as something to be overcome, conquered, or tamed? Americans historically considered nature as something to be overcome or improved. In line with this, animals were either destroyed as enemies or romanticized and made into heroes and pets. Dogs, for example, are pets in the United States, and few Americans would feel comfortable consuming them as food. However, they are a common food source in some countries, such as Korea and China.

Most Northern European countries place a very high value on the environment. Packaging and other environmental regulations are stronger in these countries than in America. In turn, Americans and Canadians appear to place a higher value on the environment than the Southern European countries and most developing countries (though this may reflect variations in the financial ability to act on this value rather than in the value itself).[23]

These differences in attitudes are reflected in consumer's purchase decisions, consumption practices, and recycling efforts. The average number of categories of items regularly recycled per household across a number of European countries shown below illustrates this point:[24]

Austria	5.1	Luxembourg	3.9
Belgium	3.0	Netherlands	4.1
Denmark	3.8	Norway	2.8
France	2.0	Portugal	0.7
Germany	4.8	Spain	0.7
Greece	0.3	Sweden	4.1
Ireland	0.7	Switzerland	5.0
Italy	3.0	United Kingdom	2.2

The power of environmental concern in countries such as Germany can be seen by the success of Greuner Frosch (Green Frog) household cleaners. The family-owned firm launched the line of environmentally friendly cleaners in 1985. Despite its small size and limited advertising, the firm has captured market share from such multinationals as Unilever, P&G, Henkel, and Colgate-Palmolive by offering products less harmful to the environment. For example while P&G, Unilever, and Henkel sell a concentrated detergent that uses one-third less powder and packaging than standard detergents, the Gruener Frosch brand uses only one-half as much.

Self-Oriented Values

Active/Passive Are people expected to take a physically active approach to work and play? Are physical skills and feats valued more highly than less physical performances? Is emphasis placed on doing? Americans are much more prone to engage in physical activities and to take an action-oriented approach to problems. ''Don't just stand there, DO SOMETHING,'' is a common response to problems in America. Active exercise is rare among women in most countries other than the United States. This is true even in European countries.[25] While this obviously limits the market for exercise equipment in these countries, it also affects advertising themes and formats. For example, the ad shown in Managerial Application 1–4 (page 14) would not be appropriate in most countries.

Material/Nonmaterial Is the accumulation of material wealth a positive good in its own right? Does material wealth bring more status than family ties, knowledge, or other activities? The data below show the percents of people from various European countries who agree with the statement: ''In the next 10 years most people will rather have more leisure than more money.''[26]

Austria	62%	Great Britain	41%
Belgium	57	Greece	34
Denmark	45	Ireland	45
Finland	66	Italy	39
France	64	Luxembourg	47

MANAGERIAL APPLICATION 2–2

The Appeal of Achievement and Status as Reflected in Material Possessions Are Effective in Many Cultures

Netherlands	73	Sweden	51
Norway	42	Switzerland	40
Portugal	36	West Germany	39
Spain	38		

The Chrysler ad from a German magazine shown in Managerial Application 2–2 appeals to the desire for status associated with material possessions. This German ad is very similar to ads used in America, as both cultures are relatively materialistic.

There are two types of materialism. **Instrumental materialism** is the acquisition of things to enable one to do something. Skis can be acquired to allow one to ski. **Terminal materialism** is the acquisition of items for the sake of owning the item itself. Art is generally acquired for the pleasure of owning it rather than as a means to another goal. Cultures differ markedly in their relative emphasis on these two types of materialism. For example, a substantial percentage of advertisements in both the United States and Japan have a materialistic theme. However, instrumental materialism is most common in U.S. advertising, while terminal materialism is predominant in Japanese ads.[27]

A further description of cultural variation in the meaning of material items is presented in the section on nonverbal communications.

Hard Work/Leisure Is work valued for itself, independent of external rewards, or is work merely a ''means to an end''? Will individuals continue to work hard even when their minimum economic needs are satisfied, or will they opt for more leisure time? In parts of Latin America, work is viewed as a necessary evil. However, in much of Europe work is considered essential for a full life. Labor-saving products and instant food often met with failure in countries such as Switzerland and Italy.

Postponed Gratification/Immediate Gratification Is one encouraged to ''save for a rainy day,'' or should one ''live for today''? Is it better to secure immediate benefits and pleasures, or is it better to suffer in the short run for benefits in the future (or in the hereafter or for future generations)?

This value has implications for distribution strategies, efforts to encourage savings, and the use of credit.[28] For example, in Germany and the Netherlands, buying on credit is widely viewed as living beyond one's means. In fact, the word for debt in German (*schuld*) is the same word used for ''guilt.''

Sensual Gratification/Abstinence Is it acceptable to pamper oneself, to satisfy one's desires for food, drink, or sex beyond the minimum requirement? Is one who forgoes such gratification considered virtuous or strange? Muslim cultures are very, very conservative on this value. Advertisements, packages, and products must carefully conform to Muslim standards. Polaroid's instant cameras gained rapid acceptance because they allowed Arab men to photograph their wives and daughters without fear that a stranger in a film laboratory would see the women unveiled.

In contrast, Brazilian advertisements contain nudity and blatant (by U.S. standards) appeals to sensual gratification. Consider the following prime-time television ad for women's underwear:

> A maitre d' hands menus to a couple seated at a restaurant table. When the man opens his menu to the ''chef's suggestion,'' he has a ''vision'' of a woman's bare torso and arms. She then pulls on a pair of panties.
>
> ''What a dish!'' he exclaims, only to have another ''vision,'' this time of a woman unclasping her front-closing bra to fully expose her breasts.
>
> The man slumps under the table to the consternation of both his wife and the waiter.[29]

Humor/Serious Is life a serious and frequently sad affair, or is it something to be taken lightly and laughed at when possible? Cultures differ in the extent to which humor is accepted and appreciated and in the nature of what qualifies as humor.[30] Americans see little or no conflict between humor and serious communication. The Japanese do see a conflict. In their view, if a person is serious, the talk is completely serious; when a person tells jokes or funny stories, the entire situation is to be taken lightly.[31] Personal selling techniques and promotional messages should be developed with an awareness of a culture's position on this value dimension.

Clearly, the preceding discussion has not covered all of the values operating in the various cultures. However, it should suffice to provide a feel for the importance of cultural values and how cultures differ along value dimensions.

CULTURAL VARIATIONS IN NONVERBAL COMMUNICATIONS

Differences in verbal communication systems are immediately obvious to anyone entering a foreign culture. An American traveling in Britain or Australia will be able to communicate, but differences in pronunciation, timing, and meaning will be readily apparent. For example, to "table a report or motion" in the United States means to postpone discussion, while in England it means to give the matter priority. These differences are easy to notice and accept because we realize that language is an arbitrary invention. The meaning assigned to a particular group of letters or sounds is not inherent in the letters or sounds. A word means what a group of people agree that it will mean.

Attempts to translate marketing communications from one language to another can result in ineffective communications, as Ford Motor Company is painfully aware:

> Fiera (a low-cost truck designed for developing countries) faced sales problems since *fierra* means "ugly old woman" in Spanish. The popular Ford car Comet had limited sales in Mexico, where it was named Caliente. The reason—*caliente* is slang for a streetwalker. The Pinto was briefly introduced in Brazil without a name change. Then it was discovered that *pinto* is slang for a "small male sex organ." The name was changed to Corcel, which means horse.[32]

Coca-Cola Company avoided the problems Ford encountered by realizing that *enjoy*, which is part of its famous logo *Enjoy Coca-Cola*, has sensual connotations in Russian and several other languages. As Managerial Application 2–1 (page 38) indicates, Coca-Cola solved this problem by changing the logo to *Drink Coca-Cola* where appropriate.

Exhibit 2–3 indicates that Ford is not the only company to encounter translation problems. The problems of literal translations and slang expressions are compounded by symbolic meanings associated with words, the absence of certain words from key languages, and the difficulty of pronouncing certain words:

- Taco Time recently expanded into the Japanese market but had to position its menu as American Western rather than Mexican, because the Japanese have a negative image of Mexico.
- Mars addressed the problem of making the M&M's name pronounceable in France, where neither ampersands nor the apostrophe "s" plural form exists, by advertising extensively that M&M's should be pronounced "aimainaimze." Whirlpool is facing a similar problem in Spain, as its name is virtually unpronounceable in Spanish.
- In the Middle East, consumers often refer to a product category by the name of the leading brand. Thus, all brands of vacuum cleaners are referred to as Hoovers and all laundry detergents are Tide.
- To market its Ziploc food storage bags in Brazil, Dow Chemical had to use extensive advertising to create the word "zipar," meaning to zip, since there was no such term in Portuguese.

In addition, such communication factors as humor and preferred style and pace vary across cultures, even those speaking the same basic language.[33] Nonetheless, verbal language translations generally do not present major problems as long as we are careful. What many of us fail to recognize, however, is that each culture also has nonverbal communication systems or languages that, like verbal languages, are specific to each culture. Unlike verbal languages, most of us think of our nonverbal languages as being innate or natural rather than learned. Therefore, when we encounter a foreign culture, we tend to assign our own culture's meanings to the nonverbal signs being utilized by the other culture. The

EXHIBIT 2–3 Translation Problems in International Marketing

- An American airline operating in Brazil advertised the plush "rendezvous lounges" on its jets only to discover that *rendezvous* in Portuguese means a room hired for lovemaking.
- General Motors' "body by Fisher" was translated as "corpse by Fisher" in Flemish.
- Colgate's Cue toothpaste had problems in France as *cue* is a crude term for "butt" in French.
- In Germany, Pepsi's advertisement, "Come alive with Pepsi," was presented as "Come alive out of the grave with Pepsi."
- Sunbeam attempted to enter the German market with a mist-producing curling iron named the Mist-Stick. Unfortunately, *mist* translates as "dung" or "manure" in German.
- Pet milk encounters difficulties in French-speaking countries where *pet* means, among other things, "to break wind."
- Fresca is a slang word for "lesbian" in Mexico.
- Esso found that its name phonetically meant "stalled car" in Japanese.
- Kellogg's Bran Buds translates to "burned farmer" in Swedish.
- United Airline's inflight magazine cover for its Pacific Rim routes showed Australian actor Paul Hogan in the outback. The caption stated, "Paul Hogan Camps It Up." Unfortunately, "camps it up" is Australian slang for "flaunts his homosexuality."
- A car wash was translated into German as "car enema."
- China attempted to export Pansy brand men's underwear to America.

problem is compounded by the fact that the "foreigner" is interpreting our nonverbal cues by the "dictionary" used in his or her own culture. The frequent result is misunderstanding, unsuccessful sales calls and advertising campaigns, and, on occasion, long-lasting bitterness.

The following discussion examines seven variables (shown in Figure 2–5) we consider to be nonverbal languages: time, space, friendship, agreements, things, symbols, and etiquette.[34]

Time

The meaning of time varies between cultures in two major ways. First is what we call time perspective: this is a culture's overall orientation toward time. The second is the interpretations assigned to specific uses of time.[35]

Time Perspective Americans and Canadians tend to view time as inescapable, linear, and fixed in nature. It is a road reaching into the future with distinct, separate sections (hours, days, weeks, and so on). Time is seen almost as a physical object: we can schedule it, waste it, lose it, and so forth. We believe a person does one thing at a time. We have a strong orientation toward the present and the short-term future. This is known as a **monochronic** view of time.

Factors Influencing Nonverbal Communications

FIGURE 2-5

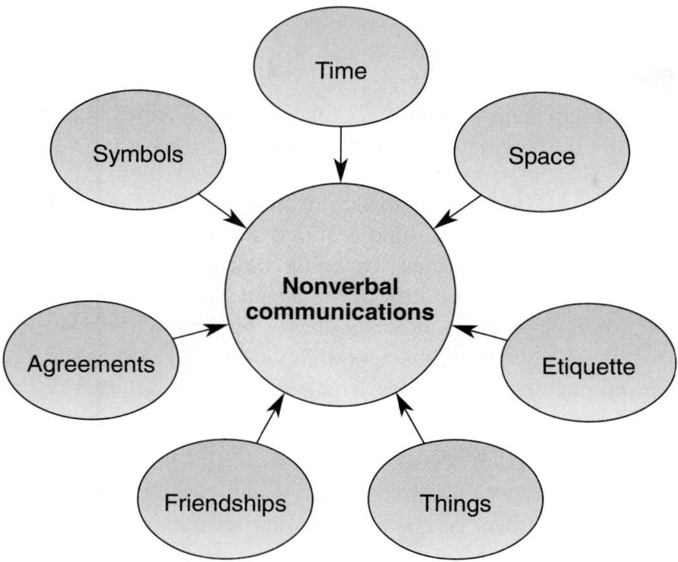

Other cultures have different time perspectives. Latin Americans tend to view time as being less discrete and less subject to scheduling. They view simultaneous involvement in many activities as natural. People and relationships take priority over schedules, and activities occur at their own pace rather than according to a predetermined timetable. They have an orientation toward the present and the past. This is known as a **polychronic** time perspective.

Some of the important differences between individuals with a monochronic perspective and those with a polychronic perspective are listed below.[36]

Monochronic Culture	Polychronic Culture
Do one thing at a time	Do many things at once
Concentrate on the job	Highly distractible and subject to interruptions
Take deadlines and schedules seriously	Consider deadlines and schedules secondary
Committed to the job or task	Committed to people and relationships
Adhere religiously to plans	Change plans often and easily
Emphasize promptness	Base promptness on the relationship
Accustomed to short-term relationships	Prefer long-term relationships

As the following examples illustrate, time perspectives affect marketing practice in a variety of ways:

- An American firm introduced a filter-tip cigarette into an Asian culture. However, it soon became evident that the venture would fail. One of the main advertised advantages of filter cigarettes was that they would provide future benefits in the form of reduced risks of lung cancer. However, future benefits were virtually meaningless in this society, which was strongly oriented to the present.

- The high value that Americans place on ''saving time'' is not shared by all other cultures. This has made convenience or timesaving products less valued in many cultures. For example, fast-food outlets including Wimpy, Kentucky Fried Chicken, Jack in the Box, and McDonald's have found the Latin American markets difficult to penetrate.
- In contrast, the high value assigned to time by the Japanese has made them very receptive to many timesaving convenience goods.

Meanings in the Use of Time Specific uses of time have varying meanings in different cultures. In much of the world, the time required for a decision is proportional to the importance of the decision. Americans, by being well prepared with ''ready answers,'' may adversely downplay the importance of the business being discussed. Likewise, both Japanese and Middle Eastern executives are put off by Americans' insistence on coming to the point directly and quickly in business transactions. Greek managers find the American habit of setting time limits for business meetings to be insulting. Consider the following advice from a business consultant:

> In many countries we are seen to be in a rush; in other words, unfriendly, arrogant, and untrustworthy. Almost everywhere, we must learn to wait patiently and never to push for deadlines. Count on things taking a long time, the definition of ''a long time'' being at least *twice* as long as you would imagine.[37]

The lead time required for scheduling an event varies widely. One week is the minimum lead time for most social activities in America. However, a week represents the maximum lead time in many Arabic countries.

Promptness is considered very important in America and Japan. Furthermore, promptness is defined as being on time for appointments, whether you are the person making the call or the person receiving the caller. The variation in waiting time between cultures is illustrated in this story:

> Arriving a little before the hour (the American respect pattern), he waited. The hour came and passed; 5 minutes—10 minutes—15 minutes. At this point he suggested to the secretary that perhaps the minister did not know he was waiting in the outer office . . . 20 minutes—25 minutes—30 minutes—45 minutes (the insult period)!
>
> He jumped up and told the secretary that he had been ''cooling his heels'' in an outer office for 45 minutes and he was ''damned sick and tired'' of this type of treatment.
>
> The principal source of misunderstanding lay in the fact that in the country in question, the five-minute delay interval was not significant. Forty-five minutes, on the other hand, instead of being at the tail end of the waiting scale, was just barely at the beginning. To suggest to an American's secretary that perhaps her boss didn't know you were there after waiting 60 seconds would seem absurd, as would raising a storm about ''cooling your heels'' for five minutes. Yet this is precisely the way the minister registered the protestations of the American in his outer office.[38]

Space

The use people make of space and the meanings they assign to their use of space constitute a second form of nonverbal communication. In America, ''bigger is better.'' Thus, office space in corporations generally is allocated according to rank or prestige rather than need. The president will have the largest office, followed by the executive vice president, and so on. The fact that a lower echelon executive's work may require a large space seldom plays a major role in office allocation.

Americans tend to separate the offices of supervisors from the work space of subordinates. The French tend to place supervisors in the midst of subordinates. In the United States, the chief executive offices are on the top floor, and production, maintenance, or "bargain basements" are located on the lowest floor. In Japanese department stores, the bargain "basement" is located on an upper floor.

Americans tend to personalize their work space and consider it their own. Few Americans would be comfortable in the following environment:

> In Tokyo, office space is four times as expensive as in Manhattan. In response, IBM Japan provides only 4,300 desks for its 5,000 sales representatives since at least 700 are generally out on a sales call at any point in time. When sales representatives arrive at the office, they check a computer to see which desk is empty, take their personal filing cabinet from storage and roll it to the available desk where they work until they need to visit a customer. Each time they leave, they clear the desk and return their file cabinet to storage.[39]

A second major use of space is **personal space**. It is the nearest that others can come to you in various situations without your feeling uncomfortable. In the United States normal business conversations occur at distances of 5 to 8 feet and highly personal business from 18 inches to 3 feet. In parts of Northern Europe the distances are slightly longer, while in most of Latin America, they are substantially shorter.

An American businessperson in Latin America will tend to back away from a Latin American counterpart in order to maintain his or her preferred personal distance. In turn, the host will tend to advance toward the American in order to maintain his or her personal space. The resulting "chase" would be comical if it were not for the results. Both parties generally are unaware of their actions or the reasons for them. Furthermore, each assigns a meaning to the other's actions based on what the action means in his or her own culture. Thus, the North American considers the Latin American to be pushy and aggressive. The Latin American, in turn, considers the North American to be cold, aloof, and snobbish.

Friendship

The rights and obligations imposed by friendship are another nonverbal cultural variable. Americans, more so than most other cultures, make friends quickly and easily and drop them easily also. In large part, this may be due to the fact that America has always had a great deal of both social and geographic mobility. People who move every few years must be able to form friendships in a short time period and depart from them with a minimum of pain. In many other parts of the world, friendships are formed slowly and carefully because they imply deep and lasting obligations. As the following quote indicates, friendship and business are intertwined in most of the world:

> To most Asians and Latin Americans, good personal relationships and feelings are all that really matter in a long-term agreement. After all, the written word is less important than personal ties. Once personal trust has been established, cooperation increases. The social contacts developed between the parties are often far more significant than the technical specifications and the price. In many countries the heart of the matter, the major point of the negotiations, is getting to know the people involved. Brazilians and many Latin Americans cannot depend on their own legal system to iron out conflicts, so they must depend on personal relationships.

> Americans negotiate a contract, the Japanese negotiate a relationship. In many cultures, the written word is used simply to satisfy legalities. In their eyes, emotion and personal relations are more important than cold facts. The key issue is, "can I get along with these people and their company and do I want to sell (or buy) their products?" rather than "can I make money on this deal?" They are particularly interested in the sincerity of those with whom they are negotiating. The Japanese are especially unwilling to do business with someone they think may be arrogant or unpleasant: "I do not do business with someone who does not like us!" The Japanese do not separate personal feelings from business relationships.
>
> Personal affinity is also immensely important to Mexicans and other Latin Americans. The goal is to nurture a mutual confidence, engage in informal discussions, and seek solutions to problems. Therefore, personal rapport, preliminary meetings, telephone conversations, and social activities are necessary.[40]

Attempts to imitate Avon's American success in Europe were unsuccessful. Avon's use of homemakers to sell beauty products to their friends and neighbors was not acceptable in much of Europe, in part because of a strong reluctance to sell to friends at a profit. However, in Mexico the approach was very successful as the Mexican homemaker found the sales call an excellent opportunity to socialize.

Friendship often replaces the legal or contractual system for ensuring that business and other obligations are honored. In countries without a well-established and easily enforceable commercial code, many people insist on doing business only with friends. An international business consultant offers the following advice on this point:

> Product and pricing and clear contracts are not as important as the *personal relationship and trust* that is developed carefully and sincerely over time. The marketer must be established as simpatico, worthy of the business, and dependable *in the long run*. Contracts abroad often do not mean what they do here, so interpersonal understanding and bonds are important. Often business is not discussed until after *several* meetings, and in any one meeting business is only discussed after lengthy social conversation. The American must learn to sit on the catalog until the relationship has been established.[41]

Agreements

Americans rely on an extensive and, generally, highly efficient legal system for ensuring that business obligations are honored and for resolving disagreements. Many other cultures have not evolved such a system and rely instead on friendship and kinship, local moral principles, or informal customs to guide business conduct. For example, in China the business relationship is subordinate to the moralistic notion of a friendship. Under the American system, we would examine a proposed contract closely. Under the Chinese system, we would examine the character of a potential trading partner closely.

When is an agreement concluded? Americans consider the signing of a contract to be the end of negotiations. However, to many Greeks and Russians such a signing is merely the signal to begin serious negotiations that will continue until the project is completed. At the other extreme, presenting a contract for a signature can be insulting to an Arab, who considered the verbal agreement to be completely binding.

We also assume that, in almost all instances, prices are uniform for all buyers, related to the service rendered, and reasonably close to the going rate. We order many products such as taxi rides without inquiring in advance about the cost. In many Latin American and Arab countries the procedure is different. Virtually all prices are negotiated *prior* to the sale. If a product such as a taxi ride is consumed without first establishing the price, the customer must pay whatever fee is demanded by the seller. Likewise, decision processes, negotiating styles, and risk strategies vary across cultures.[42]

Things

Items conveying dependability and respectability to the English would often seem out-of-date and backward to Americans. Japanese homes would seem empty and barren to many Americans. In addition to assigning different meanings to the possession of various objects, cultures differ in the degree to which they value the acquisition of goods as an end in itself (terminal materialism) or as a means to an end, such as acquisition of a graphite racket to play tennis (instrumental materialism). Such differences lead to problems in determining salary schedules, bonuses, gifts, product designs, and advertising themes.

The differing meanings that cultures attach to things, including products, make gift-giving a particularly difficult task.[43] The business and social situations that call for a gift, and the items that are appropriate gifts, vary widely. For example, a gift of cutlery is generally inappropriate in Russia, Taiwan, and West Germany. In Japan, small gifts are required in many business situations, yet in China they are inappropriate. In China, gifts should be presented privately but in Arab countries they should be given in front of others.

Symbols

If you were to see a baby wearing a pink outfit, you would most likely assume the child is female. If the outfit were blue, you would probably assume the child is male. These assumptions would be accurate most of the time in the United States but would not be accurate in many other parts of the world such as Holland. Failure to recognize the meaning assigned to a color or other symbols can cause serious problems:

- A manufacturer of water-recreation products lost heavily in Malaysia because the company's predominant color, green, was associated with the jungle and illness.
- A leading U.S. golf ball manufacturer was initially disappointed in its attempts to penetrate the Japanese market. Its mistake was packaging its golf balls in sets of four. Four is a symbol of death in Japanese.
- Pepsi-Cola lost its dominant market share in Southeast Asia to Coke when it changed the color of its coolers and vending equipment from deep "regal" blue to light "ice" blue. Light blue is associated with death and mourning in Southeast Asia.
- Most Chinese business travelers were shocked during the inauguration of United's concierge services for first-class passengers on its Pacific Rim routes. To mark the occasion, each concierge was proudly wearing a white carnation—an oriental symbol of death.
- AT&T had to change its "thumbs-up" ads in Russia and Poland where showing the palm of the hand in this manner has an offensive meaning. The change was simple. The thumbs-up sign was given showing the back of the hand.

Exhibit 2–4 presents additional illustrations of varying meanings assigned to symbols across cultures.

EXHIBIT 2–4 The Meaning of Numbers, Colors, and Other Symbols

White:	Symbol for mourning or death in the Far East; happiness, purity in United States.
Purple:	Associated with death in many Latin American countries.
Blue:	Connotation of femininity in Holland; masculinity in Sweden, United States
Red:	Unlucky or negative in Chad, Nigeria, Germany; positive in Denmark, Rumania, Argentina. Brides wear red in China, but it is a masculine color in the United Kingdom and France.
Yellow flowers:	Sign of death in Mexico; infidelity in France.
White lilies:	Suggestion of death in England.
7:	Unlucky number in Ghana, Kenya, Singapore; lucky in Morocco, India, Czechoslovakia, Nicaragua, United States.
Triangle:	Negative in Hong Kong, Korea, Taiwan; positive in Colombia.
Owl:	Wisdom in United States; bad luck in India.
Deer:	Speed, grace in United States; homosexuality in Brazil.

Etiquette

Etiquette represents generally accepted ways of behaving in social situations. Assume that an American is preparing a commercial that shows people eating an evening meal, with one person about to take a bite of food from a fork. The person will have the fork in the right hand, and the left hand will be out of sight under the table. To an American audience this will seem natural. However, in many European cultures, a well-mannered individual would have the fork in the left hand and the right hand on the table! Likewise, portraying the American custom of patting a child on the head would be inappropriate in the Orient, where the head is considered sacred.

Behaviors considered rude or obnoxious in one culture may be quite acceptable in another. The common and acceptable American habit (for males) of crossing one's legs while sitting, such that the sole of a shoe shows, is extremely insulting in many Eastern cultures. In these cultures, the sole of the foot or shoe should never be exposed to view. Yet, some American ads show managers with their feet on the desk, soles exposed!

As American trade with Japan increases, we continue to learn more of the subtle aspects of Japanese business etiquette. For example, a Japanese executive will seldom say no directly during negotiations, as this would be considered impolite. Instead, he might say,

EXHIBIT 2–5

The Exchange of Meishi (MAY-shee) in Japan

"Your meishi is your face."
"Meishi is most necessary here. It is absolutely essential."
"A man without a meishi has no identity in Japan."

The exchange of meishi is the most basic of social rituals in a nation where social ritual matters very much. It solidifies a personal contact in a nation where personal contacts are the indispensable ingredient for success in any field. The act of exchanging meishi is weighted with meaning. Once the social minuet is completed, the two know where they stand in relation to each other, and their respective statures within the hierarchy of corporate or government bureaucracy.

What is this mysterious "exchange of meishi"? It is the exchange of business cards when two people meet! A fairly common, simple activity in America, it is an essential, complex social exchange in Japan.

"That will be very difficult," which would mean no. A Japanese responding *yes* to a request often means "Yes, I understand the request," *not* "Yes, I agree to the request." Many Japanese find the American tendency to look straight into another's eyes when talking to be aggressive and rude. An example of another aspect of Japanese business etiquette, *meishi*, is provided in Exhibit 2–5.

The importance of proper, culture-specific etiquette for sales personnel and advertising messages is obvious. Although people are apt to recognize that etiquette varies from culture to culture, there is still a strong emotional feeling that "our way is natural and right."

Conclusions on Nonverbal Communications

Can you imagine yourself becoming upset or surprised because people in a different culture spoke to you in their native language, say Spanish, French, or German, instead of English? Of course not. We all recognize that verbal languages vary around the world. Yet we generally feel that our nonverbal languages are natural or innate. Therefore, we misinterpret what is being "said" to us because we think we are hearing English when in reality it is Japanese, Italian, or Russian. It is this error that marketers must and can avoid.

CROSS-CULTURAL MARKETING STRATEGY

During the 1980s, there was intense controversy over the extent to which cross-cultural marketing strategies, particularly advertising, should be standardized.[44] Standardized strategies can result in substantial cost savings. The Hanes ad shown in Managerial Application 2–3 can be used in many countries with little alteration. Campbell Soup is succeeding worldwide but the particular soups range from the traditional chicken noodle in the United States to creme of chili in Mexico, split pea with ham in Argentina, peppery tripe in Poland, and watercress and duck-gizzard in China.

Stick Ups, a room deodorizer, quickly achieved success in the United States and shortly thereafter in England. However, research produced the following changes before Stick Ups were introduced in England:

MANAGERIAL APPLICATION

2–3

Many Marketing Messages Require Little Change across Cultures

1. The strength of the product's fragrance was greatly increased to meet British preferences.
2. The U.S. cardboard twin-pack was changed to a single blister pack. The higher costs associated with the increased fragrance made this necessary to encourage trial.
3. The advertisements showed the product in less conspicuous places than had the American ads, since the British preferred an unobtrusive product.
4. The media mix was shifted away from radio and into print media and billboards.

The critical decision is whether utilizing a standardized marketing strategy, in any given market, will result in a greater return on investment than would an individualized campaign. Thus, the consumer response to the standardized campaign and to potential individualized campaigns must be considered in addition to the cost of each approach. Ford, like many other global firms, now follows a ''pattern standardization'' strategy whereby the overall strategy is designed from the outset to be susceptible to extensive modification to suit local conditions while maintaining sufficient common elements to minimize the drain on resources and management time.[45]

EXHIBIT 2–6

Key Questions in Developing a Cross-Cultural Marketing Strategy

1. Is the geographic area homogeneous or heterogeneous with respect to culture?
   Are there distinct subcultures in the geographic area under consideration? How narrow are the behavioral boundaries or norms imposed by the culture(s)?
2. What needs can this product fill in this culture?
   What needs, if any, does this product currently meet in this culture? Are there other needs it could satisfy? What products are currently meeting these needs? How important are these needs to the people in the culture?
3. Can enough of the group(s) needing the product afford the product?
   How many people need the product and can afford it? How many need it and cannot afford it? Can financing be obtained? Is a government subsidy possible?
4. What values are relevant to the purchase and use of the product?
   Is the decision maker the husband or wife? Adult or child? Will use of the product contradict any values, such as hard work as a positive good? Will ownership of the product go against any values such as a nonmaterial orientation? Will the purchase of the product require any behavior, such as financing, that might contradict a value? What values support the consumption of the product?
5. What is the distribution, political, and legal structure concerning this product?
   Where do consumers expect to buy the product? What legal requirements must the product meet? What legal requirements must the marketing mix meet?
6. In what ways can we communicate about this product?
   What language(s) can we use? What forms of nonverbal communications will affect our salespeople, packages, and advertisements? What kinds of appeals will fit with the culture's value system?
7. What are the ethical implications of marketing this product in this manner in this country?
   Might the use of this product impair the health or well-being of those using it? Will the consumption of this product divert resources from beneficial uses? Might the use or disposition of this product have negative side effects on the environment or economy?

Considerations in Approaching a Foreign Market

Exhibit 2–6 lists seven key considerations for each geographic market that a firm is contemplating. An analysis of these seven variables provides the background necessary for deciding whether or not to enter the market and to what extent, if any, an individualized marketing strategy is required. A small sample of experts, preferably native to the market under consideration, often will be able to furnish sufficient information on each variable.

MANAGERIAL APPLICATION

2–4

Anheuser-Busch's Response to Cultural Pluralism

Anheuser-Busch has successfully introduced Budweiser throughout Canada, including Quebec. It has achieved an equal penetration among both English and French Canadians. However, two distinct marketing approaches were used to reach the two cultural groups.

Since Budweiser was well known among the English-speaking Canadians (due in large part to American television viewing), the theme "This Bud's for You" was used in a manner very similar to the American campaign. The main differences were the inclusion of a Canadian flag, social references to Quebec, and stress on the fact that Canadian Bud has 5 percent alcohol (stronger than American beers but standard for Canada).

Budweiser was relatively unknown among French-speaking Canadians. Therefore, a strategy was built which tied Bud to "the positive values of American society." Since French Canadians view rock 'n' roll as a positive aspect of America, the classic song, "Rock Around the Clock," is the theme for the two French commercials. One is a *Happy Days*-type scene with young adults dancing to "Rock Around the Clock" with the words "rock, rock, rock" replaced by "Bud, Bud, Bud."

Is the Geographic Area Homogeneous or Heterogeneous with Respect to Culture? Marketing efforts are generally directed at defined geographic areas, primarily political and economic entities. Legal requirements and existing distribution channels often encourage this approach. However, it is also supported by the implicit assumption that geographical or political boundaries coincide with cultural boundaries. This assumption is incorrect more often than not.

Canada provides a clear example. Many American firms treat the Canadian market as though it were a single cultural unit despite the fact that they must make adjustments for language differences. However, studies have found French Canadians to differ from English Canadians in attitudes toward instant foods and spending money; in spending patterns toward expensive liquors, clothing, personal care items, tobacco, soft drinks, candy, and instant coffee; in television and radio usage patterns; and in eating patterns.[46] Managerial Application 2–4 describes Anheuser Busch's successful response to cultural pluralism in Canada.

What Needs Can This Product or a Version of It Fill in This Culture? While not exactly in accordance with the marketing concept, most firms examine a new market with an existing product or product technology in mind. The question they must answer is what needs their existing or modified product can fill in the culture involved. For example, bicycles and motorcycles serve primarily recreational needs in the United States, but provide basic transportation in many other countries.

General Foods has successfully positioned Tang as a substitute for orange juice at breakfast in the United States. However, in analyzing the French market, they found that the French drink little orange juice and almost none at breakfast. Therefore, a totally different positioning strategy was used; Tang was promoted as a new type of refreshing drink, for any time of the day.

Managerial Application 2–5 indicates that Toys "R" Us successfully meets the needs of consumers in many countries.

MANAGERIAL APPLICATION 2-5

Value and Selection Are Desired in Most Cultures

Can Enough of the Group(s) Needing the Product Afford the Product? This requires an initial demographic analysis to determine the number of individuals or households that might need the product and the number that can probably afford it. In addition, the possibilities of establishing credit, obtaining a government subsidy, or making a less expensive version should be considered. For example, Levi Strauss de Argentina launched a trade-in campaign in which consumers received a 50,000 peso (about $7) "reward" for turning in an old pair of jeans with the purchase of a new pair. A strong recession in Argentina prompted the action.

What Values or Patterns of Values Are Relevant to the Purchase and Use of This Product? The first section of this chapter focused on values and their role in consumer behavior. The value system should be investigated for influences on purchasing the product, owning the product, using the product, and disposing of the product. Much of the marketing strategy will be based on this analysis.

What Are the Distribution, Political, and Legal Structures for the Product? The legal structure of a country can have an impact on each aspect of a firm's marketing mix. For example, the Mexican government requested Anderson Clayton & Co. to "tone down" its commercials for Capulla mayonnaise because the advertisements were ''too aggressive.'' The aggression involved direct comparisons with competing brands (comparative advertising), which is not acceptable in Mexico (it is also illegal in Japan). Regulation of marketing activities, particularly advertising, is increasing throughout the world. Unfortunately, uniform regulations are not emerging. This increases the complexity and cost of international marketing.

The distribution channels and consumer expectations concerning where to secure products vary widely across cultures. In the Netherlands, drugstores do not sell prescription drugs (they are sold at an *apotheek*, or apothecary, which sells nothing else). Existing channels and consumer expectations generally must be considered as fixed, at least in the short run.

In What Ways Can We Communicate about the Product? This question requires an investigation into: (1) available media and who attends to each type, (2) the needs the product fills, (3) values associated with the product and its use, and (4) the verbal and nonverbal communications systems in the culture(s).[47] All aspects of the firm's promotional mix (including packaging, nonfunctional product design features, personal selling techniques, and advertising) should be based on these four factors.

For example, BSR Ltd. of Japan, an importer of phonographic turntables and changers from Britain, initially was unsuccessful because of its packaging strategy. The Japanese consumer uses a product's package as an important indicator of product quality. Thus, the standard shipping carton used by BSR, while it protected the product adequately, did not convey a high-quality image. To overcome this problem, BSR began packaging its phonograph equipment in two cartons: one for shipping and one for point-of-purchase display.

The House of Chanel was unable to use its current Chanel No. 5 campaign, which is very popular in Europe, in the United States. The television commercial features French actress Carole Bouquet seductively whispering to an unseen man: ''You hate me, don't you? Hate is a troubling emotion, very troubling. I hate you so much that I think I'm going to die of it. My love.'' Extensive testing revealed that American audiences associated the ad with violence and found it unacceptable.[48]

What Are the Ethical Implications of Marketing This Product in This Country? All marketing programs should be evaluated on ethical as well as financial dimensions. However, the ethical dimension is particularly important and complex in marketing to Third World and developing countries.[49] Consider the opening illustration of this chapter. The following questions represent the type of ethical analysis that should go into the decision:

> If we succeed, will the average nutrition level be increased or decreased?
>
> If we succeed, will the funds spent on cereal be diverted from other uses with more beneficial long-term impact for the individuals or society?
>
> If we succeed, what impact will this have on the local producers of currently consumed breakfast products?

Understanding and acting on ethical considerations in international marketing is a difficult task. However, it is also a necessary one.

SUMMARY

Culture is defined as that complex whole which includes knowledge, beliefs, art, law, morals, custom, and any other capabilities acquired by humans as members of society. Culture includes almost everything that influences an individual's thought processes and behaviors.

Culture operates primarily by setting boundaries for individual behavior and by influencing the functioning of such institutions as the family and mass media. The boundaries or *norms* are derived from *cultural values.* Values are widely held beliefs that affirm what is desirable. Cultures change when values change, the environment changes, or when dramatic events occur.

Cultural values are classified into three categories: other, environment, and self. *Other-oriented values* reflect a society's view of the appropriate relationships between individuals and groups within that society. Relevant values of this nature include *individual/collective, romantic orientation, adult/child, masculine/feminine, competitive/cooperative,* and *youth/age.*

Environment-oriented values prescribe a society's relationships with its economic, technical, and physical environments. Examples of environment values are *cleanliness, performance/status, tradition/change, risk taking/security, problem solving/fatalistic,* and *nature.*

Self-oriented values reflect the objectives and approaches to life that individual members of society find desirable. These include *active/passive, material/nonmaterial, hard work/leisure, postponed gratification/immediate gratification, sensual gratification/abstinence,* and *humor/serious.*

Differences in *verbal* communication systems are immediately obvious across cultures and must be taken into account by marketers wishing to do business in those cultures. Probably more important, however, and certainly more difficult to recognize are *nonverbal communication differences.* Major examples of nonverbal communication variables that affect marketers are *time, space, friendship, agreement, things, symbols,* and *etiquette.*

Seven questions are relevant for developing a cross-cultural marketing strategy. First, is the geographic area homogeneous with respect to culture? Second, what needs can this product fill in this culture? Third, can enough people afford the product? Fourth, what values are relevant to the purchase and use of the product? Fifth, what are the distribution, political, and legal structures concerning this product? Sixth, how can we communicate about the product? Seventh, what are the ethical implications of marketing this product in this country?

REVIEW QUESTIONS

1. What is meant by the term *culture*?
2. Does culture provide a detailed prescription for behavior in most modern societies? Why or why not?
3. What does the statement ''Culture sets boundaries on behaviors'' mean?
4. Are we generally aware of how culture influences our behavior? Why or why not?
5. What is a *norm*? From what are norms derived?
6. What is a *cultural value*?
7. What is a *sanction*?
8. How do cultures and cultural values change?
9. Cultural values can be classified as affecting one of three types of relationships—other, environment, or self. Describe each of these, and differentiate each one from the others.
10. How does a _______ orientation differ from a _______ orientation?
    a. Individual/Collective.
    b. Performance/Status.
    c. Tradition/Change.
    d. Active/Passive.
    e. Material/Nonmaterial.
    f. Hard Work/Leisure.
    g. Risk Taking/Security.
    h. Masculine/Feminine.
    i. Competitive/Cooperative
    j. Youth/Age.
    k. Problem Solving/Fatalistic.

l. Adult/Child.
m. Postponed Gratification/Immediate Gratification.
n. Sensual Gratification/Abstinence.
o. Humor/Serious.

11. What is meant by *nonverbal communications*? Why is this such a difficult area to adjust to?
12. What is meant by ______ as a form of nonverbal communication?
    a. Time.
    b. Space.
    c. Friendship.
    d. Agreements.
    e. Things.
    f. Symbols.
    g. Etiquette.
13. Give an example of how each of the variables listed in Question 12 could influence marketing practice.
14. What is the difference between *instrumental* and *terminal* materialism?
15. What are the differences between a *monochronic* time perspective and a *polychronic* time perspective?
16. What are the advantages and disadvantages of standardized international advertising?
17. What are the seven key considerations in deciding whether or not to enter a given international market?
18. What is meant by determining if a geographic area or political unit is "homogeneous or heterogeneous with respect to culture"? Why is this important?

DISCUSSION QUESTIONS

19. Why should we study foreign cultures if we do not plan to engage in international or export marketing?
20. Is a country's culture more likely to be reflected in its art museums or its television commercials? Why?
21. What are the marketing implications of Table 2–1?
22. What are the marketing implications of Table 2–2?
23. What insights can you gain from examining Tables 2–1 and 2–2 simultaneously?
24. What are the marketing implications of Figure 2–2?
25. What are the marketing implications of Table 2–3?
26. Based on Table 2–3, which European Community countries represent the best market for (a) wine, (b) mountain bikes, (c) jewelry? Justify your answer.
27. Are the cultures of the world becoming more similar or more distinct?
28. Why do values differ across cultures?
29. The text lists 18 cultural values of relevance to marketing practice. Describe and place into one of the three categories four additional cultural values that have some relevance to marketing practice.
30. Select two cultural values from each of the three categories. Describe the boundaries (norms) relevant to that value in your society and the sanctions for violating those norms.
31. What are the most relevant cultural values affecting the consumption of ______? Describe how and why these values are particularly important.
    a. Movies.
    b. Sports cars.
    c. Health food.
    d. Dishwashers.
    e. Perfume.
    f. Scotch whiskey.
32. What variations between the United States and other societies, *other than cultural variations*, may affect the relative level of usage of ______?
    a. Movies.
    b. Sports cars.
    c. Health food.
    d. Dishwashers.
    e. Perfume.
    f. Scotch whiskey.
33. The text suggested that variations in environmental actions by individuals and countries might reflect differing financial conditions rather than differing values. Do you agree with this? Why?
34. Why do Japanese ads focus more on terminal materialism while American ads focus more on instrumental materialism?
35. Is the European Community (EC) likely to become a relatively homogeneous culture by 2010?
36. What are the marketing implications of the

differences in the *adult/child orientation* across the 17 European countries shown in the text (page 41)?

37. What are the marketing implications of the differences in the *masculine/feminine orientation* across the 17 European countries shown in the text (pages 41–42)?
38. What are the marketing implications of the differences in the *cleanliness orientation* across the 17 European countries shown in the text (page 42)?
39. What are the marketing implications of the differences in the *environmental orientation* across the 16 European countries shown in the text (page 44)?
40. What are the marketing implications of the differences in the *material/nonmaterial orientation* across the 17 European countries shown in the text (pages 44–45)?
41. Why do nonverbal communication systems vary across cultures?
42. What, if any, nonverbal communication factors might be relevant in the marketing of ________?
    a. Health food.
    b. Perfume.
    c. Scotch whiskey.
    d. Laundry detergent.
    e. Toothpaste.
    f. Mountain bikes.
43. The text provides a seven-step procedure for analyzing a foreign market. Using this procedure, analyze your country as a market for:
    a. Automobiles from Indonesia.
    b. Shoes (women's) from Mexico.
    c. Perfume from Poland.
    d. Wine from Canada.
44. What are the major ethical issues in introducing prepared foods such as breakfast cereals to Third World countries?

PROJECT QUESTIONS

45. Interview two students from two different cultures. Determine the extent to which ________ are used in those cultures and the variations in the values of those cultures that relate to the use of ________.
    a. Bicycles.
    b. Perfume.
    c. Beer.
    d. Health food.
    e. Cigarettes.
    f. Television viewing.
46. Interview two students from two different foreign cultures. Report any differences in nonverbal communications they are aware of between their culture and your culture.
47. Interview two students from two different foreign cultures. Report their perceptions of the major differences in cultural values between their culture and your culture.
48. Interview a Korean and a Japanese student. Ask each to contrast his or her culture to the other's culture.
49. Interview a student from Mexico. Report on the advice that the student would give an American firm marketing consumer products in Mexico.
50. Interview two students from EC countries. Report on the extent to which they feel the EC will be a homogeneous culture by 2010.
51. Imagine you are a consultant working with your state or province's tourism agency. You have been asked to advise the agency on the best promotional themes to use to attract foreign tourists. What would you recommend if Korea and France were the two target markets?
52. Analyze a foreign culture of your choice and recommend a marketing program for a brand of ________ made in your country.
    a. Bicycle.
    b. Perfume.
    c. Beer.
    d. Health food.
    e. Automobile.
    f. Personal computer.
53. Examine foreign magazines and newspapers in your library or bookstore.
    a. Comment on any differences you notice in advertising from various countries. What causes this difference?
    b. Copy or describe ads from the same company that differ across countries. Explain the differences.

REFERENCES

[1]S. C. Jain, *International Marketing Management* (Boston: Kent Publishing, 1987), pp. 403–6.

[2]For another approach, see J. R. Wills, Jr., A. C. Samli, and L. Jacobs, "Developing Global Products and Marketing Strategies," *Journal of the Academy of Marketing Science*, Winter 1991, pp. 1–10; L. S. Amine, "Linking Consumer Behavior Constructs to International Marketing Strategy," and A. C. Samli, J. R. Wills, Jr., and L. Jacobs, "A Rejoinder," both in *Journal of the Academy of Marketing Science*, Winter, 1993, pp. 71–77 and 79–83.

[3]R. Bartos, "International Demographic Data? Incomparable!" *Marketing and Research Today*, November 1989, pp. 205–12.

[4]See J. F. Sherry, Jr., "The Cultural Perspective in Consumer Research," in *Advances in Consumer Research, XIII*, ed. R. J. Lutz (Chicago: Association for Consumer Research, 1986), pp. 573–75.

[5]See D. K. Tse, R. W. Belk, and N. Zhou, "Becoming a Consumer Society," *Journal of Consumer Research*, March 1989, pp. 457–72.

[6]For a treatment of the role of culture in international business, see V. Terpstra and K. David, *The Cultural Environment of International Business* (Cincinnati: South-Western Publishing, 1985) and D. A. Ricks, *Big Business Blunders* (Homewood, Ill.: Dow Jones-Irwin, 1983).

[7]S. P. Galante, "U. S. Companies Seek Advice on Avoiding Cultural Gaffes Abroad," *The Wall Street Journal*, European ed., July 20, 1984, sec. 1, p. 7.

[8]P. Kotler, "Global Standardization: Courting Danger," *Journal of Consumer Marketing*, Spring 1986, p. 13.

[9]J. S. Hill and J. M. Winski, "Goodbye Global Ads," *Advertising Age*, November 16, 1987, p. 22.

[10]S. P. Galante, "Clash Courses," *The Wall Street Journal*, European ed., July 20, 1984, p. 1.

[11]For a different value set, see K. G. Grunert, S. C. Grunert, and S. E. Beatty, "Cross-Cultural Research on Consumer Values," *Marketing and Research Today*, February 1987, pp. 30–39; the special issue on values, *Journal of Business Research*, March 1990; and S. E. Beatty, L. R. Kahle, and P. Homer, "Personal Values and Gift-Giving Behaviors," *Journal of Business Research*, March 1991, pp. 149–57.

[12]K. L. Miller, "You Just Can't Talk to These Kids," *Business Week*, April 19, 1993, pp. 104–6.

[13]See Ricks, footnote 6, p. 63.

[14]B. Oliver, "A Little Romance," *Advertising Age*, June 24, 1985, p. 39.

[15]*Reader's Digest Eurodata—A Consumer Survey of 17 European Countries* (Pleasantville, N.Y.: The Reader's Digest Association, Inc., 1991), p. 26.

[16]P. Duggan, "Feeding China's 'Little Emperors,'" *Forbes*, August 6, 1990, pp. 84–85.

[17]See footnote 15, p. 26.

[18]See footnote 12, p. 106.

[19]See footnote 15, p. 19.

[20]N. Giges, "Europeans Buy Outside Goods," *Advertising Age*, April 27, 1992, p. I:26.

[21]Ibid.

[22]See Terpstra and David, footnote 6, p. 133.

[23]See G. Levin, "Too Green for Their Own Good," *Advertising Age*, April 12, 1993, p. 29.

[24]*Trends in Europe: Consumer Attitudes & the Supermarket* (Washington, D.C.: Food Marketing Institute, 1992), p. 56.

[25]C. Miller, "No Exercise, And They Like to Smoke," *Marketing News*, August 17, 1992, p. 13.

[26]See footnote 15, p. 26.

[27]R. W. Belk and R. W. Pollay, "Materialism and Status Appeals in Japanese and U.S. Print Advertising," in *Comparative Consumer Psychology*, eds. A. Woodside and C. Keown (Washington, D.C.: American Psychological Association, 1985). See also E. C. Hirschman and P. A. LaBarbera, "Dimensions of Possession Importance," *Psychology & Marketing*, Fall 1990, pp. 215–33.

[28]See L. R. Kahle and P. Kennedy, "Using the List of Values (LOV) to Understand Consumers," *The Journal of Consumer Marketing*, Summer 1989, pp. 5–12.

[29]J. Michaels, "Nudes Dress Up Brazil Undies Ads," *Advertising Age*, August 3, 1987, p. 42.

[30]D. L. Alden, W. D. Hoyer, and C. Lee, "Identifying Global and Culture-Specific Dimensions of Humor in Advertising," *Journal of Marketing*, April 1993, pp. 64–75.

[31]T. Holden, "The Delicate Art of Doing Business in Japan," *Business Week*, October 2, 1989, p. 120.

[32]See Ricks, footnote 6, p. 39.

[33]J. P. King, "Cross-Cultural Reactions to Advertising," *European Research*, February 1988, pp. 10–16.

[34]See E. T. Hall, *The Silent Language* (New York: Fawcett World Library, 1959), p. 39; E. T. Hall, "The Silent Language in Overseas Business," *Harvard Business Review*, May–June 1960, pp. 87–96; and E. T. Hall and M. R. Hall, *Hidden Differences* (New York: Doubleday, 1987).

[35]See C. J. Kaufman and P. M. Lane, "The Intensions and Extensions of the Time Concept," in *Advances in Consumer Research XVII*, eds. M. E. Goldberg, G. Gorn, and R. W. Pollay (Provo: Association for Consumer Research, 1990), pp. 895–901.

[36]See E. T. Hall and M. R. Hall, footnote 34, pp. 18–19.

[37]L. Copeland "Foreign Markets: Not for the Amateur," *Business Marketing*, July 1984, p. 116. See also P. A. Herbig and H. E. Kramer, "Do's and Don'ts of Cross-Cultural Negotiations," *Industrial Marketing Management*, no. 4, 1992, pp. 287–98.

[38]Adapted from E. T. Hall, *The Hidden Dimension* (Garden City, N.Y.: Doubleday Publishing, 1966).

[39]S. Smith, "The Sales Force Plays Musical Chairs at IBM Japan," *Fortune*, July 3, 1989, p. 14.

[40]See Herbig and Kramer, footnote 37, p. 293.

[41]See Copeland, footnote 37.

[42]See J. L. Graham et al., "Buyer-Seller Negotiations Around the Pacific Rim," *Journal of Consumer Research*, June 1988, pp. 48–54; and D. K. Tse et al., "Does Culture Matter?" *Journal of Marketing*, October 1988, pp. 81–95.

[43]See R. T. Green and D. L. Alden, ''Functional Equivalence in Cross-Cultural Consumer Behavior,'' *Psychology & Marketing*, Summer 1988, pp. 155–68.

[44]A. Kanso, ''International Advertising Strategies,'' *Journal of Advertising Research*, January/February 1992, pp. 10–14; and W. L. James and J. S. Hill, ''International Advertising Messages,'' *Journal of Advertising Research*, June/July 1991, pp. 65–71.

[45]R. E. Hite and C. Fraser, ''International Advertising Strategies of Multinational Corporations,'' *Journal of Advertising Research*, August/September 1988, pp. 9–17.

[46]See C. M. Schaninger, J. C. Bourgeois, and W. C. Buss, ''French-English Canadian Subcultural Consumption Differences,'' *Journal of Marketing*, Spring 1985, pp. 82–92.

[47]See F. Zandpour, C. Chang, and J. Catalano, ''Stories, Symbols, and Straight Talk''; C. A. di Benedetto, M. Tamate, and R. Chandran, ''Developing Creative Advertising Strategy for the Japanese Marketplace''; J. Ramaprasad and K. Hasegawa, ''Creative Strategies in American and Japanese TV Commercials''; and B. D. Cutler, and R. G. Javalgi, ''A Cross-Cultural Analysis of the Visual Components of Print Advertising,'' all in *Journal of Advertising Research*, January/February 1992, pp. 25–38, 39–48, 59–67, and 71–80; T. Nevett, ''Differences Between American and British Television Advertising''; and A. Biswas, J. E. Olsen, and V. Carlet, ''A Comparison of Print Advertisements from the United States and France,'' both in *Journal of Advertising*, December 1992, pp. 61–71 and 73–81.

[48]P. Rowlands, ''Global Approach Doesn't Always Make Scents,'' *Advertising Age*, January 17, 1994, p. I:1.

[49]R. W. Belk and N. Zhou, ''Learning to Want Things,'' in *Advances in Consumer Research XIV*, ed. M. Wallendorf and P. Anderson (Provo: Association for Consumer Research, 1987), pp. 478–81; N. Dholakia and J. F. Sherry, Jr., ''Marketing and Development,'' in *Research in Marketing IX*, ed. J. N. Sheth (Greenwich, Conn.: JAI Press, 1987), pp. 119–43; and R. W. Pollay, D. K. Tse, and Z. Y. Wang, ''Advertising Propaganda and Value Change in Economic Development,'' *Journal of Business Research* 20 (1990), pp. 83–95.

THE CHANGING AMERICAN SOCIETY: VALUES AND DEMOGRAPHICS

The Gillette Company, like other firms that market shaving products, had traditionally focused on the men's market. Razors were designed by and for men. While all major razor manufacturers had long marketed "women's razors," most were merely slight variations on razors designed primarily for men. According to a Gillette executive: "the general approach was to take a man's razor, change the handle a bit, color it pink, and say, 'Here, honey, this is for you.' " Most women shunned this approach and simply used the razor their husband used.

Several years ago, Gillette gave one of the industrial designers in its shaving division, Jill Shurtleff, the task of reassessing the women's shaving market. Shurtleff first tried all the women's razors on the market and concluded that none worked well: "They were ergonomically terrible."

The next step was to conduct research to answer the question, "How do women shave?" The answer was—"differently from men." The average woman shaves 9 times more surface area than a man, shaves 2.5 times a week, and changes the blade 10 times a year. While men generally shave in front of a well-lit mirror, most women shave in a slippery, often poorly lit, shower or tub. Women also shave parts of the body that they cannot see well, such as underarms and backs of thighs. Not surprisingly, many women complained of nicks and cuts and considered shaving an unpleasant task.

Shurtleff concluded that blade razor features, such as the T-shape, were excellent for shaving men's faces but were inappropriate for women's needs. Therefore she developed the radically new *Sensor for Women.* A distinct break with the pink women's razors of the past was achieved with a white and aqua design, to evoke a clean, watery feeling. A traditional naming strategy would have produced *Lady Sensor*; however, *Sensor for Women* was chosen—as a more direct statement. When men, including the Gillette managers, saw the new product, they were skeptical at best. Women, however, quickly saw its advantages. The *Sensor for Women* produced $40 million in sales in its first six months on the market for a 60 percent market share![1]

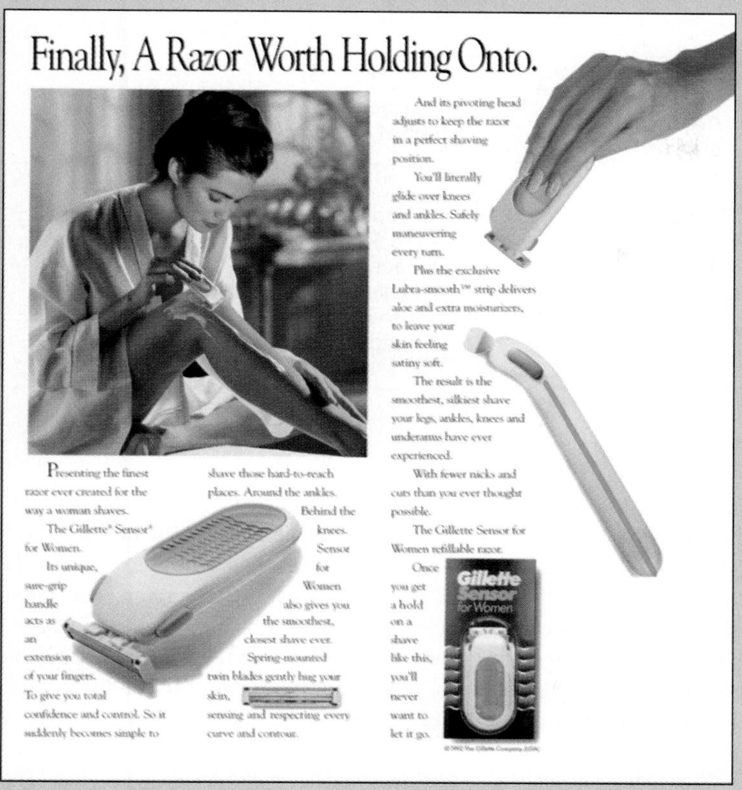

In Chapter 2, we discussed how variations in values influence consumption patterns *across* cultures. In this chapter, we will describe how changes in values over time influence consumption patterns *within* cultures. Cultural values are not constant. Rather, they evolve over time. Twenty years ago, Gillette simply used "pink men's razors" for the female market. However, America's values and beliefs concerning gender-based behaviors have changed radically, as have gender-related products and marketing activities. Other values are evolving more slowly. In the first section of this chapter we will examine the evolution of American values in general. We will then take a more in-depth look at changes in gender roles.

As Figure 3–1 indicates, values are not the only aspect of American society that is changing. America's demographics, such as the size and distribution of the population and its age, education, income, and occupation structure, are also changing. The last section of this chapter examines these changes. In Chapter 4, we will explore ongoing changes in America's subcultures.

CHANGES IN AMERICAN VALUES

Observable shifts in behavior, including consumption behavior, often reflect underlying shifts in values. Therefore, it is necessary to understand the underlying *value shifts* in order to understand current and future behavior.

While we discuss American values as though every American has the same values, the opposite is more accurate. There is substantial variance in values across individuals and groups. In addition, changes in values tend to occur slowly and unevenly across individuals

FIGURE 3–1

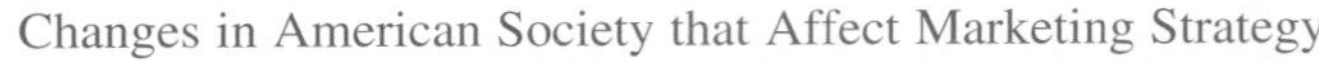
Changes in American Society that Affect Marketing Strategy

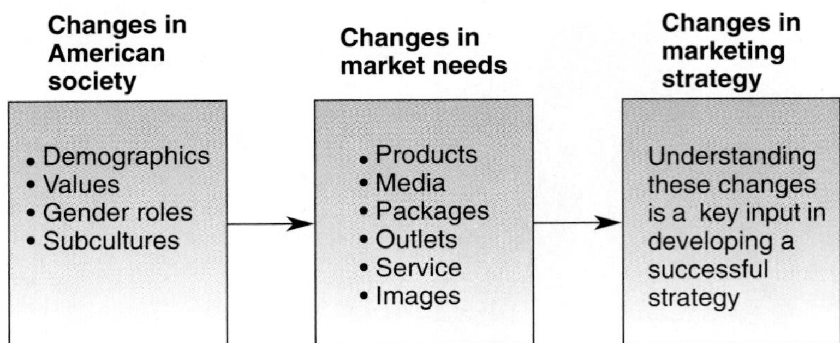

and groups. Thus, while the popular press often trumpets "the new values of the 90s," sound studies of these "new," or changing, values generally indicate less change than is implied by the popular press. For example, a "return to traditional values" is often described as a major change in the early 1990s. However, the percent who regard religion as important or who attend church once a month has not increased noticeably, while the percent in favor of living together before marriage and in favor of legalized abortions has remained constant or increased.[2] Thus, marketers must carefully analyze value shifts of relevance to their products and markets before developing strategy based on assumed changes.

Figure 3–2 presents our estimate of how American values are changing. These are the same values used to describe different cultures in Chapter 2. It must be emphasized that Figure 3–2 is based on the authors' subjective interpretation of the American society. You should feel free to challenge these judgments.

Self-Oriented Values

Traditionally, Americans have been active, materialistic, hard-working, humorous people inclined toward abstinence and postponed gratification. Beginning after the end of World War II and accelerating rapidly during the 1970s and early 1980s, Americans placed increasing emphasis on leisure, immediate gratification, and sensual gratification. An examination of American advertising, product features, and personal debt levels indicates that these changes have significantly affected consumers' behaviors and marketing practice.

It appears that several of these trends are now reversing direction and moving back toward their traditional positions. The most notable shift is in sensual gratification. While it is still perfectly acceptable to consume products for the sensual pleasures they provide, the range of products and occasions for which this is acceptable has narrowed.[3] This has produced some interesting marketing opportunities and challenges. For example, consumption of both frozen nonfat yogurt *and* a super-premium, high-fat ice cream has increased, while consumption of regular ice cream has declined. It appears that many consumers are indulging themselves less frequently but more lavishly.

Hard work is being valued more now than in the recent past. This is undoubtedly influenced by the difficulty of obtaining employment in the past few years. Americans also appear to be more willing to postpone gratification. Concern about personal debt is at a 15-year high,[4] and more consumers are shopping for value and waiting for sales.

FIGURE 3–2

Traditional, Current, and Emerging American Values

Self-Oriented		
Active	ECT	Passive
Material	T C E	Nonmaterial
Hard work	T E C	Leisure
Postponed gratification	T E C	Immediate gratification
Sensual gratification	C E T	Abstinence
Humorous	TC E	Serious
Environment-Oriented		
Maximum cleanliness	TCE	Minimum cleanliness
Performance	T E C	Status
Tradition	E C T	Change
Risk taking	T E C	Security
Problem solving	T CE	Fatalistic
Admire nature	E C T	Overcome nature
Other-Oriented		
Individual	T EC	Collective
Romantic	T CE	Nonromantic
Adult	T EC	Child
Competition	T C E	Cooperation
Youth	T C E	Age
Masculine	T C E	Feminine

T = Traditional E = Emerging C = Current

Environment-Oriented Values

Environment-oriented values prescribe a society's relationship with its economic, technical, and physical environments. Americans have traditionally admired cleanliness, change, performance, risk taking, problem solving, and the conquest of nature. While this cluster of values remains basically intact, there are some significant shifts occurring.

Our risk-taking orientation seems to have changed somewhat over time. There was an increased emphasis on security during the period from 1930 through the mid-1980s. This attitude was a response to the tremendous upheavals and uncertainties caused by the Depression, World War II, and the Cold War. However, risk taking remains highly valued. It appears to be regaining appreciation as we look to entrepreneurs for economic growth and to smaller firms and self-employment to obtain desired lifestyles.

Americans are shifting back to a focus on performance rather than status. While consumers are still willing to purchase "status" brands, these brands must provide style and functionality in addition to the prestige of the name. This has led to substantial increases in sales at various types of discount stores, and for retailer and other private-label brands.[5] It has caused Procter & Gamble to completely alter its pricing and promotion strategy away from periodic discounts and coupons toward "everyday low prices."[6] Stores, such as Kmart, that position themselves as providing good quality and stylish merchandise at low prices are well positioned to take advantage of this shift.

Americans have always been very receptive to change. *New* has traditionally been taken to mean *improved.* While still appreciative of change, Americans are now less receptive to change for its own sake. New-product recalls, the expense and the failure of many new government programs, and the energy required to keep pace with rapid technological changes are some of the reasons for this shift.

Traditionally, nature was viewed as an obstacle. We attempted to bend nature to fit our desires without realizing the negative consequences this could have for both nature and humanity. This attitude has shifted dramatically over the past 25 years.

Recent surveys report that nearly 80 percent of the public is concerned about the condition of the environment. One survey found that 64 percent would pay more for environmentally sound grocery products, 76 percent would boycott manufacturers of polluting products, and 81 percent would sacrifice some convenience to save natural resources.[7] Another poll found over 90 percent stating they would (1) make a special effort to buy products from companies that protect the environment, (2) give up some convenience for environmentally safer products or packaging, and (3) pay more for such products.[8] These values are being translated into actions. A recent study found that 25 percent of the respondents had stopped buying the products of at least one firm they believed was not a good environmental citizen.[9]

Marketers have responded to Americans' increasing concern for the environment with an approach called **green marketing**. Green marketing generally involves one or more strategies: (1) producing products in a manner less harmful to the environment than traditional processes, (2) producing products whose production, use, or disposition is less harmful to the environment than the traditional versions of the product, (3) developing products that have a positive impact on the environment, or (4) tying the purchase of a product to an environmental organization or event. An example of each approach follows.

- Although it increased their costs, Celestial Seasonings replaced its chlorine-bleached tea bags with oxygen-bleached bags. The process of chlorine bleaching creates dioxin, a carcinogen which sometimes enters the groundwater around the pulp mills where the bleaching occurs. Managerial Application 3–1 shows Wrangler's "green" jeans, which are also manufactured in a more environmentally friendly manner.
- Wal-Mart has launched an "eco-store." The store carries Wal-Mart's usual merchandise mix but highlights environmentally superior products. Recycling is the theme. The store recycles much of its own waste and provides recycling services for its customers. The store itself is designed to be energy efficient and uses recycled materials both in its construction and in the shopping bags it provides for consumers.
- Organic fertilizers, such as those produced by Ringer Corp., can have a positive effect on the environment. Organic fertilizers now have a 10 percent market share despite costing about twice as much as chemical fertilizers. The Church & Dwight Company, Inc. developed sodium bicarbonate products to help purify wastewater and to restore lakes damaged by acid rain.
- Americans also spend hundreds of millions of dollars on the environment through their support of environmental groups such as the Nature Conservancy, the National Audubon Society, the National Park Foundation, and Greenpeace. Managerial Application 3–2 illustrates a successful tie-in between Church & Dwight's Arm & Hammer and the National Audubon Society. Chevrolet's Geo plants a tree in the buyer's name when a Geo is purchased. Since the Geo is the most fuel efficient car in America, the environmental tie-in makes sense to consumers and works effectively.

Marketers need to be cautious when making environmental claims. While specific environmental claims enhance consumers' attitudes toward the product and advertiser, vague environmental claims have a negative impact. Consumers consider a specific environmen-

MANAGERIAL APPLICATION 3–1

A Product with a Production Process that Reduces Environmental Harm

tal claim to be one that (1) provides detailed, useful information, (2) has environmental benefits superior to competing products, and (3) will clearly improve the environment.[10] Managerial Application 3–3 describes several successful green marketing activities.

Other-Oriented Values

Other-oriented values reflect a society's view of the appropriate relationships between individuals and groups within that society. Historically, America was an individualistic, competitive, romantic, masculine, youth, and parent-oriented society. Several aspects of this orientation are undergoing change.

Children have always played an important role in our society, though traditionally they were secondary to the adult members of the household. This orientation changed radically during the 20th century, particularly after World War II. While our focus appears to be shifting back toward adults, children are still very important.

Traditionally, age has been highly valued in almost all cultures. Older people were considered wiser than young people and were, therefore, looked to as models and leaders.

MANAGERIAL APPLICATION

3–2

An Example of Green Marketing by Tying a Brand to an Environmental Association

This has never been true in American culture, probably because transforming a wilderness into a new type of producing nation required characteristics such as physical strength, stamina, youthful vigor, and imagination. This value on youth continued as we became an industrial nation. Since World War II, it has increased to such an extent that products such as cars, clothing, cosmetics, and hairstyles seem designed for and sold only to the young!

However, there is a slow reversal of this value on youth. Because of their increasing numbers and disposable income, older citizens have developed political and economic clout and are beginning to use it. Retirement communities excluding younger people are being developed in large numbers. There are cosmetics, medicines, and hair care products being marketed specifically to older consumers. Middle-aged consumers now constitute the largest single market segment, and this segment has lifestyles distinct from the youth markets. In Managerial Application 3–7 (page 82), one of the Maybelline cosmetics ads shown is aimed at a mature woman.

American society, like most others, has reflected a very masculine orientation for a long time. This chapter's opening story indicates how this orientation is changing. The marketing implications resulting from changes in this value are so vast that the next section of this chapter is devoted to this topic.

MANAGERIAL APPLICATION

3–3

Green Marketing Activities

- Procter & Gamble recently introduced a refillable container for Downy fabric softener.
- Heinz changed the formula of its squeezable plastic ketchup containers to make them more readily recyclable.
- Estēe Lauder launched, under the *Origins* label, a complete line of cosmetics that are made of natural ingredients, are not tested on animals, and are packaged in recyclable containers.
- Cannon USA gives the Nature Conservancy 50 cents for each laser-printer toner container that is returned for recycling. This is producing over $750,000 for the conservancy annually.
- Church & Dwight eliminated the plastic overwrap and converted to 100 percent recycled paperboard the boxes for its Arm & Hammer Carpet Deodorizer.
- Tension Envelope Corp. developed the Send-'N-Return envelope that easily converts from an outgoing mailing to a return envelope.
- Eveready Battery Co. is testing Green Power, a ''zero mercury-added'' battery for household uses.
- *Good Housekeeping* magazine added a monthly Green Watch editorial and an annual environmental section—in addition to making extensive use of recycled paper.
- Wrangler's Earth Wash Jeans are ''made with low-sulfide dyes, biodegradable enzymes and less water to help protect our rivers and streams.''

Marketing Strategy and Values

We have examined a number of marketing implications associated with values and changes in values. It is critical that *all aspects of the firm's marketing mix be consistent with the value system of its target market.* Different groups will have differing value systems and marketers must adjust their activities to the values of their target group. Marketers must change their marketing mix as the value systems of their target groups evolve. Fortunately, values generally change slowly. Firms will have time to evolve their practices if they monitor customer values. Firms can conduct their own monitoring surveys or subscribe to one of the many commercial surveys that measure values. However, caution should be used in responding to popular press declarations of major value shifts.

GENDER ROLES IN AMERICAN SOCIETY

Until recently, the prevailing stereotype of an automobile purchase involved a male making the purchase alone. If accompanied by his wife or girlfriend, she only offered suggestions concerning color and interior features.

Today, research indicates that women influence 80 percent of all automobile purchases, buy 45 percent of all new cars (and this is projected to grow to 60 percent by 2000), and are the predominant buyers of many models, including Nissan Pulsars, Cadillac Cimarrons, Toyota SR5s, Pontiac Fieros, and Ford Escort EXPs. Marketers who have clung to the outdated stereotype by either ignoring women purchasers or by focusing on excessively ''feminine'' themes have lost substantial sales opportunities. For example, one of Chevrolet's first ads aimed at women backfired because it contained limited product feature information but showed lots of pinks and lavenders. Likewise, Chrysler failed with a model named ''La Femme'' that was designed for the stereotyped woman of yesterday.

MANAGERIAL APPLICATION 3–4

An Automobile Ad Aimed at Women

Although surveys consistently indicate that women want the same basic features in a car as males do, there are subtle differences. For example, many automobiles have radios, heaters, and other accessories that are difficult to operate with long fingernails. Likewise, women find unrealistic role portrayals in automobile advertising offensive and are frequently frustrated in their attempts to deal with auto sales personnel who don't treat them seriously. They are also more attentive to the showroom environment. Like male buyers women car buyers are heterogeneous. One study identified six segments: value seekers, driving enthusiasts, comfort seekers, luxury seekers, budget buyers, and voluntary minimalists.[11]

Managerial Application 3–4 contains a Lumina Minivan advertisement from *Know-How*, a magazine focused on the modern woman (as described below). Note that the ad does not have an overly feminine ''flavor.'' The only obviously feminine feature is the woman's hand with the remote power sliding-door control. However, a power sliding door is a feature that women are particularly likely to appreciate.

Gender roles, the behaviors considered appropriate for males and females, have undergone massive changes over the past 20 years. The general nature of this shift has been for behaviors previously considered appropriate primarily for men to be acceptable for women, too.

Gender roles are **ascribed roles**. An ascribed role is based on *an attribute over which the individual has little or no control.* This can be contrasted with **achievement roles**, which are based on *performance criteria over which the individual has some degree of control.* Individuals can, within limits, select their occupational roles (achievement roles), but they cannot influence their gender (ascribed role).

Researchers categorize women into traditional or modern orientations based on their preference for one or the other of two contrasting lifestyles:

> *Traditional:* A marriage with the husband assuming the responsibility for providing for the family, and the wife running the house and taking care of the children.

Modern: A marriage where husband and wife share responsibilities. Both work, and they share homemaking and child care responsibilities.

In a 1977 survey, 65 percent of the adult respondents expressed a preference for a traditional lifestyle. By 1991, this figure had dropped to 41 percent. Further, while 69 percent of Americans over 60, and 44 percent of those between 45 and 60, prefer the traditional lifestyle, only 30 percent of those under 45 prefer it. In addition to varying by age, preference for a traditional lifestyle varies with geographic region (it is lowest on the West Coast) and education (it decreases as education level increases).[12]

While males and females both express strong preferences for modern lifestyles as a general concept, attitudes and behaviors toward specific aspects of that lifestyle remain very conservative. For example, a majority of both sexes believes that "a woman with young children should not work outside the home." Studies consistently find that many men resent and resist housework even if their spouses are employed. For example, in traditional households women spend 26 hours per week on household chores and men spend 8 hours. In dual wage-earning households, the woman's time on household chores drops to 18 hours but the male's remains below 10.[13] Married men indicate that primary responsibility for most household tasks belongs to the wife:[14]

Task	Husband	Wife
Making shopping list	10%	82%
Grocery shopping	15	77
Cooking	12	82
Washing dishes	11	75
Caring for children	5	60

Thus, we find a pattern typical of a changing value: growing acceptance of the change, but not for all aspects of it, and substantial resistance to the new behaviors from the more traditional groups or those who stand to lose as the new value is accepted. In the following sections we examine some of the marketing implications of this value shift.

Market Segmentation

Neither the women's nor the men's market is as homogeneous as it once was. At least four significant female market segments exist.[15]

1. *Traditional Housewife:* Generally married. Prefers to stay at home. Very home- and family-centered. Desires to please husband and/or children. Seeks satisfaction and meaning from household and family maintenance as well as volunteer activities. Experiences strong pressures to work outside the home and is well aware of forgone income opportunity. Feels supported by family and is generally content with role.
2. *Trapped Housewife:* Generally married. Would prefer to work, but stays at home due to small children, lack of outside opportunities, or family pressure. Seeks satisfaction and meaning outside the home. Does not enjoy most household chores. Has mixed feelings about current status and is concerned about lost opportunities.
3. *Trapped Working Woman:* Married or single. Would prefer to stay at home, but works for economic necessity or social/family pressure. Does not derive satisfaction or meaning from employment. Enjoys most household activities, but is frustrated by lack of time. Feels conflict about her role, particularly if younger children are home. Resents missed opportunities for family, volunteer, and social activities. Is proud of financial contribution to family.

4. *Career Working Woman:* Married or single. Prefers to work. Derives satisfaction and meaning from employment rather than, or in addition to, home and family. Experiences some conflict over her role if younger children are at home, but is generally content. Views home maintenance as a necessary evil. Feels pressed for time.

While the above descriptions are oversimplified, they indicate the diverse nature of the adult female population. Clearly, a single brand-positioning strategy for a household cleaner or similar products that would appeal to all four segments would be difficult to achieve.

As female roles have changed, so have male roles, though at a much slower pace. Men have begun to assume more household responsibility and have become more active in taking care of the children. Like women, men differ in their acceptance of changes in gender roles. In general, younger and more highly educated males are most accepting of the modern orientation.

Product Strategy

Many products are losing their traditional gender typing. Guns, cars, cigarettes, motorcycles, and many other once-masculine products are now designed with women in mind. Gillette's Sensor for Women, whose development we described earlier, is an example.

Smith & Wesson recently launched LadySmith, a line of guns designed specifically for women. Other manufacturers had attempted to reach the female market by "feminizing" men's guns with colored handles and engraved roses on the side plates. Smith & Wesson found through research that "if a woman is going to pull out a gun for personal protection, she doesn't want a cute gun." Smith & Wesson redesigned the guns to fit women's hands and has a very successful new line.

Women are taking a much more active approach to leisure than in the past. Competitive sports, once a male domain, are rapidly gaining popularity with women. This has opened substantial new markets for a wide range of products—from sports bras to special magazines. For example, Everfresh is test marketing Cool Down, a post-workout drink for women who don't like Gatorade. According to Everfresh's vice president of marketing: "The great surprise is that the American jock is not a male, it's a female. She's the one who's exercising twice a week."[16]

A few years ago, a new Barbie doll that reflected the changing role of women generated a substantial amount of publicity. Introduced with the theme "We girls can do anything, right, Barbie?" the Home and Office Barbie represented the career woman. This new Barbie had a calculator, business card, credit card, newspaper, and business magazines. A dollhouse-like accessory package provided an office desk with a personal computer terminal. However, her business suit was a feminine pink with white accents. Today, Army Barbie (in combat fatigues), Navy Barbie, and Policewoman Barbie look completely natural on the shelf next to Beach Barbie.

Marketing Communications

As gender roles evolve, it is increasingly necessary to communicate how an existing product or brand is appropriate for the gender that traditionally did not use it. Beer ads, once targeted exclusively at males, are now targeted at females as well (see Managerial Application 6–1, page 144). Miller, Budweiser, Michelob, and Coors have all launched advertising campaigns aimed at female consumers, and females now consume over 20 percent of domestic beer volume.

MANAGERIAL APPLICATION 3–5

An Example of the Changing Role of Men

State Farm Insurance targets working mothers who have children or who are expecting a child as prospects for their life insurance products. It runs ads in magazines such as *Working Mother*, *Working Woman*, and *American Baby*. The ads feature a picture of a woman life insurance agent with her own child. The copy from one ad is:

> *A MOTHER'S LOVE KNOWS NO BOUNDS.* AND THERE'S NO BETTER WAY TO SHOW HOW MUCH YOU LOVE THEM THAN WITH STATE FARM LIFE INSURANCE. NOBODY KNOWS BETTER THAN GAIL COLEMAN—A STATE FARM AGENT AND MOM. WHEN SHE SITS DOWN WITH YOU TO TALK ABOUT LIFE INSURANCE, SHE KNOWS YOU NEED A PLAN DESIGNED FOR WORKING MOMS. ONE THAT WILL GROW AS YOUR NEEDS GROW. AND SHE'S ALWAYS THERE TO ANSWER YOUR QUESTIONS. SO WHEN IT COMES TO LIFE THERE ARE TWO THINGS YOU CAN ALWAYS COUNT ON. A MOTHER'S LOVE AND YOUR STATE FARM AGENT. LIKE A GOOD NEIGHBOR, STATE FARM IS THERE.®

Marketing communications, particularly advertising, have become increasingly difficult as the male and female markets both have become more fragmented. Advertisements portraying women must not offend any of the various segments. For example, an ad that implied that housework was unimportant or that women who work outside the home are somehow superior to those who do not, could insult many traditional housewives.[17] Ads that show women primarily as decoration or as clearly inferior to males tend to produce negative responses across all female segments.[18]

There are relatively few ads showing men using products traditionally designed for women or performing tasks traditionally performed by women. Managerial Application 3–5 shows an exception. One advertising agency offers the following advice for portraying men performing household tasks:

> It is important to keep in mind that most men, while they do some housework, resent having to do it. Therefore, the houseworking husband should be shown as a no-nonsense person knocking off a job because it has to be done. The pleasure is in the completion of the task, not in the act of doing it.
>
> The husband should not be shown as doing the wife a favor by helping her out. While this might appeal to the husband, it may well alienate the wife. As more and more women pursue careers, they will expect the sharing of household tasks as a right and obligation, not as a favor on the part of their mates.[19]

Retail Strategy

Men are increasingly shopping for household products, and females are shopping for "masculine" products such as lawn mowers and hammers. According to one estimate, men bought 25 percent of the groceries in 1991. When men shop for household items for the family, they generally select which brand for items such as soups, and soft drinks but serve primarily as purchasing agents for other items such as cleaning and baby products.[20] However, retailers such as Kmart are showing very masculine men shopping for such products as baby shampoo at their stores. Campbell soup has begun advertising its Chunky Soup in *Sports Illustrated* and *Field & Stream.*

As men increasingly shop in supermarkets and other stores traditionally dominated by women shoppers, astute marketers will alter their product mix, operating hours, and general decor to appeal to males as well as to females. For example, supermarkets are expanding their garden, hardware, and automotive sections. Similar changes are occurring at hardware stores such as Home Depot and Builders Square, which now have a clientele that is almost half female.

DEMOGRAPHICS

Just as our value structure is changing, so are our demographics. **Demographics** are used to describe a population in terms of its size, distribution, and structure. *Size* means the number of individuals in a population, while *structure* describes the population in terms of age, income, education, and occupation. *Distribution* of the population describes the location of individuals in terms of geographic region and rural, urban, or suburban location. Each of these factors influences the behavior of consumers and contributes to the overall demand for various products and services. Managerial Application 3–6 shows how firms can use demographics to develop marketing strategies.

Population Size and Distribution

As shown in Figure 3–3, the size of the U.S. population has grown steadily and is projected to continue growing in the immediate future. This continued and steady growth allowed some industries to survive and others to grow. For example, coffee consumption has declined steadily from 3.5 cups per day in the 1960s to an average of less than 1.5 cups today. However, the addition of 80 million people during this period enabled the industry to maintain its total sales.

Thus, population growth can have dramatic effects on an industry. If the growth of the U.S. population slows or stops, many industries will face stable or declining demand. This could lead to the failure of firms, increased diversification, a more competitive environment, and increased emphasis on export sales.

In addition to growth of a population, it is important for marketers to know where this growth is likely to take place. For example, Arizona is predicted to grow in population 23 percent from 1990 to 2000. This creates a tremendous marketing opportunity for those

MANAGERIAL APPLICATION 3-6

Frito-Lay's Use of Demographic-Based Marketing Strategy

Frito-Lay recently developed a Light product line, including Cheetos Light, Doritos Light, and Ruffles Light. Marketing research identified the primary target market as age 35 to 54, college-educated, white-collar workers with annual incomes above $35,000. While Frito-Lay will use its knowledge of the values, attitudes, and media habits of this group to structure its communication campaign, its most creative use of demographics has been in distribution.

Frito-Lay used Market Metrics—a firm with a database on 30,000 supermarkets. Market Metrics defines trading areas around each supermarket, considering distance and the presence of travel barriers such as freeways or rivers. It then uses Census Bureau data to profile the demographics of the shoppers in each store's trade area. Market Metrics took Frito-Lay's target demographics and ranked the 30,000 supermarkets in terms of how well they matched the target market.

This approach has allowed Frito-Lay to focus maximum sales, point-of-purchase, and promotional efforts on those specific stores with the greatest market potential based on demographics. They plan to increase their use of this approach in the future: ''If we wanted to target Hispanics or Italians or married couples with children under the age of five, we could do it with this program.''

Source: J. Lawrence, ''Frito's Micro Move,'' *Advertising Age*, February 12, 1990 p. 44.

U.S. Population: 1960–2010

FIGURE 3-3

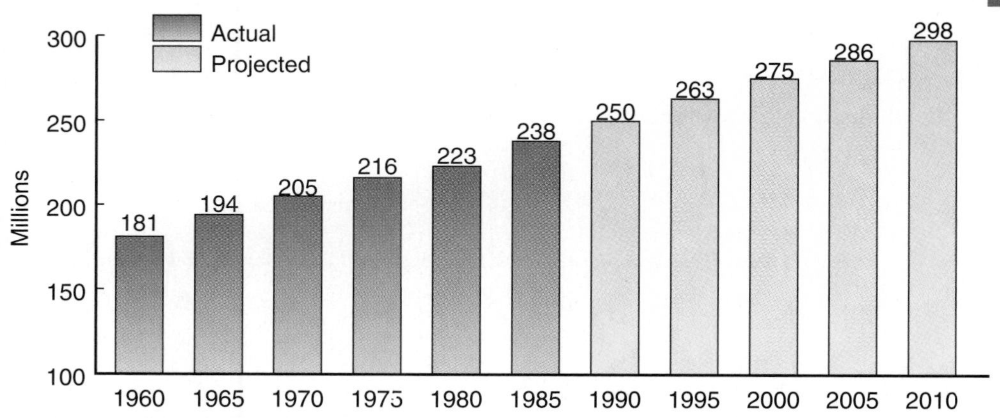

Source: *Projections of the States by Age, Sex, and Race*, Bureau of the Census, Series P-25

who understand the needs of people likely to make up this population growth. Likewise, California, Florida, Georgia, Hawaii, Nevada, New Mexico, and Texas are expected to grow in population while Illinois, Indiana, Iowa, Ohio, and Pennsylvania will decrease.

Occupation

The number of white-collar workers grew three times faster than the number of blue-collar workers over the past 25 years. And within the white-collar segment, professionals and technicians grew from approximately 8 million in the early 60s to over 20 million in the early 90s. Because our occupation influences the clothes we wear, cars we drive, and foods

TABLE 3-1 Occupational Influences on Consumption*

	Professional/ Manager	Technical/ Clerical/ Sales	Precision/ Craft
Products			
Imported beer	111	86	112
Piano/organ	170	123	63
Cigarettes	78	99	133
Diet colas	116	112	83
Activities			
Snow skiing	226	124	46
Bowling	100	114	181
Dinner parties	158	118	71
State lottery	89	111	124
Shopping			
Best	157	102	73
Ames	95	102	132
Toys "R" Us	129	115	85
Health food store	133	114	70
Media			
Playboy	80†	95	202
The New Yorker	284†	95	42
"Monday Night Football"	86†	99	155
"L.A. Law"	111†	111	83

*100 = Average level of use, purchase, or consumption.

†Professional only.

Source: *1991 Study of Media & Markets* (New York: Simmons Market Research Bureau, Inc., 1991).

we eat, products that serve the white-collar worker have experienced greater growth in demand than those targeted at the blue-collar worker.

Differences in consumption between occupational classes have been found for products such as beer, detergents, dog food, shampoo, and paper towels. Media preferences, hobbies, and shopping patterns are also influenced by occupational class (see Table 3–1). These implications are discussed in depth in Chapter 5.

Education

The level of education in the United States continues to rise. The percentage of the population age 25 and over completing high school and college is going up, while the percentage with only some high school or elementary education is decreasing. Unfortunately, the high school dropout rate is also increasing and is particularly high in disadvantaged

Education Level Influences on Consumption*

TABLE 3–2

	Graduated College	Attended College	Graduated High School	Did Not Graduate High School
Products				
Champagne	150	125	93	47
Chewing tobacco	57	72	95	172
Book club	137	118	94	62
Computer	150	118	87	64
Instant coffee	64	73	105	143
Activities				
Tennis	155	145	80	47
State lottery	75	92	122	91
Attends stock car races	69	78	128	97
Cook for fun	130	113	100	63
Shopping				
Wal-Mart	90	99	98	113
Marshalls'	159	121	93	43
Chinese take-out	131	117	100	59
Convenient food mart	68	101	107	114
Media				
National Enquirer	47	85	123	145
National Geographic	186	123	78	52
"FBI: Untold Stories"	81	93	102	133
"Wings"	109	101	102	92

*100 = Average level of use, purchase, or consumption.

Source: *1991 Study of Media & Markets* (New York: Simmons Market Research Bureau, Inc., 1991).

populations. Further, years of schooling completed does not always reflect education level accurately.

As education levels increase, we can expect to see many changes in preference to occur in the demand for beverages, automobiles, media, and home computers (see Table 3–2). Marketers will have to recognize the education level of target markets to effectively reach and communicate with them. The impact of education on consumption behavior is discussed in detail in Chapter 5.

Income

A household's income level combined with its accumulated wealth determines its purchasing power. While a great many purchases are made on credit, one's ability to buy on credit is ultimately determined by one's current and past (wealth) income. Since income enables us consumers to meet our needs by purchasing products, it is no surprise that marketers consider income to be a critical demographic variable.

With the exception of the Depression in the 1930s, modern American history has been characterized by consistently increasing per capita incomes. While per capita income is still increasing, for many it has not kept pace with increased expenses. This is particularly true for younger households and for those without specialized skills. A decade of economic uncertainty as well as limited or no increase in purchasing power for many has helped produce the "value shopper" described earlier. Consumers at virtually all income levels are demanding products that deliver value—significant performance for the price. Lower-income consumers seek value in lower-priced products such as the Hyundai, while Buick advertises that it provides the same performance as several luxury imports for "thousands less."

Sales and Marketing Management magazine prepares an annual study that attempts to measure the buying power of the cities and regions in America. Many firms find its **Buying Power Index (BPI)** very useful for outlet location decisions, sales force and advertising allocations, and product introduction targets. Exhibit 3–1 describes this index.

EXHIBIT 3–1 Using the Buying Power Index (BPI) to Estimate Market Demand

Trading Area	Population (millions)	Buying Income (billions)	Retail Sales (billions)	Buying Power Index (percent)	BPI Economy Priced Products (percent)	BPI Moderate Priced Products (percent)	BPI Premium Priced Products (percent)
Cincinnati, Ohio	1.466	22.408	11.302	.6024	.5773	.5821	.5956
Austin, Tex.	.819	12.816	6.523	.3439	.3678	.3464	.3493
Orlando, Fla.	1.139	16.778	10.430	.4867	.4204	.5201	.4799
Chicago, Ill.	6.109	106.693	47.661	2.6926	2.0027	2.1107	2.9323
Denver, Colo.	1.653	28.087	13.431	.7281	.6363	.6876	.7704
San Francisco, Calif.	1.631	33.999	15.335	.8371	.5884	.6163	.9379
Phoenix, Ariz.	2.224	31.271	17.241	.8787	.9425	.9929	.8899
Little Rock, Ark.	.521	7.216	4.171	.2064	.2126	.2324	.2116
New York, N.Y.	8.627	149.120	48.759	3.4832	3.4255	2.7850	3.8375

Buying Power Index (BPI) and Market Demand

The buying power index is an index for a given trading area based on size of population, buying income, and retail sales. The BPI for Cincinnati, Ohio, is 0.6024 percent. This means that we would expect 0.006024 of the total demand for a product to occur in Cincinnati if there are no regional influences on the consumption of the product.

Price Influence on Market Demand

Because some trading areas are more sensitive to price and quality differences, the buying power index is also computed for products sold in three price categories—economy, moderate, and premium. Note that in Austin, Texas, the BPI is highest for economy-priced products (0.3678 percent) and lowest for premium-priced products (0.3493 percent). In San Francisco, the BPI is highest for premium-priced products (0.9379 percent) and lowest for economy products (0.5884 percent).

Source: *Survey of Buying Power Demographics, 1992, Sales and Marketing Management Magazine* (January 1993).

Age Structure

Age has been found to affect the consumption of products ranging from beer to toilet paper to vacations. Our age shapes the media we use, where we shop, how we use products, and how we think and feel about marketing activities. Table 3–3 illustrates some consumption behaviors that vary with age. Managerial Application 3–7 shows how Maybelline approaches two distinct age segments. Figure 3–4 provides the estimated age distribution of the U.S. population in 1995 and 2005. Some of the profound marketing implications of the shift in age structure over the next 10 years are:

- Demand for children's products, such as toys, diapers, and clothes, will remain constant as the population under 15 years of age will be stable over this period.
- Products consumed by young adults will decline as this population group grows smaller. This will have significant implications for the overall economy as well as for specific products, as this is the age of initial household formation and first purchases. Housing construction, appliances, automobiles, and similar products will suffer unless use increases among older groups.
- The largest impact will be caused by the huge increase in individuals between 45 and 64. This is the age of highest earning, so luxury items should do well. As children

TABLE 3–3

Age Influences on Consumption*

	18–24	25–34	35–44	45–54	55–64	>64
Products						
Tequila	143	135	114	82	64	32
Scotch	74	100	107	116	118	87
Records/disks/tapes	125	117	118	99	82	44
Laxatives	48	78	91	100	140	175
Activities						
Cruise vacation	87	90	96	115	127	99
Aerobics	142	127	131	94	58	19
Flower gardening	61	87	112	116	122	107
Cookout parties	95	116	124	108	89	50
Shopping						
Woolworth	87	95	104	111	98	105
Burger King	125	119	116	97	70	53
Use store brands	98	117	112	104	88	68
Convenience stores	112	116	113	104	83	58
Media						
Reader's Digest	53	73	104	112	137	141
People	127	116	124	91	79	44
"Murder, She Wrote"	86	79	83	105	127	143
"In Living Color"	136	127	124	73	67	45

100 = Average level of use, purchase, or consumption.

Source: *1991 Study of Media & Markets* (New York: Simmons Market Research Bureau, Inc., 1991).

MANAGERIAL APPLICATION

3–7 Approaching Two Age Groups with the Same Product Line

FIGURE 3–4 The Changing Age Structure of the United States: 1995 to 2005

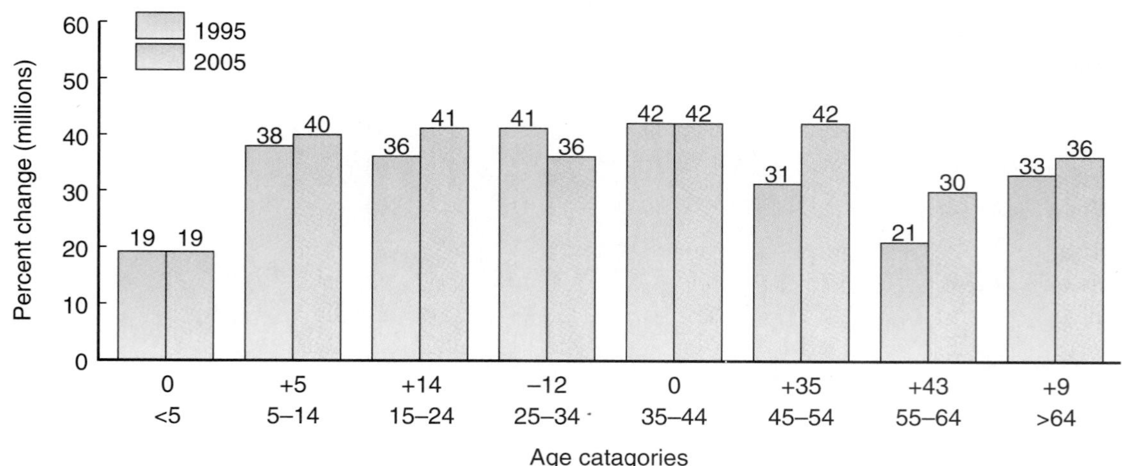

Source: *Projections of the Population of the United States*, Bureau of the Census, Series P-25.

leave home, vacations, restaurants, and financial services aimed at the mature market should flourish. Television programs will change to meet the interests of this mature market. With over half of the population 45 or older, the general ''tone'' of the American society will undoubtedly change significantly.

The age structure of a population is best understood through generation or **cohort analysis**. A generation or age cohort is a group of persons who have experienced a common social, political, historical, and economic environment.[21] For example, the pre-Depression generation (those over 65) spent their childhood in the depression of the 1930s, their adolescence or early adulthood during World War II, and their middle years during the Cold War. It is not surprising that they are more conservative and security conscious than the younger generations.

Cohort analysis allows us to understand the behaviors of existing market segments. It also increases our ability to forecast the needs and desires of future segments. For example, in 2010 the baby boom generation will be entering retirement. However, it would be a mistake to assume that retiring baby boomers will behave like the pre-Depression generation does today. The forces that shaped the lives of these generations were different and their behaviors will differ throughout their life cycles. In the following sections, we will examine the four generations that compose the adult American market.

Pre-Depression Generation The pre-Depression generation, often termed the *mature market* or *seniors*, refers to those individuals born before 1930. About 30 million Americans are in this generation. These individuals grew up in traumatic times. They have witnessed radical social, economic, and technological change. As a group, they are conservative and concerned with financial and personal security.

As with all generations, the pre-Depression generation is composed of many distinct segments.[22] Marketing to the senior market requires a segmented strategy. For example, 70 percent of the younger members of this market are married and 63 percent of these have no activity limitations, while only 24 percent of the oldest members are married and 57 percent have activity limitations. The poorest 20 percent have an average net worth less than $3,500 while the wealthiest 20 percent has an average net worth of almost $300,000.

Products related to the unique needs of mature consumer segments range from vacations to health services to serving sizes. Communications strategies involve both media selection and message content. Most adult consumers report feeling 70 to 85 percent of their chronological age. This suggests using spokespersons somewhat younger than the target segment. However, evidence on the effectiveness of this approach is limited.[23]

In general, age should not be the point of the message.[24] As one experienced marketer stated: ''It's important to appeal to the things they are interested in, rather than appealing to the age they've reached—because they aren't thinking about age.'' It is also important to pretest advertisements aimed at this market.

Depression Generation This is the cohort born between 1930 and 1946 so they are now 50 to 65 years of age. There are about 33 million individuals in this group. They are at the height of their earning power and they dominate the top positions in both business and government. They are beginning to notice the physical effects of aging. Comfort as well as style is important. Levi's Action Slacks have been a major success with this generation. These slacks, which have an elastic waistband, are cut for the less lean, more mature body. This generation has given rise to many of the products low in fat, sugar, salt, and/or cholesterol on the market today.

Retirement planning is important to this group and they are concerned about the ability of the Social Security system to fulfill its promises. Firms such as Merrill Lynch have developed products and services to meet these needs.

Baby Boom Generation The baby boom generation refers to those individuals born during the dramatic increase of births between the end of World War II and 1964. There are about 80 million baby boomers. Most of this group grew up during the prosperous 1950s and 1960s. They were heavily influenced by the Kennedy assassination, the Vietnam War, recreational drugs, the sexual revolution, the energy crisis, and the Cold War, as well as rock and roll and the Beatles.

One reason for the focus on youth in advertising and product developments has been the size of this segment and the fact that, until recently, it was young. It *is* the mass market, and as it ages, marketers will have to deal with a much more mature market. One aspect of this change is the fact that most (60 percent) baby boomers are now parents. Parenthood provides a consistency of lifestyle between the older and younger members of this generation.

Baby boomers are characterized by high education levels, high incomes, and dual-career households. However, they are also characterized by time poverty as they try to manage two careers and family responsibilities. Many are now facing economic hardships and uncertainties as the economy remains sluggish and many companies continue reducing the size of their workforces, including middle management.

In 2000, this generation will be aged 36 to 54. This is an age range characterized by a family and home orientation. It also involves the need to save for, or to pay for, children's college and marriages. In addition, it is the time that individuals begin to plan for retirement.[25] This is a particular concern as there are doubts about the ability of the Social Security system to handle the large influx of demand that this generation will produce.

Baby Bust Generation The baby bust generation, often referred to as Generation X, was born between 1965 and 1980. It is a smaller generation than its predecessor. This generation reached adulthood during difficult economic times that show no signs of abating. They are the first generation to be raised mainly in dual-career or single parent households. They are the first American generation to seriously confront the issue of ''reduced expectations.'' These reduced expectations are based on reality for many ''busters'' as the data below show:[26]

18- to 29-year-olds who had:	1978	1992
A second car	26%	17%
A house	31	24
A yard	34	25

This generation faces a world racked by ''regional conflicts,'' an environment that continues to deteriorate, an economy that offers them less hope than at any time since the 1930s, an AIDS epidemic that threatens their lives, and a staggering national debt. It tends to blame the ''me generation'' and the materialism associated with the baby boom generation for the difficult future it sees for itself. Recent headlines provide a feel for this generation's mood: *Move Over Boomers—The Busters Are Here and They Are Angry* and *Why Busters Hate Boomers.*[27]

Until recently, this generation has largely been ignored both by marketers and by the mass media as they have focused on the baby boomers. However, the baby bust generation is a $125 billion market, and it is vital for products such as beer, fast food, cosmetics, and electronics. As it enters the household formation age over the next 10 years, it will be critical for cars, appliances, and children's products. However, it is not an easy generation to reach. It is both cynical and sophisticated about products, ads, and shopping. It is materialistic and impatient. In many aspects, its tastes are "not baby boom." Thus, the grunge look and grunge music are currently fashionable, new magazines such as *Spin*, *Details*, and *YSP* are popular, and irreverence in advertising works. For example, almost half of those aged 18 to 24 preferred Coca-Cola's *Polar Bear* ads to its previous campaign, while less than a fifth of those aged 45 to 54 did.[28]

Busters need value because many have low-paying jobs, and they want products and messages designed uniquely for their tastes and lifestyles.[29] Marketers are increasingly targeting this group. Apple's decision to advertise computers on MTV and MCI's 1-800-COLLECT service are both targeted at baby busters. Managerial Application 3–8 shows MCI's ad from *Spy* magazine aimed at this group. Note how this ad follows the general observations made above.

MANAGERIAL APPLICATION 3–8

Appealing to the Baby Busters

SUMMARY

American values have and will continue to evolve. In terms of those values that influence an individual's relationship with *others*, Americans are slightly less individualistic than in the past. We have substantially less of a masculine orientation now than in the past. We also place a greater value on older persons and on cooperation. Families appear to be returning to a parent-centered orientation.

Values that affect our relationship to our *environment* have become somewhat more performance oriented and less oriented toward change. There is a strong and growing value placed on protecting the natural environment.

Self-oriented values have also undergone change. In particular, hard work is regaining respect as an end in itself. We also place slightly less emphasis on sensual gratification, and we are more content to delay our rewards than in the recent past.

Values are not embraced equally by all individuals and groups in America. For example, the baby bust generation appears to be more materialistic and to have less respect for work as an end in itself than the older generations have.

Roles are prescribed patterns of behavior expected of a person in a situation. *Gender roles* are *ascribed roles* based on the sex of the individual rather than on characteristics the individual can control. In contrast, an *achievement role* is acquired based on performance over which an individual does have some degree of control.

Gender roles, particularly the female role, have undergone radical changes in the past 20 years. The fundamental shift has been for the female role to become more like the traditional male role. Virtually all aspects of our society, including marketing activities, have been affected by this shift.

American society is described in part by its demographic makeup, which includes a population's size, distribution, and structure. The structure of a population refers to these elements: gender, age, income, education, and occupation. Demographics are not static. At present, the rate of population growth is slowing, average age is increasing, southern and western regions are growing, the workforce contains more women and white-collar workers than ever before, and per capita income is growing slowly. Since demographics affect all aspects of the consumption process, marketers must anticipate these shifts and adjust their marketing mixes accordingly.

A particularly useful form of demographic analysis is cohort or generation analysis. A generation or age cohort is a group of persons who have experienced a common social, political, historical, and economic environment. Their behaviors and values differ from those of other generations as they evolve through their life cycle. The present adult American market consists of four major generations: pre-Depression, Depression, baby boom, and baby bust. They differ sharply in many aspects of their lives, including their behavior as consumers.

REVIEW QUESTIONS

1. What is a *cultural value*? Are cultural values shared by all members of a culture?
2. Describe the current American culture in terms of the following values:
   a. Individual/Collective.
   b. Performance/Status.
   c. Tradition/Change.
   d. Masculine/Feminine.
   e. Competitive/Cooperative.
   f. Youth/Age.
   g. Active/Passive.
   h. Material/Nonmaterial.
   i. Hard work/Leisure.
   j. Risk taking/Security.

k. Problem solving/Fatalistic.
l. Admire nature/Overcome nature.
m. Adult/Child.
n. Postponed gratification/Immediate gratification.
o. Sensual gratification/Abstinence.
p. Humorous/Serious.
q. Romantic/Nonromantic.
r. Cleanliness.

3. What is *green marketing*?
4. How does an *ascribed role* differ from an *achievement role*?
5. What is a *gender role*?
6. What is happening to male and female gender roles?
7. What is the difference between a traditional and a modern gender role orientation?
8. Describe a segmentation system for the female market based on employment status and gender role orientation.
9. What are some of the major marketing implications of the changing role of women?
10. What are *demographics*?
11. What trend(s) characterizes the size of the American population?
12. Why is *population growth* an important concept for marketers?
13. What trend(s) characterizes the geographic distribution of the American population?
14. What trend(s) characterizes the occupational structure of the United States?
15. What trend(s) characterizes the level of education in the United States?
16. What trend(s) characterizes the level of income in the United States?
17. What trend(s) characterizes the age distribution of the American population?
18. What is *cohort analysis*? Why is it useful?
19. Describe the major generation groups in America.

DISCUSSION QUESTIONS

20. Describe additional values you feel could (or should) be added to Figure 3–2. Describe the marketing implications of each.
21. Pick the three values you feel the authors were most inaccurate about in describing the *current* American values. Justify your answers.
22. Pick the three values you feel the authors were most inaccurate about in describing the *emerging* American values. Justify your answers.
23. Which values are most relevant to the purchase and use of a ______? Are they currently favorable or unfavorable for ______ ownership? Are they shifting at all? If so, is the shift in a favorable or unfavorable direction?
    a. Dog
    b. Sierra Club contribution
    c. Dishwasher
    d. *MTV*
    e. Golf club membership
    f. American Express card
24. Do you believe Americans' concern for the environment is a stronger value than their materialism?
25. Do you think housewives may become "defensive" or "sensitive" about not having employment outside of the home? If so, what implications will this have for marketing practice?
26. Develop an advertisement for a ______ for each of the four female market segments described in the chapter.
    a. Casual restaurant
    b. Vacuum cleaner
    c. Laundry detergent
    d. Moderate-priced wine
    e. American Express card
    f. Cosmetic
27. Name five products that are now primarily associated with the:
    a. Male role but will increasingly be used by females.
    b. Male role but will *not* increasingly be used by females.
    c. Female role but will increasingly be used by males.
    d. Female role but will *not* increasingly be used by males.
28. Which demographic shifts, if any, do you feel will have a noticeable impact on the market for ______ in the next 10 years? Justify your answer.

a. Automobiles
b. Vacations
c. Fast food restaurants
d. Soft drinks
e. "Green" products
f. Television programs

29. Given the shift in population shown in Figure 3–3, name five products that will face increasing demand and five that will face declining demand.
30. Will the increasing median age of our population affect the general "tone" of our society? In what ways?
31. Use the buying power index in Exhibit 3–1 (see page 87) to estimate the annual soft drink consumption of Chicago. Assume that U.S. consumption is 800 million gallons and that soft drinks are considered to be a moderate-priced product.
32. How would your response to question 31 change if soft drinks were considered an economy-priced product? Why?
33. What types of products, media, messages, and outlets will appeal to the ______ generation in 2005?
    a. Pre-Depression
    b. Depression
    c. Baby boom
    d. Baby bust

APPLICATION ACTIVITIES

34. Interview a salesperson at a ______ and obtain a description of the "average" purchaser in demographic terms. Are the demographic shifts predicted in the text going to increase or decrease the size of this average-purchaser segment?
    a. BMW or Mercedes dealership
    b. Waterbed outlet
    c. Travel agent (vacation travel)
    d. Pharmacy
    e. Golf equipment outlet
    f. Video rental
35. Find and copy or describe an advertisement for an item that reflects Americans' position on the ______ value.
    a. active—passive
    b. material—nonmaterial
    c. hard work—leisure
    d. postponed—immediate gratification
    e. sensual gratification—abstinence
    f. humorous—serious
    g. cleanliness
    h. performance—status
    i. tradition—change
    j. risk taking—security
    k. problem solving—fatalistic
    l. admire—overcome nature
    m. individual—collective
    n. romantic—nonromantic
    o. adult—child
    p. competition—cooperation
    q. youth—age
    r. masculine—feminine
36. Interview a salesperson who has been selling ______ for at least 10 years. See if this individual has noticed a change in the purchasing roles of women over time.
    a. Automobiles
    b. Expensive wine
    c. Do-it-yourself equipment
    d. Life insurance.
37. Interview a career-oriented workwife and a traditional housewife of a similar age. Report on differences in attitudes toward shopping, products, and so forth.
38. Find one advertisement you think is particularly appropriate for each of the female market segments (traditional housewife, trapped housewife, trapped working woman, career working woman). Copy or describe each ad and justify its selection.
39. Interview a ______ salesperson. Ascertain the interest shown in ______ by males and females. Determine if males and females are concerned with different characteristics of ______ and if they have different purchase motivations.
    a. Stereo equipment
    b. Computer
    c. Automobile
    d. Golf equipment
    e. Refrigerator
    f. Flower
40. Interview 10 male and 10 female students. Ask each to describe a typical ______ owner or

consumer. If they do not specify, ask for the gender of the typical owner. Then probe to find out why they think the typical owner is of the gender they indicated. Also determine the perceived marital and occupational status of the typical owner and the reasons for these beliefs.

a. Cat
b. Expensive wine
c. Mountain bike
d. Compact disk player
e. United Way contributor
f. Waterbed

41. Read "Move Over Boomers" by L. Zinn, *Business Week*, December 14, 1992, pp. 74–82. Write a brief report indicating the extent to which you feel it is an accurate portrayal of the baby bust generation.

42. Interview a member of each generation described in the text. Ask about their values, hopes, and concerns as well as their product and media use. Write a brief report indicating any differences you found across the generations.

43. Find and copy or describe an advertisement you think is particularly appropriate for each generation described in the text. Explain why you chose each ad.

REFERENCES

[1]M. Maremont, "A New Equal Right: The Close Shave," *Business Week*, March 29, 1993, pp. 58–59.

[2]J. W. Winski, "Who We Are," *Advertising Age*, January 20, 1992, pp. 16, 18.

[3]F. Rose, "If It Feels Good, It Must Be Bad," *Fortune*, October 21, 1991, pp. 91–108.

[4]Winski, "Who We Are."

[5]S. Sherman, "How to Prosper in the Value Decade," *Fortune*, November 30, 1992, pp. 90–103; F. Rice, "What Intelligent Consumers Want," *Fortune*, December 28, 1992, pp. 56–60; and "Economy Puts Focus on Value," *Advertising Age*, July 26, 1993, pp. 1+.

[6]"P&G Plays Pied Piper on Pricing," *Advertising Age*, March 9, 1992, p. 6.

[7]S. Hayward, "The Environmental Opportunity," *Marketing Research*, December 1989, pp. 66–67.

[8]S. Hume and P. Strnad, "Consumers Go 'Green'," *Advertising Age*, September 25, 1989, p. 3.

[9]L. Freeman and J. Dagnoli, "Green Concerns Influence Buying," *Advertising Age*, July 30, 1990, p. 19. See also A. Atwood, "Environmental Issues and Consumers' State of Mind"; C. Obermiller, "Teaching Environmentally Conscious Consumer Behavior"; T. J. Olney and W. Bryce, "Environmentally Based Product Claims and the Erosion of Consumer Trust," *Advances in Consumer Behavior 18*, ed. R. H. Holman and M. R. Solomon (Provo: Association for Consumer Research, 1991), pp. 693–94; and "Is Green Marketing Dead?" *Advertising Age*, June 29, 1992, pp. S.1–S.11.

[10]J. L. Davis, "Strategies for Environmental Advertising," *Journal of Consumer Marketing*, no. 2, 1993, pp. 19–36. See also J. S. Scerbinski, "Consumers and the Environment," *Journal of Business Strategy*, September/October 1991, pp. 44–47; J. A. Ottman, "Industry's Response to Green Consumerism," and R. J. Gillespie, "Pitfalls and Opportunities for Environmental Marketers," both in *Journal of Business Strategy*, July/August, 1992, pp. 3–7 and 14–17; and J. K. Ross III, L. T. Patterson, and M. A. Stutts, "Consumer Perceptions of Organizations that Use Cause-Related Marketing," *Journal of the Academy of Marketing Science*, Winter 1992, pp. 93–97.

[11]B. J. Snyder and R. Serafin, "Auto Makers Set New Ad Strategy to Reach Women," *Advertising Age*, September 23, 1985, pp. 3, 80; "Women and the Auto Market," *Advertising Age*, September 15, 1986, sec. S; "Women Help Select Cars," *Marketing News*, October 9, 1987, p. 18; F. Curtindale, "Marketing Cars to Women," *American Demographics*, November 1988, pp. 28–31; and T. Triplett, "Automakers Recognizing Value of Women's Market," *Marketing News* (April 11, 1994), pp. 1–2.

[12]J. S. Grigsby, "Women Change Places," *American Demographics*, November 1992, p. 48.

[13]R. Deaton, *Work and Family Life* (Des Moines: *Better Homes and Gardens*, 1986). See also W. T. Anderson, L. L. Golden, U. N. Umesh, and W. A. Weeks, "Timestyles," *Psychology & Marketing*, March 1992, pp. 101–22.

[14]S. Hayward, "Men Beginning to Redefine Roles," *Advertising Age*, November 18, 1991, p. 20.

[15]These segments are similar to the four categories popularized by Bartos. See R. Bartos, *The Moving Target* (New York: The Free Press, 1982); and R. Bartos, *Marketing to Women Around the World* (Cambridge, Mass.: Harvard University Press, 1989).

[16]L. Zinn, "This Bud's for You," *Business Week*, November 4, 1991, p. 90.

[17]N. Darnton, "Mommy vs. Mommy," *Newsweek*, June 4, 1990, p. 60.

[18]For recent research in these areas, see L. J. Jaffe, "Impact of Positioning and Sex-Role Identity on Women's Responses to Advertising," and J. A. Bellizzi and L. Milner, "Gender Positioning of a Traditionally Male-Dominant Product," both in *Journal of Advertising Research*, June/July 1991, pp. 57–64 and 72–70; V. Prakash, "Sex Roles and Advertising Preferences," *Journal of Advertising Research*, May/June 1992, pp. 43–52; and M. L. Klassen, C. R. Jasper, and A. M. Schwartz, *Journal of Advertising Research*, pp. 30–39.

[19]"Males Don't Like New Women: DDB," *Advertising Age*, October 20, 1980, p. 60. See also A. W. Fawcett, "Ads Awaken to Fathers' New Role in Family Life" *Advertising Age*, January 10, 1994, p. S-8.

[20]*Men in the Marketplace* (Emmaus, Penn.: Rodale Press, 1989).

[21]L. G. Pol, "Demographic Contributions to Marketing," *Journal of Marketing Science*, Winter 1991, p. 56. See W. Strauss and N. Howe, "The Cycle of Generations," *American Demographics*, April 1991, pp. 26–34, and J. Waldrop, "Secrets of the Age Pyramid," *American Demographics*, August 1992, pp. 46–52.

[22]C. F. Longino, Jr., and W. H. Crown, "Older Americans," *American Demographics*, August 1991, pp. 48–52; L. G. Pol, M. G. May, and F. R. Hartranft, "Eight Stages of Aging," *American Demographics*, August 1992, pp. 54–57; and T. S. Gruca and C. D. Schewe, "Researching Older Consumers," *Marketing Research*, September 1992, pp. 18–23.

[23]G. P. Mosschis, "Marketing to Older Adults," *Journal of Consumer Marketing*, Fall 1991, pp. 33–41; and D. W. Wolfe, "The Key to Marketing to Older Consumers," *Journal of Business Strategy*, November 1992, pp. 14–19. See also N. Stephens, "Cognitive Age," *Journal of Advertising*, December 1991, pp. 37–48.

[24]See G. P. Moschis, A. Mathur, and R. K. Smith, "Older Consumers' Orientations Toward Age-Based Marketing Stimuli," *Journal of the Academy of Marketing Science*, Summer 1993, pp. 195–205.

[25]For details, see B. Townsend, "Boomers Facing 50," *Marketing Research*, June 1992, pp. 48–49.

[26]W. B. Fay, "Understanding Generation X," *Marketing Research*, Spring 1993, p. 55.

[27]L. Zinn, "Move Over Boomers," *Business Week*, December 14, 1992, pp. 74–82; and S. Ratan, "Why Busters Hate Boomers," *Fortune*, October 4, 1993, pp. 56–70.

[28]A. W. Fawcett, "CAA Ads Make Big Splash with Youth, Women," *Advertising Age*, April 12, 1993, p. 1.

[29]Ibid.; also see E. M. Crimmins, R. A. Easterlin, and Y. Saito, "What Young Adults Want," *American Demographics*, July 1991, pp. 24–33; W. Dunn, Hanging Out with American Youth," *American Demographics*, February 1992, pp. 24–35; and P. Herbig, W. Koehler, K. Day, "Marketing to the Baby Bust Generation," *Journal of Consumer Marketing*, no. 1, 1993, pp. 4–9, and J. B. Kim, "Generation X Gets Comfortable," *Advertising Age*, January 10, 1994, p. S-2.

CHAPTER 4

THE CHANGING AMERICAN SOCIETY: SUBCULTURES

Until the late 1980s, Hills Bros® did not specifically market its MJB or Hills Bros brands of coffee to the Hispanic market. Focus groups and quantitative research both revealed a strong market opportunity for coffee, particularly instant. Many Mexican Hispanics in California used instant coffee to make *cafe con leche*—a mixture of warm milk and coffee. This drink is consumed by adults and children. In addition, adult Hispanics are heavy users of regular coffee, consuming 30 percent more than Anglos.

At this time, Hills Bros' general strategy relied heavily on couponing. However, this was not considered a sound method for an initial approach to the Hispanic market. A 30-second Spanish-language radio ad was developed for each brand and run on four Los Angeles radio stations with Hispanic audiences from August to December.

The MJB ad in which a mother takes an instant-coffee break after sending her children off to school and her husband off to work uses the theme: "When it's time for coffee, savor the moment with a rich, delicious cup of MJB." The ad attempts to capture the importance of the mother's role in the close-knit Hispanic family.

The second Hills Bros' commercial focused on Hispanic women as gracious hostesses. During a discussion of the just-finished dinner, the hostess says her recipe for coffee was simple: Hills Bros instant. The guests agree that the coffee was perfect for *sobremesa*, the time spent talking at the table after the meal is complete.

Sales of both brands increased over 15 percent.[1]

In the previous chapter, we described how changes in American values and demographics were creating challenges and opportunities for marketers. Another extremely important aspect of the American society is its numerous subcultures. Although the American society has always contained numerous subcultures, until recently many marketers treated it as a homogeneous culture based primarily on Western European values. Though this view of America was never accurate, it is even less so today as non-European immigration, differential birth rates, and increased ethnic identification accentuate the heterogeneous nature of our society.

American society is characterized by an array of racial, ethnic, nationality, religious, and regional groups or subcultures. These subcultures are growing at different rates and are themselves undergoing change. As Figure 4–1 shows, identification with a subculture produces unique market behaviors.

FIGURE 4–1 Identification with a Subculture Produces Unique Market Behaviors

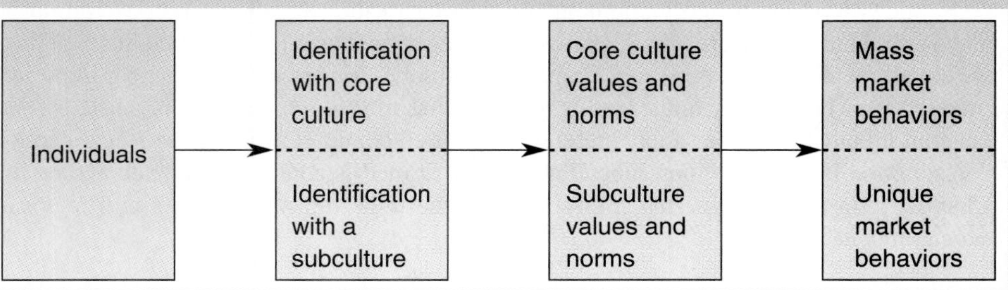

In this chapter we describe the more important groups from a marketing perspective. We also highlight the marketing strategy implications of a heterogeneous rather than a homogeneous society.

THE NATURE OF SUBCULTURES

A **subculture** is *a segment of a larger culture whose members share distinguishing patterns of behavior.* The unique patterns of behavior shared by subculture group members are based on the social history of the group as well as on its current situation. Subculture members are also part of the larger culture in which they exist. Subculture members generally share many behaviors and beliefs with the core culture. As Figure 4–1 indicates, the degree to which an individual behaves in a manner unique to a subculture depends on the extent to which the individual identifies with the subculture.

While there are a number of bases for subcultures, most attention is focused on racial, ethnic, and nationality groups. The traditional view was that America was a melting pot or a soup bowl. Immigrants from various countries would come to America and quickly (at least by the second generation) surrender their old languages, values, behaviors, and even religions. In their place, they would acquire American characteristics that were largely a slight adaptation of Western European, particularly British features. The base American culture was vast enough that new immigrants did not change the flavor of the mixture to any noticeable extent. While this view was a reasonable approximation for most Western European immigrants, it was never very accurate for African, Hispanic, or Asian immigrants. Nor did it accurately describe the experience of the American Indian.

Today, America is often described as a salad rather than a melting pot or a soup bowl. When a small amount of a new ingredient is added to soup, it generally loses its identity completely and blends into the overall flavor of the soup. In a salad, each ingredient retains its own unique identity while adding to the color and flavor of the overall salad. The soup analogy is probably most accurate for European immigrants and nationality groups, while the salad analogy most closely describes the experience of non-European immigrants and nationality groups. However, even in the salad bowl analogy we should add a large serving of salad dressing that represents the core American culture and that blends the diverse groups into a cohesive society.[2]

Astute marketers are aggressively pursuing opportunities created by increased diversity in the market. AT&T runs broadcast and print ads in 20 different languages in the United States! Chrysler advertises its New Yorker model by stressing safety features to the general market, styling to African-Americans, and aspiration and achievement to Hispanics. However, marketing to ethnic groups requires a thorough understanding of the attitudes and values of each group. For example, a New York Life Insurance ad designed to appeal to Koreans was a disaster because it used a Chinese model. More subtly, Citibank had to withdraw a holiday TV ad aimed at Chinese consumers due to complaints about the sexual innuendo of corks popping out of champagne bottles.[3]

Ethnic groups are the most commonly described subcultures, but generations, religions, and geographic regions are also the bases for strong subcultures in the United States. Thus, we are all members of several subcultures. Our attitudes toward new products or imported products may be strongly influenced by our regional subculture, our taste in music by our generation subculture, our food preferences by our ethnic subculture, and our alcohol consumption by our religious subculture. We described generation-based subcultures in Chapter 3. In the sections that follow here we describe the major ethnic and regional subcultures in America.

ETHNIC SUBCULTURES

The Bureau of the Census uses the terms *black*, *white*, *Asian*, *Pacific Islander*, and *American Indian* to describe America's major racial groups. *Hispanic* is used as an ethnic term to describe individuals from Spanish-speaking countries. However, we will define **ethnic subcultures** broadly as *those whose members' unique shared behaviors are based on a common racial, language, or nationality background.* Figure 4–2 provides the current and projected sizes of the major ethnic groups in America. As this figure makes clear, non-European ethnic groups constitute a significant and growing part of our population (from 24 percent in 1990 to 32 percent by 2010). The percentages shown in the figure understate the importance of these ethnic groups to specific geographic regions. Ethnic groups tend to concentrate in relatively few areas of the country. Thus Hispanics are the largest population group in parts of southern California, south Texas, and Florida, while Asian-Americans are the largest group in Honolulu, and African-Americans are a majority in parts of the South.

The relatively faster growth rate of non-European groups is due in part to a higher birthrate among these groups (they have a relatively young age distribution; see Figure 4–3) and to greater immigration. Immigration accounted for 11 percent of America's

FIGURE 4–2

Ethnic Subcultures in the United States: 1990–2010

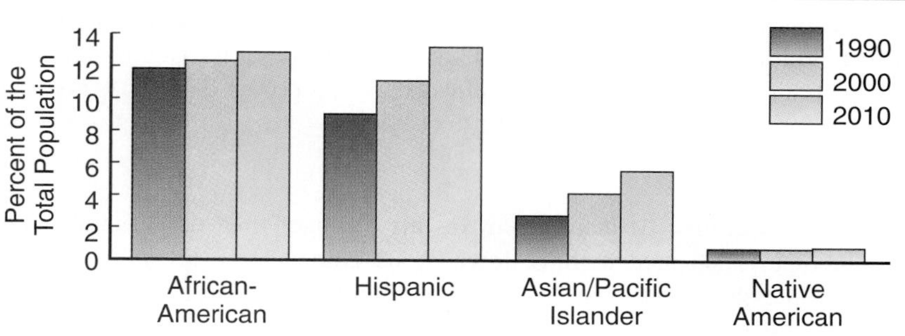

FIGURE 4–3

Age Distribution of the Major Ethnic Groups

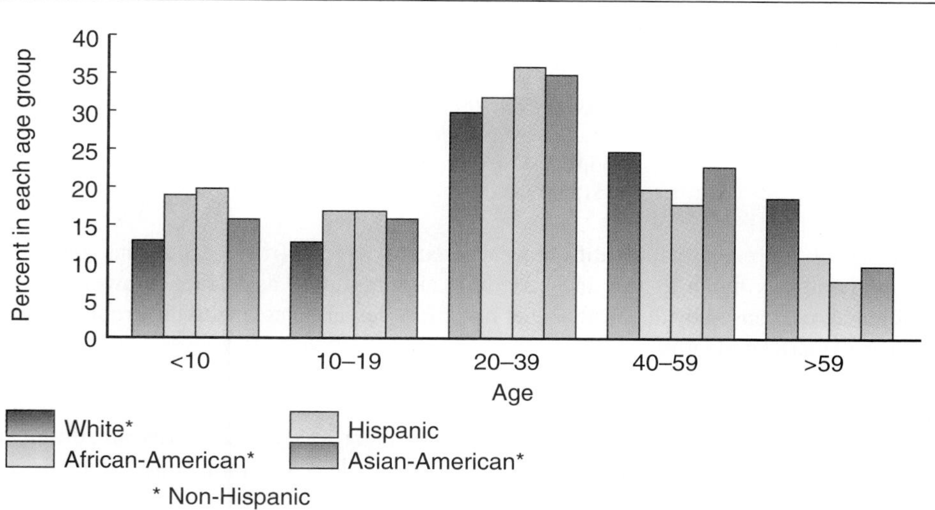

growth during the 1960s, 33 percent in the 1970s, and 39 percent in the 1980s. There were almost nine million legal and probably two million illegal immigrants during the 1980s.[4] Between 1971 and 1991, the sources of these immigrants were:

Asia	35.2%
Mexico	23.7
Caribbean	13.1
Europe	12.0
Central/South America	11.1
Canada	1.8
Elsewhere	3.1

Clearly, immigration patterns have fueled the growth of ethnic subcultures. The influx of ethnic immigrants not only increases the size of the ethnic subcultures, it also reinforces the unique behaviors and attitudes derived from the group's home culture. In the following sections we describe the major ethnic subcultures. It is critical to remember that all subcultures are very diverse and general descriptions do not apply to all of the members.

AFRICAN-AMERICANS

African-Americans, or blacks (surveys do not indicate a clear preference for either term among African-Americans[5]), constitute 12 percent of the American population. Concentrated in the South and the major metropolitan areas outside of the South, African-Americans have more than $250 billion in combined spending power. Thus, it is not surprising that marketers are very interested in this group.

Demographics

As Figure 4–3 indicates, African-Americans are younger than the general population. African-Americans also tend to have lower household income levels ($19,758 versus $31,435 for whites) and to be single-parent households.[6] However, stereotyping African-Americans as poverty ridden would not be accurate, as the data below indicate:

African-American Family Household Income	Percent
>$99,999	1.4%
$75,000–$99,999	3.1
$50,000–$74,999	10.3
$25,000–$49,999	29.3
$15,000–$24,999	18.4
<$15,000	37.5

Many of the consumption differences noted between African-Americans and other groups relates as much to age and economic circumstances as to race. However, other differences are caused by differing values and lifestyles associated with the group's unique African-American identity.

Consumer Groups

Market Segment Research recently conducted a major study of the African-American, Hispanic, and Asian-American markets in America.[7] This study identified four distinct consumer groups among African-Americans.

Contented (37 percent) This is the largest group and it is the oldest (mean age = 44). Forty percent of the group are married; 32 percent are widowed or divorced. The average household size is 2.3. Fifty-six percent are female. Half are not employed. Three-fourths finished high school and 13 percent completed college.

This is a mature segment that is basically content with life. They are not concerned with social appearances or status. They are not impulsive. They prefer to stay at home and they are moderately health conscious. They tend to save and are followers rather than leaders. They are the least optimistic about their financial future.

Upwardly Mobile (24 percent) This group has an average age of 37. Slightly more than half are male. Sixty-two percent are married; less than 10 percent are widowed or divorced. The average household size is 3.1. Over 80 percent are employed and 50 percent attended college.

This segment is composed of active, status-oriented professionals. They have materialistic aspirations and are quality oriented. They are impulsive shoppers but are also smart shoppers. They are financially secure, health conscious, and optimistic about the future.

Living for the Moment (21 percent) This is the youngest group; two-thirds are less than 34. Fifty-eight percent are male; 61 percent are single. The average household size is 2.4. Almost 80 percent are employed and 90 percent completed high school.

This segment is self-oriented and lives for the moment. They are not concerned with social issues or responsibility. They are socially active, carefree, and image conscious.

Living Day-to-Day (18 percent) This group has the lowest income and the largest average household size (5.4) although only a third are married. Its average age is 36, and 56 percent are female. Only half are employed and over a fourth have less than a high school education.

This is basically an unskilled poverty group. They are not status conscious nor are they socially active. They are most concerned with price and least concerned with quality. They are not health conscious and they are not optimistic about their financial future.

The four segments described above are not the only ways the African-American subculture could be segmented. However, they do indicate the diversity that exists within this population.

Media Usage

African-Americans make greater use of mass media than do whites and they have strongly different preferences. Table 4–1 shows the top 10 television shows among African-Americans along with their ratings with general audiences and the top 10 shows overall and their ratings with African-Americans. Clearly, African-Americans prefer shows with African-American themes or performers. Likewise, radio stations that play music popular with African-Americans and magazines focused on African-American concerns receive most of the attention from this segment.

Marketing to African-Americans

Marketing to African-Americans should be based on the same principles as marketing to any other group. That is, the market should be carefully analyzed, relevant needs should be identified among one or more segments of the market, and the entire marketing mix should be designed to meet the needs of the target segments. At times the relevant segment of the African-American market will require a unique product. At other times it will require a unique package, advertising medium, or message. Or, no change may be required from

TABLE 4–1 The Top 10 Television Shows among African-Americans

Top 10 Shows Among Blacks	Rating among Blacks	Rating among Gen'l aud.	Top 10 Prime-Time Shows	Rating among Gen'l aud.	Rating among Blacks
A Different World (NBC)	43.6	18.0	Cheers (NBC)	21.6	26.4
The Bill Cosby Show (NBC)	39.0	17.4	60 Minutes (CBS)	20.6	18.7
Fresh Prince of Bel Air (NBC)	34.2	13.2	Roseanne (ABC)	18.2	15.1
In Living Color (Fox)	31.1	10.4	A Different World (NBC)	17.9	43.6
In the Heat of the Night (NBC)	27.7	15.2	The Bill Cosby Show (NBC)	17.4	39.0
Family Matters (ABC)	27.3	15.8	Murphy Brown (CBS)	16.9	12.8
Blossom (NBC)	27.1	11.3	America's Funniest Home Videos (ABC)	16.9	7.1
Cheers (NBC)	26.4	21.5	Empty Nest (NBC)	16.7	19.9
Amen (NBC)	25.5	10.1	Designing Women (CBS)	16.7	13.9
Ferris Bueller (NBC)	25.4	11.1	America's Funniest People (ABC)	16.7	10.5

Source: Nielsen Media Research

the marketing mix used to reach the overall market. However, it is critical that the decision on how to appeal to this market be based on a sound understanding of the needs of the selected segments.

Products African-Americans have different skin tones and hair from white Americans. Cosmetics and similar products developed for white consumers are often inappropriate for black consumers. Recent recognition of this fact by major firms has created aggressive competition for the $600 million that African-American women spend each year on cosmetics.

Estée Lauder's subsidiary, Prescriptives, recently launched a product line called *All Skins* with 115 different shades designed to reach this market. Maybelline introduced *Shades of You* to meet the unique needs of this market. Managerial Application 4–1 show a print advertisement for Maybelline's *Shades of You* targeted at African-American women and an ad for the regular Maybelline lipstick targeted at the mass market. Note that the advertising message and approach are the same for both products. The differences are in the magazines in which the ads appear and the product characteristics. The underlying desire for beauty is the same for both segments. However, due to physiological differences, different product formulations are required and black-oriented media are used to reach the African-American market segment.

Other manufacturers have found it worthwhile to alter their products to meet unique social needs of African-Americans. Hallmark has introduced a *Mahogany* line of greeting cards that features black characters and sayings. Mattel had considerable success with a black version of *Barbie*. However, the firm has done even better with *Shani*, a Barbie-type doll with broader facial features and slightly fuller hips as well as a dark skin. Managerial Application 4–2 shows several of Tyco Toys' African-American dolls.

Blacks often use the same product as whites but use it in a different way. Carnation's *Instant Breakfast Drink* is popular with black consumers. However, while whites use it as a low-calorie substitute for breakfast, African-Americans often consume it with breakfast because they enjoy the taste.

MANAGERIAL APPLICATION 4–1

A Product Designed to Appeal to Unique Physiological Needs of African-American Consumers and a Similar Product Designed for Whites

MANAGERIAL APPLICATION 4–2

Products Designed to Appeal to Unique Social Needs of African-American Consumers

Communications A common mistake when communicating with any ethnic group is to assume that its members are the same as the larger culture except for superficial differences. However, as one expert says: "Black people are not dark-skinned white people."[8] Failure to recognize this fact often produces commercials "targeted" at African-Americans that

MANAGERIAL APPLICATION

4–3

Advertisements Using Universal Appeals and African-American Models

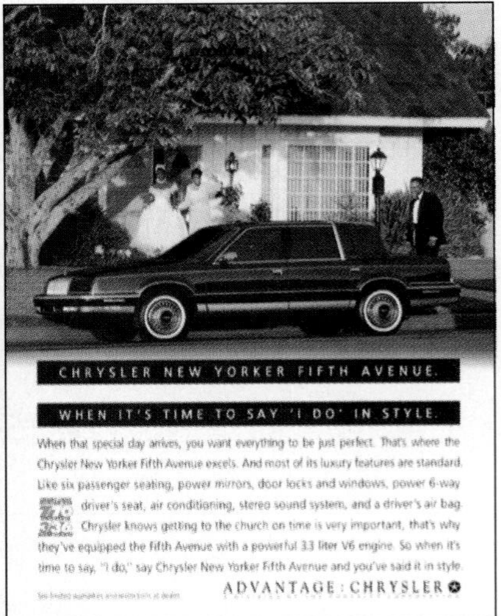

simply place the firm's standard ad in black media or that replace white actors with black actors, without changing the script, language, or setting. For example, Greyhound Bus targeted blacks by placing its standard commercials on black radio stations. Unfortunately, the soundtrack for the commercials was country-western, which is not popular with black audiences.

Not all messages targeted at African-Americans need differ significantly from those targeted at other groups. As we saw in Managerial Application 4–1, Maybelline's appeal to the desire to feel beautiful is the same for whites and blacks though the product and model are different. Managerial Application 4–3 contains two ads from African-American-oriented magazines that use black models but are otherwise similar to the firm's standard ads. Both ads are sound because the appeal to status and achievement (Chrysler) and security (State Farm) are appropriate to the targeted segments of both white and black subcultures.

In contrast, the ad for *Stove Top Stuffing* shown in Managerial Application 4–4 is used specifically to target African-Americans. Research revealed that many African-Americans refer to foods of this type as dressing rather than stuffing. Thus, in ads targeting this segment the word *dressing* is used. Note also the use of the term *Mama* and the outdoor basketball court setting.

Retailing J. C. Penney Co. has had great success with its *Authentic African* boutiques in its stores located near significant African-American populations. These small shops located inside J. C. Penney stores feature clothing, handbags, hats, and other accessories imported from Africa.

Kmart advertises in black media to attract customers to its stores. A recent radio commercial features a woman's voice saying:

MANAGERIAL APPLICATION 4–4

An Advertisement Created Specifically for the African-American Market

> Check this out and don't tell anyone. I went to Kmart the other day to get a lamp and accidentally went down the wrong aisle. Uh-huh, the one where the clothes are . . . Girl, I couldn't believe my eyes. I went out and looked at the store name again. It was Kmart, all right.

KFC has launched a ''neighborhood program'' to tie its neighborhood outlets to the character of the neighborhood in which they operate. In African-American neighborhoods this involves having the employees wear traditional African style uniforms, piping in up-tempo rhythm & blues music, and offering additional menu items that reflect local tastes such as soul sides—red beans and rice, sweet potato pie, Honey BBQ Wings, and Mean Greens.

Summary on the African-American Subculture

African-Americans are a large, growing, diverse market. They share many needs and desires with the larger culture. However, African-Americans are also a distinct group with unique needs, values, expressions, media habits, and so forth. They constitute an important segment for a great many products. They should be approached with careful attention to their unique attributes as well as recognition that they are Americans and share many desires in common with the larger market.

HISPANICS

The Bureau of the Census defines **Hispanic** as *a person of any race whose primary language, or the primary language of an ancestor, is Spanish.*[9] The use of the Spanish language among Hispanic-Americans is increasing rather than decreasing. The percent of Hispanics who use Spanish at home increased from 57 percent in 1988 to 70 percent in

1992. Extensive immigration is one reason for the increased use of Spanish. It is estimated that over 70 percent of Hispanic-Americans were born outside the United States.[10] Another reason is the growth of self-contained Spanish-speaking communities, coupled with the impact of national Spanish-language media.

Like any large group in America, Hispanics are diverse. Many marketers feel that the Hispanic subculture is not a single ethnic subculture but instead is three main and several minor nationality subcultures: Mexican-Americans (60 percent), Puerto Ricans (12 percent), Cubans (5 percent), and other Latinos, mainly from Central America (23 percent). Each group speaks a slightly different version of Spanish and has somewhat distinct values and lifestyles. Further, each group tends to live in distinct regions of the country: Mexican-Americans in the Southwest and California, Puerto Ricans in New York and New Jersey, Cubans in Florida, and other Latinos in California, New York, and Florida. Income levels also vary widely across the groups:

	1990 Income
Non-Hispanic families	$36,334
Mexican	$23,240
Puerto Rican	$18,008
Cuban	$31,439
Central/South American	$23,266
Other Hispanic	$27,382[11]

Others argue that while one must be sensitive to nationality-based differences, the common language, common religion (Roman Catholic for most Hispanics), and the emergence of national Spanish-language media and entertainment figures create sufficient cultural homogeneity for many products and advertising campaigns. Thus, the decision to treat Hispanics as a single ethnic subculture or several nationality subcultures depends on the product and the nature of the intended communication.

Identification with Traditional Hispanic Culture

Another way to segment the Hispanic market is by degree of identification with the traditional Hispanic culture. The Market Segment Research study identified three groups based on this dimension:

- Strong Hispanic Identification: This group is almost entirely Spanish-speaking. They tend to live in areas populated exclusively by Hispanics. They are recent arrivals and retain close ties to family and friends "at home." They are generally low on all measures of social status. Their media usage is heavily Spanish language. About 60 percent of all Hispanic nationality groups except Puerto Ricans (38 percent) are in this group.
- Moderate Hispanic Identification: This group speaks both Spanish and English but is most comfortable with Spanish. They live in areas of moderate Hispanic density. Most have been in the United States for 12 years or more. They have average levels of income and social status. Their ties to the "old country" are moderate. They use both Spanish-language and English media. About 25 percent of all Hispanic nationality groups except Puerto Ricans (35 percent) are in this group.
- Limited Hispanic Identification: This group speaks both Spanish and English. It is very comfortable with English. They live in areas dominated by non-Hispanics. They have lived in the United States for a long time and many are second- or third-generation Americans. Their ties to their country of origin are limited. They tend to use English language media. Their income and social status are relatively high. About 18 percent of all Hispanic nationality groups except Puerto Ricans (27 percent) are in this group.[12]

As the above discussion indicates, most Hispanics identify more or less strongly with a Hispanic culture. This culture is heavily influenced by the Roman Catholic religion. It is very family oriented, with the extended family playing an important role. It is also a very masculine culture. This masculine orientation manifests itself in many ways, including "macho" rules for interaction between males and between males and females. Sports are very important to Hispanics, particularly boxing, baseball, and soccer. Nationality tends to determine which of these is most popular (soccer for Mexican Americans, baseball for Cubans and Puerto Ricans).

While most Hispanics identify with their Hispanic roots, most also view themselves first and foremost as Americans. Many are quite conservative on issues such as increased immigration and bilingual education.[13] Thus, communicating with Hispanics is not a simple task.

Consumer Groups

The Market Segment Research study described earlier identified five unique consumer groups among the overall Hispanic market. Table 4–2 provides an overview of the demographics of each segment. The values and attitudes of each group are described in the following sections.

Demographic Characteristics of Hispanic Consumer Groups **TABLE 4–2**

Characteristic	Middle of the Road	Empty Nesters	Social Climbers	Living for the Moment	Recent Arrivals
Average family size	3.4	2.8	3.7	4.9	6.5
Average age	36	44	35	29	37
Male	46%	43%	61%	58%	38%
Married	59	61	68	47	19
Employed full-time	38	30	72	38	38
High school graduate	38	36	82	45	24
Attended college	7	15	43	11	2
From Mexico	59	51	53	57	81
From Puerto Rico	11	10	10	14	4
From Cuba	9	17	9	10	2
Speak Spanish only	63	60	31	37	68
Primarily Spanish	17	22	23	25	22
Spanish and English	19	16	39	34	10
Prefer Spanish media	61	64	38	47	68
Strong Hispanic ID.	60	67	41	40	78
Moderate Hispanic ID.	24	20	31	37	14
Limited Hispanic ID.	16	13	28	23	8

Source: *The 1993 MSR Minority Market Report* (Coral Gables, Florida: Market Segment Research, Inc., 1993).

Middle of the Road (26 percent) As their name indicates, this is an average group. They are moderately concerned about their finances and they try to balance spending and saving. Though somewhat impulsive, they are basically followers. They try to balance price and quality in their purchases. They are health conscious and are comfortable at home and at social gatherings.

Empty Nesters (25 percent) This is an established, older group with many retired members. They are financially conservative, budget conscious, and focused on saving. They are not impulsive. They are oriented toward the home and are not concerned with social appearances or trends. They are not socially active but are politically active. They are health conscious and are generally content.

Social Climbers (23 percent) This group has the least identification with the Hispanic culture. It is composed of upwardly mobile achievers. They are financially secure and have strong materialistic aspirations. They are optimistic about their economic outlook. They are more concerned with quality than price and they are impulsive shoppers. They are active in many areas and are very socially conscious.

Living for the Moment (14 percent) These young people have limited goals and are focused on the here and now. They are not concerned with financial security nor with broader issues such as the environment or social issues. They are socially active and optimistic about their future economic status.

Recent Arrivals (12 percent) This group has not been in the country very long. They are traditional and conservative. They are family oriented and are not socially active. They are seeking financial security and are optimistic that they will obtain it. However, most are unemployed and have limited education and training. They are careful, budget shoppers and are not concerned about trends or social status.

Marketing to Hispanics

Marketing to Hispanics requires the same attention to subsegment needs described earlier for African-Americans. Since the Hispanic market is estimated to be worth over $170 billion and is the most rapidly growing segment of our population, it is somewhat surprising that many marketers are just beginning to devote attention to it (in 1990 only $750 million was spent on Spanish-language advertising).[14] However, as the chapter opening example indicates, well-designed programs can result in substantial sales gains. Managerial Application 4–5 provides additional examples of successful approaches to this market.

As we saw earlier, most Hispanics speak Spanish most of the time and prefer Spanish-language media. Therefore, although it is possible to reach part of this market on mass media, any serious attempt to target Hispanics must use Spanish-language media.[15] Fortunately, this is a straightforward task. There are two Spanish-language television networks (Telemundo and Univision),[16] numerous Spanish-language magazines, including Spanish versions of *Cosmopolitan* and *Reader's Digest*,[17] and many Spanish-language radio stations and newspapers.

The first step in marketing to Hispanics is to determine which segment(s) to target. This decision is based on the same criteria used for any segmentation decision. The next step is to determine if one message will be sufficient or if unique messages will be required for the various nationality groups. Language and imagery are the important components of this decision. For example, an ad using sports in any way should consider the differences in sports preferences between the nationality groups.

MANAGERIAL APPLICATION 4–5

Successful Approaches to the Hispanic Market

- ''It's tough to get Hispanics to switch brands. And while the general buyer looks at price first, Hispanics are willing to pay extra to purchase quality products for their family. So handing out coupons or reducing price is not an effective way to get them to try our products. A far better approach is to do in-store promotions to get Hispanics to sample our product.'' Martin Serna, president of the firm that does Borden's promotions in the Hispanic community.
- Associating your firm with the Hispanic community is often effective. Anheuser-Busch, Campbell Soup, and Coca-Cola sponsor the nine-day Carnival Miami, one of the largest Hispanic festivals in America. Adolph Coors sponsors a variety of events, including community cook-offs and *Cinco de Mayo* celebrations. American Honda Motor Company helped fund the U.S. tour of Mexico City's Ballet Folklorico. Ford has helped fund many soccer teams in Hispanic communities.
- See's Candies shows ads on Spanish television that feature a tour of their manufacturing plant. The fact that 70 percent of their workforce is Hispanic is apparent and shows their support of the Hispanic community.
- Tiangus, a grocery chain aimed at the Mexican-American market in Los Angeles, was launched with a fiesta atmosphere. Stands served a wide variety of Mexican foods, the walls were splashed with bright colors, and shoppers were serenaded with mariachi bands. The shelves were stocked with empanadas, handmade tortillas, and other items typically found only in specialty stores. Tiangus has become a major success.
- Pepsi developed an advertisement that appealed to all the Hispanic nationality groups. It produced a Spanish version of its Pepsi-generation campaign that focuses on a ''sweet 15'' party, the *quinceanera*, which celebrates the coming of age for Hispanic girls. In contrast, Nestlé had to depart from their normal one-ad approach for Butterfinger candy. They found that peanut butter was *mantequilla de mani* for Hispanics from the Caribbean and *crema de cacahuate* for those from Mexico. Therefore, they created two different sets of copy for their Spanish-language ads.

Source: S. Livingston, ''Marketing to the Hispanic-American Community,'' *Journal of Business Strategy*, March–April 1992, pp. 54–57.

As the opening example and Managerial Application 4–5 illustrate, successfully marketing to Hispanic consumers involves more than translating ad copy from English to Spanish. However, even direct translations are not necessarily simple. Tang introduced itself in its Spanish ads as jugo de chino, which worked well with Puerto Ricans who knew it meant orange juice. However, the phrase had no meaning to most other Hispanics. Exhibit 4–1 provides additional examples of translation difficulties.

Most successful marketing to Hispanics moves beyond accurate translations into unique appeals and symbols. Sears recognized the importance of the extended family in a successful ad for baby furniture. In the English ad, a husband and wife are shown selecting the furniture. In the Spanish ad, the expectant couple are joined by a teenage daughter and the grandparents. Prego spaghetti sauce recognized the traditional Hispanic family role structure in its advertising. In its English ad, a father and son are shown alone in the kitchen preparing dinner. In the Spanish language ad, the entire family—mother, father, and child—are shown in the kitchen. Showing men cooking would not appeal to many traditional Hispanics. However, such unique appeals are not always necessary:

EXHIBIT 4–1

Advertising to Hispanics Requires Accurate Translation of Ad Copy

- Frank Perdue's chicken slogan, "It Takes a Tough Man to Make a Tender Chicken," was directly translated and read, "It Takes a Sexually Excited Man to Make a Chick Affectionate."
- Budweiser's slogan ended up being, "The Queen of Beers," while another brand was "Filling; Less Delicious."
- A candy marketer wanted to print a statement on its package, bragging about its 50 years in the business. When a tilde did not appear over the appropriate "n," the package claimed it contained 50 anuses.
- One food company's burrito became *burrada*, a colloquialism for "big mistake."
- Coors' beer slogan, "Get loose with Coors" came out as "Get the runs with Coors."

Source: "Marketing to Hispanics," *Advertising Age*, February 8, 1987, p. S–23; and M. Westerman, "Death of the Frito Bandito," March 1989, p. 28–32.

> Saturn developed "a Saturn commercial that happened to be Spanish." The commercial used the standard Saturn format of a pleased owner commenting on the car or firm. In this case, Christina Mendoza of San Antonio delivers the testimonial in Spanish. The commercial is shown in regions of the country with heavy Hispanic populations not only on Spanish-language stations but also on English language stations (with English subtitles).[18]

Other than specialty food products, few marketers have developed unique products or services for the Hispanic market. Managerial Application 4–6 describes a recent exception. The reaction of several Hispanic women to Bunuelitos were:

> When I first saw the box of Bunuelitos, I instantly thought of my own mother making bunuelos for the family. In my traditional Mexican home, bunuelos are a treat that is only made twice a year—at Christmas and for New Year's.
>
> The cereal people are telling me that I matter. They are catering to my roots and my taste. My kids and I had to accept and adjust to the taste of Fruit Loops. Now I feel important and catered to and my children can eat something they're familiar with.
>
> The cereal will give Hispanics the opportunity to buy a product that has a familiar name and taste, plus it gives Hispanics the opportunity to expose others to our traditional flavors and tastes.[19]

MCI Communications recently launched *Servicio Llamame* (Call Me Service) targeting U.S. Hispanics with family and friends in Mexico. The service costs $5 per month. The U.S. customer is provided a residential toll-free number plus a four-digit security code that may be given to friends and family in Mexico. This allows the Mexican residents to dial the U.S. resident directly. The call is billed to the U.S. resident (who generally has more disposable income) at a significant discount from the normal collect-call rate. The new service was launched with Spanish-language television ads featuring boxer Oscar De La Hoya receiving calls from friends in Mexico critiquing his last fight.[20]

MANAGERIAL APPLICATION 4–6

Developing a Product for the Hispanic Market

Hispanic consumers, both adults and children, are above-average consumers of sweetened cereals. Many Hispanics are also very fond of cinnamon flavoring. *Bunuelos* are sweet, cinnamon-flavored Mexican pastries that are used to celebrate special occasions. Thus bunuelos have both a desirable flavor and warm emotional connotations for many Mexican-Americans. General Mills has utilized this in creating a major product targeted primarily at Hispanics. General Mills developed a sweetened, cinnamon-flavored corn puff cereal that tastes like bunuelos. They named it the diminutive of bunuelos, *Bunuelitos* (little bunuelos). While initially targeted at Hispanics (primarily Mexican-Americans) and introduced with Spanish-language advertising, the packaging is in English. This is to emphasize the fact that it is an American product. It is also based on General Mills' desire to expand Bunuelitos into the mainstream cereal market.

ASIAN-AMERICANS

Although substantially smaller than the African-American and Hispanic subcultures, Asian-Americans are the fastest growing subculture, due primarily to immigration. Asian-Americans have the highest average income of any ethnic group ($36,784 compared to $31,435 for whites).[21] It is also the most diverse group with numerous different nationalities, languages, and religions. Figure 4–4 shows that Chinese and Filipinos are the two largest nationality groups. However, Koreans, Vietnamese, and others (primarily Laotian, Cambodian, and Thai) are the most rapidly growing. Figure 4–5 illustrates the tendency to retain the native language across the various groups. Asian-Americans are concentrated in the West and in New York. More than half live in California, New York, and Hawaii.

Consumer Groups

The Market Segment Research study identified three groups of Asian-Americans, based on their demographics and attitudes: traditionalist, established, and live-for-the-moment.

FIGURE 4–4

National Background of Asian-Americans

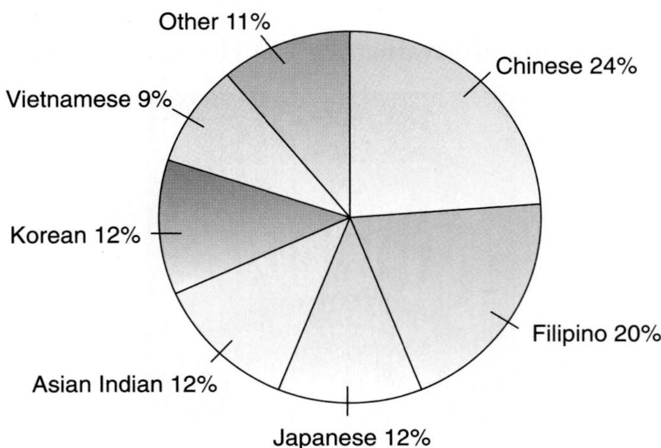

FIGURE 4–5

Native-Language Use by Asian-American Nationalities

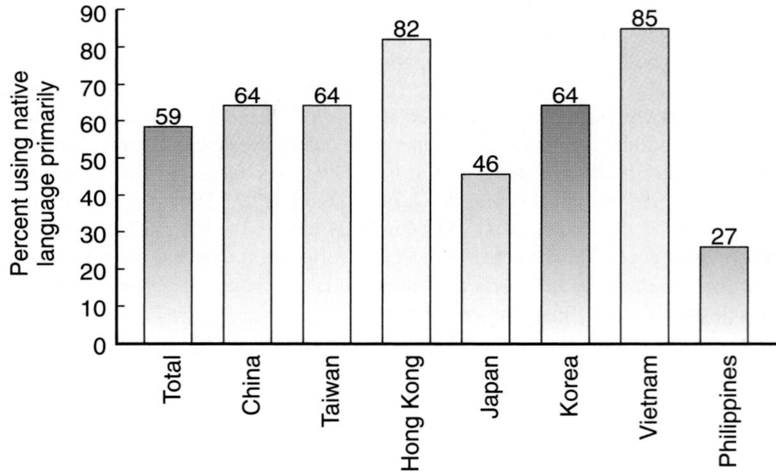

Traditionalist (49 percent) This group has an average age of 41 but almost 40 percent are over 50. Seventy percent are married. Almost half are unemployed but a large number of these are retired. They are relatively uneducated with 50 percent having a high school diploma or less. Their average household size is small (3.1).

Traditionalists have a strong identification with their original culture. Almost half speak their native language exclusively and three-fourths speak only their native language at home. They are not status conscious. They are not highly concerned with price or quality when shopping. While not concerned with financial security, they are also not optimistic about their financial future.

Established (27 percent) This group's average age of 40 is almost the same as the Traditionalists', but only 22 percent are over 50. Eighty percent are married and 60 percent are employed full-time. Seventy-three percent have at least some college and over half have a college degree. Their average household size is relatively large (4.1).

Members of this group have relatively weak identification with their native cultures. Only a fourth speak their native language exclusively and less than half prefer native-language television programming.

This is a conservative, professional group. They are financially secure and optimistic about their financial futures. They are quality oriented and are willing to pay a premium for high quality.

Live for the Moment (24 percent) This is the youngest of the three segments (average age = 35). Most (70 percent) are married and half are employed full-time. Almost half have at least some college. Their average household size is 4.0.

This group has a moderate level of identification with their traditional cultures. About 30 percent speak their native language exclusively, though two-thirds do so at home. This is a spontaneous, materialistic group. They are impulsive shoppers and are concerned about status and quality. They are spenders rather than savers.

Marketing to Asian-Americans

As the preceding discussion indicates, there is not a single Asian-American market. Rather there are several Asian-American markets, based primarily on nationality and language. Each of these in turn can be further segmented based on lifestyle and other variables. Thus, while the number and average income of Asian-Americans makes them attractive to marketers, the diversity of languages and cultures has precluded major marketing efforts focused on them as a group. Also, the relatively small size of the individual nationality groups has resulted in limited marketing activity focused on each group.

There are, however, opportunities to market effectively to the nationality subgroups.[22] As mentioned earlier, these groups tend to be clustered in limited geographic regions (half live in just three states). Where there is a concentration of any of the nationality groups, there are native language television and radio stations, as well as newspapers. Thus, targeted nationalities can be efficiently reached with native-language ads. Marketing activities targeted at Asian-Americans, as well as those for Hispanics and African-Americans, should be developed using the same principles described in Chapter 2 for marketing to other cultures. That is, one should be sensitive to the verbal and nonverbal differences between the core American culture and the targeted subculture.

REGIONAL SUBCULTURES

In the early 1980s a book by J. Garreau, *The Nine Nations of North America*, became a best seller. Its central theme was that North America comprised nine distinct cultural regions whose boundaries did not coincide with state or other political boundaries. Behaviors, values, and consumption patterns were similar within each of the nine regions and distinct across the regions. The distinct cultures within each region arose due to climatic conditions, the natural environment and resources, the characteristics of the various immigrant groups that have settled in each region, and significant social and political events.

Though Garreau's contention that North America was splitting into nine distinct nations seems to have been a significant overstatement, there is no doubt that regional subcultures exert a strong influence on all aspects of our consumption patterns. However, regional

TABLE 4–3 Regional Consumption Differences*

	Northeast[1]	Midwest[2]	South[3]	West[4]
Magazines				
Cosmopolitan	124	78	97	106
Outdoor Life	62	159	94	78
True Story	69	90	149	61
Omni	91	98	83	141
Television				
Doogie Howser, MD	132	81	98	91
Quantum Leap	89	120	97	92
American Detective	86	94	121	87
Top Cops	82	94	105	117
Hobbies/Activities				
Hunting	74	167	85	73
Racquet ball	86	93	85	150
Movie attendance**	148	85	83	97
Product Use				
Imported wine**	177	71	82	85
Cigarettes	90	99	112	91
Diet Cola drinks**	85	118	111	76
Regular Cola drinks**	74	88	124	100
TV dinners**	76	96	107	118
Restaurants/Shopping				
Fast food restaurants**	127	112	96	64
Kmart	81	129	98	90
Montgomery Ward	40	96	101	165
J.C. Penney	84	121	92	106
Sears	118	107	93	85

*100 = Average consumption or usage.
**Based on heavy users.

[1]Connecticut, Maine, Massachusetts, New Hampshire, New Jersey, New York, Pennsylvania, Rhode Island, Vermont.

[2]Illinois, Indiana, Iowa, Kansas, Michigan, Minnesota, Missouri, Nebraska, North Dakota, Ohio, South Dakota, Wisconsin.

[3]Alabama, Arkansas, Delaware, Florida, Georgia, Kentucky, Louisiana, Maryland, Mississippi, North Carolina, Oklahoma, South Carolina, Tennessee, Texas, Virginia, Washington, D.C., West Virginia.

[4]Arizona, California, Colorado, Idaho, Montana, Nevada, New Mexico, Oregon, Utah, Washington, Wyoming.

Source: *1991 Study of Media and Markets* (New York: Simmons Market Research Bureau, 1991)

subcultures involve much smaller geographic areas than the nine proposed by Garreau. For example, Anheuser-Busch divided Texas into several regions and developed unique marketing programs for Budweiser in each. In the northern part of the state they used a cowboy image, while in the southern region a Hispanic identity was stressed. Market share rose from 23 percent to 37 percent.[23] Other examples of successful regional marketing include:

- Campbell Soup's original pork and beans did not sell well in the Southwest. In response, they removed the pork and added chili pepper and ranchero beans. Sales increased dramatically. A Campbell's subsidiary developed Zesty Pickles for the Northeast because consumers there prefer sourer pickles than do other Americans.
- Ford Motor Co. decided to try a one-price, one-set-of-options strategy for its Escort. In the Southeast, the $9,995 Escorts had a cassette player rather than the rear window defroster that was on cars bound for other regions.
- Mercedes Benz has half of its total advertising budget controlled by its four regional divisions. Chevrolet allocates 20 percent of its advertising budget to regional ads, some of which are targeted at the state level (Suburbans are advertised in Texas as the "national car of Texas"). Coca-Cola has developed specific ad campaigns for Texas and Minnesota. In addition, Coca-Cola bottlers conduct extensive local advertising campaigns.
- Frito Lay potato chips are darker and oilier in the Northeast and lighter-tasting, heavier textured in the Southeast.
- McDonald's Egg McMuffin was an instant success in most of the country but was a disaster in the Southeast where most people had never heard of eggs Benedict and English muffins were not commonly consumed. Only after the Southeastern McDonald's franchisees developed a customized regional marketing strategy to explain the new product in a humorous way did Eggs McMuffin become a nationwide success.[24]

While the most effective regional marketing strategies are often based on very small geographic areas, we can observe significant consumption differences across much larger regions. Table 4–3 illustrates some of the consumption differences across the four U.S. census regions. Given such clear differences in consumption patterns, marketers are beginning to realize that, for at least some product categories, the United States is no more a single market than is the European Community (see Chapter 2). Since specialized (regional) marketing programs generally cost more than standardized (national) programs, marketers must balance potential sales increases against increased costs.[25] This decision process is exactly the same as described in the section on multinational marketing decisions in Chapter 2.

SUMMARY

The United States, like many other countries, is becoming increasingly diverse. Much of this diversity is fueled by immigration and an increase in ethnic pride and by identification with non-European heritages among numerous Americans. Most members of a culture share most of the core values, beliefs, and behaviors of that culture. However, most individuals also belong to one or more subcultures. A subculture is a segment of a larger culture whose members share distinguishing patterns of behavior. American society is characterized by an array of racial, ethnic, nationality, religious, and regional subcultures. The existence of these subcultures provides marketers the opportunity to develop unique marketing programs to match the unique needs of each.

Ethnic subcultures are defined broadly as those whose members' unique shared behaviors are based on a common racial, language, or nationality background. Non-European ethnic groups constitute a significant and growing part of U.S. population (from 24 percent in 1990 to 32 percent by 2010).

African-Americans are the largest non-European ethnic group, with 12 percent of the U.S. population. While African-Americans are, on average, younger and poorer than the general population, they are a large, diverse group with many subsegments. Given the size and total income of this group, it is not surprising that marketers are beginning to develop unique products and communications campaigns focused on the unique needs and media habits of African-Americans.

Hispanics are the second largest non-European ethnic group and they are predicted to surpass African-Americans in numbers by 2010. While Hispanics have a variety of national backgrounds (Mexico = 60%, Puerto Rico = 12%, Cuba = 5%), the use of the Spanish language, a common religion (Roman Catholic), and national Spanish-language media and entertainment figures has created a somewhat homogeneous Hispanic subculture. The use of Spanish as the primary language is growing among Hispanics due to substantial immigration, fully developed Spanish-language media, and self-contained Hispanic communities. Thus, any serious attempt to market to Hispanics must make use of the Spanish language and Spanish media. Like African-Americans, Hispanics are diverse in terms of their demographics, lifestyles, and extent of Hispanic identification.

Asian-Americans are the most diverse of the major ethnic subcultures. They are characterized by a variety of nationalities, languages, and religions. From a marketing perspective, it is not appropriate to consider Asian-Americans as a single group. Instead, Asian-Americans are best approached as a number of nationality subcultures. Thus, while the high average income and rapid growth rate of Asian-Americans makes the group appear very attractive, its highly fragmented nature has prevented most firms from developing specific programs aimed at this market. The fact that the various Asian-American nationality groups tend to be concentrated geographically does present opportunities to reach them economically with local media.

Marketing to ethnic groups in the United States requires the same types and levels of analysis as used to communicate with cultural groups outside of the United States (see Chapter 2).

Regional subcultures arise due to climatic conditions, the natural environment and resources, the characteristics of the various immigrant groups that have settled in each region, and significant social and political events. Regional subcultures affect all aspects of consumption behavior, and sophisticated marketers recognize that the United States is composed of numerous regional markets.

REVIEW QUESTIONS

1. What is a *subculture*?
2. What types of subcultures influence consumption behaviors in the United States?
3. What determines the degree to which a subculture will influence an individual's behavior?
4. Is the American culture more like a soup or a salad?
5. What is an *ethnic subculture*?
6. How large are the major ethnic subcultures in America? Which are growing most rapidly?
7. Are non-European ethnic groups evenly distributed throughout the United States?
8. What percent of America's recent growth has been caused by immigration?

9. What countries/regions are the major sources of America's immigrants?
10. How does the age distribution of the major non-European ethnic groups compare to that of non-Hispanic whites?
11. Are the various ethnic subcultures homogeneous or heterogeneous?
12. Describe the income distribution of African-Americans. What are the marketing implications of this distribution?
13. Describe the four African-American consumer groups found by the Market Segmentation Research study.
14. How does African-American media use differ from that of the general population?
15. What are the basic principles that should be followed in marketing to an African-American market segment?
16. Provide four examples of successful or unsuccessful marketing to African-Americans and indicate the cause of success or failure.
17. To what extent is the Spanish language used by American Hispanics?
18. What are the major nationality groups from which American Hispanics originated?
19. Can Hispanics be treated as a single market?
20. Describe the five Hispanic consumer groups identified by the Market Segment Research study.
21. Provide four examples of successful or unsuccessful marketing to Hispanics and indicate the cause of success or failure.
22. How homogeneous are Asian-Americans?
23. What are the major nationality groups from which Asian-Americans originated?
24. To what extent do Asian-Americans use their native language?
25. Describe the three Asian-American consumer groups identified by the Market Segment Research study.
26. What is a regional subculture?
27. What causes regional subcultures?
28. Provide four examples of successful or unsuccessful marketing to regional subcultures and indicate the cause of success or failure.
29. How does one decide whether to use a regional or a national marketing program?

DISCUSSION QUESTIONS

30. Do you agree that America is becoming more "like a salad than a soup" in terms of the integration of ethnic groups?
31. Most new immigrants to America are non-European and have limited English-language skills. What opportunities does this present to marketers?
32. The major non-European ethnic groups have a younger age distribution than the European-based population (see Figure 4–3). What are the marketing implications of this fact?
33. A significant number of African-Americans live in inner cities or rural areas and have household incomes below the poverty level. What are the marketing implications of this fact? Does a firm's social responsibility play a role here? If so, what?
34. While many African-Americans have very limited incomes, others are quite prosperous. Does marketing to prosperous African-Americans require a marketing mix different from the one used to reach other prosperous consumers?
35. Describe how each of the following firms' product managers should approach the African-American market.
    a. Budweiser
    b. TGI Fridays
    c. CBS television
    d. *Time* magazine
    e. United Way
    f. Sony televisions
    g. Sears
    h. Crest toothpaste
36. Describe how each of the following firms' product managers should approach each of the four African-American consumer groups identified by the Market Segment Research study.
    a. Budweiser
    b. TGI Fridays
    c. CBS television
    d. *Time* magazine
    e. United Way
    f. Sony television
    g. Sears
    h. Crest toothpaste
37. While many Hispanics have very limited incomes, others are quite prosperous. Does marketing to prosperous Hispanics require a marketing mix different from the one used to reach other prosperous consumers?
38. For what types of products can the nationality differences among Hispanics be ignored? Why?

39. Describe how each of the following firms' product managers should approach the Hispanic market.
    a. Pepsi Cola
    b. Burger King
    c. CBS television
    d. *Time* magazine
    e. United Way
    f. Ford
    g. Kmart
    h. Crest toothpaste
40. Describe how each of the following firms' product managers should approach each of the five Hispanic consumer groups identified by the Market Segment Research study.
    a. Pepsi Cola
    b. Burger King
    c. CBS television
    d. *Time* magazine
    e. United Way
    f. Ford
    g. Kmart
    h. Crest toothpaste
41. While many Asian-Americans are very prosperous, others have very limited incomes. Does marketing to prosperous Asian-Americans require a marketing mix different from the one used to reach other prosperous consumers?
42. For what types of products can the nationality differences among Asian-Americans be ignored? Why?
43. Describe how each of the following firms' product managers should approach the Asian-American market.
    a. Coca-Cola
    b. McDonald's
    c. NBC television
    d. *Time* magazine
    e. United Way
    f. Buick
    g. Wal-Mart
    h. Crest toothpaste
44. Describe how each of the following firms' product managers should approach each of the three Asian-American consumer groups identified by the Market Segment Research study.
    a. Coca-Cola
    b. McDonald's
    c. NBC television
    d. *Time* magazine
    e. United Way
    f. Buick
    g. Wal-Mart
    h. Crest toothpaste
45. Will regional subcultures become more or less distinct over the next 20 years? Why?
46. Select one product, service, or activity from each category in Table 4–3 and explain the differences in consumption for the item across the regions shown.
47. What regional consumption differences, if any, should managers of the following firms or products be concerned about?
    a. Coca-Cola
    b. McDonald's
    c. NBC television
    d. *Time* magazine
    e. United Way
    f. Buick
    g. Wal-Mart
    h. Crest toothpaste

APPLICATION ACTIVITIES

48. Watch two hours of prime-time major network (ABC, CBS, or NBC) television. What subculture groups are portrayed in the programs? Describe how they are portrayed. Do these portrayals match the descriptions in this text? How would you explain the differences? Repeat these tasks for the ads shown during the programs.
49. Pick a product of interest and examine the Simmons Market Research Bureau or Media-Mark studies in your library (these are often in the Journalism Library) on the product and determine the extent to which its consumption varies by ethnic group and region. Does consumption also vary by age, income, or other variables? Are the differences in ethnic and regional consumption due primarily to these causes or to the fact that the ethnic group or region is older, richer, or otherwise different from the larger culture?
50. Examine several magazines and/or newspapers aimed at a non-European ethnic or nationality group. What types of products are advertised? Why?
51. Develop a brief description of the consumer groups within each of the major ethnic subcultures as found in the Market Segment Research study. Interview three ______, present them with the description of their subculture, and ask them to indicate the accuracy of the segments identified for their subculture.
    a. African-Americans
    b. Asian-Americans
    c. Hispanics
52. Interview three ______ and ascertain their opinions of how their ethnic and/or nationality

group is portrayed on network television shows and in national ads.
   a. African-Americans
   b. Asian-Americans
   c. Hispanics
53. Interview three Hispanics and ascertain the extent to which they identify with the core American culture, the Hispanic subculture within America, or their nationality subculture. Also determine the extent to which they feel other Hispanics feel as they do and the reasons for any differences.
54. Interview three Asian-Americans and ascertain the extent to which they identify with the core American culture, the Asian-American subculture within America, or their nationality subculture. Also determine the extent to which they feel other Asian-Americans feel as they do and the reasons for any differences.
55. Interview three Asian-Americans and determine how they would react to a major marketer such as Coca-Cola or Ford using an Asian-American as an advertising spokesperson from a nationality group that is other than their own.
56. Interview two students from other regions of the United States and determine the differences they have noticed between their home and your present location. Try to determine the causes of these differences.

REFERENCES

[1]A. Z. Cuneco, "Hills Bros. Push Percolator from Bottom to Top," *Advertising Age*, February 1990, p. S–1.

[2]M. F. Riche, "We're All Minorities Now," *American Demographics*, October 1991, pp. 6–34.

[3]T. McCarroll, "It's a Mass Market No More," *Time*, Fall 1993, p. 80.

[4]M. J. Mandel and C. Farrell, "The Immigrants," *Business Week*, July 13, 1992, pp. 114–22.

[5]E. Morris, "The Difference in Black and White," *American Demographics*, January 1993, p. 46.

[6]L. McAllister, "Ethnic Customs Influence How Ethnic-Americans Gift," *Gifts & Decorative Accessories*, July 1993, p. 53.

[7]*The 1993 Minority Market Report* (Coral Gables, Florida: Market Segment Research, Inc., 1993).

[8]H. Schlossberg, "Many Marketers Still Consider Blacks 'Dark-skinned' Whites," *Marketing News*, January 19, 1993, p. 1.

[9]For a thorough discussion of this issue, see G. R. Soruco and T. P. Myer, "The Mobile Hispanic Market," *Marketing Research*, Winter 1993, p. 8.

[10]P. Braus, "What Does Hispanic Mean?" *American Demographics*, June 1993, pp. 46–50.

[11]See footnote 6, p. 25.

[12]See footnote 6, pp. 41–43. For data on how identification with the Hispanic culture influences information search, see C. Webster, "The Effects of Hispanic Subcultural Identification on Information Search Behavior," *Journal of Advertising Research*, September–October 1992, pp. 54–62.

[13]See footnote 8.

[14]See footnote 9, p. 7.

[15]For a strong opposing view, see C. Palmeri and J. Levine, "No Habla Espanol," *Forbes*, December 1991, pp. 140–42.

[16]C. Fisher, "Hispanic TV Networks Take the Gloves Off," *Advertising Age*, November 8, 1993, p. 44.

[17]Ibid., "*Mas* Death Opens Hispanic Hole," *Advertising Age*, May 31, 1993, p. 31.

[18]R. Serafin, "Saturn's Spanish-Language Ad Is Not for Hispanics Only," *Advertising Age*, July 28, 1993, p. 10.

[19]C. Lee, "Cereal Targets Ethnic Group," *Amarillo Daily News*, July 7, 1993, p. 10.

[20]S. Hume, "MCI Seeks Mexican Friends and Family," *Advertising Age*, March 8, 1993, p. 7.

[21]See footnote 5.

[22]See B. Townsend, "Inside the Asian-American Market," *Marketing Research*, September 1991, pp. 75–78.

[23]T. Moore, "Different Strokes for Different Folks," *Fortune*, September 16, 1985, p. 68.

[24]S. L. Hapoienu, "The Rise of Micromarketing," *The Journal of Business Strategy*, November–December 1990, p. 3.

[25]R. E. Linneman and J. L. Stanton, Jr., "A Game Plan for Regional Marketing," *Journal of Business Strategy*, November–December 1992, pp. 19–25.

CHAPTER 5

SOCIAL STRATIFICATION

Chinese economists describe five consumption classes in the Chinese society as follows:

"The highest are the super rich. They are mainly the bosses of successful private enterprises or Sino-foreign joint businesses. They have millions of yaun. They often dine in restaurants and they buy whatever they like without asking the price. They are fond of foreign goods.

Second are the rich. Most are senior managerial staff and technicians of Sino-foreign joint ventures, senior intellectuals, performers doing extra work, people with rich relatives abroad, and contractors of medium and small projects. They have a fat income. They often dine at restaurants on festival days or Sundays and they buy the best thing regardless of price. They often buy fashion or precious goods to boast their economic strength and status.

The third group is the well-to-do. This includes medium-level managerial staff at Sino-foreign joint ventures, intellectuals doing a second job, individual industrial or commercial people and contractors. They may have bank deposits of several thousand yaun. They live comfortably and can afford meat and fish every day. They have all kinds of electrical appliances and sometimes have a meal at a restaurant. They are able to go after fashion but are practical as well.

The fourth group is those who live a decent life. They are wage earners in well-run enterprises. They have small bank deposits. They have to plan for a few years to buy a big electrical appliance. Their psychology on consumption is cheap and utility. They often go window-shopping rather than actually buying. They have a high demand for durability and after-sale service.

The last is the poor. They have no bank deposits and can barely make both ends meet. They work in poorly run state enterprises and have many children. They just buy cheap daily necessities, regardless of brand, style, or color.[1]

China worked for decades to produce a classless, egalitarian society. However, as the above description indicates, classes exist in China despite years of stringent government policy to eliminate them. In fact, variations in social standing appear to exist in all societies of any size. This is certainly true for the United States and Canada, which both pride themselves on being egalitarian.

We are all familiar with the concept of social class, but most of us would have difficulty explaining our class system to a foreigner. The following quotes illustrate the vague nature of social class in America and Canada:

> Like it or not, all of us are largely defined, at least in the eyes of others, according to a complex set of criteria—how much we earn, what we do for a living, who our parents are, where and how long we attended school, how we speak, what we wear, where we live, and how we react to the issues of the day. It all adds up to our socioeconomic status, our ranking in U.S. society.[2]
>
> I would suppose social class means where you went to school and how far. Your intelligence. Where you live. The sort of house you live in. Your general background, as far as clubs you belong to, your friends. To some degree the type of profession you're in—in fact, definitely that. Where you send your children to school. The hobbies you have. Skiing, for example, is higher than the snowmobile. The clothes you wear . . . all of that. These are the externals. It can't be (just) money, because nobody ever knows that about you for sure.[3]

Americans and Canadians use the words *social class* and *social standing* interchangeably to mean *societal rank*. How do we obtain a social standing? Your social standing is a result of characteristics you possess that others in society desire and hold in high esteem. Your education, occupation, ownership of property, income level, and heritage (racial/ethnic background, parents' status) influence your social standing as shown in Figure 5–1. Social standing ranges from the lower class, those with few or none of the socioeconomic

FIGURE 5–1

Social Standing Is Derived and Influences Behavior

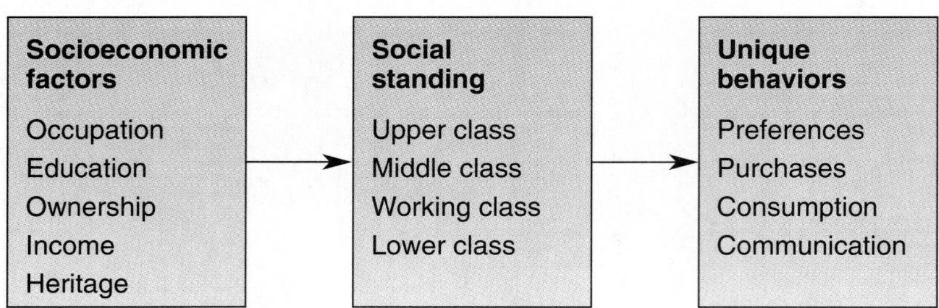

FIGURE 5–2

Not All Behaviors within a Social Class Are Unique

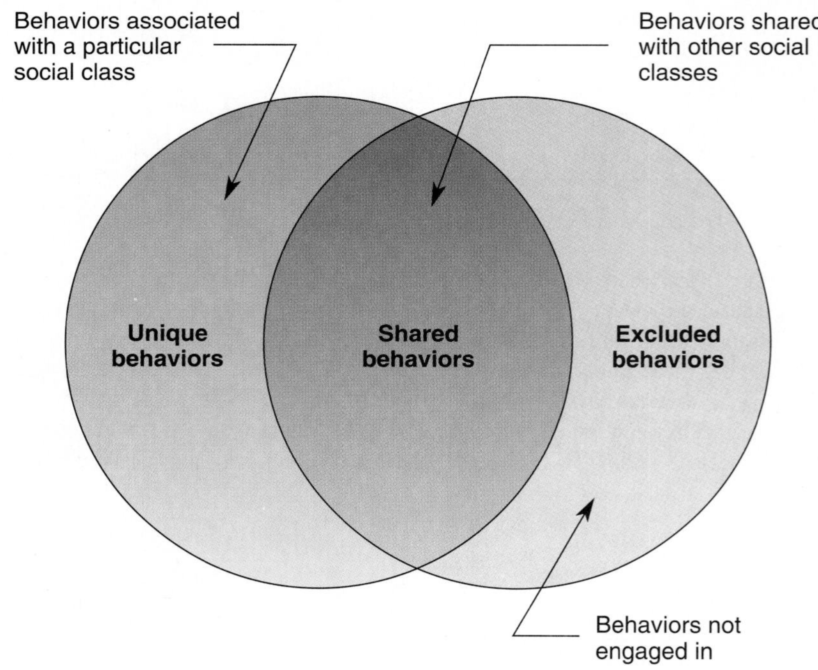

factors desired by society, to the upper class, who possess many of the socioeconomic characteristics considered by society as desirable and high in status. Individuals with different social standings tend to have different needs and consumption patterns.

Because individuals with different social standings are likely to live their lives differently, a **social class system** can be defined as:

> A hierarchical division of a society into relatively distinct and homogeneous groups with respect to attitudes, values, and lifestyles.

The fact that members of each social class have a set of unique behaviors makes the concept relevant to marketers. It is important for marketers to understand when social class is an influencing factor and when it is not. As shown in Figure 5–2, not all behaviors differ between social strata; many are shared. Therefore, we should recognize that the applicability of social class in the formulation of marketing strategies is product-specific (e.g., expensive china and crystal) and often situation-specific (e.g., entertaining).

THE CONCEPT OF SOCIAL CLASS

For a social class system to exist in a society, the individual classes must meet five criteria: they must be (1) bounded, (2) ordered, (3) mutually exclusive, (4) exhaustive, and (5) influential. *Bounded* means that there are clear breaks between each social class. In other words, it is necessary that a rule be devised for each class that will include or exclude any particular individual. *Ordered* means that the classes can be arrayed or spread out in terms of some measure of prestige or status from highest to lowest. *Mutually exclusive* means that an individual can only belong to one social class (though movement from one class to another over time is possible). Requiring social classes to be *exhaustive* means that every member of a social system must fit into some class. Finally, the social classes must be *influential*. That is, there must be behavioral variations between the classes.

Based on these five criteria, it is clear that a strict and tightly defined social class system does not exist in most industrialized nations. The first criteria, that the classes be distinctly bounded, obviously is not so in the United States. The two classic studies of social class in America developed differing numbers of classes (and other researchers have reported yet other breakdowns).[4] If there were indeed firm boundaries, reasonably careful researchers would identify the same number of classes. Likewise, various criteria of social class will place individuals into differing categories. That is, a person may be considered upper middle class if education is the placement criterion but upper lower if income is used. This casts doubt on the ability to construct mutually exclusive social classes.

Status Crystallization

''Pure'' social classes do not exist in the United States or most other industrialized societies. However, it is apparent that these same societies do have hierarchical groups of individuals and that individuals in those groups do exhibit some unique behavior patterns that are different from behaviors in other groups.

What exists is *not a set of social classes*, but a *series of status continua*.[5] These status continua reflect various dimensions or factors that the overall society values. In an achievement-oriented society such as the United States, achievement-related factors constitute the primary status dimensions. Thus, education, occupation, income, and, to a lesser extent, quality of residence and place of residence are important status dimensions in the United States. Race and gender are *ascribed* dimensions of social status that are not related to achievement. Likewise, the status characteristics of a person's parents are an ascribed status dimension that appears to exist in the United States. However, heritage is a more important dimension in a more traditional society such as England.

The various status dimensions are related to each other both functionally and statistically. In a functional sense, the status of one's parents or one's race influences one's education, which in turn influences occupation that generates income, which sets limits on one's lifestyle. Does this mean that an individual with high status based on one dimension will have high status based on the other dimensions? This is a question of **status crystallization**.

The more consistent an individual is on all status dimensions, the greater the degree of status crystallization for the individual. Status crystallization is relatively low in the United States. For example, many blue-collar workers (such as plumbers and electricians) earn higher incomes than many professionals (such as public school teachers).

SOCIAL STRUCTURE IN THE UNITED STATES

The low degree of status crystallization in the United States is support for the contention that a social class system is not a perfect categorization of social position. However, this does not mean that the population cannot be subdivided into status groups that share similar lifestyles, at least with respect to particular product categories or activities. Furthermore, there are many people with high levels of status crystallization who exhibit many of the behaviors associated with a class system. It is useful for the marketing manager to know the characteristics of these relatively pure class types, even though the descriptions represent a simplified abstraction from reality.

A number of different sets of social classes have been proposed to describe the United States. We will use the one developed by R. P. Coleman and L. Rainwater. Coleman and Rainwater base their social class structure on "reputation," relying heavily on the "man in the street" imagery. A reputationalist approach:

> is designed to reflect popular imagery and observation of how people interact with one another—as equals, superiors, or inferiors. Personal and group prestige is at its heart.[6]

In their system, shown in Exhibit 5–1, the *upper class* (14 percent) is divided into three groups primarily on differences in occupation and social affiliations. The *middle class* (70 percent) is divided into a middle class (32 percent) of average-income white- and blue-collar workers living in better neighborhoods, and a working class (38 percent) of average-income blue-collar workers who lead a "working-class lifestyle." The *lower class* (16 percent) is divided into two groups, one living just above the poverty level and the other visibly poverty-stricken. These groups are described in more detail in the following sections.

Upper Americans (14 Percent)

The Upper-Upper Class Members of the upper-upper social class are aristocratic families who make up the social elite. Members with this level of social status generally are the nucleus of the best country clubs and sponsors of major charitable events. They provide leadership and funds for community and civic activities and often serve as trustees for hospitals, colleges, and civic organizations.

The Lower-Upper Class The lower-upper class is often referred to as "new rich—the current generation's new successful elite." These families are relatively new in terms of upper-class social status and have not yet been accepted by the upper crust of the community. In some cases, their income is greater than those of families in the upper-upper social strata. However, their consumption is often more conspicuous and acts as an important symbol of their social status.

Families in the lower-upper social strata are major purchasers of large homes, luxury automobiles, and more expensive clothing, food, vacations, and furniture. Together, the upper-upper and lower-upper constitute less than 2 percent of the population. However, because they are a visible symbol of social status, their behavior and lifestyle can influence individuals in lower social strata. The ad shown in Managerial Application 5–1 would appeal to the lower-upper class.

EXHIBIT 5–1

The Coleman–Rainwater Social Class Hierarchy

Upper Americans

- Upper-Upper (0.3%). The "capital S society" world of inherited wealth, aristocratic names.
- Lower-Upper (1.2%). The newer social elite, drawn from current professional, corporate leadership.
- Upper-Middle Class (12.5%). The rest of college graduate managers and professionals; lifestyle centers on private clubs, causes, and the arts.

Middle Americans

- Middle Class (32%). Average pay white-collar workers and their blue-collar friends; live on "the better side of town," try to "do the proper things."
- Working Class (38%). Average pay blue-collar workers; lead "working-class lifestyle" whatever the income, school background, and job.

Lower Americans

- Upper-Lower (9%). "A lower group of people but not the lowest"; working, not on welfare; living standard is just above poverty; behavior judged "crude," "trashy."
- Lower-Lower (7%). On welfare, visibly poverty-stricken, usually out of work (or have "the dirtiest jobs"); "bums," "common criminals."

Typical Profile

Social Class	Percent	Income	Education	Occupation
Upper Americans				
Upper-upper	.3%	$600,000	Master's degree	Board chairman
Lower-upper	1.2	450,000	Master's degree	Corporate president
Upper-middle	12.5	150,000	Medical degree	Physician
Middle Americans				
Middle class	32.0	28,000	College degree	High school teacher
Working class	38.0	15,000	High school	Assembly worker
Lower Americans				
Upper-lower	9.0	9,000	Some high school	Janitor
Lower-lower	7.0	5,000	Grade school	Unemployed

Source: R. P. Coleman, "The Continuing Significance of Social Class to Marketing," *Journal of Consumer Research*, December 1983, p. 267.

MANAGERIAL APPLICATION

5–1

A Product Aimed at the Upper Classes

The Upper-Middle Class The upper-middle class consists of families who possess neither family status derived from heritage nor unusual wealth. Their social position is achieved primarily by their occupation and career orientation. Occupation and education are key aspects of this social stratum as it consists of successful professionals, independent businesspeople, and corporate managers. As shown in Exhibit 5–1, members of this social class are typically college graduates, many of whom have professional or graduate degrees. They buy fine homes, expensive automobiles, quality furniture, good wines, and so forth. Managerial Application 5–2 contains an advertisement aimed at this group.

While this segment of the U.S. population is small (approximately 12.5 percent), it is highly visible and many Americans would like to belong to it. Because it is aspired to by many, it is an important positioning variable for some products.

Figure 5–3 illustrates this "upward pull" strategy. This pull strategy works well for the manufacturer of expensive fashion items such as Gucci. Gucci, high in social status, is attractive to those middle-class consumers wishing to improve their social status or to enjoy elements of the upper-middle-class lifestyle.

MANAGERIAL APPLICATION 5–2

A Product Positioned for the Upper-Middle Class

''Upward Pull'' Strategy Targeted at Middle Class

FIGURE 5–3

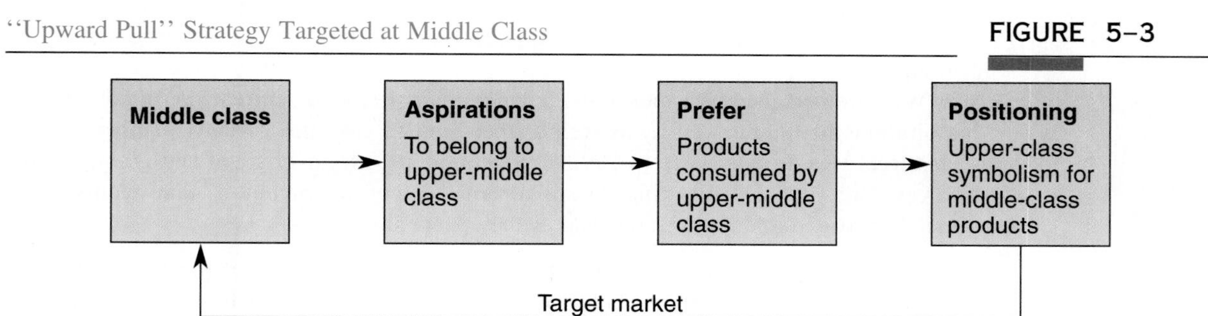

The ad for Kahlua shown in Managerial Application 5–3 illustrates this approach. Kahlua, a relatively inexpensive liqueur, is shown being consumed in very elegant surroundings. Thus, a product readily affordable by the middle and working class is positioned as one that will allow its users to experience some elements of the upper-middle-class lifestyle. However, as we discuss later, this ''upward pull'' strategy will not work for all products or groups.

MANAGERIAL APPLICATION

5–3

A Product Using an Upward Pull Strategy

Middle Americans (70 Percent)

The Middle Class The middle class is relatively large (approximately 32 percent of the population) and is composed of white-collar workers (office workers, school teachers) and high-paid blue-collar workers (plumbers, factory supervisors). Thus, the middle class represents the majority of the white-collar group and the top of the blue-collar group.

Members of the middle class have respectable incomes and often college educations and some management responsibility. The middle-class core is typically a college-educated, white-collar worker or a factory supervisor with average income. They generally live in modest suburban homes, avoid elegant furniture, and are likely to get involved in do-it-yourself projects. They represent the primary target market for the goods and services of home improvement centers, garden shops, automotive parts houses, as well as mouthwashes and deodorants. Managerial Application 5–4 shows a product targeted at this group.

With limited incomes, they must balance their desire for current consumption with aspirations for future security as well as their limited cash flow. Many members of this class feel very insecure due to 1990s' reductions in both government and private workforces. Consider the following description of "downward mobility" that haunts many members of the middle class (as well as the upper-middle class):

- Well-paying jobs in large corporations are permanently disappearing for many managers, professionals, and technical workers. Only a quarter of them will be reemployed in big companies. The rest will work for smaller companies, consult, or "temp"—at 20 to 50 percent less pay.
- You see friends, relatives, and neighbors losing their jobs and failing to find new ones. But "my company is too profitable; I'm too important to the organization. At any rate, I could quickly get a new job with my skills and background."
- Then you lose your job. You spend months trying to find another job as good as the one you just lost. You use up all your savings. You get another job at a smaller firm at half the pay, but that doesn't last long either. This time you get no severance package.

MANAGERIAL APPLICATION 5–4

A Product Targeted at Middle Americans

- You face reality and realize your family income will be drastically reduced for years. Kiss the credit cards and vacations good-bye. Everybody in the family works—your spouse, your kids. You turn to your church or synagogue for networking, mortgage money, maybe even soup.
- You change tactics as your job expectations change. You go to school at night and do interim jobs in the day. You go into the family business or start a new one. Like struggling generations before you, you focus family resources on your kids' education.[7]

The Working Class The working class (38 percent) is the largest social-class segment in the U.S. population, although it is declining in relative size. It is solidly blue collar and consists of skilled and semiskilled factory workers. Though some households in this social stratum seek advancement, members of this stratum are more likely to seek security for and protection of what they already have. The ad shown in Managerial Application 5–5 would appeal to those members of this class seeking advancement as well as those concerned about downward mobility due to workforce reductions.

Many "working-class aristocrats" dislike the upper-middle class and prefer products and stores positioned at their social-class level (see Figure 5–4).[8] They are heavy consumers of pickups and campers, hunting equipment, power boats, and beer. Miller Brewing Company recently gave up attempts to attract a broad audience for its Miller High Life beer. Instead, it is targeting working-class aristocrats with ads that feature bowling alleys, diners, and country music.

Lower Americans (16 Percent)

The Upper-Lower Class Approximately 9 percent of the U.S. population can be categorized as members of the upper-lower class. The upper-lower class consists of individuals who are poorly educated, have very low incomes, and work as unskilled laborers (janitor, laborer in a bottling plant, and so on).

MANAGERIAL APPLICATION 5-5

A Product Aimed at the Working Class

FIGURE 5-4 Positioning within Social Class

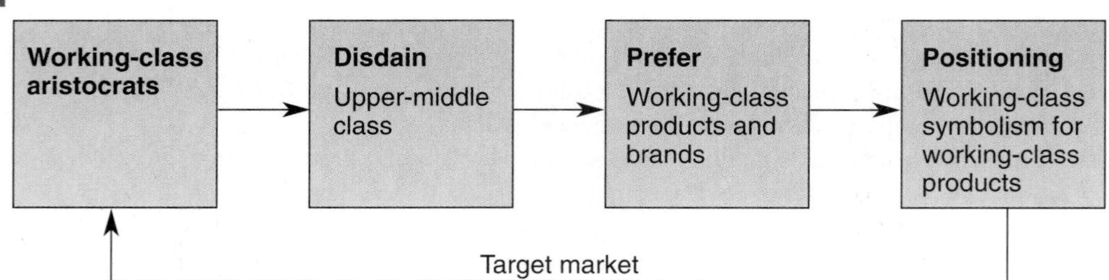

Because of their limited education, members in this social stratum have a difficult time moving up in occupation, and hence, social status. Painfully aware of the lifestyle of the class below them, they strive to avoid slipping into the ranks of the society-dependent, lower-lower class. Yet, without sufficient education or occupational training, they are unable to move up. As one author put it: "They are in bondage—to monetary policy, rip-off advertising, crazes and delusions, mass low culture, fast foods, consumer schlock."[9]

However, sophisticated chain retailers such as Dollar General Corporation have begun to meet the unique needs of this segment.

The Lower-Lower Class The lower-lower social stratum (7 percent), the poverty class, or the ''bottom layer'' as Coleman and Rainwater have categorized them, has the lowest social standing in society. They have very low incomes and minimal education. This segment of society is often unemployed for long periods of time and is the major recipient of government support and services provided by nonprofit organizations.

The poor are an important concern for public policymakers attempting to eliminate or at least minimize poverty. Likewise, serving the poor has been viewed as a problem for the marketing system as a whole and for individual firms. As the income, and thus expenditures, of the nonpoverty group grows, it will be increasingly easy to ignore the low-income segment of the market. To ignore this segment completely is to forgo a large and potentially profitable market segment. Marketers should at least examine the possibility of developing marketing strategies for this market segment. The motive for such decisions can be profit instead of, or in addition to, social responsibility.

Conclusions on Social Structure in the United States

The descriptions provided above are brief. In part, this reflects our belief that it is relatively unproductive to attempt to provide very specific descriptions for social classes. The complexity and variety of behaviors and values involved precludes doing a thorough job. Rather, marketing managers must investigate the various status dimensions to determine which, if any, affect the consumption process for their products. In the next section, we discuss how this can be done.

THE MEASUREMENT OF SOCIAL STATUS

As described earlier, education, occupation, income, and, to a lesser extent, place of residence are the primary achievement-based status dimensions used to determine social standing. Race, gender, and parents' status are ascribed (nonachievement) status dimensions. How do we measure the primary achievement dimensions in the most useful manner? There are two basic approaches:

1. A single dimension: a single-item index.
2. A combination of several dimensions: a multi-item index.

Single-Item Indexes

Single-item indexes estimate social status based on a single dimension. Since an individual's overall status is influenced by several dimensions, single-item indexes are generally less accurate at predicting an individual's social standing or position in a community than are well-developed multi-item indexes. However, single-item indexes allow one to estimate the impact of specific status dimensions on the consumption process. The three most common single-item indexes are (1) education, (2) occupation, and (3) income.

Education Education has traditionally been highly valued in our culture. It has served as the primary path for upward social mobility. Thus, education is a direct measure of status and is used as a component in several of the multiple-item indexes. In addition, education influences an individual's tastes, values, and information-processing style.

As Table 3–2 (page 81) indicates, education level influences all aspects of one's lifestyle and consumption patterns. However, education seldom provides a complete explanation for consumption patterns. For example, college graduates earning $30,000 per year have different lifestyles from college graduates earning $100,000 per year, despite similar educational backgrounds.

Occupation Occupation is the most widely used single-item index in marketing studies. In fact, occupation is probably the most widely used single cue that allows us to evaluate and define individuals we meet. That this is true should be obvious when you stop to think of the most common bit of information we seek from a new acquaintance, "What do you do?" Almost invariably we need to know someone's occupation to make inferences about his/her probable lifestyle. Occupation is associated with education and income, although the association is not as strong as it once was. The type of work one does and the types of individuals one works with directly influence one's preferred lifestyle and all aspects of the consumption process (see Table 3–1, page 80).

A number of approaches are used to assign scores or rankings to the hundreds of occupational categories that exist in an industrial society. By far the most widely used today is the **socioeconomic index (SEI)**. This scale is based on the educational attainments and income of individuals in various occupations. The weight given each component was derived so that the score given each occupation was similar to the "standing" assigned that occupation by a large sample of the public. Once the appropriate weights were derived, any occupation could be ranked.

This scale has been revised several times and is the most up-to-date scale available. Exhibit 5–2 provides the SEI scores for a number of job titles.

Income Income has traditionally been used as a measure of both purchasing power and status. Historically, the association between income and status has been high. However, this association is not as strong today as in the past. Correlations between income and education of 0.33 and income and occupational category of 0.4 have been reported (where a 1.0 represents a perfect association and a 0 represents no association between the variables).

Using income poses a number of measurement problems. Basically, the researcher must decide which income to measure. This involves such decisions as:

EXHIBIT 5–2

SEI Scores for Selected Occupations

Occupation	SEI Score	Occupation	SEI Score
Accountant	65	Marketing manager	58
Aerospace engineer	84	Marketing professor	83
Athlete	49	Mail carrier	28
Auto mechanic	21	Plumber	27
Bartender	24	Police	38
Chemist	78	Registered nurse	46
Dentist	89	Sales, Apparel	25
Elementary school teacher	70	Sales, Engineer	78
Housekeeper	15	Stevedore	22

Source: G. Stevens and J. H. Cho, "Socioeconomic Indices," *Social Science Research* 14, 1985, pp. 142–68.

- Individual or family income.
- Before or after taxes.
- Salary or total income.

Many individuals may not have accurate knowledge of their incomes as defined by the researcher (i.e., total family pre-tax income). In addition, individuals are often reluctant to reveal their income, and if they do respond, they may not provide an accurate answer.

Income is clearly necessary to maintain a lifestyle. Likewise, there is a higher status attached to higher incomes than to lower incomes. Still, income does not explain lifestyles completely. A college professor or lawyer may have the same income as a truck driver or plumber. Nonetheless, it is likely that their consumption processes for a variety of products will differ. As we will see shortly, income relative to other variables such as occupation may be quite useful, and a number of studies have found it useful when used alone. Table 5–1 shows the impact of income on the consumption of several product categories.

Income Levels and Consumption

TABLE 5–1

	Income Level (000s)					
Item	**<$10**	**$10–19**	**$20–29**	**$30–39**	**>$40**	**>$60**
Media						
"Coach"	77	92	96	107	108	109
"L.A. Law"	77	82	90	105	116	117
"Knots Landing"	131	117	111	111	77	71
"FBI"	138	116	103	101	82	76
New Yorker	47	60	60	65	159	230
True Story	158	138	112	106	63	51
Products						
Domestic beer*	98	121	113	106	85	84
Imported wine*	45	66	65	116	137	169
Scotch whiskey	60	67	98	95	126	136
PC at home	53	51	80	106	138	143
Catsup*	99	108	97	98	99	99
Canned stew	130	107	93	107	86	87
Kraft mayonnaise	121	107	119	92	82	69
Best mayonnaise	88	94	120	93	99	106
Activities						
State lottery	68	86	102	109	110	119
Bowling	44	73	94	116	122	122
Smoke cigarettes*	123	124	110	88	85	72
Golf						

100 = Average level of use, purchase, or consumption.

*Heavy user.

Source: *1991 Study of Media & Markets* (New York: Simmons Market Research Bureau, 1991).

Relative Occupational Class Income Thus far we have been discussing the relative merits of one status dimension over another. However, in some cases it may be more productive to consider using one status dimension *in conjunction with another*. This is what the concept of **relative occupational class income** (ROCI) involves. ROCI is the "relationship of a family's total income to the median income of other families in the same occupational class."[10] Thus, occupational class is viewed as setting the basic lifestyle, while relative income provides (1) excess funds, (2) neither excess nor deficient funds, or (3) deficient funds for the desired lifestyle. The three categories are referred to as overprivileged, average, and underprivileged, respectively. It has been found to influence the consumption of such products as coffee and automobiles. Relative class income (used with Coleman's multi-item index) influences the types of stores shopped.[11]

A closely related concept is **subjective discretionary income** (SDI). SDI is an estimate by the consumer of how much money he or she has available to spend on nonessentials.[12] One study operationalized this concept by using the responses on a 1-to-6, agree-to-disagree scale to the following statements:

1. No matter how fast our income goes up, we never seem to get ahead.
2. We have more to spend on extras than most of our neighbors do.
3. Our family income is high enough to satisfy nearly all our important desires.

In this large-scale study, SDI was found to add considerable predictive power to total family income (TFI) measures and, for some product categories, to predict purchases when family income does not. Some of the interesting findings include:

FIGURE 5–5 Social Class and Media Usage

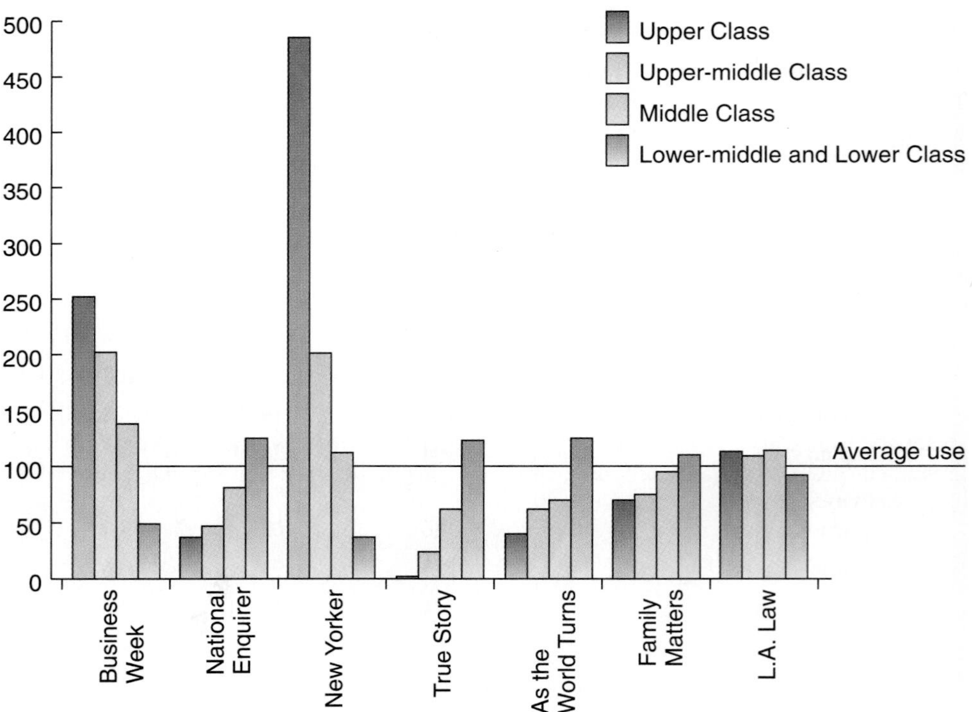

Source: *1991 Study of Media & Markets* (New York: Simmons Market Research Bureau, Inc., 1991).

- Investments, such as mutual funds, IRAs, stocks, and luxury cars require relatively high levels of *both* TFI and SDI.
- Loans and second mortgages are associated with relatively high TFI (necessary to qualify) but low levels of SDI (a felt need for extra cash).
- Fast-food restaurant patronage is predicted by relatively high TFI but relatively low SDI.
- Consumption of low-cost foods, such as bologna and packaged spaghetti, is not predicted by TFI but is associated with a low SDI.

Multi-Item Indexes

The use of social class as an explanatory consumer behavior variable has been heavily influenced by two studies, each of which developed a multi-item index to measure social class.[13] The basic approach in each of these studies was to determine, through a detailed analysis of a relatively small community, the classes into which the community members appeared to fit. Then, more objective and measurable indicators or factors related to status were selected and weighted in a manner that would reproduce the original class assignments.

Hollingshead Index of Social Position The Hollingshead Index of Social Position (ISP), is a two-item index that is well developed and widely used. The item scales, weights, formulas, and social-class scores are shown in Exhibit 5–3. Using Hollingshead's Index of Social Position, significant differences in the rates of consumption are shown for various television programs and magazines in Figure 5–5.

It is important to note that this scale, like most multi-item indexes, was designed to measure or reflect an individual family's overall social position within a community. Because of this, it is possible for a high score on one variable to offset a low score on another. Thus, the following three individuals would all be classified as middle class: (1) someone with an eighth-grade education who is a successful owner of a medium-sized firm; (2) a four-year college graduate working as a salesperson; and (3) a graduate of a junior college working in an administrative position in the civil service. All of these individuals may well have similar standing in the community. However, it seems likely that their consumption processes for at least some products will differ, pointing up the fact that overall status may mask or hide potentially useful associations between individual status dimensions and the consumption process for particular products.

Warner's Index of Status Characteristics Another widely used multi-item scale of social status is Warner's Index of Status Characteristics (ISC). Warner's system of measurement is based on four socioeconomic factors: occupation, source of income, house type, and dwelling area. Each of these dimensions of status is defined over a range of seven categories and each carries a different weight. This system classifies individuals into one of six social status categories.

Census Bureau's Index of Socioeconomic Status A three-factor social status index based on occupation, income, and education is used by the U.S. Bureau of the Census. This scale, referred to as the Socioeconomic Status scale (SES), produces four social status categories.

EXHIBIT 5–3 Hollingshead Index of Social Position (ISP)

Occupation Scale (Weight of 7)

Description	Score
Higher executives of large concerns, proprietors, and major professionals	1
Business managers, proprietors of medium-sized businesses, and lesser professionals	2
Administrative personnel, owners of small businesses, and minor professionals	3
Clerical and sales workers, technicians, and owners of little businesses	4
Skilled manual employees	5
Machine operators and semiskilled employees	6
Unskilled employees	7

Education Scale (Weight of 4)

Description	Score
Professional (M.A., M.S., M.E., M.D., Ph.D., LL.B., and the like)	1
Four-year college graduate (B.A., B.S., B.M.)	2
One to three years college (also business schools)	3
High school graduate	4
Ten to 11 years of school (part high school)	5
Seven to nine years of school	6
Less than seven years of school	7

ISP score = (Occupation score × 7) + (Education score × 4)

Classification System

Social Strata	Range of Scores
Upper	11–17
Upper-middle	18–31
Middle	32–47
Lower-middle	48–63
Lower	64–77

Source: Adapted from A. B. Hollingshead and F. C. Redlich, *Social Class and Mental Illness* (New York: John Wiley & Sons, 1958).

Which Scale Should Be Used?

The selection of a measure of social status or prestige is not as complex a problem as it might appear. What must be realized is that there is no one, unidimensional status or class continuum. Thus, the problem is not one of selecting the best measure. Rather, it is to select the most appropriate prestige or status dimension for the problem at hand. When an individual's total personal status is the dimension of concern, perhaps in a study of opinion leadership, a multi-item index such as the Warner or Hollingshead index would be most appropriate. Studies of taste and intellectually oriented activities such as magazine readership or television viewing should consider education as the most relevant dimension. Occupation might be most relevant for studies focusing on leisure-time pursuits.

The task of the marketing manager is to think the problem through and select the measure of social stratification that is conceptually most relevant to the problem.

SOCIAL STRATIFICATION AND MARKETING STRATEGY

While social stratification does not explain all consumption behavior, it is certainly relevant for some product categories. For clear evidence of this, visit a furniture store in a working-class neighborhood and then an upper-class store such as Ethan Allen Galleries.[14]

Figure 5–6 indicates the steps involved in using social stratification to develop marketing strategy. The first task managers must preform is to determine, for their product categories, which aspects of the consumption process are affected by social status. This will generally require research in which relevant measures of social class are taken and associated with product/brand usage, purchase motivation, outlet selection, media usage, and so forth.

Product/brand utilization often varies widely across social strata. Income clearly restricts the purchase of some products such as expensive sports cars and boats. Education often influences consumption of fine art. Occupation appears to be related closely to leisure profits.

The consumption of imported wine, liqueurs, and original art varies with social class. Beer is consumed across all social classes, but Michelob is more popular at the upper end and Pabst is more popular at the lower end. A product/brand may have different meanings to members of different social strata. Blue jeans may serve as economical, functional clothing items to working-class members and as stylish, self-expressive items to upper-class individuals. Likewise, different purchase motivations for the same product may exist between social strata. Individuals in higher social classes use credit cards for convenience (pay off the entire balance each month), while individuals in lower social classes use them for installment purchases (do not pay off the entire bill at the end of each month).

Using Social Stratification to Develop Marketing Strategy

FIGURE 5–6

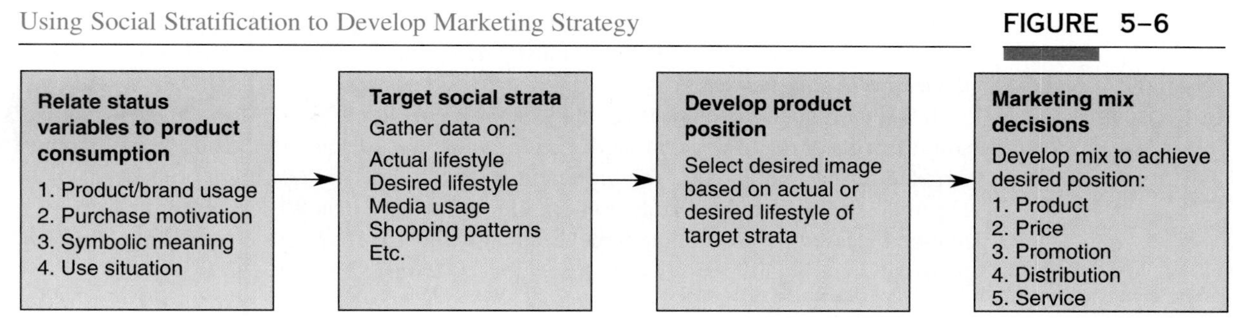

FIGURE 5–7 Anheuser-Busch Positioning to Social Class Segments

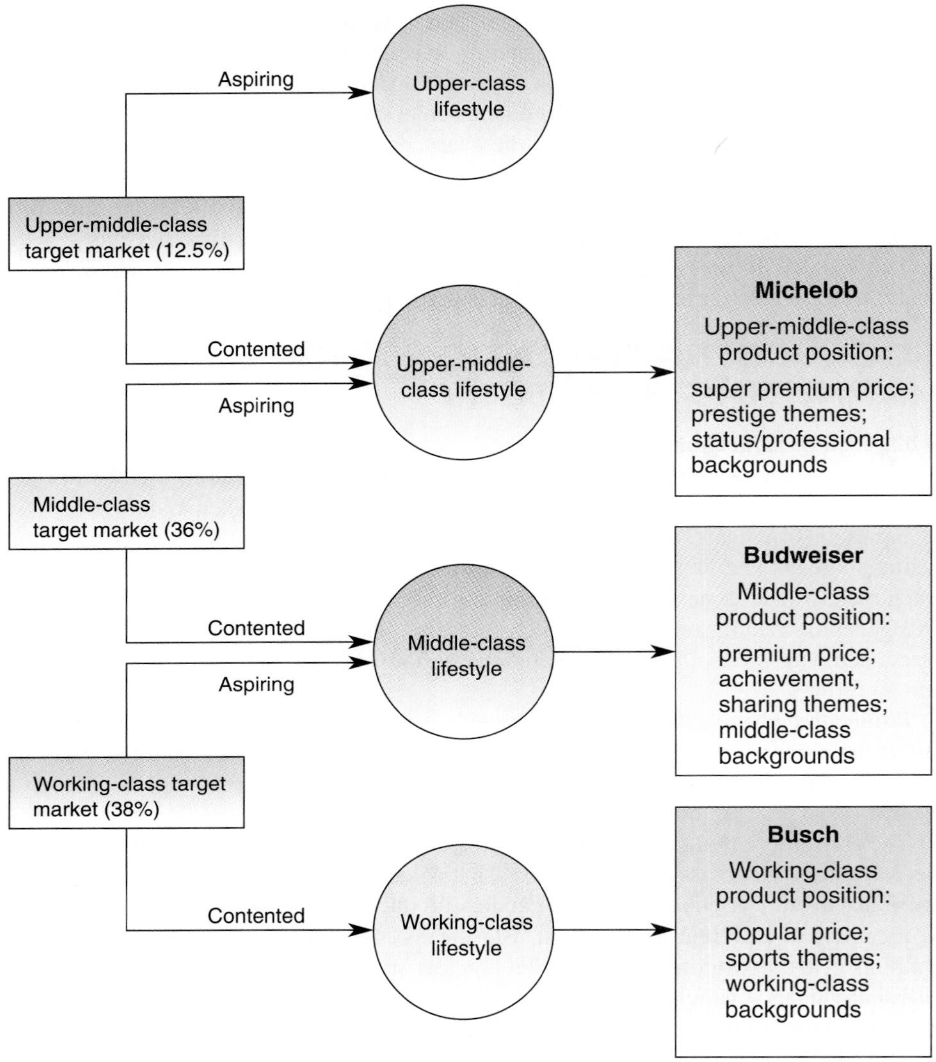

For products such as those described above, social class represents a useful segmentation variable. Having selected a segment based on usage rate, purchase motivation, or product/brand meaning, the marketer must position the brand in a manner consistent with the desired target market.

It is important to remember that many members of various social strata desire to emulate some aspects of the lifestyle of higher social strata at least some of the time. Thus, a brand targeted at the middle class might benefit from an upper middle-class product position. Figure 5–7 illustrates how Anheuser-Busch covers more than 80 percent of the U.S. population by carefully positioning three different brands. Table 5–2 indicates that consumers perceive these brands very clearly in social class terms.

Perceived Social Class Appeal of Various Brands of Beer

TABLE 5-2

	Social Class*				
Brand	Upper/ Upper Middle	Middle	Lower Middle	Upper Lower/ Lower	All Classes
Coors	22	54	16	2	3
Budweiser	4	46	37	7	4
Miller	14	50	22	6	6
Michelob	67	23	4	1	2
Old Style†	3	33	36	22	1
Bud Light	22	53	14	3	5
Heineken	88	9	1	—	1

*Percent classifying the brand as most appropriate for a particular social class.

†Local beer on tap.

Source: K. Grønhaug and P. S. Trapp, ''Perceived Social Class Appeals of Branded Goods,'' *Journal of Consumer Marketing*, Winter 1989, p. 27.

SUMMARY

A *social class system* is defined as the hierarchical division of a society into relatively permanent and homogeneous groups with respect to attitudes, values, and lifestyles.

For a social class system to exist in a society, the individual classes must meet five criteria. They must be (1) *bounded*, (2) *ordered*, (3) *mutually exclusive*, (4) *exhaustive*, and (5) *influential*. Using these criteria, it is obvious that a strict and tightly defined social class system does not exist in the United States. What does seem to exist is a series of status continua that reflect various dimensions or factors that the overall society values. Education, occupation, income, and, to a lesser extent, type of residence are important status dimensions in this country. *Status crystallization* refers to the consistency of individuals and families on all relevant status dimensions (e.g., high income, high educational level).

While pure social classes do not exist in the United States, it is useful for marketing managers to know and understand the general characteristics of major social classes. Using Coleman and Rainwater's system, we described American society in terms of seven major categories (*upper-upper, lower-upper, upper-middle, middle, working class, upper-lower, and lower-lower*).

Based on this stratification, each social class is different in occupation, education, income, ownership, and affiliations. Because of these differences, the lifestyles and consumption behavior of individuals in one social stratum can be quite different from those in other strata. These differences often provide marketers with useful insights into the consumption behavior of certain segments of our population. This allows marketing managers to develop more effective marketing programs directed at these groups.

There are two basic approaches to the measurement of social classes: (1) use a combination of several dimensions, a *multi-item index*, or (2) use a single dimension, a *single-item index*. Multi-item indexes are designed to measure an individual's overall rank or social position within the community. Problems occur in doing this because of differences—inconsistencies—between status items. Single-item indexes estimate status based on a single-status dimension. *Income*, *education*, and *occupation* are the most frequently used measures of social status.

Since there is no one, unidimensional status or class continuum, it is impossible to state which is the best measure. Rather, the choice of the measure to be used should depend on its appropriateness or relevance to the problem at hand. Increasingly, the use of one status dimension in conjunction with another seems appropriate. *Relative occupational class income (ROCI)* is a good example of such an approach. *Subjective discretionary income (SDI)*, which measures how much money consumers feel they have available for nonessentials, is also useful to marketers.

REVIEW QUESTIONS

1. What is a *social class system*?
2. Describe the five criteria necessary for a social class system to exist.
3. Does a tightly defined social class system exist in the United States? Explain your answer.
4. What is meant by the statement, "What exists is not a set of social classes, but a series of status continua"?
5. What underlying cultural value determines most of the status dimensions in the United States?
6. What status dimensions are common in the United States?
7. What is meant by *status crystallization*? Is the degree of status crystallization relatively high or low in the United States? Explain.
8. What are the two basic approaches used by marketers to measure social class?
9. What are the advantages of multi-item indexes? The disadvantages?
10. Describe the Hollingshead two-factor index.
11. What are the primary advantages of single-item indexes?
12. What are the problems associated with using income as an index of status?
13. Why is education sometimes used as an index of status?
14. What are the advantages of using occupation as an indication of status?
15. How should a marketing manager select the most appropriate measure of status?
16. What is meant by *relative occupational class income*? Why is the general idea behind this concept particularly appealing?
17. What is meant by *subjective discretionary income*? How does it affect purchases?
18. Briefly describe the primary characteristics of each of the classes listed below (assume a high level of status crystallization):
    a. Upper-upper.
    b. Lower-upper.
    c. Upper-middle.
    d. Middle class.
    e. Working class.
    f. Upper-lower.
    g. Lower-lower.
19. How does a manager develop marketing strategy based on social status?

DISCUSSION QUESTIONS

20. Which status variable, if any, is most related to
    a. Subscribing to *Time*.
    b. Owning inline skates.
    c. Extensive television viewing.
    d. Luxury car ownership.
    e. Type of pet owned.
    f. Charity contributions.
21. How could a knowledge of social stratification be used in the development of a marketing strategy for
    a. A shopping center.
    b. A new magazine.
    c. A golf course.
    d. Toothpaste.

   e. Cruise vacations.
   f. Energy conservation.
22. Do you think the United States is becoming more or less stratified over time?
23. Which status continuum do you think conveys the most status?
24. Did your parents have a high or low level of status crystallization? Explain.
25. Based on the Hollingshead two-factor index, what social class would your father be in? Your mother?
26. Name four products for which each of the three following single-factor indexes would be most appropriate as measurements of status. Justify your answer.
   a. Income.
   b. Education.
   c. Occupation.
27. What are some of the marketing implications of Table 5–1? 5–2?
28. Name four products in addition to automobiles for which the *relative occupational class income concept* would be particularly useful.
29. Evaluate the *subjective discretionary income* concept. How does it differ from ROCI? Which is most useful? Why?
30. How should marketers approach the lower-lower class?
31. Is it ethical for marketers to use the mass media to promote products that most members of the lower class and working class cannot afford?
32. Would your answer to Question 31 change if the products were limited to children's toys?
33. Name five products for which the "upward pull strategy" shown in Figure 5–3 would be appropriate. Name five for which it would be inappropriate. Justify your answer.
34. What causes the results shown in Table 5–2?
35. What causes the results shown in Figure 5–5?
36. What causes the results shown in Table 5–1?
37. Why did social classes evolve in China despite government opposition?

APPLICATION ACTIVITIES

38. Interview salespersons from stores carrying differing quality levels of furniture. Determine the social class or status characteristics of his or her customers, and the marketing strategies used by the store.
39. Using *Standard Rate and Data* or Simmons Research Bureau studies, pick three magazines that are oriented toward different social classes. Comment on the differences in content and advertising.
40. Interview a salesperson from an expensive, moderate, and an inexpensive outlet for ________. Ascertain their perceptions of the social classes or status of their customers. Determine if their sales approach differs with differing classes.
   a. Men's clothing.
   b. Women's clothing.
   c. Automobiles.
   d. Jewelry.
   e. Appliances.
41. Examine a variety of magazines/newspapers and clip or describe an advertisement which positions a product as appropriate for one of the seven social classes described in the text.
42. Using Figures 5–3 and 5–4, find advertisements that are examples of these marketing strategies. Explain the strategy of each ad in terms of the target market, product positioning, and periodical used to reach this target market.
43. Interview an electrician, schoolteacher, retail clerk, and successful businessperson. Measure their social status using one of the multi-item measurement devices. Evaluate their status crystallization, unique and similar consumer behaviors.
44. Visit a bowling alley and a tennis club parking lot. Analyze the differences in the types of cars, dress, and behaviors of those patronizing these two sports.
45. Secure a newspaper from a city you have not lived in (a Sunday paper is best). Select five or six ads from retail outlets such as furniture stores. Estimate the social class the ads are aimed at. What cues in the ads led you to your estimate?
46. Volunteer to work two days or evenings at a homeless shelter, soup kitchen, or other program aimed at very low income families. Write a brief report on your experiences and reactions.

REFERENCES

[1]Y. Yigang, ''Five Levels of Consumption,'' *Trade Promotion* (China Council for the Promotion of International Trade & China Chamber of International Commerce, no. 16, 1993, p. 10–11.

[2]K. Labich, ''Class in America,'' *Fortune*, February 7, 1994, p. 114.

[3]R. P. Coleman and L. Rainwater, *Social Standing in America: New Dimensions of Class* (New York: Basic Books, 1978), p. 18.

[4]See A. B. Hollingshead, *Elmstown's Youth* (New York: John Wiley & Sons, 1949); and W. L. Warner, M. Meeker, and K. Eels, *Social Class in America: A Manual of Procedure for the Measurement of Social Status* (Chicago: Science Research Associates, 1949).

[5]J. E. Fisher, ''Social Class and Consumer Behavior,'' in *Advances in Consumer Research XIV*, ed. M. Wallendorf and P. Anderson (Provo, Utah: Association for Consumer Research, 1987), pp. 492–96.

[6]R. Coleman, ''The Continuing Significance of Social Class in Marketing,'' *Journal of Consumer Research*, December 1983, p. 265.

[7]B. Nussbaum, ''Downward Mobility,'' *Business Week*, March 23, 1992, pp. 56–57. See also G. J. Duncan, T. M. Smeeding, and W. Rodgers, ''The Incredible Shrinking Middle Class,'' *American Demographics*, May 1992, pp. 34–38.

[8]See J. P. Dickson and D. L. MacLachlan, ''Social Distance and Shopping Behavior,'' *Journal of the Academy of Marketing Science*, Spring 1990, pp. 153–62.

[9]P. Fussell, *Class* (New York: Ballantine Books, 1984), p. 38.

[10]W. H. Peters, ''Relative Occupational Class Income: A Significant Variable in the Marketing of Automobiles,'' *Journal of Marketing*, April 1970, p. 74.

[11]S. Dawson, B. Stern, and T. Gillpatrick, ''An Empirical Update and Extension of Patronage Behaviors Across the Social Class Hierarchy,'' in *Advances in Consumer Research XVII*, eds. M. E. Goldberg, G. Gorn, and R. W. Pollay (Provo, Utah: Association for Consumer Research, 1990), pp. 833–38.

[12]T. C. O'Guinn and W. D. Wells, ''Subjective Discretionary Income,'' *Marketing Research*, March 1989, pp. 32–41.

[13]See footnote 4.

[14]See also R. Prus, *Pursuing Customers* (Newbury Park, California: Sage, 1989).

CHAPTER 6

GROUP INFLUENCES ON CONSUMER BEHAVIOR

Reebok is one of the most successful shoe firms in the world. Sales in America grew rapidly through the mid and late 1980s.

How did the firm accomplish this dramatic growth during a time when shoe sales, particularly sales of athletic shoes, were flat?

A large part of the firm's initial success was due to its association with aerobics. In 1983, aerobics was a minor sport with limited participation and no custom products such as shoes. Paul Fireman, who had U.S. distribution rights for Reebok, recognized the potential appeal of aerobics to women, particularly younger, upscale, active women. Equally important, Fireman recognized that group pressures would strongly influence the clothing worn during aerobics sessions and that style as well as function would be important.

Therefore, in addition to developing a functional shoe designed specifically for aerobics, Reeboks were stylish, trendy, and unique. Reebok also helped develop the sport of aerobics by publishing newsletters, sponsoring seminars, developing an aerobics teacher-certification program, and providing a clearinghouse for information on injury prevention. Sales of Reebok shoes grew rapidly as aerobics gained popularity. They became ''the'' shoe to wear for aerobics, and, increasingly, in other contexts as well.[1]

When you decided what to wear to the last party you attended, you probably based your decision in part on the anticipated responses of the other individuals at the party. Likewise, your behavior at an anniversary celebration for your grandparents probably would differ from your behavior at a graduation party for a close friend. These behaviors are responses to group influences as shown in Figure 6–1.

The term **group**, considered in its broadest sense, refers to *two or more individuals who share a set of norms, values, or beliefs and have certain implicitly or explicitly defined relationships to one another such that their behaviors are interdependent.* Almost all consumer behavior takes place within a group setting. In addition, groups serve as one of the primary agents of consumer socialization and learning. Therefore, understanding how groups function is essential to understanding consumer behavior. As the Reebok example illustrates, marketers use knowledge of group influences when developing marketing strategy.

This chapter examines the manner in which groups function. Our first concern is with the various ways groups can be classified. Next, we analyze the impact reference groups have on the consumption process and how marketers can develop strategies based on these influences. Roles—behaviors associated with a position in a group—are then described and their implications for marketing strategy discussed.

FIGURE 6–1

Groups Influence Consumption

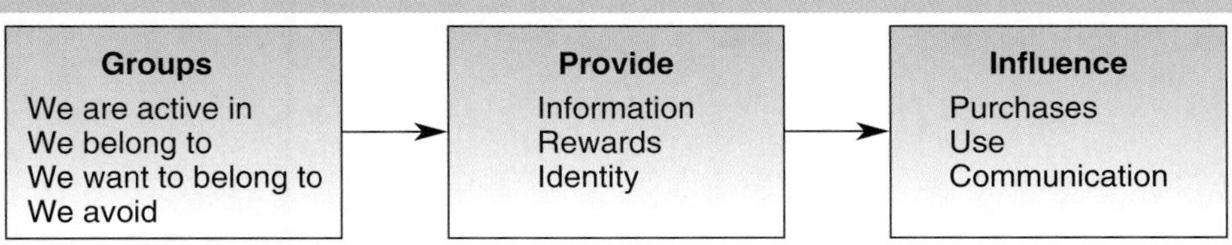

TYPES OF GROUPS

The terms *group* and *reference group* need to be distinguished. A group was defined earlier as two or more individuals who share a set of norms, values, or beliefs and have certain implicitly or explicitly defined relationships to one another such that their behaviors are interdependent. A **reference group** is *a group whose presumed perspectives or values are being used by an individual as the basis for his or her current behavior.* Thus, a reference group is simply a group that an individual uses as a guide for behavior in a specific situation.

Most of us belong to a number of different groups and perhaps would like to belong to several others. When we are actively involved with a particular group, it generally functions as a reference group. As the situation changes we may base our behavior on an entirely different group which then becomes our reference group. We may belong to many groups simultaneously, but we generally use only one group as a point of reference in any given situation. This is illustrated in Figure 6–2.

Groups may be classified according to a number of variables. Marketers have found three classification criteria to be particularly useful:

1. Membership.
2. Type of contact.
3. Attraction.

The *membership* criterion is dichotomous: either one is a member of a particular group or one is not a member of that group. Of course, some members are more secure in their membership than others are. That is, some members feel they really ''belong'' to a group

FIGURE 6–2 Reference Groups Change as the Situation Changes

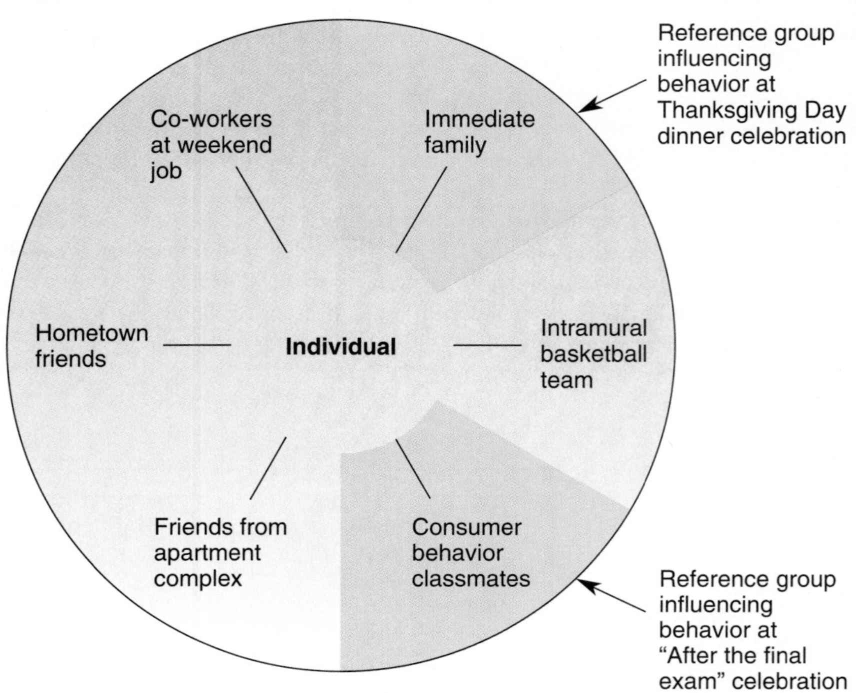

while others lack this confidence. However, membership is generally treated as an either/or criterion for classification purposes.

Degree of contact refers to how much interpersonal contact the group members have with each other. As group size increases, interpersonal contact tends to decrease. For example, you probably have less interpersonal contact with all other members of the American Marketing Association or your university than you have with your family or close friends. Degree of contact is generally treated as having two categories. Groups characterized by frequent interpersonal contact are called **primary groups**. Groups characterized by limited interpersonal contact are referred to as **secondary groups**.

Attraction refers to the desirability that membership in a given group has for the individual. This can range from negative to positive. Groups with negative desirability can influence behavior just as do those with positive desirability. For example, at one time motorcycles in the United States became associated with disreputable groups such as the Hell's Angels. Sales of motorcycles were limited because many people did not want to use a product associated with such groups. Thus, motorcycle gangs served as negative reference groups for those individuals. (However, they were a positive reference group for individuals identifying with the Hell's Angels.) It took extensive advertising by firms such as Honda ("You meet the nicest people on a Honda") to change this image and increase market acceptance of motorcycles.

Nonmembership groups with a positive attraction, **aspiration reference groups**, exert a strong influence on desired products. That is, individuals may purchase products thought to be used by the desired group in order to achieve actual or symbolic membership in the group. The following theme from an ad for *Financial World* illustrates this:

> Surveys show that one of four *Financial World* readers is a millionaire. Our average reader is worth over $628,000. Join this select group who rely on *Financial World* for investment news, information, and insights.

Figure 6–3 illustrates the various types of groups that commonly influence consumer behavior. The ways they influence behavior are described in the next section of this chapter. Managerial Application 6–1 shows Bud Light as appropriate for consumption in a group setting.

REFERENCE GROUP INFLUENCES ON THE CONSUMPTION PROCESS

We all conform in a variety of ways to numerous groups. For example, the fact that we wear clothes when attending class is conforming to a basic societal norm. By the same token, shorts, sandals, and no shirt would be inappropriate to wear to most worship services. Note that we, as individuals, do not generally consider these behaviors to constitute conformity. Normally, we conform without even being aware of doing so, though we also frequently face conscious decisions on whether or not to go along with the group. When we respond to group expectations, we are reacting to either *role expectations* (discussed in the next section) or *group norms.*

Norms are *general expectations about behaviors that are deemed appropriate for all persons in a social context, regardless of the position they hold.* Norms arise quickly, often without verbal communication or direct thought, anytime a group exists. Norms tend to cover all aspects of behavior relevant to the group's functioning, and violation of the norms can result in sanctions.

Reference groups have been found to influence a wide range of consumption behaviors. Before examining the marketing implications of these findings, we need to examine the nature of reference group influence more closely.

FIGURE 6-3 Types of Groups

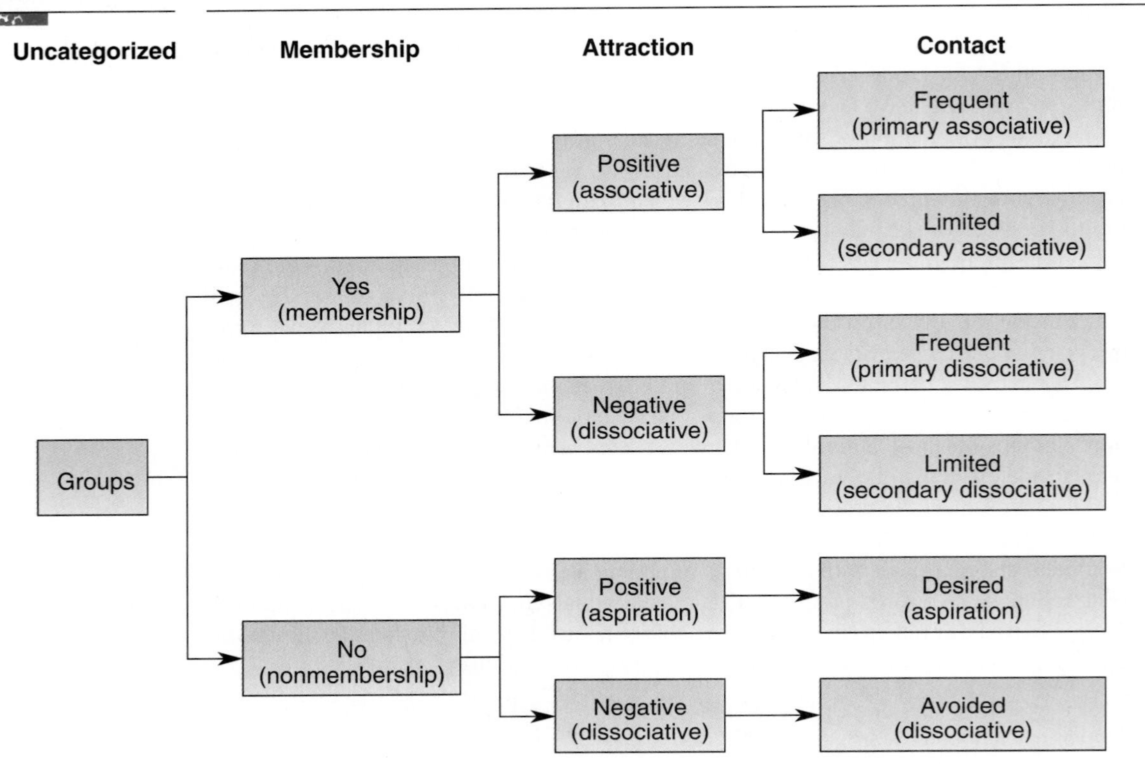

MANAGERIAL APPLICATION

6-1

Group-Based Consumption Behavior

Three Types of Group Influence

FIGURE 6–4

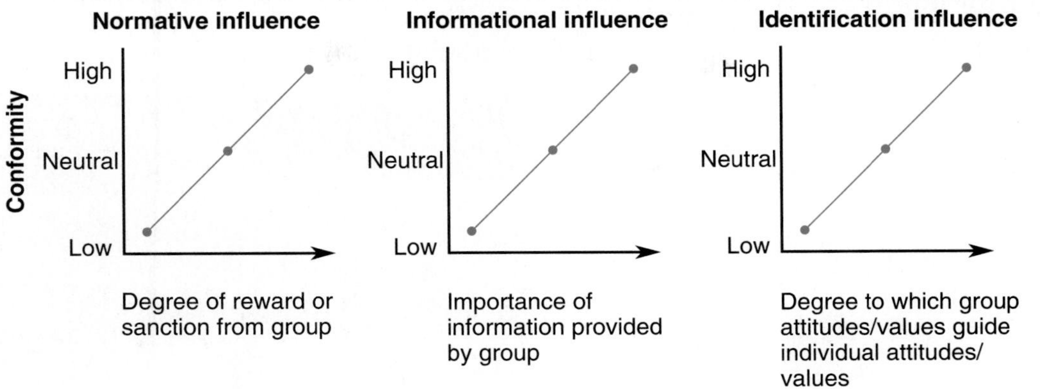

The Nature of Reference Group Influence

Conformity is not a unidimensional concept.[2] Three types of group influence are illustrated in Figure 6–4. It is important to distinguish among these types since the marketing strategy required depends on the type of influence involved.

Informational influence occurs when an individual uses the behaviors and opinions of reference group members as potentially useful bits of information. Thus, a person may notice several members of a given group using a particular brand of coffee. He or she may then decide to try that brand simply because there is evidence (its use by friends) that it may be a good brand. Or, one may decide to see a particular movie because a friend with similar tastes in movies recommends it. In these cases, conformity is simply the result of information shared by the group members. Managerial Application 6–2 illustrates the nature of informational influence.

Normative influence, sometimes referred to as *utilitarian* influence, occurs when an individual fulfills group expectations to gain a direct reward or to avoid a sanction. You may purchase a given brand of coffee to win approval from a spouse or a neighborhood group. Or you may refrain from wearing the latest fashion for fear of teasing by friends.

Identification influence, also called *value-expressive* influence, occurs when individuals use the perceived group norms and values as a guide for their own attitudes or values. Thus, the individual is using the group as a reference point for his or her own self-image. Peer reference groups appear to have a particularly important identification influence on adolescents.

Figure 6–5 on page 149 illustrates a series of consumption situations and the type of reference group influence that is operating in each case. While this table indicates the wide range of situations in which groups influence the consumption process, there are other situations in which groups have at most a limited, indirect effect.[3] For example, purchasing a particular brand of aspirin or noticing a billboard advertisement generally are not subject to group influence.

Degree of Reference Group Influence

Reference groups may have no influence in a given situation or they may influence usage of the product category, the type of product used, and/or the brand used. Brand influence is most likely to be a category influence rather than a specific brand. That is, a group is

MANAGERIAL APPLICATION

6–2

Informational Group Influence

Drs. Junkins, Kwiatkowski, Cuervo, and Huang haven't been doctors long enough to know they're supposed to drive one of those overpriced luxury imports.

When Ed, Janet, Beth, and Jim emerged, successfully, from medical school, they felt the gratification of having achieved a lifelong goal, while also confronting a hard reality common to most young doctors—a ton of student loan debt. (You could buy five Saturns with what a new M.D. typically owes.)

In Ed's case, that hard reality also included his 10-year-old car—nobody could tell him how much time it had left. Since a pediatric resident's life is ruled by a beeper (and because you can't tell a sick kid that the tow truck was late), Ed bit the bullet and went looking for a new car.

Say ahh! Our hunch is that at least 9 out of 10 doctors would really love how easy Saturns are to take care of. (But don't quote us on that. Ask your doctor.)

While he was making the rounds of the car dealerships in town, Ed discovered Saturn. Where, along with the simple, painless way one shops at our showrooms, he liked the rather healthy range of standard features offered and (especially) the fact that the price of a Saturn did not put him into a state of shock.

SATURN

Since then, mostly on his referral, many of Ed's colleagues have been filling the hospital parking lot with new Saturns. (Apparently, the people who pay most attention to a doctor's advice are other doctors.)

The Saturn SL1

A Different Kind *of* Company. A Different Kind *of* Car.

likely to approve (or disapprove) a range of brands such as imported beers or luxury automobiles.

Exhibit 6–1 shows how two consumption situation characteristics—necessity/nonnecessity and visible/private consumption—combine to influence the degree of reference group influence likely to operate in a specific situation.[4] In the following paragraphs we will discuss these two, and three additional determinants of reference group influences.

1. Group influence is strongest *when the use of product or brand is visible to the group.* For a product such as aerobic shoes, the product category (shoes), product type (aerobic), and brand (Reebok) are all visible. A dress is visible in terms of product category and product type (style), but the brand is less obvious. The consumption of other products such as vitamins is generally private. Reference group influence typically affects only those aspects of the product (category, type, or brand) that are visible to the group.
2. Reference group influence is higher *the less of a necessity an item is.* Thus, reference groups have strong influence on the ownership of nonnecessities such as sailboats, but much less influence on necessities such as refrigerators.

Consumption Situations and Reference Group Influence

FIGURE 6–5

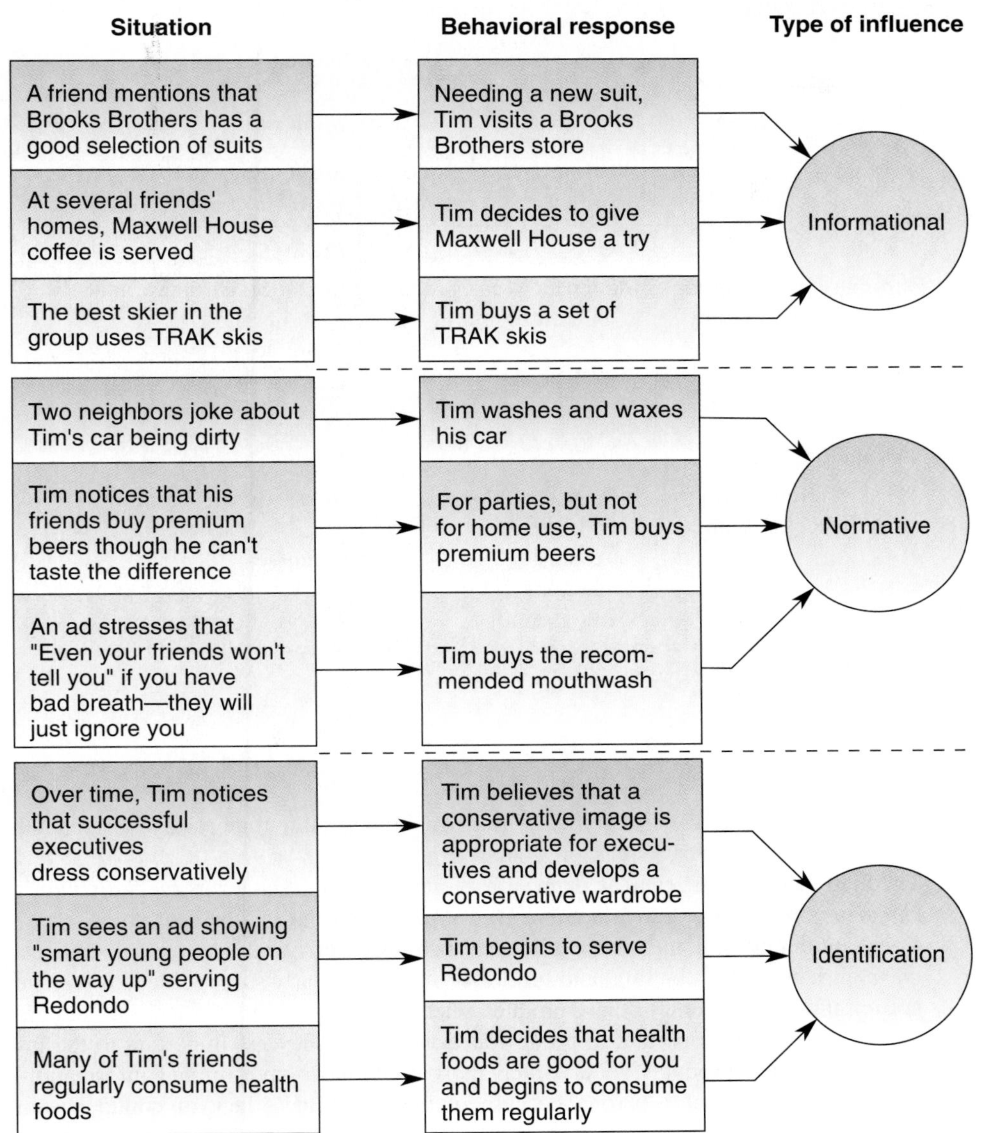

3. In general, *the more commitment an individual feels to a group, the more the individual will conform to the group norms.* We are much more likely to consider group expectations when dressing for a dinner with a group we would like to join (stay with) than for dinner with a group that is unimportant to us.
4. The fourth factor influencing the impact of a reference group on an individual's behavior is *the relevance of the behavior to the group.* The more relevant a particular activity is to the group's functioning, the stronger the pressure to conform to the group norms concerning that activity. Thus, style of dress may be important to a social group

EXHIBIT 6–1 Two Consumption Situation Characteristics and Product/Brand Choice

Consumption	**Degree Needed** **Necessity**	**Nonnecessity**
	Weak reference group influence on product	Strong reference group influence on product
Visible Strong reference group influence on brand	*Public necessities* Influence: Weak product and strong brand Examples: Wristwatch Automobile	*Public luxuries* Influence: Strong product and brand Examples: Snow skis Sailboat
Private Weak reference group influence on brand	*Private necessities* Influence: Weak product and brand Examples: Mattress Refrigerator	*Private luxuries* Influence: Strong product and weak brand Examples: TV game Trash compactor

Source: Adapted from W. D. Bearden and M. J. Etzel, "Reference Group Influence on Product and Brand Purchase Decision," *Journal of Consumer Research*, September 1982, p. 185.

that frequently eats dinner together at nice restaurants and unimportant to a reference group that meets for basketball on Thursday nights.

5. The final factor that affects the degree of reference group influence is *the individual's confidence in the purchase situation*. One study found the purchase of color televisions, automobiles, home air conditioners, insurance, refrigerators, medical services, magazines or books, clothing, and furniture to be particularly susceptible to reference group influence. Several of these products such as insurance and medical services are neither visible nor important to group functioning. Yet they are important to the individual and are products about which most individuals have limited information. Thus, group influence is strong because of the individual's lack of confidence in purchasing these products. In addition to confidence in the purchase situation, there is evidence that individuals differ in their tendency to be influenced by reference groups.[5]

MARKETING STRATEGIES BASED ON REFERENCE GROUP INFLUENCES

Figure 6–6 summarizes the manner in which reference groups influence product and brand usage. Marketing managers can use this structure to determine the likely degree of group influence on the consumption of their brand.

The first task the manager faces in using reference group influence is to determine the degree and nature of reference group influence that exists, *or can be created*, for the product in question. Figure 6–6 provides the starting point for this analysis.

Consumption Situation Determinants of Reference Group Influence

FIGURE 6–6

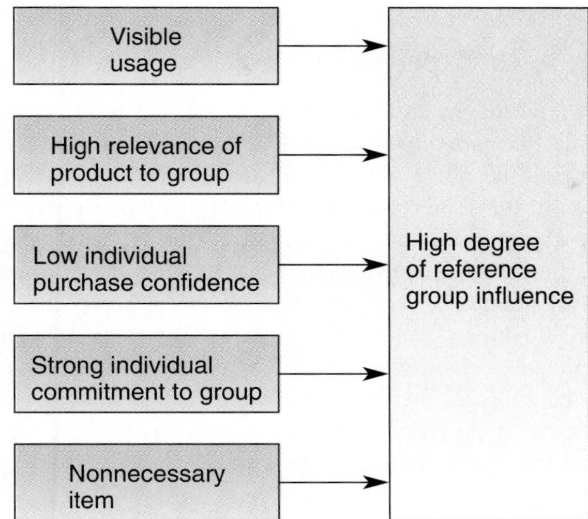

Personal Sales Strategies

The power of group norms has been demonstrated in a series of studies now generally referred to as the Asch experiments or the **Asch phenomenon**. The basic Asch study is described in Exhibit 6–2.

This study has been repeated in a variety of formats and has generally achieved the same results. Interviews with respondents after the experiments found that many changed their beliefs concerning which answers were correct. Thus, more than verbal conformity occurs. In addition, many respondents who expressed correct judgments indicated doubts about their own accuracy afterward. Note that the conformity being obtained was among strangers with respect to a discrete, physical task that had an objective, correct answer. Imagine how much stronger the pressures to conform are among friends or when the task is less well defined, such as preferring one brand or style over another.

Exhibit 6–2 also illustrates one way that the Asch phenomenon has been used by marketers in a personal selling situation.

Tupperware and other firms using ''party'' sales situations rely on situations in which reference group behavior encourages sales. Tupperware products are ones for which we would not normally predict a strong level of reference group influence—private usage, limited relevance to the group, fairly high individual purchase skills, and a necessary item. However, by making the *purchase itself* part of a party *at a friend's home*, the situation is dramatically changed. Now the *purchase act* is the focus of attention, and it is visible and highly relevant to the party group to which the individual usually has a fair degree of commitment.[7]

Advertising Strategies

Marketers use all three types of reference group influence when developing advertisements. Managerial Application 6–3 on page 153 shows an ad based on identification influence. Ads showing group members praising or admiring another group member for purchasing or using a particular product (normative influence) are also common.

EXHIBIT 6–2 Utilization of the Asch Phenomenon in Personal Selling

The Classic Asch Experiment

Eight subjects are brought into a room and asked to determine which of a set of three unequal lines are closest to the length of a fourth line shown some distance from the other three. The subjects are to announce their judgments publicly. Seven of the subjects are working for the experimenter, and they announce incorrect matches.

The order of announcement is arranged so that the naive subject responds last. In a control situation, 37 naive subjects performed the task 18 times each without any information about others' choices. Two of the 37 subjects made a total of three mistakes. However, when another group of 50 naive subjects responded *after* hearing the unanimous but *incorrect* judgment of the other group members, 37 subjects made a total of 194 errors, all of which were in agreement with the mistake made by the group.[6]

The Asch Format in Personal Selling

A group of potential customers—owners and salesmen of small firms—are brought together in a central location for a sales presentation. As each design is presented, the salesman scans the expressions of the people in the group, looking for the one who shows approval (e.g., head nodding) of the design. He then asks that person for an opinion, since the opinion is certain to be favorable. The person is asked to elaborate. As he does so, the salesman scans the faces of the other people, looking for more support. He then asks for an opinion of the next person now showing most approval. He continues until he reaches the person who initially showed the most disapproval. In this way, by using the first person as a model, and by social group pressure on the last person, the salesman gets all or most of the people in the group to make a positive public statement about the design.

ROLES

Roles are defined and enacted within groups. A **role** is *a prescribed pattern of behavior expected of a person in a given situation by virtue of the person's position in that situation.* Thus, while an individual must perform in a certain way, the expected behaviors are based on the position itself and not on the individual involved. For example, in your role as a student, certain behaviors are expected of you, such as attending class and studying. The same general behaviors are expected of all other students. Roles are based on positions, not individuals.

While all students in a given class are expected to exhibit certain behaviors, the manner in which these expectations are fulfilled varies dramatically from individual to individual. Some students arrive at class early, take many notes, and ask numerous questions. Others come to class consistently, but never ask questions. Still others come to class only occasionally. **Role style** refers to these *individual variations in the performance of a given*

MANAGERIAL APPLICATION 6–3

Identification Group Influence in Advertising

role. **Role parameters** represent the *range of behavior acceptable within a given role.* The role of college student has wide parameters while the role of a private in the U.S. Marines carries very narrow parameters.

Sanctions are *punishments imposed on individuals for violating role parameters.* A student who fails to attend class or disrupts the conduct of the class generally is subject to sanctions ranging from mild reprimands to dismissal from school. The most severe sanction for most role violations is disqualification from that role. Therefore, an individual's **role commitment** or desire to continue in the role position is an important determinant of the effectiveness of the sanctions and the likelihood that the individual will remain within the role parameters.

All of us fulfill numerous roles, which is known as **role load**. When an individual attempts to fill more roles than the available time, energy, or money allows, **role overload** occurs.[8] Occasionally two roles demand different behaviors. Consider the individual represented in Figure 6–7. In numerous situations, this fairly typical student will face incompatible role demands. For example, the basketball team member role may require practice one evening while the student role requires library research. This is known as **role conflict**.

FIGURE 6–7 One Student's Role Set

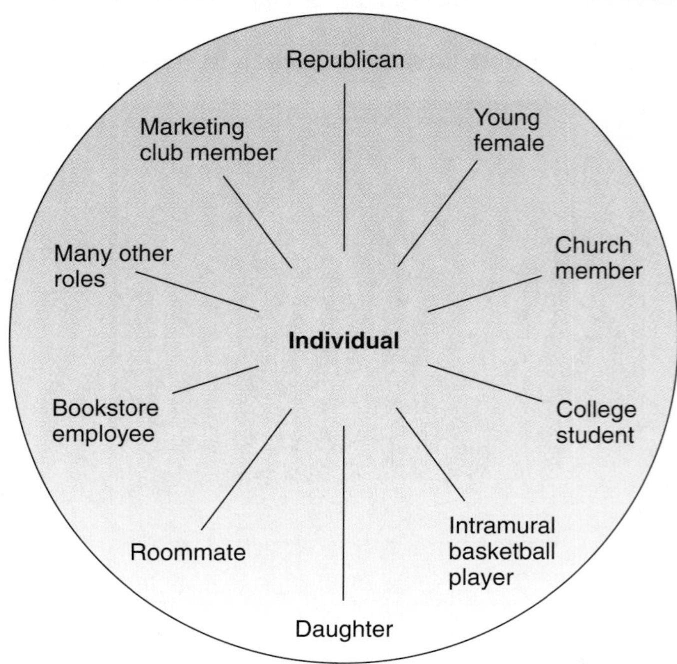

Most career-oriented individuals experience conflicts between their role as family member (husband, wife, father, or mother) and their career.

The set of roles that an individual fulfills over time is not static. Individuals acquire new roles, **role acquisition**, and drop existing roles, **role deletion**. Since roles often require products, individuals must learn which products are appropriate for their new roles. For example, the student in Figure 6–7 may soon drop her roles as college student, intramural basketball player, and bookstore employee. She may acquire additional roles such as assistant brand manager, wife, and tennis club member. To be effective in her new roles, she will have to learn new behaviors and consume different products.

Roles themselves are not static over time. **Role evolution** occurs. The behaviors and products appropriate for a given role change with time. For example, in Chapter 3 we discussed the changes associated with gender role evolution.

A **role stereotype** is a shared visualization of the ideal performer of a given role. Most of us share a common view of the physical and behavioral characteristics of a doctor, lawyer, or grade school teacher. Close your eyes and imagine any of these occupational types. Chances are that your mental image is similar to the image held by your classmates. The fact that large numbers of people share such common images is quite useful to marketing managers.

Application of Role Theory in Marketing Practice

Role-Related Product Cluster *A* **role-related product cluster** (sometimes referred to as a consumption constellation) is *a set of products generally considered necessary to properly fulfill a given role.*[9] The products may be functionally necessary to fulfill the role or they may be symbolically important. For example, the boots associated with the cowboy

MANAGERIAL APPLICATION

Positioning a Camera as Part of the Parent Product Cluster

6–4

role originally were functional. The pointed toe allowed the foot to enter the stirrup quickly and easily while the high heel prevented the foot from sliding through the stirrup. The high sides of the boot protected the rider's ankles from thorns. Today, the "cowboy" role still calls for boots, although few urban cowboys spend much time in the saddle. The boot now is symbolically tied to the cowboy role.

Role-related product clusters are important because they define both appropriate and inappropriate products for a given role. Since many products are designed to enhance role performance, marketing managers must be sure that their products fit with existing and evolving roles. Managerial Application 6–4 indicates that the Pentax camera is an appropriate part of the parent product cluster.

Evolving Roles As roles evolve and change, challenges and opportunities are created for marketers. For example, the shifting role of women now includes active sports. In response, numerous companies have introduced sports clothes and equipment for women. Likewise, the increasing number of businesswomen has resulted in garment bags designed to hold dresses. The location and operating hours of many retail outlets now reflect the changed shopping patterns caused by widespread female participation in the workforce. Marketers must be prepared to adjust product, promotion, and distribution to stay in tune with evolving roles.

Role Conflict and Role Overload As roles evolve and change, new types of role conflicts come into existence. These role conflicts offer opportunities for marketers. For example, many airlines have altered their pricing policies and promote, "take your spouse along on your business trip," in an attempt to capitalize on conflicts between career and family roles. Students are frequently advised of the existence of speed-reading courses which promise to improve classroom performance and reduce conflict between the student

MANAGERIAL APPLICATION

6–5

Role Overload Reduction as a Product Benefit

role and other roles, by reducing the time required for studying. The following advertisement copy from an Evelyn Wood Reading Dynamics bulletin reflects this theme:

> Why let the responsibilities that college demands deprive you of enjoying the college life? With Reading Dynamics you can handle both all the reading you're expected to do and know, plus still have time to do what you want to do.

With increasing participation of women in the workforce, role overload has become more common for both females and males. The ad in Managerial Application 6–5 positions *Trek Fitness Cycles* as a solution to role overload.

Role Acquisition and Transition Role acquisitions and transitions present marketers with the opportunity to associate their products or brands with the new role.[10] This is a particularly useful approach when major role changes occur for significant numbers of people. For example, the role change from young single to young married person happens to most people in our society and requires a significant shift in role-related behaviors. The ad in Managerial Application 6–6 clearly positions the Mazda Miata as a car to have *before* the transition to the parenthood role.

SUMMARY

A *group* in its broadest sense includes two or more individuals who share a set of norms, values, or beliefs, and have certain implicit or explicit relationships such that their behaviors are interdependent. Groups may be classified on the basis of membership, nature of contact, and attraction.

MANAGERIAL APPLICATION

Product Positioning Based on Role Transitions

6–6

Before
the spouse,
the house,
the kids,
you get
one chance.

mazda
IT JUST FEELS RIGHT

Some groups require *membership*; others (e.g., aspiration groups) do not. The *nature of contact* is based on the degree of interpersonal contact. Groups that have frequent personal contact are called *primary groups*, while those with limited interpersonal contact are called *secondary groups*. *Attraction* refers to the degree of positive or negative desirability the group has to the individual.

Norms are general expectations about behaviors that are deemed appropriate for all persons in a social context, regardless of the position they hold. Norms arise quickly and naturally in any group situation. The degree of conformity to group norms is a function of: (1) the visibility of the usage situation, (2) the level of commitment the individual feels to the group, (3) the relevance of the behavior to the functioning of the group, (4) the individual's confidence in his or her own judgment in the area, and (5) the necessity/nonnecessity nature of the product.

Group influence varies across situations. *Informational influence* occurs when individuals simply acquire information shared by group members. *Normative influence* is stronger because an individual conforms to group expectations to gain approval or avoid disapproval. *Identification conformity* is still stronger, because an individual uses the group norms and identifies with them as a part of his or her self-concept and identity.

A *role* is defined as a prescribed pattern of behavior expected of a person in a given situation by virtue of the person's position in that situation. Thus, roles are based on positions and situations and not on individuals. Many characteristics affect role behavior, such as *role style* and *parameters*, one's *commitment* to a certain role, and *role conflict*. An important use of role theory in marketing revolves around the fact that there is usually a set of products considered necessary to properly fulfill a given role—in other words, a *role-related product cluster*. Marketers also structure strategies around *role conflict*, *role acquisition*, *role evolution*, and *role overload*.

REVIEW QUESTIONS

1. What is a *negative attraction reference group*? In what way can negative attraction reference groups influence consumer behavior?
2. What criteria are used by marketers to classify groups?
3. What is an *aspiration reference group*? How can an aspiration reference group influence behavior?
4. How does a *group* differ from a *reference group*?
5. What is the *Asch phenomenon*?
6. What factors determine the degree of influence a reference group will have on a given consumer decision?
7. What types of group influence exist? Why must a marketing manager be aware of these separate types of group influence?
8. What product characteristics appear to influence the type of reference group influence that will exist in a given situation?
9. How can personal sales strategies use a knowledge of reference group influence?
10. How can a marketer use a knowledge of reference group influences to develop advertising strategies?
11. What is a *role*?
12. How does *role style* relate to *role parameters*?
13. How does a *role sanction* relate to a *role parameter*?
14. How does *role commitment* relate to *role sanctions*?
15. What is *role conflict*? How can marketers use role conflict in product development and promotion?
16. What is a *role stereotype*? How do marketers use role stereotypes?
17. What is a *role-related product cluster*? Why is it important to marketing managers?
18. How does a *group norm* differ from a *role*?
19. What is meant by *role acquisition*? How can marketers use this phenomenon?
20. What is *role evolution*? Why is this concept important to marketing managers?
21. What is *role load*? *Role overload?*

DISCUSSION QUESTIONS

22. Using college students as the market segment, describe the most relevant reference group(s) and indicate the probable degree of influence for each of the following decisions:
    a. Brand of toothpaste.
    b. Purchase of health insurance.
    c. Contribution to a charity.
    d. Purchase of a stereo system.
    e. Magazine subscription.
23. Answer the following questions for: (1) beer, (2) video rentals, (3) automobile insurance, (4) vitamins, (5) a pet, or (6) joining a conservation organization.
    a. How important are reference groups to the purchase of ________? Would their influence also affect the brand or model? Would their influence be informational, normative, or identification? Justify your answers.
    b. What reference groups would be relevant to the decision to purchase a ________ (based on students on your campus)?
    c. What are the norms of the social groups of which you are a member concerning ________?
    d. Could an Asch-type situation be used to sell ________?
    e. How could ________ be associated with the student role on your campus?
24. Describe five groups to which you belong and give an example of a purchase instance when each served as a reference group.
25. Describe two groups that serve as aspiration reference groups for you. In what ways, if any, have they influenced your consumption patterns?
26. Describe two groups to which you belong. For each, give two examples of instances when the

group has exerted (a) informational, (b) normative, and (c) identification influence on you.

27. Why is reference group influence weak on product ownership (use) of necessities and strong on nonnecessities?
28. Describe the role-related product cluster for students in your major on your campus. In what ways will this product cluster change when you begin your career?
29. Describe three situations in which you have experienced role conflict.
30. Describe a situation in which you have violated a group norm with respect to product ownership or use. What sanctions, if any, were applied?
31. Describe a recent role acquisition that you have engaged in. What new functional products were required? Were any symbolic products required?
32. Describe your role load. Do you experience role overload? How do you deal with role overload?

PROJECT QUESTIONS

33. Find three advertisements that use reference groups in an attempt to gain patronage.
    a. Describe the advertisement.
    b. Describe the type of reference group being used.
    c. Describe the type of conformity being sought.
34. Find three advertisements that use role stereotypes and describe the type of role being portrayed.
35. Find and describe an advertisement, product, or other use of the marketing mix based on role conflict.
36. Perform the following activities for: (1) beer, (2) soft drink, (3) health food, (4) Christian Children's Fund, (5) mouthwash, or (6) vitamins.
    a. Develop an advertisement using an informational reference group influence.
    b. Develop an advertisement using a normative reference group influence.
    c. Develop an advertisement using an identification reference group influence.
    d. Develop an advertisement using a role-related product cluster approach.
    e. Develop an advertisement using a role conflict approach.
    f. Develop an advertisement using a role acquisition approach.
37. Interview: (a) five students, (b) five working women, or (c) five working men with children at home to determine the types of role conflicts they face. What marketing opportunities are suggested by your results?
38. Interview five recently married males and five recently married females to determine how their consumption patterns have changed as a result of their role change. What marketing opportunities are suggested by your results?
39. Interview five recent college graduates now employed in a management or sales position to determine how their consumption patterns have changed as a result of their role change. What marketing opportunities are suggested by your results?
40. Find two advertisements that use the role-related product cluster approach. What role is being used? Is the advertisement effective? Why?
41. Interview two new (within one year) mothers or fathers. Determine who serves as a reference group for child-related purchases.
42. Interview an (a) ______ salesperson. Determine the extent to which he or she feels that reference groups influence the purchase or use of the product. Is the salesperson able to utilize this?
    a. Automobile.
    b. Furniture.
    c. Bicycle.
    d. Ski.
    e. Computer.

REFERENCES

[1]Adapted from G. Lazaras, *Marketing Immunity* (Homewood, Ill.: Dow Jones-Irwin, 1988), pp. 48–49.

[2]See W. O. Bearden, R. G. Netemeyer, and J. E. Teel, ''Measurement of Consumer Susceptibility to Interpersonal Influence,'' *Journal of Consumer Research*, March 1989, pp. 473–481; W. O. Bearden, R. G. Netemeyer, and J. E. Teel, ''Further Validations of the Consumer Susceptibility to Influence Scale'' in M. E. Goldberg et al., *Advances in Consumer Research XVII*, Provo, Utah: Association for Consumer Research, 1990, pp. 770–76; and O. A. J. Mascarenhas and M. A. Higby, ''Peer, Parent, and Media Influences in Teen Apparel Shopping,'' *Journal of the Academy of Marketing Science*, Winter 1993, pp. 53–58.

[3]P. W. Miniard and J. P. Cohen, ''Modeling Personal and Normative Influences on Behavior,'' *Journal of Consumer Research*, September 1983, pp. 169–80. See also D. F. Midgley, G. R. Dowling, and P. D. Morrison, ''Consumer Types, Social Influence, Information Search and Choice,'' in *Advances in Consumer Research XVI*, ed. T. K. Srull (Provo, Utah: Association for Consumer Research, 1989), pp. 137–43.

[4]See also T. L. Childers and A. R. Rao, ''The Influence of Familial and Peer-based Reference Groups on Consumer Decisions,'' *Journal of Consumer Research*, September 1992, pp. 198–211.

[5]R. C. Becherer, W. F. Morgan, and L. M. Richard, ''Informal Group Influence among Situationally/Dispositionally Oriented Customers,'' *Journal of the Academy of Marketing Science*, Summer 1982, pp. 269–81; and see footnote 2.

[6]Adapted from S. E. Asch, ''Effects of Group Pressure upon the Modification and Distortion of Judgments,'' in *Readings in Social Psychology*, ed. E. E. MacCoby et al. (New York: Holt, Rinehart & Winston, 1958), pp. 174–83.

[7]J. K. Frenzen and H. L. Davis, ''Purchasing Behavior in Embedded Markets,'' *Journal of Consumer Research*, June 1990, pp. 1–12.

[8]See A. C. Burns and E. R. Foxman, ''Some Determinants of the Use of Advertising by Married Working Women,'' *Journal of Advertising Research*, November 1989, pp. 57–63.

[9]See M. R. Solomon and B. Buchanan, ''A Role-Theoretic Approach to Product Symbolism,'' *Journal of Business Research*, March 1991, pp. 95–109.

[10]See M. Solomon and P. Anand, ''Ritual Costumes and Status Transition,'' in *Advances in Consumer Research XII*, ed. E. Hirschman and M. Holbrook (Provo, Utah: Association for Consumer Research, 1985), pp. 315–18; A. Andreasen, ''Life Status Changes and Changes in Consumer Preferences and Satisfaction,'' *Journal of Consumer Research*, December 1984, pp. 784–94; and J. McAlexander, ''Divorce, The Disposition of the Relationship and Everything''; J. Schouten, ''Personal Rites of Passage and the Reconstruction of Self''; M. Young, ''Disposition of Possessions During Role Transitions''; and S. Roberts, ''Consumption Responses to Involuntary Job Loss''; all in R. H. Holman and M. Soloman, *Advances in Consumer Research XVIII* (Provo, Utah: Association for Consumer Research, 1991), pp. 33–51.

CHAPTER

7

GROUP COMMUNICATIONS

Two high school friends, Michael Crete and Stuart Brewley, pooled their savings and, at age 27, started a company in an abandoned farm labor camp. Four years later their sales hit $100 million! The product, California Cooler, is a mixture of lightly carbonated wine and fruit juice. Their impressive sales were obtained at a time when U.S. wine and beer sales where showing virtually no growth.

The entrepreneurs began with a 15-gallon keg of the cooler made from a recipe Crete had used for beach parties during his college days. In their first year, the two claimed to represent an established firm and sold 700 cases from the back of a pickup. The second year, several Coors distributors agreed to handle the product and sales increased to 80,000 cases. In the third year, 5.4 million gallons ($25 million wholesale) were sold. Numerous competitors began entering the market in year four.

Crete and Bewley did a number of innovative things. First, the product itself was new, though wine coolers were often mixed and served at parties. Second, California Cooler was packaged in 12-ounce bottles and sold 4 to the pack or 24 to the case. Third, the product was generally sold chilled in the cold beer racks of retail outlets. Thus, the cooler is a wine-based product, but is packaged and sold much like a beer product. Unlike either the beer or wine industries, California Cooler relied on word-of-mouth communications rather than advertising to spread the news of the product. However, when strong competition entered the market, Crete and Bewley added a substantial advertising budget.[1]

As this example illustrates, new products—*innovations*—are an important and exciting part of our economic life. It also shows the tremendous power of word-of-mouth communications—5.4 million gallons of California Cooler were sold in one year without advertising. This chapter examines both of these critical concepts.

COMMUNICATION WITHIN GROUPS

Since California Cooler was not advertised, consumers could only learn about it through in-store exposure or from other individuals. While many consumers undoubtedly tried the product after seeing it in a store, most learned about it from friends. This is referred to as **word-of-mouth** (WOM) communications.[2] We learn about new products from our friends and other reference groups by (1) observing or participating with them as they use the product, or (2) by seeking or receiving advice and information from them.

An analyst with Morgan Stanley & Company characterizes Wal-Mart as ''a company built on word-of-mouth reputation.'' What does this mean? By providing ''everyday low prices before they were popular, along with a broad selection of merchandise, fully stocked shelves, and superior customer services, Wal-Mart was able to generate excitement among its customers who, in turn, told their friends about the store. Based on this, Wal-Mart has become America's largest retailer. However, it spends just 0.5 percent of its sales on advertising (compared to 2.5 percent for Kmart and 3.8 percent for Sears). This translates into a *billion dollars more profit* per year compared to Sears' performance.[3]

Figure 7–1 illustrates the relative importance of various information sources to purchasers of home video game hardware. Several findings shown in this table are noteworthy. First, a variety of information sources was considered important. However, reference group

FIGURE 7–1

Relative Importance of Information Sources for Purchasers of Home Video Game Hardware

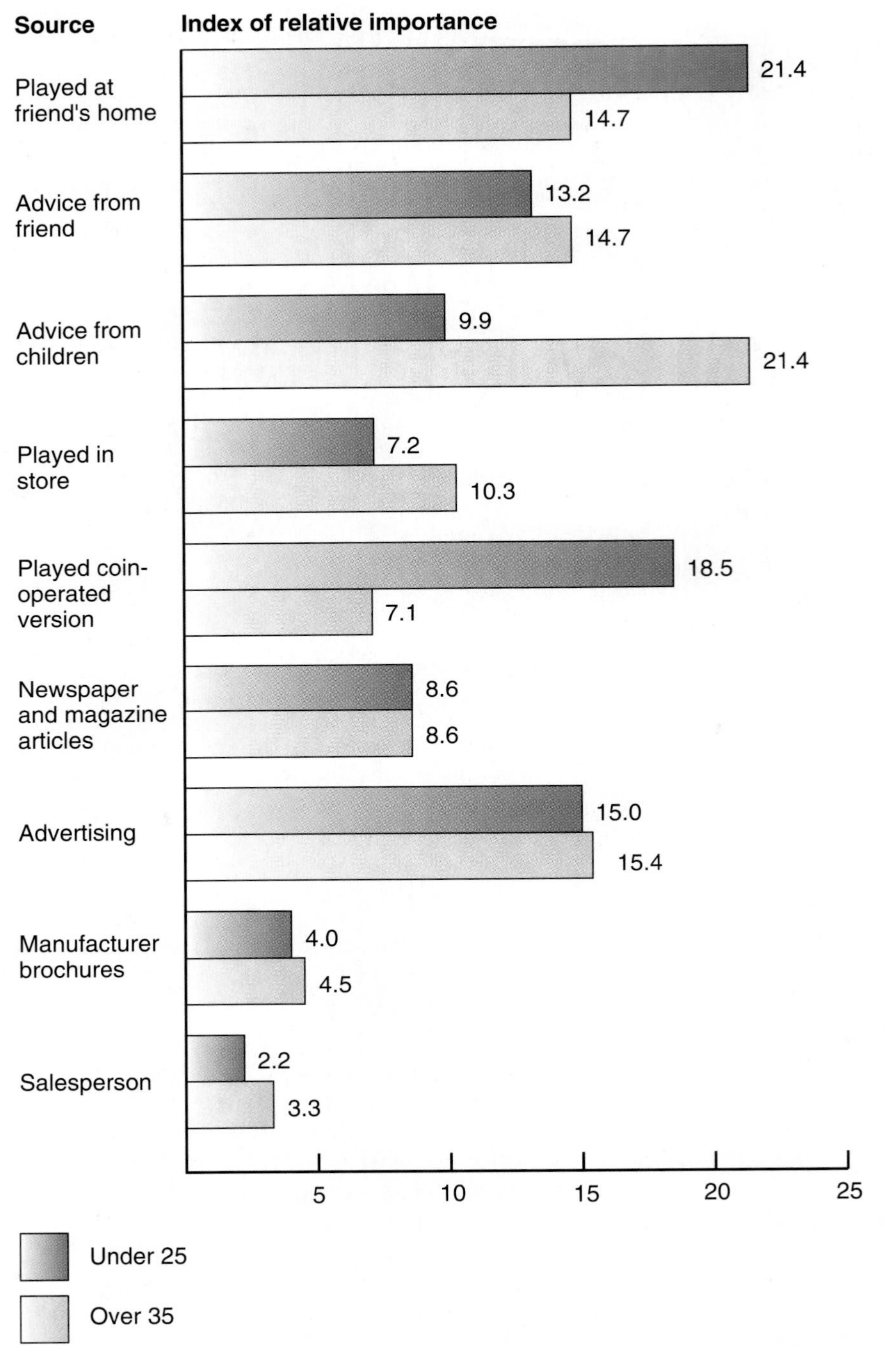

Source: Derived from "1982–83 Newsweek Study of Home Video Game Hardware Purchasers," *Newsweek Magazine*, 1983.

sources were as important as all other sources combined. This is not unusual in situations involving a major purchase.

A second common finding is that the relative importance of information sources is not the same for all groups. Not surprisingly, children have a much smaller influence on young adults than on older adults (who are likely to have more and older children at home). Obviously, different sources of information are used for different products. For example, children are not likely to be an information source for life insurance.

Another key aspect shown in Figure 7–1 is the fact that using the product at a friend's home was an important source of information. This information source no doubt was vital for California Cooler as well.

Figure 7–1 indicates the clear importance that personal sources of information have in at least some purchase decisions. Individuals who supply consumption-related information to others are referred to as *opinion leaders*.

OPINION LEADERSHIP

Information is the primary tool that marketers use to influence consumer behavior. While information is ultimately processed by an individual, in a substantial number of cases one or more group members filter, interpret, or provide the information for the individual. The person who performs this task or role is known as an **opinion leader**. The process of one person receiving information from the mass media or other marketing sources and passing that information on to others is known as the **two-step flow of communications**. The two-step flow explains some aspects of communication within groups, but it is too simplistic to account for most communication flows. What usually happens is a **multistep flow of communication**.[4] Figure 7–2 contrasts the direct flow with a multistep flow of mass communications.

The multistep flow involves opinion leaders for a particular product area who actively seek relevant information from the mass media as well as other sources. These opinion leaders process this information and transmit their interpretations of it to some members of their groups. These group members also receive information from the mass media as well as from group members who are not opinion leaders. The figure also indicates that these nonopinion leaders often initiate requests for information and supply feedback to the opinion leaders.[5]

FIGURE 7–2

Mass Communication Information Flows

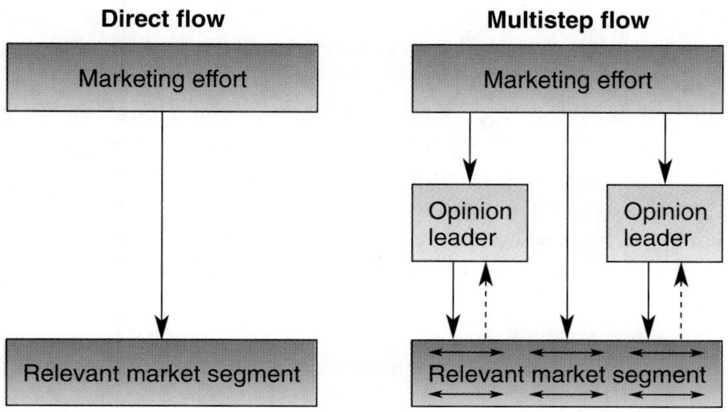

FIGURE 7–3 Likelihood of Seeking an Opinion Leader

Product/purchase involvement	Product knowledge	
	High	Low
High	Moderate	High
Low	Low	Moderate

Situations in which Opinion Leadership Occurs

The exchange of advice and information between group members can occur when: (1) one individual seeks information from another, (2) one individual volunteers information; and (3) as a by-product of normal group interaction.

Imagine that you are about to make a purchase in a product category with which you are not very familiar. Further imagine that the purchase is important to you—perhaps a new stereo system, skis, or a bicycle. How would you go about deciding what type and brand to buy? Chances are you would, among other things, consult someone you know who you believe to be knowledgeable about the product category. This person would be an opinion leader for you. Notice that we have described a *high-involvement* purchase situation in which the purchaser had limited product knowledge.

High-involvement purchases often involve extended decision making, which may include seeking an opinion leader. Figure 7–3 illustrates the factors that would lead to this situation. Of course, both product involvement and knowledge will vary across consumers.

Industrial and retail buyers behave in a manner similar to consumers when seeking information from members of their reference groups (other purchasing agents and businesspeople). For example, one study found such personal information sources to be significantly more important for retail buyers when purchasing a complex item that when purchasing a relatively simple item.[6]

In a low-involvement purchase, one is less likely to seek an opinion leader. (Imagine seeking out a friend and asking which brand of wood pencil is best!) However, opinion leaders may well volunteer information on low-involvement products. Of course, such products and purchases would not be low involvement for the opinion leader. For example, most of us would consider canned peas an unimportant (low-involvement) purchase. However, a person concerned with health might be highly involved with food purchases. Such a person might well seek out information and provide unsolicited opinions on the nutritional value of canned vegetables.

In addition to *explicitly* seeking or volunteering information, group members provide information to each other through observable behaviors. For example, suppose you visit a friend's house and a camcorder is used to film part of the evening. Obviously, you have learned that your friend likes this product and you have gained personal experience with it.

Opinion Leader Characteristics

What characterizes opinion leaders? The most salient characteristic is greater long-term involvement with the product category than the nonopinion leaders in the group. This is referred to as **enduring involvement**, and it leads to enhanced knowledge about and experience with the product category or activity.[7] This knowledge and experience makes opinion leadership possible. Thus, an individual tends to be an opinion leader only for specific product or activity clusters.

Opinion leadership functions primarily through interpersonal communications and observation. These activities occur most frequently among individuals with similar demographic characteristics. Thus, it is not surprising that opinion leaders are found within all demographic segments of the population and seldom differ significantly on demographic variables from the people they influence.

There is limited evidence that opinion leaders are somewhat more gregarious than others. A personality trait, public individuation, also seems to characterize opinion leaders. **Public individuation** is a willingness to act differently from one's peers even if it attracts attention.[8] Opinion leaders also have higher levels of exposure to relevant media than do nonopinion leaders.

In addition to the above individual characteristics associated with opinion leadership, a very important situational characteristic has been identified: product (or store) dissatisfaction. Substantial research evidence indicates that dissatisfied consumers are highly motivated to tell others about the reasons for their dissatisfaction, and these negative messages influence the recipients' attitudes and behaviors (see Chapter 19).

This phenomenon makes imperative both consistent product quality and quick, positive responses to consumer complaints.

The Market Maven Opinion leaders are generally product or activity specific. However, some individuals appear to have information about many kinds of products, places to shop, and other aspects of markets. They both initiate discussions with others about products and shopping and respond to requests for market information. They are referred to as **market mavens**.

Market mavens provide significant amounts of information to others across a wide array of products, including durables and nondurables, services, and store types. They provide information on product quality, sales, usual prices, product availability, store personnel characteristics, and other features of relevance to consumers. Like opinion leaders, market mavens do not differ demographically from those they provide information to except they are more likely to be female.

Although market mavens are demographically similar to others, they have unique media habits. They are extensive users of media, particulariy direct mail and homemaking magazines. They also watch television more and listen to the radio more than others. These media patterns provide an avenue for marketers to communicate with this important group.[9]

Marketing Strategy and Opinion Leadership

The importance of opinion leadership varies radically from product to product and from target market to target market. Therefore, the initial step in using opinion leaders is to determine—through research, experience, or logic—the role opinion leadership has in the situation at hand. Once this is done, marketing strategies can be devised to make use of opinion leadership.

Product Quality and Customer Complaints An obvious fact that has been confirmed by research is: consumers talk to other consumers about their experiences with products, stores, and services. Therefore it is absolutely essential that marketers meet or exceed customer expectations concerning their products. When customer expectations are not met, the firm must respond quickly and fairly to customer complaints. Both these issues are discussed in detail in Chapter 19.

Identifying Opinion Leaders Utilizing knowledge of opinion leadership and the multistep flow of communication is complicated by the fact that opinion leaders are difficult to identify. They tend to be similar to those they influence. While opinion leaders can be identified by using sociometric techniques, key informants, and self-designating questionnaires, these methods are seldom practical for marketing applications.

The fact that opinion leaders are heavily involved with the mass media, particularly media that focus on their area of leadership, provides a partial solution to the identification problem. For example, Nike could assume that many subscribers to *Runners World* serve as opinion leaders for jogging and running shoes. Likewise, the fact that opinion leaders are gregarious and tend to belong to clubs and associations suggests that Nike could also consider members, and particularly officials, of local running clubs to be opinion leaders.

Some product categories have professional opinion leaders. For products related to livestock, county extension agents are generally very influential. Barbers and hairstylists serve as opinion leaders for hair care products. Pharmacists are important opinion leaders for a wide range of health care products. Computer science majors may be natural opinion leaders for other students considering purchasing a personal computer.

Thus, for many products it is possible to identify individuals who have a high probability of being an opinion leader. Once these individuals are identified, what should the marketer do?

Marketing Research Since opinion leaders receive, interpret, and relay marketing messages to others, marketing research should focus on opinion leaders rather than "representative" samples in those product categories and groups in which opinion leaders play a critical role. Thus, product-use tests, pretests of advertising copy, and media preference studies should be conducted on samples of individuals likely to be opinion leaders. It is essential that these individuals be exposed to, and respond favorably to, the firm's marketing mix. Of course, for those product categories or groups in which opinion leadership is not important, such a strategy would be unwise.

Product Sampling Sampling—sending a sample of a product to a group of potential consumers—is an effective means of generating interpersonal communications concerning the product. In one study, 33 percent of a randomly selected group of women who received a free sample of a new brand of instant coffee discussed it with someone outside their immediate family within a week.[10] Instead of using a random sample, a marketer should attempt to send the product to individuals likely to be opinion leaders.

Retailing/Personal Selling Numerous opportunities exist for retailers and sales personnel to use opinion leadership. Clothing stores can create "fashion advisory boards" composed of likely style leaders from their target market. An example would be cheerleaders and class officers for a store catering to teenagers. Restaurant managers can send special invitations, 2-for-1 meal coupons, and menus to likely leaders in their target markets, such as officers in Junior League, League of Women Voters, and Rotary.

Retailers and sales personnel can encourage their current customers to pass along information to potential new customers. For example, an automobile salesperson, or the

MANAGERIAL APPLICATION 7–1

Sage Advance's Program to Encourage Word-of-Mouth Communications

SAGE ADVANCE CORPORATION
"JUST REWARDS" PROGRAM

We at Sage Advance Corporation have discovered that our satisfied customers have been giving very positive testimonials for our product and referring new customers to us. Our "Just Rewards" Program acknowledges the value of your word-of-mouth referrals. The program also offers you another means to recoup the cost of your Copper Cricket solar water heating system.

WHAT IS THE "JUST REWARDS" PROGRAM?

Sage Advance Corporation will pay a $100 reward to any owner of a Copper Cricket system who introduces the Copper Cricket to another person IF that introduction results in the sale of a new system to that person.

HOW DOES THE PROGRAM WORK?

1. You must be a Copper Cricket Owner.

2. The new purchaser of a Copper Cricket system must identify you as the person who introduced them to the system. The only way to do this is to have the new purchaser fill out the "Just Rewards" card which they then present to the Sage Advance representative at time of purchase. If there is no Sage Advance representative in their area, call Sage Advance direct (503) 485-1947, and we will record your claim in the customer file.

3. You are eligible for the "Just Rewards" Program for two (2) years from the date of your purchase of the Copper Cricket System.

4. The new purchaser can reside in any state of the U.S.A.

5. This $100 reward per system sale is not a rebate or otherwise a part of the sales price of the system.

Sage Advance Corporation is committed to establishing a sustainable energy future. We welcome your assistance in reaching this goal. The rewards for us and you are many. Not only can you help reduce our national dependency on fossil fuels and nuclear energy, you can also reduce your living expenses and make a personal statement about your concern for the future. Pure, safe, renewable solar energy has been, and will continue to be, the public's choice. So, call a friend and share the rewards.

SAC 5/1/90

Courtesy Sage Advance Corporation

dealership, might provide a free car wash or oil change to current customers who send friends in to look at a new car. Real estate agents might send a coupon good for a meal for two at a nice restaurant to customers or other contacts who send them new clients. Managerial Application 7–1 illustrates Sage Advance's efforts in this area.

MANAGERIAL APPLICATION

7–2

Using an Acknowledged Opinion Leader to Endorse a Brand

Advertising Advertising attempts to both *stimulate* and *simulate* opinion leadership. Stimulation involves themes designed to encourage current owners to talk about the product/brand or prospective owners to ask current owners for their impressions.[11] Before such a campaign is used, the firm needs to be certain that there is a high degree of satisfaction among existing owners.

Simulating opinion leadership involves having an acknowledged opinion leader—such as Florence Joyner or Carl Lewis for running equipment—endorse a brand. Managerial Application 7–2 is an example of this approach. Or, it can involve having an apparent opinion leader recommend the product in a ''slice of life'' commercial. These commercials involve an ''overheard'' conversation between two individuals in which one person provides brand advice to the other.

DIFFUSION OF INNOVATIONS

The manner by which a new product is accepted or spreads through a market is basically a group phenomenon. In this section, we will examine this process in some detail.[12]

Nature of Innovations

An **innovation** is *an idea, practice, or product perceived to be new by the relevant individual or group.* Whether or not a given product *is* an innovation is determined by the perceptions of the potential market, not by an objective measure of technological change. Polaroid's 600 System camera, which will ''automatically blend strobe light and existing light to a degree previously impossible,'' represents a major engineering accomplishment.

Categories of Innovations

FIGURE 7–4

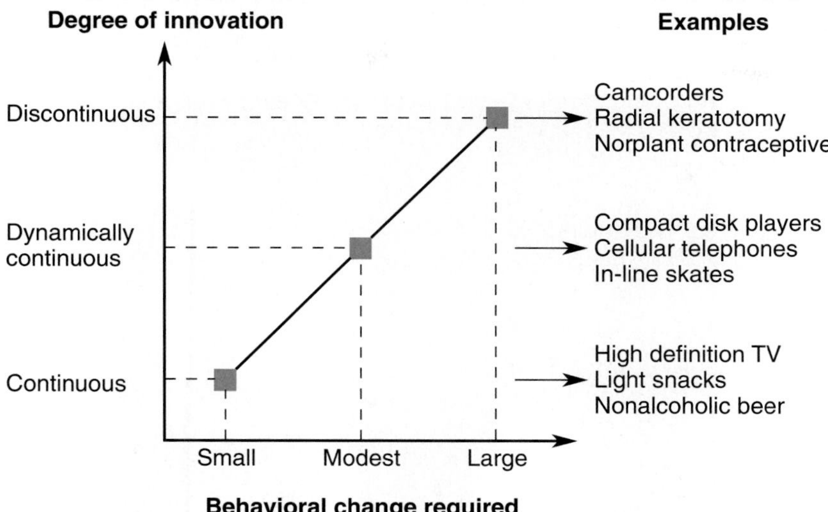

Yet, unless consumers interpret it as a change, they will not respond to it as an innovation. One analyst states Polaroid's problem as follows: "The average instant photographer does not understand what is going on to begin with, so how is he going to understand the significance of these technical improvements?"[13]

Categories of Innovations

Try to recall new products that you have encountered in the past two or three years. As you reflect on these, it may occur to you that there are degrees of innovation. For example, a compact disk player is more of an innovation than light beer. We can picture any given product as falling somewhere on a continuum ranging from no change to radical change, depending on the target market's response to the item. This is shown in Figure 7–4.

Behavior change in Figure 7–4 refers to changes required in the consumer's behavior (including attitudes and beliefs) if the innovation is adopted or utilized. It does not refer to technical or functional changes in the product. Thus, shifting to Crystal Pepsi from regular Pepsi would not require a significant change in behavior. However, purchasing and using a home computer requires significant behavior changes.

Also indicated in Figure 7–4 are three categories into which it is useful to classify a given innovation as viewed by a specific market segment. Each of these categories is described below. Note that no boundaries are shown between the categories. This is because there are no distinct breaks between each category.

1. Continuous Innovation Adoption requires relatively minor changes in behavior. Examples include Kraft Free salad dressings (oil free), Frito-Lay's Doritos Light, and Farberware's never-stick Millenium cookware, which will not scratch like Teflon. Managerial Application 7–3 is another example of a continuous innovation.

2. Dynamically Continuous Innovation Adoption requires a major change in an area of behavior that is relatively unimportant to the individual. Examples would include compact disk players, cellular telephones, and in-line skates.

MANAGERIAL APPLICATION

7–3

A Continuous Innovation

3. Discontinuous Innovation Adoption requires major changes in behavior in an area of importance to the individual or group. Examples would include Norplant contraceptive, radial keratotomy (eye surgery), and facsimile machines. Managerial Application 7–4 shows a discontinuous innovation that has achieved rapid success.

Most of the thousands of new products or alterations introduced each year tend toward the no-change end of the continuum. Much of the theoretical and empirical research, however, has been based on discontinuous innovations. For example, individual consumers presumably go through a series of very distinct steps or stages known as the **adoption process** when purchasing a new innovation. These stages are shown in Figure 7–5.

Figure 7–5 also shows the steps in extended decision making described in Chapter 1. As can be seen, the adoption process is basically a term used to describe extended decision making when a new product is involved. As we will discuss in detail in Chapter 15, extended decision making occurs when the consumer is *highly involved* in the purchase. High purchase involvement is likely for discontinuous innovations, and most studies of innovations of this nature have found that consumers use extended decision making.

However, it would be a mistake to assume that all innovations are evaluated using extended decision making (the adoption process). In fact, most continuous innovations

MANAGERIAL APPLICATION 7–4

A Discontinuous Innovation

Adoption Process and Extended Decision Making

FIGURE 7–5

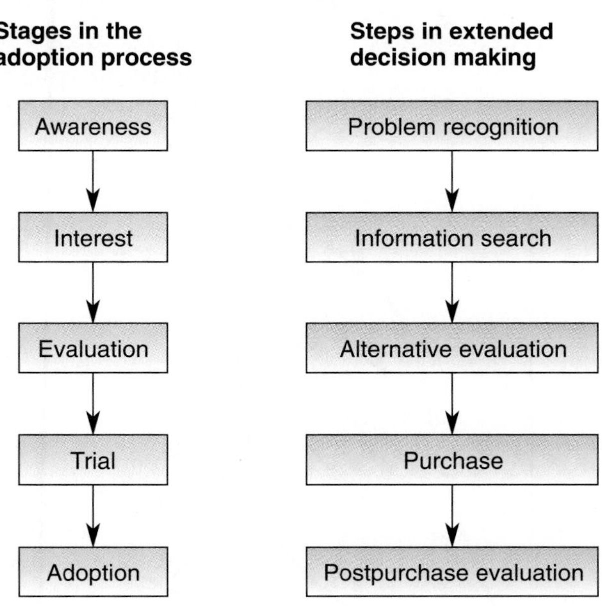

probably trigger limited decision making. That is, as consumers we generally don't put a great deal of effort into deciding to purchase such innovations as Hershey Food's new Marabou Milk chocolate rolls or Heublein's new bottled drink, Espree.

Thus, we have a situation where diffusion theory and research have focused on discontinuous innovations while most new consumer products are continuous innovations. The following material is most valid for discontinuous innovations and least applicable for continuous innovations.

Diffusion Process

The **diffusion process** is *the manner in which innovations spread throughout a market.* The term *spread* refers to purchase behavior in which the product is purchased with some degree of continuing regularity.[14] The market can range from virtually the entire society (for a new soft drink, perhaps) to the students at a particular junior high (for an automated fast-food and snack outlet).

No matter which innovation is being studied or which social group is involved, the diffusion process appears to follow a similar pattern over time: a period of relatively slow growth, followed by a period of rapid growth, followed by a final period of slower growth. This pattern is shown in Figure 7-6. However, there are exceptions to this pattern. In particular, it appears that for continuous innovations such as new ready-to-eat cereals, the initial slow-growth stage may be skipped.

An overview of innovation studies reveals that the time involved from introduction until a given market segment is saturated (i.e., sales growth has slowed or stopped) varies from a few days or weeks to years. This leads to two interesting questions: (1) *What determines how rapidly a particular innovation will spread through a given market segment?* and (2) *In what ways do those who purchase innovations relatively early differ from those who purchase them later?*

FIGURE 7-6 Diffusion Rate of an Innovation over Time

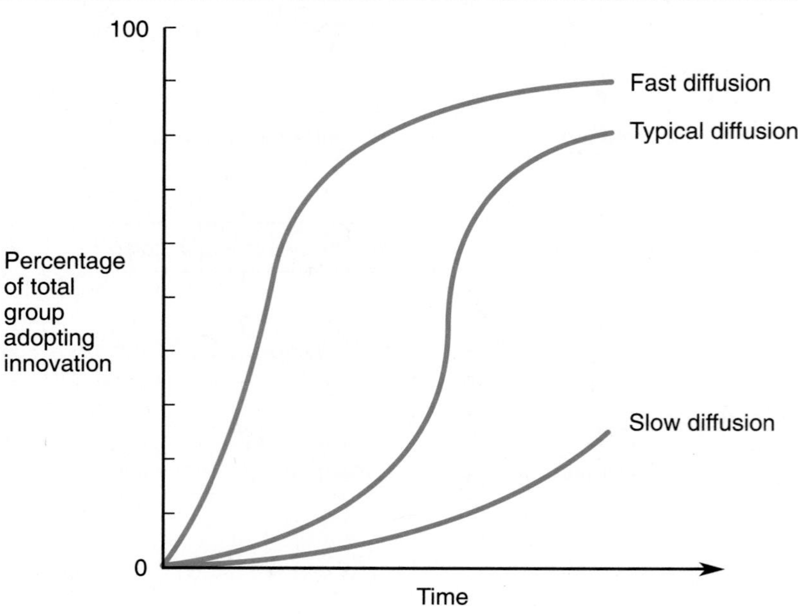

Factors Affecting the Spread of Innovations The rate at which an innovation is diffused is a function of 10 factors:

1. ***Type of group.*** Some groups are more accepting of change than others. In general, young, affluent, and highly educated groups accept change, including new products, readily. Thus, the target market for the innovation is an important determinant of the rate of diffusion.
2. ***Type of decision.*** The type of decision is basically an individual versus collective dimension. The fewer individuals involved in the decision, the more rapidly the innovation will spread. Therefore, innovations likely to involve two or more household members will generally spread slower than innovations that affect primarily one individual.
3. ***Marketing effort.*** The rate of diffusion is influenced by the extent of marketing effort involved. That is, the rate of diffusion is not completely beyond the control of the firm. A good example of this is provided by Apple Computer's expenditure of $180 million on advertising and sales promotion to promote the Macintosh computer, which became a huge success. Without such major expenditures as a $2 million Super Bowl commercial, the acceptance of this innovative new computer would have been much slower.
4. ***Fulfillment of felt need.*** The more manifest or obvious the need that the innovation satisfies, the faster the diffusion. One of the difficulties the Polaroid 600 System faced (described earlier) was the fact that consumers did not feel a strong need for the performance improvement the system offered.
5. ***Compatibility.*** The more the purchase and use of the innovation is consistent with the individual's and group's values or beliefs, the more rapid the diffusion. Camcorders are quite compatible with the existing values of large segments of the American society, while boxed or canned wine is not.
6. ***Relative advantage.*** The better the innovation is perceived to meet the relevant need compared to existing methods, the more rapid the diffusion. For example, a Weed Eater appears to offer substantial advantages over hand trimming a lawn. Included in relative advantage is *price*. Thus, while a Weed Eater enjoys a tremendous advantage over hand trimming in terms of effort involved, this aspect of relative advantage is somewhat offset by the higher cost.

   In contrast, most fax machines provide poorer-quality copies than overnight delivery services but, if many messages are sent, they are less expensive (as well as faster). To succeed, an innovation must have either a performance advantage or a cost advantage. It is the combination of these two that we call relative advantage.
7. ***Complexity.*** The more difficult the innovation is to understand and use, the slower the diffusion. The key to this dimension is ease of use, *not* complexity of product. For example, compact disk players, while very complex products, are very simple for most stereo owners to use. Complexity involves both attribute complexity and trade-off complexity.[15] **Attribute complexity** deals with the difficulty encountered in understanding or using the attributes of a product. A home computer has a high level of attribute complexity for many older consumers. **Trade-off complexity** refers to the degree and number of conflicting benefits. A microwave oven has a high degree of trade-off complexity for many consumers because it contains such conflicting attributes as speed of cooking versus quality of cooking, cost of purchase versus economy of operation, and convenience versus space requirements.
8. ***Observability.*** The more easily consumers can observe the positive effects of adopting an innovation, the more rapid its diffusion will be. Cellular telephones are

relatively visible. Radial keratotomy and compact disk players, while less visible, are often the topic of conversation. On the other hand, headache remedies, such as Advil, are less obvious and generally less likely to be discussed.

9. ***Trialability.*** The easier it is to have a low-cost or low-risk trial of the innovation, the more rapid its diffusion. The diffusion of such products as radial keratotomy and cellular telephones has been hampered by the difficulty of trying out the product. This is much less of a problem with low-cost items such as headache remedies, or such items as in-line skates or camcorders that can be rented, borrowed, or tried at a retail outlet.
10. ***Perceived risk.*** The more risk associated with trying an innovation, the slower the diffusion. Risk can be financial, physical, or social. It is a function of three dimensions: (1) the probability that the innovation will not perform as expected; (2) the consequences of its not performing as expected; and (3) the ability to reverse, and the cost of reversing, any negative consequences. Thus, many consumers feel a need for the benefits offered by a radial keratotomy and view the probability of its working successfully as being quite high. However, they perceive the consequences of failure as being extreme and irreversible and therefore do not adopt this innovation.

    An additional type of risk exists for durable technological innovations such as compact disk players and high-density television. Consumers have observed that such products are typically characterized by rapid performance improvements and price declines. Thus they see a risk in adopting such products too early and paying ''too much'' and/or having a product that is soon out of date.[16]

Figure 7–7 summarizes the impact of these determinants on the rate of diffusion when all are favorable.

Characteristics of Individuals Who Adopt an Innovation at Varying Points in Time
The curves shown in Figure 7–6 are cumulative curves that illustrate the increase in the percentage of adopters over time. If we change those curves from a cumulative format to one that shows the percentage of a market that adopts the innovation at any given point in time, we will have the familiar bell-shaped curves shown in Figure 7–8.

Figure 7–8 reemphasizes the fact that a few individuals adopt an innovation very quickly, another limited group is very reluctant to adopt the innovation, and the majority of the group adopts at some time in between the two extremes. As shown, the total time involved varies by product.

Researchers have found it useful to divide the adopters of any given innovation into five groups based on the relative time at which they adopt. These groups, called **adopter categories**,[17] are shown in Figure 7–8 and are defined below:

Innovators:	The first 2.5 percent to adopt an innovation.
Early adopters:	The next 13.5 percent to adopt.
Early majority:	The next 34 percent to adopt.
Late majority:	The next 34 percent to adopt.
Laggards:	The final 16 percent to adopt.

How do these five groups differ? The first answer is: It depends on the product category being considered. Exhibit 7–1 illustrates the rather dramatic differences between early purchasers of home computers and VCRs.[18] Thus, while we propose some broad generalizations, they may not hold true for a particular product category. Indeed, they should be treated as hypotheses or ideas to test for the product category you are involved with rather than as established facts.

Determinants of a Rapid Rate of Diffusion

FIGURE 7–7

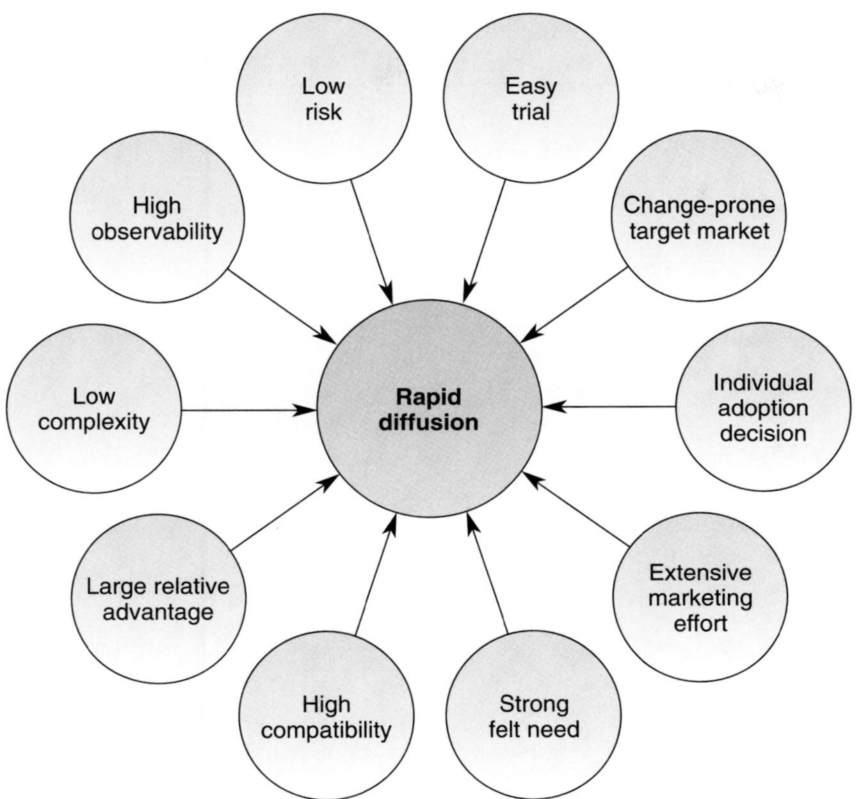

Adoptions of an Innovation over Time

FIGURE 7–8

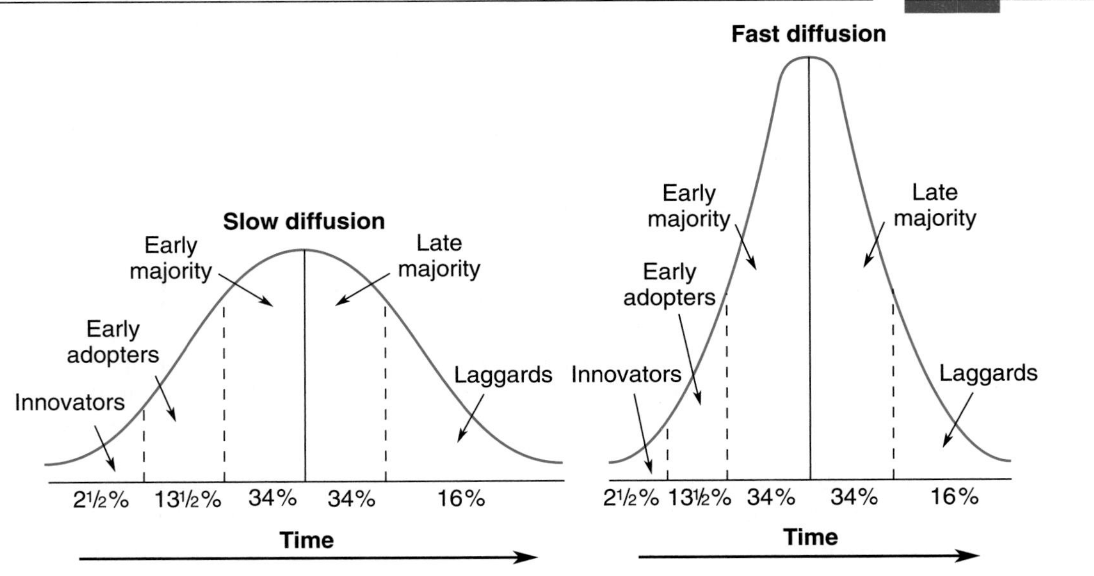

EXHIBIT 7–1

Early Purchasers of Home Computers and VCRs

	Home Computer	VCR
*Age**		
18–24	103	163
25–34	113	91
35+	94	84
*Education**		
College graduate	179	152
Attended college	125	86
High school	77	92
*Marital status**		
Married	209	92
Single	107	136
Products owned†		
Tennis clothing	0	+
Squash racquet	0	–
Water skis	–	+
Target gun	–	+
Bowling ball	–	+
Ski boots	–	0
Luxury car	–	0
Men's diamond ring	–	+
Classical folk records/tapes	0	–
Contemporary jazz records/tapes	–	0
Book club	0	–
Solar heating	+	–
Food dehydrator	+	–
Electric ice cream maker	–	+

*Results are index numbers where 100 equals average consumption.

†+ = Heavy consumption; 0 = Moderate consumption; and – = Light consumption.

Source: A. J. Kover, "Somebody Buys New Products Early—But Who?" Unpublished paper prepared for Cunningham & Walsh, Inc.

Innovators are venturesome risk-takers. They are capable of absorbing the financial and social costs of adopting an unsuccessful product. They are cosmopolitan in outlook and use other innovators rather than local peers as a reference group. They tend to be younger, better educated, and more socially mobile than their peers. Innovators make extensive use of commercial media, sales personnel, and professional sources in learning of new products.

Early adopters tend to be opinion leaders in local reference groups. They are successful, well educated, and somewhat younger than their peers. They are willing to take a calculated risk on an innovation but are concerned with failure. Early adopters also use commercial, professional, and interpersonal information sources, and they provide information to others.[19]

Early majority consumers tend to be cautious with respect to innovations. They adopt sooner than most of their social group but also after the innovation has proven successful with others. They are socially active but seldom leaders. They tend to be somewhat older, less well educated, and less socially mobile than the early adopters. The early majority relies heavily on interpersonal sources of information.

Late majority members are skeptical about innovations. They often adopt more in response to social pressures or a decreased availability of the previous product than because of a positive evaluation of the innovation. They tend to be older and have less social status and mobility than those who adopt earlier.

Laggards are locally oriented and engage in limited social interaction. They tend to be relatively dogmatic and oriented toward the past. Innovations are adopted only with reluctance.

Marketing Strategies and the Diffusion Process

Market Segmentation The fact that earlier purchasers of an innovation differ from later purchasers suggests a "moving target market" approach. That is, after a general target market is selected, the firm should initially focus on those individuals within the target market most likely to be innovators and early adopters.[20] As the product gains acceptance, the focus of attention should shift to the early and late majority. This means that both media and advertising themes may need to change as a product gains market acceptance.

Diffusion Enhancement Strategies Exhibit 7–2 provides a framework for developing strategies to enhance the market acceptance of an innovation. The critical aspect of this process is to analyze the innovation *from the target market's perspective.* This analysis will indicate potential obstacles—*diffusion inhibitors*—to rapid market acceptance. The manager's task is then to overcome these inhibitors with *diffusion enhancement strategies.*[21] Exhibit 7–2 lists a number of potential enhancement strategies. Many others are possible.

Suppose a proposed innovation scores high (favorably) on all attributes except compatibility. What marketing strategy does this suggest? The firm's communications, particularly advertising, will have to minimize this problem. For example, "light" (diet) beers were introduced successfully by relating them to active, masculine individuals and avoiding direct references to diet, which many "real beer drinkers" felt to be for women and sissies. Likewise, the fact that the relative advantage of Polaroid's 600 System was not readily observable meant that its introductory advertising budget was "twice as much as any other previous Polaroid product introduction."[22]

SUMMARY

Communication within groups is a major source of information about certain products. It is a particularly important source when an individual has a high level of *purchase involvement* and a low level of *product knowledge.* In such cases, the consumer is likely to seek information from a more knowledgeable group member. This person is known as an *opinion leader.* Opinion leaders are sought out for information, and they also volunteer information. Of course, substantial product information is exchanged during normal group interactions.

Opinion leaders are product-category or activity-group specific. They tend to have greater product knowledge, more exposure to relevant media, and more gregarious

EXHIBIT 7–2 Innovation Analysis and Diffusion Enhancement Strategies

Diffusion Determinant	Diffusion Inhibitor		Diffusion Enhancement Strategies
1. Nature of group	Conservative	→	Search for other markets Target innovators within group
2. Type of decision	Group	→	Choose media to reach all deciders Provide conflict reduction themes
3. Marketing effort	Limited	→	Target innovators within group Use regional rollout
4. Felt need	Weak	→	Extensive advertising showing importance of benefits
5. Compatibility	Conflict	→	Stress attributes consistent with values and norms
6. Relative advantage	Low	→	Lower price Redesign product
7. Complexity	High	→	Distribute through high service outlets Use skilled sales force Use product demonstrations Extensive marketing efforts
8. Observability	Low	→	Use extensive advertising
9. Trialability	Difficult	→	Use free samples to early adopter types Special prices to rental agencies Use high service outlets
10. Perceived risk	High	→	Success documentation Endorsement by credible sources Guarantees

personalities than their followers. They tend to have demographics similar to their followers. A situational variable, *product dissatisfaction*, motivates many individuals to become temporary opinion leaders. The term *market maven* is used to describe individuals who are opinion leaders about the shopping process in general.

Marketers attempt to identify opinion leaders primarily through their media habits and social activities. Identified opinion leaders then can be used in marketing research, product sampling, retailing/personal selling, and advertising.

Groups, because of their interpersonal interaction and influence, greatly affect the diffusion of innovations. *Innovations* vary in degree of behavioral change required and the rate at which they are diffused. The first purchasers of an innovative product or service are termed *innovators*; those who follow over time are known as *early adopters*, *early majority*, *late majority*, and *laggards*. Each of these groups, which differ in the time of adoption of an innovation, differ in terms of personality, age, education, and reference group membership. These characteristics help marketers identify and appeal to different classes of adopters at different stages of an innovation's diffusion.

The time it takes for an innovation to spread from innovators to laggards is affected by several factors: (1) nature of the group involved; (2) type of innovation decision required; (3) extent of marketing effort; (4) strength of felt need; (5) compatibility of the innovation with existing values; (6) relative advantage; (7) complexity of the innovation; (8) ease in observing usage of the innovation; (9) ease in trying the innovation; and (10) perceived risk in trying the innovation.

REVIEW QUESTIONS

1. What is an *opinion leader*? How does an opinion leader relate to the *multistep flow of communication*?
2. How do the information sources for video game equipment differ between younger and older purchasers?
3. What characterizes an opinion leader?
4. How does a *market maven* differ from an *opinion leader*?
5. What determines the likelihood that a consumer will seek information from an opinion leader?
6. How can marketing managers identify opinion leaders?
7. How can marketers utilize opinion leaders?
8. How can opinion leaders be used in personal selling?
9. What is an *innovation*? Who determines whether a given product is an innovation?
10. What are the various categories of innovations? How do they differ?
11. What is the *diffusion process*? What pattern does the diffusion process appear to follow over time?
12. Describe the factors that affect the diffusion rate for an innovation. How can these factors be utilized in developing marketing strategy?
13. What are *adopter categories*? Describe each of the adopter categories.
14. How can a marketer use a knowledge of adopter categories?

DISCUSSION QUESTIONS

15. Answer the following questions for: (1) clear cola drinks, (2) in-line skates, (3) Sony's Mini Disc (MD), (4) Panasonic's 300 Interactive Multiplayer, or (5) antioxidant multivitamin pills.
    a. Is ________ an innovation? Justify your answer.
    b. Assume ________ becomes widely used on your campus. Speculate on the characteristics of the adopter categories.
    c. Using the student body on your campus as a market segment, evaluate the perceived attributes of ________.
    d. Who on your campus would serve as opinion leaders for ________?

e. Will the early adopters of ______ use the adoption process (extended decision making), or is a simpler decision process likely?

16. Describe two situations in which you have served as an opinion leader. Are these situations consistent with the text?
17. Describe two situations in which you have sought information from an opinion leader. Are these situations consistent with the text?
18. Are you aware of market mavens on your campus? Describe their characteristics, behaviors, and motivation.
19. The figure at the bottom of this page approximates the diffusion rate for television sets and automatic washers in the Milwaukee area. On an after-the-fact basis, analyze the attributes of each product to see if such an analysis would predict their relative rates of diffusion.
20. Assume that you are a consultant to firms with new products. You have members of the appropriate market segments rate the innovation on the 10 characteristics described in the chapter. Based on these ratings you develop marketing strategies. Assume that a rating of 9 is extremely favorable (strong relative advantage or a lack of complexity), and 1 is extremely unfavorable. Develop appropriate strategies for each of the following products.

	Product								
Attribute	**A**	**B**	**C**	**D**	**E**	**F**	**G**	**H**	**I**
Fulfillment of felt need	8	9	9	7	3	8	8	5	7
Compatibility	9	8	8	8	8	8	9	2	8
Relative advantage	8	8	9	2	8	9	7	8	9
Complexity	8	7	9	9	9	9	9	3	8
Observability	8	8	8	8	9	1	9	4	8
Trialability	2	9	8	9	8	9	9	2	9
Nature of group	7	3	3	8	7	8	9	9	7
Type of decision	3	7	3	7	8	8	6	7	7
Marketing effort	8	7	6	7	8	7	8	6	3
Perceived risk	8	5	3	8	7	7	3	7	8

21. Identify a recent (a) continuous innovation, (b) dynamically continuous innovation, and (c) discontinuous innovation. Justify your selections.
22. Analyze each of the products identified in Question 21 in terms of the determinants in Exhibit 7–2 and suggest appropriate marketing strategies.
23. Describe an innovation you adopted and for which you went through each of the steps in the adoption process. Describe another for which you did not explicitly use each step. Why did you use differing processes in the two situations?

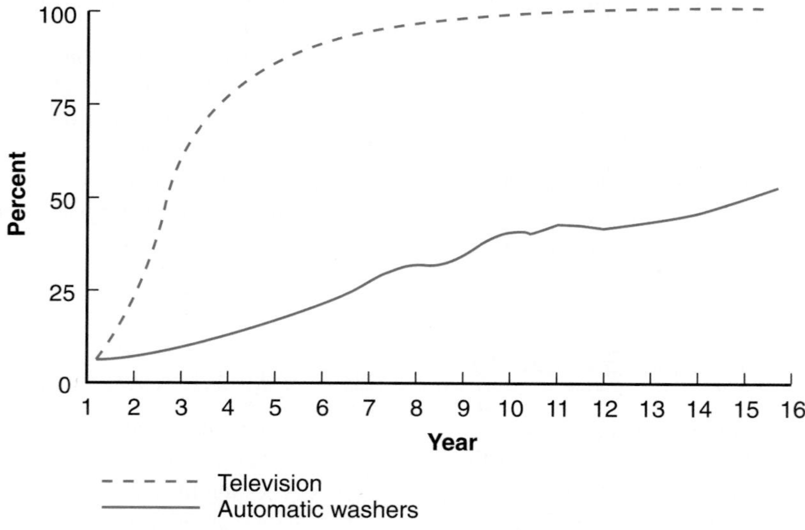

APPLICATION EXERCISES

24. Identify and interview several innovators on your campus for:
    a. Clothing styles.
    b. Recreation equipment.
    c. Stereo equipment.
    d. Computer equipment.

    To what extent do they match the "ideal profile" of an innovator?
25. Repeat Question 24 for early adopters.
26. Find and interview two opinion leaders for one of the product categories listed in Question 24. To what extent do they match the description provided in the chapter?
27. Interview two ______ salespersons. Determine the role that opinion leaders play in the purchase of their product. To what extent, if any, do they utilize opinion leaders?
    a. Bicycle
    b. Fashion clothing
    c. Computer
    d. Insurance.
    e. In-line skates
    f. Stereo equipment
28. Look in the first issue of a recent month's *Advertising Age* or *Fortune* at the section entitled "New Products." Categorize the new products as continuous, dynamically continuous, or discontinuous innovations. Interpret the results.
29. Interview two students who have recently made major purchases. Determine the role, if any, played by opinion leaders.
30. Interview two students who have recently purchased an innovation. Determine and describe the decision processes they used.

REFERENCES

[1]"The Concoction That's Raising Spirits in the Wine Industry," *Business Week*, October 8, 1984, pp. 182, 186.

[2]W. R. Wilson and R. A. Peterson, "Some Limits on the Potency of Word-of-Mouth Information," in *Advances in Consumer Research XVI*, ed. T. K. Srull (Provo, Utah: Association for Consumer Research, 1989), pp. 23–29. See also J. E. Swan and R. L. Oliver, "Postpurchase Communications by Consumers," *Journal of Retailing*, Winter 1989, pp. 516–33; and P. M. Herr, F. R. Kardes, and J. Kim, "Effects of Word-of-Mouth and Product-Attribute Information on Persuasion," *Journal of Consumer Research*, March 1991, pp. 454–62.

[3]C. Fisher, "Wal-Mart's Way," *Advertising Age*, February 18, 1991, p. 3.

[4]P. H. Reingen and J. B. Kernan, "Analysis of Referral Networks in Marketing," *Journal of Marketing Research*, November 1986, pp. 370–78.

[5]L. F. Feick, L. L. Price, and R. A. Higie, "People Who Use People," in *Advances in Consumer Research XIII*, ed. R. J. Lutz (Provo, Utah: Association for Consumer Research, 1986), pp. 301–5; and P. H. Reingen, "A Word-of-Mouth Network," in *Advances in Consumer Research XIV*, ed. M. Wallendorf and P. Anderson (Provo, Utah: Association for Consumer Research, 1987), pp. 213–17.

[6]G. D. Upah, "Product Complexity Effects on Information Source Preference by Retail Buyers," *Journal of Business Research*, First Quarter 1983, pp. 107–26.

[7]M. L. Richins and P. H. Bloch, "After the New Wears Off," *Journal of Consumer Research*, September 1986, pp. 280–85; M. P. Venkatraman, "Opinion Leaders, Adopters, and Communicative Adopters," *Psychology and Marketing*, Spring 1989, pp. 51–68; and M. P. Venkatraman, "Opinion Leadership, Enduring Involvement and Characteristics of Opinion Leaders," in *Advances in Consumer Research XVII*, eds. M. E. Goldberg, G. Gorn, and R. W. Pollay (Provo, Utah: Association for Consumer Research, 1990), pp. 60–67.

[8]K. K. Chan and S. Misra, "Characteristics of the Opinion Leader," *Journal of Advertising*, no. 3, 1990, pp. 53–60.

[9]L. F. Feick and L. L. Price, "The Market Maven," *Journal of Marketing*, January 1987, pp. 83–97; see also R. A. Higie, L. F. Feick, and L. L. Price, "Types and Amount of Word-of-Mouth Communications about Retailers," *Journal of Retailing*, Fall 1987, pp. 260–78; and M. E. Slama and T. G. Williams, "Generalization of the Market Maven's Information Tendency across Product Categories," in *Advances XVII*, eds. Goldberg, Gorn, and Pollay, pp. 48–52.

[10]J. H. Holmes and J. D. Lett, Jr., "Product Sampling and Word of Mouth," *Journal of Advertising Research*, October 1977, pp. 35–40.

[11]B. L. Bayus, "Word of Mouth: The Indirect Effects of Marketing Efforts," *Journal of Advertising Research*, June/July 1985, pp. 31–35.

[12]L. A. Brown, *Innovation Diffusion* (Methuen, 1981); and A. M. Kennedy, "The Adoptions and Diffusion of New Industrial Products," *European Journal of Marketing*, Third Quarter, 1983, pp. 31–85; E. M. Rogers, *Diffusion of Innovations* (New York: The Free Press, 1983); H. Gatignon and T. S. Robertson, "A Propositional Inventory for New Diffusion Research," *Journal of Consumer Research*, March 1985, pp. 849–67; and V. Mahajan, E. Muller, and F. M. Bass, "New Product Diffusion Models in Marketing," *Journal of Marketing*, January 1990, pp. 1–26.

[13]L. A. Fanelli, "Polaroid Shows, but Can It Tell (and Sell)?" *Advertising Age*, June 6, 1981, p. 3, p. 86.

[14]See J. H. Antil, "New Product or Service Adoption," *Journal of Consumer Marketing*, Spring 1988, pp. 5–16.

[15]K. Derow, "Classify Consumer Products with Perceptual Complexity, Observation, Difficulty Model," *Marketing News*, May 14, 1982, p. 16.

[16]S. L. Holak, D. R. Lehmann, and F. Sultan, "The Role of Expectations in the Adoption of Innovative Consumer Durables," *Journal of Retailing*, Fall 1987, pp. 243–59.

[17]For a different scheme see V. Mahajan, E. Muller, and R. K. Srivastava, "Determination of Adopter Categories by Using Innovation Diffusion Models," *Journal of Marketing Research*, February 1990, pp. 37–50.

[18]See also M. D. Dickerson and J. W. Gentry, "Characteristics of Adopters and Non-Adopters of Home Computers," *Journal of Consumer Research*, September 1983, pp. 225–35; W. D. Danko and J. M. MacLachlon, "Research to Accelerate the Diffusion of a New Innovation," *Journal of Advertising Research*, June/July 1983, pp. 39–43; and M. P. Venkatraman, "The Impact of Innovativeness and Innovation Type on Adoption," *Journal of Retailing*, Spring 1991, pp. 51–67.

[19]L. L. Price, L. F. Feick, and D. C. Smith, "A Re-examination of Communication Channel Usage by Adopter Categories," in *Advances in Consumer Research XIII*, ed. R. J. Lutz (Provo, Utah: Association for Consumer Research, 1986), p. 409.

[20]See R. E. Goldsmith and C. F. Hofaker, "Measuring Consumer Innovativeness," *Journal of the Academy of Marketing Science*, Summer 1991, pp. 209–21.

[21]For a similar but distinct approach see J. N. Sheth, "Consumer Resistance to Innovations," *Journal of Consumer Marketing*, Spring 1989, p. 5–14.

[22]See footnote 13.

CHAPTER 8

HOUSEHOLD CONSUMPTION BEHAVIOR

How do you market automobiles, grocery stores, coffee, hair spray, and similar items to a family with younger children (aged 4–12)? Most would say: *Focus on the relevant adult in considering both product design and advertising message.* However, research indicates that children not only spend $9 billion dollars on their own, they influence the purchase of over $130 billion dollars worth of "adult" goods and services!

Part of the reason for the tremendous influence of children on household purchase decisions is the rapid expansion of single parent and dual-income homes. Thus, younger children often have the time and exposure to media required to be relatively knowledgeable consumers. Marketers are initiating numerous programs to capitalize on children's influence in purchase decisions (we will examine the ethical aspects of some of these activities in Chapter 21).

Hyatt Hotels offers a kids' program called Camp Hyatt. It offers sports lessons, pottery classes, movies, and video games. It also sends Camp Hyatt "graduates" news of contests and certificates for coming events. According to Hyatt's vice president for marketing: *There's nothing like a seven-year-old asking 19 times "When are we going back to that hotel?" to get parents to go back.*

More than two dozen major corporations have started kids' clubs since 1989. Kraft General Foods Group has one for macaroni and cheese eaters, while Delta Airlines has 700,000 children in its Fantastic Flyer Club. Burger King has 2.7 million members in its Kids Club. The children receive six newsletters annually "written" by various cartoon characters, iron-on T-shirt logos, and activity booklets.

Retailers are also actively trying to attract children (and thus their parents). The Great Atlantic & Pacific Tea Co. (A&P) has installed child-size shopping carts in 100 of its outlets. The objectives are to occupy the children and make their visit to the store fun (which will also increase the parents' pleasure) and to get the children involved in the shopping process. Piggly Wiggly is starting Piggly Wiggly Pals Clubs in many of its outlets. Children can get their membership cards stamped at the store and receive such items as the Earth Pals kit which includes tree seedlings.[1]

The household is the basic consumption unit for most consumer goods.[2] Major items such as housing, automobiles, and appliances are consumed more by household units than by individuals. Furthermore, the consumption patterns of individual household members seldom are independent from those of other household members. For example, deciding to grant a child's request for a bicycle may mean spending discretionary funds that could have been used to purchase an evening out for the parents, new clothing for a sister or brother, or otherwise used by another member of the household. Therefore, it is essential that marketers understand the household as a consumption unit as shown in Figure 8–1.

Households are important not only for their direct role in the consumption process, but also for the critical role they perform in socializing children. The family household is the primary mechanism whereby cultural and social class values and behavior patterns are passed on to the next generation. Purchasing and consumption patterns are among those attitudes and skills strongly influenced by the family household unit.

This chapter examines: (1) the nature and importance of households in contemporary American society; (2) the household life cycle; (3) the nature of the household decision process; and (4) consumer socialization. Households, particularly family households, are even more important in most other societies.

THE NATURE OF AMERICAN HOUSEHOLDS

Types of Households

The term *household* designates a variety of distinct social groups. This variety can cause confusion unless each type of household unit is distinguished clearly. The Census Bureau defines a **family household** as *a household unit that consists of two or more related*

FIGURE 8–1

The Household Influences Most Consumption Decisions

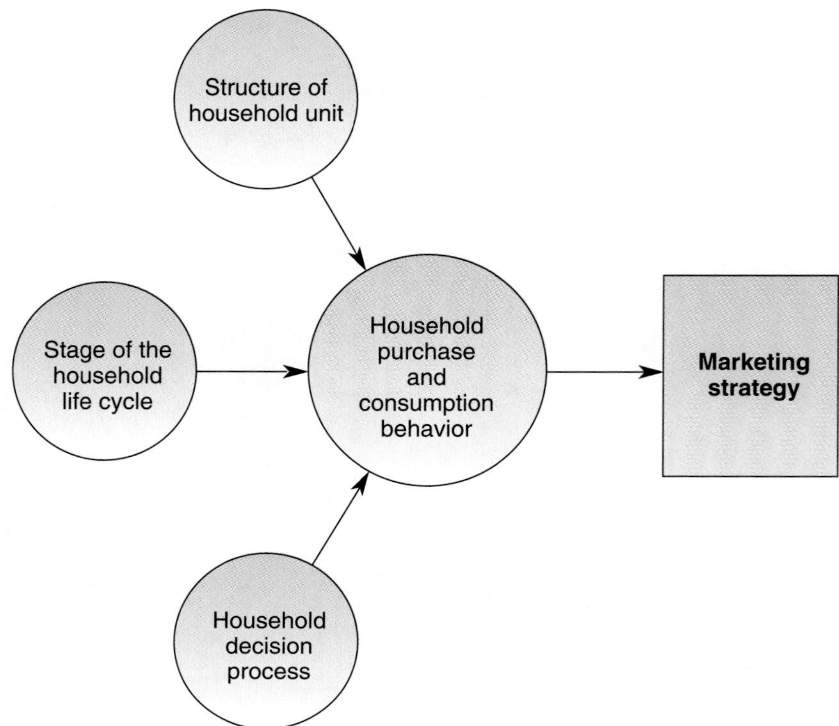

persons, one of whom (i.e., the householder) owns or rents the living quarters. The **nuclear family** consists of two adults of opposite sex, living in a socially approved sex relationship with their own or adopted children. The nuclear family is important in virtually every culture.

The nuclear family described above represents the *prescriptive* (culturally desirable) and *descriptive* (most common) version of the nuclear family (see Table 8–1). However, there are several variations of the nuclear family. The most common variation in the United States is the single-parent family household created by the death of one spouse, or, more commonly, divorce. In either case, the children and the mother are likely to remain together as a nuclear family.

The **extended family household** is a household that includes the nuclear family plus additional relatives. The most common form of the extended family involves the inclusion of one or both sets of grandparents. In addition, aunts, uncles, cousins, in-laws, and other relatives may be included. This is not common in America but is very common in other countries, such as China and India.

Household units that are not families also have several variations. The Census Bureau defines a **nonfamily household** as *households made up of householders who either live alone or with others to whom they are not related.* In 1995, 30 percent of all households are nonfamily households and this percentage is growing.

Family and Nonfamily Households: 1995–2005

TABLE 8–1

Type of Household	1995 Number	1995 Percent	2005 Number	2005 Percent	Percent Change 1995–2005
All households	98,872	100.0	111,040	100.0	12.3
Families	68,937	69.7	76,100	68.5	10.4
Married couples	53,408	54.0	58,269	52.5	9.1
with children under 18 at home	24,410	24.7	23,807	21.4	(2.5)
without children under 18 at home	28,998	29.3	34,462	31.0	18.8
Single fathers	1,366	1.4	1,598	1.4	17.1
Single mothers	7,238	7.3	7,607	6.9	5.1
Other families	6,925	7.0	8,626	7.8	24.6
Nonfamilies	29,935	30.3	34,940	31.5	16.7
Men living alone	9,983	10.1	11,751	10.6	17.7
Women living alone	15,153	15.3	17,397	15.7	14.8
Other nonfamilies	4,802	4.9	5,792	5.2	20.6

Source: Adapted from "The Future of Households," *American Demographics*, December 1993, p. 27.

Changes in Household Structure

Households, family or nonfamily, are important to marketing managers because they constitute consumption units, and therefore represent the proper unit of analysis for many aspects of marketing strategy. The fact that the number of household units is growing and is projected to continue to grow, is more important than population growth for marketers of refrigerators, televisions, telephones, and other items purchased primarily by household units. Equally important to home builders, appliance manufacturers, and automobile manufacturers are the *structure* and *size* of households. Between 1995 and 2005, changes such as those cited below will have a major impact on a wide variety of marketing practices.

- Family households will grow by 7 million, but all of that growth will be in single-parent households or in households with no children at home.
- Nonfamily households will grow by 6 million and will constitute almost a third of all households.

These changes in household structure are reflected in the reduced average size of households, as shown in Figure 8–2. This decline has been caused by an increase in single-parent and single-person households as well as by a decline in the birth rate.

The age of the householder also plays a role in purchase and consumption behavior. The greatest household growth during the 1990s will occur in those with householders in the 45 to 54 age category. The kinds of household products this age group consumes are different from products consumed by younger and older householders. This growth implies a strong demand for upgraded household furnishings, vacations, luxury items, and sports and entertainment items targeted at a more mature market. The fact that much of this growth is coming from single-person households suggests that apartments, appliances, and food containers should be produced in sizes appropriate for the single individual.

FIGURE 8–2

Average Size of Household and Family Units

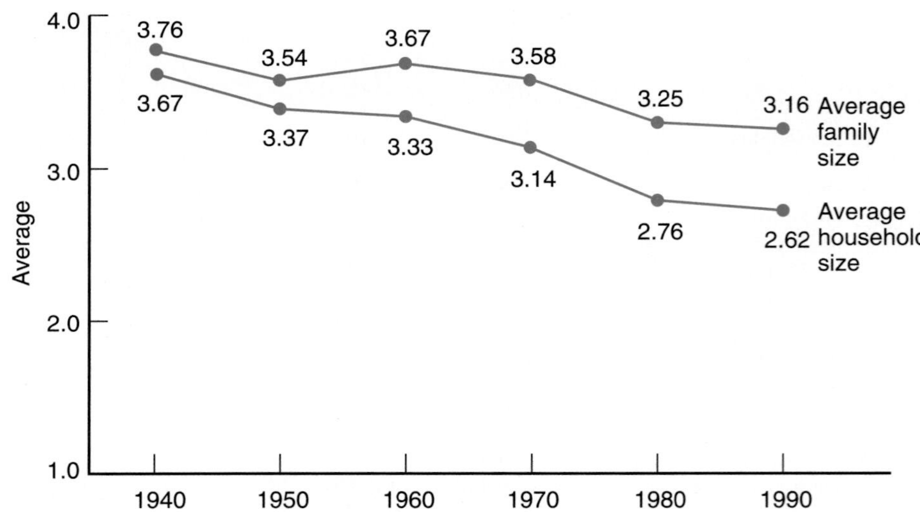

Source: Adapted from U.S. Department of Commerce, ''Households, Families, Marital Status, and Living Arrangements: March 1986,'' *Population Characteristics*, Series P-20, no. 441 (November 1989), p. 3; and J. Waldrop and T. Exter, ''What the 1990 Census Will Show,'' *American Demographics*, January 1990, p. 27.

The growth in single-parent families also implies a need for convenience items, day care centers, and appliances which relatively young children can operate. The timing and content of advertising aimed at singles and single-parent families may need to differ from what is aimed at the traditional nuclear families. As with most variables affecting consumer behavior, the marketing manager must examine the shifts in the American family structure for specific product category implications.

THE HOUSEHOLD LIFE CYCLE

The structure of most family and nonfamily households changes over time. As you move from being single to married, then through various stages of child rearing, you move through discernible changes in family structure. To better understand and describe these structural differences, the concept of **family life cycle** was developed. The basic assumption underlying the family life cycle approach is that most families pass through an orderly progression of stages, each with its own characteristics, financial situation, and purchasing patterns. However, since 30 percent of all households are nonfamily households, it is important to extend the family life cycle concept to a **household life cycle**. There are several similar versions of the household life cycle (HLC).[3] The version used in this text is shown in Figure 8–3.

The HLC applies to both *family* and *nonfamily households*. It assumes that these entities, like individuals, move through a series of relatively distinct and well-defined stages with the passage of time. Each stage in the household life cycle poses a series of problems which household decision makers must solve. The solution to these problems is bound intimately to the selection and maintenance of a lifestyle and, thus, to product consumption. For example, all young married couples with no children face a need for relaxation or recreation. Solutions to this common problem differ. Some couples opt for an outdoors-oriented lifestyle and consume camping equipment and related products. Others choose a

Stages in the Household Life Cycle

FIGURE 8–3

Stage	Marital status		Children at home	
	Single	Married	No	Yes
Younger (under 35)				
Single	■		■	
Young married		■	■	
Full nest I		■		■
Single parent I	■			■
Middle-aged (35–64)				
Single	■		■	
Full nest II		■		■
Single parent II	■			■
Empty nest I		■	■	
Older (over 64)				
Single	■		■	
Empty nest II		■	■	

sophisticated urban lifestyle and consume tickets to the theater and opera, restaurant meals, and so forth. As these families move into another stage in the HLC, generally the ''full nest I'' stage, the problems they face also change. The amount of time and resources available for recreation usually diminishes. New problems related to raising a family become more urgent.

Each stage presents unique needs and wants as well as financial conditions and experiences. Thus, the HLC provides marketers with relatively homogeneous household segments that share similar needs with respect to household-related problems and purchases.

The remainder of this section describes each stage of the HLC and some of the consumption problems encountered in each stage.

Young Single The young single is characterized by age (under 35) and marital status (single). This group can be subdivided into those who live with their family (75 percent) and those who are independent. At-home singles have an average income of $7,900 and an average age of 22. They have few cares and lead an active, social life. They go to bars, movies, and concerts, and purchase sports equipment, clothes, and personal care items.

The independent singles have an average income of $17,800 and an average age of 26. Two-thirds live in multi-individual households. However, they have more financial obligations and must invest more time in household management than at-home singles. They are a good market for the same types of products as the at-home singles as well as convenience-oriented household products. The ads shown in Managerial Application 8–1 are aimed at both groups.

MANAGERIAL APPLICATION

8–1

Advertising to the Young Single Segment

Young Married: No Children The decision to marry (or to live together) brings about a new stage in the household life cycle. The lifestyles of two young singles are generally altered as they develop a joint lifestyle. Joint decisions and shared roles in household responsibilities are in many instances new experiences. Savings, household furnishings, major appliances, and more comprehensive insurance coverage are among the new areas of problem recognition and decision making to which a young married couple must give serious consideration.

Like the young single stage, the time spent by a young couple in this stage of the HLC has grown as couples either delay their start in having children or choose to remain childless. Eighty-five percent of all households in this group have dual incomes and are thus relatively affluent. Compared to Full Nest I families, this group spends heavily on theater tickets, expensive clothes, luxury vacations, restaurant meals, and alcoholic beverages.

Full Nest I: Young Married with Children The addition of a child to the young married family creates many changes in lifestyle and consumption. Naturally, new purchases in the areas of baby clothes, furniture, food, and health care products occur in this stage. Lifestyles are also greatly altered. The couple may have to move to another place of

MANAGERIAL APPLICATION 8–2

Advertising to the Full Nest I and the Single Parent I Segments

residence since many apartments do not permit children. Likewise, choices of vacations, restaurants, and automobiles must be changed to accommodate young children. McDonald's, for example, attempts to occupy children in a restaurant environment by providing recreational equipment at their outlets that cater heavily to families with young children. Income tends to decline as one spouse often stays home with young children (only 61 percent have dual incomes). Discretionary funds are also reduced by the need to spend on child-related necessities. However, the increasing average age of parents before the birth of the first child and the smaller families common today have reduced this impact. Managerial Application 8–2 contains two ads aimed at this market segment.

Single Parent I: Young Single Parents Divorce continues to be a significant part of American society, so marketers cannot ignore the needs of young single parents. One in every three marriages will end in divorce, and this occurs most frequently at earlier points in a marriage. While most divorced individuals eventually remarry, almost 9 percent of American households are single-parent households, and 30 percent of U.S. children live in single-parent households. This type of family situation creates many unique needs in the areas of child care, easy-to-prepare foods, and residence. Individuals in this situation often face severe financial difficulties which greatly intensify the problems associated with purchasing the products and services needed to support their families' desired lifestyles. Financial burdens are intensified by the need for child care and time shortages if the household head works. The ads in Managerial Application 8–2, particularly the Kemper ad, would also appeal to this segment.

Middle-Aged Single The middle-aged single category is made up of those who have never married, and individuals who are divorced and have no child-rearing responsibilities. These individuals are in the 35 to 64 age category. This group is relatively small, consisting of about 2 percent of the U.S. adult population. The needs of middle-age singles in many ways reflect those of young singles. But middle-age singles are likely to have more money to spend on their lifestyles. Thus, they may live in nice condominiums, frequent expensive restaurants, and travel often.

Empty Nest I: Middle-Aged Married with No Children The lifestyle changes in the 1970s and 1980s influenced many young couples to not have children. As a result, numerous American households are middle-aged married couples without children. In other cases, these households represent second marriages in which children from a first marriage are not living with the parent. This group also includes married couples whose children have left home. Both adults typically will have jobs, so they will be short on time but have money to spend on dining out, expensive vacations, and time-saving services such as house-cleaning, laundry, and shopping.

Full Nest II: Middle-Aged Married with Children at Home Because it includes people 35 to 64, in most cases the children of this group are over six years and are less dependent than the children of the young married couple. However, the fact that the children are older creates another set of unique consumption needs. Families with children six and older are the primary consumers of lessons of all types (piano, dance, gymnastics, and so on), dental care (orthodontics, braces, fillings), soft drinks, presweetened cereals, and a wide variety of snack foods. Greater demands for space create a need for larger homes and cars. This, coupled with heavy demand for clothing, places a considerable financial burden on households in this stage of the household life cycle.

The teenage members of this segment, as well as those in the Single Parent II segment, are important consumers. Marketers target them as individual consumers and as purchasers for the household. Nabisco, Quaker Oats, Kellogg, and Procter & Gamble advertise household products to teens on MTV, while Chef Boyardee's canned pasta, Swiss Miss Cocoa Mix, Mazola Cooking Oil, and Gorton's Frozen Seafood are advertised on major network programs aimed at teenagers.[4]

Communicating with teenagers is challenging as the words and symbols acceptable to them change rapidly. As one expert says, by the time a popular teenage expression can be incorporated into an advertisement it will no longer be "in" with teenagers. For example, by the time advertisers were using *awesome*, teenage boys had shifted to *dope* and teenage girls to *cool beans*. As of summer 1993, the term *cool* was:

swanky to pre-teen boys
stylin' or *saweet* to pre-teen girls
wicked to teenage boys
Bonus! to teenage girls[5]

Single Parent II: Middle-Aged Single with Children at Home Single individuals in the 35 to 64 age group who have children often are faced with tremendous financial pressures. The same demands that are placed on the middle-aged married couple with children are present in the life of a middle-aged single with children—except that the single person generally is the sole supporter and completely responsible for all household duties. Besides financial stress, a tremendous time burden is placed on this segment of the population. Many individuals in this position are thus inclined to use time-saving alternatives, such as ready-to-eat food, and are likely to eat at fast-food restaurants. The children of this segment are given extensive household responsibilities.

Empty Nest II: Older Married Couples This group represents individuals with the head of household more than 64 years of age. The head of household may still be working, but for the most part couples in the over-64 age group are either fully or partially retired from full-time employment. Because of age, social orientation, and weakening financial status (due to retirement), the older married couple has unique needs in the areas of health care, housing, food, and recreation. For example, this group has a great deal of time but not a great deal of money. This has made the sale of travel trailers and group vacations very attractive to many older married couples (a popular bumper sticker on the back of travel vehicles reads: "I'm spending my children's inheritance"). Managerial Application 8–3 shows an ad for a product designed to meet one of this segment's needs.

MANAGERIAL APPLICATION 8–3

Products Designed for the Empty Nest II Segment

Older Single The older single represents more than 2 percent of our adult population. Older singles typically are female, since females tend to outlive males. Again, the conditions of being older (over 64), single, and generally not working create many unique needs for housing, socialization, travel, and recreation. Many financial firms have set up special programs to work with these individuals. They often have experienced a spouse's death and now are taking on many of the financial responsibilities once cared for by the other person.

MARKETING STRATEGY BASED ON THE HOUSEHOLD LIFE CYCLE

The preceding sections have illustrated the power of the HLC as a segmentation variable. The purchase and consumption of many products is driven by the HLC. The reason for this is the fact that each stage in the HLC poses unique problems/opportunities to the household members. The resolution of these problems often requires the consumption of products. Our earlier discussion and Managerial Applications illustrated how marketers are responding to the unique needs of each segment (stage in the HLC).

While stage in the HLC provides many of the problems/opportunities individuals confront as they mature, it does not provide solutions. Thus, while all Full Nest I families face similar needs and restrictions with respect to recreation, how they will meet those needs is heavily influenced by their social class. As we saw in Chapter 5 social class provides consumption-related attitudes and values as well as the financial resources required to enact a desired lifestyle. Social class provides solutions to many of the problems posed as one moves through the various stages of the HLC.

Exhibit 8–1 presents the **HLC/Social Stratification Matrix**. One axis is the stages in the HLC (which determines the problems the household will likely encounter) and the other is a set of social strata (which provide a range of acceptable solutions). Any set of social strata may be used.

This matrix can be used to segment the market for many products and to develop appropriate marketing strategies for the targeted segments. An effective use of the matrix is to isolate an activity or problem of interest to the firm such as preparing the evening meal, snacks, weekend recreation, and so forth. Research, often in the form of focus group interviews, is used to determine the following information for each relevant cell in the matrix:

1. What products or services are now being used to meet the need or perform the activity.
2. What, if any, symbolic or social meaning is associated with meeting the need or using the current products?
3. Exactly how are the current products or services being used?
4. How satisfied are the segment members with the current solutions and what improvements would be desired?

This approach has been used to select target markets and develop successful marketing strategies for such products as regional bakeries, movies, and financial services.

HOUSEHOLD DECISION MAKING

Decision making by a group such as a household differs in many ways from decisions made by an individual. Consider the purchase of a breakfast cereal that children, and perhaps the adults, will consume. How is a type and brand selected? Does everyone consider the same attributes? The parents typically make the actual *purchase*; does that mean

EXHIBIT 8–1

Household Life Cycle/Social Stratification Matrix

Stage of Household Life Cycle	Blue Collar	White Collar	Managerial-Professional	Student
Younger (<35) Single				
Young married				
Married (children)				
Single parent				
Middle-aged (35–64) Single				
Married/children				
Single parent				
Married (no children)				
Older (>64) Single				
Married				

that they also make the *choice*? Or, is the choice made by the children? Or, is it a joint decision? Figure 8–4 illustrates the five roles that frequently occur in household decision making, using the cereal purchase as an example.[6] It is important to note that individuals will play various roles for different decisions:

- **Information gatherer(s).** The individual who has expertise and interest in a particular purchase. Different individuals may seek information at different times or on different aspects of the purchase.
- **Influencer(s).** The person who influences the alternatives evaluated, the criteria considered, and the final choice.
- **Decision maker(s).** The individual who makes the final decision. Of course, joint decisions also are likely to occur.
- **Purchaser(s).** The household member who actually purchases the product. This is typically an adult or teenager.
- **User(s).** The user of the product. For many products there are multiple users.

In many household purchase decisions, the primary product users are neither the decision maker nor the purchaser. For example, women (wives and girlfriends) purchase 70 percent of the fragrances used by men.[7] Thus, marketers must decide who in the household plays which role before they can affect the household decision process. After careful examination of the household decision process, Crayola® shifted its advertising budget from children's television to women's magazines. Their research revealed that mothers rather than children were more likely to recognize the problem, evaluate alternatives, and

FIGURE 8–4 The Household Decision–Making Process for Children's Products

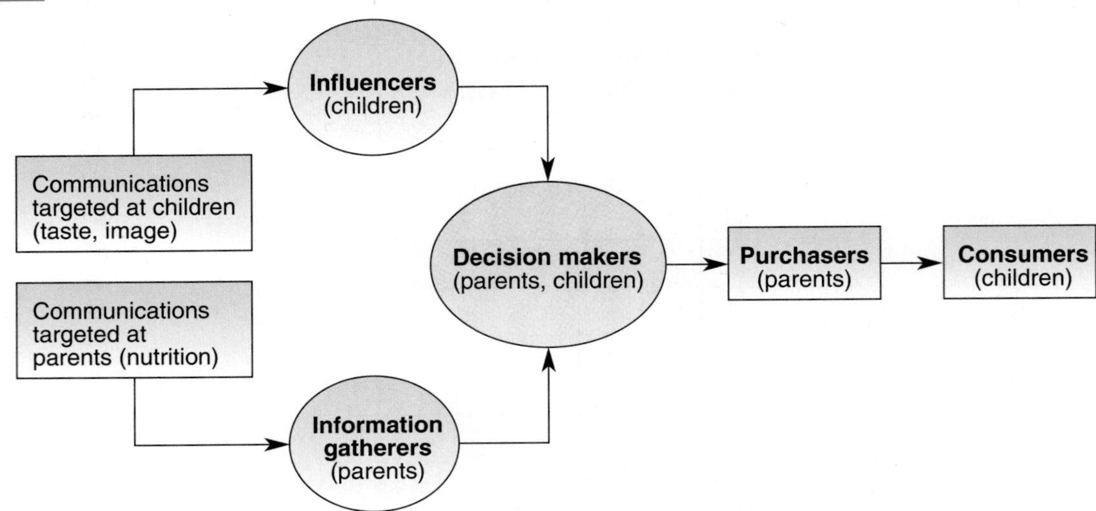

make the purchase. Managerial Application 8–4 shows a product designed for use by children that is generally selected and purchased by parents.

Household decision making is generally categorized as husband-dominant, wife-dominant, joint-decision (syncretic), or individualized decision (autonomic).[8] Husband-dominant decisions generally occur with the purchase of such products as automobiles, liquor, and life insurance. Wife-dominant decisions are more likely to occur in the purchase of furniture, food, and appliances. Joint decisions are likely to occur when buying a house, living room furniture, and vacations. These areas will undoubtedly change as marital roles continue to evolve.

How household members interact in a purchase decision is largely dependent on the *role specialization* of different household members and the degree of *involvement* each has in the product area of concern.[9]

Over time, each spouse develops more specialized roles as a part of their household lifestyle and household responsibilities. Husbands are often expected to play a more significant role in automotive repairs and maintenance and, therefore, have a more specialized role in establishing criteria and evaluating alternatives in an automobile purchase (as we saw in Chapter 3, this is changing rapidly). Wives often have a more specialized role in certain aspects of child rearing and, as a result, have a more specialized role in buying children's clothing and food. Because role specialization within any household takes time to develop, younger couples often engage in greater degrees of joint decision making than more established households. The greater the role specialization and the more closely related the product is to the area of specialization, the less likely a shared or syncretic decision will be made.

Involvement in a product area is another major factor that has an impact on how a household purchase decision will be made. Naturally, the more involved a spouse is with a product area, the more likely he or she will be to exert influence over other family members during a purchase in that product area. For example, a spouse very interested in electronics as a hobby probably would greatly influence the purchase of a stereo, television,

MANAGERIAL APPLICATION 8–4

A Children's Product Advertised to Parents

or home computer. Likewise, children's influence increases the more the product relates to their interests and activities.

Studies of household decisions have focused on direct influence and ignored indirect influence. For example, a wife might report purchasing an automobile without discussing it with any member of her family. Yet she might purchase a blue station wagon to meet her perceptions of the demands of the family rather than the red sports car that she personally would prefer. Most research studies would classify the above decision as strictly wife-dominated. Clearly, however, other household members influenced the decision.

To date, most studies have focused not on household decision making but on husband–wife decision making. The influence of children has been largely ignored. Yet, children often exert a substantial influence on the consumption process.

Household decision making allows different household members to become involved at different stages of the process. Figure 8–5 shows the influence of wives, husbands, and teenage children at each stage of the decision process for a variety of products.

Household decisions also allow different members to make specific subdecisions of the overall decision. When an individual makes a decision, he or she evaluates all the relevant attributes of each alternative and combines these evaluations into a single decision. In a family decision, different members often focus on specific attributes. For example, a child may evaluate the color and style of a bicycle while one or both parents evaluate price, warranty, and safety features.

Much remains to be learned about household decision making. But we can offer five general conclusions:

FIGURE 8–5 Family Member Influence by Stage of the Decision Process*

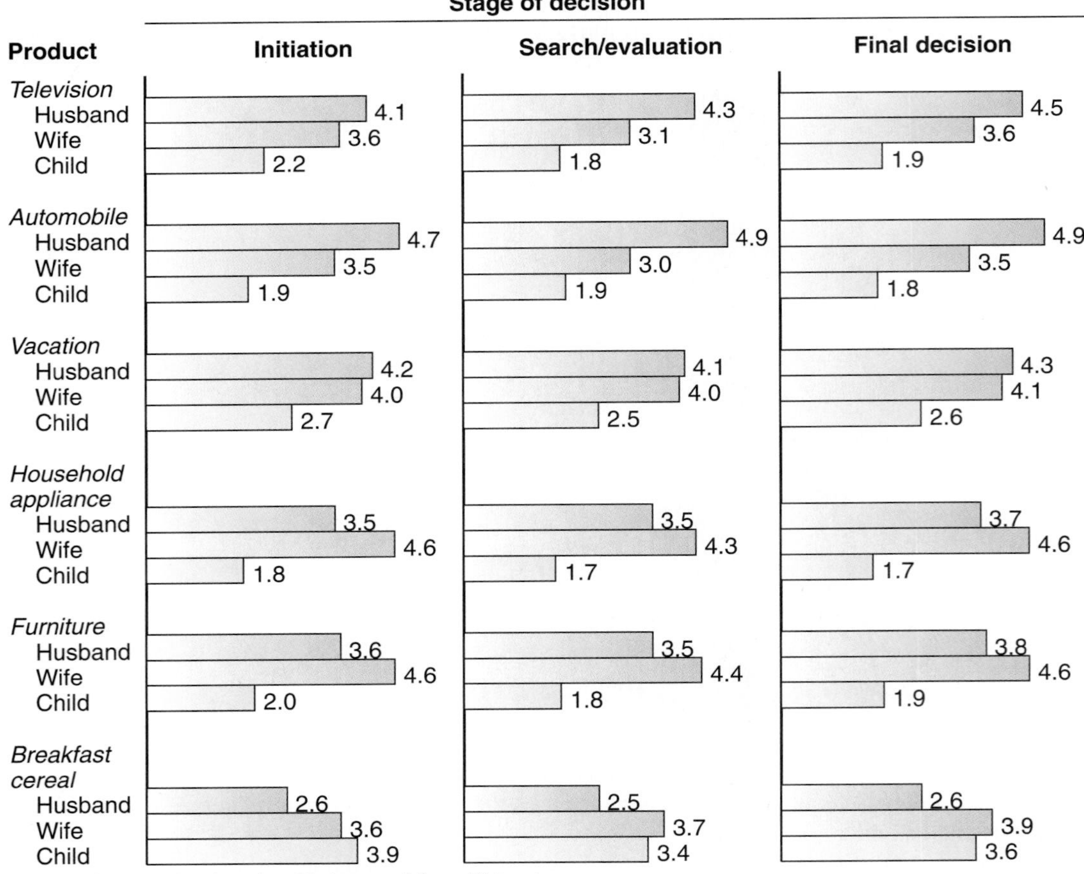

*Measured on a scale where 1 = No input and 6 = All input.
All children were over 13, and their mean age was 17.

Source: G. E. Belch, M. A. Belch, and G. Ceresino, "Parental and Teenage Child Influences in Family Decision Making," *Journal of Business Research*, April 1985, p. 167.

1. Different household members are often involved at different stages of the decision process.
2. Different household members often evaluate different attributes of a product or brand.
3. The direct involvement of household members in each stage of the decision process represents only a small part of the picture. Taking into account the desires of other household members is also important, though seldom studied.
4. Who participates at each stage of the decision process and the method by which conflicts are resolved are primarily a function of the product category, and secondarily a function of the characteristics of the individual household members and the characteristics of the household. The product category is important because it is closely related to who uses the product.
5. Overt conflicts in decision making are less common than agreement. Conflicts are most frequently resolved through problem solving and negotiation.

EXHIBIT 8–2

Marketing Strategy Based on the Household Decision-Making Process

Segment: ______________

Stage in the Decision Process	Household Members Involved	Household Members' Motivation and Interests	Marketing Strategy and Tactics
Problem recognition			
Information search			
Alternative evaluation			
Purchase			
Use/Consumption			
Disposition			
Evaluation			

MARKETING STRATEGY AND HOUSEHOLD DECISION MAKING

Formulating an effective marketing strategy for most consumer products requires a thorough understanding of the household decision-making process with respect to that product. Exhibit 8–2 provides a framework for such an analysis.

The household decision-making process often varies across market segments such as stages in the household life cycle or social class. Therefore, it is essential that we analyze household decision making *within* each of our defined target markets. Within each market, we need to determine which household members are involved at each stage of the decision process and what their motivations and interests are. For example, younger children are often involved in the problem recognition stage related to breakfast. They may note a new cartoon-character-based cereal or discover that their friends are eating a new cereal. They are interested in identifying with the cartoon character or being like their friends. When they request the new cereal, one or both parents may become interested but they are more likely to focus on nutrition and price.

Once we have determined who is involved at each stage and the nature of their motivation, we must put together a marketing program that will meet the needs of all the participants. An examination of Managerial Application 8–4 reveals a product and package that children will appreciate coupled with a communications campaign aimed at the parents who make the purchase decision and buy the product.

CONSUMER SOCIALIZATION

The household unit provides the basic framework in which *consumer socialization* occurs. **Consumer socialization** is defined as *the process by which young people acquire skills, knowledge, and attitudes relevant to their functioning as consumers in the marketplace.*

Learning, including acquiring consumption-related knowledge, is a lifelong process. However, the quantity and nature of learning that take place before early adulthood (around 18), as well as its impact on subsequent learning, are sufficiently unique to justify focusing on this time period.[11]

We are concerned with understanding both what behaviors children learn and how those behaviors are associated with the purchase and use of goods and services. The *what* of consumer learning refers to the content of learning, and the *how* refers to the methods by which that content is acquired.

The content of consumer learning can be broken down into two categories: *directly relevant* and *indirectly relevant. Directly relevant* aspects of consumer learning are those necessary for purchase and use to actually take place. In other words, a person has to learn particular skills, such as how to shop, how to compare similar brands, how to budget available income, and so forth.[12] Knowledge and attitudes about stores, products, brands, salespeople, clearance sales, advertising media, and coupons are examples of directly relevant consumer learning content.

Indirectly relevant consumer learning content refers to everything that has been learned which motivates purchase and use behavior. In other words, it is the knowledge, attitudes, and values which cause people to want certain goods or services and allow them to attach differential evaluations to products and brands. For example, some consumers know (have learned) that Calvin Klein is a prestigious brand name, and they may respond positively to various products carrying this name. This information about Calvin Klein's prestige is not necessary to carry out the actual purchase (directly relevant), but it is extremely important in deciding *to* purchase and *what* to purchase (indirectly relevant).

Advertising and other marketing activities have a strong influence on consumer socialization. We will examine the ethical implications of this influence in some detail in Chapter 21. However, the family remains the primary source of consumer socialization through instrumental training, modeling, and mediation.[13]

Instrumental training occurs when a parent, or sibling, specifically and directly attempts to bring about certain responses through reasoning or reinforcement. In other words, a parent may try directly to teach a child which snack foods should be consumed by explicitly discussing nutrition. Or, rules may be established which limit the consumption of some snack foods and encourage the consumption of others.[14]

Managerial Application 8–5 illustrates how easy it is to inadvertently teach children dysfunctional behavior. The Chef Boyardee ad (one of a series of such ads) provides a value service by alerting parents to the danger of using food as a reward for positive behavior.

Modeling occurs when a child learns appropriate (or inappropriate) consumption behaviors by observing others. Modeling frequently, though not always, occurs without direct instruction from the role model and even without conscious thought or effort on the part of the child. Modeling is an extremely important way for children to learn relevant skills, knowledge, and attitudes. Children learn both positive and negative consumption patterns through modeling. For example, children whose parents smoke are more likely to start smoking than are children whose parents do not smoke.

Mediation can easily be seen in the following example:

CHILD Can I have one of those? See, it can walk!

PARENT No. That's just an advertisement. It won't really walk. They just make it look like it will so kids will buy them.

MANAGERIAL APPLICATION 8–5

Unintended Consumer Socialization

Chef Boyardee Child Development Series

"If you'll just be quiet till we get to Grandma's, you can have a cookie."

Have you ever found yourself saying something like this? Or been tempted to?

Kids aren't always angels, and somehow it seems that when you want them to behave their best, they misbehave the most. And often, a favorite food is a quick way to get them to quiet down.

But it's not the best way.

Children who continually are given food to pacify them or reward them or coax them to do something can come to regard food as comfort in times of stress. They may begin to eat whenever they feel anxious and, consequently, may develop weight problems, since they are eating for reasons other than hunger.

Although foods shouldn't be used as rewards, that doesn't mean foods shouldn't be fun. That's the whole idea behind the interesting shapes of Chef Boyardee® Sharks,™ Chef Boyardee Dinosaurs,™ and Teenage Mutant Ninja Turtles® Pastas. Each is made from ripe tomatoes and enriched wheat flour. They have no preservatives, and kids just love them. You want to make sure your child eats a good, balanced diet. Chef Boyardee wants to make it easier.

"Thank goodness for Chef Boyardee."

The advertisement illustrated a product attribute and triggered a desire, but the parent altered the belief in the attribute and in the believability of advertising in general. This is not to suggest that family members mediate all commercials, or for all product categories, or even for all children. However, children often learn about the purchase and use of products during interactions with other family members. Thus, the firm wishing to influence children must do so in a manner consistent with the values of the rest of the family.

SUMMARY

The household is the basic purchasing and consuming unit in American society and is, therefore, of great importance to marketing managers of most products. Family households also are the primary mechanism whereby cultural and social class values and behavior patterns are passed on to the next generation.

The *family household* consists of two or more related persons living together in a dwelling unit. *Nonfamily households* are dwelling units occupied by one or more unrelated individuals.

The *household life cycle* is the classification of the household into stages through which it passes over time. Households, family and nonfamily, change over time at relatively predictable intervals based largely on demographic (and thus readily measurable) variables. The household life cycle is, therefore, a very valuable marketing tool because its stages provide marketers with segments that face similar consumption problems.

The demographic variables most frequently used to define household life cycle are age and marital status of the head of the household, and the presence and age of children. Using these variables, specific stages can be determined and described. One common form of the life cycle lists the following stages: young single, young married, full nest I, single parent I, middle-aged single, empty nest I, full nest II, single parent II, empty nest II, and older single.

Household decision making involves consideration of some very important and very complex questions. Who buys, who decides, and who uses are only a few of the questions that marketers must ask when dealing with products purchased and used by and for households.

Marketing managers must analyze the household decision process separately for each product category within each target market. Household member involvement in the decision process varies by involvement with the specific product as well as by stage in the decision process. Role specialization within the family also influences which household members are most likely to be directly involved in a purchase decision.

Consumer socialization deals with the processes by which young people (from birth until 18 years of age) learn how to become functioning consumers. How children become socialized (learn their own culture with respect to consumption) is very important to marketers interested in selling products to young people now or in the future. Consumer socialization deals with the learning of both directly relevant purchasing skills (budgeting, shopping) and indirectly relevant skills (symbols of quality and prestige, for example). Families influence consumer socialization through direct instrumental training, modeling, and mediation.

REVIEW QUESTIONS

1. The household is described as ''the basic consumption unit for consumer goods.'' Why?
2. What is a *nuclear family*? Can a single-parent family be a nuclear family?
3. How does a *nonfamily household* differ from a *family household*?
4. What is an *extended family household*?
5. Why are households important to marketing managers?
6. How has the distribution of household types in the United States been changing? What are the implications of these shifts?
7. What is meant by the *household life cycle*? How do family and nonfamily households progress through this cycle?
8. What is meant by the statement: ''Each stage in the household life cycle poses a series of problems which household decision makers must solve''?
9. Describe the general characteristics of each of the following stages in the household life cycle:
   - a. Young single.
   - b. Young married.
   - c. Full nest I.
   - d. Single parent I.
   - e. Middle-aged single.
   - f. Full nest II.
   - g. Single parent II.
   - h. Empty nest I.
   - i. Older single.
   - j. Empty nest II.
10. Describe the HLC/social stratification matrix.
11. What is meant by *household decision making*? How can different members of the household

be involved with different stages of the decision process?

12. The text states that the marketing manager must analyze the household decision process separately within each target market. Why?
13. What factors influence involvement by a household member in a purchase decision?
14. What is meant by *role specialization* with respect to household purchase decisions?
15. What is *consumer socialization*? How is knowledge of it useful to marketing managers?
16. What do we mean when we say that children learn *directly relevant* and *indirectly relevant* consumer skills and attitudes?
17. How do children learn to become consumers?
18. In what ways does the family influence children's consumption learning?

DISCUSSION QUESTIONS

19. Rate the stages of the household life cycle in terms of their probable purchase of ______. Justify your answer.
    a. New van.
    b. Portable compact disk player.
    c. In-line skates.
    d. Expensive perfume.
    e. Piano.
    f. Home entertainment center.
20. Pick two stages in the household life cycle (HLC). Describe how your marketing strategy for ______ would differ depending on which group was your primary target market.
    a. Toothpaste. c. Camcorder.
    b. Large-screen TV. d. Breakfast cereal.
21. Do you think the trend toward nonfamily households will continue? Justify your response.
22. What are the primary marketing implications of Table 8–1?
23. How would the marketing strategies for ______ differ by stage of the HLC (assume each stage is the target market)?
    a. Multi-vitamin. d. Mouthwash.
    b. Resort hotel. e. Washing machine.
    c. Expensive wine. f. Furniture polish.
24. Create two different household structure/social status matrixes using different measures of structure and status. How would the segments identified by these matrixes differ from each other and from the ones in the text?
25. What are the marketing implications of Figure 8–2?
26. What are the marketing implications of Figure 8–4?
27. What are the marketing implications of Figure 8–5?
28. Evaluate the ads shown in ______.
    a. Managerial Application 8–1.
    b. Managerial Application 8–2.
    c. Managerial Application 8–3.
    d. Managerial Application 8–4.
    e. Managerial Application 8–5.
29. Complete Exhibit 8–2 for ______ if the target market is Full Nest I and (1) blue-collar, (2) white-collar, or (3) managerial-professional.
    a. Breakfast cereal. c. Toothpaste.
    b. Vacation. d. New car.
30. Complete Exhibit 8–2 for the items in Question 29 if the target market is:
    a. Single.
    b. Young married, no children.
    c. Single parent I.
    d. Middle-aged single.
    e. Full Nest II.
    f. Single parent I.
    g. Empty Nest I.
    h. Older single.
    i. Empty Nest II.
31. Describe four types of activities or situations in which *direct instrumental training* is likely to occur.
32. Describe four types of activities or situations in which *modeling* is likely to occur.
33. Describe four types of activities or situations in which *mediation* is likely to occur.

APPLICATION EXERCISES

34. Interview a junior high or high school student who owns a snowboard or pair of in-line skates. Determine and describe the household decision process involved in the purchase.
35. Interview two furniture salespersons from different outlets. Try to ascertain which stages in the household life cycle constitute their primary markets and why this is so.
36. Interview one individual from each stage in the household life cycle. Determine and report the extent to which these individuals conform to the descriptions provided in the text.
37. Interview a family with at least one child under 13 at home. Interview both the parents and the child, but interview the child separately. Try to determine the influence of each family member on the following products *for the child's use.* In addition, ascertain what method(s) of conflict resolution are used.
    a. Toothpaste.
    b. Shoes.
    c. Snacks.
    d. Major "toys," such as a bicycle.
    e. Television viewing.
    f. Restaurant meals.
38. Interview a couple that has been married ______. Ascertain and report the degree and nature of role specialization that has developed with respect to their purchase decisions.
    a. Less than 1 year.
    b. 1–5 years.
    c. 6–10 years.
    d. Over 10 years.
39. Examine five different magazines and count the ads that appear to portray each stage of the HLC. What do you conclude?
40. Watch three hours of prime-time television and count the ads that appear to portray each stage of the HLC. What do you conclude?
41. Pick a product and market segment of interest and interview five households. Collect sufficient data to complete Exhibit 8–2.
42. Pick a product of interest and with several fellow students complete enough interviews to fill the relevant cells in Exhibit 8–1. Develop an appropriate marketing strategy based on this information.

REFERENCES

[1]C. Power, "Getting 'Em While They're Young," *Business Week*, September 9, 1991, pp. 94–95; and J. U. McNeal, "The Littlest Shoppers," *American Demographics*, February 1992, pp. 48–53.

[2]See F. L. Williams, "The Family as an Economic System," *Psychology & Marketing*, March/April 1993, pp. 111–20.

[3]See C. M. Schaninger and W. D. Danko, "A Conceptual and Empirical Comparison of Alternative Household Life Cycle Models," *Journal of Consumer Research*, March 1993, pp. 580–94.

[4]G. Hauser, "How Teenagers Spend the Family Dollar," *American Demographics*, December 1986, pp. 38–41. See also H. H. Stipp, "Children as Consumers," *American Demographics*, February 1988, pp. 27–32.

[5]A. W. Fawcett, "When Using Slang in Advertising," *Advertising Age*, August 23, 1993, p. S-6.

[6]C. Lackman and J. M. Lanasa, "Family Decision-Making Theory," *Psychology & Marketing*, March/April 1993, pp. 81–113.

[7]P. Sloan, "Matchabelli Name Readied for Men's Fragrance Line," *Advertising Age*, April 21, 1980, p. 69.

[8]W. J. Qualls, "Household Decision Behavior," *Journal of Consumer Research*, September 1987, pp. 264–79; M. B. Menasco and D. J. Curry, "Utility and Choice," *Journal of Consumer Research*, June 1989, pp. 87–97; K. P. Corfman, "Measures of Relative Influence in Couples," and I. R. Foster and R. W. Olshavsky, "An Exploratory Study of Family Decision Making Using a New Taxonomy of Family Role Structure," both in *Advances in Consumer Research XVI*, ed. T. K. Srull (Provo, Utah: Association for Consumer Research, 1989), pp. 659–64 and 665–70.

[9]For a view based on relative power, see D. J. Burns, "Husband-Wife Innovative Consumer Decision Making," *Psychology & Marketing*, May/June 1992, pp. 175–89.

[10]See footnote 1; W. R. Swinyard and C. P. Sim, "Perception of Children's Influence on Family Decision Processes," *Journal of Consumer Marketing*, Winter 1987, pp. 25–37; L. Isler, E. T. Popper, and S. Ward, "Children's Purchase Requests and Parental Responses," *Journal of Advertising Research*, November 1987, pp. 28–39; E. R. Foxman, P. S. Tansuhaj, and K. M. Ekstrom, "Family Members' Perceptions of Adolescents' Influence in Family Decision Making," *Journal of Consumer Research*, March 1989, pp. 482–91; and T. F. Mangleburg, "Children's Influence in Purchase Decisions," in *Advances in Consumer Behavior XVII*, eds. M. E. Goldberg, G. Gorn, and R. W. Pollay (Provo, Utah: Association for Consumer Research, 1990), pp. 813–25.

[11]See S. Ward, D. M. Klees, and D. B. Wackman, ''Consumer Socialization Research,'' in Goldberg, Gorn, and Pollay, *Advances XVII*; footnote 10, pp. 798–803.

[12]B. B. Reece and T. C. Kinnear, ''Indices of Consumer Socialization for Retailing Research,'' *Journal of Retailing*, Fall 1986, pp. 267–80; and B. B. Reece, ''Children and Shopping,'' *Journal of Public Policy and Marketing*, vol. 5 (1986), pp. 185–94.

[13]See G. P. Moschis, ''The Role of Family Communication in Consumer Socialization,'' *Journal of Consumer Research*, March 1985, pp. 898–913; S. Grossbart, L. Carlson, and A. Walsh, ''Consumer Socialization and Frequency of Shopping with Children,'' *Journal of the Academy of Marketing Science*, Summer 1991, pp. 155–64; and O. A. J. Mascarenhas and M. A. Higby, ''Peer, Parent, and Media Influences in Teen Apparel Shopping'' *Journal of the Academy of Marketing Science*, Winter 1993, pp. 53–58.

[14]See L. Carlson and S. Grossbart, ''Parental Style and Consumer Socialization of Children,'' *Journal of Consumer Research*, June 1988, pp. 77–94; and J. L. Haynes, D. C. Burts, A. Dukes, and R. Cloud, ''Consumer Socialization of Pre-schoolers and Kindergarteners,'' *Psychology & Marketing*, March/April 1993, pp. 151–66.

SECTION 2 CASES

Case 2–1 Europe 2005

At the end of 1992, the 12 nations of the European Community (EC) removed most of the trade barriers that separated them. Between-country tariffs were dropped, most trade restrictions were removed, relatively common commercial laws were established, and some movement toward a common currency and monetary policy was occurring.

Will the removal of many political and most trade barriers between the 12 EC nations create a single market? Experts have differing opinions.

> ''We are moving fast (to a single market). People who don't want to believe that are living in the wrong century. Europe is really no more diverse than the United States. Look at Alaska and Hawaii.'' Yves Franchet, director general, Eurostat (statistical office of the EC)

> ''Too many Americans are looking at Europe as being homogeneous. It will never be. In fact, I believe Europe will be even more fragmented tomorrow than it is today. Removing all the economic barriers will bring a return of old regional borders. We are looking at the return of regions.'' Jean Quatrezooz, president of INRA (a major European consulting group)*

TABLE A Expenditure Patterns across European Community (EC) Count

	Country												
Product	**All EC**	**W. Germany**	**Italy**	**G. Britain**	**France**	**Spain**	**Netherlands**	**Belgium**	**Portugal**	**Greece**	**Denmark**	**Ireland**	**Luxembourg**
Usually in Home (%)													
Breakfast Cereal	47	51	17	90	39	25	36	42	34	15	70	87	48
Coffee (beans/ground)	78	93	93	40	87	69	97	93	26	88	96	17	89
Coffee (instant)	47	33	15	90	49	59	27	36	60	56	16	76	51
Butter	80	89	83	66	93	59	82	87	68	73	87	89	60
Margarine	71	87	39	88	63	57	90	86	78	49	95	70	82
Frozen pizza	26	38	8	41	23	14	25	19	10	9	24	32	26
Frozen vegetables	47	54	29	71	40	34	49	44	16	36	82	43	41
Window cleaners	74	64	83	70	92	76	41	53	69	87	64	76	74
Floor polish	36	24	52	27	43	48	22	46	35	48	10	29	47

(Continued on following page)

Expenditure Patterns across European Community (EC) Countries (Continued)

TABLE A

Product	All EC	W. Germany	Italy	G. Britain	France	Spain	Netherlands	Belgium	Portugal	Greece	Denmark	Ireland	Luxembourg
Consumed Last Week													
Beer	40	52	37	40	29	37	44	47	39	36	67	42	33
Wine	44	40	59	28	61	32	32	35	46	29	53	11	41
Spirits	24	29	13	28	37	16	19	15	20	17	40	21	14
No alcoholic drink	32	29	28	35	26	44	31	35	39	44	16	43	42
Generally Used (Women)													
Face powder	27	24	27	46	14	23	29	34	10	21	36	30	32
Facial moisturisers	58	67	51	65	66	46	56	49	25	33	80	62	46
Lipstick/gloss	63	59	59	79	60	63	68	57	39	48	78	74	55
Eye Cosmetics	48	43	46	60	46	50	59	51	24	44	58	45	28
Perfume	36	37	10	56	44	30	42	49	39	6	37	42	44
Generally Used (Men)													
Electric shaver	42	63	30	43	35	35	61	60	21	10	59	32	60
Hair dressings	24	23	26	34	27	11	30	29	9	9	22	13	24
Splash-on lotion	52	69	71	32	62	49	24	50	23	11	9	26	56
Skincare preparations	18	38	15	15	13	12	17	13	3	2	35	4	15
Have/Own													
Bank account	77	89	57	81	88	69	87	81	68	56	94	63	87
Cheque book	55	57	39	70	84	22	65	56	53	3	43	33	70
Cash dispenser card	39	38	16	60	53	30	61	51	22	2	43	30	40
Credit card(s)	21	10	6	41	39	13	19	18	7	8	15	14	31
Whole-life insurance*	32	34	10	57	33	10	40	37	17	7	36	43	24
Term life insurance*	24	39	12	40	17	4	17	18	5	8	19	23	23
Private medical ins.*	30	25	5	16	79	12	65	34	8	8	16	35	21
Stock*	14	10	5	22	23	6	12	22	4	2	40	9	9
Attitudes toward EC													
We should be a member	72	78	73	63	84	57	80	79	75	68	55	65	75
Know the 12 members	34	27	24	17	58	42	28	42	63	56	42	15	55
Good for Europe's future	61	60	63	61	65	48	65	62	65	65	54	64	52

Source: Reproduced from *Reader's Digest Eurodata—a Consumer Survey of 17 European Countries*, (Pleasantville, NY: The Reader's Digest Association, Inc., 1991).

*Someone in household has.

Examine Table A (pp. 208, 209) in this case; Table 2–3 (p. 35) in Chapter 2; and the material on value differences across the EC countries in Chapter 2 (pp. 37–46). Which, if either, of the two views expressed above is accurate?

Discussion Questions

1. What explains the large differences among the 12 EC countries?
2. Will these differences diminish significantly by 2005?
3. Does a "single market" require similar expenditure patterns throughout?
4. What pressures will push the EC toward a number of regional markets? Do similar pressures exist in the United States/Canada?
5. What pressures will push the EC toward a single market? Do similar pressures exist in the United States/Canada?
6. How should the following firms/products position themselves to prosper in the EC in 2005?
   a. Procter & Gamble—cosmetics.
   b. Chrysler—automobiles.
   c. Sony—home electronics.
   d. General Electric—appliances.
   e. Domino's—fast food.
   f. Visa—financial services.

B. Cutler, "Reaching the Real Europe," *American Demographics*, October 1990, pp. 38–43.

Case 2–2 The Copper Cricket

Bob Block, president of Sage Advance, which manufactures and markets the Copper Cricket (a patented geyser-pumping solar water heater for home use), describes the history of the firm as follows:

> By November 1986, after working for three years with only enough compensation to keep us in debt, Eldon Haines and I were looking over the edge of frustration. Eldon, a nuclear chemist from the Jet Propulsion Lab, had invented geyser pumping with a friend in 1979. He dabbled with it for a few years and in 1983 we built the first working prototype. By the end of 1984, we had a patent and were searching for licensees for the technology. During the previous 10 years of solar tax credits a hurricane of mediocre technologies had swept the solar industry. Infinitely more innovation was directed at how to sell solar and tax credits than was directed toward improving technologies. When we offered the geyser pump to most of the larger solar companies, we were laughed at. "It sounds like you guys have relegislated the laws of physics," was what one solar engineer said when we described our no-moving-parts downward pumper. Like many innovators we heard a lot of "it will never work," and from some of the more diplomatic industry leaders we were told that the end of the federal tax credits was imminent and that they couldn't afford to develop any new products.
>
> In 1985, the worst fears of the solar industry were realized; the tax credits were canceled, and within the next year 85 percent of the solar manufacturers disappeared. We were ready with our new product and no one was around to manufacture it. We built about 30 systems and sold them to individuals who had written to us after reading about the technology in *New Shelter Magazine*. All of those systems are still out there and working perfectly.
>
> While walking one rainy autumn night, around midnight I realized that we had to do something. Our intentions were honorable; we were working in solar because we knew that it was one of the ways to wean our energy-dependent society away from its environmentally destructive nuclear and fossil fuel addictions. What we were missing was a way to disseminate our technology. Why wasn't the world

beating a path to our door? Solar energy is older than the mousetrap, and we had made the first real innovation in solar water heating since the advent of glass. I realized that the only people who will beat a path to your door are the ones who know they can profit from the visit, and nobody was making any money in solar in 1986. We were at the lowest point in the solar market in 20 years and yet we had a great new technology. Our altruistic investors were morally supportive but didn't have any more discretionary capital to invest on our rapidly decaying personal energy. Our board of directors had effectively disbanded, and we were two scientists with no desire to become businessmen.

The next day I offered a plan to Eldon: we should start a new company to manufacture the geyser pump, join up with some businesspeople who know marketing and manufacturing, build a production prototype and write a business plan. We found two people who were perfect; one had just lost his own solar manufacturing company to the tax credits and the other had a still-successful solar engineering and sales firm. We put together $10,000 that we borrowed from family and friends and wrote our plan.

The new firm was named Sage Advance and the geyser-pump-driven solar hot water system was named the Copper Cricket. Despite Bob and Eldon's enthusiasm and the experience of their new partners, the firm was not at the break-even sales level as of January 1, 1994.

The Product

The product is described in Exhibit A. The geyser pump is protected by a strong patent. The absence of moving parts, zero maintenance requirements, and the fact that it is freezeproof are significant advantages over all other systems on the market.

The Copper Cricket, at about $2,100, costs somewhat more than competitive systems. It can provide over half the hot water used by a family of four (47 percent in Boston to 95 percent in Phoenix), it saves $100 per year in electricity bills in Portland, Oregon (those figures vary, depending on the climate and utility rates), and it protects the environment (by reducing electrical consumption). Thus, a $2,100 investment that generates a minimum of $100 in nontaxable energy savings each year is earning at least a 5 percent tax-free return.

The Copper Cricket **EXHIBIT A**

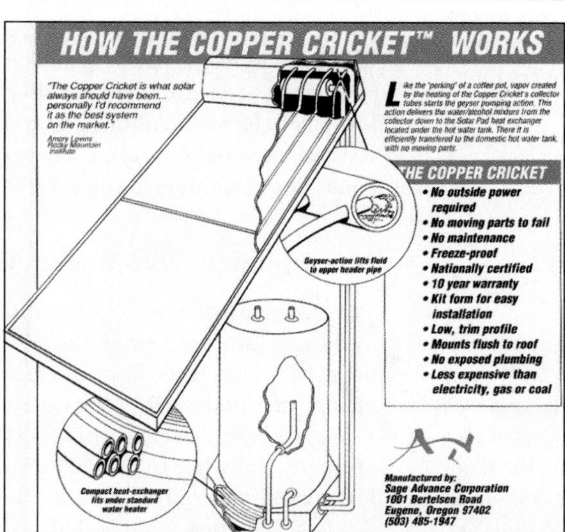

The Copper Cricket can be easily installed in an existing home. In fact, many are installed by do-it-yourselfers. Of course, they can also be installed in new construction.

The virtues of the Copper Cricket have been widely recognized. *Popular Science* named it one of 1989's "Greatest Achievements in Science and Technology." Christopher Flavin of the World Watch Institute describes it as "the most cost-effective solar hot water system to be developed in the last decade." Amory Lovins, director of the Rocky Mountain Institute, says: "It's what solar always should have been. Personally, I'd recommend it as the best system on the market." A recent survey of Copper Cricket owners found that 98 percent would recommend the product to a friend.

The Environment

The energy crises of the late 1970s and early 1980s coupled with the federal government's (and many states') tax credit program created a huge market for solar energy systems, particularly solar water heating systems. Hundreds of firms began to produce such systems. Unfortunately, many of them produced systems that were inefficient, flawed, subject to freezing, or that required extensive maintenance. The easing of the energy crisis and the removal of the federal tax credit program in 1985 devastated the industry. Within a year, approximately 90 percent of the solar water heater producers dropped out of the business. Unfortunately, tens of thousands of poorly performing systems had been sold. Both consumers and distributors were left holding the bag.

In December 1993, the market picture was uncertain. The environment was a major concern, and both nuclear- and coal-based energy generation were under attack. However, in recent elections, most "green" initiatives nationwide had failed (many by two to one). The Persian Gulf crisis had increased fuel prices but they were again quite low. The lingering recession had consumers nervous about capital outlays.

Marketing Efforts

The firm's marketing efforts have been extremely limited due to its severe cash flow problems.

A significant percent of the firm's sales occur in Oregon, where the firm is headquartered. Oregon also has an energy tax credit program. In Oregon, the Copper Cricket has been advertised in newspapers, on radio, and via direct mail. The product is also shown at home shows, which appears to be particularly effective.

Sage Advance has developed a high-quality four-page brochure and a one-page ad slick for mass mailings and to hand out at trade and home shows. It has also developed a direct mail program and newspaper ads for its dealers to use.

Unfortunately, Sage's attempts to attract dealers have not been very successful. It attempts to secure distributors (individuals) who will both sell the system to homeowners and set up a group of retail dealers within a defined geographic area. Despite a training program and generous commissions, few effective distributors have signed on. (Two large manufacturers who survived the 1985 shakeout have substantial distribution and sales despite having a less advanced product.)

At the national and regional levels, the product and company have received substantial publicity. Two articles on the Copper Cricket appeared in *Popular Science* in 1989 (July and December). They produced over 1,000 inquiries. The product has also appeared in the *Environmental Products Resource Guide*, *Brown's Business Reports*, *Pacific Northwest Magazine*, and numerous newspapers and trade periodicals.

To encourage word-of-mouth communications, Sage will pay Copper Cricket owners $100 for a referral that results in a sale (see Managerial Application 7–1, p. 167). So far, this has produced relatively few sales.

Sage is also working with a number of large electrical utilities. Many utilities now sponsor programs to conserve energy, and several are evaluating the Copper Cricket as a means to this end. A standard program would involve the utility's underwriting part of the cost of the system and/or providing financing at a very low rate. However, utilities generally make such decisions only after observing a new system in use under controlled conditions for several years.

The January 1994 Board Meeting

The board of directors left the January 1994 board meeting with mixed emotions. They were thrilled that Sage had shown its first quarterly profit in the last quarter of 1993. Sales projections were also strong for 1994. However, cash was perilously low and the management team had not been paid their full salaries for several years. This resulted in a large "deferred salaries" liability on the balance sheet which was hampering new fund raising efforts. Management remained convinced that all that stood between the firm and significant success was enough cash to launch a major marketing program.

There was some concern among the board members about launching a sizable program. Current sales were strong only in Oregon, though they were projected to expand significantly into other states in the Northwest. Pacific Power recently certified the Copper Cricket as the first solar water heater eligible for an $800 rebate under its *Super Good Cents* program. While this was good news, the board was concerned about the permanence of Pacific Power's program and Sage's inability to successfully market the Copper Cricket in the absence of government or utility rebates. The need for a profitable 1994 appeared essential for the future of Sage Advance.

Discussion Questions

1. Conduct an innovation analysis of the Copper Cricket.
2. What insights does the innovation analysis provide into its slow sales growth?
3. What strategies does the innovation analysis suggest to increase the diffusion of the Copper Cricket?
4. Evaluate Sage's attempt to increase word-of-mouth communications (see Managerial Application 7–1, p. 167). How would you improve its effectiveness?
5. Who do you think the innovators are for this product? How will they differ from the early adopters? The early majority?
6. Would an environmental theme or an economic theme be most effective for the Copper Cricket in 1994 (fewer than 1,800 total units have been sold in total)?
7. Evaluate the effectiveness of an appeal that, for a particular region of the country, would claim a $2,000 purchase of a Copper Cricket is better than a certificate of deposit (or savings account) paying 9 percent *tax free* because the Copper Cricket will save $200 per year in electricity (a 10 percent tax-free return).
8. What should Sage do to be profitable in 1994?

Norelco Electric Shavers

Case 2–3

For the fourth-quarter 1992, all but one of the major marketers of electric razors planned substantial increases in their advertising expenditures. Remington planned to double 1991 expenditures to $8 million, Panasonic will increase 10 percent to $4.5 million, Norelco plans a "substantial" increase from 1991's $29 million, while Gillette's spending for Braun will be flat at $14 million. Electric razor marketers generally spend most of their annual advertising budgets during the fourth quarter because about half of their annual sales are for holiday gifts.*

About a third of U.S. males use electric shavers and even fewer females use them. Electric shaver sales reached an annual high of 7.1 million units for men and 1.8 million units for women in 1987 but dropped back to 6.8 and 1.7 million units by 1991. This represented a $400 million dollar market in 1991. Norelco had a market share of 47 percent in the men's segment, followed by Remington (25 percent), Braun (15 percent), and Panasonic (8 percent). Remington led the women's segment with 35 percent, followed by Norelco (31 percent), Panasonic (29 percent), and Braun (1 percent).

Exhibit A provides demographic data from Simmons Market Research Bureau on the users of electric razors, disposable razors, and replaceable-blade razors. Exhibit B provides similar data on the users of Remington and Norelco electric shavers.

Discussion Questions

1. Prepare a two-page summary (accompanied by no more than four graphs) that conveys the key information in the two exhibits to a manager.
2. Describe the typical user of an electric razor, a disposable razor, and a blade razor, in one paragraph each.

EXHIBIT A

Demographics and Razor Use

Variable	Males			Females		
	Electric†	Disposable‡	Blades‡	Electric†	Disposable‡	Blades‡
Percent Adults Using	31.2	46.3	45.7	15.5	54.4	31.3
Age*						
18–24 years	90	100	99	77	111	113
25–34	93	115	100	85	113	115
35–44	93	103	105	104	118	104
45–54	102	102	103	113	102	106
55–64	106	92	102	133	90	97
>64	127	73	89	101	60	64
Education*						
College graduate	111	86	106	105	108	101
Some college	110	98	109	107	111	104
High school graduate	98	108	97	104	102	104
No degree	84	102	92	83	81	88
Occupation*						
Professional/Manager	108	85	109	91	113	105
Technical/Clerical/Sales	109	99	100	112	114	109
Precision/Craft	91	113	97	74	104	130
Other employed	90	113	104	90	103	102
Race*						
White	107	99	100	106	104	105
Black	50	113	94	47	77	70
Other	76	95	113	126	79	66
Region*						
Northeast	98	94	94	73	87	88
Midwest	121	96	99	116	108	103
South	78	111	105	97	105	104
West	113	92	99	114	95	102
Household Income*						
<$10,000	79	95	85	56	71	73
$10,000–19,999	89	107	90	89	97	88
$20,000–29,999	99	106	97	106	102	102
$30,000–39,999	100	114	103	119	108	106
>$40,000	108	92	105	111	108	112
>60,000	111	82	108	108	110	108

(Continued on following page)

EXHIBIT A

Demographics and Razor Use* (Continued)

Variable	Males			Females		
	Electric	Disposable	Blades	Electric	Disposable	Blades
Household Structure*						
1 person	101	91	93	62	80	48
2 people	108	92	102	120	92	102
3 or more people	100	105	101	98	111	109
5 or more people	83	110	99	101	109	123
No children	105	93	100	105	90	96
Child < 2 years	86	114	96	84	111	95
Child 2–5 years	97	104	97	78	109	109
Child 6–11 years	89	112	97	95	112	109
Child 12–17 years	93	115	104	101	122	110

*100 = Average use or consumption.
†Used in last seven days.
‡Used in last 30 days.
Source: *1991 Study of Media and Markets* (New York: Simmons Market Research Bureau, 1991).

EXHIBIT B

Demographics and Brand of Razor Used

Variable	Males		Females	
	Norelco†	Remington†	Norelco†	Remington†
Percent Adults Using	16.8	9.1	5.5	4.8
Age*				
18–24 years	80	94	59‡	83‡
25–34	85	108	87	91
35–44	96	81	107	106
45–54	107	88	111	115
55–64	111	112	134	127
>64	138	124	110	89
Education*				
College graduate	101	133	124	106
Some college	118	106	97	111
High school graduate	96	94	100	117
No degree	91	73	85	55

(Continued on following page)

EXHIBIT B Demographics and Brand of Razor Used* (Continued)

Variable	Males Norelco	Males Remington	Females Norelco	Females Remington
Occupation*				
Professional/Manager	101	111	90	105
Technical/Clerical/Sales	107	127	97	110
Precision/Craft	94	85	30‡	121‡
Other employed	91	87	95	72‡
Race*				
White	108	106	107	107
Black	44	55‡	55‡	29‡
Other	61‡	75‡	84‡	186‡
Region*				
Northeast	88	94	70	79
Midwest	145	110	120	124
South	75	93	95	87
West	100	106	115	116
Household Income*				
<$10,000	68	76	61‡	17‡
$10,000–19,999	85	91	91	80
$20,000–29,999	107	93	102	137
$30,000–39,999	104	100	115	132
>$40,000	107	110	112	111
>60,000	103	108	108	107
Household Structure*				
1 person	89	109	36	59
2 people	112	112	145	129
3 or more people	98	98	96	93
5 or more people	86	73	76‡	95‡
No children	106	110	105	115
Child < 2 years	77	109	69‡	104‡
Child 2–5 years	95	87	91	57‡
Child 6–11 years	95	77	102	81
Child 12–17 years	89	85	87	97

*100 = Average use or consumption.
†Used in last seven days.
‡Sample size too small for reliability.
Source: *1991 Study of Media and Markets* (New York: Simmons Market Research Bureau, 1991).

3. Which of the demographic factors are most relevant for developing marketing strategy for electric razors?
4. What additional demographic data would you like to have in order to develop marketing strategy for Norelco electric shavers? Justify your answer.
5. Based on the available data, develop a marketing strategy for ______.
   a. Norelco.
   b. Remington.
   c. Braun.
   d. Panasonic.
6. Interview three ______ and determine what influenced the type of razor they shave with (or plan to shave with) and how they feel about shaving. Report your results and the marketing implications associated with them.
   a. Male college students.
   b. Female college students.
   c. Male high school students.
   d. Female high school students.
   e. Male junior high students.
   f. Female junior high students.
   g. Male preteens (age 10–12).
   h. Female preteens (age 10–12).

*R. A. Davis, ''Electric Razors Plan Aggressive Fourth-Quarter,'' *Advertising Age*, October 12, 1992, p. 20.

Sony versus Philips

Case 2–4

In the early 1980s, Sony Corp. of Japan attempted to make its Betamax format the standard for videocassette recorders. Despite what many believed to be a superior technology, Sony's Betamax format lost to VHS, which was promoted by Matsushita, JVC, and others. Most attribute Sony's failure in the American market to superior marketing on behalf of the VHS format.

A similar battle is now occurring between Sony and Philips over the next generation of audiocassettes. Sony recently launched its Mini Disc which offers near-CD sound and allows listeners to record music. Sony invested about $100 million in Mini Disc development and plant retooling.

Philips Electronic of the Netherlands launched an alternative product called the Digital Compact Cassette (DCC) at about the same time (see Managerial Application 1–5). Philips spent $55 million developing its technology in conjunction with Matsushita. It also offers near-CD sound and recording capability with the added advantage of coming in the traditional cassette format which allows owners to play their current analog tapes on the system. A brief comparison of the products follows.

	Sony	Philips
Features	Near-CD sound, ability to shuffle among tunes, portable, erasable, and recordable	Near-CD sound, can play existing tapes, portable, erasable and recordable
Price	$650–$800	$799
Backers	Sanyo, Denon, Aiwa will produce players. EMI, Columbia, and Epic will issue music	Matsushita, Denon, and Sanyo will produce players. Bertelsmann, Polygram, and Columbia will issue music.

The stakes are very high. In 1991, U.S. cassette player sales were roughly $2 billion; prerecorded and blank tapes were $3.2 billion. Worldwide sales are, of course, much larger. While Philips, which codeveloped the technology with Sony, is the leading supplier of CD players in Europe, Sony currently dominates the U.S. CD market. Sony has 30 percent of the in-home CD player sales and 60 percent of the portable player sales. It also has 50 percent of the portable cassette player sales, 15 percent of the home cassette deck sales, and 17 percent of the car cassette deck sales.

Retailers are currently carrying both lines and waiting for consumer preferences to develop.

According to Robert Heilblim, president of Denon America Inc. which will make players for both technologies, technological superiority will not determine success: "This war will be won over marketing."

Exhibit A provides demographic data on current CD player users.

EXHIBIT A

Demographics and Stereo Equipment Ownership

Variable	CD Player	Compact/Console Stereo	DAT Player
Percent adults ever bought	9.3	15.8	2.4
Gender*			
Female	82	99	86
Male	119	101	115
Age*			
18–24 years	129	92	139
25–34	120	105	123
35–44	124	125	106
45–54	101	121	108
55–64	78	98	66
>64	28	50	40†
Education*			
College graduate	170	125	123
Some college	129	113	118
High school graduate	82	102	114
No degree	47	64	40†
Occupation*			
Professional/Manager	167	135	134
Technical/Clerical/Sales	123	127	123
Precision/Craft	109	106	146†
Other employed	89	95	99
Race*			
White	107	102	104
Black	53	92	73†
Other	90	82	87†

(Continued on following page)

Demographics and Stereo Equipment Ownership* (Continued)

EXHIBIT A

Variable Percent	CD Player	Compact/Console Stereo	DAT Player
Region*			
Northeast	100	102	100
Midwest	98	100	114
South	84	98	98
West	129	101	87
Household Income*			
<$10,000	23	47	40†
$10,000–19,999	43	86	65†
$20,000–29,999	97	109	107
$30,000–39,999	100	113	102
>$40,000	144	111	127
>$60,000	155	112	100
Household Structure*			
1 person	76	88	70
2 people	99	93	101
3 or 4 people	112	107	111
5 or more people	91	105	94†
No children	93	90	96
Child < 2 years	102	114	76†
Child 2–5 years	106	101	114
Child 6–11 years	96	114	87
Child 12–17 years	110	121	112

*100 = Average ownership.
†Sample size too small for reliability.
Source: *1991 Study of Media and Markets* (New York: Simmons Market Research Bureau, 1991).

Discussion Questions

1. What type of innovation do each of these products represent?
2. Define one or more target markets based on the demographic data available in Exhibit A. What additional demographic data would you like to have?
3. Based on an innovation analysis (Exhibit 7–2), will either of these achieve rapid diffusion? Which one? Why?
4. Based on your analysis for Question 3, develop a set of diffusion-enhancement strategies for ________.
   a. Sony.
   b. Philips.
5. Interview a salesperson at each of two stores that sell these products. Determine which is most successful and why. What are the marketing strategy implications of the information you gained?

6. Interview five students who own one or the other of these products. Do they fit the description of innovator or early adopters provided in the text? What decision process did they use? What reference group influences, if any, were important? What are the marketing implications of this information?

Source: L. Therrien, ''The Sound and Fury at Sony and Philips,'' *Business Week*, June 15, 1992, p. 42; ''Philips V. Sony,'' *Economist*, November 7, 1992, p. 9; and B. Jorgensen, ''Digital Audio Format War Heats Up,'' *Electronic Business*, December 1992, pp. 68–70.

Case 2–5 Frito-Lay's Sunchip

Frito-Lay's new snack, the Sunchip, had record test-market results and produced sales in excess of $100 million in its first year. Frito-Lay spent $30 million introducing Sunchips in April 1991 and another $20 million in 1992. Sunchips are made from whole wheat, corn, other grains, and canola or sunflower oil.

Dwight Riskey, vice president of marketing at Frito-Lay explains the strategy behind Sunchips:

> The aging baby boomers were a very significant factor. We were looking for new products that would allow them to snack. But we were looking for ''better-for-you'' aspects in products and pushing against that demographic shift.

After enthusiastic response from consumers, retailers, and its own sales force during test market, Frito-Lay launched the product nationally. Initial advertising evolved around the Beatles' song, *Good Day Sunshine*, which was sung by Carly Simon in a 30-second TV commercial.

Sunchips have an unusually high repeat purchase rate once people try the product. According to Riskey:

> Our advertising focuses less against pure product sell and more on awareness. The area where we have been least successful is in trial. I attribute this to the fact that this is truly a new category and people are skeptical. My personal challenge for 1992 is to double trial rates.

Exhibit A contains demographic data relevant to the consumption of chips.

Discussion Questions

1. What type of innovation is Sunchips?
2. Analyze Sunchips, using the innovation analysis methodology of Exhibit 7–2.
3. What values might explain Sunchip's success?
4. Based on the demographic material available, what target market(s) would you select? What additional demographic data would you like to have? How would you use it?
5. How should Frito-Lay proceed in introducing Sunchips to _______?
   a. the European Community.
   d. Taiwan.
   b. Japan.
   e. Hong Kong.
   c. Mexico.
   f. Indonesia.
6. What role, if any, do you feel group communications played in the success of Sunchips?
7. What role, if any, do you feel reference group influences played in the success of Sunchips?
8. Which stage in the family life cycle is the best market for this product? Why?
9. What would you do to double the trial rates?
10. Develop a marketing strategy for Sunchips, from its national launch through its fourth year.

Source: J. Lawrence: ''The Sunchip Also Rises,'' *Advertising Age*, April 27, 1992, p. S-2.

EXHIBIT A

Demographics and Snack Use*

Variable	Pop-corn	Potato Chips	Corn Chips†	Doritos	Doritos Light	Salted Pretzels	Unsalted Pretzels
Age							
18–24 years	87	102	101	86	77	97	82
25–34	104	105	115	106	96	110	92
35–44	112	107	134	128	130	117	85
45–54	112	104	98	127	132	117	113
55–64	100	95	83	84	79	95	127
>64	77	83	51	54	69	57	110
Education							
College graduate	110	99	83	118	120	106	119
Some college	106	101	100	112	124	108	105
High school graduate	101	103	102	97	94	111	104
No degree	85	96	112	81	74	69	73
Occupation							
Professional/Manager	111	100	86	111	117	115	118
Technical/Clerical/Sales	109	103	104	108	120	120	102
Precision/Craft	101	107	104	110	72	103	89
Other employed	102	107	121	109	114	100	97
Race							
White	103	100	95	101	104	106	105
Black	86	100	132	89	68	67	76
Other	81	99	127	109	102	54	60
Region							
Northeast	84	93	63	76	50	120	158
Midwest	114	105	89	103	110	124	73
South	99	101	124	99	106	78	98
West	101	100	112	125	132	86	73
Household Income							
<$10,000	79	91	112	66	79	58	87
$10,000–19,999	90	100	104	93	79	81	100
$20,000–29,999	104	102	104	102	103	99	89
$30,000–39,999	102	100	88	97	119	106	84
>$40,000	111	102	96	117	110	124	117
>$60,000	113	104	96	127	111	131	126

(Continued on following page)

EXHIBIT A — Demographics and Snack Use* (Continued)

Variable	Pop-corn	Potato Chips	Corn Chips†	Doritos	Doritos Light	Salted Pretzels	Unsalted Pretzels
Household Structure							
1 person	79	84	55	66	64	67	89
2 people	97	97	67	81	94	89	104
3 or more people	113	109	135	121	128	122	112
5 or more people	107	112	171	152	102	125	71
No children	93	93	67	81	87	86	109
Child < 2 years	104	110	118	110	99	120	78
Child 2–5 years	112	111	133	105	105	118	80
Child 6–11 years	111	114	168	136	110	121	84
Child 12–17 years	113	112	176	151	147	128	76

*Based on principal shoppers; 100 = Average use or consumption.
†Heavy users.
Source: *1991 Study of Media and Markets*, New York, Simmons Market Research Bureau, 1991.

Case 2–6 Nintendo

Nintendo holds more than an 80 percent market share in a market with a retail sales of $5 billion projected for 1990. For its system, Nintendo expects sales of 9 million units in 1990. This means that there will be 29 million households with Nintendo Entertainment Systems (the control deck that connects to the television set), approximately one-third of all U.S. households.

To further fuel sales growth, Nintendo introduced a hand-held video game in June 1989 called Game Boy. Nintendo expects to sell 5 million units of Game Boy in 1990 (in six months in 1989, Nintendo sold 1 million units). Nintendo and its licensees expect to sell 20 million game cartridges in 1990, with a retail value to $1 billion, or one-fourth of Nintendo's total company sales.

New product expansion such as the introduction of Game Boy is only one way to grow sales. Nintendo has also sought to grow sales through expanding marketing activities. While Nintendo's core market is 6- to 17-year-olds, consumer market research showed that many adults play Nintendo games, particularly Game Boy. About 40 percent of Nintendo's Game Boy sales were to adults.

Based on this research, efforts were made to address the adult market with advertising focused on adults who were parents. In 1989, Nintendo introduced television advertisements stressing that "it's not the child introducing an adult to a child's toy, it's really positioning it as an adult way to have fun."

However, this target market misses a great many American households: young singles over 18 years of age, young married couples without children, and middle-aged singles and 18- to 49-year-old couples without children. Because 60 percent of its adult consumers are male, Nintendo decided to focus on males in these additional household life cycle categories. In

Market Segmentation of the Home Video Market

FIGURE A

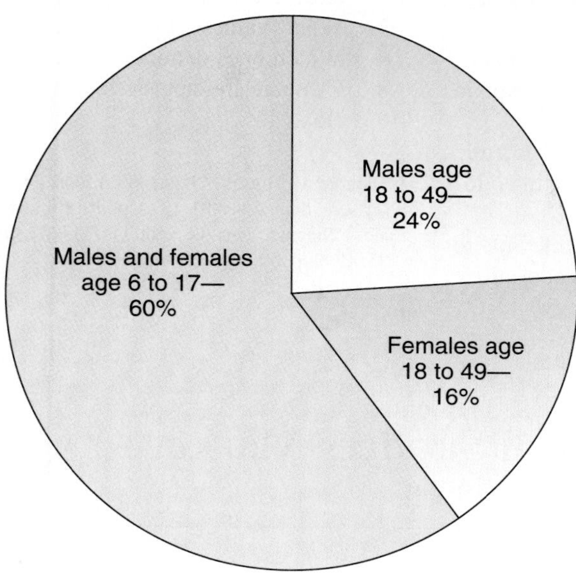

1990, Nintendo will allocate $15 million to Game Boy advertising targeted at male adults in the 18- to 49-year-old age category. Figure A summarizes the current segmentation of the market demand for Nintendo-type video products.

The adult advertising will feature the theme "Never Get Old." The ads will show adult men in a variety of professional situations where symphonic music gives way to wild guitar music and the men begin playing Game Boy. Two messages appear on the screen:

> "You don't stop playing because you are old," followed by "But you could get old if you stop playing."

The intent is to create an ad that says "It's OK for adults to play video games." To reach this adult market, Nintendo will run these ads nationally on the Fox network and in 10 spot markets during prime time, late night, and sports shows.

Advertisements targeted at the 6- to 17-year-old market will run on syndicated programs and cable television. For this market, Nintendo has created a new video game called Spot, developed by Nintendo in conjunction with 7UP. Spot is an animated soft-drink character. This joint venture will enable both companies to further extend the way they communicate to consumers.

In total, Nintendo will spend $120 million in 1990 on advertising and sales promotion, or 3 percent of the retail sales value for all Nintendo products. As shown below, Nintendo's communication strategy involves a wide range of communication channels.

- $35 million to $40 million for Nintendo Entertainment System and Game Boy.
- $10 million to advertise *Nintendo Power*, a monthly magazine published by Nintendo with a paid subscription of 1.5 million.
- $7 million to $8 million in joint promotions that will feature tie-in promotions with other companies' products.
- $40 million to $45 million in cooperative advertising with retailers, which is funded 100 percent by Nintendo.
- $17 million to $18 million on in-store merchandising.

Discussion Questions

1. How will the ad copy for adult-targeted Nintendo advertising differ from kid-targeted Nintendo advertising?

2. Should Nintendo advertise differently to females age 18 to 49 than to males age 18 to 49? Explain your position.
3. Should Nintendo consider new channels of distribution to better reach the adult market? Explain your position.
4. Is adult Nintendo a fad, or is adult use of Nintendo a sustainable market opportunity for Nintendo? Explain your position.
5. What types of group influence are relevant to games like Nintendo? How can Nintendo utilize these influences in its marketing strategy?
6. What roles support adult use of Nintendo? Which ones detract from it?
7. What values support adult use of Nintendo? Which ones detract from it?
8. Evaluate the appropriateness of the name Game Boy.

*Source: C. Horton, ''Nintendo Adopts Dual Strategy,'' *Advertising Age*, September 10, 1990, p. 40; J. Lawrence and K. Fitzgerald, ''Nintendo Hits the Spot with 7UP,'' *Advertising Age*, June 25, 1990, p. 59.

Case 2–7 Financial Services Market Opportunities

Though the financial holdings of female investors are enormous, it was not until recently that financial services companies recognized the unique needs of different female investors. Some facts were well known. The financial wealth controlled by females was in the billions of dollars and larger than that held by males. In addition to financial assets controlled throughout the life cycle, women outlive men and acquire a large quantity of stocks, bonds, mutual funds, certificates of deposit, and so on in the latter stages of the household life cycle.

However, until recently the female investor market was largely ignored and was not targeted as an important market opportunity. Consumer analysis of the female investor market uncovered a variety of differences with respect to needs, demographics, lifestyles, income, and awareness and knowledge of investment alternatives. Other differences, such as media habits, pointed out the fact that there is tremendous diversity among this group of investors. A quantitative analysis of this information uncovered the existence of three market segments, each unique in terms of needs for financial services, demographics, consumer lifestyle, awareness and knowledge of financial services, and media habits.

Each of these female investor segments represents a unique market opportunity. To design an effective marketing strategy for any or all of these segments, it is first necessary to understand the unique aspects of each female investor segment.

The Career Woman

This segment of the female investor market is the smallest but is growing rapidly. These investors are younger (30 to 40 years old), college educated, and actively pursuing a career. Their incomes are high relative to incomes of other working women and growing as they progress in their careers. This group includes single and married females, but the majority did not have children living in their households.

While their demographics are unique, equally important differences exist in their needs for financial services. Women in this segment have higher incomes and pay considerable taxes because they are single or, if married, have two sources of income. As a result, their needs focus on ways to increase their financial holdings without incurring additional tax obligations. Also, because they do not need current income, they have a greater need for long-term capital appreciation rather than current interest or dividend income.

The Single Parent

This segment is the second largest in size and also growing. These female investors are middle aged (35 to 45 years old), unmarried, but have children living at home. Their single-parent status could be the result of divorce or death of a spouse. Because these events tend to happen more often at middle age, this particular female investor is often thrust into managing money without much experience. Current income is generally under pressure and money affairs have to be carefully budgeted.

For this segment, security is first. With parental responsibility and limited income, they want to make sure their money will be there in the future. As a result, they prefer investments that offer secure growth. This investment will be a source of income later in life and/or used for their children's education. In either case these consumers do not want to risk their futures.

The Older Investor

This segment is the largest of the female market for financial services. These female investors are older (55 and up) and typically single. Unlike the "Single Parent," these female investors do not have children at home and often have more discretionary income. Also, many of these investors have considerable knowledge and experience with the many financial alternatives that exist.

A need for current income makes this segment of female investors different from the other two segments. In many instances, these women support themselves from interest and dividends on their investments. Because investments are often their sole source of income, they seek safety and minimum risk in the investments they hold. Thus, their ideal investment portfolio would include a variety of secure investments that yield good current income.

While many differences exist among the many female investors, these three female investor segments capture important differences in basic needs, demographics, and lifestyle as summarized in Figure A. Based on these differences, individualized marketing strategies could be developed for each segment. The degree to which such strategies will succeed will depend on how well each strategy satisfies the specific needs of each segment in terms of both product offerings and market communications.

Discussion Questions

1. Discuss how different demographic situations (i.e., age, income, marital status, etc.) contribute to different financial needs among female investors.
2. How might each of these segments be further segmented demographically? What would be the advantages and disadvantages of further segmentation of this market?
3. For the three segments described, prepare an ad concept for each, such that the ad copy communicates products that fit the target segments' financial needs and also matches their demographics and lifestyles. Also specify which print media you would recommend to reach each target segment.
4. How could the channels of distribution for presenting and selling financial services be designed to best meet the needs of each target segment?

Summary of Female Investor Segmentation

FIGURE A

Segment	Basic Needs	Experience	Key Demographics
Career woman	Tax avoidance, long-term growth	Limited to average	Educated, working at career, between 25 and 40
Single parent	Security, future income	None to limited	Unmarried with children, between 35 and 55
Older investor	Current income, security	Limited to extensive	Typically single, 55 and older

Case 2–8 Kellogg's Global Challenge

Kellogg Company has distribution in over 150 countries and yet is still "unknown to half the world's population," according to Arnold Langbo, Kellogg's CEO. Mr. Langbo plans to change that during the 1990s.

Kellogg is building a company-owned cereal plant in Latvia and currently has sales in Poland, Hungary, and Czechoslovakia. It has also started construction on a plant in India and has plans to enter China soon. These efforts will greatly expand non-U.S. sales, which in 1991 were 53 percent of total volume and 41 percent of total revenue. However, international expansion and the development of global brands will not be easy.

To become more international, the firm recently reorganized into four divisions: North America, Latin America, Europe, and Australasia. According to Langbo:

> The way we used to be organized, we were a U.S.-based multinational—a company with a big domestic business and, by the way, some international business. That was the way we were thinking; that's the way the organization was structured.
>
> Today, if you talk to customers in the U.K., Canada, or Australia, they think of Kellogg as being based in the U.K. or Canada or Australia. We're global in organizational structure and business but also multidomestic.
>
> We now have a number of truly global brands (Frosted Flakes and Corn Flakes, with Froot Loops and Rice Krispies close, and Frosted Mini-Wheats and Honey Nut Loops moving rapidly). There used to be slight variations in our food around the world, but now you'll recognize the product wherever you go.

Advertising for Frosted Flakes is now global and that for other brands may follow. Expanding into many markets will involve more than trying to gain share from other cereal marketers. It will require altering long-held traditions:

> In Eastern Europe it's going to be pretty slow because we're going to have to go in there and literally create the habit—much as we did in Germany 25 years ago or France 20 years ago. Cereal is a whole new breakfast concept for these people. However, they do eat breakfast in those countries and they eat fairly substantial breakfasts.
>
> In Asia, consumers are used to eating something warm, soft, and savory for breakfast—and we're going to sell them something that's cold, crisp, and sweet or bran tasting. That's quite a difference.

The challenge is made greater by the presence of aggressive competition in many developed or developing markets. Competition is particularly intense in Europe where Nestlé and General Mills formed a joint venture called Cereal Partners Worldwide. Langbo characterizes the new competitor this way:

> They are a very formidable competitor with Nestlé's distribution strength and knowledge of the European market and General Mills' technology and cereal marketing expertise.

The result of the entry of the new competitor, which spent an estimated $35 to $50 million in advertising in the top six European markets, and the response of existing firms, such as Kellogg, was an increase in the growth rate of total cereal sales as well as share erosion among the weaker brands.

Competition is strong even in some countries where consumption is low. For example, in Japan, with consumption at four bowls per year per person compared to 10 *pounds* in the United States, there are more than 100 products fighting for shelf space.

Discussion Questions

1. What type of innovation would cold cereal be to a country not accustomed to this type food?
2. Conduct an innovation analysis based on Exhibit 7–2 for cold cereal in China.

3. What values are involved in the consumption of a product such as breakfast cereal?
4. What values would support and what values would harm the chances of Kellogg succeeding with cold cereal in ______. What other factors would be important?
   a. China.
   b. Russia.
   c. Mexico.
   d. Japan.
5. What nonverbal communications factors would be important in developing an advertising campaign for a cold cereal?
6. Develop a marketing program to market one of Kellogg's cold cereals in ______.
   a. China.
   b. Russia.
   c. Mexico.
   d. Japan.

Source: J. Liesse, ''Kellogg Chief to Push Harder for Int'l Growth,'' *Advertising Age*, August 24, 1992, p. 4.

Folgers and the Hispanic Market Case 2–9

Hispanics are quality conscious as opposed to price conscious when selecting a store. This can be attributed to the importance they place on pleasing and providing what is best for their families. Despite their limited budgets, many feel that purchasing a lower-priced item may cost them more in the end if their families are not satisfied with its performance.*

Folgers recently began a national program to increase its sales to the Hispanic market. A major part of this effort is its sponsorship of ''Primera Hora,'' the first national morning news and talk show on Hispanic television (on the Telemundo network). Folgers' Hispanic ad theme, ''*Despeirtan lo mejor en ti*'' (Wake up the best in you) ties in with the morning show. It is also repeated on ''shelf-talkers'' in Hispanic area supermarkets (see Exhibit A).

Exhibit B provides information on Hispanic shopping patterns relevant to coffee.

Folgers Hispanic Shelf-Talker

EXHIBIT A

EXHIBIT B Hispanic Shopping Patterns Relevant to Coffee Consumption

1. Frequency of shopping for groceries:
   At least once a week = 57%
   Once every two weeks = 27%
   Less frequently = 13%
   Mean number of times per month = 3.1
2. Most important factor in selecting a store:
   Quality = 72%
   Price = 28%
3. Repeat purchasing behavior:
   Generally purchase the same brand = 64
   Purchase whatever brand is on sale = 36
4. When in a store, I often buy an item on the spur of the moment.
   Strongly agree/Agree = 40%
   Strongly disagree/Disagree = 35%
5. When I go to the supermarket, I shop based on a budget.
   Strongly agree/Agree = 69%
   Strongly disagree/Disagree = 16%
6. I definitely/probably would make a purchase based on:
   Buy 1—Get 1 free = 57%
   Cents-off coupon = 46%
   In-store samples = 42%
   Rebates = 37%
   Sweepstakes = 25%
   Used cents-off coupon in past 30 days = 36%
   Language of coupons Used:
      Spanish = 52%
      English = 15%
      Both = 33%
   Source of coupons:
      Newspaper = 67%
      Mail = 62%
      In-store = 12%
7. Purchased coffee in past month:
   Regular = 73%
   Decaffeinated = 20%

*Source: *The 1993 MSR Minority Market Report* (Coral Gables, Fla.: Market Segment Research, Inc., 1993).

Discussion Questions

1. Which of the Hispanic market segments described in Chapter 4 would be the best target market(s) for Folgers?
2. Would it make more sense to treat Hispanics as several nationality groups or as a single Hispanic group (perhaps with demographic submarkets)? Why?
3. Develop a complete marketing strategy for Folgers to use to gain sales among Hispanic consumers.

*Source: *The 1993 MSR Minority Market Report* (Coral Gables, Fla.: Market Segment Research, Inc., 1993).

A.1. Steak Sauce and the African-American Market

Case 2–10

A.1. Steak Sauce has a flavor that complements many of the dishes that are popular with African-American cooks.

Management is interested in expanding the sales of A.1. Steak Sauce to this consumer group for several reasons. First, the size of this group is growing faster than the general population. Food preferences have been shifting away from steaks and other red meats toward lighter meals with fewer sauces. While this trend is affecting all segments, the traditional food preferences of many African-American consumers still involve red meats and sauces.

Exhibit A contains a recent ad for A.1. Steak Sauce aimed at African-American consumers. Exhibit B contains information relevant to the purchase of A.1. by African-Americans. Exhibit C provides information on the general demographics of steak sauce users.

Discussion Questions

1. Which of the African-American segments described in Chapter 4 would be the best target market(s) for A.1. Steak Sauce?
2. Does it make sense to treat African-Americans as a separate segment for this product? Why?
3. Develop a complete marketing strategy for A.1. Steak Sauce to use to gain sales among African-American consumers. What additional data would you like to have to develop your strategy?
4. Based on the data in Exhibit C, what would be the best target markets for A.1. Steak Sauce among the general population? Why?

An A.1. Steak Sauce Ad Targeted at African-American Consumers

EXHIBIT A

EXHIBIT B African-American Shopping Patterns Relevant to A.1. Steak Sauce*

1. Frequency of shopping for groceries:
   At least once a week = 35%
   Once every two weeks = 30%
   Less frequently = 31%
   Mean number of times per month = 2.4
2. Most important factor in selecting a store:
   Quality = 76%
   Price = 24%
3. Repeat purchasing behavior:
   Generally purchase the same brand = 57%
   Purchase whatever brand is on sale = 43%
4. When in a store, I often buy an item on the spur of the moment.
   Strongly agree/Agree = 47%
   Strongly disagree/Disagree = 33%
5. When I go to the supermarket, I shop based on a budget.
   Strongly agree/Agree = 64%
   Strongly disagree/Disagree = 21%
6. I definitely/probably would make a purchase based on
   Buy 1—Get 1 free = 58%
   Cents-off coupon = 54%
   In-store samples = 48%
   Rebates = 34%
   Sweepstakes = 29%
   Used cents-off coupon in past 30 days = 43%
   Source of coupons:
      Newspaper = 79%
      Mail = 42%
      In-store = 17%
7. I prefer lighter foods to heavy meals.
   Strongly agree/Agree = 53%
   Strongly disagree/Disagree = 27%
8. Major leisure activities:
   Watching TV = 66%
   Going shopping = 50%
   Reading = 48%
   Going to parties = 39%
   Cooking for pleasure = 37%
   Hanging out with friends = 36%
   Eating out at restaurants = 31%

*Source: *The 1993 MSR Minority Market Report* (Coral Gables, Fla.: Market Segment Research, Inc., 1993).

EXHIBIT C

Demographics and Steak Sauce Use*

Variable	All Users	Heavy Users	A.1. Users	Heinz 57 Users
Age				
18–24 years	92	95	91	76
25–34	116	118	107	112
35–44	109	103	109	106
45–54	110	96	123	115
55–64	94	96	97	93
>64	67	80	68	81
Education				
College graduate	101	90	96	102
Some college	103	77	106	89
High school graduate	108	104	108	103
No degree	82	120	84	102
Occupation				
Professional/Manager	102	90	100	102
Technical/Clerical/Sales	111	94	111	106
Precision/Craft	123	108	124	133
Other employed	111	114	116	112
Race				
White	101	96	101	99
Black	101	130	100	107
Other	82	104	75	93
Region				
Northeast	79	73	81	58
Midwest	110	115	111	124
South	110	118	105	124
West	93	78	97	76
Household Income				
<$10,000	71	118	70	86
$10,000–19,999	95	91	94	109
$20,000–29,999	100	90	104	87
$30,000–39,999	113	106	108	112
>$40,000	109	100	110	102
>$60,000	108	88	105	97

(Continued on following page)

EXHIBIT C Demographics and Steak Sauce Use* (Continued)

Variable	All Users	Heavy Users	A.1. Users	Heinz 57 Users
Household Structure				
1 person	71	84	66	70
2 people	98	98	101	102
3 or more people	116	89	115	115
5 or more people	110	168	114	104
No children	90	87	90	95
Child < 2 years	113	122	108	86
Child 2–5 years	120	128	114	106
Child 6–11 years	120	127	113	123
Child 12–17 years	113	136	117	115

*Based on principal shoppers; 100 = Average use or consumption.

Source: *1991 Study of Media and Markets* (New York, Simmons Market Research Bureau, 1991).

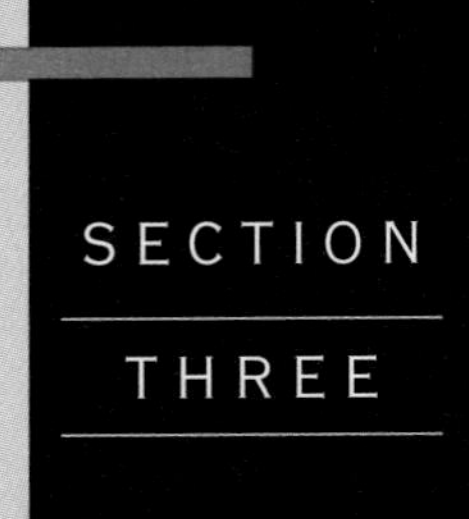

SECTION THREE

INTERNAL INFLUENCES

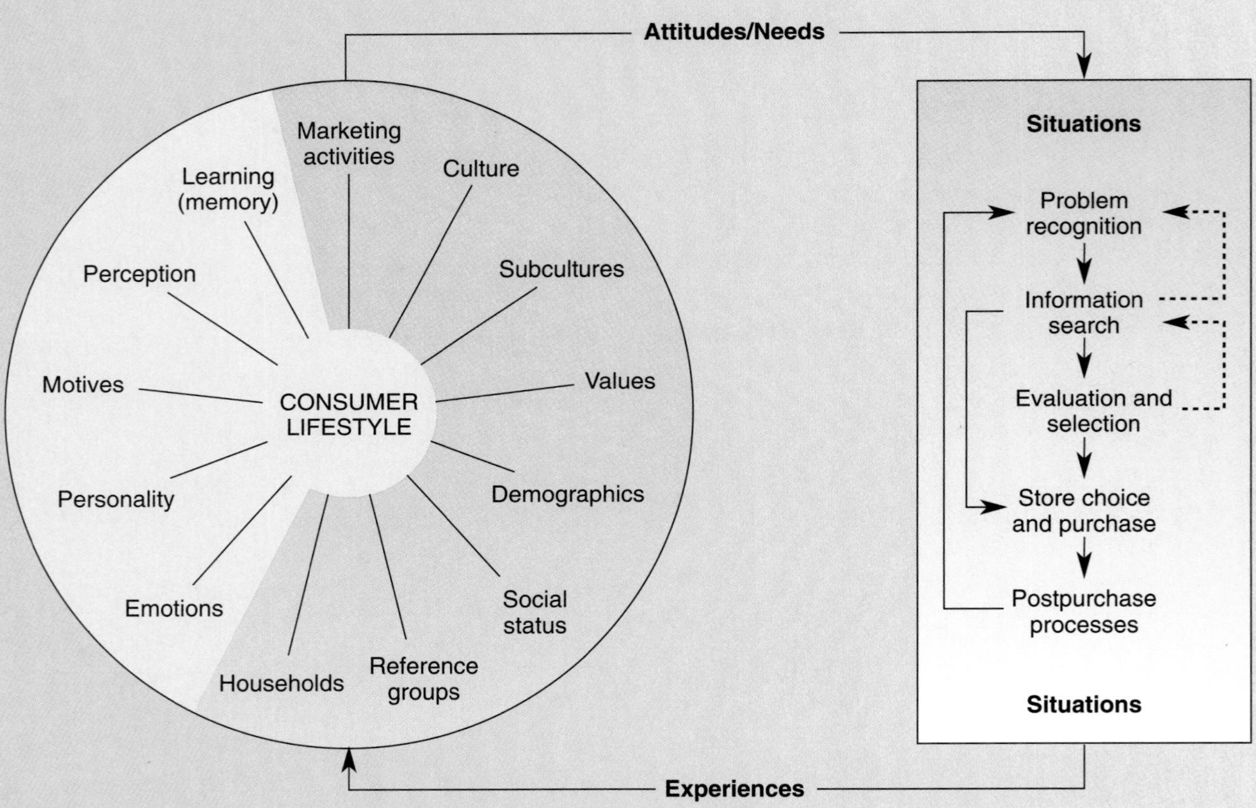

Attitudes/Needs

Marketing activities
Culture
Subcultures
Values
Demographics
Social status
Reference groups
Households
Emotions
Personality
Motives
Perception
Learning (memory)

CONSUMER LIFESTYLE

Situations

Problem recognition
Information search
Evaluation and selection
Store choice and purchase
Postpurchase processes

Situations

Experiences

The shaded area of our model shown at left is the focal point for this section of the text. That is, our attention now shifts from group influence to the processes by which individuals react to group influences, environmental changes, and marketing efforts.

The perception and processing of information for consumer decision making is the subject of Chapter 9. Then the learning process necessary for consumer behavior is discussed in Chapter 10. Next we examine motivation, personality, emotion, and self-concept in Chapter 11. Consumer lifestyle is the topic of Chapter 12. All of the previous topics tie together to influence a consumer's actual and desired lifestyle. Attitudes are the focus of Chapter 13, and we look at them as representing our basic orientations about products and marketing activities. Attitudes are brought out at this stage in the text because they are the actual manifestations of our learning about products and are the basic concept that marketers can measure and use to predict purchase tendencies. They are relatively stable clusters of knowledge, feelings, and behavioral orientations that we bring to specific purchase situations.

CHAPTER

9

PERCEPTION

Marketers often use attractive models to attract attention to their advertisements. This is particularly true when the advertisement is directed toward males. How effective is this tactic?

An eye-tracking device is a combination of computer and video technology that allows one to record eye movements in relation to a stimulus such as a package or a commercial. The respondent sits in a chair at a table and reads a magazine, watches television commercials, or observes slides of print advertisements, billboards, shelf facings, point-of-purchase displays, and so forth. Respondents control how long they view each scene. The eye-tracking device sends an unnoticeable beam of filtered light which is reflected off the respondent's eyes. This reflected beam represents the focal point and can be superimposed on whatever is being viewed. This allows the researcher to determine how long an ad or other marketing stimulus is viewed, the sequence in which it was examined, which elements were examined, and how much time was devoted to looking at each element.

RCA used an attractive model in a television ad for their Colortrack television sets. The model wore a conservative dress. Eye tracking revealed that the audience focused substantial attention on the product. Seventy-two hours later, brand name recall was 36 percent. In contrast, a similar commercial used an attractive female in a revealing dress. Eye tracking showed that the ad attracted considerable attention but most of it was focused on the attractive model. Seventy-hours later, brand name recall was only 9 percent![1]

Marketers do not want their target audience to look only at the models in their ads. They generally want to communicate something about their product as well. However, since there are many more commercials than consumers can possibly look at, marketers often use attractive models, celebrities, humor, or other factors unrelated to the product to attract the target market's interest. The opening example illustrates that if not well done these factors attract attention only to themselves, not to the advertising message.

A sound knowledge of perception is essential to avoid this and other problems encountered when communicating with various target audiences. *Perception is the critical activity that links the individual consumer to group, situation, and marketer influences.*

This chapter discusses (1) the nature of perception, (2) exposure, (3) attention, (4) interpretation, and (5) marketing applications of the perception process. The next chapter focuses on two of the outcomes of this process: learning and memory.

THE NATURE OF PERCEPTION

Information processing is *a series of activities by which stimuli are perceived, transformed into information, and stored.*

Figure 9–1 illustrates a useful information-processing model[2] having four major steps or stages: exposure, attention, interpretation, and memory. The first three of these constitute the **perception process**.

Exposure occurs when a stimulus such as a billboard comes within range of a person's sensory receptor nerves—vision for example. *Attention* occurs when the receptor nerves

FIGURE 9–1 Information Processing for Consumer Decision Making

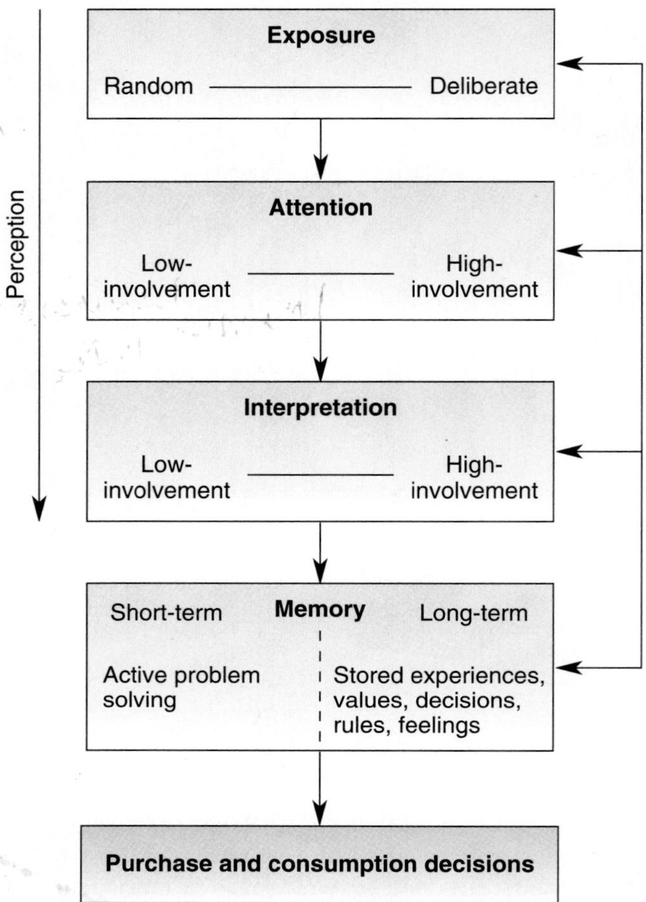

pass the sensations on to the brain for processing. *Interpretation* is the assignment of meaning to the received sensations. *Memory* is the short-term use of the meaning for immediate decision making or the longer-term retention of the meaning.

Figure 9–1 and the above discussion suggest a linear flow from exposure to memory. However, these processes occur virtually simultaneously and are clearly interactive. That is, our memory influences the information we are exposed to, attend to, and the interpretations we assign. At the same time, memory itself is being shaped by the information it is receiving.

Both perception and memory are extremely selective. Of the massive amount of information available, an individual can be exposed to only a limited amount. Of the information to which the individual is exposed, only a relatively small percentage is attended to and passed on to the central processing part of the brain for interpretation.

Much of the interpreted information will not be available to active memory when the individual needs to make a purchase decision. This is illustrated in Figure 9–2. Clearly, the marketing manager faces a challenging task when communicating with consumers.

Information Processing Is Selective

FIGURE 9–2

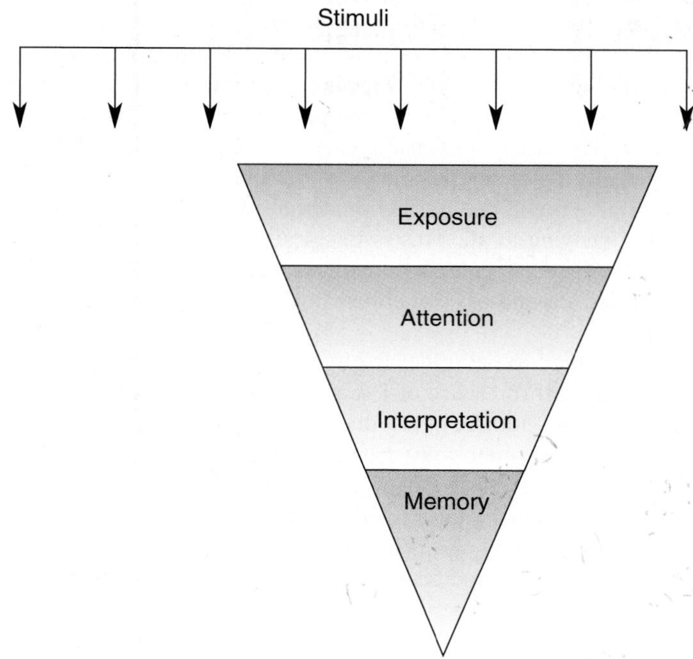

EXPOSURE

Exposure occurs *when a stimulus comes within range of our sensory receptor nerves.* For an individual to be exposed to a stimulus requires only that the stimulus be placed within the person's relevant environment. The individual need not receive the stimulus for exposure to have occurred.

As Figure 9–2 shows, an individual is generally exposed to no more than a small fraction of the available stimuli. One normally watches only one television station at a time, reads one magazine, newspaper, or book at a time, and so forth. What determines which specific stimulus an individual will be exposed to? Is it a random process or purposeful?

Why are you reading this text? Clearly you are doing so for a reason. Most of the stimuli to which an individual is exposed are "self-selected." That is, we deliberately seek out exposure to certain stimuli and avoid others.

What influences us as to which types of stimuli we will seek out? Generally, we seek *information that we think will help us achieve our goals.* These goals may be immediate or long range. Immediate goals could involve seeking stimuli such as a television program for amusement, an advertisement to assist in a purchase decision, or a compliment to enhance our self-concept. Long-range goals might involve studying this text in hopes of passing the next exam, obtaining a degree, becoming a better marketing manager, or all three. An individual's goals and the types of information needed to achieve those goals are a function of the individual's existing and desired lifestyle and such short-term motives as hunger or curiosity.

Of course, we are also exposed to a large number of stimuli on a more or less random basis during our daily activities. While driving, we may hear commercials, see billboards and display ads, and so on, that we did not purposefully seek out.

The impact of the active, self-selecting nature of exposure can be seen in the zipping and zapping of television commercials. **Zipping** occurs when one fast-forwards through a commercial on a prerecorded program. **Zapping** involves switching channels when a commercial appears. The nearly universal presence of remote controls (over 70 percent of all households) makes zipping and zapping very simple.

One study of zipping found that most commercials were zipped and most of these were zipped without any viewing at all. This is important, as it means that the advertiser has only limited ability to reduce zipping by creative advertising.[3] However, there is evidence that moderately unique ads and ads that arouse positive feelings are less subject to zipping than are other ads.[4]

Zapping has been found to be influenced by the same ad characteristics as zipping. In addition, the situation itself (presence of a remote control, a VCR time shifter, cable TV, and the amount of clutter—number of ads during a time period) and the type of household (multiple-person; higher income; with males present; with children under 18) increase zapping.[5]

Avoidance of commercials is not limited to television. A recent study found that automobile drivers avoided about half of the commercials broadcast by switching stations.[6] Newspaper readers now read only about half the daily paper compared to reading almost two-thirds 10 years ago.[7]

Of course, consumers not only avoid commercials, they also actively seek them out. Many viewers look forward to the commercials developed for the Super Bowl. More impressive is the positive response consumers have had to **infomercials**—program-length commercials (30 minutes), often with an 800 number to order the product or request additional written information. As Table 9–1 indicates, infomercials, which viewers generally must seek out, are having an impact. They have been used recently by such firms as Volvo, Ford, General Motors, Club Med, Eastman Kodak, Walt Disney World, Corning, GTE, and Bell Atlantic.

ATTENTION

Attention occurs when *the stimulus activates one or more sensory receptor nerves, and the resulting sensations go to the brain for processing*. We are constantly exposed to thousands of times more stimuli than we can process. The average supermarket has 18,000 individual items. It would take hours to attend to each of them. Therefore, we have to be selective in attending to marketing as well as to other messages.

This selectivity has major implications for marketing managers and others concerned with communicating with consumers. For example, a Federal Trade Commission staff report indicates that fewer than 3 percent of those reading cigarette ads ever notice the health warning.[8] Less than half of the direct-mail ads received are read.[9] A study conducted before television remote controls were in widespread use found that during the average prime-time commercial break, only 62 percent of the audience remains in the room and only one-third of those (22 percent of the total audience) watch the screen through the commercial.[10] As the following story illustrates, anyone wishing to communicate effectively with consumers must understand how to obtain attention after obtaining exposure.

> The Federal Crop Insurance Corporation (FCIC) spent $13.5 million over a four-year period on an advertising campaign to increase awareness and

Characteristics of Infomercial Users

TABLE 9-1

	Viewed in Past Year	Ever Purchased from Using 800 Number	Ever Purchased in Store Due to Infomercial
Gender			
Male	57%	8%	20%
Female	54	9	19
Age			
18–24	70	4	19
25–34	63	9	19
35–49	58	12	20
50–64	55	10	26
65+	33	3	13
Income			
<$15,000	53	5	23
$15–20,000	52	11	24
$20–30,000	62	8	21
$30–40,000	63	9	25
$40,000+	60	11	16
Region			
Northeast	56	7	24
North Central	52	9	14
South	57	8	21
West	55	10	17
Total	55	8	19

Source: K. Haley, ''The Infomercial Begins a New Era,'' *Advertising Age*, January 25, 1993, p. M-3.

knowledge among farmers of the federal crop insurance program. The campaign included ''direct mailings to millions of producers of crops covered by the farmers' disaster program and to FCIC policyholders; national and local news releases; feature stories in national magazines, including most state publications; a radio campaign; publication of several brochures; and formal training programs for independent agents, insurance company officials, and FCIC employees.''

However, ''farmers ended up knowing no more about this program after the ad campaign than they did before.'' J. W. Ellis, director of public affairs for the FCIC, described the problem with the program thusly: ''It was very good and very effective advertising. The trouble is that we had a hard time getting people to read it.''[11]

What determines or influences attention? At this moment you are attending to these words. If you shift your concentration to your feet, you will most likely become aware of the pressure being exerted by your shoes. A second shift in concentration to sounds will probably produce awareness of a number of background noises. These stimuli are available all the time but are not processed until a deliberate effort is made to do so. However, no matter how hard you are concentrating on this text, a loud scream or a sudden hand on your shoulder would probably get your attention. Of course, attention always occurs within the context of a situation. The *same individual* may devote different levels of attention to the *same stimulus* in *different situations.* Attention, therefore, is determined by three factors—the *stimulus*, the *individual*, and the *situation.*

Stimulus Factors

Stimulus factors are physical characteristics of the stimulus itself. A number of stimulus characteristics tend to attract our attention independently of our individual characteristics.

Size and Intensity The *size* of the stimulus influences the probability of paying attention. Larger stimuli are more likely to be noticed than smaller ones. Thus, a full-page advertisement is more likely to be noticed than a half-page advertisement. Figure 9–3 indicates the relative attention-attracting ability of various sizes of magazine ads. Another analysis of 86,000 ads found the following average number of inquiries for additional information in relation to ad size:[12]

Size	Number of Responses
Spread	107
1 page	76
⅔ page	68
½ page	56
⅓ page	47

Insertion frequency, the number of times the same ad appears in the same issue of a magazine, has an impact similar to ad size. Multiple insertions were found to increase recall by 20 percent in one study and by 200 percent in another.[13] The *intensity* (e.g., loudness, brightness) of a stimulus operates in much the same manner.

Color and Movement Both *color* and *movement* serve to attract attention with brightly colored and moving items being more noticeable. A brightly colored package is more apt to receive attention than a dull package. A study on the impact of color in newspaper advertising concluded that "median sales gains (on reduced-price items) of approximately 41 percent may be generated by the addition of one color to black-and-white in retail newspaper advertising."[14] Figure 9–4 shows the relative attention-attracting ability of black-and-white and of four-color magazine ads of different sizes. However, the impact of contrast can reverse this. That is, if all the ads in a magazine are in color, a black-and-white ad may attract substantial attention. Managerial Application 9–1 shows the impact of color on an ad for Peugeot.

Position *Position* refers to the placement of an object in a person's visual field. Objects placed near the center of the visual field are more likely to be noticed than those near the edge of the field. This is a primary reason why consumer goods manufacturers compete

FIGURE 9–3

The Impact of Size on Advertising Readership*

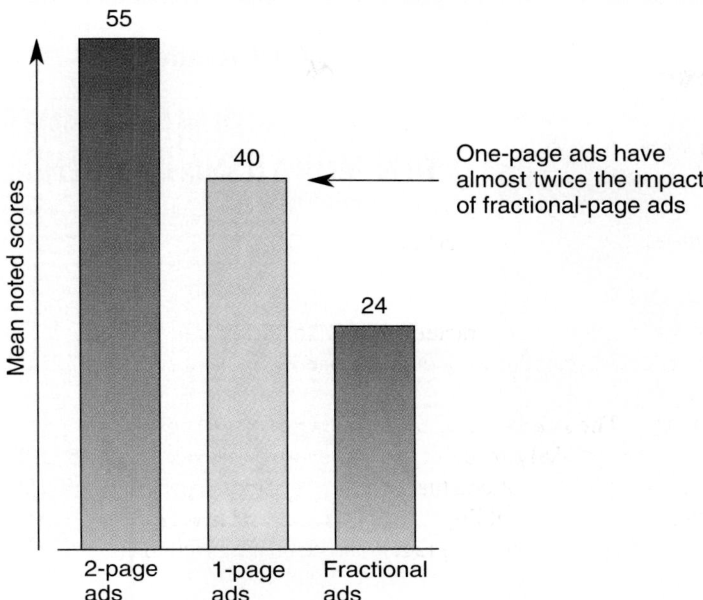

*Based on an analysis of 85,000 ads.
Source: *Cahners Advertising Research Report* 110.1B (Boston: Cahners Publishing, undated).

FIGURE 9–4

Color and Size Impact on Attention

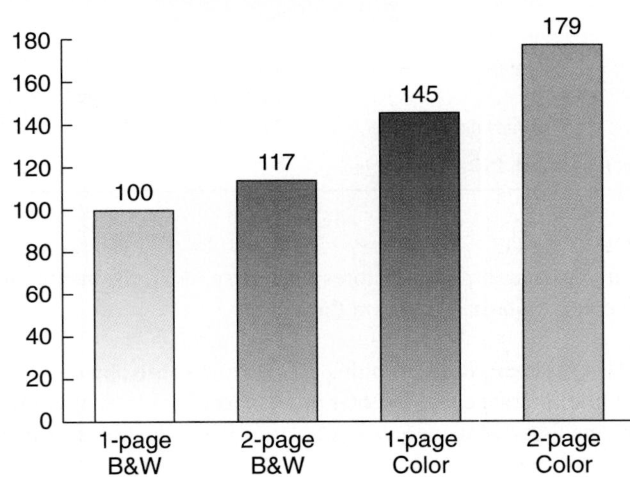

*Readership of a 1-page black-and-white ad was set at 100.
Source: ''How Important Is Color to an Ad?'' *Starch Tested Copy*, February 1989, p. 1.

MANAGERIAL APPLICATION

9–1

The Impact of Color on Ad Readership

PRESENTING THE PEUGEOT 180HP TURBO S.

The legendary BMW 325. By many car enthusiasts it's regarded as the most exhilarating performance sedan you can drive today.

But were you to spend a few minutes on a test track behind the wheel of the new Peugeot Turbo S, you might well be convinced that the legend is riding on its reputation.

With a fully-integrated, turbo-charged engine that develops 180 hp and 205 lbs./ft. of torque, the Peugeot Turbo S would rocket you from a standing start to a speed of 60 mph in a heart-pounding 7.9 seconds. Pinning you to your infinitely-adjustable, orthopedically-designed bucket seat in the process. The less muscular 121 hp 325 would require a full 10 seconds to accomplish the same task.

Next, the Turbo S would whisk you through the quarter mile in just 16.3 seconds while the 325 would need more than another second to get you across the finish line.

Of course a car that puts this kind of power at your disposal (even the sound system features 12 speakers and 200 watts of power) would be irresponsible unless it were designed to give you complete control over it. That's why the Peugeot Turbo S is equipped with fully independent suspension, precise electronically controlled, variable-assist power steering and, of course, computerized ABS braking.

The 505 Turbo S offers you a 5-year/50,000-mile power-train limited warranty and arguably the best roadside assistance plan available: AAA.* So why not call 1-800-447-2882 for the name of the Peugeot dealer nearest you, and arrange for a test drive. And if you emerge from it a little too excited, you know what to do.

IT'S TIME EUROPEAN PERFORMANCE SEDANS WERE GIVEN A LESSON IN REFINEMENT.

THE PEUGEOT 505 STX V6.

While many European performance sedans are clearly models of engineering excellence, they still have a tendency to be a little rough around the edges. For their makers' inspection, we respectfully submit the Peugeot 505 STX V-6 2.8i.

A POWERFUL V-6 ENGINE AS REFINED AS THE REST OF THE CAR.

While other European performance sedans are busy getting the most out of their in-line four and occasional six-cylinder engines, the 505 STX is debuting a more refined all-alloy, twin overhead cam, 145 hp V-6. Its uncommonly high level of torque at low revs provides a wonderfully spirited feeling.

A SUSPENSION THAT WILL SHOCK MANY PERFORMANCE SEDAN MAKERS.

To say the 505 STX is roadworthy is an understatement. It features fully-independent suspension, variable power-assisted rack-and-pinion steering, and front-ventilated disc brakes enhanced by a computerized anti-lock system.

Yet despite its superb handling characteristics, the 505 STX doesn't ask you to endure the hard ride great handling cars normally have. Because it also features unique shock absorbers that have twice as many valves as ordinary shocks. And because they are designed, built and patented by Peugeot, no other performance sedan can have the 505 STX's refined road manners ("Perhaps the nicest all-around ride in the automotive world."– *Motor Trend*).

A LEVEL OF CIVILITY THAT PUTS MOST LUXURY SEDANS TO SHAME.

Inside the 505 STX, amenities abound. Everything anyone could want is here including a new six-speaker Alpine-designed stereo cassette with anti-theft device and central locking with infra-red remote control. The orthopedically-designed seats that have helped earn Peugeot the distinction of being one of the most comfortable of all European sedans are enveloped in a sumptuous hand-fitted leather. (Speaking of comfort, we should note that the 505 STX is priced at a comparatively low $23,750.*)

ALL THE SOLIDITY OF A BOXY EUROPEAN SEDAN. WITHOUT THE BOX.

At Peugeot, we believe a car should be able to have the durability of a tank, without having to look like one. So in the 505 STX, solid unibody construction is incorporated into a body whose fluid lines were created by Pininfarina, legendary designer of the Ferrari 328 GTS.

THE ONLY ROADSIDE ASSISTANCE PROGRAM RATED AAA.

Only Peugeot offers you the comfort of AAA** service and protection. In the rare event of trouble arising on the road, you simply call AAA and help will be on the way from one of 15,000 locations.

To learn just how refined the 505 STX really is, call your local Peugeot dealer who will arrange to give you the ultimate lesson in refinement. A test drive. (He'll also be glad to give you information about our new convenient leasing program.)

For additional literature and the name of your nearest Peugeot dealer, call 800-447-2882.

PEUGEOT 505
NOTHING ELSE FEELS LIKE IT.

Noted	59%	Noted	24%
Associated	52%	Associated	24%
Read most	13%	Read most	7%

fiercely for eye-level space in grocery stores. Likewise, advertisements on the right-hand page receive more attention than those on the left.

Isolation *Isolation* is separating a stimulus object from other objects. The use of "white space" (placing a brief message in the center of an otherwise blank or white advertisement) is based on this principle. Managerial Application 9–2 illustrates effective use of this principle.

Format *Format* refers to the manner in which the message is presented. In general, simple, straightforward presentations receive more attention than complex presentations. Elements in the message that increase the effort required to process the message tend to decrease attention. Advertisements that lack a clear visual point of reference or have inappropriate movement (too fast, slow, or "jumpy") increase the processing effort and

MANAGERIAL APPLICATION 9–2

Effective Use of Isolation

decrease attention. Likewise, audio messages that are difficult to understand due to foreign accents, inadequate volume, deliberate distortions (computer voices), loud background noises, and so forth also reduce attention.[15] However, format interacts strongly with individual characteristics. What some individuals find to be complex, others find interesting. Format, like the other stimulus elements, must be developed with a specific target market in mind.

Compressed Messages Initial research indicated that speeding up a message may increase attention. Such messages are termed *compressed messages.* However, recent research suggests a more complex pattern. In general, we can say that compressed commercials do not distract from attention and may increase attention. However, attention level will vary with the type of message, the product, and the nature of the audience. The interpretation assigned the content of a compressed message will also vary and is not always favorable.[16]

Information Quantity A final stimulus factor, information quantity, relates more to the total stimulus field than to any particular item in that field. Although there is substantial variation among individuals, all consumers have limited capacities to process information. **Information overload** *occurs when consumers are confronted with so much information that they cannot or will not attend to all of it.* Instead, they become frustrated and either postpone or give up the decision, make a random choice, or utilize a suboptimal portion of the total information available.

There are no general rules or guidelines concerning how much information consumers can or will use. Marketers, the federal government, and various consumer groups want product labels, packages, and advertisements to provide *sufficient* information to allow for an informed decision. Marketers must determine the information needs of their target markets and provide the information those consumers desire. In general, the most important information should be presented first and it should be highlighted or otherwise stand out from the main part of the text. More detailed and less important data can be provided in brochures, videotapes, and infomercials that interested consumers can seek out. The regulatory implications of information overload are discussed in Chapter 21.

Individual Factors

Individual factors are characteristics of the individual. *Interest* or *need* seems to be the primary individual characteristic that influences attention. Interest is a reflection of overall lifestyle as well as a result of long-term goals and plans (e.g., becoming a sales manager) and short-term needs (e.g., hunger). Short-term goals and plans are, of course, heavily influenced by the situation. In addition, individuals differ in their *ability* to attend to information.[17]

Individuals seek out (exposure) and examine (attend to) information relevant to their current needs. For example, an individual contemplating a vacation is likely to attend to vacation-related advertisements. Individuals attending to a specialized medium such as *Runners World* or *Business Week* are particularly receptive to advertisements for related products. Parents with young children are more likely to notice and read warning labels on products such as food supplements than are individuals without young children.[18]

Situational Factors

Situational factors include stimuli in the environment other than the focal stimulus (i.e., the ad or package) and/or temporary characteristics of the individual that are induced by the environment, such as time pressures or a very crowded store.

Obviously, individuals in a hurry are less likely to attend to available stimuli than are those with extra time (if you have ever been on a long flight without a book, you may recall reading even the ads in the airline magazine). Individuals in an unpleasant environment—such as an overcrowded store or a store that is too noisy, too warm, or too cold—will not attend to many of the available stimuli as they attempt to minimize their time in such an environment.

Program Involvement Print, radio, and television ads occur in the context of a program, magazine, or newspaper. In general, the audience is attending to the medium because of the program or editorial content, not the advertisement. In fact, as we saw earlier many individuals actively avoid commercials by zapping them. Does the nature of the program or editorial content in which an ad appears influence the response that the ad will receive? The answer to this question is clearly *yes*. Table 9–2 shows that a high level of program involvement greatly increases both the viewership and the impact of television commercials.[19] Figure 9–5 makes the same point for magazines.

Contrast *Contrast* refers to our tendency to attend more closely to stimuli that contrast with their background than to stimuli that blend with it.[20] Contrast has been found to be a primary component of award-winning headlines.[21] The headline, colors, and design of the ad in Managerial Application 9–3 on page 248 contrast with expectations and will cause many to attend to the ad.

Over time we adjust to the level and type of stimuli to which we are accustomed. Thus, an advertisement that stands out when new will eventually lose its contrast effect. There is a body of knowledge called **adaptation level theory** that deals with this phenomenon.

TABLE 9-2

Television Program Involvement and Advertising Effectiveness

	Program Involvement		
	Low	Medium	High
Unaided recall	18.4%	21.0%	22.2%
Aided recall	34.0	48.0	54.0
Copy point credibility	24.0	37.0	41.0
Purchase interest	13.2	15.7	17.9
Pre/Post behavioral change	6.4	12.6	14.4

Source: Based on work done at Yankelovich Clancy Shulman as reported by K. J. Clancy, "CPMs Must Bow to 'Involvement Measurement,' " *Advertising Age*, January 20, 1992, p. 7.

FIGURE 9-5

Involvement with a Magazine and Advertising Effectiveness

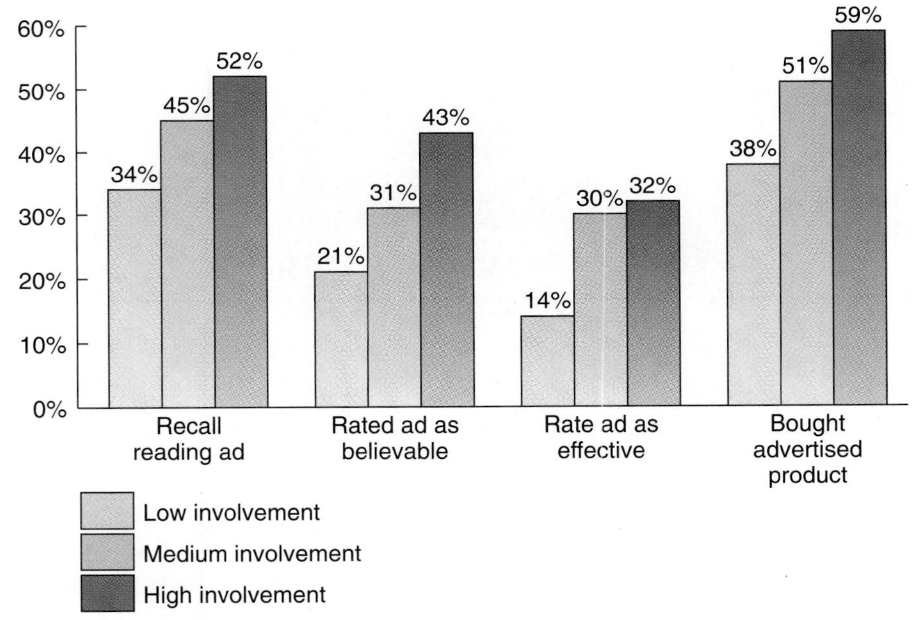

Source: *Cahners Advertising Research Report 120.1* and *120.12* (Boston: Cahners Publishing Co.).

Adaptation level theory is advanced as a major explanation for a decline in the impact of television advertising. In 1965, 18 percent of television viewers could correctly recall the brand in the last commercial aired; that figure dropped to 7 percent by the 1980s. Viewers have adapted to the presence of television and increasingly use it as "background" while doing other things.[22] The impact of adaptation on a firm's advertising can be seen in the following:

MANAGERIAL APPLICATION

9-3

Ads that Contrast with Expectations Often Capture Attention

For almost a quarter of a century, Culligan, a water treatment company, had run the same advertising campaign. It featured a ''shrewish housewife screeching, 'Hey, Culligan man!' when she experienced water problems. During the 1960s, the woman's extremely shrill voice was very effective in attracting attention. However, by the 1980s some customers began asking, ''What happened to the Culligan man?'' Research indicated that company name recognition had dropped from 64 percent in the late 1960s to 34 percent in the mid-1980s. Yet, the company was doing more advertising than ever!

Consumers had apparently adapted to the shrill tactics of the advertisement and no longer attended to it.[23]

Nonfocused Attention

Thus far, we have been discussing a fairly high-involvement attention process in which the consumer focuses attention on some aspect of the environment due to stimulus, individual, or situational factors. However, stimuli may be attended to without deliberate or conscious focusing of attention.

Hemispheric Lateralization *Hemispheric lateralization* is a term applied to activities that take place on each side of the brain. The left side of the brain is primarily responsible for verbal information, symbolic representation, sequential analysis, and the ability to be conscious and report what is happening. It controls those activities we typically call rational thought. The right side of the brain deals with pictorial, geometric, timeless, and nonverbal information without the individual being able to verbally report it. It works with images and impressions.

The left brain needs fairly frequent rest. However, the right brain can easily scan large amounts of information over an extended time period. This had led Krugman to suggest that "it is the right brain's picture-taking ability that permits the rapid screening of the environment—to select what it is the left brain should focus on."[24]

While it is a difficult area to research, the evidence indicates that there is some validity to this theory. This indicates that advertising, particularly advertising repeated over time, will have substantial effects that traditional measures of advertising effectiveness cannot detect. The nature of these effects is discussed in more detail in the next chapter. At this point, we need to stress that applied research on this topic is just beginning and much remains to be learned.[25]

Subliminal Stimuli A message presented so fast or so softly or so masked by other messages that one is not aware of "seeing" or "hearing" it is called a *subliminal message*. Subliminal stimuli have been the focus of intense study as well as public concern.

Public interest in masked subliminal stimuli has been enhanced by two books.[26] The author "documents" numerous advertisements which, once you are told where to look and what to look for, appear to continue the word *sex* in ice cubes, phalli in mixed drinks, and nude bodies in the shadows. Most, if not all, of these symbols are the chance result of preparing thousands of print ads each year (a diligent search could no doubt produce large numbers of religious symbols, animals, or whatever). Such masked symbols (deliberate or accidental) do not appear to affect standard measures of advertising effectiveness or influence consumption behavior.[27] Research on messages presented too rapidly to elicit awareness indicates that such messages have little or no effect.

Thus, though the general public is concerned about subliminal messages,[28] such messages do not appear to present a threat to the general public nor do they offer a potentially effective communications device.[29]

INTERPRETATION

Interpretation is *the assignment of meaning to sensations.* It is a function of the Gestalt or pattern formed by the characteristics of the stimulus, the individual, and the situation, as illustrated in Figure 9–6. Note that interpretation involves both a *cognitive* or factual component and an *affective* or emotional response.

Cognitive interpretation is a process whereby stimuli are placed into existing categories of meaning.[30] This is an interactive process. The addition of new information to existing categories also alters those categories and their relationships with other categories. When the compact disk player was first introduced to consumers, they most probably grouped it in the general category of record players in order to be able to evaluate it. With further experience and information, many consumers have gained detailed knowledge about the product and have formed several subcategories for classifying the various brands and types.

FIGURE 9–6

Determinants of Interpretation

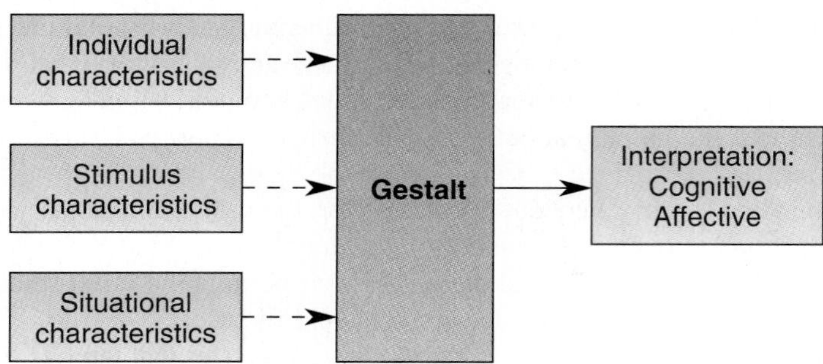

It is the individual's interpretation, not objective reality, that will influence behavior. For example, a firm may introduce a high-quality new brand at a lower price than existing brands because the firm has a more efficient production or marketing process. If consumers interpret this lower price to mean lower quality, the new brand will not be successful regardless of the objective reality.

The above example indicates the critical importance of distinguishing between **lexical** or **semantic meaning**, the conventional meaning assigned to a word such as found in the dictionary, and **psychological meaning**, the specific meaning assigned a word by a given individual or group of individuals based on their experiences and the context or situation in which the term is used.[31]

For example, the semantic meaning of the expression *on sale* is "a price reduction from the normal level." However, when applied to fashion clothes, the psychological meaning that some consumers would derive is "these clothes are, or soon will be, out of style."

Affective interpretation is the emotional or feeling response triggered by a stimulus such as an ad.[32] Like cognitive interpretation, there are "normal" (within-culture) emotional responses to an ad (e.g., most Americans experience a feeling of warmth when seeing pictures of young children with kittens). Likewise, there are also individual variations to this response (a person allergic to cats might have a very negative emotional response to such a picture).

Individual Characteristics

Marketing stimuli have meaning *only* as individuals interpret them.[33] A number of *individual characteristics* influence interpretation. For example, gender and social class affect the meaning assigned to owning various products. Likewise, gender affects the nature of the emotional response to nudity in ads.[34] Two particularly important personal variables affecting interpretation are *learning* and *expectations.*

Learning We saw in Chapter 2 that the meanings attached to such "natural" things as time, space, friendship, and colors are learned and vary widely across cultures. Even within the same culture, different subcultures assign different meanings to similar stimuli. For example, "dinner" refers to the noon meal for some social classes in some geographic regions of the United States, and to the evening meal for other social classes and geographic regions.

Likewise, many consumers have a very warm emotional response when presented with pictures of fried chicken or people frying chicken. They learned this response because of fried chicken's role in picnics and family gatherings when they were young. Of course, many other consumers would not have this response.

Marketers must be certain that the target audience has learned the same meanings that they wish to portray.

Expectations Individuals tend to interpret stimuli consistently with their *expectations.* For example, we expect dark brown pudding to taste like chocolate, not vanilla, because dark pudding is generally chocolate flavored and vanilla pudding is generally cream colored. In a recent taste test, 100 percent of a sample of college students accepted dark brown *vanilla* pudding as chocolate. Further, in comparing three versions of the vanilla pudding that differed only in degree of darkness, the students rated the darkest as having the best chocolate flavor.[35] Thus, their expectations, cued by color, led to an interpretation that was inconsistent with ''objective'' reality.

Consumers will frequently evaluate the performance of a well-known brand or a more expensive brand as higher than that of an identical product with an unknown brand name or a lower price. Before Coca-Cola introduced new Coke, consumers consistently expressed a preference for Pepsi in blind (unlabeled) taste tests, but preferred Coke when the labels were attached. Consumers also frequently attribute advertisements for new or unknown brands to well-known brands. Even an ''objective'' product feature such as price is sometimes interpreted to be closer to an expected price.[36] Likewise, brands with promotional signs on them in retail stores are interpreted as having reduced prices even when the sign does not indicate that prices have been reduced and when, in fact, prices have *not* been reduced.[37]

Situational Characteristics

A variety of situational characteristics influence interpretation. Temporary characteristics of the individual, such as hunger or loneliness, influence the interpretation of a given stimulus, as do moods.[38] The amount of time available also affects the meaning assigned to marketing messages. Likewise, physical characteristics of the situation such as temperature, the number and characteristics of other individuals present,[39] the nature of the material surrounding the message in question,[40] external distractions,[41] and the reason the message is being processed[42] affect how the message is interpreted.

Proximity refers to a tendency to perceive objects or events that are close to one another as being related. Both Coca-Cola and General Foods refuse to advertise some products during news broadcasts because they believe that ''bad'' news might affect the interpretation of their products. According to William Sharp, vice president of advertising for Coca-Cola, USA:

> It's a Coca-Cola corporate policy not to advertise on TV news because there's going to be some bad news in there, and Coke is an upbeat, fun product.[43]

Stimulus Characteristics

The stimulus sets the basic structure to which an individual responds. The structure and nature of the product, package, advertisement, or sales presentation have a major impact on the nature of the mental processes that are activated and on the final meaning assigned the message.

In recognition of the critical importance of the meaning associated with stimuli, marketers are beginning to use semiotics. **Semiotics** is the *science of how meaning is created, maintained, and altered.* It focuses on **signs**, which are *anything that conveys meaning, including words, pictures, music, colors, forms, smells, gestures, products, prices, and so forth.*[44] General principles of how meanings are learned are discussed in the next chapter.

Colors can be used to illustrate the importance of semiotics. In the previous section, we saw how color influenced taste perceptions of pudding. When Barrelhead Sugar-Free Root Beer changed the background color on its cans from blue to beige, consumers rated it as *tasting* more like old-fashioned root beer. Canada Dry's sugar-free ginger ale sales increased dramatically when the can was changed to green and white from red. Red is interpreted as a cola color and thus conflicted with the taste of ginger ale.[45]

The source of the message affects its interpretation. Price, presentation format, type of message, and the nature of the product influences how promotional claims are interpreted.[46] Previous experiences with the same or competing products or firms, and the nature of other firms' advertising campaigns also influence interpretation.[47] For example, consumers interpret quality claims for a brand in light of that brand's price relative to competing brands' prices.[48] Factors indirectly related to the product, such as its country of origin, can have a major influence on the meaning assigned the product.[49]

All aspects of the message itself influence our interpretation. This can include our reaction to the overall style, visual and auditory background, and other nonverbal and verbal aspects of the message, as well as its explicit content and even lack of content. For example, the type of background music played during an ad has been found to influence the interpretation of and response to the ad.[50]

Misinterpretation of Marketing Messages

Marketing managers and public policy officials both want consumers to interpret messages accurately, that is, in a manner consistent with what others or experts would consider to be the ''true'' or ''objective'' meaning of the messages. Having read the previous material on interpretation, you probably suspect that widespread agreement on, or accurate interpretation of, mass media messages is difficult to obtain. Several studies indicate that this is indeed the case. A study of both commercial and noncommercial television communications reached the following conclusions:

- A large proportion of the audience miscomprehends communications broadcast over commercial television.
- No communication (program content or advertisement) is immune from miscomprehension.
- An average of 30 percent of the total information was miscomprehended.
- Nonadvertising communications had higher levels of miscomprehension than did advertising messages.
- Some demographic variables appear to be slightly associated with miscomprehension.[51]

While the methodology of the study has been criticized, there is no doubt that substantial miscomprehension of television messages, including marketing messages, does occur. A second study, which focused on editorial and advertising content in general-circulation magazines, reached essentially the same conclusions.[52] Evidence also indicates that package information, including FTC-mandated disclosures, is subject to miscomprehension. Neither the consumer nor the marketer benefits from such miscomprehension.

EXHIBIT 9–1

Piaget's Stages of Cognitive Development

1. *The period of sensorimotor intelligence (0 to 2 years).* During this period, behavior is primarily motor. The child does not yet ''think'' conceptually, though ''cognitive'' development is seen.
2. *The period of preoperational thoughts (3 to 7 years).* This period is characterized by the development of language and rapid conceptual development.
3. *The period of concrete operations (8 to 11 years).* During these years the child develops the ability to apply logical thought to concrete problems.
4. *The period of formal operations (12 to 15 years).* During this period the child's cognitive structures reach their greatest level of development and the child becomes able to apply logic to all classes of problems.

We are just beginning to learn about methods to minimize miscomprehension and it is a complex task. For example, repetition does not appear to reduce miscomprehension. And while very simple television messages are less subject to miscomprehension, the same is not true for print messages. Unfortunately, we do not yet have a workable set of guidelines for eliminating this problem. Thus, marketers, public officials, and others wishing to communicate with the public should carefully pretest their messages to ensure that they are being interpreted correctly.

MEMORY

Memory plays a critical role in guiding the perception process. As Figure 9–1 indicated, memory has a long-term storage component and a short-term active component. These are not distinct entities; active memory is simply that portion of total memory that is currently activated or in use. In the next chapter, we provide a more detailed discussion of the nature of memory and the factors that influence our ability to retrieve items from long-term memory for use in consumption decisions.

CHILDREN'S INFORMATION PROCESSING

Thus far we have been discussing information processing from an adult perspective. However, there is evidence that younger children have limited abilities to process certain types of information.[53] Exhibit 9–1 shows a widely accepted set of stages of information processing or cognitive development. Piaget's approach is basically developmental. It suggests naturally occurring stages that change primarily with physiological maturation. Other researchers have suggested different stages, with learning rather than maturation as the underlying cause of observed differences. However, the general pattern of less ability to deal with abstract, generalized, unfamiliar, and/or large amounts of information by younger children is common to all approaches. As we will discuss in depth in Chapter 21, this is the basis for substantial regulation of advertising to children.

PERCEPTION AND MARKETING STRATEGY

Information is the primary raw material the marketer works with in influencing consumers. Therefore, an understanding of the perception of information is an essential guide to marketing strategy. In the following sections we discuss areas where it is particularly useful:

1. Retail strategy.
2. Brand name and logo development.
3. Media strategy.
4. Advertising and package design.
5. Advertising evaluation.

Its role in regulation of advertising is discussed in Chapter 21.

Retail Strategy

Most retail environments contain a vast array of information. Given the fact that consumers cannot process all of this information, retailers need to be concerned about information overload. That is, they do not want consumers to become frustrated or minimize their in-store information processing.

Retailers often use exposure very effectively. Store interiors are designed with frequently sought out items (canned goods, fresh fruits/vegetables, meats) separated so that the average consumer will travel through more of the store. This increases total exposure. High-margin items are often placed in high traffic areas to capitalize on increased exposure.

Shelf position and amount of shelf space influence which items and brands are allocated attention. Point-of-purchase displays also attract attention to sale and high-margin items. Stores are designed with highly visible shelves and overhead signs to make locating items (an information processing task) as easy as possible. Stores provide reference prices to increase consumers' abilities to accurately interpret price information. Unit price information by brand may be displayed on a separate sign in ascending or descending order to facilitate price comparisons. Nutrition information provided in a similar manner enhances consumers' abilities to choose nutritious brands.[54]

The total mix of in-store information cues (brands, layout, point-of-purchase displays, etc.), external building characteristics, and advertising combine to form the meaning or store image assigned the store. Semiotics has been used to design a hypermarket to meet consumer needs, merchandising requirements, and marketing strategy.[55]

Brand Name and Logo Development

Shakespeare notwithstanding, marketers do not believe that "a rose by any other name would smell the same."[56] Would you rather have a soft drink sweetened with NutraSweet or with aspartame? Lincoln-Mercury named a new model the Merkur XR4T. The name is supposed to suggest the car's German origins, but it is difficult to pronounce (Mare-Coor) and does not convey much of a visual image.

Brand names are important for both consumer and industrial products. An adhesive named *RC 601* was marketed for a number of years to equipment designers. Marketing research led to a redefinition of the target market to maintenance workers and reformulation of the product to make it easier to use. Equally important was a name change from the meaningless *RC 601* to the image-rich *Quick Metal.* Sales which were projected to be $320,000 under the old approach jumped to $2,200,000.[57]

Companies such as NameLab use linguists and computers to create names that convey the appropriate meaning for products. For example, NameLab created "Compaq" for a

EXHIBIT 9–2

Meanings Conveyed by Type Style

	Highest Quality	Best for Recording Music	Poorest Value	Preference
A. MEMOREX	**1st**	2nd	5th	2nd
B. Memorex	5th	5th	3rd	5th
C. **MEMOREX**	3rd	3rd	**1st**	3rd
D. ***Memorex***	4th	4th	2nd	4th
E. **memorex**	2nd	**1st**	4th	**1st**

Source: D.L. Masten, "Logo's Power Depends on How Well It Communicates with Target Market," *Marketing News*, December 5, 1988, p. 20.

portable computer that was originally to be called "Gateway." The focus of NameLab is the total meaning conveyed by the interaction of the meanings of the name's parts. For Compaq, *com* means computer and communications while *paq* means small. The unique spelling attracts attention and gives a "scientific" impression. In general, concrete terms with relevant, established visual images such as Mustang, Apple, or Cup-a-Soup are easier to recognize and recall than are more abstract terms.[58] However, alpha-numeric names (word and letter combinations such as Z210) are very effective for some product categories (generally technical or chemical) and target markets.[59]

The impact of the image conveyed by a name was vividly demonstrated in a recent study.[60] Three groups of consumers evaluated the same sporting goods product. The *only* difference among the three groups was the name associated with the product. The perceptual differences caused by the name include:

	Percent Attributing Feature to Product		
Feature	**Name A**	**Name B**	**Name C**
For all surfaces	11	26	17
Easy to see	8	34	19
For professionals	42	53	30
Large	38	53	18

Clearly, name selection influences how consumers interpret product features.

How a product or service's name is presented (its *logo*) is also important.[61] Exhibit 9–2 illustrates the power of type style in influencing consumers' perceptions of the attributes of Memorex audio tapes. Memorex was using style C at the time of the study and a key competitor, Maxell, was using E. The marketing implications are obvious.

Media Strategy

The fact that the exposure process is selective rather than random is the underlying basis for effective media strategies. If the process were random, a broad approach of trying to place messages randomly in the environment would make sense. Since exposure is not random, the proper approach is to determine to which media the consumers in the target market are most frequently exposed and then place the advertising messages in those media. Donald Peterson, of Ford Motor Co., has expressed this idea clearly:

> We must look increasingly for matching media that will enable us best to reach carefully targeted, emerging markets. The rifle approach rather than the old shotgun.[62]

For some products and target markets, consumers are highly involved with the product category itself and will go to considerable trouble to secure product-relevant information. This occurs most frequently among heavy users of hobby and luxury items, such as skis and mountaineering equipment or for fashion items.

For other products and target markets, consumers have limited involvement with the product category. Products such as salt or detergents are examples. In a situation such as this, the marketer must find media that the target market is interested in and place the advertising message in those media. As we learned earlier, potential target markets as defined by age, ethnic group, social class, or stage in the family life cycle have differing media preferences. Table 9–3 illustrates selective exposure to several magazines based on demographic characteristics.

Many magazine advertisers go even further and insist that their ads appear opposite certain articles or columns. Television advertisers are concerned about where within the commercial break their ad appears and the interest level aroused by the program.

TABLE 9–3 Selective Exposure to Magazines Based on Demographic Characteristics

Demographic Characteristics	United States	*Playboy*	*National Geographic*	*Family Circle*	*Forbes*
Total adults	100%	100%	100%	100%	100%
Men	47	75	51	19	67
Women	53	25	49	81	33
Age					
18–24 years	18	30	17	16	16
25–34 years	22	37	24	25	25
35–49 years	23	22	26	27	27
50–64 years	22	10	22	24	23
65 + years	15	1	10	9	9
Graduated college	15	21	28	17	51
Head of household income					
$35,000 +	11	15	19	14	36
$25,000–$35,000	15	21	22	20	22
$20,000–$25,000	14	16	15	16	12
$15,000–$20,000	15	18	14	15	13
<$15,000	45	30	31	34	17

Source: Adapted from "Average Issue Audience of Nineteen Selected Magazines," *Newsweek Marketing Report: MR 80-5, Newsweek.*

Advertisement and Package Design

Advertisements and packages must perform two critical tasks—capture attention and convey meaning. Unfortunately, the techniques appropriate for accomplishing one task are often counterproductive for the remaining task.

What should a manager do to attract attention to a package or advertisement? As with most aspects of the marketing process, it depends on the target market, the product, and the situation. If the target market is interested in the product category, or in the firm or brand, attention will not constitute much of a problem. Once consumers are exposed to the message, they will most likely attend to it. Unfortunately, most of the time consumers are not actively interested in a particular product. Interest in a product tends to arise only when the need for the product arises. Since it is difficult to reach consumers at exactly this point, marketers have the difficult task of trying to communicate with them at times when their interest is low or nonexistent.

Assume that you are responsible for developing a campaign designed to increase the number of users for your firm's toilet bowl freshener. Research indicates that the group you wish to reach has very little interest in the product. What do you do? Two strategies seem reasonable. One is to *utilize stimulus characteristics* such as full-page ads, bright colors, animated cartoons, or surrealism to attract attention to the advertisement. The second is to *tie the message to a topic the target market is interested in*. Celebrities are often used in advertisements in part for this reason, as is humor. Sex, in the form of attractive models, is also frequently used. For example, Black Velvet whiskey used ''sexy'' women in black velvet dresses in its advertising. Sales increased from 150,000 cases a year to almost 2 million, in part because ''those slinky women have given it an extremely high brand awareness among men.''[63] Managerial Application 9–4 shows a Tanqueray® ad that uses sex appeal to capture attention.

Attention-attracting features of the advertisement can also focus attention on specific parts of the ad.[64] Corporate advertising—advertising which talks about a company rather than the company's products—tends to generate a relatively high level of attention. Yet a study of more than 2,000 such advertisements has shown that about half of all people exposed to the ads do not notice the single most important bit of information in the ad—the company name. The same study found that the simplest way to avoid this problem is to place the name in the most prominent part of the ad—the headline. The following results for a Motorola corporate ad are typical:[65]

	No Name in Headline	Name in Headline
Magazine readership	4,600,000	4,500,000
Involved with ad	91% = 4,186,000	84% = 3,780,000
Involved and saw Motorola name	43% = 1,978,000	70% = 3,150,000

The Black Velvet ad illustrated how successful advertisements can be by using consumer interests unrelated to the product. However, using either stimulus characteristics or consumer interest unrelated to the product category to attract attention presents two dangers. The first danger is that the strategy will be so successful in attracting attention to the stimulus object that it will reduce the attention devoted to the sales message. The reader may observe an attractive member of the opposite sex in an advertisement and not attend to the sales message or copy. This occurred with the ad for RCA Colortrack described in this chapter's opening example.

The second risk associated with using stimulus characteristics or unrelated consumer interests to attract attention is that the *interpretation* of the message will be negatively

MANAGERIAL APPLICATION

9–4

The Use of Sex Appeal to Attract Attention

affected. For example, the use of humor to attract attention to a commercial for beer may result in the brand being viewed as appropriate for only very light-hearted, casual situations. The use of a second color (red) with large yellow-page ads, while a proven attention-attracting device, has been found to actually deter consumers from calling that advertiser.[66] Thus, caution must be used to ensure that attention-attracting devices do not have a negative impact on attention to, or interpretation of, the main message.

The Tanqueray ad shown in Managerial Application 9–4 is tied to the product through the extensive use of green which is the color of the brand's unique bottle and is featured prominently in all its ads. The product is consumed primarily by males and this ad appeared in a magazine with a predominantly male readership. Thus, it probably succeeded in both attracting attention and imparting a positive brand image. The Grand Marnier ad shown in Managerial Application 9–5 uses surrealism to attract attention. In contrast to the Tanqueray ad, the connection between the attention-attracting device (surrealism) and the brand's features or image is not clear. Ads that rely on stimulus factors not directly related to the product should be thoroughly pretested to determine how they are interpreted by the target market.

MANAGERIAL APPLICATION

The Use of Surrealism to Capture Attention

Advertising Evaluation

A successful advertisement (or any other marketing message) must accomplish four tasks:

1. *Exposure:* It must physically reach the consumer.
2. *Attention:* It must be attended to by the consumer.
3. *Interpretation:* It must be properly interpreted.
4. *Memory:* It must be stored in memory in a manner that will allow retrieval under the proper circumstances.

Advertising research covers all of these tasks. However, most of the effort is focused on attention and, to a lesser extent, on memory.

Measures of Exposure Exposure to print media is most frequently measured in terms of circulation. Data on circulation are provided by a variety of commercial firms. The major difficulty with this data is that it frequently is not broken down in a manner consistent with the firm's target market. Thus, a firm may be targeting the lower-middle social class but circulation data may be broken down by income rather than social class. Further, circulation measures are generally based on households and do not provide data on who within a household is exposed to the magazine or newspaper.

Diary reports, in which respondents record their daily listening patterns, and telephone interviews are the two methods used to determine radio listening.

Television viewing is measured primarily by **people meters**, which are electronic devices that automatically determine if a television is turned on and, if so, to which channel. They allow each household member to ''log on'' when viewing, by punching an identifying button. The demographics of each potential viewer are stored in the central computer so viewer profiles can be developed.

Measures of Attention The attention-attracting powers of commercials or packages can be partially measured in a direct manner using the techniques described in Exhibit 9–3. Of these techniques, eye tracking appears to offer the greatest potential.[67]

Indirect tests of attention (they also tap at least some aspects of memory) include theater tests, day-after recall, recognition tests, and Starch scores. **Theater tests** involve showing commercials along with television programs in a theater. Viewers complete questionnaires designed to measure which commercials (and what aspects of those commercials) attracted their attention. **Day-after recall** (DAR) is the most popular method of measuring the attention-getting power of television commercials. Individuals are interviewed the day after a commercial is aired on a program they watched. Recall of the commercial and recall of specific aspects of the commercial are interpreted as a reflection of the amount of attention.

EXHIBIT 9–3 Direct Measures of Attention

I. **Eye pupil dilation.** Changes in the size of the pupil of the eye appear to be related to the amount of attention that a person is giving a message. A pupilometer can measure these changes accurately.

II. **Eye tracking.** An eye camera can track movements of the eyes relative to the ad being read or watched. The paths of the eyes can then be mapped to determine: (1) what parts of the message were attended to, (2) what sequence was used in viewing the message, and (3) how much time was spent on each part.

III. **Tachistoscopic test.** A tachistoscope is a slide projector with adjustable projector speeds and levels of illumination. Thus, ads can be shown very rapidly and/or dimly. Ads are tested to determine at what speeds the elements, such as the product, brand, and headline, are recognized. Speed of recognition of various elements in the ads and readership (attention) are highly correlated.

IV. **Theater tests.** Theater tests involve showing commercials along with television shows in a theater. Some, such as the one maintained by ASI Market Research, have dials at each seat which viewers use to constantly indicate their interest (attention) in the show or commercial.

V. **Brain wave analysis.** There is some evidence that electroencephalographs can indicate the amount and type of attention given to an advertisement or package.

Day-after recall measures of television commercials have been criticized as favoring rational, factual, ''hard sell'' type ads and high-involvement products while discriminating against ''feeling,'' emotional, ''soft-sell'' ads. However, for many product/target market combinations the latter approach may be superior. In response, substantial work has been done to develop recognition measures for television commercials. **Recognition tests** are tests in which the commercial of interest, or key parts of it, along with other commercials are shown to target-market members. Recognition of the commercial, or key parts of the commercial, is the measure. This technique appears to work better than standard recall measures.[68]

Starch scores are the most popular technique for evaluating the attention-attracting power of print ads. The respondents are shown advertisements from magazine issues they have recently read. For each advertisement, they indicate which parts (headlines, illustrations, copy blocks) they recall reading. Three main ''scores'' are computed:

1. *Noted.* The percent who recall seeing the ad in that issue.
2. *Seen-associated.* The percent who recall reading a part of the ad that clearly identifies the brand or advertiser.
3. *Read most.* The percent who recall reading 50 percent or more of the copy.

Starch scores allow an indirect measure of attention to the overall ad and to key components of the ad.

Measures of Interpretation Marketers investigate *interpretation* primarily through the use of focus groups, theater tests, and day-after recall. **Focus groups** involve a group of 5 to 15 members of the target audience who have a relatively free-form discussion of the meaning conveyed by the advertisement. *Theater* and *day-after recall* tests measure interpretation, as well as the content of the advertisement.

One of the problems of these techniques, particularly the last two, is their tendency to produce a restatement of the verbal content of the advertisement rather than subtle meanings conveyed by the total ad. However, it is clear that consumers utilize all of the advertisement, including nonverbal visual and auditory imagery, in forming an impression of the product.

Marketers are just beginning to measure the emotional or feeling reactions or meanings that consumers assign to ads. While standard methods do not yet exist, this is clearly an important area for development (more details are provided in Chapter 11).[69]

SUMMARY

Perception consists of those activities by which an individual acquires and assigns meaning to stimuli. Perception begins with *exposure*: this occurs when a stimulus comes within range of one of our primary sensory receptors. We are exposed to only a small fraction of the available stimuli and this is usually the result of ''self-selection.''

Attention occurs when the stimulus activates one or more of the sensory receptors and the resulting sensations go into the brain for processing. Because of the amount of stimuli we are exposed to, we selectively attend to those stimuli that physically attract us (stimulus factors) or personally interest us (individual factors). *Stimulus factors* are physical characteristics of the stimulus itself, such as contrast, size, intensity, color, and movement. *Individual factors* are characteristics of the individual, such as interests and needs. Both these factors are moderated by the *situation* in which they occur.

Interpretation is the assignment of meaning to stimuli that have been attended to. Interpretation is a function of the individual as well as stimulus and situation characteristics.

Cognitive interpretation appears to involve a process whereby new stimuli are placed into existing categories of meaning. *Affective interpretation* is the emotional or feeling response triggered by the stimulus.

In general, children under age 12 or so have less developed information processing abilities than do older individuals. To protect children, a variety of formal and informal advertising guidelines have been developed.

Marketing managers use their knowledge of information processing in a variety of ways. The fact that media exposure is selective is the basis for *media strategy*. *Retailers* can enhance their operations by viewing their outlets as information environments. Both stimulus and personal interest factors are used to attract attention to *advertisements* and *packages*. Characteristics of the target market and the message are studied to ensure that accurate interpretation occurs. The meaning that consumers assign to words and parts of words is the basis for selecting *brand names*. Information processing theory guides a wide range of *advertising evaluation techniques*. Likewise, information processing theory is a basis for *regulating advertising*.

REVIEW QUESTIONS

1. What is *information processing*? How does it differ from *perception*?
2. What is meant by *exposure*? What determines which stimuli an individual will be exposed to? How do marketers utilize this knowledge?
3. What is *zipping* and *zapping*? Why are they a concern to marketers?
4. What is an *infomercial*? How effective are they?
5. What is meant by *attention*? What determines which stimuli an individual will attend to? How do marketers utilize this?
6. What stimulus factors can be used to attract attention? What problems can arise when stimulus factors are used to attract attention?
7. What is *adaptation level theory*?
8. What is an *accelerated* or *compressed message*?
9. What is *information overload*? How should marketers deal with information overload?
10. What is meant by *nonfocused attention*?
11. What is meant by *hemispheric lateralization*?
12. What is meant by *subliminal perception*? Is it a real phenomenon? Is it effective?
13. What is meant by *interpretation*?
14. What determines how an individual will interpret a given stimulus?
15. What is meant by the term *Gestalt* as it relates to interpretation? Why is it important?
16. What is the difference between *cognitive* and *affective* interpretation?
17. What is the difference between *lexical* and *psychological* meaning?
18. What is meant by *misinterpretation of a marketing message*? Is it common?
19. In what ways, if any, do children process information differently than adults?
20. Describe Piaget's stages of cognitive development.
21. How does a knowledge of information processing assist the manager in:
    a. Formulating media strategy?
    b. Formulating retail strategy?
    c. Designing advertisements and packages?
    d. Developing brand names?
    e. Evaluating advertising?
22. What is the underlying basis of media strategy?
23. Explain the differences between an eye camera, a tachistoscope, and a pupilometer.
24. What is a *Starch score*?
25. What is a *focus group*?
26. What is meant by *day-after recall*?
27. What is meant by *recognition tests*?
28. What is a *people meter*?
29. How is exposure measured? What problems are encountered in this process?

DISCUSSION QUESTIONS

30. How could a marketing manager for (a) the American Cancer Society's anti-smoking campaign, (b) in-line skates, (c) a restaurant chain, (d) bleach, or (e) toothpaste use the material in this chapter on perception to guide the development of a national advertising campaign? To assist local retailers in developing their promotional activities? Would the usefulness of this material be limited to advertising decisions? Explain your answer.
31. Anheuser-Busch test-marketed a new soft drink for adults called Chelsea. The product was advertised as a ''not-so-soft drink'' that Anheuser-Busch hoped would become socially acceptable for adults. The advertisements featured no one under 25 years of age, and the product contained one-half of 1 percent alcohol (not enough to classify the product as an alcoholic beverage).

    The reaction in the test market was not what the firm expected or hoped for. The Virginia Nurses Association decided to boycott Chelsea, claiming that it ''is packaged like a beer and looks, pours, and foams like beer, and the children are pretending the soft drink is beer.'' The Nurses Association claimed the product was an attempt to encourage children to become beer drinkers later on. The Secretary of Health, Education and Welfare urged the firm to ''rethink their marketing strategy.'' Others made similar protests. Although Anheuser-Busch reformulated the product and altered the marketing mix substantially, the product could not regain momentum and was withdrawn.

    Assuming Anheuser-Busch was in fact attempting to position Chelsea as an adult soft drink (which it appears was their objective), why do you think it failed?
32. Develop a brand name for (a) a nonalcoholic wine, (b) a national tax return service, (c) an in-line skate, (d) a magazine for junior high students, or (e) a vitamin for individuals over age 65.
33. Develop a logo for (a) a nonalcoholic beer, (b) a national housekeeping service, (c) a mountain bike, (d) a compact disk player, or (e) a magazine for high school students.
34. Evaluate the ads in this chapter. Analyze the attention-attracting characteristics and the meaning they convey. Are they good ads? What risks are associated with each?
35. To what extent, if any, and how should the government regulate advertising seen by children?
36. How should a television commercial designed to ______ change for the following age-groups: (1) 3 to 7, (2) 8 to 11, (3) 12 to 15, (4) 15 to 18? Why?
    a. Provide anti-cigarette use information and feelings.
    b. Sell a new breakfast cereal.
37. What is the best way to evaluate an advertising campaign?
38. Why might Starch scores based on a random sample of *Seventeen* magazine subscribers/readers mislead advertisers evaluating an ad for an acne medication (assume the firm's target market is young females with acne problems)?
39. What problems do you see with people meters?

APPLICATION ACTIVITIES

40. Find examples of marketing promotions that specifically use stimulus factors to attract attention. Look for examples of each of the various factors discussed earlier in the chapter, and try to find their use in a variety of promotions (e.g., point-of-purchase, billboards, print advertisements). For each example, evaluate the effectiveness of the stimulus factors used.
41. Repeat Question 40 above, but this time look for promotions using individual factors.
42. Read *Symbolic Seduction* by Wilson Bryan Key. Is the author really describing subliminal perception? Do you feel he makes a valid point?
43. Complete Discussion Question 32 and test your names on a sample of students. Justify your testing procedure.

44. Watch 10 TV commercials aimed at children under nine, and 10 aimed at adults. Analyze the differences, if any, between the commercials from an information processing perspective.
45. Visit a children's toy store and examine various types of toys that seem to be marketed to specific age-groups. Do you find any correspondence between these age groups and those postulated by Piaget? How do marketers of toys such as these appeal to their consumers?
46. Find three brand names that you feel are particularly appropriate and three that you feel are not very appropriate. Explain your reasoning for each name.
47. Find three logos that you feel are particularly appropriate and three that you feel are not very appropriate. Explain your reasoning for each logo.
48. Keep a diary of your TV viewing and radio listening for two weeks. How accurate do you feel the results are?
49. Interview 10 students about their behavior during television and radio commercial breaks. What do you conclude?
50. Answer Question 49, but use a focus group.

REFERENCES

[1]*What the Eye Does Not See, the Mind Does Not Remember* (Telecom Research, Inc., undated).

[2]For a more comprehensive model see D. J. MacInnis and B. J. Jaworski, "Information Processing from Advertisements," *Journal of Marketing*, October 1989, pp. 1–23.

[3]J. J. Cronin and N. E. Menelly, "Discrimination Vs. Avoidance," *Journal of Advertising*, June 1992, pp. 1–7.

[4]T. J. Olney, M. B. Holbrook, and R. Batra, "Consumer Responses to Advertising," *Journal of Consumer Research*, March 1991, pp. 440–50.

[5]Ibid.; F. S. Zufryden, J. H. Pedrick, and A. Sankaralingam, "Zapping and Its Impact on Brand Purchase Behavior," *Journal of Advertising Research*, January/February 1993, pp. 58–66; "Clutter Suffers Zap Attacks," *Advertising Age*, March 30, 1992, p. 38; and P. A. Stout and B. L. Burda, "Zapped Commercials," *Journal of Advertising*, no. 4, 1989, pp. 23–32.

[6]A. M. Abernethy, "Differences between Advertising and Program Exposure for Car Radio Listening," *Journal of Advertising Research*, April/May 1991, pp. 33–42.

[7]C. Fisher, "Newspaper Readers Get Choosier," *Advertising Age*, July 26, 1993, p. 22.

[8]See E. T. Popper and K. B. Murray, "Format Effects on an In-Ad Disclosure," in *Advances in Consumer Research XVI*, ed. T. K. Srull, (Provo, Utah: Association for Consumer Research, 1989), pp. 221–30; and "Researchers Say Cigarette Warnings Are Inadequate," *Marketing News*, February 13, 1989, p. 8.

[9]J. L. Rogers, "Consumer Response to Advertising Mail," *Journal of Advertising Research*, January 1990, p. 22.

[10]*Eyes On Television* (New York: *Newsweek*, 1980). See also D. Kneale, "Zapping of TV Ads Appears Pervasive," *The Wall Street Journal*, April 25, 1988.

[11]"Farm Ads Win Golden Fleece," *The Stars and Stripes*, July 10, 1984, p. 6.

[12]CARR Report No. 250.1A (Boston: Cahners Publishing Co., undated). See also K. Gronhaug, O. Kvitastein, and S. Gronmo, "Factors Moderating Advertising Effectiveness," *Journal of Advertising Research*, October/November 1991, pp. 42–50; and A. Finn, "Print Ad Recognition Scores," *Journal of Marketing Research*, May 1988, pp. 168–77.

[13]CARR Report No. 120.3 (Boston: Cahners Publishing Co., undated); and P. H. Chook, "A Continuing Study of Magazine Environment, Frequency, and Advertising Performance," *Journal of Advertising Research*, August/September 1985, pp. 23–33.

[14]N. Sparkman, Jr., and L. M. Austin, "The Effect on Sales of Color in Newspaper Advertisement," *Journal of Advertising*, Fourth Quarter, 1980, p. 42.

[15]D. Walker and M. F. von Gonten, "Explaining Related Recall Outcomes," *Journal of Advertising Research*, July 1989, pp. 11–21.

[16]D. L. Moore, D. Hausknecht, and K. Thamodaran, "Time Compression, Response Opportunity, and Persuasion," *Journal of Consumer Research*, June 1986, pp. 85–99; and J. W. Vann, R. D. Rogers, J. P. Penrod, "The Cognitive Effects of Time-Compressed Advertising," *Journal of Advertising*, no. 2, 1987, pp. 10–19; and D. R. John and C. A. Cole, "Age Differences in Information Processing," *Journal of Consumer Research*, December 1986, pp. 297–315.

[17]See D. Maheswaran and B. Sternthal, "The Effects of Knowledge, Motivation, and Type of Message on Ad Processing and Product Judgments," *Journal of Consumer Research*, June 1990, pp. 66–73; and D. J. MacInnis, C. Moorman, and B. J. Jaworski, "Enhancing and Measuring Consumers' Motivation, Opportunity, and Ability to Process Brand Information from Ads," *Journal of Marketing*, October, 1991, pp. 32–53.

[18]G. R. Funkhouser, "Consumers' Sensitivity to the Wording of Affirmative Disclosure Messages," *Journal of Public Policy and Marketing*, vol. 3, 1984, pp. 26–37.

[19]See G. L. Sullivan, "Music Format Effects in Radio Advertising," *Psychology & Marketing*, Summer 1990, pp. 97–108; D. L. Hoffman and R. Batra, "Viewer Response to Programs," *Journal of Advertising Research*, August/September 1991, pp. 46–56; and K. G. Celuch and M. Slama, "Program Content and Advertising Effectiveness," *Psychology & Marketing*, July/August 1993, pp. 285–99.

[20]See P. S. Schindler, "Color and Contrast in Magazine Advertising," *Psychology & Marketing*, Summer 1986, pp. 69–78.

[21]R. F. Beltramini and V. J. Blasko, "An Analysis of Award-Winning Headlines," *Journal of Advertising Research*, April/May 1986, pp. 48–51.

[22]L. Bogart and C. Lehman, ''The Case of the 30-Second Commercial,'' *Journal of Advertising Research*, March 1983, pp. 11–19. See also M. H. Blair, ''An Empirical Investigation of Advertising Wearin and Wearout,'' *Journal of Advertising Research*, January 1988, pp. 45–50.

[23]R. Alsop, ''Culligan Drops Familiar Voice to Broaden Appeal of Its Ads,'' *The Wall Street Journal*, August 9, 1984, p. 27.

[24]H. E. Krugman, ''Sustained Viewing of Television,'' *Journal of Advertising Research*, June 1980, p. 65; and H. E. Krugman, ''Low Recall and High Recognition of Advertising,'' *Journal of Advertising Research*, February/March 1986, pp. 79–86.

[25]See M. L. Rothschild et al., ''Hemispherically Lateralized EEG as a Response to Television Commercials,'' *Journal of Consumer Research*, September 1988, pp. 185–98; C. Janiszewski, ''Preconscious Processing Effects,'' *Journal of Consumer Research*, September 1988, pp. 199–209; J. Meyers-Levy, ''Priming Effects on Product Judgments,'' *Journal of Consumer Research*, June 1989, pp. 76–86; C. Janiszewski, ''The Influence of Print Advertisement Organization on Affect toward a Brand Name,'' *Journal of Consumer Research*, June 1990, pp. 53–65; and M. L. Rothschild and Y. J. Hyun, ''Predicting Memory for Components of TV Commercials from EEG,'' *Journal of Consumer Research*, March 1990, pp. 472–78.

[26]W. B. Key, *Subliminal Seduction* (Signet Books, 1974); and W. B. Key, *Media Sexploitation* (Signet Books, 1977).

[27]D. L. Rosen and S. N. Singh, ''An Investigation of Subliminal Embed Effect on Multiple Measures of Advertising Effectiveness,'' *Psychology & Marketing*, March/April 1992, pp. 157–73.

[28]M. Rogers and K. H. Smith, ''Public Perceptions of Subliminal Advertising,'' *Journal of Advertising Research*, March/April 1993, pp. 10–18.

[29]J. Saegert, ''Why Marketing Should Quit Giving Subliminal Advertising the Benefit of the Doubt,'' *Psychology & Marketing*, Summer 1987, pp. 107–20; and S. E. Beatty and D. I. Hawkins, ''Subliminal Stimulation,'' *Journal of Advertising*, no. 3, 1989. pp. 4–8.

[30]See J. B. Cohen and K. Basu, ''Alternative Models of Categorization,'' *Journal of Consumer Research*, March 1987, pp. 455–72.

[31]R. Friedman, ''Psychological Meaning of Products,'' *Psychology & Marketing*, Spring 1986, pp. 1–15; R. Friedman and M. R. Zimmer, ''The Role of Psychological Meaning in Advertising,'' *Journal of Advertising*, no. 1, 1988, pp. 31–40; and L. L. Golden, M. I. Alpert, and J. F. Betak, ''Psychological Meaning,'' *Psychology & Marketing*, Spring 1989, pp. 33–50. See also B. B. Stern, '' 'How Does an Ad Mean?' Language in Services Advertising,'' *Journal of Advertising*, no. 2, 1988, pp. 3–14; and K. A. Berger and R. F. Gilmore, ''An Introduction to Semantic Variables in Advertising Messages,'' in *Advances in Consumer Research XVII*, ed. M. E. Goldberg, G. Gorn, and R. W. Pollay (Provo, Utah: Association for Consumer Research, 1990), pp. 643–50.

[32]D. A. Aaker, D. M. Stayman, and R. Vezina, ''Identifying Feelings Elicited by Advertising,'' *Psychology & Marketing*, Spring 1988, pp. 1–16.

[33]See D. G. Mick and C. Buhl, ''A Meaning-Based Model of Advertising Experiences,'' *Journal of Consumer Research*, December 1992, pp. 317–38.

[34]M. S. LaTour, ''Female Nudity in Print Advertising,'' *Psychology & Marketing*, Spring 1990, pp. 65–81. See also J. J. Kellaris and R. C. Rice, ''The Influence of Tempo, Loudness, and Gender of Listener on Responses to Music'' *Psychology & Marketing*, January/February 1993, pp. 15–29.

[35]G. Tom et al., ''Cueing the Consumer,'' *Journal of Consumer Marketing*, Spring 1987, pp. 23–27. See also D. A. Aaker and D. M. Stayman, ''Implementing the Concept of Transformational Advertising,'' *Psychology & Marketing*, May/June 1992, pp. 237–53.

[36]J. G. Helgeson and S. E. Beatty, ''Price Expectation and Price Recall Error,'' *Journal of Consumer Research*, December 1987, p. 379.

[37]J. J. Inman, L. McAlister, and W. D. Hoyer, ''Promotion Signal,'' *Journal of Consumer Research*, June 1990, pp. 74–81.

[38]See D. M. Sanbonmatsu and F. R. Kardes, ''The Effects of Physiological Arousal on Information Processing and Persuasion,'' *Journal of Consumer Research*, December 1988, pp. 379–85.

[39]R. P. Hill, ''The Impact of Interpersonal Anxiety on Consumer Information Processing,'' *Psychology & Marketing*, Summer 1987, pp. 93–105.

[40]S. N. Singh and G. A. Churchill, Jr., ''Arousal and Advertising Effectiveness,'' *Journal of Advertising*, no. 1, 1987, pp. 4–10; and see footnote 19.

[41]J. E. Nelson, C. P. Duncan, and P. L. Kiecker, ''Toward an Understanding of the Distraction Construct in Marketing,'' *Journal of Business Research*, March 1993, pp. 201–21.

[42]M. Brucks, A. A. Mitchell, and R. Staelin, ''The Effects of Nutritional Informational Disclosure in Advertising,'' *Journal of Public Policy & Marketing*, vol. 3, 1984, pp. 1–25.

[43]''GF, Coke Tell Why They Shun TV News,'' *Advertising Age*, January 28, 1980, p. 39.

[44]D. G. Mick, ''Consumer Research and Semiotics,'' *Journal of Consumer Research*, September 1986, pp. 196–213; and R. D. Zakia and M. Nadin, ''Semiotics, Advertising and Marketing,'' *Journal of Consumer Marketing*, Spring 1987, pp. 5–12; and *International Journal of Research in Marketing*, vol. 4, nos. 3 and 4, 1988, which are devoted to this topic. *Marketing Signs* is a newsletter on this issue published by Research Center for Language and Semiotic Studies at Indiana University. See also P. Chao, ''The Impact of Country Affiliation on the Credibility of Product Attribute Claims,'' *Journal of Advertising Research*, May 1989, pp. 35–41; and L. M. Scott, ''Understanding Jingles and Needledrop,'' *Journal of Consumer Research*, September 1990, pp. 223–36.

[45]R. Alsop, ''Color Grows More Important in Catching Consumers' Eyes,'' *Wall Street Journal*, November 29, 1989, p. B.1.

[46]J. Gotlieb and D. Sarel, ''The Influence of Type of Advertisement, Price, and Source Credibility on Perceived Quality,'' *Journal of the Academy of Marketing Science*, Summer 1992, pp. 253–60. See also A. Biswas and E. A. Blair, ''Contextual Effects of Reference Prices,'' *Journal of Marketing*, July 1991, pp. 1–12; and A. Biswas and S. Bunton, ''Consumer Perceptions of Tensile Price Claims,'' *Journal of the Academy of Marketing Science*, Summer 1993, pp. 219–30.

[47]V. Langholz-Leymore, ''Inside Information,'' *International Journal of Research in Marketing*, no. 4, 1988, pp. 217–32.

[48]S. B. Castleberry and A. V. A. Resurreccion, ''Communicating Quality to Consumers,'' *Journal of Consumer Marketing*, Sum-

mer 1989, pp. 21–28. See also A. J. Bush and R. P. Bush, ''Should Advertisers Use Numbers-Based Copy?'' *Journal of Consumer Marketing*, Summer 1986, pp. 71–79.

[49]M. Wall, J. Liefeld, and L. A. Heslop, ''Impact of Country-of-Origin Cues on Consumer Judgments,'' *Journal of the Academy of Marketing Science*, Spring 1991, pp. 105–14; and T. A. Shimp, S. Samiee, and T. J. Madden, ''Countries and Their Products,'' *Journal of the Academy of Marketing Science*, Fall 1993, pp. 323–30.

[50]J. J. Kellaris, A. D. Cox, and D. Cox, ''The Effect of Background Music on Ad Processing,'' *Journal of Marketing*, October 1993, pp. 100–14.

[51]J. Jacoby and W. D. Hoyer, ''Viewer Miscomprehension of Televised Communications,'' *Journal of Marketing*, Fall 1982, pp. 12–31.

[52]*The Comprehension and Miscomprehension of Print Communications* (New York: The Advertising Educational Foundation, Inc., 1987). For a literature review, see J. Jacoby and W. D. Hoyer, ''The Comprehension/Miscomprehension of Print Communication,'' *Journal of Consumer Research*, March 1989, pp. 434–43.

[53]See K. D. Bahn, ''How and When Do Brand Perceptions First Form?'' *Journal of Consumer Research*, December 1986, pp. 382–93; J. Bryant and D. R. Anderson, *Children's Understanding of Television* (New York: Academic Press, 1986); D. R. John and J. C. Whitney, Jr., ''The Development of Consumer Knowledge in Children,'' *Journal of Consumer Research*, March 1986, pp. 406–17; D. R. John and M. Sujan, ''Age Differences in Product Categorization,'' *Journal of Consumer Research*, March 1990, pp. 452–460; and D. R. John and M. Sujan, ''Children's Use of Perceptual Cues in Product Categorization,'' *Psychology & Marketing*, Winter 1990, pp. 277–94. For a different view, see L. A. Peracchio, ''How Do Young Children Learn to Be Consumers?'' *Journal of Consumer Research*, March 1992, pp. 425–40.

[54]T. E. Muller, ''Structural Information Factors Which Stimulate the Use of Nutrition Information,'' *Journal of Marketing Research*, May 1985, pp. 143–57.

[55]J.-M. Floch, ''The Contribution of Structural Semiotics to the Design of a Hypermarket,'' *International Journal of Research in Marketing*, no. 4, 1988. pp. 233–52.

[56]See G. M. Zinkhan and C. R. Martin, Jr., ''New Brand Names and Inferential Beliefs,'' *Journal of Business Research*, 15, 1987, pp. 157–72; B. V. Bergh, K. Adler, and L. Oliver, ''Linguistic Distinction among Top Brand Names,'' *Journal of Advertising Research*, September 1987, pp. 39–44; and K. Robertson, ''Strategically Desirable Brand Name Characteristics,'' *Journal of Consumer Marketing*, Fall 1989, pp. 61–71.

[57]B. Abrams, ''Consumer-Product Techniques Help Lactile Sell to Industry,'' *The Wall Street Journal*, April 2, 1981, p. 29.

[58]K. R. Robertson, ''Recall and Recognition Effects of Brand Name Imagery,'' *Psychology & Marketing*, Spring 1987, pp. 3–15.

[59]T. Pavia and J. A. Costa, ''The Winning Number,'' *Journal of Marketing*, July 1993, pp. 85–98.

[60]J. N. Axelrod and H. Wybenga, ''Perceptions That Motivate Purchase,'' *Journal of Advertising Research*, June/July 1985, pp. 19–21.

[61]G. Levin, ''Some Logos Hurt Image,'' *Advertising Age*, September 13, 1993, p. 40.

[62]''Ford Boss Outlines Shift to 'Rifle' Media,'' *Advertising Age*, October 26, 1981, p. 89. See also P. Sellers, ''The Best Way to Reach Your Buyers,'' *Fortune*, Autumn/Winter 1993, pp. 13–17.

[63]C. Goldschmidt, ''Many Marketing Success Stories Are Due to Mutual Respect between Ad Agencies, Clients,'' *Marketing News*, February 19, 1982, p. 8.

[64]S. B. MacKenzie, ''The Role of Attention in Mediating the Effect of Advertising on Attribute Importance,'' *Journal of Consumer Research*, September 1986, pp. 174–95.

[65]J. Treistman, ''Will Your Audience See Your Name?'' *Business Marketing*, August 1984, pp. 88–94.

[66]D. R. Berdie and E. M. Hauff, ''Surprises Are Found in Consumer Reactions to Ads in Yellow Pages,'' *Marketing News*, September 11, 1987, p. 8.

[67]B. von Keitz, ''Eye Movement Research,'' *European Research*, 1988, pp. 217–24.

[68]S. N. Singh, M. L. Rothschild, and G. A. Churchill, Jr., ''Recognition vs. Recall as Measures of Television Commercial Forgetting,'' *Journal of Marketing Research*, February 1988, pp. 72–80.

[69]See D. S. Tull and D. I. Hawkins, *Marketing Research* (New York: Macmillan, 1993), Chap. 11; and D. I. Hawkins and D. S. Tull, *Essentials of Marketing Research* (New York: Macmillan, 1994), Chap. 11.

LEARNING, MEMORY, AND PRODUCT POSITIONING

Sewer sludge is the solid matter remaining after municipalities have processed the sewage and disposed of the effluent, generally through dumping it into rivers or oceans. The amount of sludge produced annually is growing dramatically with population increases and enhanced antipollution regulations.

Sludge is used as a soil enhancer, fertilizer, and compost. Sludge is treated by the utilities and is not a health hazard as it was in the past. However, citizen groups frequently oppose the application of sludge to farmlands or other properties. As one official stated after a citizens' group had blocked plans to apply sludge to 6,000 acres near their town: ''We kind of walked into that one blindfolded. We now realize that the public is not knowledgeable about sludge and its disposal.''

To deal with problems posed by such citizens' groups, the utilities are launching public relations campaigns to educate the public about the attributes of sludge. That is, they want the public to learn new information about sludge in the belief that such learning will lead to behavior changes.[1]

CITY/COUNTY

Tacoma turns waste into gain

TAGRO provides option for reusing city's biosolids

by Jodi Nygren
Gateway staff

Most folks flush the toilet or turn on the disposal and then forget about their wastes.

But, with landfills reaching capacity, everyone is going to have to face the biosolids disposal dilemma.

And, according to Mel Kemper, assistant manager of Tacoma's Sewer Operations Division, there's no reason why that leftover waste can't be recycled.

In fact, officials at the Tacoma utility are working to recycle everything — from biosolids to effluent to methane gas produced in the plant's anaerobic digester.

However, recycling something like biosolids, which has a rather odorous and unappealing past, can be a tough sell.

"One big problem is public perception," Kemper said.

40 years of recycling

Biosolids have been recycled at the treatment plant since it opened in 1952, according to plant officials.

In the early days, the leftover solids were dried out in lagoons and then piled near the road for local folks to load up in their trucks and use as fertilizer.

Over the years, however, the quantity of biosolids has increased with the population — and so has the technology to treat the waste.

In 1975, the Tacoma plant began a spray program, which continues to the present.

Plant employees haul tanker trucks full of a liquid form of the biosolids to farms and spray it on fields — free of charge.

They'll even mix in the seed and hydroseed in the process, according to Kemper.

Dried, "cake" biosolids are also available as soil conditioners.

Last year, 43 percent — 1,554 dry tons — of the plant's 3,577 dry tons of biosolids were used in the agriculture-land application program.

Another 39 percent was sold to Northwest Cascade for use in composting.

Gateway photo/Jodi Nygren

Tacoma Sewer Operations Division employees Gordon Behnke, left, and Mel Kemper show off their soil additive, TAGRO. Biosolids go through aerobic and anaerobic digesters and a drying process before being mixed with sandy-loam topsoil and sawdust to produce the additive.

The remaining 18 percent was used in a new product, called TAGRO, produced by the treatment plant.

TAGRO: The new wave

Designed for use in landscaping, this mix of cake biosolids, sandy-loam topsoil and sawdust can be used as a soil additive on anything from potted plants to vegetable gardens to expansive lawns.

Currently there is only a small delivery fee for the product, but Kemper said the plant probably will start charging for the material this summer — just enough to recoup some of the manufacturing costs.

TAGRO is available by "the bucket on up," said Gordy Behnke, biosolids operations supervisor.

Everyone in the treatment plant's service area contributes about 75 pounds of biosolids each year, Behnke added.

If they all would use 75 pounds of TAGRO each year, the plant would be doing well, he said.

"We're trying to change the NIMBYs (Not In My Backyard) to YIMBYs (Yes In My Backyard)," Behnke quipped.

The biosolids mix is not a replacement for topsoil, said Kemper, and to regulate the amount of nitrogen in the soil, TAGRO should be used sparingly — about four pounds per square foot.

For this reason, "Team TAGRO" employees, as they call themselves, ask each customer specific questions about how the TAGRO will be used and give them only enough to cover the area with a one-inch layer.

"That's our limit," said Behnke. "More isn't better."

Multi-use product

As a soil additive, however, TAGRO provides organic material, holds water and fluffs up the soil to allow air in, said Kemper.

In order to both display and monitor TAGRO's effectiveness, the treatment plant has a "mirror garden."

Half of the garden is treated with chemical fertilizer; the other half with TAGRO.

And for the Team TAGRO folks, even if their side is only equal to the chemical fertilizer side, it will spell victory.

Holding their own means reducing the amount of chemical fertilizer manufactured and increasing the uses for recycled biosolids, Kemper said.

Team TAGRO is on the cutting edge of the recycled biosolids industry, said Behnke.

"We're progressive enough to keep our eyes and ears open," he explained.

This openness to new ideas has put them ahead of most wastewater treatment plants in the country, he added.

Many other places use the "d-word" and i-word" to get rid of their wastes, said Kemper.

The d-word stands for "disposed of," meaning dumped in a landfill, and the i-word stands for incineration, he explained.

And some treatment facilities, like Vancouver, B.C., he added, just stockpile the biosolids.

"That seems odd to us," Kemper said. "Every day we let it pile up, the next day we have twice as much to deal with."

For information on TAGRO, the agriculture-land program or treatment plant tours, call 591-5588.

As the opening example illustrates, organizations are interested in teaching consumers and others about the nature of their products and services. In this chapter, we discuss the nature of learning and memory, conditioning and cognitive theories of learning, and general characteristics of learning. Implications for marketing managers also are examined within each section. The outcome of consumer learning about a brand and product category—product position—is discussed in the final section.

NATURE OF LEARNING

Learning is essential to the consumption process. In fact, consumer behavior is largely *learned* behavior. As illustrated in Figure 10–1, we acquire most of our attitudes, values, tastes, behaviors, preferences, symbolic meanings, and feelings through learning. Our culture and social class, through such institutions as schools and religious organizations, as well as our family and friends, provide learning experiences that greatly influence the type of lifestyle we seek and the products we consume. Marketers expend considerable effort to ensure that consumers learn of the existence and nature of their products.

Learning *is any change in the content or organization of long-term memory.*[2] Thus, learning is the result of information processing as described in the last chapter. Recall from Chapter 9 that information processing may be conscious and deliberate in high-involvement situations. Or, it may be nonfocused and even nonconscious in low-involvement situations.

FIGURE 10–1

Learning Is a Key to Consumer Behavior

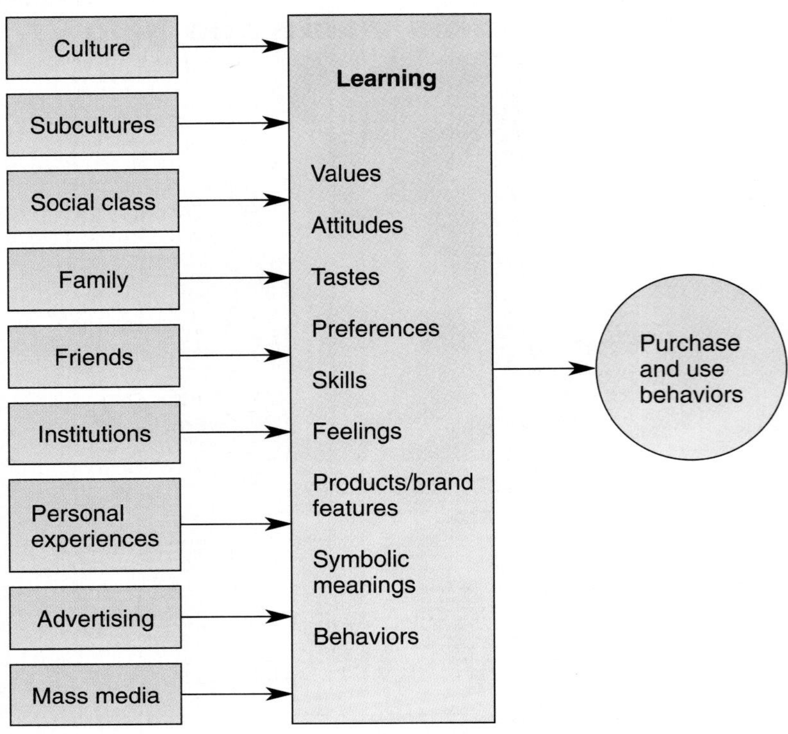

LEARNING UNDER CONDITIONS OF HIGH- AND LOW-INVOLVEMENT

Learning may occur in either a high-involvement or a low-involvement situation. A **high-involvement learning** situation is one in which the consumer is motivated to learn the material. For example, an individual reading *Consumer Reports* prior to purchasing a personal computer is probably highly motivated to learn the material dealing with the various computer brands. A **low-involvement learning** situation is one in which the consumer has little or no motivation to learn the material. A consumer whose television program is interrupted by a commercial for a product he or she doesn't currently use has little motivation to learn the material presented in the commercial. Obviously, learning involvement is not an either/or situation. Rather, it is one of degree. Managerial Application 10–1 shows one ad focused on high-involvement learning and another based on low-involvement learning.

Much, if not most, consumer learning occurs in a relatively low-involvement context. Unfortunately, we do not have a complete understanding of low-involvement learning as most of our research occurs in relatively high-involvement laboratory situations.[3] In the previous chapter, we indicated that different mental processes—the left brain versus the right brain—*may* be involved in high- versus low-involvement information processing. It appears that high- and low-involvement learning are based on similar learning principles. However, certain types of learning are more likely to occur in high-involvement situations and other types are more likely in low-involvement situations.

MANAGERIAL APPLICATION 10-1

High- and Low-Involvement Learning Ads

Low-involvement learning ad

The Economics of the Citibank Classic Visa card. How no annual fee, student discounts and Price Protection create upward growth. A variety of factors have been suggested as contributing to the economic growth of students, including (1) more lottery winners between the ages of 18 and 22, (2) a 37% increase on earnings from bottle and can returns, (3) more students doubling earnings in the lightning round of game shows, and (4) the Citibank Classic Visa® card. It's this last one, however, that affects most students. ¶ The Citibank Classic Visa card offers immediate savings to student cardmembers. You can now receive the Citibank Classic card with **No Annual Fee.** You can capitalize on a **$20 Airfare Discount** for domestic flights,[1] a low variable interest rate of 15.4%,[2] as well as savings on mail order purchases, sports equipment, music and magazines. One might even have enough savings to reinvest in a CD or two (the musical kind, of course). ¶ On the way to the record store, or any store for that matter, take stock of the 3 services concerned with purchases made on the Citibank Classic card. **Citibank Price Protection** assures one of the best prices. See the same item advertised in print for less, within 60 days, and Citibank will refund the difference up to $150.[3] **Buyers Security™** can cover these investments against accidental damage, fire or theft (ordinarily causes for Great Depressions) for 90 days from the date of purchase.[3] And **Citibank Lifetime Warranty™** can extend the warranty for the expected service life of eligible products up to 12 years.[4] ¶ But perhaps the features which offer the best protection are your eyes, your nose, your mouth, etc.—all featured on **The Photocard,** the credit card with your photo on it. Carrying it can help prevent fraud or any hostile takeover of your card. (Insiders speculate that it makes quite a good student ID, too.) Even if one's card is stolen, or perhaps lost, **The Lost Wallet™ Service** can replace your card usually within 24 hours. ¶ So never panic. As we all know, panic, such as in the Great Panics of 1837, 1857 and 1929 can cause a downswing in a market. But with **24-hour Customer Service,** there's no reason for it. A question about your account is only an 800 number away. (Panic of the sort experienced the night before Finals is something else again.) ¶ Needless to say, building a credit history with the support of such services can only be a boost. You're investing in futures—that future house, that future car, etc. And knowing the Citibank Classic Visa card is there in your wallet should presently give you a sense of security, rare in today's—how shall we say?—fickle market. ¶ To apply, call. Students don't need a job or a cosigner. And call if you'd simply like your photo added to your regular Citibank Classic Visa card. Here's the number: **1-800-CITIBANK, extension 19. (1-800-248-4226).** ¶ The Law of Student Supply and Demand states, "If a credit card satisfies more of a student's unlimited wants and needs, while reducing the Risk Factor in respect to limited and often scarce resources—with the greatest supply of services and savings possible—then students will demand said credit card." So, demand away—call.

CITIBANK CLASSIC
Linda Walker
4128 0012 3456 7890
02/94 01/31/97 CV
LINDA WALKER
VISA

Not just Visa. Citibank Visa.
Not just Visa. Citibank Visa.

Monarch Notes® Version: The Citibank Classic Visa card will be there for you with no annual fee, a low rate and special student discounts ...so your own economy will be more like a boom than a bust. Call **1-800-CITIBANK, ext. 19 (1-800-248-4226).**

[1]Offer expires 6/30/94. Minimum ticket purchase price is $100. Rebates are for Citibank student cardmembers on tickets issued by ISE Flights only. [2]The Annual Percentage Rate for purchases is 15.4% as of 12/93 and may vary quarterly. The Annual Percentage Rate for cash advances is 19.8%. If a finance charge is imposed, the minimum is 50 cents. There is an additional finance charge for each cash advance transaction equal to 2% of the amount of each cash advance transaction; however, it will not be less than $2.00 or greater than $10.00. [3]Certain conditions and exclusions apply. Please refer to your Summary of Additional Program Information. Buyers Security is underwritten by The Zurich International UK Limited. [4]Certain restrictions and limitations apply. Underwritten by the New Hampshire Insurance Company. Service life expectancy varies by product and is at least the minimum based on retail industry data. Details of coverage are available in your Summary of Additional Program Information. Monarch Notes® are published by Monarch Press, a division of Simon & Schuster, a Paramount Communications Company. Used by permission of the publisher. Citibank credit cards are issued by Citibank (South Dakota), N.A., ©1994 Citibank (South Dakota), N.A. Member FDIC.

High-involvement learning ad

Figure 10–2 shows the two general situations and the five specific learning theories that we are going to consider. The solid lines in the figure indicate that operant conditioning, vicarious learning/modeling, and reasoning are the commonly used learning strategies in high-involvement situations. Classical conditioning, iconic rote learning, and vicarious learning/modeling tend to occur in low-involvement situations. Each of these specific theories is described in the following pages.

Conditioning

Conditioning refers to learning based on *association of stimulus (information) and response (behavior or feeling)*. The word *conditioning* has a negative connotation to some and brings forth images of robotlike humans. However, conditioned learning simply means that through exposure to some stimulus and a corresponding response, one learns that they go together (or do not go together). There are two basic forms of conditioned learning—classical and operant.[4]

FIGURE 10–2 Learning Theories in High- and Low-Involvement Situations

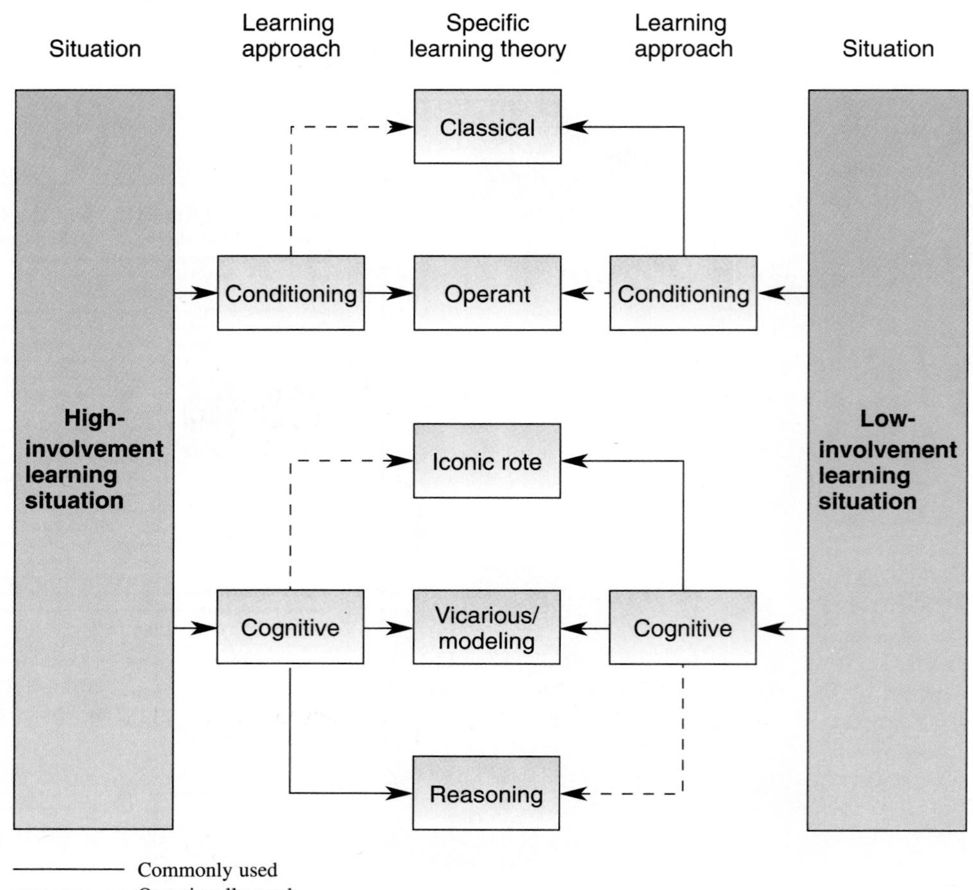

Classical Conditioning is *the process of using an established relationship between a stimulus and response to bring about the learning of the same response to a different stimulus.* Figure 10–3 illustrates this type of learning.

Hearing popular music (unconditioned stimulus) elicits a positive emotion (unconditioned response) in many individuals. If this music is consistently paired with a particular brand of pen or other product (conditioned stimulus), the brand itself may come to elicit the same positive emotion (conditioned response).

Although the ability of commercials to form associations by classical conditioning is controversial, this approach is widely used.[5] For example, Vantage cigarettes are advertised in full-page magazine ads that consist primarily of a beautiful winter snow scene, the brand name, and a picture of the cigarette package. Part of the objective of such ads is to associate the positive emotional response to the outdoor scene with the brand. This in turn will increase the likelihood that the individual will like the brand. Other marketing applications include:

- Consistently advertising a product on exciting sports programs may result in the product itself generating an ''excitement'' response.

Consumer Learning through Classical Conditioning

FIGURE 10–3

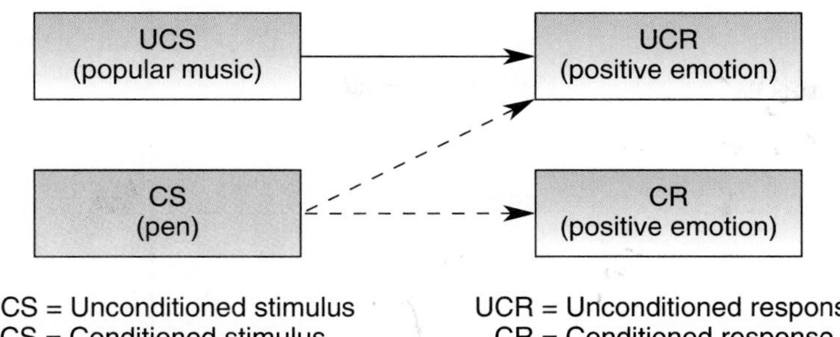

- An unknown political candidate may come to elicit ''patriotic feelings'' by consistently playing patriotic background music in his/her commercials and appearances.
- Christmas music played in stores may elicit emotional responses associated with giving and sharing, which in turn may increase the propensity to purchase.

Classical conditioning is most common in low-involvement situations. In the Vantage example described above, it is likely that many consumers devote little or no focused attention to the advertisement since cigarette ads are low-involvement messages even for most smokers. However, after a sufficient number of low-involvement ''scannings'' or ''glances at'' the advertisement, the association may be formed. It is important to note that what is learned is generally not information but emotion or an affective response. If this affective response leads to learning about the product or leads to a product trial, we have this situation:

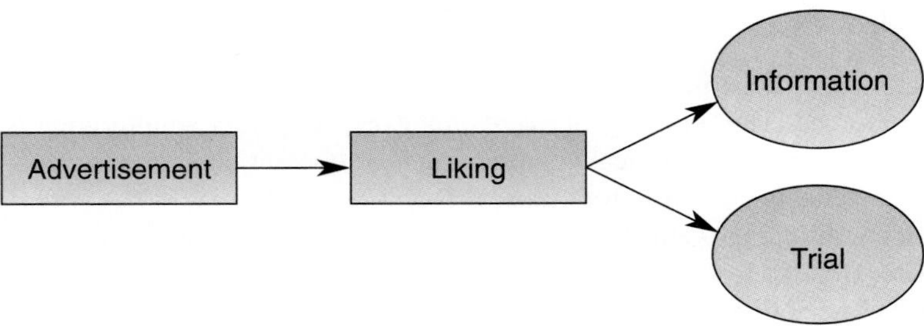

Operant Conditioning, also known as instrumental learning, differs from classical conditioning primarily in the role and timing of reinforcement.[6]

Suppose you are the product manager for Pacific Snax's *Rice Popcorn* snack. You believe your product has a light, crisp taste that consumers will like. How can you influence them to learn to consume your brand? One approach would be to distribute a large number of free samples through the mail, at shopping malls, or in stores.[7]

Many consumers would try the free sample (desired response).[8] To the extent that the taste of *Rice Popcorn* is indeed pleasant (reinforcement), the probability of continued consumption is increased. This is shown graphically in Figure 10–4.

Notice that reinforcement plays a much larger role in operant conditioning than it does in classical conditioning. Since no automatic stimulus-response relationship is involved,

FIGURE 10–4 Consumer Learning by Operant Conditioning

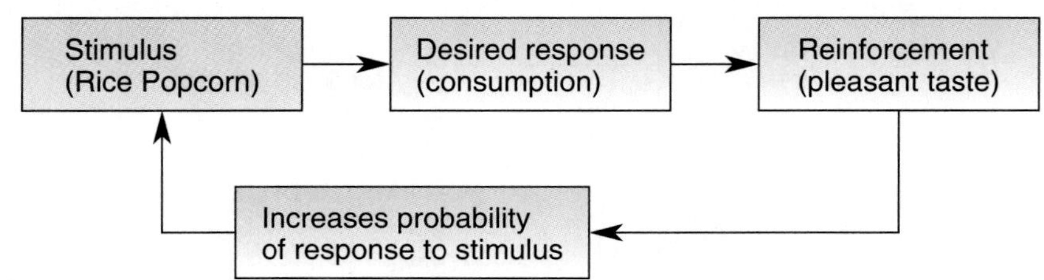

FIGURE 10–5 The Process of Shaping in Purchase Behavior

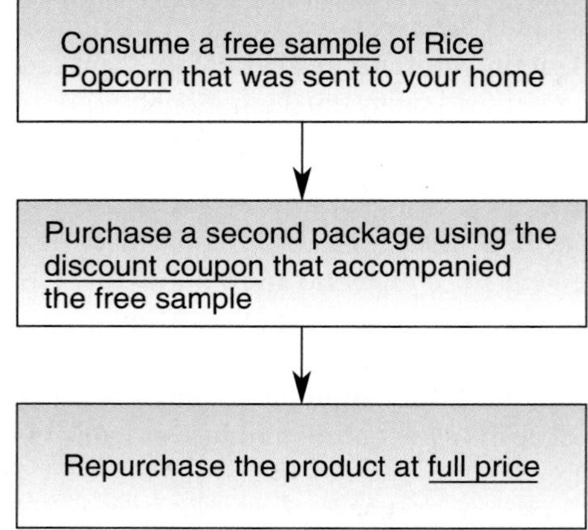

the subject must first be induced to engage in the desired behavior. Then, this behavior must be reinforced. The sequence of events involved in operant conditioning is different from that associated with classical conditioning. For operant conditioning, trial precedes liking. The reverse is often true for classical conditioning.

Operant conditioning often involves the actual usage of the product. Thus, a great deal of marketing strategy is aimed at securing an initial trial. Free samples (at home or in the store), special price discounts on new products, and contests all represent rewards offered to consumers to try a particular product or brand. If they try the brand under these conditions and like it (reinforcement), they are likely to take the next step and purchase it in the future. This process of encouraging partial responses leading to the final desired response (consume a free sample → purchase at full price) is known as **shaping**. This process is illustrated in Figure 10–5.

In a recent study, 84 percent of those given a free sample of a chocolate while in a candy store made a purchase, whereas only 59 percent of those not provided a sample made a purchase. Thus, shaping can be very effective. Managerial Application 10–2 shows an ad designed to induce trial, the first step in shaping.

While reinforcement increases the likelihood of behavior such as a purchase being repeated, a negative consequence (punishment) has exactly the opposite effect. Thus, the purchase of a brand that does not function properly greatly reduces the chances of future purchases of that brand. This underscores the critical importance of consistent product quality.

MANAGERIAL APPLICATION

10-2

An Ad Designed to Induce Trial

Operant conditioning is widely used by marketers. The most common application is to have consistent quality products so that the use of the product to meet a consumer need is reinforcing. Other applications include:

- Direct mail or personal contacts after a sale that congratulate the purchaser for making a wise purchase.
- Giving "extra" reinforcement for shopping at a store, such as trading stamps, rebates, or prizes.
- Giving "extra" reinforcement for purchasing a particular brand, such as rebates, toys in cereal boxes, or discount coupons.
- Giving free product samples or introductory coupons to encourage product trial (shaping).
- Making store interiors, shopping malls, or downtown areas pleasant places to shop (reinforcing) by providing entertainment, controlled temperature, exciting displays, and so forth.
- Advertising which reinforces product ownership or use: "The best people own. . . ."

The power of operant conditioning is demonstrated by an experiment conducted by a midwest insurance company. Over 2,000 consumers who purchased life insurance over a one-month period were randomly divided into three groups. Two of the groups received reinforcement after each monthly payment in the form of a nice "thank-you" letter or telephone call. The third group received no such reinforcement. Six months later, 10 percent of the members of the two groups receiving reinforcement had terminated their policies while 23 percent of those not receiving reinforcement had done so! Clearly, reinforcement (being thanked) lead to continued behavior (sending in the monthly premium).[9]

Operant conditioning is most likely to occur in high-involvement situations. Using a particular product implies at least some involvement. Most high-involvement purchases are followed by a conscious evaluation of the degree of reward obtained. A person who purchases a new suit is likely to devote at least some deliberate effort to evaluating both the symbolic and functional outcome of the purchase. Reinforcement (positive or negative) will have a strong impact in such a situation.

Lower-involvement purchases are generally given a deliberate evaluation only if the product performs far below expectations. Thus, while satisfactory performance is rewarding for low-involvement purchases, it's much more rewarding in high-involvement situations.

Cognitive Learning

Cognitive learning encompasses all the mental activities of humans as they work to solve problems or cope with situations. It involves learning ideas, concepts, attitudes, and facts that contribute to our ability to reason, solve problems, and learn relationships without direct experience or reinforcement. Cognitive learning can range from very simple information acquisition to complex, creative problem solving.

Iconic Rote Learning involves learning the *association between two or more concepts in the absence of conditioning*. For example, one may see an ad that states, "Advil is a headache remedy," and associate the new concept Advil with the existing concept "headache remedy." There is neither an unconditioned stimulus nor a direct reward involved.

A substantial amount of low-involvement learning involves iconic rote learning. Numerous repetitions of a simple message may result in the essence of the message being learned, probably at weak level, as a result of the consumer scanning the environment. Through iconic rote learning, consumers may form beliefs about the characteristics or attributes of products without being aware of the source of the information. When the need arises, a purchase may be made based on those beliefs.[10]

Vicarious Learning/Modeling is another important manner by which consumers learn.[11] It is not necessary for consumers to directly experience a reward or punishment to learn. Instead, we can observe the outcomes of others' behaviors and adjust our own accordingly. Likewise, we can use imagery to anticipate the outcome of various courses of action.

This type of learning is common in both low- and high-involvement situations. In a high-involvement situation such as purchasing a new suit shortly after taking a job, a consumer may deliberately observe the styles worn by others at work or by role models from other environments, including advertisements.

A substantial amount of modeling also occurs in low-involvement situations. Throughout the course of our lives we observe people using products and behaving in a great variety of situations. Most of the time we pay limited attention to these behaviors. However, over time, we learn that certain behaviors (and products) are appropriate in some situations while others are not.

Reasoning represents the most complex form of cognitive learning. In reasoning, individuals engage in creative thinking to restructure and recombine existing information as well as new information to form new associations and concepts. The Roche ad in Managerial Application 10–3 requires the reader to think about the relationship between diet, health, and vitamin supplements.

Summary on Learning Theories

Theories of learning help us understand how consumers learn across a variety of situations. We have examined five specific learning theories: operant conditioning, classical conditioning, iconic rote learning, vicarious learning/modeling, and reasoning. Each of these

MANAGERIAL APPLICATION 10-3

An Ad Requiring Reasoning

learning theories can operate a high- or a low-involvement situation. Exhibit 10–1 summarizes these theories and provides examples from both high- and low-involvement contexts.

GENERAL CHARACTERISTICS OF LEARNING

Regardless of which approach to learning is applicable in a given situation, several general characteristics of learning are relevant and of interest to marketing managers. Five of the most important are strength of learning, extinction (or forgetting), stimulus generalization, stimulus discrimination, and the response environment.

Strength of Learning

What is required to bring about a strong and long-lasting learned response? How can the promotion manager of Pepsi teach you the advantages of this brand so that you will not forget them? The *strength of learning* is heavily influenced by four factors: *importance, reinforcement, repetition,* and *imagery.* Generally, learning comes about more rapidly and lasts longer (*a*) the more important the material to be learned, (*b*) the more reinforcement

EXHIBIT 10–1 Summary of Learning Theories with Examples of Involvement Level

Theory	Description	High-Involvement Example	Low-Involvement Example
Classical conditioning	A response elicited by one object will be elicited by the second object if both objects frequently occur together.	The favorable emotional response elicited by the word *America* comes to be elicited by the brand Chrysler after a consumer reads that Chrysler plans to use only American-made parts.	The favorable emotional response elicited by a picture comes to be elicited by a brand name that is consistently shown with that picture, even though the consumer does not "pay attention" to the advertising.
Operant conditioning	A response that is given reinforcement is more likely to be repeated when the same situation arises in the future.	A suit is purchased and the purchaser finds that it does not wrinkle and generates several compliments. A sport coat made by the same firm is then purchased.	A familiar brand of peas is purchased without much thought. They taste "all right." The consumer continues to purchase this brand.
Iconic rote learning	Two or more concepts become associated without conditioning.	A jogger learns about various brands of running shoes as a result of closely reading many shoe advertisements which he/she finds enjoyable.	A consumer learns that Apple makes home computers, without ever really "thinking" about Apple advertisements or products.
Vicarious learning or modeling	Behaviors are learned by watching the outcomes of others' behaviors or by imagining the outcome of a potential behavior.	A consumer watches the reactions people have to her friend's new short skirt before deciding to buy one.	A child learns that men don't wear dresses without ever really "thinking" about it.
Reasoning	Individuals use thinking to restructure and recombine existing information to form new associations and concepts.	A consumer believes that baking soda removes odors from the refrigerator. Noticing an unpleasant aroma in the carpet, the consumer decides to sweep some baking soda into the carpet.	Finding that the store is out of black pepper, a consumer decides to substitute white pepper.

MANAGERIAL APPLICATION

An Example of Negative Reinforcement

10–4

(or punishment) received during the process, (*c*) the greater the number of stimulus repetitions (or practice) that occurs, and (*d*) the more imagery contained in the material.

Importance refers to the value that the consumer places on the information to be learned. The more important it is for you to learn a particular behavior or piece of information, the more effective and efficient you become in the learning process.[12]

Importance is the dimension that separates high-involvement learning situations from low-involvement situations. Therefore, high-involvement learning tends to be more complete than low-involvement learning. As we will see, high involvement with the learning situation reduces the need for reinforcement, repetition, and imagery. Unfortunately, marketers are most often confronted with consumers in low-involvement learning situations.

Reinforcement is anything which increases the likelihood that a given response will be repeated in the future. While learning frequently occurs in the absence of reinforcement (or punishment), reinforcement has a significant impact on the speed at which learning occurs and the duration of its effect.

A **positive reinforcement** is a pleasant or desired consequence. A thirsty person purchases and consumes a Sprite, which quenches the thirst. Sprite is now more likely to be purchased and consumed the next time the person is thirsty. A **negative reinforcement** involves the removal or the avoidance of an unpleasant consequence. In Managerial Application 10–4, Advil promises to relieve muscle aches. If the ad convinces a consumer to try it and it does relieve the pain, this consumer is likely to continue using Advil due to negative reinforcement.

Punishment is the opposite of reinforcement. It is any consequence which decreases the likelihood that a given response will be repeated in the future. A consumer who tries the *Rice Popcorn* snack described earlier and finds the taste unpleasant would be unlikely to continue buying the product.

From the above discussion, we can see that there are two very important reasons for marketers to determine precisely what reinforces specific consumer purchases. First, to obtain repeat purchases the product must satisfy the goals sought by the consumer. Second, to induce the consumer to make the first purchase, the promotional messages must promise the appropriate type of reinforcement; that is, satisfaction of the consumer's goals.

Repetition (or practice) increases the strength and speed of learning. Quite simply, the more times we are exposed to information or practice a behavior, the more likely we are to learn it. The effects of repetition are, of course, directly related to the importance of the information and the reinforcement given. In other words, less repetition of an advertising message is necessary for us to learn the message if the subject matter is very important or if there is a great deal of relevant reinforcement. Since many advertisements do not contain information of current importance to consumers or direct rewards for attention, repetition plays a critical role in the promotion process for low-involvement products and messages.

Figure 10–6, based on a study of 16,500 respondents, shows the impact of various levels of advertising repetition over a 48-week period on brands that had either high or low levels of initial awareness. Several features stand out. First, the initial exposure has the largest impact. Second, frequent repetition (once a week) outperforms limited repetition (once every other week or every four weeks). This advantage grows the longer the campaign lasts. Finally, relative gains are much greater for unknown brands.

Both the number of times a message is repeated and the timing of those repetitions affect the extent and duration of learning.[13] Figure 10–7 illustrates the relationship between repetition timing and product recall for a food product. One group of homemakers, represented by the curved line in the figure, was exposed to a food product advertisement once a week for 13 consecutive weeks. For this group, product recall (learning) increased rapidly and reached its highest level during the 13th week, forgetting occurred rapidly, and recall was virtually zero by the end of the year.

A second group of homemakers was exposed to the same 13 direct-mail advertisements. However, they received one ad every four weeks. The recall pattern for this group is shown by the zigzag line in the figure. Here learning increased throughout the year, but with substantial forgetting between message exposures.

Placing multiple insertions of the same ad in the single issue of a magazine enhances learning. Three insertions generate more than twice the impact of one insertion.[14] Concentrating one's messages during a single television broadcast has a similar effect. Compared to one showing of a Miller Lite Beer commercial, three showings during a championship baseball game produced two and one-third times the recall, with 20 percent more positive attitudes and 50 percent fewer negative attitudes.[15] The results below are based on the number of times another commercial appeared during an NFC championship game:

Number of Times Commercial Shown	Average Recall (percent)
1	28%
2	32
3	41
4	45

Impact of Repetition on Brand Awareness for High- and Low-Awareness Brands

FIGURE 10–6

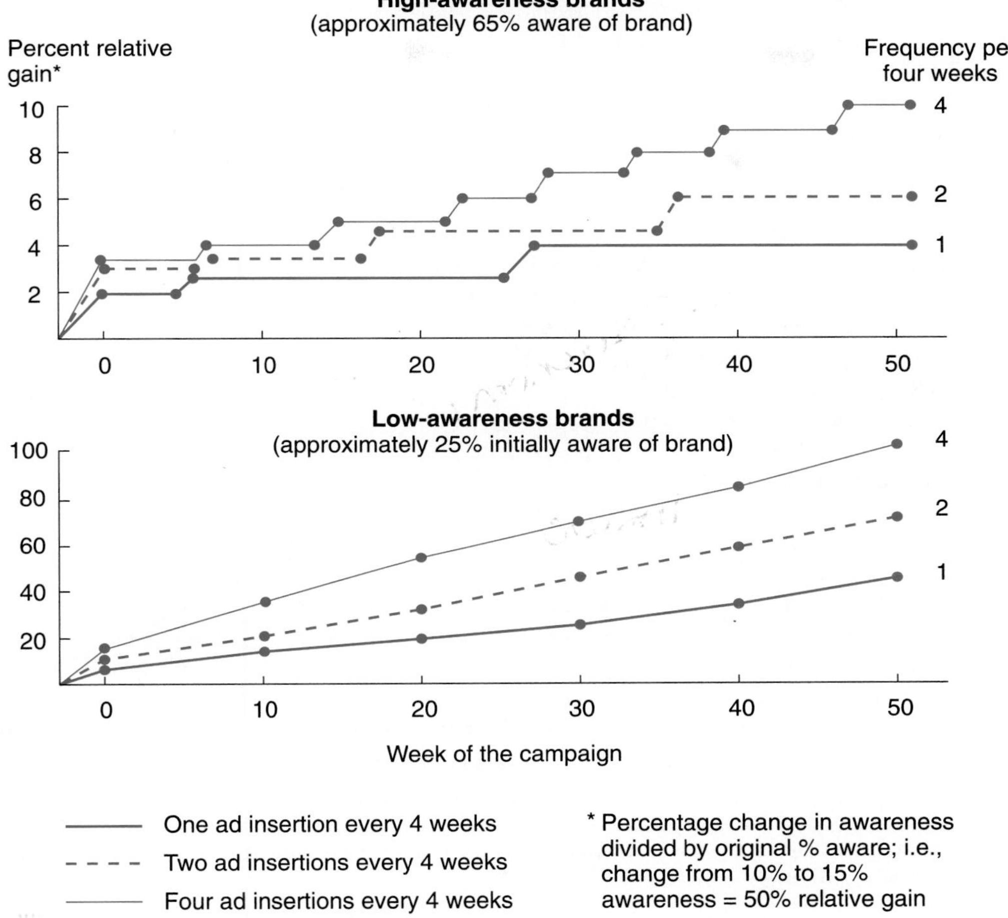

Source: *A Study of the Effectiveness of Advertising Frequency in Magazines* (Time Inc., 1982).

Any time it is important to produce widespread knowledge of the product rapidly, frequent (close together) repetitions should be used. This is referred to as **pulsing**. Thus, political candidates frequently hold back a significant proportion of their media budgets until shortly before the election and then use a ''media blitz'' to ensure widespread knowledge of their desirable attributes. More long-range programs, such as store image development, should use more widely spaced repetitions. In either case, learning is likely to be enhanced if different variations of the same basic message are used.[16]

Consumers frequently complain about repetition in advertising, and some even declare that because of excess repetition, ''I will never buy that brand!'' Thus, there is a fine line for the marketer to balance in terms of repetition. Too much repetition can cause people to actively shut out the message, evaluate it negatively, or pay no attention to it.[17]

Imagery Words, whether a brand name or corporate slogan, create certain images.[18] For example, brand names such as Camel and Rabbit evoke sensory images or well-defined

FIGURE 10–7

Repetition Timing and Advertising Recall

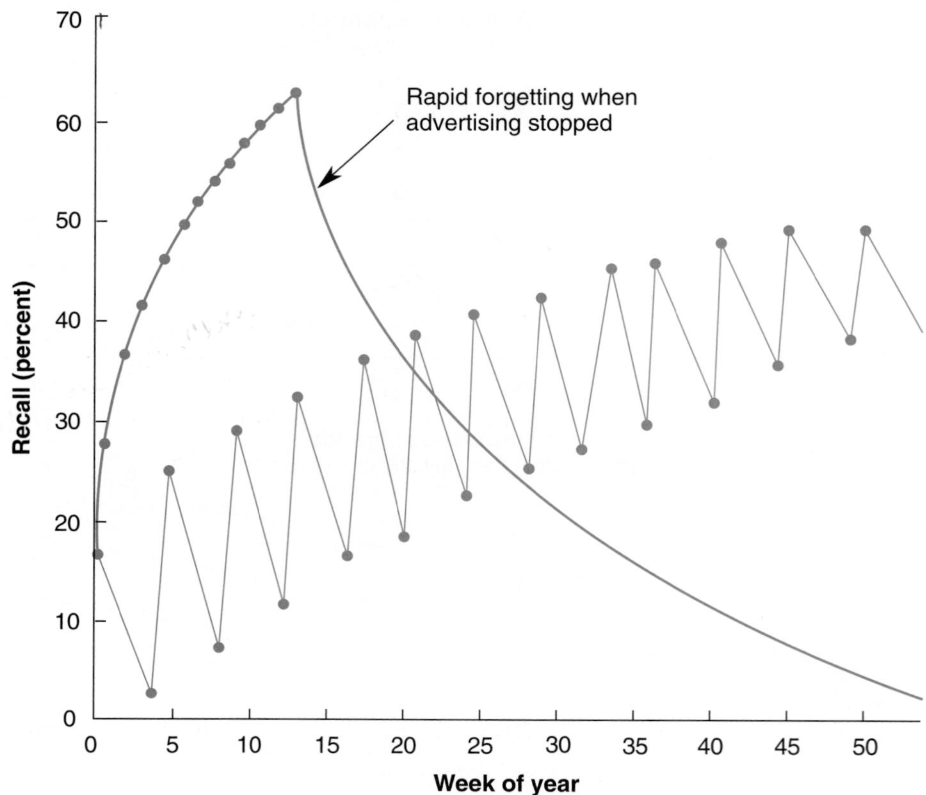

Source: Reprinted from H. J. Zielske, "The Remembering and Forgetting of Advertising," *Journal of Marketing*, January 1959, p. 240, with permission from the American Marketing Association. The actual data and a refined analysis are in J. L. Simon, "What Do Zielski's Data Really Show about Pulsing," *Journal of Marketing Research*, August 1979, pp. 415–20.

mental pictures. As a result these words possess a high degree of imagery or mental visibility. This aids learning, as words high in imagery are substantially easier to learn and remember than low-imagery words. The theory behind the imagery effect is that high-imagery words leave a dual code since they can be stored in memory on the basis of both verbal and pictorial dimensions, while low-imagery words can only be coded verbally.[19] Since imagery greatly enhances the speed and nature of learning, the imagery of a brand name represents a critical marketing decision.

Pictures *are* images and thus, by definition, have a high level of imagery. Compared to verbal content, pictorial components of advertisements appear to enhance learning.[20] Pictures enhance the consumer's visual imagery, which is a particularly effective learning device. They also appear to assist consumers in encoding the information into relevant chunks. Thus, the key communication points of an ad should be in the images elicited by its pictorial component, as this is what will be learned most quickly and firmly.

There is also evidence that **echoic memory**, memory of sounds including words, has characteristics distinct from visual memory.[21] Background music which conveys meanings congruent with the meaning being conveyed by the verbal message has been found to increase learning.[22]

Extinction

Liggett & Myers's share of the cigarette market slid from 20 percent to less than 4 percent. Much of this decline appears to have resulted from limited marketing activities. As one executive stated:

> Some time after the company moved away from advertising and marketing, it became clear that people would quickly forget about our products if we didn't support them in the marketplace.[23]

The above quote emphasizes that marketers want consumers to learn *and* remember positive features, feelings, and behaviors associated with their brands. However, **extinction**, or forgetting as it is more commonly termed, occurs when the reinforcement for the learned response is withdrawn, or the learned response is no longer used.

Figure 10–8 illustrates a commonly found rate-of-forgetting (decay) curve for advertising. In this study, aided and unaided recall of four advertisements from *American Machinist* magazine were measured. As can be seen, recall dropped rapidly after five days, then stabilized.

The rate at which extinction occurs is inversely related to the strength of the original learning. That is, the more important the material, the more reinforcement, the more repetition, and the greater the imagery, the more resistant the learning is to extinction.

At times, marketers or regulatory groups desire to accelerate extinction. For example, the American Cancer Society and other organizations offer programs designed to help individuals ''unlearn'' smoking behavior. Manufacturers want consumers to forget unfavorable publicity or outdated product images.[24] A recent national study found that American automobiles are seen as bland, less prestigious than their European competitors, and less reliable than Japanese cars. They were rated low on ''sporty,'' ''fun,'' and ''innovative'' dimensions.[25] Clearly, American car manufacturers need to help consumers ''unlearn'' these negative aspects of their image and learn new, positive material.

Corrective advertising, a government requirement that firms remove inaccurate learning caused by past advertising, is described in detail in Chapter 21.

Stimulus Generalization

Stimulus generalization (often referred to as the *rub-off effect*) occurs when a response to one stimulus is elicited by a similar but distinct stimulus. Thus, a consumer who learns that Nabisco's *Oreo Cookies* taste good and therefore assumes that their new *Oreo Chocolate Cones* will also taste good, has engaged in stimulus generalization. Stimulus generalization is often used by marketers to develop brand extensions such as *Oreo Chocolate Cones*.

Brand Equity is a value consumers assign to a brand above and beyond any specific functional characteristics of the product (though it is generally derived from such features).[26] It is nearly synonymous with the reputation of the brand. However, the term *equity* implies economic value. Thus, brands with ''good'' reputations have the potential for high levels of brand equity, while unknown brands or brands with weak reputations do not.

Brand leverage (often termed *family branding, brand extensions,* or *umbrella branding*) refers to marketers capitalizing on brand equity by placing the existing brand name

FIGURE 10–8 Forgetting over Time: Magazine Advertisement

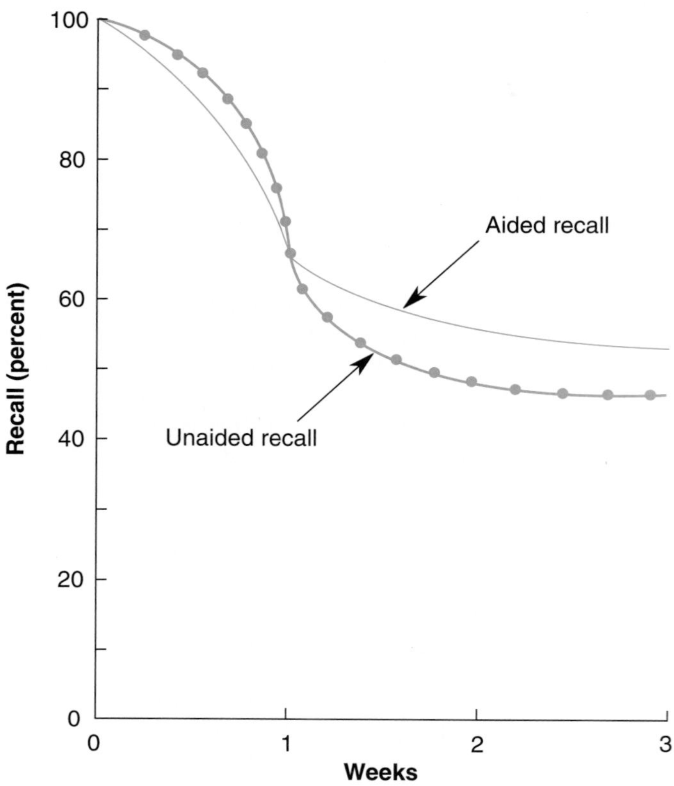

Source: LAP Report #5260.1 (New York: Weeks McGraw-Hill, undated.) Used with permission.

onto new products. If done correctly, consumers will assign some of the characteristics of the existing brand to the new brand. This is based on stimulus generalization.

However, stimulus generalization does not occur just because two products have the same brand name. There must be a connection between the products. Bacardi is particularly conservative in using its name for fear of adversely affecting sales of Bacardi rum, the world's largest-selling distilled spirit. However, they successfully launched Bacardi Tropical Fruit Mixers (frozen nonalcoholic drinks) based on the following rationale:

> Our research found that tropical drinks—piña coladas and frozen daiquiris—are highly associated with Bacardi rum. We already have credibility in that area, which made this new venture right. Bacardi has a lot of equity in its name; it means quality in areas related to rum. . . . But we feel the name wouldn't have that equity in another area. Bacardi wine, for example, wouldn't mean a lot because rum has nothing to do with wine.[27]

In contrast, Campbell's was not able to introduce a spaghetti sauce under the Campbell's name (it used *Prego* instead). Consumer research found that

> Campbell's, to consumers, says it isn't authentic Italian. Consumers figured it would be orangy and runny like our tomato soup.[28]

MANAGERIAL APPLICATION 10–5

A Successful Brand Extension

Successful brand leverage requires that the original brand have a strong positive image and that the new product fit with the original product on at least one of four dimensions:

1. *Complement*—the two products are used together.
2. *Substitute*—the new product can be used instead of the original.
3. *Transfer*—the new product is seen by consumers as requiring the same manufacturing skills as the original.
4. *Image*—the new product shares a key image component with the original.[29]

Porsche has a high-quality, sporty image among many consumers. It could logically extend its name to tires (complement), motorcycles (substitute), ski boats (transfer), or sunglasses (image). Eddie Bauer is known for providing rugged but stylish outdoor wear. It has a loyal following among upscale consumers. Recently it sought to leverage the reputation associated with its clothing by launching a line of men's cologne and related products such as soap. The cologne will be named *Adventurer* to tie it to Bauer's general image (see Managerial Application 10–5). Other examples of successful and unsuccessful brand extensions include:

- Gillette was unsuccessful with a facial moisturizer line under the *Silkience* brand name. Silkience's excellent reputation in haircare simply did not translate to face creams.
- Harley-Davidson has applied its name successfully to a wide variety of products, but its Harley-Davidson wine coolers were not successful.
- Levi Strauss failed in its attempt to market Levi's tailored suits for men.
- Country Time could not expand from lemonade to apple cider.
- Life Savers gum did not succeed.
- Welch's prune juice was not a success.
- Ivory Soap has expanded to Ivory Shampoo.

- Coleman expanded from camping stoves and lanterns into a complete line of camping equipment.
- Oil of Olay bar soap is successful in large part due to the equity of the Oil of Olay lotion.

One must remember that if favorable brand attributes can be learned via generalization, so can unfavorable ones. Witness the case of Bon Vivant soups. The company had a line of soups, among which was a vichyssoise. Unfortunately, a number of food poisonings were traced to a shipment of Bon Vivant's vichyssoise. Naturally, the product was withdrawn from the market, but consumers also generalized to all of the other soups under the Bon Vivant brand, and sales for the entire line were drastically affected.

Stimulus Discrimination

Stimulus discrimination refers to the process of learning to respond differently to somewhat similar stimuli.[30] At some point, stimulus generalization becomes dysfunctional because less and less similar stimuli are still being grouped together. At this point consumers must begin to be able to differentiate among the stimuli. For example, the management of Bayer aspirin feels that consumers should not see their aspirin as being just like every other brand. In order to develop a brand-loyal market for Bayer, consumers had to be taught to differentiate among all the similar brands.

Marketers have a number of ways to do this, not the least obvious of which is advertising that specifically points out brand differences, real or symbolic. The product itself is frequently altered in shape or design to help increase product differentiation.

For example, Nuprin did not gain market share with ads showing research indicating that two Nuprins gave more headache relief than Extra Strength Tylenol. The campaign was changed to focus on the color of Nuprin (''*Little—Yellow—Different—Better*'') with a picture of the yellow Nuprin capsules. The campaign made Nuprin the segment's fastest-growing brand. According to the advertising director:

> That Nuprin is yellow is superficial to the superiority, yet it opens people's minds that this product is different.[31]

Response Environment

It appears that consumers generally have learned more information than they can readily retrieve. That is, we frequently have relevant information stored in memory that we cannot access when needed. One factor that influences our ability to retrieve stored information is the strength of the original learning. The stronger the original learning, the more likely relevant information will be retrieved when required.

A second factor affecting retrieval is the similarity of the retrieval environment to the original learning environment. Thus, the more the retrieval situation offers cues similar to the cues present during learning, the more likely effective retrieval is to occur. (This suggests that exam performance might be enhanced by studying at a deck in a quiet environment rather than on a sofa with music playing.) While we still have much to learn about this, it appears that marketers should do one of two things: (1) configure the learning environment to resemble the most likely retrieval environment, or (2) configure the retrieval environment to resemble the original learning environment.

Matching the retrieval and learning environments requires an understanding of when and where consumers make brand or store decisions. Decisions on brand or store made at home do not have the same set of cues that are available at a retail outlet or in a shopping mall. Suppose a firm teaches consumers to have a positive feeling toward its brand of gum by consistently pairing the pronouncement of its brand name with a very pleasant, fun scene in a television ad (classical conditioning). However, it does not show the package, and the name is presented visually only briefly. In the purchase situation, the consumer faces a shelf with many packages but no auditory presentation of brand name. Thus, the retrieval environment is not conducive to triggering the learned response.

Quaker Oats applied this concept in a very direct manner. It developed and ran an extremely popular advertising campaign for Life cereal. As the popularity of the campaign became evident, Quaker placed a photo of a scene from the commercial on the front of the Life cereal package. This enhanced the ability of consumers to recall both affect and information from the commercial and was very successful.[32]

Conclusions on Consumer Learning

Thus far, we have examined specific theories and approaches to learning. Knowledge of learning theories can be used to structure communications that will assist consumers in learning relevant facts, behaviors, and feelings about our products. We will now turn our attention to an outcome of learning, memory.

MEMORY

Memory is the total accumulation of prior learning experiences. It consists of two interrelated components: short-term and long-term memory. These are *not* distinct physiological entities. Instead, *short-term memory* is that portion of total memory that is currently activated or in use. In fact, it is often referred to as *working memory.*

Long-Term Memory

Long-term memory is viewed as an unlimited, permanent storage. It can store numerous types of information such as concepts, decision rules, processes, affective (emotional) states, and so forth. Marketers are particularly interested in **schematic memory** (frequently termed *semantic memory*), which is the stored representations of our generalized knowledge about the world we live in.[33] It is this form of memory that is concerned with the association and combinations of various ''chunks'' of information.

Figure 10–9 provides an example of a schema by showing how one might associate various concepts with Zima to form a complete network of meaning for that brand. Notice that our hypothetical schema contains *product characteristics*, *usage situations*, and *affective reactions.* The schematic memory of a brand is the same as the brand image. It is what the consumer thinks of *and* feels when the brand name is mentioned.

What do you think of when you see the word *thirst*? The various things, including brands, that come to mind constitute the schema for thirst. Pepsi-Cola exerts substantial marketing efforts in an attempt to become part of the schema associated with thirst. Brands in the schematic memory for a consumer problem such as thirst are known as the *evoked set.* We will discuss the way consumers and marketers use the evoked set in Chapter 16.

Memory of an action sequence, such as purchasing and drinking a soft drink in order to relieve thirst, is a special type of schemata known as a **script** (sometimes referred to as *episodic memory*). Marketers and public policy officials want consumers to develop scripts for appropriate product acquisition, use, and disposal behavior.

Short-Term Memory

Short-term memory has been described in terms of two basic kinds of information processing activities—maintenance rehearsal and elaborative activities. **Maintenance rehearsal** is the continual repetition of a piece of information in order to hold it in current memory for use in problem solving or transferral to long-term memory. While extensive rehearsal generally strengthens retention in long-term memory, it is not essential for a strong long-term memory.

FIGURE 10–9 Schematic Memory for Zima

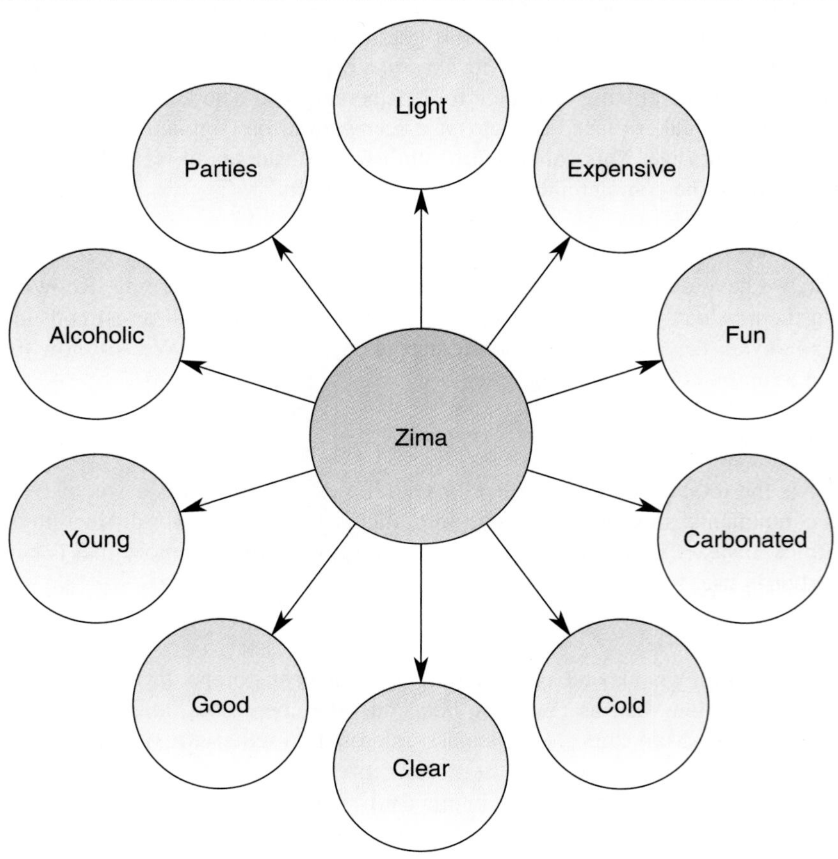

Elaborative activities are the use of previously stored experiences, values, attitudes, beliefs, and feelings to interpret and evaluate information in *working* memory as well as add relevant previously stored information. Elaborative activities serve to redefine or add new elements to memory. Thus, the interpretation process described in Chapter 9 is based on elaborative activities.

Short-term memory is closely analogous to what we normally call thinking. It is an active, dynamic process, not a static structure.

Our previous discussion implies that working memory operates primarily by activating and processing schemata in a discursive or descriptive manner—that is, by *symbol* manipulation. While this accounts for a significant amount of the activities in working memory, *imagery* is also important.[34] Imagery involves concrete sensory representations of ideas, feelings, and objects. It permits a direct recovery of past experiences. Thus, imagery processing involves the recall and mental manipulation of sensory images including sight, smell, taste, and tactile situations. The two tasks below will clarify the distinctions between schema and imagery in working memory:

- Write down the first 10 *words* that come to mind when I say ''romantic evening.''
- Imagine a ''romantic evening.''

Obviously, marketers often want to elicit imagery responses rather than verbal ones. While we are just beginning to study imagery responses, they are a significant part of consumers' mental activities.

PRODUCT POSITIONING STRATEGY

A **product position** refers to the schematic memory of a brand in relation to competing brands, products, or stores.[35] **Brand image**, a closely related concept, is the schematic memory of a brand without reference to competing brands. However, the terms are often used interchangeably.

Anheuser-Busch, Inc., has developed unique product positions for its Michelob, Budweiser, and Busch beers. Each beer is differentiated physically on the basis of price and taste. Busch ad copy stresses quality and price while using baseball as a theme. Budweiser ad copy stresses fun, fellowship, and quality while using football and hockey themes. Michelob ad copy emphasizes superior quality and uses country club sports.

The importance of a proper position is readily apparent in the following quote attributed to a former Schlitz marketing executive:

> Beer is not a drink; it's a symbol. When a guy goes into a bar and orders a Bud or a Miller, he's making a statement about himself. Schlitz's image is so bad that, regardless of taste, the consumer doesn't want to be seen drinking that product.[36]

The stimuli that marketing managers employ to influence a product's interpretation and thus its position can be quite subtle.[37] Sunkist Growers has a pectin-based (a carbohydrate obtained from orange and lemon peels) candy available in various fruit flavors. It contains no preservatives and less sugar than most fruit jelly candies. Originally, the candy was available in restaurants, hospitals, and, to a limited extent, supermarket candy sections.

Now, Sunkist Growers is actively promoting the candy, called Sunkist Fruit Gems, as a ''healthful, natural'' snack. The company hopes to attract adults as well as children. As part of the overall marketing strategy, Sunkist is attempting to distribute the candy through the produce departments of supermarkets. Notice how the distribution plan supports the desired product position or image. A consumer receiving a message that this is a healthful, natural product may agree when the product is found near other healthful, natural products such as apples and oranges.

Marketing managers frequently fail to achieve the type of product image or position they desire because they fail to anticipate or test for consumer reactions. Toro's initial light-weight snow thrower was not successful. Why? It was named the Snowpup, and consumers interpreted this to mean that it was a toy or lacked sufficient power. Sales success came only after a more macho, power-based name was utilized—first Snowmaster and later Toro.

Product positions are developed and evolve over time. Therefore, the messages consumers receive from the firm must be consistent, or change in a deliberate manner to reflect a desired change in a brand's position. Unfortunately, many firms have a tendency to alter promotional themes, prices, and other aspects of the marketing mix in response to short-run sales objectives and competitor tactics. One survey of large firms found that 55 percent developed advertising campaigns focusing solely on achieving short-term results, 34 percent concentrated on long-term results, and 11 percent sought a balance.[38] Such overemphasis on immediate sales results can easily detract from a firm's ability to develop or maintain a sound product position.

FIGURE 10–10 Perceptual Map for Automobiles

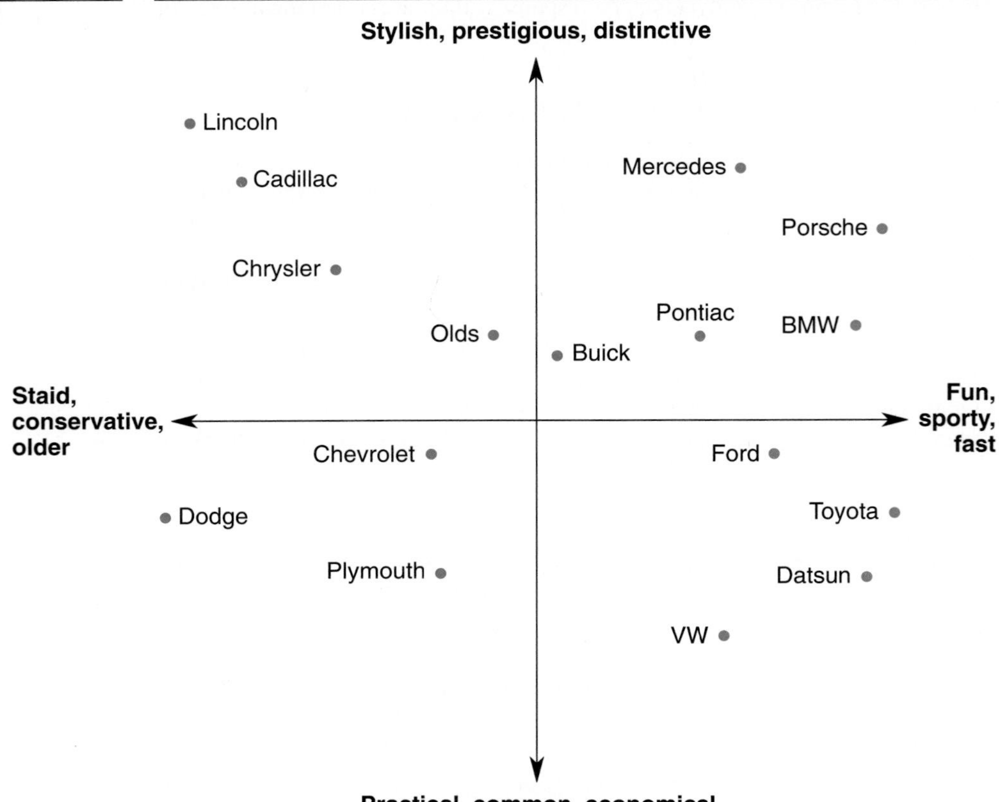

Perceptual mapping offers marketing managers a useful technique for measuring and developing a product's position.[39] Perceptual mapping takes consumers' perceptions of how similar various brands or products are to each other and relates these perceptions to product attributes. Figure 10–10 is a perceptual map for several automobile manufacturers. The marketing implications of the positions held by Olds and Buick are serious. Not only are they viewed as being rather unexciting, they also appear to compete primarily with each other rather than with the products of other manufacturers.

Successful product positioning requires careful attention to all aspects of information processing. Consumers must be exposed to the firm's messages through appropriate media and outlets. They must attend to the message using either low- or high-involvement processes. The total message sent must be structured in a manner that will lead to the desired interpretation. Thus, all aspects of the marketing mix—price, product design and quality, outlets, and advertising messages—must be consistent. Sufficient repetitions, rewards, and so forth must be offered to ensure that the desired interpretation (product position) is learned.

Managerial Application 10–6 shows an ad for *Game Boy* from *Men's Journal.* The ad attempts to position *Game Boy* as an appropriate product for adults to carry and use when delayed in travel or otherwise have unexpected free time (many notebook computers use a similar positioning strategy). While *Game Boy's* positioning strategy seems sound, the product's name may not be consistent with the image adult males prefer.

MANAGERIAL APPLICATION 10-6

A Product Positioning Ad

SUMMARY

Consumers must learn almost everything related to being a consumer—product existence, performance, availability, values, preference, and so forth. Marketing managers, therefore, are very interested in the nature of consumer learning.

High-involvement learning occurs when an individual is motivated to acquire the information. *Low-involvement learning* occurs when an individual is paying only limited or indirect attention to an advertisement or other message. Low-involvement learning tends to be limited due to a lack of elaborate activities. Nonetheless, it explains a substantial amount of consumer learning. While all of the learning theories may operate in a low-involvement situation, classical conditioning, iconic rote learning, and modeling are most common.

Learning is defined as any change in the content or organization of long-term memory. Two basic types of learning, *conditioning* and *cognition*, are used by consumers.

There are two forms of conditioned learning—classical and operant. *Classical conditioning* refers to the process of using an existing relationship between a stimulus and response to bring about the learning of the same response to a different stimulus.

In *operant conditioning*, *reinforcement* plays a much larger role than it does in classical conditioning. No automatic stimulus-response relationship is involved, so the subject must first be induced to engage in the desired behavior and then this behavior must be reinforced.

The *cognitive* approach to learning encompasses the mental activities of humans as they work to solve problems, cope with complex situations, or function effectively in their environment. It includes *iconic rote learning* (forming associations between unconditioned stimuli without rewards), *vicarious learning/modeling* (learning by imagining outcomes or observing others), and *reasoning*.

The strength of learning depends on four basic factors: importance, reinforcement, repetition, and imagery. *Importance* refers to the value that the consumer places on the information to be learned—the greater the importance, the greater the learning. *Reinforcement* is anything that increases the likelihood that a response will be repeated in the future—the greater the reinforcement, the greater the learning. *Repetition* or practice refers to the number of times that we are exposed to the information or that we practice a behavior. Repetition increases the strength and speed of learning. *Imagery* is the degree to which concepts evoke well-defined mental images. High-image concepts are easier to learn.

Corrective advertising is designed to increase the rate of extinction for incorrect material that consumers have learned.

Stimulus generalization is one way of transferring learning by generalizing from one stimulus situation to other, similar ones. Leveraging brand equity is an example of the use of stimulus generalization by marketers. *Stimulus discrimination* refers to the opposite process of learning—to respond differently to somewhat similar stimuli. Marketers interested in building brand-loyal customer segments must bring about the ability to discriminate between similar brands.

Extinction, or forgetting, is also of interest to marketing managers. Extinction is directly related to the strength of original learning, modified by continued repetition.

Memory is the result of learning. Most commonly, information goes directly into *short-term memory* for problem solving or elaboration where two basic activities occur—maintenance rehearsal and elaborative activities. *Maintenance rehearsal* is the continual repetition of a piece of information in order to hold it in current memory. *Elaborative activities* are the use of stored experiences, values, attitudes, and feelings to interpret and evaluate information in current memory.

Long-term memory is information from previous information processing that has been stored for future use. It undergoes continual restructuring as new information is acquired. Information is retrieved from retention for problem solving, and the success of the retrieval process depends on how well the material was learned and the match between the retrieval and learning environment.

Product positioning, a brand's position in a consumer's schematic memory in relation to competing brands, is a major focus of marketing activity. It is the final outcome of the consumer's information processing activities for a product category.

REVIEW QUESTIONS

1. What is *learning*?
2. Describe *low-involvement learning*. How does it differ for *high-involvement learning*?
3. What do we mean by *cognitive learning*, and how does it differ from the *conditioning theory* approach to learning?
4. Distinguish between learning via classical conditioning and that which occurs via operant conditioning.
5. What is *iconic rote learning*? How does it differ from classical conditioning? Operant conditioning?
6. Define *modeling*.
7. What is meant by *learning by reasoning*?
8. What factors affect the strength of learning?
9. What is *imagery*?
10. What is meant by *stimulus generalization*? When is it used by marketers?
11. What is *brand equity*?
12. What is meant by *leveraging brand equity*?
13. Define *stimulus discrimination*. Why is it important?
14. Explain *extinction* and tell why marketing managers are interested in it.

15. What is *corrective advertising*?
16. Why is it useful to match the retrieval and learning environments?
17. What is *memory*?
18. Define *short-term memory* and *long-term memory*?
19. What is *schematic memory*?
20. How does a *schema* differ from a *script*?
21. What is *echoic memory*?
22. What is an *evoked set*?
23. What is *maintenance rehearsal*?
24. What is meant by *elaborative activities*?
25. What is meant by *imagery* in working memory?
26. What is *product positioning strategy*? What is it based on?
27. What is *perceptual mapping*?

DISCUSSION QUESTIONS

28. How would you ensure that consumers learn a favorable product position for:
    a. A candidate for the U.S. Senate.
    b. A motorcycle made by General Motors.
    c. A nonprofit organization focused on saving endangered insect specifics.
    d. A cavity-preventive gum.
    e. A vitamin-fortified soft drink.
    f. A nonalcoholic wine.
29. Is low-involvement learning really widespread? Which products are most affected by low-involvement learning?
30. Almex and Company introduced a new coffee-flavored liqueur in direct competition with Hiram Walker's tremendously successful Kahlua brand. Almex named its new entry Kamora and packaged it in a bottle similar to that of Kahlua, using a pre-Columbian label design. The ad copy for Kamora reads: ''If you like coffee—you'll love Kamora.'' Explain Almex's marketing strategy in terms of learning theory.
31. Discuss stimulus generalization and discrimination with respect to a firm's branding strategy. Identify five brand names that encourage learning by utilizing stimulus generalization, and five brand names that avoid this type of learning. Why would the marketers of these respective products either encourage or discourage stimulus generalization?
32. Describe the product position the following ''brands'' have among students on your campus.
    a. Sting.
    b. Your state's governor.
    c. Zima.
    d. Bose stereo components.
    e. Sierra Club.
    f. The College of Business.
33. In what ways, if any, would these positions differ with different groups, such as (a) middle-aged professionals, (b) young blue-collar workers, (c) high school students, and (d) retired couples?
34. What is the relationship between imagery and schema?
35. Why do a majority of large advertisers design campaigns based exclusively on short-term goals?
36. Evaluate Managerial Application ______ in light of its apparent objectives and target market.
    a. 10–1
    b. 10–2
    c. 10–3
    d. 10–4
    e. 10–5
    f. 10–6

APPLICATION EXERCISES

37. Fulfill the requirements of Question 32 by interviewing five male and five female students.
38. Answer Question 33 based on interviews with five individuals from each group.
39. Pick a consumer convenience product, perhaps a personal care product such as a deodorant or mouthwash, and create advertising copy stressing: (a) a positive reinforcement, (b) a negative reinforcement, and (c) a punishment.
40. Pick a small sample of friends and interview them to find out which type of reinforcement appeal (from Question 39 above) would be

most effective. To do this, you might present each friend with one of the appeals and then ask him/her to respond to the following questions:

What is your overall reaction to this advertisement?

Unfavorable ___ : ___ : ___ : ___ : ___ : ___ : ___ Favorable

How likely would you be to try this product based on this advertising appeal?

Very likely ___ : ___ : ___ : ___ : ___ : ___ : ___ Very unlikely

41. Identify three advertisements, one based on cognitive learning, another based on operant conditioning, and the third based on classical conditioning. Discuss the nature of each advertisement and how it utilizes a certain type of learning.
42. Identify three advertisements which you believe are based on low-involvement learning and three which are based on high-involvement learning. Justify your selection.
43. Select a product and develop an advertisement based on low-involvement learning and one based on high-involvement learning. When should each be used (be specific)?
44. Select a product that you feel has a good product position and one that has a weak position. Justify your selection. Find an ad or package for each product and indicate how it affects the product's position.
45. Select a product, store, or service of relevance to students on your campus. Using a sample of students, measure its product position. Develop a marketing strategy to improve its position.
46. Develop a campaign to reduce the risk of AIDS for students on your campus by teaching them the value of ______.
    a. Abstinence from sex outside of marriage.
    b. "Safe" sex.
47. Find two recent brand extensions that you feel will be successful and two that you feel will fail. Explain each of your choices.

REFERENCES

[1]"PR Campaign Seeks to Improve Image of Sludge," *Marketing News*, October 23, 1987, p. 6.

[2]A. A. Mitchell, "Cognitive Processes Initiated by Exposure to Advertising," in *Information Processing Research in Advertising*, ed. R. Harris (Lawrence Erlbaum Associates, 1983), pp. 13–42.

[3]See S. A. Hawkins and S. J. Hoch, "Low-Involvement Learning," *Journal of Consumer Research*, September 1992, pp. 212–25; and N. M. Alperstein, "The Verbal Content of TV Advertising and Its Circulation in Everyday Life," *Journal of Advertising* no. 2, 1990, pp. 15–22.

[4]W. R. Nord and J. P. Peter, "A Behavior Modification Perspective on Marketing," *Journal of Marketing*, Spring 1980, pp. 36–47.

[5]See E. W. Stuart, T. A. Shimp, and R. W. Engle, "Classical Conditioning of Consumer Attitudes," *Journal of Consumer Research*, December 1987, pp. 334–49; J. J. Kellaris and A. D. Cox, "The Effects of Background Music in Advertising," *Journal of Consumer Research*, June 1989, pp. 113–18; E. W. Stuart, T. A. Shimp, and R. W. Engle, "Classical Conditioning of Negative Attitudes," in *Advances in Consumer Research XVII*, ed. M. E. Goldberg, G. Gorn, and R. W. Pollay (Provo, Utah: Association for Consumer Research, 1990), pp. 536–40; and T. A. Shimp, E. W. Stuart, and R. W. Engle, "A Program of Classical Conditioning Experiments," *Journal of Consumer Research*, June 1991, pp. 1–12.

[6]For details, see M. L. Rothschild and W. C. Gaidis, "Behavioral Learning Theory: Its Relevance to Marketing and Promotions," *Journal of Marketing*, Spring 1981, pp. 70–78; and J. P. Peter and W. R. Nord, "A Clarification and Extension of Operant Conditioning Principles in Marketing," *Journal of Marketing*, Summer 1982, pp. 102–7.

[7]S. Hume, "Sampling Wins Over More Marketers," *Advertising Age*, July 27, 1992, p. 12.

[8]H. B. Lammers, "The Effect of Free Samples on Immediate Consumer Purchase," *Journal of Consumer Marketing*, Spring 1991, pp. 31–37.

[9]B. J. Bergiel and C. Trosclair, "Instrumental Learning," *Journal of Consumer Marketing*, Fall 1985, pp. 23–28. See also W. Gaidis and J. Cross, "Behavior Modification as a Framework for Sales Promotion Management," *Journal of Consumer Marketing*, Spring 1987, pp. 65–74.

[10]See J. R. Rossiter and L. Percy, "Visual Communication in Advertising," in Harris, footnote 2, pp. 83–126; also see footnote 3.

[11]See footnote 4.

[12]See R. Weijo and L. Lawton, "Message Repetition, Experience, and Motivation," *Psychology & Marketing*, Fall 1986, pp. 165–79.

[13]See D. W. Schumann, R. E. Petty, and D. S. Clemons, "Predicting the Effectiveness of Different Strategies of Advertising Variation," *Journal of Consumer Research*, September 1990, pp. 192–202; S. Park and M. Hahn, "Pulsing in a Discrete Model of Advertising Competition," *Journal of Marketing Research*, November 1991, pp. 397–405; and S. N. Singh and C. A. Cole, "The Effects of Length, Content, and Repetition on Television Commer-

cial Effectiveness'' *Journal of Marketing Research*, February 1993, pp. 91–104.

[14]P. H. Chook, ''A Continuing Study of Magazine Environment, Frequency, and Advertising Performance,'' *Journal of Advertising Research*, August/September 1985, pp. 23–33.

[15]J. O. Eastlack, Jr., ''How to Get More Bang from Your Television Bucks,'' *Journal of Consumer Marketing*, Third Quarter 1984, pp. 25–34. Conflicting results are in G. F. Belch, ''The Effects of Television Commercial Repetition on Cognitive Response and Message Acceptance,'' *Journal of Consumer Research*, June 1982, pp. 56–65.

[16]H. R. Unnava and R. E. Burnkrant, ''Effects of Repeating Varied Ad Executions on Brand Name Memory,'' *Journal of Marketing Research*, November 1991, pp. 406–16.

[17]See A. J. Rethans, J. L. Swasy, and L. J. Marks, ''Effects of Television Commercial Repetition, Receiver Knowledge, and Commercial Length,'' *Journal of Marketing Research*, February 1986, pp. 50–61; M. H. Blair, ''An Empirical Investigation of Advertising Wearin and Wearout,'' *Journal of Advertising Research*, January 1988, pp. 45–50; and G. D. Hughes, ''Real-Time Response Measures Redefine Advertising Wearout,'' *Journal of Advertising Research*, May/June 1992, pp. 61–77.

[18]G. M. Zinkhan and C. R. Martin, Jr., ''New Brand Names and Inferential Beliefs,'' *Journal of Business Research*, April 1987, pp. 157–72.

[19]K. R. Robertson, ''Recall and Recognition Effects on Brand Name Imagery,'' *Psychology & Marketing*, Spring 1987, pp. 3–15. See also J. Meyers-Levy, ''The Influence of a Brand Name's Association Set Size and Word Frequency on Brand Memory,'' *Journal of Consumer Research*, September 1989, pp. 197–207.

[20]J. Kisielus and B. Sternthal, ''Examining the Vividness Controversy,'' *Journal of Consumer Research*, March 1986, pp. 418–31; M. P. Gardner and M. J. Houston, ''The Effects of Verbal and Visual Components of Retail Communications,'' *Journal of Retailing*, Spring 1986, pp. 64–78; T. L. Childers, S. E. Heckler, and M. J. Houston, ''Memory for the Visual and Verbal Components of Print Advertisements,'' *Psychology & Marketing*, Fall 1986, pp. 137–50; D. J. MacInnis and L. L. Price, ''The Role of Imagery in Information Processing,'' *Journal of Consumer Research*, March 1987, pp. 473–91; and M. J. Houston, T. L. Childers, and S. E. Heckler, ''Picture-Word Consistency and the Elaborative Processing of Advertisements,'' *Journal of Marketing Research*, November 1987, pp. 359–69.

[21]T. Clark, ''Echoic Memory Explored and Applied,'' *Journal of Consumer Marketing*, Winter 1987, pp. 39–46. See also C. E. Young and M. Robinson, ''Video Rhythms and Recall,'' *Journal of Advertising Research*, July 1989, pp. 22–25.

[22]J. J. Kellaris, A. D. Cox, and D. Cox, ''The Effect of Background Music on Ad Processing,'' *Journal of Marketing*, October 1993, pp. 114–25. See also D. W. Stewart, K. M. Farmer, and C. I. Stannard, ''Music as a Recognition Cue in Advertising Tracking Studies,'' *Journal of Advertising Research*, August/September 1990, pp. 39–48.

[23]''L&M Lights Up Again,'' *Marketing & Media Decisions*, February 1984, p. 69.

[24]For an example of how to combat an unfavorable rumor, see A. M. Tybout, B. J. Calder, and B. Sternthal, ''Using Information Processing Theory to Design Marketing Strategies,'' *Journal of Marketing Research*, February 1981, pp. 73–79.

[25]''U.S. Car Makers Weak on Image,'' *Advertising Age*, September 14, 1987, p. 108.

[26]See K. L. Keller, ''Conceptualizing, Measuring, and Managing Customer-Based Brand Equity,'' *Journal of Marketing*, January 1993, pp. 1–22.

[27]L. Freeman and P. Winters, ''Franchise Players,'' *Advertising Age*, August 18, 1986, pp. 3, 61.

[28]H. Schlossberg, ''Slashing through Market Clutter,'' *Marketing News*, March 5, 1990, p. 6.

[29]D. A. Aaker and K. L. Keller, ''Consumer Evaluations of Brand Extensions,'' *Journal of Marketing*, January 1990, pp. 27–41; A. L. Baldinger, ''Defining and Applying the Brand Equity Concept,'' *Journal of Advertising Research*, July 1990, RC.2–RC.5; D. A. Aaker, ''Brand Extensions,'' *Sloan Management Review*, Summer 1990, pp. 47–56; C. W. Park, S. Milberg, R. Lawson, ''Evaluation of Brand Extensions,'' *Journal of Consumer Research*, September 1991, pp. 185–93; D. A. Aaker, ''The Value of Brand Equity,'' *Journal of Business Strategy*, July/August 1992, pp. 27–32; D. C. Smith, ''Brand Extensions and Advertising Efficiency,'' *Journal of Advertising Research*, November 1992, pp. 11–20; A. Rangaswamy, R. R. Burke, and T. A. Oliva, ''Brand Equity and the Extendability of Brand Names,'' and L. Sunde and R. J. Brodie, ''Consumer Evaluations of Brand Extensions,'' both in *International Journal of Research in Marketing* (no. 10, 1993), pp. 47–53 and 61–75; and B. Loken and D. R. John, ''Diluting Brand Beliefs,'' *Journal of Marketing*, July 1993, pp. 71–85.

[30]See M. Sujan and J. R. Bettman, ''The Effects of Brand Positioning Strategies on Consumers' Brand and Category Perceptions,'' *Journal of Marketing Research*, November 1989, pp. 454–67.

[31]P. Winters, ''Color Nuprin's Success Yellow,'' *Advertising Age*, October 31, 1988, p. 28.

[32]K. L. Keller, ''Memory Factors in Advertising,'' *Journal of Consumer Research*, December 1987, pp. 316–33. See also C. J. Cobb and W. D. Hoyer, ''The Influence of Advertising at the Moment of Brand Choice,'' *Journal of Advertising*, no. 4, 1985, pp. 5–12; and G. Tom, ''Marketing with Music,'' *The Journal of Consumer Marketing*, Spring 1990, pp. 49–53.

[33]R. A. Smith, M. J. Houston, and T. L. Childers, ''The Effects of Schematic Memory on Imaginal Information Processing,'' *Psychology & Marketing*, Spring 1985, pp. 13–29.

[34]MacInnis and Price, ''The Role,'' see footnote 20.

[35]See C. W. Park, B. J. Jaworski, and D. J. MacInnis, ''Strategic Brand Concept-Image Management,'' *Journal of Marketing*, October 1986, pp. 135–45; J. F. Durgee and R. W. Stuart, ''Advertising Symbols and Brand Names that Best Represent Key Product Meanings,'' *Journal of Consumer Marketing*, Summer 1987, pp. 15–24; H. Barich and P. Kotler, ''A Framework for Marketing Image Management,'' *Sloan Management Report* (Winter 1991), pp. 94–104; and E. W. Anderson and S. M. Shogan, ''Repositioning for Changing Preferences,'' *Journal of Consumer Research*, September 1991, pp. 219–32.

[36]J. Neher, ''Schlitz to Taste-Test,'' *Advertising Age*, December 8, 1980, p. 90.

[37]D. Mazursky and J. Jacoby, ''Exploring the Development of Store Images,'' *Journal of Retailing*, Summer 1986, pp. 145–65.

[38]L. Freeman, ''Short-term Focus Hurts Reputation of Brands,'' *Advertising Age*, December 14, 1987, p. 12.

[39]R. Friedmann, ''Psychological Meaning of Products,'' *Psychology & Marketing*, Spring 1986, pp. 1–15; W. R. Dillon, T. Dormzal, and T. J. Madden, ''Evaluating Alternative Product Positioning Strategies,'' *Journal of Advertising Research*, August/September 1986, pp. 29–35; W. DeSarbo and V. R. Rao, ''A Constrained Unfolding Methodology for Product Positioning,'' *Marketing Science*, Winter 1986, pp. 1–19; and R. S. Winer and W. L. Moore, ''Evaluating the Effects of Marketing-Mix Variables on Brand Positioning,'' *Journal of Advertising Research*, March 1989, pp. 39–45.

MOTIVATION, PERSONALITY, EMOTION, AND SELF-CONCEPT

One of the fastest selling new products today is a ''food'' product that has no calories, additives, or artificial coloring. In addition, it is essential to everyone's diet. This miracle product is water.

Water is virtually cost-free from municipal agencies, yet millions of consumers now pay 1,000 times the price of municipal water to purchase bottled water. While heavily advertised brands such as Perrier are well known, bulk water, delivered to homes and offices in five-gallon containers, makes up half the market.

Why do consumers pay to purchase a virtually free item? There appear to be three major purchase motives. Health concerns focusing on nutrition and fitness motivate some users. These individuals want natural, untreated, ''pure'' water. Safety motivates other purchases. Many consumers are concerned with ground water contamination and reports of deteriorating water quality levels. The third motivating factor is ''snob appeal'' or status. Ordering or serving Perrier is more chic and higher status than plain water. The marketing strategy implications of these differing motivations are:

Safety: Show danger of municipal water. Stress filtration, safe source, low price, home/office delivery.

Health: Stress purity and taste, no additives or treatments, moderate price, home/office delivery.

Status: Stress quality, usage situations, exclusive taste, high price; retail, restaurant, and bar outlets.

As the opening example illustrates, a variety of motives may underlie the consumption of even a basic product such as water. This chapter focuses on consumer motivation and three closely related concepts: personality, emotion, and self-concept.

Consumer *motivation* is the energizing force that activates behavior and provides purpose and direction to that behavior. *Personality* reflects the common responses (behaviors) that individuals make to a variety of recurring situations. *Emotions* are strong, relatively uncontrollable feelings that affect our behavior. The three concepts are closely interrelated and are frequently difficult to separate. For example, consumers who are self-confident (a personality characteristic) are more likely to have a need for assertion (a characteristic of motivation) and to seek situations that allow them to feel powerful (an emotional response). Our *self-concept* is our perception of ourselves and our feelings toward ourselves. It includes and influences our motivation, personality, and emotions.

THE NATURE OF MOTIVATION

Motivation is *the reason for behavior.* A **motive** is a *construct representing an unobservable inner force that stimulates and compels a behavioral response and provides specific direction to that response.* A motive is why an individual does something.

To illustrate the nature of consumer motivation, consider consumer motives in the purchase of clothing. At one level, many clothing purchases are partially motivated by a physiological need (for shelter) or a safety need (avoidance of arrest/harassment). In addition, consumers may be motivated to purchase clothing that expresses or symbolizes status because they have a strong need to express that aspect of their self-concept (or desired self-concept) to others. On the other hand, consumers with a strong need for

EXHIBIT 11–1 Marketing Strategies and Maslow's Motive Hierarchy

I. PHYSIOLOGICAL: Food, water, sleep, and, to a limited extent, sex, are physiological motives.

Products: Health foods, medicines, special drinks, low-cholesterol foods, and exercise equipment.

Specific themes:
- Campbell's Soup—"Soup is good food."
- Kellogg's All-Bran—"At last, some news about cancer you can live with."
- NordicTrack—"Only NordicTrack gives you a total-body workout."

II. SAFETY: Seeking physical safety and security, stability, familiar surroundings, and so forth are manifestations of safety needs.

Products: Smoke detectors, preventive medicines, insurance, social security, retirement investments, seat belts, burglar alarms, safes.

Specific themes:
- Sleep Safe—"We've designed a travel alarm that just might wake you in the middle of the night—because a fire is sending smoke into your room. You see, ours is a smoke alarm as well as an alarm clock."
- Chrysler—"Airbags as standard equipment—advantage Chrysler."
- General Electric—"Taking a trip usually means leaving your troubles behind. But there are times when you just might need help or information on the road. And that's when you need HELP, the portable CB from GE."

III. BELONGINGNESS: Belongingness motives are reflected in a desire for love, friendship, affiliation, and group acceptance.

Products: Personal grooming, foods, entertainment, clothing, and many others.

affiliation may purchase a certain wardrobe in order to feel more comfortable in their relationships with people they want to be liked by.[1]

While these motivations may be strong, they are still dependent on the situation. For example, a consumer with a high need for affiliation may not be guided by that motivation in a purchase of underwear if the purchase or use of this product is unlikely to be observed by others. Therefore, we need to keep in mind that motives directing behavior in one situation may be quite different from motives shaping behavior in another situation.

THEORIES OF MOTIVATION

There are numerous theories of motivation and many of them offer potentially useful insights for the marketing manager. This section describes two particularly useful approaches to understanding consumer motivation. The first approach, Maslow's motive hierarchy, is a macro theory designed to account for most human behavior in general

Marketing Strategies and Maslow's Motive Hierarchy (Continued)

EXHIBIT 11–1

Specific themes:
- Atari—''Atari brings the computer age home,'' with a picture of a family using an Atari home computer.
- Oil of Olay—''When was the last time you and your husband met for lunch?''
- J.C. Penney—''Wherever teens gather, you'll hear it. It's the language of terrific fit and fashion. . . .''

IV. ESTEEM: Desires for status, superiority, self-respect, and prestige are examples of esteem needs. These needs relate to the individual's feelings of usefulness and accomplishment.

Products: Clothing, furniture, liquors, hobbies, stores, cars, and many others.

Specific themes:
- Sheaffer—''Your hand should look as contemporary as the rest of you.''
- St. Pauli Girl—''People who know the difference in fine things know the difference between imported beer and St. Pauli Girl. . . .''
- Cadillac—''. . . those long hours have paid off. In recognition, financial success, and in the way you reward yourself. Isn't it time you owned a Cadillac?''

V. SELF-ACTUALIZATION: This involves the desire for self-fulfillment, to become all that one is capable of becoming.

Products: Education, hobbies, sports, some vacations, gourmet foods, museums.

Specific themes:
- U.S. Army—''Be all you can be.''
- U.S. Home—''Make the rest of your life . . . the best of your life.''
- Outward Bound School—''Challenges, adventure, growth.''

terms. The second approach, based on McGuire's psychological motives, uses a fairly detailed set of motives to account for a limited range of consumer behavior.

Maslow's Hierarchy of Needs

Maslow's hierarchy of needs approach is based on four premises:

1. All humans acquire a similar set of motives through genetic endowment and social interaction.
2. Some motives are more basic or critical than others.
3. The more basic motives must be satisfied to a minimum level before other motives are activated.
4. As the basic motives become satisfied, more advanced motives come into play.[2]

Thus, Maslow proposes a motive hierarchy shared by all. Exhibit 11–1 illustrates this hierarchy, briefly describes each level, and provides marketing examples.

MANAGERIAL APPLICATION

11-1

An Appeal to Physiological Motives

Maslow's theory is a good guide to general behavior. It is not an ironclad rule, however. Numerous examples exist of individuals who sacrificed their lives for friends or ideas, or who gave up food and shelter to seek self-actualization. However, we do tend to regard such behavior as exceptional, which indicates the general validity of Maslow's overall approach. It is important to remember that any given consumption behavior can satisfy more than one need. Likewise, the same consumption behavior can satisfy different needs at different times. For example, the consumption of Perrier could satisfy both physiological and esteem needs, just physiological needs, or just esteem needs (or perhaps social needs or even safety needs). Managerial Application 11–1 shows an appeal for *evian* bottled water based on *physiological* needs.

McGuire's Psychological Motives

McGuire has developed a motive classification system that is more specific than Maslow.'s.[3] McGuire's motives that are of most use to marketing are briefly described in the following sections.

Need for Consistency A basic desire is to have all facets or parts of oneself consistent with each other. These facets include attitudes, behaviors, opinions, self-images, views of others, and so forth. Look back at Managerial Application 10–6 (page 291). Game Boy may have a difficult time persuading traveling businesspeople to use Game Boy on planes and similar surroundings—because the name and the product are inconsistent with the image of a businessperson.

Need to Attribute Causation This set of motives deals with our need to determine who or what causes the things that happen to us. Do we attribute the cause of a favorable or unfavorable outcome to ourselves or to some outside force?

The need to attribute cause has led to an area of research known as *attribution theory*.[4] This approach to understanding the reasons consumers assign particular meanings to the behaviors of others has been used primarily for analyzing consumer reactions to promotional messages (in terms of credibility). Thus, when consumers attribute a sales motive to advice given by a salesperson or advertising message, they tend to discount the advice.

Need to Categorize We have a need to be able to categorize and organize information and experiences in some meaningful yet manageable way. So we establish categories or mental partitions which allow us to process large quantities of information. Prices are often categorized such that different prices connote different categories of goods. Automobiles over $20,000 and automobiles under $20,000 may elicit two different meanings because of information categorized on the basis of price level. Many firms price items at $9.95, $19.95, $49.95, and so forth. A reason is to avoid being categorized in the *over* $10.00, $20.00, or $50.00 group.

Need for Cues These motives reflect needs for observable cues or symbols which enable us to infer what we feel and know. Impressions, feelings, and attitudes are subtly established by viewing our own behavior and that of others and drawing inferences as to what we feel and think. In many instances, clothing plays an important role in presenting the subtle meaning of a desired image and consumer lifestyle.[5] This is so critical at companies such as Anheuser-Busch that it uses a special clothing consulting firm to tailor clothes for its executives that are consistent with the firm's desired image.

Need for Independence An individual's need for independence or feeling of self-government is derived from a need to establish a sense of self-worth and meaning by achieving self-actualization. Marketers have responded to this motive by providing products that suggest that you "do your own thing" and "be your own person."

Need for Novelty We often seek variety and difference simply out of a need for novelty. This may be a prime reason for brand switching and so-called impulse purchasing.[6] The need for novelty is curvilinear and changes over time. That is, individuals experiencing rapid change generally become satiated and desire stability while individuals in stable environments become "bored" and desire change. The travel industry segments the vacation market in part by promoting "adventure" vacations or "relaxing" vacations to groups, depending on their likely need for novelty.[7]

Need for Self-Expression This motive is externally oriented and deals with the need to express one's identity to others. We feel the need to let others know by our actions (which include the purchase and display of goods) who we are and what we are. The purchase of many products, particularly clothing and automobiles, allows consumers to express an identity to others since these products have symbolic or expressive meanings. Thus, the purchase of the latest in ski wear may reflect much more than a desire to remain warm while skiing.

Need for Ego-Defense The need to defend our identities or egos is another important motive. When our identity is threatened, we are motivated to protect our self-concept and utilize defensive behaviors and attitudes. Many products can provide ego-defense. A consumer who feels insecure may rely on well-known brands for all socially visible products to avoid any chance of making a socially incorrect purchase.

Need for Assertion The need for assertion reflects a consumer's need for engaging in those types of activities that will bring about an increase in self-esteem, as well as esteem in the eyes of others.[8] Individuals with a strong need for assertion are more likely to complain when dissatisfied with a purchase.

Need for Reinforcement We quite often are motivated to act in certain ways because we were rewarded for doing so. Products designed to be used in public situations (clothing, furniture, and artwork) are frequently sold on the basis of the amount and type of reinforcement that will be received. Keepsake diamonds uses this motive with an advertisement that states: ''*Enter a room and you are immediately surrounded by friends sharing your excitement.*''

Need for Affiliation Affiliation is the need to develop mutually helpful and satisfying relationships with others. The need here is to share and to be accepted by others. As we saw in Chapter 6, group membership is a critical part of most consumers' lives, and many consumer decisions are based on the need to maintain satisfying relationships with others. Marketers frequently use such affiliation-based themes as, ''Your kids will love you for it,'' in advertisements.[9] Managerial Application 11–2 is focused on this motive.

Need for Modeling The need for modeling reflects a tendency to base behavior on that of others. Modeling is a major means by which children learn to become consumers. The tendency to model explains some of the conformity that occurs within reference groups. Marketers utilize this motive by showing desirable types of individuals using their brands. For example, some Rolex ads devote most of their copy to a description of Arnold Palmer. They then state that he owns a Rolex.

MOTIVATION THEORY AND MARKETING STRATEGY

Beck's and *Heineken* are imported beers that are consumed primarily by confident, upscale, professional men. However, BBDO (a major advertising agency) found through its motivation research that *Heineken* consumption is driven by a desire for status, whereas *Beck's* is associated with a desire for individuality. Likewise, both *Classico* and *Newman's Own* spaghetti sauces are consumed by upscale, sophisticated adults. However, *Classico* buyers are motivated by indulgence and romance while *Newman's Own* buyers are showing ambition and individuality. Clearly, each of these brands requires distinct marketing and advertising programs.[10]

Consumers do not buy products. Instead they buy motive satisfaction or problem solutions. Thus, a consumer does not buy a perfume (or a chemical compound with certain odoriferous characteristics): she buys ''atmosphere and hope and the feeling she is something special.''[11] Managers must discover the motives that their products and brands can satisfy and develop their marketing mixes around these motives.

As an example, consumers often buy products and services as a gift for themselves, though they may feel some guilt at being self-indulgent. Motivation research has found that women make such purchases for a variety of motives, including rewarding themselves for an accomplishment.[12] The *Keepsake* ad shown in Managerial Application 11–3 on page 306 directly addresses the appropriateness of self-gifts as a reward.

MANAGERIAL APPLICATION

11-2

An Appeal to the Need for Affiliation

The preceding section provided a number of examples of firms appealing to specific consumer motives. We often find that multiple motives are involved in consumption behavior. In the following sections we examine: (1) how to discover which motives are likely to affect the purchase of a product category by a particular target market; (2) how to develop strategy based on the total array of motives that are operating; and (3) how to reduce conflict between motives.

Marketing Strategy Based on Multiple Motives

Suppose a marketing researcher interviewed you and asked why you wear designer jeans (or drink Heineken, or ski, or whatever). Odds are you would offer several reasons such as "They're in style," "My friends wear them," "I like the way they fit," and "They look good on me." However, there may be other reasons which you are reluctant to admit to or perhaps are not even aware of: "They show that I have money," "They make me sexually desirable," or "They show I'm still young." All or any combination of the above motives could influence the purchase of a pair of designer jeans.

MANAGERIAL APPLICATION

11–3

An Ad Justifying Self-Gifts as a Reward

The first group of motives above were known to the consumer and admitted to the researcher. Motives that are known and freely admitted are called **manifest motives**. Any of the motives we have discussed can be manifest. However, motives that conform to a society's prevailing value system are more likely to be manifest than are those that are in conflict with such values.

The second group of motives described above were either unknown to the consumer or were such that the consumer was very reluctant to admit them. Such motives are **latent motives**. Both latent and manifest motives may influence a purchase or only manifest motives may be operating. Figure 11–1 illustrates how the two types of motives might influence a purchase.

Given that a variety of manifest and latent motives may be operative in a particular purchase such as that shown in Figure 11–1, the first task of the marketing manager is to determine the combination of motives influencing the target market. Manifest motives are relatively easy to determine. Direct questions (Why did you buy a Mercedes?) will generally produce reasonably accurate assessments of manifest motives.

Determining latent motives is substantially more complex. Sophisticated analytical techniques, such as multidimensional scaling, can sometimes provide insights into latent motives. ''Motivation research'' or projective techniques are designed to provide information on latent motives. Exhibit 11–2 describes some of the more common projective techniques.[13]

Once the market manager has isolated the combination(s) of motives influencing the target market, the next task is to design the marketing strategy around the appropriate set of motives. This task involves everything from product design to marketing communications. The nature of these decisions is most apparent in the communications area. Suppose that the motives shown in Figure 11–1 are an accurate reflection of a desired target market. What communications strategy should the manager use?

Latent and Manifest Motives in a Purchase Situation

FIGURE 11–1

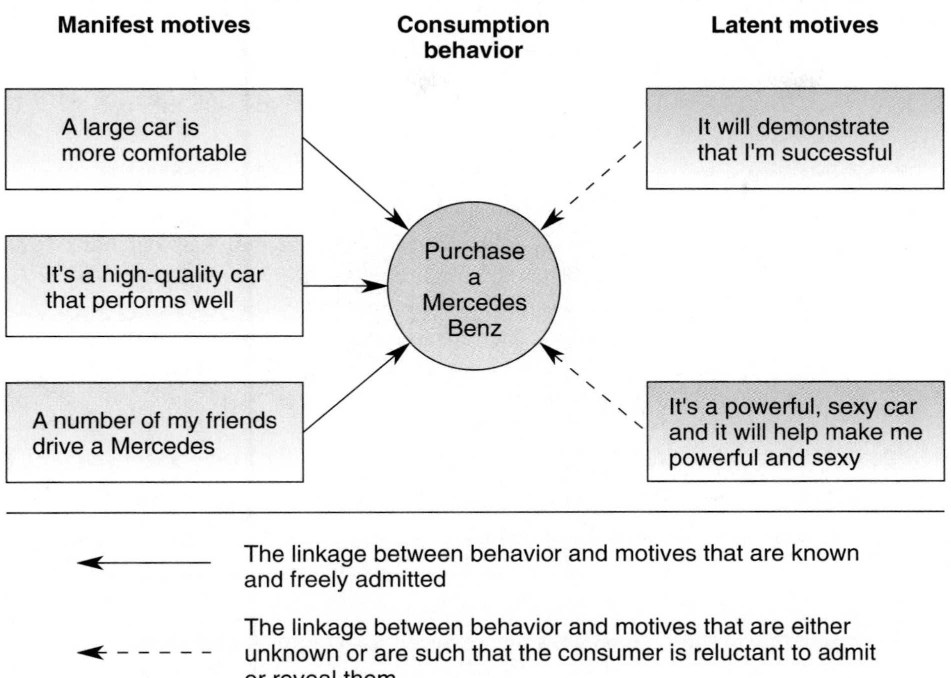

First, to the extent that more than one motive is important, the product must provide more than one benefit and the advertising for the product must communicate these multiple benefits. Communicating manifest benefits is relatively easy. For example, an advertisement for Cadillac states, ''From the triple-sanded finish (once with water and twice with oil) to that superbly refined Cadillac ride, the quality comes standard on Cadillac.'' This is a direct appeal to a manifest motive for product quality. *Direct appeals* are generally effective for manifest motives since these are motives that consumers are aware of and will discuss.

However, since latent motives often are less than completely socially desirable, *indirect appeals* frequently are used. The bulk of the copy of the Cadillac ad referred to above focused on the quality of the product. However, the artwork (about 60 percent of the ad) showed the car being driven by an apparently wealthy individual in front of a luxurious club. Thus, a *dual appeal* was used. The direct appeal in the copy focused on quality while the indirect appeal in the artwork focused on status.

While any given advertisement for a product may focus on only one or a few purchasing motives, the campaign needs to cover all the important purchase motives of the target market. In essence, the overall campaign attempts to position the product in the schematic memory of the target market in a manner that corresponds with the target market's manifest and latent motives for purchasing the product.

Marketing Strategies Based on Motivation Conflict

With the many motives we have and the many situations in which these motives are activated, there are frequent conflicts between motives. The resolution of a motivational conflict often affects consumption patterns. In many instances the marketer can analyze situations which are likely to result in a motivational conflict, provide a solution to the

EXHIBIT 11–2 Motivation Research Techniques

I. ASSOCIATION TECHNIQUES

Word association	Consumers respond to a list of words with the first word that comes to mind.
Successive word association	Consumers give the series of words that come to mind after hearing each word on the list.
Analysis and use	Responses are analyzed to see if negative associations exist. When the time to respond (response latency) is also measured, the emotionality of the word can be estimated. These techniques tap semantic memory more than motives and are used for brand name and advertising copy tests.

II. COMPLETION TECHNIQUES

Sentence completion	Consumers complete a sentence such as "People who buy a Mercedes ______________________________."
Story completion	Consumers complete a partial story.
Analysis and use	Responses are analyzed to determine what themes are expressed. Content analysis—examining responses for themes and key concepts—is used.

III. CONSTRUCTION TECHNIQUES

Cartoon techniques	Consumers fill in the words and/or thoughts of one of the characters in a cartoon drawing.
Third-person techniques	Consumers tell why "an average woman," "most doctors," or "people in general" purchase or use a certain product. Shopping lists (describe a person who would go shopping with this list) and lost wallets (describe a person with these items in his wallet) are also third-person techniques.
Picture response	Consumers tell a story about a person shown buying or using a product in a picture or line drawing.
Analysis and use	Same as for completion techniques.

motivational conflict, and attract the patronage of those consumers facing the motivational conflict. There are three types of motivational conflict of importance to marketing managers: approach-approach conflict, approach-avoidance conflict, and avoidance-avoidance conflict.

Approach–Approach Motivational Conflict faces a consumer with a choice between two attractive alternatives. The more equal this attraction, the greater the conflict. A consumer who recently received a large income tax refund (situational variable) may be torn between a vacation in Hawaii (perhaps powered by the novelty motive) and a compact disk player (perhaps powered by the need for self-expression). This conflict could be resolved by a timely advertisement designed to encourage one or the other action. Or, a price modification, such as "fly now, pay later," could result in a resolution whereby both alternatives are selected.

Approach–Avoidance Motivational Conflict faces the consumer with both positive and negative consequences in the purchase of a particular product. A consumer who is concerned about gaining weight yet likes beer faces this conflict. The development of lower-calorie beers reduces this conflict and allows the weight-sensitive beer consumer to drink beer and also control calorie intake. Nonalcoholic beers reduce the conflict between liking beer and being concerned about alcohol consumption.

Avoidance–Avoidance Motivational Conflict faces the consumer with two undesirable alternatives. When a consumer's old washing machine fails, this conflict may occur. The person may not want to spend money on a new washing machine or go without one. The availability of credit is one way of reducing this motivational conflict. Advertisements stressing the importance of regular maintenance, such as oil filter changes, also use this type of motive conflict: "Pay me now, or pay me (more) later."

PERSONALITY

While motivations are the energizing and directing force that makes consumer behavior purposeful and goal directed, the personality of the consumer guides and directs the behavior chosen to accomplish goals in different situations. **Personality** *is an individual's characteristic response tendencies across similar situations.*

We can easily (though perhaps not always accurately) describe our own personality or the personality of a friend. For example, you might say that one of your friends is "fairly aggressive, very opinionated, competitive, outgoing, and witty." What you have described are the behaviors your friend has exhibited over time across a variety of situations. These characteristic ways of responding to a wide range of situations should, of course, also include responses to marketing strategies.

There is controversy as to the exact nature of personality, the value of studying such a broad area, and the problems with measurement.[14] However, the concept is a very real and meaningful one to all of us on a daily basis. People do have personalities! Personality characteristics exist in those we know, and help us to describe and differentiate between individuals. Personality characteristics also can be used to help structure marketing strategies. Personality theories can be categorized as being either individual theories or social learning theories. Understanding these two general approaches to personality will provide an appreciation of the potential uses of personality in marketing decisions.

Individual Personality Theories

All individual personality theories have two common assumptions: (1) that all individuals have internal characteristics or traits, and (2) that there are consistent and measurable differences between individuals on those characteristics. The external environment or events around us (situations) are not considered in these theories. Most of these theories state that the traits or characteristics are formed at a very early age and are relatively unchanging over the years. Differences between individual theories center around the definition of which traits or characteristics are the most important.

EXHIBIT 11–3 Cattell's Personality Traits*

Reserved: detached, critical, aloof, stiff	versus	*Outgoing:* warmhearted, easy-going, participating
Affected by feeling: emotionally less stable	versus	*Emotionally stable:* mature, faces reality, calm
Humble: stable, mild, easily led, docile, accommodating	versus	*Assertive:* aggressive, competitive, stubborn
Sober: taciturn, serious	versus	*Happy-go-lucky:* enthusiastic
Expedient: disregards rules	versus	*Conscientious:* persistent, moralistic, staid
Shy: timid, threat-sensitive	versus	*Venturesome:* uninhibited, socially bold
Tough-minded: self-reliant, realistic	versus	*Tender-minded:* sensitive, clinging, overprotected
Practical: down-to-earth	versus	*Imaginative:* bohemian, absent-minded
Forthright: unpretentious, genuine, but socially clumsy	versus	*Astute:* polished, socially aware
Self-assured: placid, secure, complacent, serene	versus	*Apprehensive:* self-reproaching, insecure, worrying, troubled
Conservative: respecting traditional ideas, conservatism of temperament	versus	*Experimenting:* liberal, free-thinking, radicalism
Group dependent: a joiner and sound follower	versus	*Self-sufficient:* resourceful, prefers own decisions
Undisciplined: lax, follows own urges, careless of social rules	versus	*Controlled:* exacting will-power, socially precise, compulsive, following self-image
Relaxed: tranquil, torpid, unfrustrated, composed	versus	*Tense:* frustrated, driven, overwrought

*The source trait is in italics.

Source: Adapted from R. B. Cattell, H. W. Eber, and M. M. Tasuoka, *Handbook for the Sixteen Personality Factor Questionnaire* (Champaign, Ill.: Institute for Personality and Ability Testing, 1970), pp. 16–17.

Cattell's theory is a representative example of the individual approach. Cattell believes that traits are acquired at an early age through learning, or are inherited. A unique aspect of his approach is the delineation of surface traits or observable behaviors that are similar and cluster together, and source traits that represent the causes of those behaviors. Cattell felt that if one could observe the surface traits that correlate highly with one another, they would identify an underlying source trait. For example, a source trait of assertiveness may account for the surface traits of aggressiveness, competitiveness, and stubbornness. Exhibit 11–3 gives examples of some of Cattell's major source traits and corresponding surface traits.

While Cattell's theory is representative of multitrait personality theories (more than one trait influences behavior), there are a number of single-trait theories. Single-trait theories stress one trait as being of overwhelming importance. Some examples of single-trait theories are those that deal with dogmatism, authoritarianism, anxiety, locus of control, and social character (tradition-, inner-, and other-directed).

Social Learning Theories

Social learning theories, as opposed to individual theories, emphasize the environment as the important determinant of behavior.[15] Hence, there is a focus on external versus internal factors. Also, there is little concern with variation between individuals in terms of individual traits. Systematic differences in situations, in stimuli, or in social settings are the major interest of social theorists—not differences in traits, needs, or other properties of individuals. Rather than classifying individuals, the social theorists classify situations.

Social learning theories deal with how people learn to respond to the environment and the patterns of responses they learn. As situations change, individuals change their reactions. In the extreme case, every interpersonal interaction may be viewed as a different situation, with the result being a different response pattern. Some people may see you as an extrovert and others as an introvert. Each can be accurate in his assessment of your personality because individuals express different aspects of their personalities to each person.

A Combined Approach

In essence, the differences between individual and social theories of personality can be defined as state versus trait. Individual or trait theorists see behavior as largely determined by internal characteristics common to all persons but existing in differing amounts within individuals. Social or state theories claim just the opposite—situations that people face are the determinants of behavior, and different behaviors among people are the result of differing situations. We take the position that behavior is a result of both individual traits or characteristics and situations that people face.

While research seems to indicate that individual traits are not good predictors of behavior, our basic intuitions disagree and we look for and expect to see some basic stability in individual behavior across situations. For example, a person who is assertive will probably tend to exhibit assertive behaviors in a variety of situations. Certainly some situations would result in less assertive behavior than others, but it seems reasonable to assume that the assertive person will generally act in a more assertive way than a shy person would in the same situation. Thus, the situation modifies the general trait and together they affect behavior.

THE USE OF PERSONALITY IN MARKETING PRACTICE

While we each have a variety of personality traits and become involved in many situations which activate different aspects of our personality, some of these traits or characteristics are more desirable than others and some may even be undesirable. That is, in some situations we may be shy when we wish we were bold, or timid when we would like to be assertive. Thus, we all can find some areas of our personality that need bolstering or improvement.

Like individuals, many consumer products also have a "personality."[16] One brand of perfume may project youth, sensuality, and adventure, while another perfume may be viewed as modest, conservative, and aristocratic. In this example, each perfume has a distinct personality and is likely to be purchased by a different type of consumer or for a different situation. Consumers will tend to purchase the product with the personality that most closely matches their own *or* that strengthens an area the consumer feels weak in.

The impact of personality can be seen in a study by Anheuser-Busch. The firm created four commercial advertisements for four new brands of beer. Each commercial represented one of the new brands and was created to portray the beer as appropriate for a specific "drinker personality." For example, one brand was featured in a commercial that portrayed the "reparative drinker," a self-sacrificing, middle-aged person who could have achieved more if he had not sacrificed personal objectives in the interest of others. For this consumer, drinking a beer serves as a reward for sacrifices. Other personality types—such as the "social drinker" who resembles the campus guzzler, and the "indulgent drinker" who sees himself as a total failure—were used to develop product personalities for the other new brands of beer in the study.

These commercials were watched by 250 beer consumers who then tasted all four brands of beer. After given sufficient time to see each commercial and sample each beer, they were asked to state a brand preference and complete a questionnaire which measured their own "drinker personality." The results showed that most consumers preferred the brand of beer that matched their own drinker personality. Furthermore, the effect of personality on brand preferences was so strong that most consumers also felt that at least one brand of beer was not fit to drink. Unknown to these 250 consumers was the fact that all four brands were the same beer. Thus, the product personalities created in these commercials attracted consumers with like personalities.[17]

EMOTION

Earlier we defined **emotion** as *strong, relatively uncontrolled feelings that affect our behavior.* All of us experience a wide array of emotions. Think for a moment about a recent emotional experience. What characterized this experience? All emotional experiences tend to have several elements in common.

Emotions are generally triggered by *environmental events.* Anger, joy, and sadness are most frequently a response to a set of external events. However, we can also initiate emotional reactions by internal processes such as imagery. Athletes frequently use imagery to "psych" themselves into a desired emotional state.

Emotions are accompanied by *physiological changes.* Some characteristic changes are: (1) eye pupil dilation, (2) increased perspiration, (3) more rapid breathing, (4) increased heart rate and blood pressure, and (5) enhanced blood sugar level.

Another characteristic feature of an emotional experience is *cognitive thought.* Emotions generally, though not necessarily, are accompanied by thinking. The types of thoughts and our ability to think "rationally" vary with the type and degree of emotion. Extreme emotional responses are frequently used as an explanation for inappropriate thoughts or actions: "I was so mad I couldn't think straight."

Emotions also have associated *behaviors.* While the behaviors vary across individuals, and within individuals across time and situations, there are unique behaviors characteristically associated with different emotions: fear triggers fleeing responses; anger triggers striking-out; grief triggers crying, and so forth.

Finally, and most important, emotions involve *subjective feelings.* In fact, it is the feeling component we generally refer to when we think of emotions. Grief, joy, anger, jealousy, and fear *feel* very differently to us. These subjectively determined feelings are the essence of emotion.

These feelings have a specific component that we label as the emotion, such as sad or happy. In addition, emotions carry an evaluative or a like/dislike component. While the

FIGURE 11–2

Nature of Emotions

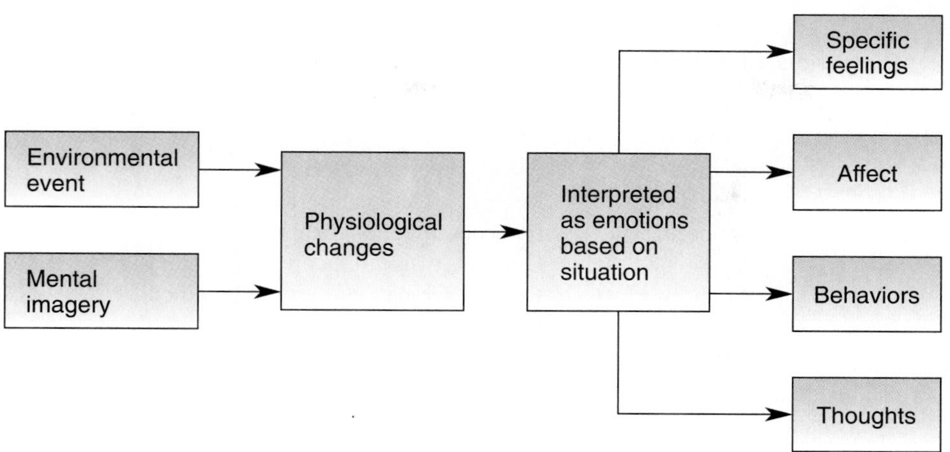

terms are used inconsistently in the literature, we use the term *emotion* to refer to the identifiable, specific feeling, and the term *affect* to refer to the liking/disliking aspect of the specific feeling.[18] While emotions are generally evaluated (liked and disliked) in a consistent manner across individuals, and within individuals over time, there is some individual and situational variation. For example, few of us generally want to be sad or afraid yet we occasionally enjoy a movie or book that scares or saddens us.

Figure 11–2 reflects current thinking on the nature of emotions.

Types of Emotions

If asked, you could doubtless name numerous emotions. A group of 20 or so people can generally name or describe several hundred emotions. Thus, it is not surprising that researchers have attempted to categorize or ''type'' emotions into more manageable clusters. Plutchik lists eight basic emotional categories: (1) fear, (2) anger, (3) joy, (4) sadness, (5) acceptance, (6) disgust, (7) expectancy, and (8) surprise. According to Plutchik, all other emotions are secondary emotions and represent combinations of these basic categories.[19] For example, delight is a combination of surprise and joy, and contempt is composed of disgust and anger.

Other authors have suggested that three basic dimensions—pleasure, arousal, and dominance (PAD)—underlie all emotions. Specific emotions reflect various combinations and levels of these three dimensions.[20] Consumer researchers use both typologies. Exhibit 11–4 lists the three primary PAD dimensions, a variety of emotions or emotional categories associated with each dimension, and indicators or items that can be used to measure each emotion. Exhibit 11–5 provides the same information for a 12-emotion typology developed by Batra and Holbrook.

EMOTIONS AND MARKETING STRATEGY

While marketers have always used emotions to guide product positioning, sales presentations, and advertising on an intuitive level, the deliberate, systematic study of the relevance of emotions in marketing strategy is new. In this section we will briefly describe strategies focused on emotion arousal as a product benefit, emotion reduction as a product benefit, and emotion arousal in the context of advertising.

EXHIBIT 11–4 Emotional Dimensions, Emotions, and Emotional Indicators

Dimension	Emotion	Indicator/Feeling
Pleasure	Duty	Moral, virtuous, dutiful
	Faith	Reverent, worshipful, spiritual
	Pride	Proud, superior, worthy
	Affection	Loving, affectionate, friendly
	Innocence	Innocent, pure, blameless
	Gratitude	Grateful, thankful, appreciative
	Serenity	Restful, serene, comfortable, soothed
	Desire	Desirous, wishful, craving, hopeful
	Joy	Joyful, happy, delighted, pleased
	Competence	Confident, in control, competent
Arousal	Interest	Attentive, curious
	Hypoactivation	Bored, drowsy, sluggish
	Activation	Aroused, active, excited
	Surprise	Surprised, annoyed, astonished
	Déjà vu	Unimpressed, uninformed, unexcited
	Involvement	Involved, informed, enlightened, benefited
	Distraction	Distracted, preoccupied, inattentive
	Surgency	Playful, entertained, lighthearted
	Contempt	Scornful, contemptuous, disdainful
Dominance	Conflict	Tense, frustrated, conflictful
	Guilt	Guilty, remorseful, regretful
	Helplessness	Powerless, helpless, dominated
	Sadness	Sad, distressed, sorrowful, dejected
	Fear	Fearful, afraid, anxious
	Shame	Ashamed, embarrassed, humiliated
	Anger	Angry, initiated, enraged, mad
	Hyperactivation	Panicked, confused, overstimulated
	Disgust	Disgusted, revolted, annoyed, full of loathing
	Skepticism	Skeptical, suspicious, distrustful

Source: Adapted from M.B. Holbrook and R. Batra, ''Assessing the Role of Emotions as Mediators of Consumer Responses to Advertising,'' *Journal of Consumer Research*, December 1987, pp. 404–20.

Emotion Arousal as a Product Feature

Emotions are characterized by positive or negative evaluations. Consumers actively seek products whose primary or secondary benefit is emotion arousal. While positive emotions are sought the majority of the time, this is not always the case (''The movie was so sad, I cried and cried. I loved it. You should see it.'').[21]

Many products feature emotion arousal as a primary benefit. Movies, books, and music are the most obvious examples. Las Vegas, Atlantic City, and Disney World are positioned as emotion-arousing destinations, as are various types of adventure travel programs. Long-distance telephone calls have been positioned as emotion-arousing products (''Reach out

Batra and Holbrook's Emotions and Indicators (Adjectives)*

EXHIBIT 11–5

Emotion	**Indicator**
Activation	Arousal, active, excited
Skepticism	Skeptical, suspicious
Anger	Angry, enraged, mad
Restful	Restful, serene
Bored	Bored, (un)involved, unimpressed, unexcited
Fear	Fearful, afraid
Desire	Desirous, wishful, full of craving
Social affection	Loving, affectionate, pure
Gratitude	Grateful, thankful, benefited
Sadness	Sad, remorseful, sorrowful
Irritation	Disgusted, irritated, annoyed
Surgency	Playful, entertained, lighthearted

*Administered as "I felt not at all (adjective)/very (adjective)" (seven-point scale).

Source: Adapted from R. Batra and M. B. Holbrook, "Developing a Typology of Affective Responses to Advertising," *Psychology & Marketing*, Spring 1990, p. 22. These authors use term *affect*; *emotion* is used in this table to be consistent with the text.

and touch someone"). Several brands of soft drinks and beers stress excitement and fun as primary benefits. Even automobiles are sometimes positioned as emotion-arousing products: Toyota—"Oh What a Feeling"; and Pontiac—"We Build Excitement."

Emotion Reduction as a Product Benefit

As a glance at Exhibit 11–4 or 11–5 indicates, many emotional states are unpleasant to most individuals most of the time. Few of us like to feel sad, powerless, humiliated, or disgusted. Responding to this, marketers design and/or position many products to prevent or reduce the arousal of unpleasant emotions.

The most obvious of these products are the various over-the-counter medications designed to deal with anxiety or depression. Shopping malls, department stores, and other retail outlets are often visited to alleviate boredom or to experience activation, desire, or surgency.[22] Flowers are heavily promoted as an antidote to sadness. Weight-loss products and other self-improvement products are frequently positioned primarily in terms of guilt, helplessness, shame, or disgust reduction benefits. Personal grooming products often stress anxiety reduction as a major benefit.

Emotion in Advertising

Emotion arousal is often used in advertising even when emotion arousal or reduction is not a product benefit. Managerial Application 11–4 provides examples of such ads. We are just beginning to develop a sound understanding of how emotional responses to advertising influence consumer responses,[23] as well as what causes an ad to elicit particular emotions.[24] Therefore, the general conclusions discussed below must be regarded as tentative.

Emotional content in advertisements *enhances their attention attraction and maintenance capabilities.* Advertising messages that trigger emotional reactions of joy, warmth,

MANAGERIAL APPLICATION

11-4

Emotion Arousing Ads

or even disgust are more likely to be attended to than are more neutral ads. As we saw in Chapter 9, attention is a critical step in the perception process.

Emotions are characterized by a state of heightened physiological arousal. Individuals become more alert and active when aroused. Given this enhanced level of arousal, *emotional messages may be processed more thoroughly* than neutral messages. More effort and increased elaboration activities may occur in response to the emotional state.

Emotional advertisements that *trigger a positively evaluated emotion enhance liking of the ad itself.* For example, ''warmth'' is a positively valued emotion that is triggered by experiencing directly or vicariously a love, family, or friendship relationship. Ads high in warmth, such as the McDonald's ad showing father–daughter and father–son relationships, trigger the psychological changes described previously. In addition, warm ads such as these are liked more than neutral ads. Liking an ad has a positive impact on liking the product (see Chapter 13).

Emotional ads *may be remembered better than neutral ads.*[25] As discussed in Chapter 9, recognition measures, rather than recall measures, may be required to measure this enhanced memory. The improvement in memory may be due to the increased processing mentioned above, or it may reflect message structure elements, differing levels of message involvement, or other factors.

Pictures Used to Measure Emotional Reactions

EXHIBIT 11–6

Repeated exposure to positive-emotion-eliciting ads may *increase brand preference through classical conditioning*. Repeated pairings of the unconditioned response (positive emotion) with the conditioned stimulus (brand name), may result in the positive affect occurring when the brand name is presented.

Brand liking may also occur in a direct, high-involvement manner. A person having a single or few exposures to an emotional ad may simply ''decide'' that the product is a good, or likable, product. This is a much more conscious process than implied by classical conditioning. For example, viewing warmth-arousing ads has been found to increase purchase intentions, an outcome of liking a product.

Advertising using emotion-based appeals is gaining popularity. For example, Warner-Lambert recently dropped its fact-based comparative ad campaign for its e.p.t. Stick Test home pregnancy test in favor of a strong emotional campaign. Their 30-second TV spots capture the moment when a young husband learns his wife is pregnant. The wife playfully hints at the news of her pregnancy by chanting the lines from familiar songs that use the word ''baby,'' such as ''Baby Face,'' until her husband catches on.

BBDO, a major ad agency, has a list of 26 emotions they believe can be triggered by advertising. To measure the emotions triggered by an ad, they developed the Emotional Measurement System. Starting with 1,800 pictures of six actors portraying various emotions, the firm used extensive research to narrow the list to 53 that reflect the 26 emotions of interest. Exhibit 11–6 shows the types of pictures used.

To test a commercial, respondents quickly sort through the 53 pictures and set aside all that reflect how they *felt* while watching the commercial. The percent of respondents selecting particular pictures provides a profile of the emotional response to the commercial.

The system has been used for such companies as Gillette, Pepsi-Cola, Polaroid, and Wrigley. The Gillette commercial—''The Best a Man Can Get''—arouses feelings of ''pride'' and ''confidence'' among men and ''happiness'' and ''joyfulness'' among women.[26]

SELF-CONCEPT

Self-concept can be defined *as the totality of the individual's thoughts and feelings having reference to him- or herself as an object.*[27] In other words, your self-concept is composed of the attitudes you hold toward yourself.

The self-concept is really divided into four basic parts, as shown in Exhibit 11–7: actual versus ideal, and private versus social. The actual/ideal distinction refers to your perception

EXHIBIT 11–7 Dimensions of a Consumer's Self-Concept

Dimensions of self-concept	Actual self-concept	Ideal self-concept
Private self	How I actually see myself	How I would like to see myself
Social self	How others actually see me	How I would like others to see me

FIGURE 11–3 The Self-Concept and Consumption Behavior

of *who I am now* (actual) and *who I would like to be* (ideal). The private self refers to *how I am or would like to be to myself* (private self), while the social self is *how I am seen by others or how I would like to be seen by others* (social self).

As Figure 11–3 indicates, there is a very definite relationship between the actual and ideal private self-concept and between the actual and ideal social self-concept. In both cases, we strive to move our real (actual) self-concept toward our ideal self-concept. Attempts to obtain our ideal self-concept (or maintain our actual self-concept) often involve the purchase and consumption of products, services, and media.[28]

Measuring Self-Concept

Utilizing self-concept requires that we be able to measure it. The most common measurement approach is the semantic differential (see Appendix A in this book). Malhotra has developed a set of 15 pairs of adjectives that offer promise of being applicable across a variety of settings. These terms, shown in Exhibit 11–8, were found effective in describing ideal, actual, and social self-concepts, automobiles, and celebrities. Thus, they could be used to ensure a match between the self-concept (actual or ideal) of a target market, the product concept, and the characteristics of an advertising spokesperson.

Using Self-Concept to Position Products

The use of the self-concept by marketing managers is explained by the following logical sequence that leads to a relationship between the self-concept and product purchase:

- An individual has a self-concept. The self-concept is formed through interaction with parents, peers, teachers, and significant others.
- One's self-concept is of value to the individual.

Measurement Scales for Self-Concepts, Person Concepts, and Product Concepts

EXHIBIT 11–8

1. Rugged	....	Delicate
2. Excitable	....	Calm
3. Uncomfortable	....	Comfortable
4. Dominating	....	Submissive
5. Thrifty	....	Indulgent
6. Pleasant	....	Unpleasant
7. Contemporary	....	Noncontemporary
8. Organized	....	Unorganized
9. Rational	....	Emotional
10. Youthful	....	Mature
11. Formal	....	Informal
12. Orthodox	....	Liberal
13. Complex	....	Simple
14. Colorless	....	Colorful
15. Modest	....	Vain

Source: N. K. Malhotra, ''A Scale to Measure Self-Concepts, Person Concepts, and Product Concepts,'' *Journal of Marketing Research*, November 1981, p. 462.

The Relationship between Self-Concept and Brand Image Influence

FIGURE 11–4

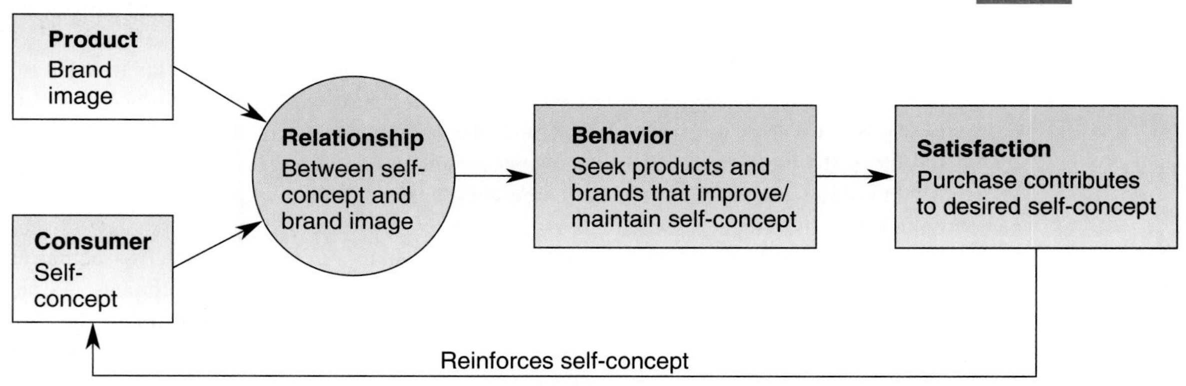

- Because the self-concept is valued, individuals strive to enhance their self-concept.
- Certain products serve as social symbols and communicate social meaning about those who own or use such products.
- The use of products as symbols communicates meaning to one's self and to others, causing an impact on the individual's private and social self-concept.
- As a result, individuals often purchase or consume products, services, and media to maintain or enhance a desired self-concept.

As shown in Figure 11–4, before self-concept can be a relevant marketing tool there has to be a relationship between self-concept and brand image. Furthermore, for this to

MANAGERIAL APPLICATION

11–5

Ads Appealing to the Self-Concept

impact purchase and consumption there has to be both expected and actual satisfaction. That is, the brand purchased must help deliver the desired self-concept.

While it has been shown that consumers prefer brands that are similar to their self-concepts (actual or ideal, private or social), the degree to which they would be attracted to a product varies with the *symbolism* and *conspicuousness* of that product class. Furthermore, the interaction between self-concept and product image is situation specific. That is, the situation may heighten or lessen the degree to which a product or store would enhance an individual's self-image.

In summary then, the self-concepts that individuals have of themselves—actual and ideal, private and social—serve as a guide for many product and brand choices. As marketing managers strive to develop new products and new appeals for consumers, they need to keep in mind this important variable. Products seen as expressive of self-image will be judged by consumers on "how well they help make me what I want to be, and how I want others to see me."

Managerial Application 11–5 contains two ads that appeal to specific self-concepts.

SUMMARY

Consumer motivations are energizing forces that activate behavior and provide purpose and direction to that behavior. In terms of specific product purchases, consumer motivations are dependent on the situation at hand. It is necessary, therefore, to understand what motives and behaviors are influenced by specific situations in which consumers engage in goal-directed behavior.

There are numerous motivation theories. *Maslow's need hierarchy* states that basic motives must be minimally satisfied before more advanced motives are activated. It proposes five levels of motivation: physiological, safety, belongingness, esteem, and self-actualization.

McGuire has developed a more detailed set of motives: consistency, causation, categorization, cues, independence, and curiosity, self-expression, ego-defense, assertion, reinforcement, affiliation, and modeling.

Consumers are often aware of and will admit to the motives causing their behavior. These are *manifest motives.* They can be discovered by standard marketing research techniques such as direct questioning. Direct advertising appeals can be made to these motives. At other times, consumers are unable or are unwilling to admit to the motives that are influencing them. These are *latent motives.* They can be determined by *motivation research techniques* such as word association, sentence completion, and picture response. While direct advertising appeals can be used, indirect appeals are often necessary. Both manifest and latent motives are operative in many purchase situations.

Because of the large number of motives and the many different situations that consumers face, *motivational conflict* can occur. In an *approach–approach conflict,* the consumer faces a choice between two attractive alternatives. In an *approach–avoidance conflict,* the consumer faces both positive and negative consequences in the purchase of a particular product. And finally, in the *avoidance–avoidance conflict* the consumer faces two undesirable alternatives.

The *personality* of a consumer guides and directs the behavior chosen to accomplish goals in different situations. Personality is the relatively long-lasting personal quality that allows us to respond to the world around us. Though there are many controversies in the area of personality research, personalities do exist and are meaningful to consumers and, therefore, to marketing managers.

There are two basic approaches to understanding personality. *Individual theories* have two common assumptions: (1) all individuals have internal characteristics or traits, and (2) there are consistent differences between individuals on these characteristics or traits that can be measured. Most of the individual theories state that traits are formed at an early age and are relatively unchanging over the years. *Social learning theories* emphasize the environment as the important determinant of behavior. Therefore, the focus is on external (situational) versus internal factors.

Brands, like individuals, have personalities, and consumers tend to prefer products with personalities that are pleasing to them. It is also apparent that consumers prefer advertising messages that portray their own or a desired personality. However, for most product categories, personality plays only a limited role in brand selection.

Emotions are strong, relatively uncontrollable feelings that affect our behavior. Emotions occur when environmental events or our mental processes trigger physiological changes including increased perspiration, eye pupil dilation, increased heart and breath rate, and elevated blood sugar level. These changes are interpreted as specific emotions based on the situation. They affect consumers' thoughts and behaviors. Marketers design and position products to both arouse and reduce emotions. Advertisements include emotion-arousing material to increase attention, degree of processing, remembering, and brand preference through classical conditioning or direct evaluation.

The self-concept is one's beliefs and feelings about one's self. There are four types of self-concept: actual private self-concept, actual social self-concept, ideal private self-concept, and ideal social self-concept. The self-concept is important to marketers because consumers purchase and use products to express, maintain, and enhance their self-concepts.

REVIEW QUESTIONS

1. What is a *motive*?
2. What is meant by a *motive hierarchy*? How does Maslow's hierarchy of needs function?
3. Describe each level of Maslow's hierarchy of needs.
4. Describe each of McGuire's motives.
5. What is meant by *motivational conflict*, and what relevance does it have for marketing managers?
6. What is a *manifest motive*? A *latent motive*?
7. How do you measure manifest motives? Latent motives?
8. How do you appeal to manifest motives? Latent motives?
9. Describe the following motivation research techniques:
   a. Association.
   b. Completion.
   c. Construction.
10. What is *personality*?
11. Describe the *individual* and the *social learning* approaches to personality.
12. What do we mean by *single-trait* and *multiple-trait individual theories*? How can knowledge of personality be used to develop marketing strategy?
13. What is an *emotion*?
14. What triggers an emotion?
15. What physiological changes accompany emotional arousal?
16. What is the relationship between emotions and physiological changes?
17. What factors characterize emotions?
18. How can we type or categorize emotions?
19. How do marketers use emotions in product design and positioning?
20. What is the role of emotional content in advertising?
21. Describe BBDO's Emotional Measurement System.
22. What is the self-concept?
23. What is the difference between the private and social self-concept? The actual and ideal self-concept?

DISCUSSION QUESTIONS

24. How could Maslow's motive hierarchy be used to develop marketing strategy for:
    a. Mothers Against Drunk Driving.
    b. Cosmetics.
    c. A pet store.
    d. Boy Scouts.
    e. A candidate for governor.
    f. Women's deodorant.
25. Which of McGuire's motives would be useful in developing a promotional campaign for: _______. Why?
    a. United Way.
    b. Hair salon.
    c. Mountain bike.
    d. Toothpaste.
    e. Salt.
    f. Compact disk player.
26. Describe how motivational conflict might arise in purchasing [or giving to]:
    a. United Way.
    b. Discount store.
    c. Expensive restaurant.
    d. Compact disk player.
    e. Mountain bike.
    f. Dress.
27. Describe the manifest and latent motives that might arise in purchasing, shopping at, or giving to:
    a. Christian Children's Fund.
    b. Compact disk player.
    c. Sports car.
    d. Toothpaste.
    e. B&B (a liqueur).
    f. A cat.
28. How might a knowledge of personality be used to develop an advertising campaign for:
    a. The Sierra Club.
    b. A candidate for the U.S. Senate.
    c. In-line skates.
    d. A tax service.
    e. A micro-brewery.
    f. A sports car.
29. Using Exhibit 11–3, discuss how you would

use one of the personality source traits in developing a package design for a nonalcoholic beer.

30. How would you use emotion to develop marketing strategy for the products listed in Discussion Question _______?
    a. 24.
    b. 25.
    c. 26.
    d. 27.
    e. 28.
31. List all the emotions you can think of. Which ones are not explicitly mentioned in Exhibit 11–4? Where would you place them in this table?
32. What products or brands, other than those described in the chapter, arouse or reduce emotions?
33. How would you use self-concept to market _______?
    a. Christian Children's Fund.
    b. B&B (a liqueur).
    c. Condoms.
    d. A mountain bike.
    e. Fat-free yogurt.
    f. A micro-brewery beer.
    g. A sports car.
    h. A multivitamin for senior citizens.
34. What is your _______? Why are there differences between these?
    a. Actual private self-concept.
    b. Actual social self-concept.
    c. Desired private self-concept.
    d. Desired social self-concept.

APPLICATION EXERCISES

35. Develop an advertisement for two of the items in Discussion Question _______ based on relevant motives from McGuire's set.
    a. 24.
    b. 25.
    c. 26.
    d. 27.
    e. 28.
36. Repeat Question 35 using Maslow's need hierarchy.
37. Repeat Question 35 using emotions.
38. Repeat Question 35 using the self-concept.
39. Find two advertisements that appeal to each level of Maslow's hierarchy. Explain why the ads appeal to the particular levels and speculate on why the firm selected these levels to appeal to.
40. Find two ads that contain direct appeals to manifest motives and indirect appeals to latent motives. Explain how the ads are using indirect appeals.
41. Select a product of interest and use motivation research techniques to determine the latent purchase motives for 5 consumers.
42. Have 5 students describe the personality of _______. To what extent are the descriptions similar? Why are there differences?
    a. Harvard University.
    b. Bud Light beer.
    c. Mercedes Benz.
    d. Apple MacIntosh.
    e. A local restaurant.
    f. The University bookstore.
43. Find and copy two ads with strong emotional appeals, and two ads from the same product categories with limited emotional appeals. Why do the companies use different appeals?
    a. Have 10 students rank or rate the ads in terms of their preferences and then explain their rankings or ratings.
    b. Have 10 different students talk about their reactions to each ad as they view it. What do you conclude?
44. Use 5 students and measure their actual private self-concept and their ideal private self-concept. What type purchases is each likely to make in the future?
45. Repeat the Anheuser-Busch study (described on page 312) using bottled water or a soft drink as the product.
46. Do number 45 above but use self-concept and product image instead of personality.

REFERENCES

[1]See G. D. McCracken and V. J. Roth, ''Does Clothing Have a Code?'' *International Journal of Research in Marketing*, September 1989, pp. 13–33.

[2]A. H. Maslow, *Motivation and Personality*, 2nd ed. (New York: Harper & Row, 1970).

[3]W. J. McGuire, ''Psychological Motives and Communication Gratification,'' in *The Uses of Mass Communications*, ed. J. G. Blumler and C. Katz (Beverly Hills, Calif.: Sage Publications, 1974), pp. 167–96; and W. J. McGuire, ''Some Internal Psychological Factors Influencing Consumer Choice,'' *Journal of Consumer Research*, March 1976, pp. 302–19.

[4]V. S. Folkes, ''Recent Attribution Research in Consumer Behavior,'' *Journal of Consumer Research*, March 1988, pp. 548–65.

[5]S. Dawson and J. Cavell, ''Status Recognition in the 1980s,'' *Advances in Consumer Research XIV*, ed. M. Wallendorf and P. Anderson (Provo, Utah: Association for Consumer Research, 1987) pp. 487–91; and R. Belk and R. Pollay, ''Images of Ourselves,'' *Journal of Consumer Research*, March 1985, pp. 887–97.

[6]J. M. Lattin and L. McAlister, ''Using a Variety-Seeking Model,'' *Journal of Marketing Research*, August 1985, pp. 330–39; and B. E. Kahn, M. U. Kalwani, and D. G. Morrison, ''Measuring Variety-Seeking and Reinforcement Behaviors,'' *Journal of Marketing Research*, May 1986, pp. 89–100; and I. Simonson, ''The Effect of Purchase Quantity and Timing on Variety-Seeking Behavior,'' *Journal of Marketing Research*, May 1990, pp. 150–62. See also N. Hanna and J. S. Wagle, ''Who Is Your Satisfied Customer?'' *Journal of Consumer Marketing*, Winter 1989, pp. 19–23; and M. P. Venkatraman and L. L. Price, ''Differentiating between Cognitive and Sensory Innovativeness,'' *Journal of Business Research*, June 1990, pp. 293–314.

[7]D. C. Bellow and M. J. Etzel, ''The Role of Novelty in the Pleasure Travel Experience,'' *Journal of Travel Research*, Summer 1985, pp. 20–26.

[8]See J. F. Durgee, ''Self-Esteem Advertising,'' *Journal of Advertising*, no. 4, 1986, pp. 21–27.

[9]See G. M. Zinkhan, J. W. Hong, and R. Lawson, ''Achievement and Affiliation Motivation,'' *Journal of Business Research*, March 1990, pp. 135–43.

[10]C. Miller, ''Spaghetti Sauce Preference,'' *Marketing News*, August 31, 1992, p. 5.

[11]J. Birnbaum, ''Pricing of Products Is Still an Art Often Having Little Link to Costs,'' *The Wall Street Journal*, November 25, 1981, p. 29.

[12]G. D. Mick, M. DeMoss, and R. J. Faber, ''A Projective Study of Motivations and Meanings of Self-Gifts,'' *Journal of Retailing*, Summer 1992, pp. 122–44.

[13]For details see D. S. Tull and D. I. Hawkins, *Marketing Research* (New York: Macmillan, 1993), pp. 452–60; and D. I. Hawkins and D. S. Tull, *Essentials of Marketing Research* (New York: Macmillan, 1994), pp. 313–20.

[14]J. L. Lastovicka and E. A. Joachimsthaler, ''Improving the Detection of Personality-Behavior Relationships in Consumer Research,'' *Journal of Consumer Research*, March 1988, pp. 583–87; and G. R. Foxall and R. E. Goldsmith, ''Personality and Consumer Research,'' *Journal of the Market Research Society*, no. 2, 1988, pp. 111–25.

[15]See F. Buttle, ''The Social Construction of Needs,'' *Psychology & Marketing*, Fall 1989, pp. 196–210.

[16]J. J. Plummer, ''How Personality Makes a Difference,'' *Journal of Advertising Research*, January 1985, pp. 27–31; R. S. Duboff, ''Brands, Like People, Have Personalities,'' *Marketing News*, January 3, 1986, p. 8; and J. F. Durgee, ''Understanding Brand Personality,'' *The Journal of Consumer Marketing*, Summer 1988, pp. 21–23.

[17]R. L. Ackoff and J. R. Emsoff, ''Advertising at Anheuser-Busch, Inc.,'' *Sloan Management Review*, Spring 1975, pp. 1–15.

[18]See M. B. Holbrook and J. O'Shaughnessy, ''The Role of Emotion in Advertising,'' *Psychology & Marketing*, Summer 1984, pp. 45–63; and R. Batra and M. L. Ray, ''Affective Responses Mediating Acceptance of Advertising,'' *Journal of Consumer Research*, September 1986, pp. 234–49.

[19]R. Plutchik, *Emotion: A Psychoevolutionary Synthesis* (New York: Harper & Row, 1980).

[20]W. J. Havlena and M. B. Holbrook, ''The Varieties of Consumption Experience,'' *Journal of Consumer Research*, December 1986, pp. 394–404; D. M. Zeitlin and R. A. Westwood, ''Measuring Emotional Response,'' *Journal of Advertising Research*, October/November 1986, pp. 34–44; W. J. Havlena, M. B. Holbrook, and D. R. Lehmann, ''Assessing the Validity of Emotional Typologies,'' *Psychology & Marketing*, Summer 1989, pp. 97–112. See also P. A. Stout and J. D. Leckenby, ''Measuring Emotional Response to Advertising,'' *Journal of Advertising*, no. 4, 1986, pp. 53–57; T. J. Page et al., ''Measuring Emotional Response to Advertising''; P. A. Stout and J. D. Leckenby, ''The Nature of Emotional Response to Advertising,'' both in *Journal of Advertising*, no. 4, 1988, pp. 49–52 and 53–57; M. B. Holbrook and R. Batra, ''Toward a Standardized Emotional Profile (SEP) Useful in Measuring Responses to the Nonverbal Components of Advertising,'' in *Nonverbal Communication in Advertising*, ed. S. Hecker and D. W. Stewart (Lexington, Mass: D. C. Heath, 1988); and E. Day, ''Share of Heart,'' *Journal of Consumer Marketing*, Winter 1989, pp. 5–12.

[21]See C. Campbell, *The Romantic Ethic and the Spirit of Modern Consumerism* (Oxford: Blackwell, 1987).

[22]See R. A. Westbrook and W. C. Black, ''A Motivation-Based Shopper Typology,'' *Journal of Retailing*, Spring 1985, pp. 78–103; T. C. O'Guinn and R. W. Belk, ''Heaven on Earth,'' *Journal of Consumer Research*, September 1989, pp. 227–38; and footnote 12.

[23]T. J. Olney, M. B. Holbrook, and R. Batra, ''Consumer Responses to Advertising,'' *Journal of Consumer Research*, March 1991, pp. 440–53; S. P. Brown and D. M. Stayman, ''Antecedents and Consequences of Attitude toward the Ad,'' *Journal of Consumer Research*, June 1992, pp. 34–51; G. Biehal, D. Stephens, and E. Curlo, ''Attitude toward the Ad and Brand Choice,'' *Journal of Advertising*, September 1992, pp. 19–36; and P. A. Stout and R. T. Rust, ''Emotional Feelings and Evaluative Dimensions of Advertising,'' *Journal of Advertising*, March 1993, pp. 61–71. See also footnote 8 in Chapter 13.

[24]S. Lee and J. H. Barnes, Jr., "Using Color Preferences in Magazine Advertising," *Journal of Advertising Research*, January 1990, pp. 25–29; and A. L. Biel and C. A. Bridgwater, "Attributes of Likable Television Commercials," *Journal of Advertising Research*, July 1990, pp. 38–44.

[25]M. Friestad and E. Thorson, "Emotion-Eliciting Advertising," in *Advances in Consumer Research XIII*, ed. R. J. Lutz (Provo, Utah: Association for Consumer Research, 1986), pp. 111–16.

[26]G. Levin, "Emotion Guides BBDO's Ad Tests," *Advertising Age*, January 29, 1990, p. 12.

[27]M. J. Sirgy, "Self-Concept in Consumer Behavior," *Journal of Consumer Research*, December 1982, pp. 287–300. For a differing conceptualization, see R. W. Belk, "Possessions and the Extended Self," *Journal of Consumer Research*, September 1988, pp. 139–68.

[28]M. Sirgy and J. Danes, "Self-Image/Product-Image Congruence Models: Testing Selected Models," in *Advances in Consumer Research*, ed. A. Mitchell (Chicago: Association for Consumer Research, 1982), pp. 556–61; M. J. Sirgy, "Using Self-Congruity and Ideal Congruity to Predict Purchase Motivation," *Journal of Business Research*, June 1985, pp. 195–206; and S. Onkvisit and J. Shaw, "Self-Concept and Image Congruence," *Journal of Consumer Marketing*, Winter 1987, pp. 13–23.

CHAPTER 12

LIFESTYLE

A marketing study identified five consumer lifestyles in relation to outdoor activities.[1] What are the marketing implications of this study for Prince tennis equipment, Schwinn bicycles, Jazzercise Inc., and Old Town canoes?

- **Excitement-seeking competitives (16 percent):** Like risk, some danger, and competition, though they also like social and fitness benefits. Participate in team and individual competitive sports. Half belong to a sports club or team. Median age of 32, two-thirds are male. Upper-middle class, and about half are single.
- **Getaway actives (33 percent):** Like the opportunity to be alone or experience nature. Active in camping, fishing, and birdwatching. Not loners; focus on families or close friends. Half use outdoor recreation to reduce stress. Median age of 35, equally divided between men and women.
- **Fitness-driven (10 percent):** Engage in outdoor activities strictly for fitness benefits. Walking, bicycling, and jogging are popular activities. Upscale economically. Median age of 46, over half of which are women.
- **Health-conscious sociables (33 percent):** Relatively inactive despite stated health concerns. Most involved with spectator activities such as sightseeing, driving for pleasure, visiting zoos, and so forth. Median age 49, two-thirds are female.
- **Unstressed and unmotivated (8 percent):** Not interested in outdoor recreation except as an opportunity for the family to be together. Median age of 49, equally divided between males and females.

As Figure 12–1 indicates, our lifestyle is basically how we live. It is determined by our past experiences, innate characteristics, and current situation. It influences all aspects of our consumption behavior. In this chapter we will discuss the meaning of lifestyle and the role it plays in developing marketing strategies. We will also examine ways in which lifestyle is measured and examples of how lifestyle is being used to develop well-targeted marketing programs.

THE NATURE OF LIFESTYLE

Lifestyle is defined simply as *how one lives*.[2] One's lifestyle is a function of inherent individual characteristics that have been shaped and formed through social interaction as one moves through the life cycle. Thus, lifestyle is influenced by the factors discussed in the past 11 chapters—culture, values, demographics, subculture, social class, reference groups, family, and individual characteristics such as motives, emotions, and personality. Individuals and households both have lifestyles. While household lifestyles are in part determined by the individual lifestyles of the household members, the reverse is also true.

Our desired lifestyle influences our needs and attitudes and thus our purchase and use behavior. It determines many of our consumption decisions which, in turn, reinforce or alter our lifestyle. Thus, we view lifestyle as central to the consumption process.

Lifestyle analysis can be used by marketers with respect to specific areas of consumers' lives, such as outdoor recreation. This is a common, very applied approach. Many firms have conducted lifestyle studies focused on those aspects of individual or household

FIGURE 12–1 Lifestyle and the Consumption Process

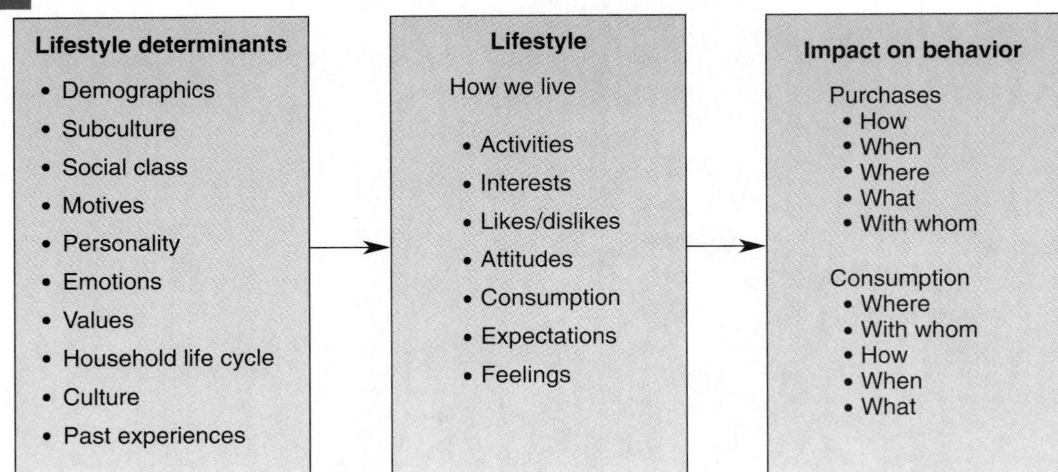

lifestyles of most relevance to their product or service. A second approach is to capture the general lifestyle patterns of a population. This approach is also widely used in practice.

Consumers are seldom explicitly aware of the role lifestyle plays in their purchase decisions. For example, few consumers would think, "I will buy High Point instant coffee to maintain my lifestyle." However, individuals pursuing an active lifestyle might purchase High Point because of its convenience, since time is important in an active lifestyle. Thus, lifestyle frequently provides the basic motivation and guidelines for purchases but generally does so in an indirect, subtle manner. Of course, some products and marketing strategies focus on an explicit recognition of a particular lifestyle.

The Club Med® ad shown in Managerial Application 12–1 would have a strong appeal to individuals classified as "excitement seeking competitives" in this chapter's opening example. The ad appeared in *Outside* magazine, whose readers are likely to be "excitement seeking competitives."

In this chapter we will first discuss the measurement of lifestyles, starting with an activity-specific lifestyle segmentation study. In the next sections, we will describe the primary commercial lifestyles system, VALS 2, and a geo-lifestyle system—PRIZM. The final section will describe the emerging work in developing international lifestyle systems.

MEASUREMENT OF LIFESTYLE

Attempts to develop quantitative measures of lifestyle were initially referred to as **psychographics**. In fact, psychographics and lifestyle are frequently used interchangeably. Psychographic research attempts to place consumers on psychological—as opposed to purely demographic—dimensions. Psychographics originally focused on individuals' activities (behaviors), interests, and opinions. The initial measurement instrument was an AIO (activities, interests, and opinions) inventory. These inventories consist of a large number (often as many as 300) of statements with which large numbers of respondents express a degree of agreement or disagreement. Exhibit 12–1 lists some of the components of AIO inventory.

MANAGERIAL APPLICATION 12-1

A Lifestyle-Oriented Ad

EXHIBIT 12-1

Several Components of AIO Questionnaires

Activities	Interests	Opinions
Work	Family	Themselves
Hobbies	Home	Social issues
Social events	Job	Politics
Vacation	Community	Business
Entertainment	Recreation	Economics
Club membership	Fashion	Education
Community	Food	Products
Shopping	Media	Future
Sports	Achievement	Culture

FIGURE 12–2 Continuum for Lifestyle Measurements

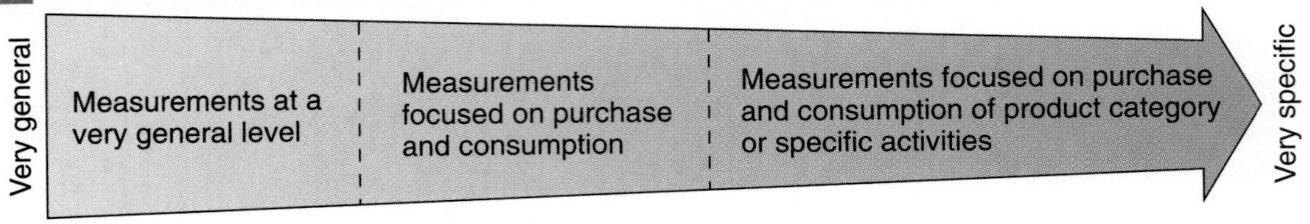

While it is a useful addition to demographic data, marketers found the original AIO inventories too narrow. Now psychographics or lifestyle studies typically include the following:

- *Attitudes:* evaluative statements about other people, places, ideas, products, and so forth.
- *Values:* widely held beliefs about what is acceptable and/or desirable.
- *Activities and interests:* nonoccupational behaviors to which consumers devote time and effort, such as hobbies, sports, public service, and church.
- *Demographics:* age, education, income, occupation, family structure, ethnic background, gender, and geographic location.
- *Media patterns:* which specific media the consumers utilize.
- *Usage rates:* measurements of consumption within a specified product category. Often consumers are categorized as heavy, medium, light, or nonusers.

A large number of individuals, often 500 or more, provide the above information. Statistical techniques are used to place them into groups.[3] Most studies use the first two or three dimensions described above to group individuals. The other dimensions are used to provide fuller descriptions of each group. Other studies include demographics as part of the grouping process.

As illustrated in Figure 12–2, lifestyle measurements can be constructed with varying degrees of specificity. At one extreme are very general measurements dealing with general ways of living. At the other, measurements are product or activity specific.[4] For example, a manufacturer of floor tiles might include items on home entertainment, the behavior and role of children in the home, pet ownership, usage of credit, interest in fashion, and so forth. The value of such lifestyle information on a particular target market is easy to understand. General or ''product free'' lifestyles can be used to discover new product opportunities, while product-specific lifestyle analysis may help reposition existing brands.

Exhibit 12–2 presents a small portion of a lifestyle analysis of British women between the ages of 15 and 44. This was an activity/product-specific analysis focused on appearance, fashions, exercise, and health. Six groups were formed based solely on their attitudes and values with respect to the four areas mentioned. *After* the groups were formed, very significant differences were found in terms of product usage, shopping behaviors, media patterns, and demographics. Attempts to segment the market using demographics alone produced much less useful results.

The value of this type of data is obvious. For example, how would you develop a marketing strategy to reach the conscience-stricken segment?

While product- or activity-specific lifestyle studies are very useful, many firms have found general lifestyle studies to be of great value also. Two popular general systems are described next.

Lifestyle Analysis of the British Cosmetics Market

EXHIBIT 12-2

COSMETIC LIFESTYLE SEGMENTS

1. *Self-aware*—concerned about appearance, fashion, and exercise.
2. *Fashion-direct*—concerned about fashion and appearance, not about exercise and sport.
3. *Green goddesses*—concerned about sport and fitness, less about appearance.
4. *Unconcerned*—neutral attitudes to health and appearance.
5. *Conscience-stricken*—no time for self-realization, busy with family responsibilities.
6. *Dowdies*—indifferent to fashion, cool on exercise, and dress for comfort.

BEHAVIORS AND DESCRIPTORS

	Cosmetic Use Index*	Blush Use Index*	Retail Outlets* Wallis	Miss Selfridge	Etam	C&A	Age† (15–44)	Social Class‡
Self-aware	162	188	228	189	151	102	51%	60%
Fashion-directed	147	166	153	165	118	112	43	56
Green goddesses	95	76	74	86	119	103	32	52
Unconcerned	82	81	70	89	74	95	44	64
Conscience-stricken	68	59	53	40	82	99	24	59
Dowdies	37	19	17	22	52	85	20	62

* 100 = Average usage.

† Read as "____ percent of this group is between 15 and 44."

‡ Read as "____ percent of this group is in the working and lower middle class."

Source: T. Bowles, "Does Classifying People by Lifestyle Really Help the Advertiser?" *European Research*, February 1988, pp. 17–24.

THE VALS LIFESTYLES

By far the most popular application of lifestyle and psychographic research by marketing managers is SRI International's Value and Lifestyles (VALS) program. Introduced in 1978, VALS provided a systematic classification of American adults into nine distinct value and lifestyle patterns. Despite widespread use, many managers found it difficult to work with. For example, VALS classified about two-thirds of the population into two groups, which made the other seven groups too small to be interesting to many firms. In addition, the maturing of the American market during the 1980s and VALS' heavy reliance on demographics reduced its utility somewhat.[5]

For these reasons, SRI introduced a new system called **VALS 2** in 1989.[6] VALS 2 has more of a psychological base than the original, which was more activity and interest based. The psychological base attempts to tap relatively enduring attitudes and values. It is measured by 42 statements with which respondents state a degree of agreement or disagreement such as:

- I am often interested in theories.
- I often crave excitement.
- I liked most of the subjects I studied in school.
- I like working with carpentry and mechanical tools.
- I must admit that I like to show off.
- I have little desire to see the world.
- I like being in charge of a group.
- I hate getting grease and oil on my hands.

The questions are designed to classify respondents according to their *self-orientation*, which serves as one of VALS 2's two dimensions. SRI has identified three primary self-orientations:

- *Principle-oriented*—these individuals are guided in their choices by their beliefs and principles rather than by feelings, events, or desire for approval.
- *Status-oriented*—these individuals are heavily influenced by the actions, approval, and opinions of others.
- *Action-oriented*—these individuals desire social or physical activity, variety, and risk-taking.

These three orientations determine the types of goals and behaviors that individuals will pursue.

The second dimension, termed *resources*, reflects the ability of individuals to pursue their dominant self-orientation. It refers to the full range of psychological, physical, demographic, and material means on which consumers can draw. Resources generally increase from adolescence through middle age and then remain relatively stable until they begin to decline with older age.

Based on these two concepts, SRI has identified eight general psychographic segments, as shown in Figure 12–3. Each of these segments is described briefly in Exhibit 12–3. Table 12–1 provides a demographic description of each segment. Tables 12–2, 12–3, and 12–4 provide information on segment product ownership, activities, and media use, respectively. VALS 2 is linked with numerous major data bases. Both Simmons Market Research Bureau and Mediamark Research classify their respondents into VALS 2 categories, which allows additional product and media use analyses. National Family Opinion and the NPD Group also classify members of their national consumer panels using VALS 2. Finally, the VALS 2 system is linked to all the major geo-demographic systems, such as PRIZM (described in the next section of this chapter).

VALS 2 appears to share some of the shortcomings of the original. Several concerns are:

- VALS 2 are *individual* measures, but most consumption decisions are *household* decisions or are heavily influenced by other household members.
- Few individuals are "pure" in terms of self-orientation. While one of the three themes SRI has identified may be dominant for most individuals, the degree of dominance will vary as will the orientation that is second in importance.
- The types of values and demographics measured by VALS 2 may be inappropriate for particular products or situations. Product- or activity-specific lifestyles may provide more useful information. For example, VALS 2 seems most useful for important or ego-involving purchases. Will it work well for laundry detergent?

VALS 2 Lifestyle System

FIGURE 12–3

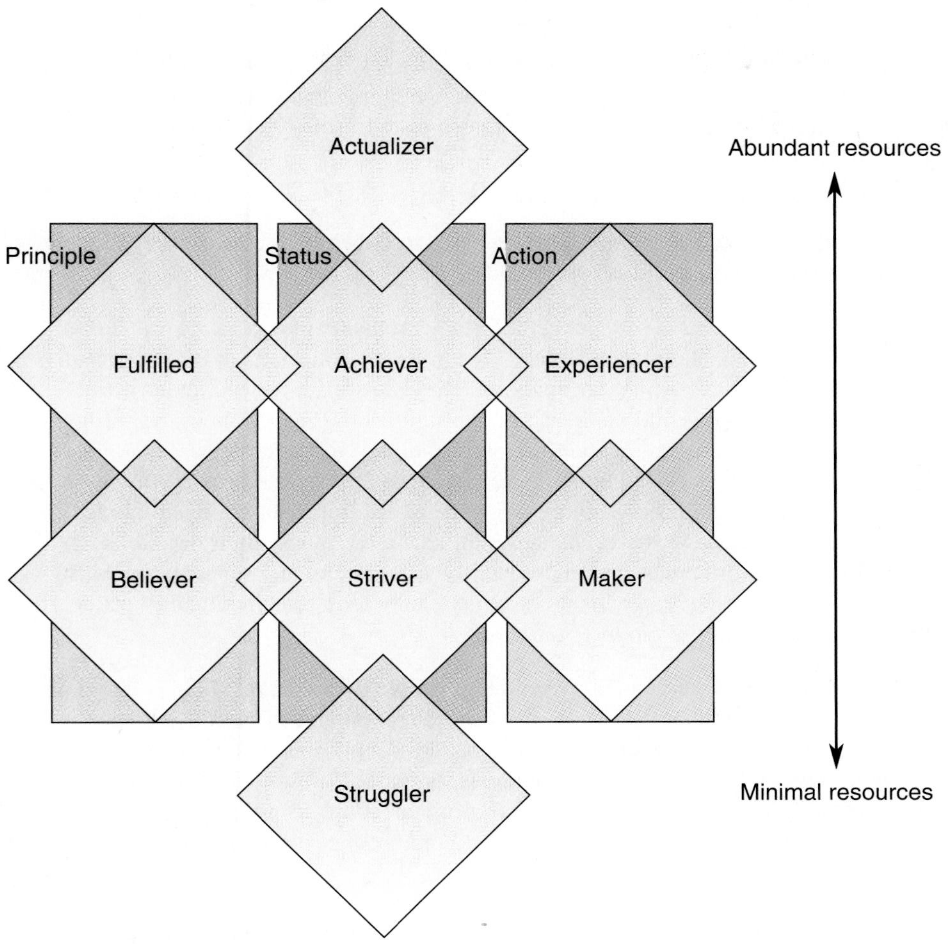

Source: SRI International.

VALS 2 Segments

EXHIBIT 12–3

ACTUALIZERS

Actualizers are successful, sophisticated, active, "take-charge" people with high self-esteem and abundant resources. They are interested in growth and seek to develop, explore, and express themselves in a variety of ways—sometimes guided by principle, and sometimes by a desire to have an effect, to make a change. Image is important to Actualizers, not as evidence of status or power, but as an expression of their taste, independence, and character. Actualizers are among the established and emerging leaders in business and

EXHIBIT 12–3 VALS 2 Segments (*continued*)

government, yet they continue to seek challenges. They have a wide range of interests, are concerned with social issues, and are open to change. Their possessions and recreation reflect a cultivated taste for the finer things in life.

FULFILLEDS AND BELIEVERS: PRINCIPLE-ORIENTED

Principle-oriented consumers seek to make their behavior consistent with their views of how the world is or should be.

Fulfilleds are mature, satisfied, comfortable, reflective people who value order, knowledge, and responsibility. Most are well educated, and in (or recently retired from) professional occupations. They are well-informed about world and national events and are alert to opportunities to broaden their knowledge. Content with their careers, families, and station in life, their leisure activities tend to center around the home. Fulfilleds have a moderate respect for the status quo institutions of authority and social decorum, but are open-minded about new ideas and social change. Fulfilleds tend to base their decisions on strongly held principles and consequently appear calm and self-assured. Fulfilleds are conservative, practical consumers; they look for functionality, value, and durability in the products they buy.

Believers are conservative, conventional people with concrete beliefs based on traditional, established codes: family, church, community, and the nation. Many Believers express moral codes that are deeply rooted and literally interpreted. They follow established routines, organized in large part around their homes, families, and social or religious organizations to which they belong. As consumers, they are conservative and predictable, favoring American products and established brands.

ACHIEVERS AND STRIVERS: STATUS-ORIENTED

Status-oriented consumers have or seek a secure place in a valued social setting. They make choices to enhance their position or to facilitate their move to another, more desirable group. Strivers look to others to indicate what they should be and do, whereas Achievers, more resourceful and active, seek recognition and self-definition through achievements at work and in their families.

Achievers are successful career- and work-oriented people who like to, and generally do, feel in control of their lives. They value consensus, predictability, and stability over risk, intimacy, and self-discovery. They are deeply committed to work and family. Work provides them with a sense of duty, material rewards, and prestige. Their social lives reflect this focus and are structured around family, church, and career. Achievers live conventional lives, are politically conservative, and respect authority and the status quo. Image is important to them; they favor established, prestige products and services that demonstrate success to their peers.

VALS 2 Segments (*continued*)

EXHIBIT 12-3

Strivers seek motivation, self-definition, and approval from the world around them. They are striving to find a secure place in life. Unsure of themselves and low on economic, social, and psychological resources, Strivers are concerned about the opinions and approval of others. Money defines success for Strivers, who don't have enough of it and often feel that life has given them a raw deal. Strivers are easily bored and impulsive. Many of them seek to be stylish. They emulate those who own more impressive possessions, but what they wish to obtain is generally beyond their reach.

EXPERIENCERS AND MAKERS: ACTION-ORIENTED

Action-oriented consumers like to affect their environment in tangible ways. Makers do so primarily at home and with constructive activity, Experiencers in the wider world through adventure and vivid experiences.

Experiencers are young, vital, enthusiastic, impulsive, and rebellious. They seek variety and excitement, savoring the new, the offbeat, and the risky. Still in the process of formulating life values and patterns of behavior, they quickly become enthusiastic about new possibilities but are equally quick to cool. At this stage of their lives, they are politically uncommitted, uninformed, and highly ambivalent about what they believe. Experiencers combine an abstract disdain for conformity with an outsider's awe of others' wealth, prestige, and power. Their energy finds an outlet in exercise, sports, outdoor recreation, and social activities. Experiencers are avid consumers and spend much of their income on clothing, fast food, music, movies, and video.

Makers are practical people who have constructive skills and value self-sufficiency. They live within a traditional context of family, practical work, and physical recreation and have little interest in what lies outside that context. Makers experience the world by working on it—building a house, raising children, fixing a car, or canning vegetables—and have sufficient skill, income, and energy to carry out their projects successfully. Makers are politically conservative, suspicious of new ideas, respectful of government authority and organized labor, but resentful of government intrusion on individual rights. They are unimpressed by material possessions other than those with a practical or functional purpose (e.g., tools, pick-up trucks, or fishing equipment).

STRUGGLERS

Strugglers' lives are constricted. Chronically poor, ill-educated, low-skilled, without strong social bonds, elderly and concerned about their health, they are often resigned and passive. Because they are limited by the need to meet the urgent needs of the present moment, they do not show a strong self-orientation. Their chief concerns are for security and safety. Strugglers are cautious consumers. They represent a very modest market for most products and services, but are loyal to favorite brands.

TABLE 12–1 VALS 2 Segment Demographics

Segment	Percent of Population	Sex (M)	Median Age	Median Income	Education (College)	Occupation (White Collar)	Married
Actualizer	8%	59%	43	$58,000	95%	68%	72%
Fulfilled	11	47	48	38,000	81	50	73
Believer	16	46	58	21,000	6	11	70
Achiever	13	39	36	50,000	77	43	73
Striver	13	41	34	25,000	23	19	60
Experiencer	12	53	26	19,000	41	21	34
Maker	13	61	30	23,000	24	19	65
Struggler	14	37	61	9,000	3	2	47

Source: SRI International.

TABLE 12–2 VALS 2 Segment Product Ownership

Item	Segment							
	Actualizer	Fulfilled	Believer	Achiever	Striver	Experiencer	Maker	Struggler
Own SLR camera	163	124	80	138	83	88	115	29
Own bicycle >$150	154	116	90	33	83	120	88	43
Own compact disk player	133	108	119	97	96	94	94	69
Own fishing equipment	87	91	114	87	84	113	142	67
Own backpacking equipment	196	112	64	100	56	129	148	29
Own home computer	229	150	59	136	63	82	109	20
Own <$13K import car	172	128	80	143	68	109	89	44
Own >$13K import car	268	105	70	164	79	119	43	32
Own medium/small car	133	117	89	101	112	92	112	54
Own pickup truck	72	96	115	104	103	91	147	52
Own sports car	330	116	43	88	102	112	90	5

Note: Figures under each segment are the index for each segment (100 = Base rate usage).

Source: SRI International.

VALS 2 Segment Activities

TABLE 12-3

Item	Segment							
	Actualizer	Fulfilled	Believer	Achiever	Striver	Experiencer	Maker	Struggler
Barbecue outdoors	125	93	82	118	111	109	123	50
Do gardening	155	129	118	109	68	54	104	80
Do gourmet cooking	217	117	96	103	53	133	86	47
Drink coffee daily	120	119	126	88	87	55	91	116
Drink domestic beer	141	88	73	101	87	157	123	50
Drink herbal tea	171	125	89	117	71	115	81	68
Drink imported beer	238	93	41	130	58	216	88	12
Do activities with kids	155	129	57	141	112	89	116	32
Play team sports	114	73	69	104	110	172	135	34
Do cultural activities	293	63	67	96	45	154	63	14
Exercise	145	114	69	123	94	143	102	39
Do home repairs	161	113	85	82	53	88	171	58
Camp or hike	131	88	68	95	84	156	158	33
Do risky sports	190	48	36	52	59	283	171	7
Socialize weekly	109	64	73	90	96	231	94	62

Note: Figures under each segment are the index for each segment (100 = Base rate usage).

Source: SRI International.

VALS 2 Segment Media Use

TABLE 12-4

Item	Segment							
	Actualizer	Fulfilled	Believer	Achiever	Striver	Experiencer	Maker	Struggler
Read automotive magazines	92	105	50	79	50	254	157	22
Read business magazines	255	227	74	179	37	71	33	8
Read commentary magazines	274	173	106	87	66	109	49	15
Read *Reader's Digest*	58	143	150	90	63	57	87	130
Read fish and game magazines	56	83	119	46	37	130	209	79
Read general sports magazines	73	75	96	90	88	186	134	49
Read health magazines	108	135	168	98	62	53	75	96

TABLE 12-4 VALS 2 Segment Media Use (*continued*)

Item	Actualizer	Fulfilled	Believer	Achiever	Striver	Experiencer	Maker	Struggler
	Segment							
Read home and garden magazines	116	153	141	99	71	53	89	80
Read human-interest magazines	83	115	113	129	93	135	86	46
Read literary magazines	533	120	29	77	44	105	45	31
Watch "Face the Nation"	161	199	161	62	42	35	37	126
Watch "Family Ties"	54	84	77	108	138	131	111	85
Watch "Golden Girls"	65	96	137	82	101	71	92	135
Watch "L.A. Law"	96	113	132	114	109	71	89	70
Watch "McGyver"	35	50	126	57	92	104	153	140

Note: Figures under each segment are the index for each segment (100 = Base rate usage).

Source: SRI International.

Despite these problems, VALS 2 is the most complete general segmentation system available. It will be widely used by marketing managers. Managerial Application 12–2 contains two ads, one that appeals to the *experiencer* segment, and one that would appeal to the *achiever* and, to a lesser extent, the *striver* segments.

GEO-LIFESTYLE ANALYSIS (PRIZM)

Claritas, a leading firm in this industry, describes the logic of geo-demographic analysis:

> People with similar cultural backgrounds, means, and perspectives naturally gravitate toward one another. They choose to live amongst their peers in neighborhoods offering affordable advantages and compatible lifestyles.
>
> Once settled in, people naturally emulate their neighbors. They adopt similar social values, tastes, and expectations. They exhibit shared patterns of consumer behavior toward products, services, media and promotions.[7]

Analyses of this type are known as **geo-demographic** analyses. They focus on the demographics of geographic areas based on the belief that lifestyle, and thus consumption, is largely driven by demographic factors, as described above. The geographic regions analyzed can be quite small, ranging from standard metropolitan statistical areas, through five-digit ZIP codes, census tracts, and down to census blocks (averaging only 340 households). Such data are used for target market selection, promotional emphasis, and so forth, by numerous consumer goods marketers.

Claritas has taken geo-demographic analysis one step further and incorporated extensive data on consumption patterns. The output is a set of 40 lifestyle clusters organized into 12 broad social groups, as briefly described in Appendix 12–A (at the end of this chapter, page 348). This is called the **PRIZM** system. Every neighborhood in the United States can be profiled in terms of these 40 lifestyle groups. For example, one of the authors lives

MANAGERIAL APPLICATION

12-2

Ads Aimed at Distinct VALS 2 Segments

Appealing to experiencers

Appealing to achievers

outside of Eugene, Oregon, in a large ZIP code area that includes part of the city. Its profile is:

Towns and gowns	37.9%
Young influentials	26.3
Blue-blood estates	10.7
Bohemian mix	8.9
Smalltown downtown	6.5
Money and brains	5.3
Single-city blues	4.4

Unlike the VALS 2 typology, PRIZM does not measure values or attitudes (though the distribution of VALS 2 types within each geographic area covered by PRIZM is available). It is primarily driven by demographics with substantial support from consumption and media usage data. Claritas and its competitors are widely used by consumer marketing firms such as General Motors and Hertz.[8] To illustrate how firms can use such data, we will describe an application for a hypothetical imported beer, Brinker.[9]

Brinker had stable sales in the United States for several years. Annual surveys indicated that 65 percent of the consumers were male, 80 percent were under 50 years of age, and

58 percent had above-average household incomes. Thus, the firm defined its target market as males, age 21 to 49, with above-average incomes. This target-market definition includes 30 percent of the brand's consumers (.65 × .80 × .58 = .30).

While this target definition was workable for media planning, it did not function well for market expansion, or for estimating and targeting potential Brinker consumers by geographic markets. Nearly *all* major markets show similar concentrations of males between 21 and 49. Should Brinker target solely by household income? And what of the remaining 70 percent of brand drinkers? In short, where was the real potential for growth?

Based on Brinker's survey data, its consumers were categorized by the PRIZM lifestyle clusters. Figure 12–4 shows the 40 clusters arrayed from left to right in descending social rank. The height of each cluster bar shows its concentration of brand drinkers relative to the U.S. average (100).

Fourteen lifestyle clusters appeared to represent good target markets. Further analysis suggested three major targets. The seven upscale clusters in groups S1, S2, and S3 buy Brinker to drink and serve at home. These were labeled the "Suburban Entertainers." The six heavy-user clusters in U1 and U2 consume Brinker at home and in bars and taverns. The firm called these the "Singles Bar Trade." Finally, Cluster 9 in U3 was labeled "Urban Hispanics." They appear to have a strong taste preference for Brinker and other imports. The market segmentation strategy was as follows:

Selected PRIZM Target Groups	Percent Total Adults	Percent Brand Drinkers	Index Concentration
Primary (main-thrust marketing)			
G1—Suburban entertainers	15.6%	24.2%	156
G2—Singles bar trade	12.4	19.4	155
Subtotal	28.0	43.6	155
Secondary (special market promos)			
G3—Urban Hispanics	1.6%	2.2%	135

FIGURE 12–4 Brinker Beer Drinker Index*

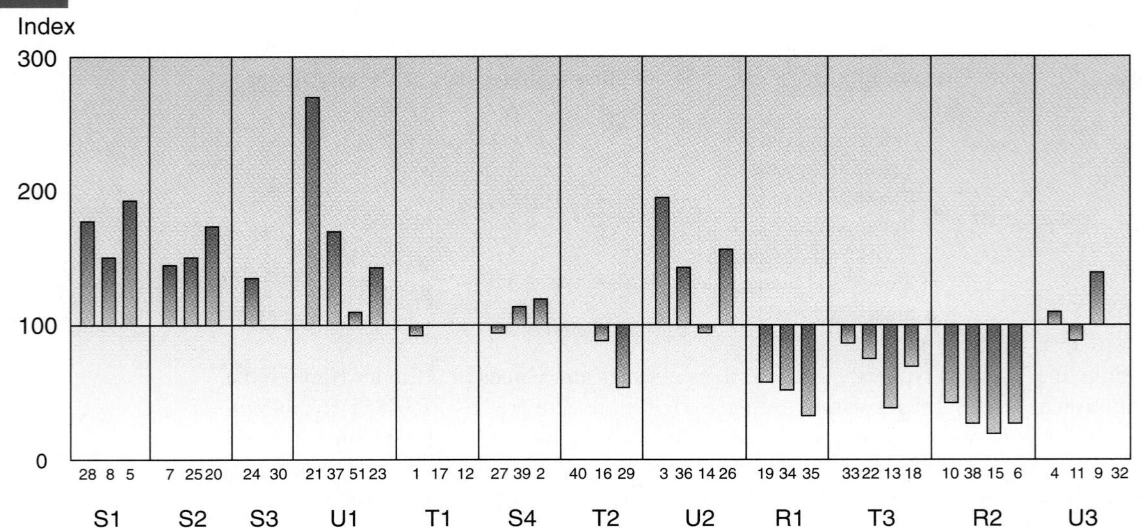

*The 40 clusters shown are arrayed from left to right in descending social rank, and the height of each cluster bar shows its concentration of brand drinkers relative to the U.S. average (100).

INTERNATIONAL LIFESTYLES: GLOBAL SCAN

Both VALS 2 and PRIZM are oriented to the United States. However, as we saw in Chapter 2, marketing is increasingly a global activity. If there are discernible lifestyle segments that cut across cultures, marketers can develop cross-cultural strategies around these segments. Although language and other differences would exist, individuals pursuing similar lifestyles in different cultures should be responsive to similar product features and communication themes.

Not surprisingly, a number of attempts have been made to develop such systems.[10] Large, international advertising agencies have provided much of the impetus behind these efforts. We will describe a system developed by Backer Spielvogel Bates Worldwide (BSBW).

BSBW's **GLOBAL SCAN** is based on annual surveys of 15,000 consumers in 14 countries (Australia, Canada, Colombia, Finland, France, Germany, Hong Kong, Indonesia, Japan, Mexico, Spain, the United Kingdom, the United States, and Venezuela). It measures over 250 value and attitude components in addition to demographics, media usage, and buying preferences.

Based on the combination of lifestyle and purchasing data, BSBW found five global lifestyle segments, as described in Exhibit 12–4. While these segments exist in all 14

EXHIBIT 12–4

Five Global Lifestyle Segments Identified by GLOBAL SCAN

- *Strivers* (26%)—young people on the run. Their median age is 31, and their average day is hectic. They push hard to achieve success, but they're hard-pressed to meet all their goals. They're materialistic, they look for pleasure, and they insist on instant gratification. Short of time, energy, and money, they seek out convenience in every corner of their lives.
- *Achievers* (22%)—slightly older and several giant steps ahead of the Strivers—affluent, assertive, and on the way up. Opinion leaders and style-setters, Achievers shape our mainstream values. They led the way to the fitness craze and still set the standard for what we eat, drink, and wear today. Achievers are hooked on status and fixated on quality, and together with Strivers, create the youth-oriented values that drive our societies today.
- *Pressured* (13%)—downtrodden people with more than their share of problems. Largely women from every age group, the Pressured face economic and family concerns that drain their resources and rob much of the joy from their lives.
- *Adapters* (18%)—may be an older crowd, but these folks are hardly shocked by the new. Content with themselves and their lives, they respect new ideas without rejecting their own standards. And they are all ready to take up whatever activities will enrich their golden years.
- *Traditionals* (16%)—embody the oldest values of their countries and cultures. Conservative, rooted in the heartland, and tied to the past, Traditionals prefer the tried and true, the good old ways of thinking, eating, and living their lives.

FIGURE 12-5 GLOBAL SCAN Segment Sizes across Countries

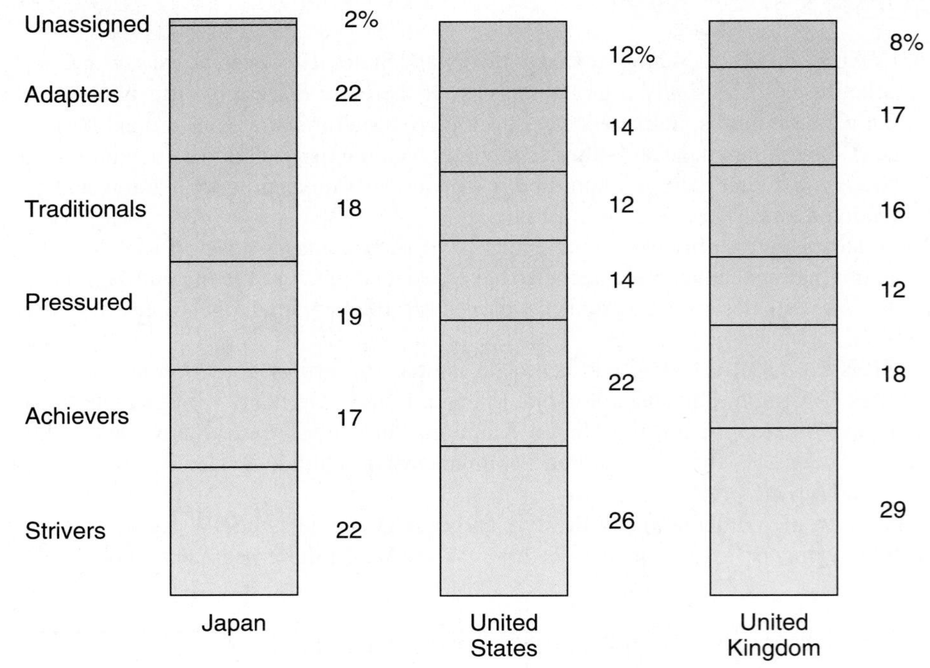

FIGURE 12-6 Within-Segment Differences across Countries—Live-Together-Before-Marriage Strivers

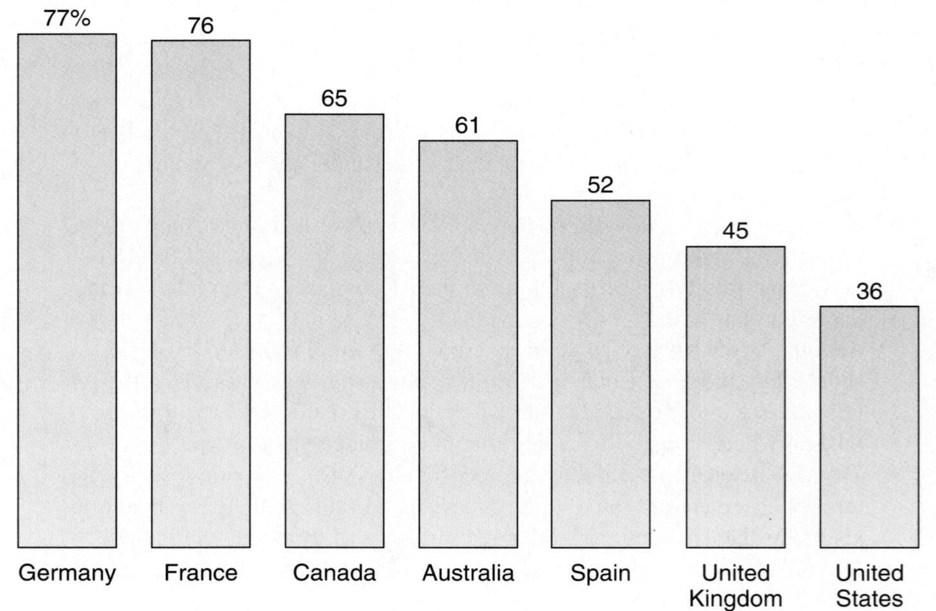

MANAGERIAL APPLICATION 12–3

An Ad that Appeals to the GLOBAL SCAN Striver Segment

countries studied thus far, the percentage of the population in each group varies by country, as shown in Figure 12–5. While the lifestyle segments share many common characteristics and behaviors across cultures, there are also differences on important cultural values. Figure 12–6 provides a clear example of this.

Suppose you were developing an international strategy for Whirlpool Appliances. You would notice that strivers are the largest global segment, although this is not true in all countries. A product line targeted at this group would need to be relatively inexpensive and readily available, would require access to credit, and should have a maximum number of convenience features (perhaps at the expense of durability if this is necessary to keep costs low). The communications theme would stress convenience, gratification, and value. Promotional efforts would be allocated disproportionately to those countries with concentrations of strivers. Managerial Application 12–3 shows an international ad that would appeal to *strivers.*

SUMMARY

Lifestyle, a major factor that influences the consumer decision-making process, can be defined simply as how one lives. Lifestyle is a function of one's inherent individual characteristics that have been shaped through social interaction as one moves through one's life cycle.

Psychographics is the primary way that lifestyle is made operationally useful to marketing managers. This is a way of describing the psychological makeup or lifestyle of consumers by assessing such lifestyle dimensions as activities, interests, opinions, values, and demographics. Lifestyle measures can be macro and reflect how individuals live in general, or micro and describe their attitudes and behaviors with respect to a specific product category or activity.

The VALS 2 system, developed by SRI, divides the United States into eight groups—actualizers, fulfilled, believers, achievers, strivers, experiencers, makers, and strugglers. These groups were derived based on two dimensions. The first dimension is self-orientation with three categories: *principle-oriented* (those guided by their basic beliefs and values); *status-oriented* (those influenced by the actions, approval, and opinions of others); and *action-oriented* (those who seek social or physical activity, variety, and risks). The second dimension is the physical, mental, and material resources to pursue one's dominant self-orientation.

Geo-lifestyle analysis is based on the premise that individuals with similar lifestyles tend to live near each other. PRIZM is one system that has analyzed demographic and consumption data down to the census block. It has developed profiles of each block in terms of 40 lifestyle clusters.

In response to the rapid expansion of international marketing, a number of attempts have been made to develop lifestyle measures applicable across cultures. GLOBAL SCAN is the largest of these. It has found five segments that exist across the 14 countries it has analyzed to date.

REVIEW QUESTIONS

1. What do we mean by *lifestyle*? What factors determine and influence that lifestyle?
2. What relationship exists between consumer lifestyle and consumer decision making?
3. What is *psychographics*?
4. What types of variables do marketing managers use to construct a psychographic instrument?
5. When is a product- or activity-specific psychographic instrument superior to a general one?
6. What are the dimensions on which VALS 2 is based? Describe each.
7. Describe the VALS 2 system and each segment in it.
8. What is *geo-demographic analysis*?
9. Describe the PRIZM system.
10. What is an international lifestyle system?
11. Describe the GLOBAL SCAN system.

DISCUSSION QUESTIONS

12. Does VALS 2 make sense to you? What do you like or dislike about it?
13. How would one use VALS 2 to develop a marketing strategy?
14. Develop a marketing strategy based on VALS 2 for:
    a. Christian Children's Fund.
    b. In-line skates.
    c. Bose stereo equipment.
    d. *Time* magazine.
    e. A new TV series.
    f. A new restaurant chain.
15. Develop a marketing strategy for *each* of the eight VAL 2 segments for:
    a. Perfume. d. TV series.
    b. Resort. e. Automobile.
    c. Mouthwash. f. A new magazine.
16. Does PRIZM make sense to you? What do you like or dislike about it? Is it really a measure of lifestyle?
17. How would one use PRIZM to develop a marketing strategy?
18. Develop a marketing strategy based on PRIZM for the products in Question 14.
19. Develop a marketing strategy for each of five (you choose) PRIZM segments for:
    a. Perfume. d. TV series.
    b. Resort. e. Automobile.
    c. Mouthwash. f. A new magazine.
20. Does GLOBAL SCAN make sense to you?
21. How would you use GLOBAL SCAN to develop marketing strategy?
22. Develop a marketing strategy based on

GLOBAL SCAN for the products in Question 14.

23. Develop a marketing strategy for each of the five GLOBAL SCAN segments for the six products in Question 15.
24. The following quote is from Paul Casi, president of Glenmore distilleries:

    > Selling cordials is a lot different from selling liquor. Cordials are like the perfume of our industry. You're really talking high fashion and you're talking generally to a different audience—I don't mean male versus female—I'm talking about lifestyle.

    a. In what ways do you think the lifestyle of cordial drinkers would differ from those who drink liquor, but not cordials?
    b. How would you determine the nature of any such differences?
    c. Of what use would knowledge of such lifestyle differences be to a marketing manager introducing a new cordial?
25. How is one likely to change one's lifestyle at different stages of one's household life cycle? Over one's life, is one likely to assume more than one of the VALS 2 lifestyle profiles described? PRIZM's? GLOBAL SCAN's?
26. To which VALS 2 category do you belong? To which do your parents belong? Which will you belong to when you are your parents' age?
27. Repeat Question 26 for PRIZM.
28. Based on the outdoor activity lifestyles described in the chapter opening example, develop a marketing strategy for:
    a. A resort.
    b. A fitness club.
    c. In-line skates.
    d. Schwinn bicycles.
    e. Jazzercize Inc.
    f. Old Town canoes.
29. Develop a marketing strategy for the items below for *each* of the outdoor activity lifestyles described in the chapter opening example.
    a. A resort.
    b. The local YMCA.
    c. Schwinn bicycles.
    d. A fitness club.
30. Using Exhibit 12–2, develop a cosmetics line and marketing program targeting the _______ segment.
    a. Self-aware.
    b. Fashion-directed.
    c. Green goddesses.
    d. Unconcerned.
    e. Conscience-stricken.
    f. Dowdies.

APPLICATION EXERCISES

31. Develop your own psychographic instrument (set of relevant questions) that measures lifestyle of college students.
32. Using the psychographic instrument developed in Question 31, interview 10 students (using the questionnaire instrument). Based on their responses categorize them into lifestyle segments.
33. Develop 15 statements related to the attitudes, interests, and opinions of students on your campus. Using a five-category agree–disagree scale, interview five other students not enrolled in the class. Then, using all the information collected by the entire class, divide up the individuals surveyed into groups based on similarity. For two groups of reasonable size that are dissimilar in agreement with AIO statements (activities, interests, opinions), discuss what campus activities would appeal most to each group. Are there new activities these groups would enjoy using if available?
34. Find and copy or describe ads that would appeal to each of the eight VALS 2 segments.
35. Repeat Question 34 for the five GLOBAL SCAN segments.
36. Identify a male and a female TV personality or role played on television that fits each of the eight VALS 2 profiles outlined.
37. Repeat Question 36 for the five GLOBAL SCAN segments.

REFERENCES

[1]B. E. Bryant, ''Built for Excitement,'' *American Demographics*, March 1987, pp. 39–42.

[2]For a review and different definition, see W. T. Anderson and L. L. Golden, ''Lifestyle and Psychograpics,'' in *Advances in Consumer Research XI*, ed. T. C. Kinnear (Provo, Utah: Association for Consumer Research, 1984), pp. 405–11.

[3]See A. Boste, ''Interactions in Psychographics Segmentation: Implications for Advertising,'' *Journal of Advertising*, 1984, pp. 4–48; J. L. Lastovicka, ''On the Validation of Lifestyle Traits: A Review and Illustration,'' *Journal of Marketing Research*, February 1982, pp. 126–38; and E. H. Demby, ''Psychographics Revisited,'' *Marketing News*, January 2, 1989, p. 21.

[4]J. A. Lesser and M. A. Hughes, ''The Generalizability of Psychographic Market Segments across Geographic Locations,'' *Journal of Marketing*, January 1986, pp. 18–27.

[5]See L. R. Kahle, S. E. Beatty, and P. Homer, ''Alternative Measurement Approaches to Consumer Values,'' *Journal of Consumer Research*, December 1986, pp. 405–9; J. L. Lastovicka, J. P. Murry, Jr., and E. Joachimsthaler, ''Evaluating the Measurement Validity of Lifestyle Typologies with Qualitative Measures and Multiplicative Factoring,'' *Journal of Marketing Research*, February 1990, pp. 11–23; T. P. Novak and B. MacEvoy, ''On Comparing Alternative Segmentation Schemes,'' *Journal of Consumer Research*, June 1990, pp. 105–9; and M. F. Riche, ''Psychographics for the 1990s,'' *American Demographics*, July 1989, pp. 25+.

[6]Values and Lifestyles Program. *Descriptive Materials for the VALS 2 Segmentation System* (Menlo Park, Calif.: SRI International, 1989).

[7]*How to Use PRIZM* (Alexandria, Va.: Claritas, 1986), p. 1.

[8]B. Morris, ''Marketing Firm Slices U.S. into 240,000 Parts to Spur Clients' Sales,'' *The Wall Street Journal*, November 3, 1986, p. 1.

[9]Copyrighted by and used with permission of Claritas.

[10]For example, see R. Bartos, *Marketing to Women around the World* (Cambridge, Mass.: Harvard Business School, 1989).

APPENDIX 12A

PRIZM LIFESTYLE CLUSTERS

S1

Educated, Affluent Executives and Professionals in Elite Metro Suburbs

The three clusters in Group S1 are characterized by top socioeconomic status, college-plus educations, executive and professional occupations, expensive owner-occupied housing, and conspicuous consumption levels for many products. Representing 5 percent of U.S. households, Group S1 contains about 32 percent of the nation's $75K+ household incomes, and an estimated third of its personal net worth.

Blue-Blood Estates (28) are America's wealthiest socioeconomic neighborhoods, populated by super-upper established managers, professionals, and heirs to ''old money,'' accustomed to privilege and living in luxurious surroundings.

Money and Brains (8) have the nation's second highest socioeconomic rank. These neighborhoods are typified by swank, shipshape townhouses, apartments, and condos. This group has relatively few children and is dominated by childless couples and a mix of upscale singles. They are sophisticated consumers of adult luxuries—apparel, restaurants, travel, and the like.

Furs and Station Wagons (5) is typified by ''new money,'' living in expensive new neighborhoods in the greenbelt suburbs of the nation's major metros, coast to coast. These are well-educated, mobile professionals and

S2

Pre- and Post-Child Families and Singles in Upscale, White-Collar Suburbs

The three clusters of Group S2 typify pre- and post-child communities, with predominantly one- and two-person households. While significantly below S1 in socioeconomic levels, S2s display all of the characteristics of success, including high-end educations, incomes, home values, and white-collar occupations, with consumption levels to match.

Pools and Patios (7) once resembled Furs and Station Wagons, being upscale greenbelt suburbs in a late child-rearing mode. But today, these children are grown, leaving aging couples in empty nests too costly for young homemakers. Good educations, high white-collar employment levels, and double incomes assure ''the good life'' in these neighborhoods.

Young Influentials (20) could be imagined as tomorrow's Money & Brains. These are young, metropolitan sophisticates, with exceptional high-tech, white-collar employment levels. Double incomes afford high spending, and lifestyles are open, with singles, childless couples, and unrelated adults predominating in expensive one- and two-person homes, apartments, and condos.

Two More Rungs (25) has a high concentration of foreign-born European

S3

Upper-Middle, Child-Raising Families in Outlying, Owner-Occupied Suburbs.

The two clusters of Group S3 represent our newest minority—the traditional family—Mom, Dad, and the kids. In this case, the families are upscale. Both clusters show high indices for married couples, school-age children, double incomes, two or more cars, and single-unit, owner-occupied, suburban housing. In short, S3 is the essence of the traditional American Dream.

Young Suburbia (24) is one of our largest clusters, found coast to coast in most major markets. It runs to large, young families, and ranks second in incidence of married couples with children. These neighborhoods are distinguished by their relative affluence and high white-collar employment levels. As a result, they are strong consumers of most family products.

Blue-Chip Blues (30) ranked fourth in married couples with children, is similar to Young Suburbia on most dimensions except social rank. Its predominant high school educations and blue-collar occupations are reflected in fewer high-end incomes and lower home values. However, high employment and double incomes yield similar discretionary spending patterns, and make this cluster an outstanding market.

managers with the nation's highest incidence of teenage children. They are winners—big producers and big spenders.

ethnics and is somewhat older, with even fewer children. It is also more dense, with a higher incidence of renters in multiple-unit, high-rise housing, and has a northeastern geocenter. Two More Rungs neighborhoods show a high index for professionals, and somewhat conservative spending patterns.

U1

Educated, White-Collar Singles and Couples in Upscale, Urban Areas

With minor exceptions for Black Enterprise, Group U1 is characterized by millions of young, white-collar couples and singles (many divorced and separated), dense mid- and high-rise housing, upscale socioeconomic status, cosmopolitan lifestyles, big-city universities and students, high concentrations of foreign born, and an undeniable panache and notoriety.

Urban Gold Coast (21) is altogether unique. It is the most densely populated per square mile, with the highest concentration of one-person households in multi-unit, high-rise buildings, and the lowest incidence of auto ownership. Other mosts: most white collar, most childless, and most New York. Urban Gold Coast is the top in Urbania, a fit address for the 21 Club.

Bohemian Mix (37) is America's Bohemia, a largely integrated, singles-dominated, high-rise hodge-podge of white collars, students, divorced persons, actors, writers, artists, aging hippies, and races.

Black Enterprise (31) neighborhoods are nearly 70 percent black, with median black household incomes well above average and with consumption behavior to match. It is the most family-oriented of the U1 clusters. A few downscale pockets can be found, but the majority of blacks in these neighborhoods are educated, employed, and solidly set in the upper middle class.

New Beginnings (23) is represented in nearly all markets, but shows its

T1

Educated, Young, Mobile Families in Exurban Satellites and Boom Towns

The three clusters share a lot of American geography, most of it around our younger boom towns or in the satellite towns and exurbs far beyond the beltways of major metros. Other shared characteristics are young, white-collar adults, extremely high mobility rates, and new, low-density single-unit housing.

God's Country (1) contains the highest socioeconomic, white-collar neighborhoods primarily located outside major metros. These are well-educated frontier types, who have opted to live away from the big metros in some of our most beautiful mountain and coastal areas. They are highly mobile, and are among the nation's fastest-growing neighborhoods. God's Country is an outstanding consumer of both products and media.

New Homesteaders (17) is much like God's Country in its mobility, housing, and family characteristics. The big difference is that these neighborhoods are nine rungs down on the socioeconomic scale, with all measures of education and affluence being significantly lower. It shows peak concentrations of military personnel, and has a strong Western skew. It is one of our largest and fastest-growing clusters.

Towns and Gowns (12) contains hundreds of mid-scale college and university towns in nonmetropolitan America. The population ratio is three quarters local (''towns'') to one quarter students (''gowns''), giving this

S4

Middle-Class, Post-Child Families in Aging Suburbia and Retirement Areas

The three clusters of Group S4, while each distinct, all represent a continuing U.S. trend toward post-child communities. As a group, S4s include many aging married couples, widows, and retirees on pensions and Social Security incomes. Except Gray Power, they are tightly geo-centered in the Northeast.

Levittown USA (27) was formed when the post-WWII baby boom caused an explosion of tract housing in the late 40s and 50s—brand new suburbs for young white-collar and well-paid blue-collar families. The children are now largely grown and gone. Aging couples remain in comfortable, middle-class, suburban homes. Employment levels are still high, including double incomes, and living is comfortable.

Gray Power (39) represents nearly two million senior citizens who have chosen to pull up their roots and retire amongst their peers. Primarily concentrated in sunbelt communities of the South Atlantic and Pacific regions, these are the nation's most affluent elderly, retired, and widowed neighborhoods, with the highest concentration of childless married couples, living in mixed multi-units, condos, and mobile homes on nonsalaried incomes.

Rank and File (2) is a blue-collar version of Levittown, U.S.A., five rungs down on the socioeconomic scale. This cluster contains many traditional, blue-collar family neighborhoods where

strongest concentrations in the West. It provides new homes to many victims of the divorce boom in search of new job opportunities and lifestyles. The predominant age is 18 to 34, and the mode is pre-child with employment concentrated in lower-level white-collar and clerical occupations.

cluster its name and unique profile. It shows extreme concentrations of age 18 to 24 singles and students in group quarters, very high educational, professional, and technical levels, and a taste for prestige products in contrast with modest income and home values.

children have grown and departed, leaving an aging population. Rank and File shows high concentrations of protective-service and blue-collar workers living in aged duplex rows and multi-unit ''railroad'' flats. It leads the nation in durable manufacturing.

T2

Mid-Class, Child-Raising, Blue-Collar Families in Remote Suburbs and Towns

The three clusters might be characterized as America's blue-collar baby factories (equivalent to white-collar Furs and Station Wagons and Young Suburbia). These neighborhoods are very middle class and married. They show high indices for large families, household incomes close to the U.S. mean, and owner-occupied single-unit houses in factory towns and remote suburbs of industrial metros. While anchored in the Midwest, T2s are broadly distributed across the nation.

Blue-Collar Nursery (40) leads the nation in craftsmen, the elite of the blue-collar world. It is also No. 1 in married couples with children and households of three or more. These are low-density satellite towns and suburbs of smaller industrial cities. They are well paid and very stable.

Middle America (16) is composed of mid-sized, middle-class satellite suburbs and towns. It is at center on the socioeconomic scale, and is close to the U.S. average on most measures of age, ethnicity, household composition and life cycle. It is also centered in the Great Lakes industrial region, near the population geo-center of the United States.

Coalburg and Corntown (29) fits a popular image of the Midwest, being concentrated in small peaceful cities with names like Terre Haute, Indiana, and Lima, Ohio, surrounded by rich farmland, and populated by solid,

U2

Mid-Scale Families, Singles and Elders in Dense, Urban Row and High-Rise Areas

The four clusters encompass densely urban, middle-class neighborhoods, composed of duplex rows and multi-unit rented flats built more than 30 years ago in second-city centers and major-market fringes. U2s show high concentrations of foreign-born, working women, clerical and service occupations, singles and widows in one-person households, continuing deterioration, and increasing minority presence.

New Melting Pot (3) neighborhoods are situated in the major ports of entry on both coasts. The original European stock of many old urban neighborhoods has given way to new immigrant populations, often with Hispanic, Asian, and Middle-Eastern origins.

Old Yankee Rows (36) matches the New Melting Pot in age, housing mix, family composition, and income. However, it has a high concentration of high-school educated Catholics of European origin with very few minorities. These are well paid, mixed blue/white-collar areas, geo-centered in the older industrial cities of the Northeast.

Emergent Minorities (14) is almost 80 percent black, the remainder largely Hispanics and other minorities. Unlike other U2s, Emergent Minorities shows above-average concentrations for children, almost half of them with single parents. It also shows below-average levels of education and white-collar employment.

R1

Rural Towns and Villages amidst Farms and Ranches across Agrarian Mid-America

The three clusters are geo-centered in a broad swath across the Corn Belt, through the wheat fields of the Great Plains states, and on into ranch and mining country. R1 clusters share large numbers of sparsely populated communities, lower-middle to downscale socioeconomic levels, high concentrations of German and Scandinavian ancestries, negligible black presence, high incidence of large families headed by married parents, low incidence of college educations, and maximum stability.

Shotguns and Pickups (19) aggregates hundreds of small, outlying townships and crossroad villages which serve the nation's breadbasket and other rural areas. It has a more easterly distribution than other R1s, and shows peak indices for large families with school-age children, headed by blue-collar craftsmen, equipment operators, and transport workers with high-school educations. These areas are home to many dedicated outdoorsmen.

Agri-Business (34) is geo-centered in the Great Plains and mountain states. These are, in good part, prosperous ranching, farming, lumbering, and mining areas. However, the picture is marred by rural poverty where weather-worn old men and a continuing youth exodus testify to hard living.

Grain Belt (35) is a close match to Agri-Business on most demographic

blue-collar citizens raising sturdy, Tom Sawyer-ish children in decent, front-porch houses.

Single City Blues (26) represents the nation's densely urban, downscale singles areas. Many are located near city colleges, and the cluster displays a bimodal education profile. With very few children and its odd mixture of races, classes, transients, and night trades, Single City Blues could be aptly described as the poor man's Bohemia.

measures. However, these areas show a far higher concentration of working farm owners and less affluent tenant farmers. Tightly geo-centered in the Great Plains and mountain states, these are the nation's most stable and sparsely populated rural communities.

T3

Mixed Gentry and Blue-Collar Labor in Low-Mid Rustic, Mill and Factory Towns

The four clusters in Group T3 cover a host of predominantly blue-collar neighborhoods in the nation's smaller industrial cities, factory, mining, and mill towns, and rustic coastal villages. The T3 clusters share broad characteristics such as lower-middle incomes, limited educations, and (except Small-town Downtown) single units and mobile homes in medium- to low-density areas. However, it is the differences between clusters which make Group T3 interesting.

Golden Ponds (33) includes hundreds of small, rustic towns and villages in coastal resort, mountain, lake, and valley areas, where seniors in cottages choose to retire amongst country neighbors. While neither as affluent nor as elderly as Gray Power, Golden Ponds ranks high on all measures of retirement.

Mines and Mills (22) gathers hundreds of mining and mill towns scattered throughout the Appalachian mountains, from New England to the Pennsylvania-Ohio industrial complex and points south. It ranks first in total manufacturing and blue-collar occupations.

Norma Rae-Ville (13) is concentrated in the South, with its geo-center in the Appalachian and Piedmont regions. These neighborhoods include hundreds of industrial suburbs and mill towns, a great many in textiles and other light industries. They are country folk with

R2

Landowners, Migrants and Rustics in Poor Rural Towns, Farms and Uplands

The four clusters in group R2 pepper rural America and blanket the rural South with thousands of small agrarian communities, towns, villages and hamlets. As a group, R2s have long shared such characteristics as very low population densities, low socioeconomic rankings, minimal educations, large, highly stable households with widowed elders, predominantly blue-collar/farm labor, and peak concentrations of mobile homes. Since 1970, they have also shared rapid short-term growth and economic gains.

Back-Country Folks (10) abounds in remote rural towns, geo-centered in the Ozark and Appalachian uplands. It is strongly blue collar, with some farmers, and leads all clusters in concentration of mobile homes and trailers.

Sharecroppers (38) is represented in 48 states but is deeply rooted in the heart of Dixie. Traditionally, these areas were devoted to such industries as tenant farming, chicken breeding, pulpwood, and paper milling, etc. But sunbelt migration and a ready labor pool have continued to attract light industry and some population growth.

Tobacco Roads (15) is found throughout the South with its greatest concentrations in the river basins and coastal, scrub-pine flatlands of the Carolinas, Georgia, and the Gulf states. These areas are above average for children of all ages, nearly a third in single-parent households, and unique among the R2s

U3

Mixed, Unskilled Service and Labor in Aging, Urban Row and Hi-Rise Areas

The four clusters of Group U3 represent the least advantaged neighborhoods of urban America. They show peak indices for minorities, high indices for equipment operators, service workers and laborers, very low income and education levels, large families headed by solo parents, high concentrations of singles (widowed, divorced, separated, and never married), peak concentrations of renters in multi-unit housing, and chronic unemployment.

Heavy Industry (4) is much like Rank and File, nine rungs down on the socioeconomic scale and hard hit by unemployment. It is chiefly concentrated in the older industrial markets of northeastern United States and is very Catholic, with an above-average incidence of Hispanics. These neighborhoods have deteriorated rapidly during the past decade. There are fewer children and many broken homes.

Downtown Dixie-Style (11) has a southern geo-center. These middle-density urban neighborhoods are nearly 70 percent black and fall between Emergent Minorities and Public Assistance in relative affluence. Unemployment is high, with service occupations dominating amongst the employed.

Hispanic Mix (9) represents the nation's Hispanic barrios and is, therefore, chiefly concentrated in the Mid-Atlantic and West. These neighborhoods feature dense, row-house areas containing large families with minimal educations, unique amongst the T3s in having a high index for blacks, and lead the nation in nondurable manufacturing.

Smalltown Downtown (18) is unique among the T3s in the relatively high population densities. A hundred-odd years ago, our nation was laced with railroads and booming with heavy industry. All along these tracks, factory towns sprang up to be filled with laborers, in working-class row-house neighborhoods. Many can be seen today in Smalltown Downtown, mixed with the aging, downtown portions of other minor cities and towns.

with a large black population. Dependent upon agriculture, Tobacco Roads ranks at the bottom in white-collar occupations.

Hard Scrabble (6) neighborhoods represent our poorest rural areas, from Appalachia to the Ozarks, Mexican border country, and the Dakota Bad Lands. Had Scrabble leads all other clusters in concentration of adults with less than eight years of education, and trails all other clusters in concentration of working women.

small children, many headed by solo parents. They rank second in percentage of foreign born, first in short-term immigration, and are essentially bilingual neighborhoods.

Public Assistance (32) with 70 percent of its households black, represents the Harlems of America. These are the nation's poorest neighborhoods. These areas have been urban-renewal targets for three decades and show large, solo-parent families in rented or public high-rise buildings interspersed with aging tenement rows.

CHAPTER 13

ATTITUDES AND INFLUENCING ATTITUDES

What do you think of when you see the word *plastic*? Would you be pleased to know that the body of a car you are considering purchasing is primarily plastic, or would you prefer metal? Do you feel more comfortable using and recycling a paper cup or a Styrofoam cup? Many consumers think of plastic as cheap, artificial, weak, breakable, nondegradable, environmentally harmful, and otherwise undesirable. These negative *attitudes* affect consumers' willingness to purchase products containing plastic and their willingness to support legislation restricting the ways plastic is used.

The American Plastics Council recently spent $18 million on a six-month advertising campaign to improve consumers' and legislators' attitudes toward plastic. About $12 million was spent on television advertising, with the rest split between print and radio.

One of the four spots began at a grocery checkout where the clerk sees a shopper with numerous plastic containers and says: *When you look at plastic, you know how it helps things stay fresh and safe and unbreakable and easy to carry. But take another look.* (The checkout stand is passed by a moving car and then the stand itself seems to pass in front of a suburban home.) *Plastic also saves energy because it helps make cars lighter and saves gas. And plastic insulation helps save energy at home.* (Now the clerk grabs two plastic bags full of groceries.) *Even these strong plastic bags, because they take less energy than other grocery bags.* The ad closes with the slogan: *Take another look at plastic.*

Will this campaign succeed? Jackie Prince, a scientist with the Environmental Defense Fund, does not think so:

> *People don't dislike plastics; they just don't know what to do with them when they're done. An advertising campaign that focuses on perceptions, on plastics' advantages, is not going to work. You've got to change the underlying reality.*

While Ms. Prince feels that no advertising campaign can make plastics acceptable to environmentally concerned consumers, advertising expert Bob Garfield is critical of this specific approach to changing attitudes:

For a campaign such as this to have impact, it must confront consumer mistrust and then convert it, saying, in effect "We know you think we're scum. Here's why you're wrong." Then it could enumerate various plastics myths and one by one explode them, or exhaust viewers with an endless litany of products, from plastic replacement heart valves to Vibram soles, that they cannot live without. A great plastics campaign would first shame us for obsessing about liter bottles to the exclusion of the myriad ways plastic has improved the lives of billions, and then impress us about how the industry, in its own self-interest, is spending millions to make bottle recycling work.[1]

An **attitude** is *an enduring organization of motivational, emotional, perceptual, and cognitive processes with respect to some aspect of our environment.* It is "a learned predisposition to respond in a consistently favorable or unfavorable manner with respect to a given object."[2] Thus, an attitude is the way we think, feel, and act toward some aspect of our environment such as a retail store, television program, or product.

Attitudes are formed as the result of all the influences we have been describing in the previous chapters, and they represent an important influence on and reflection of an

FIGURE 13–1 Attitude Components and Manifestations

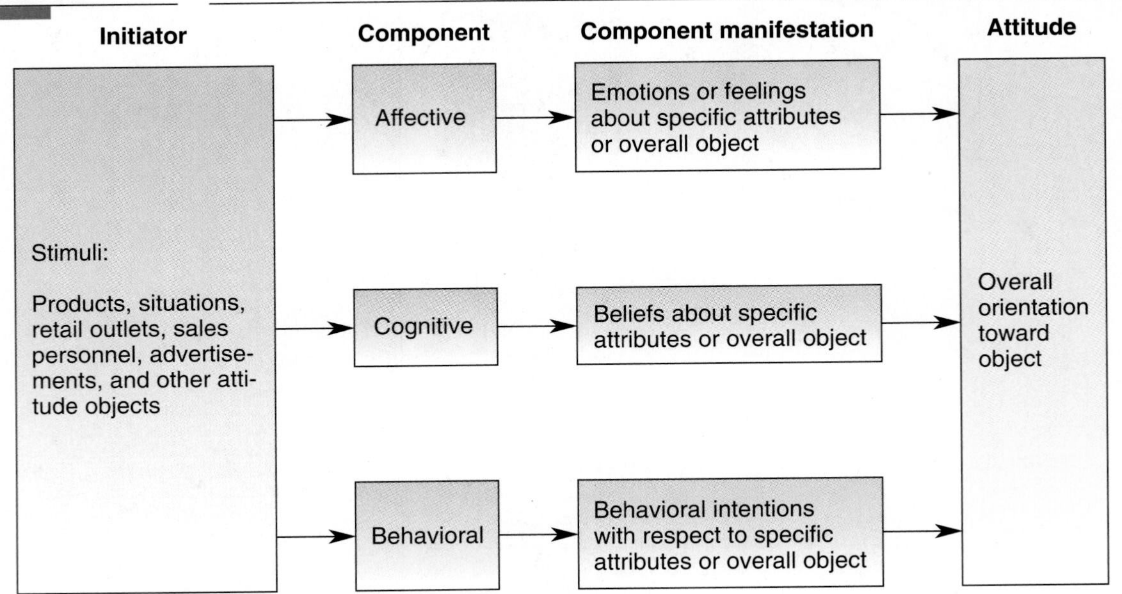

individual's lifestyle. Because of their importance, attitudes are the focal point for a substantial amount of marketing strategy as our opening example indicates.

In this chapter we will examine attitude components, the general strategies that can be used to change attitudes, and the effect of marketing communications on attitudes.

ATTITUDE COMPONENTS

As Figure 13–1 illustrates, it is useful to consider attitudes as having three components: cognitive, affective, and behavioral. Each of these attitude components is discussed in more detail below.

Cognitive Component

The **cognitive component** *consists of a consumer's beliefs about an object.* For most attitude objects, we have a number of beliefs. For example, we may believe that Diet Coke

- Has almost no calories.
- Contains caffeine.
- Is competitively priced.
- Is made by a large company.

The total configuration of beliefs about this brand of soda represents the cognitive component of an attitude toward Diet Coke. It is important to keep in mind that beliefs need not be correct or true; they only need to exist.

Many beliefs about attributes are evaluative in nature. That is, high gas mileage, attractive styling, and reliable performance are generally viewed as positive beliefs. The more positive beliefs there are associated with a brand and the more positive each belief is, the more favorable the overall cognitive component is presumed to be. And, since all of the components of an attitude are generally consistent, the more favorable the overall attitude is. This logic underlies what is known as the **multiattribute attitude model**.

There are several versions of this model. The simplest is:

$$A_b = \sum_{i=1}^{n} X_{ib}$$

where

A_b = The consumer's attitude toward a particular brand b.

X_{ib} = The consumer's belief about brand b's performance on attribute i.

n = The number of attributes considered.

This version assumes that all attributes are equally important in determining our overall evaluation. However, a moment's reflection suggests that for some products a few attributes such as price, quality, or style are more important than others. Thus, it is often desirable to add an importance weight for each attribute:

$$A_b = \sum_{i=1}^{n} W_i X_{ib}$$

where

W_i = The importance the consumer attaches to attribute i.

This version of the model is useful in a variety of situations. However, it assumes that more (or less) is always better. This is frequently the case. More miles to the gallon is always better than fewer miles to the gallon, all other things being equal. This version is completely adequate for such situations.

For some attributes, more (or less) is good up to a point but then further increases (decreases) become bad. For example, adding salt to a saltless pretzel will generally improve our attitude toward the pretzel up to a point. After that point, additional amounts of salt will decrease our attitude. In such situations, we need to introduce an "ideal point" into the multiattribute attitude model:

$$A_b = \sum_{i=1}^{n} W_i |I_i - X_{ib}|$$

where

I_i = The consumer's ideal level of performance on attribute i.

Since multiattribute attitude models are widely used by marketing researchers and managers, we will work through an example using the weighted, ideal point model. The simpler models would work in a similar manner.

Assume that a segment of consumers perceive Diet Coke to have the following levels of performance on four attributes:

	(1)	(2)	(3)	(4)	(5)	(6)	(7)	
Low price			I	X				High price
Sweet taste		I				X		Bitter taste
High status			I		X			Low status
Low calories	IX							High calories

This segment of consumers believes (the X's) that Diet Coke is average priced, very bitter in taste, somewhat low in status, and extremely low in calories. Their ideal soda (the I's) would be slightly low priced, very sweet in taste, somewhat high in status, and extremely low in calories. Since these attributes are not equally important to consumers, attributes are assigned weights based on the relative importance a segment of consumers attaches to each attribute. A popular way of measuring importance weights is with a 100-point **constant-sum scale**. For example, the importance weights shown below express the relative importance of four soft-drink attributes such that the total adds up to 100 points.

Attribute	Importance
Price	10
Taste	30
Status	20
Calories	40
	100 points

In this case, calories is considered the most important attribute with taste slightly less important. Price is given little importance.

From this information we can index this segment's attitude toward Diet Coke as follows:

$$\begin{aligned} A_{Diet\ Coke} &= (10)(|3 - 4|) + (30)(|2 - 6|) + (20)(|3 - 5|) \\ &\quad + (40)(|1 - 1|) \\ &= (10)(1) + (30)(4) + (20)(2) + (40)(0) \\ &= 170 \end{aligned}$$

This involves taking the absolute difference between the consumer's ideal soft-drink attributes and beliefs about Diet Coke's attributes and multiplying these differences times the importance attached to each attribute. In this case, the attitude index is computed as 170. Is this good or bad?

An attitude index is a relative measure, so in order to fully evaluate it, we must compare it to attitudes toward competing products or brands. However, if Diet Coke were perceived as their ideal soft drink, then all their beliefs and ideals would be equal and an attitude index of zero would be computed, since there would be no difference between what is desired and what the consumers believe to be provided. Thus, the closer an attitude index calculated in this manner is to zero, the better.

We have been discussing the multiattribute view of the cognitive component as though consumers explicitly and consciously went through a series of deliberate evaluations and summed them to form an overall impression. However, this level of effort would occur only in *very* high-involvement purchase situations. In general, the multiattribute attitude model merely *represents* a nonconscious process that is much less precise and structured than implied by the model.

Affective Component

Our feelings or emotional reactions to an object represent the **affective component** of an attitude. A consumer who states, "I like Diet Coke," or "Diet Coke is a terrible soda," is expressing the results of an emotional or affective evaluation of the product. This overall evaluation may be simply a vague, general feeling developed without cognitive information or beliefs about the product. Or, it may be the result of several evaluations of the product's performance on each of several attributes. Thus, the statements, "Diet Coke tastes bad," and "Diet Coke is overpriced," imply a negative affective reaction to specific aspects of the product which, in combination with feelings about other attributes, will determine the overall reaction to this brand of soft drink.

Most beliefs about a product have associated affective reactions or evaluations. For example, the belief that Diet Coke costs $3.49 for six could produce a positive reaction (affective statement or feeling) of ''this is a bargain,'' a negative feeling of ''this is overpriced,'' or a neutral feeling of ''this is an average price.'' The emotion or feeling attached to a given belief depends on the individual and the situation.

Since products, like other objects we react to, are evaluated in the context of a specific situation, a consumer's affective reaction to a product (as well as beliefs about the product) may change as the situation changes. For example, a consumer may believe that (1) Diet Coke has caffeine and (2) caffeine will keep you awake. These beliefs may cause a positive affective response when the consumer needs to stay awake to study for an exam, and a negative response when he wants to drink something late in the evening that won't keep him awake later.

Due to unique motivations and personalities, past experiences, reference groups, and physical conditions, individuals may evaluate the same belief differently. Some individuals may have a positive feeling toward the belief that ''Diet Coke has a strong taste,'' while others could respond with a negative reaction. Despite individual variations, most individuals within a given culture react in a similar manner to beliefs that are closely associated with cultural values. For example, beliefs and feelings about a restaurant with respect to cleanliness are likely to be very similar among individuals in the United States since this value is important in our culture. Thus, there often is a strong association between how a belief is evaluated and a related value that is of importance within a culture.[3]

While feelings are often the result of evaluating specific attributes of a product, they can precede and influence cognitions. As we discuss in depth in the next section, one may come to like a product *without acquiring any cognitive beliefs about the product.* Indeed, our initial reaction to a product may be one of like or dislike without any cognitive basis for the feeling. This initial affect can then influence how we react to the product itself.[4]

Behavioral Component

The **behavioral component** of an attitude *is one's tendency to respond in a certain manner toward an object or activity.* A series of decisions to purchase or not purchase Diet Coke or to recommend it or other brands to friends would reflect the behavioral component of an attitude. As we will see in the next section, the behavioral component provides response tendencies or behavioral intentions. Our actual behaviors reflect these intentions as they are modified by the situation in which the behavior will occur.

Since behavior is generally directed toward an entire object, it is less likely to be attribute specific than are either beliefs or affect. However, this is not always the case, particularly with respect to retail outlets. For example, many consumers buy canned goods at discount or warehouse-type grocery outlets but purchase meats and fresh vegetables at regular supermarkets. Thus, for retail outlets it is possible and common to react behaviorally to specific beliefs about the outlet. This is generally difficult to do with products because we have to either buy or not buy the complete product.

Component Consistency

Figure 13–2 illustrates a critical aspect of attitudes: all three components tend to be consistent. This means that a change in one attitude component tends to produce related changes in the other components. This tendency is the basis for a substantial amount of marketing strategy.

FIGURE 13-2

Attitude Component Consistency

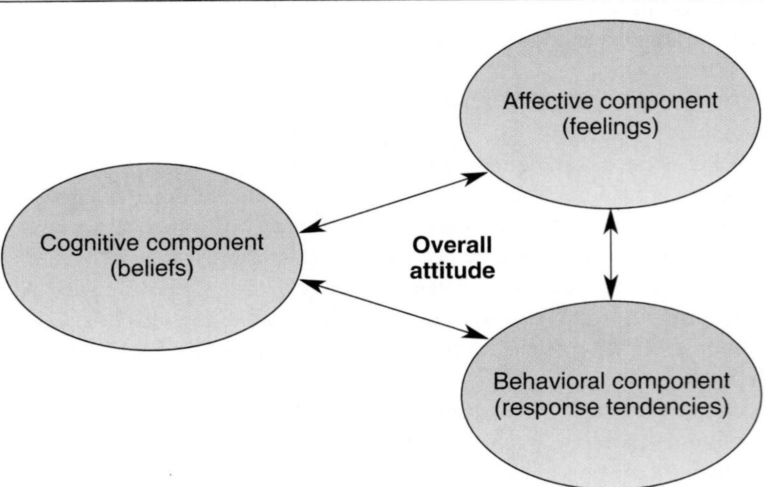

As marketing managers, we are ultimately concerned with influencing behavior. However, it is often difficult to influence behavior directly. That is, we are frequently unable to directly cause consumers to buy our products. However, consumers will often listen to our sales personnel, attend to our advertisements, or examine our packages. We can, therefore, indirectly influence behavior by providing information, music, or other stimuli that influence a belief or feeling about the product *if* the three components are indeed consistent with each other.

A number of research studies have found only a limited relationship among the three components.[5] Let's examine the sources of this inconsistency by considering an example. Suppose an individual has a set of positive beliefs toward the Macintosh computer and also has a positive affective response to this brand and model. Further, suppose that these beliefs and affect are more favorable toward the Macintosh than any other computer. Our customer responds to a questionnaire and indicates these positive beliefs and feelings. However, the consumer does not own a Macintosh, or purchases another brand or model. Thus, a researcher might conclude that the three components are not consistent.

At least seven factors can operate to reduce the consistency between measures of beliefs and feelings and observations of behavior.

First, a favorable attitude requires a need or motive before it can be translated into action. Thus, our consumer may not feel a need for a computer or might already own an acceptable, though less preferred, brand.

Second, translating favorable beliefs and feelings into ownership requires ability. One might not own a computer or might purchase a less expensive model due to insufficient funds to purchase a Macintosh.

Third, we measured attitudes only toward computers. Purchases often involve trade-offs both within and between product categories. Thus our consumer might purchase a less expensive computer in order to save resources to buy new skis, a camera, or an automobile.

Fourth, if the cognitive and affective components are weakly held, and if the consumer obtains additional information while shopping, then the initial attitudes may give way to new ones.

Fifth, we measured an individual's attitudes. However, as we saw in Chapter 8, many purchase decisions involve other household members either directly or indirectly. Thus, our shopper may purchase a simpler computer so that other family members can operate it.

Sixth, we generally measure brand attitudes independent of the purchase situation. However, many items are purchased for, or in, specific situations.[6] A very inexpensive computer might be purchased if the consumer anticipates access to more sophisticated equipment in the near future.

Seventh, it is difficult to measure all of the relevant aspects of an attitude. Consumers may be unwilling or unable to articulate all of their feelings and beliefs about various products or brands. Therefore, attitude components are sometimes more consistent than our measures suggest them to be.

In summary, attitude components—cognitive, affective, and behavioral—tend to be consistent. However, the degree of apparent consistency between measures of cognitions and affect and observations of behavior may be reduced by a variety of factors as mentioned above.

Measurement of Attitude Components

Purchase and use behavior at the brand level are predicted most accurately by overall measures of brand liking or affect. However, since components of attitudes are often an integral part of a marketing strategy, it is important that we be able to measure each component. Approaches to measuring the components are shown in Exhibit 13–1, with details provided in Appendix A of this book.

ATTITUDE CHANGE STRATEGIES

Examine Managerial Application 1–6 (p. 18). The attitude change induced by manipulating the marketing mix for Marlboro is a classic in marketing history. As this example illustrates, managers can form and change attitudes toward products and brands. It also raises ethical questions concerning how firms use this knowledge.

As we saw in Figure 13–2, changing any one attitude component is likely to produce related changes in the other components. Therefore, managers may focus on any one or more of the components as they attempt to develop favorable attitudes toward their brands.

Change the Affective Component

It is increasingly common for a firm to influence consumers' liking of their brand without directly influencing either beliefs or behavior. If the firm is successful, increased liking will tend to lead to increased positive beliefs, which could lead to purchase behavior should a need for the product category arise. Or, perhaps more commonly, increased liking will lead to a tendency to purchase the brand should a need arise, with purchase and use leading to increased positive beliefs. Both of these outcomes are shown in Figure 13–3 on page 363. Marketers use three basic approaches to directly increase affect: classical conditioning, affect toward the ad itself, and "mere" exposure.

Classical Conditioning One way of directly influencing the affective component is through classical conditioning (Chapter 10, pp. 272–73). In this approach, a stimulus the audience likes, such as music, is consistently paired with the brand name. Over time some of the positive affect associated with the music will transfer to the brand. Other "liked" stimuli, such as pictures, are frequently used for this reason.[7]

Affect toward the Ad As we saw in Chapter 11, liking the advertisement increases the tendency to like the product.[8] Positive affect toward the ad may increase liking of the brand through classical conditioning, or it may be a more high-involvement, conscious process. Using humor, celebrities, or emotional appeals increases affect toward the ad.

EXHIBIT 13–1 Measuring Attitude Components

Cognitive Component (Measuring Beliefs about Specific Attributes)

Diet Coke

Strong taste	—	—	—	—	—	—	—	Mild taste
Low priced	—	—	—	—	—	—	—	High priced
Caffeine free	—	—	—	—	—	—	—	High in caffeine
Distinctive in taste	—	—	—	—	—	—	—	Similar in taste to most

Affective Component (Measuring Feelings about Specific Attributes or the Overall Brand)

	Strongly Agree	Agree	Neither Agree nor Disagree	Disagree	Strongly Disagree
I like the taste of Diet Coke.	______	______	______	______	______
Diet Coke is overpriced.	______	______	______	______	______
Caffeine is bad for your health.	______	______	______	______	______
I like Diet Coke.	______	______	______	______	______

Behavioral Component (Measuring Actions or Intended Actions)

Have you ever purchased Diet Coke?

- ☐ Yes (how often? __)
- ☐ No

What is the likelihood you will buy Diet Coke the next time you purchase a soft drink?

- ☐ Definitely will buy
- ☐ Probably will buy
- ☐ Might buy
- ☐ Probably will *not* buy
- ☐ Definitely will *not* buy

Each is discussed in the last section of this chapter. Managerial Applications 13–1 and 11–4 (page 316) contain ads that rely on positive affect.

Mere Exposure While controversial, there is evidence that affect may also be increased by "mere exposure."[9] That is, simply presenting a brand to an individual on a large number of occasions might make the individual's attitude toward the brand more positive. Thus, the continued repetition of advertisements for low-involvement products may well increase liking and subsequent purchase of the advertised brands *without* altering the initial belief structure.

FIGURE 13-3

Attitude Change Strategy Focusing on Affect

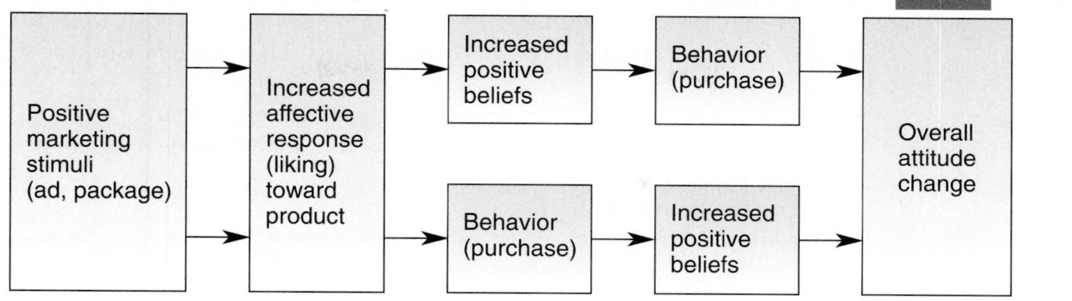

MANAGERIAL APPLICATION 13-1

Ads that Rely on a Positive Affect toward the Ad

The fact that advertising may alter affect directly and, by altering affect, indirectly alter purchase behavior *without* first changing beliefs, has a number of important implications:

- Ads designed to alter affect need not contain any cognitive (factual or attribute) information.
- Classical conditioning principles should guide such campaigns.
- Attitudes (liking) toward the ad itself are critical for this type of campaign (unless ''mere exposure'' is being used).
- Repetition is critical for affect-based campaigns.
- Traditional measures of advertising effectiveness focus on the cognitive component and are inappropriate for affect-based campaigns.

Change the Behavioral Component

Behavior, specifically purchase or consumption behavior, may precede the development of cognition and affect. Or, it may occur in contrast to the cognitive and affective components. For example, a consumer may dislike the taste of diet soft drinks and believe that artificial sweeteners are unhealthy. However, rather than appear rude, the same consumer may accept a diet drink when offered one by a friend. Drinking the beverage may alter her perceptions of its taste and lead to liking; this in turn may lead to increased learning, which changes the cognitive component. Evidence suggests that attitudes formed as a consequence of product trial are strongly held.[10]

Figure 13–4 illustrates this approach. Behavior can lead directly to affect, to cognitions, or to both simultaneously. Consumers frequently try new brands or types of low-cost items in the absence of prior knowledge or affect. Such purchases are as much for information (''will I like this brand'') as for satisfaction of some underlying need such as hunger.

Changing behavior prior to changing affect or cognition is based primarily on operant conditioning (Chapter 10, pp. 273–76). Thus, the key marketing task is to induce people to purchase or consume the product while ensuring that the purchase/consumption will indeed be rewarding. Coupons, free samples, point-of-purchase displays, tie-in purchases, and price reductions are common techniques for inducing trial behavior. Since behavior often leads to strong positive attitudes toward the consumed brand, a sound distribution system (limited stockouts) is important to prevent current customers from trying competing brands.

Change the Cognitive Component

A common and effective approach to changing attitudes is to focus on the cognitive component.[11] Thus, to change attitudes toward cigarette smoking, the American Cancer Society has presented information on the negative health consequences of smoking. The theory is that by influencing this belief, affect and behavior will then change. This sequence is shown in Figure 13–5. It is also possible for a changed cognition to lead directly to purchase which could then lead to increased liking. This is also shown in Figure 13–5.

Four basic marketing strategies are used for altering the cognitive structure of a consumer's attitude.

Change Beliefs This strategy involves shifting beliefs about the performance of the brand on one or more attributes. For example, many consumers believe that American cars are not as well made as Japanese cars. A substantial amount of advertising for American automobiles is designed to change this belief. Attempts to change beliefs generally provide ''facts'' or statements about performance. Managerial Application 13–2 shows an ad for

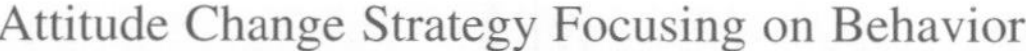

Attitude Change Strategy Focusing on Behavior

FIGURE 13–4

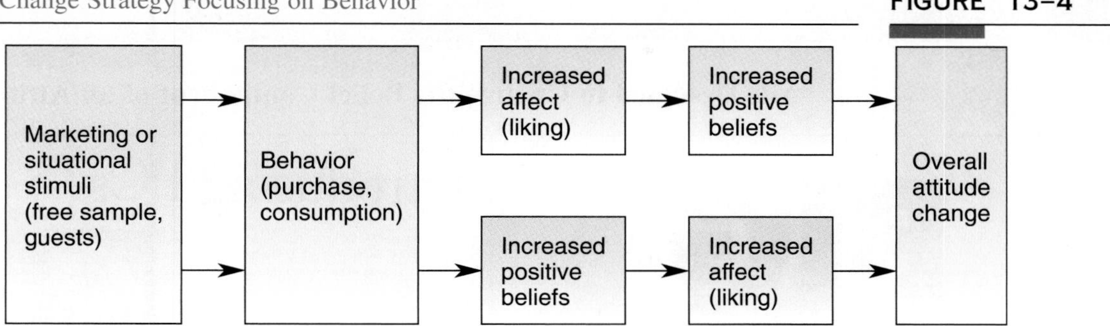

Attitude Change Strategy Focusing on Cognitions

FIGURE 13–5

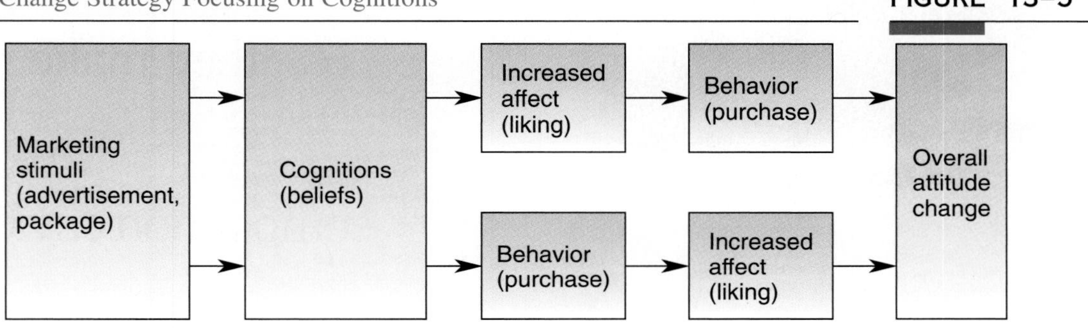

Kellogg's Low Fat Granola designed to change the belief held by many consumers that all granolas are very high in fat content.

Shift Importance Most consumers consider some product attributes to be more important than others. Marketers often try to convince consumers that those attributes on which they are relatively strong are the most important. For example, Chrysler was one of the first automobile manufacturers to have air bags as standard equipment. It then advertised this feature heavily in an attempt to make it more important to consumers.

Add Beliefs Another approach to changing the cognitive component of an attitude is to add new beliefs to the consumer's belief structure. The ad for Digital PCs in Managerial Application 13–2 is attempting to add a belief about the energy consumption of PCs to the cognitive structure consumers have of this product category (it also attempts to make this attribute more important among those who already consider this attribute).

Change Ideal The final strategy for changing the cognitive component is to change the perceptions of the ideal brand. Thus, many conservation organizations strive to influence our beliefs about the ideal product in terms of minimal packaging, nonpolluting manufacturing, extensive use of recycled materials, and nonpolluting disposition after its useful life.

MANAGERIAL APPLICATION

13-2

Ads Designed to Change the Belief Component of an Attitude

An Attempt to Change a Belief

An Attempt to Add a Belief

COMMUNICATION CHARACTERISTICS THAT INFLUENCE ATTITUDE FORMATION AND CHANGE

Attitudes are influenced most strongly when the brand has something unique to offer and the unique benefits of the brand are the focus of the commercial.[12] In this section, we describe techniques that enhance attitude change when unique brand features are present and that also can be used to influence attitudes when a brand does not have unique benefits.

Source Characteristics

Source Credibility Influencing attitudes is easier when the source of the message is viewed as highly credible by the target market. This is referred to as **source credibility**.

Source credibility appears to be composed of two basic dimensions: *trustworthiness* and *expertise.*[13] A source that has no apparent reason to provide other than complete, objective, and accurate information would generally be considered as trustworthy. Most

MANAGERIAL APPLICATION 13–3

An Ad Using a Credible Source to Support a Claim

of us would consider our good friends trustworthy on most matters. However, our friends might not have the knowledge necessary to be credible in a certain area. While sales personnel and advertisers often have ample knowledge, many consumers doubt the trustworthiness of sales personnel and advertisements because it might be to their advantage to mislead the consumer.

Such organizations as the American Dental Association (ADA), which is widely viewed as both trustworthy and expert, can have a tremendous influence on attitudes. The remarkable success of Crest toothpaste is largely attributable to the ADA endorsement. Underwriters Laboratories, *Good Housekeeping*, and other trustworthy and expert sources are widely sought for their endorsements. Managerial Application 13–3 shows the use of an occupational group—pediatricians—as a credible source for *Yoplait* yogurt.

Celebrity Sources The source of a communication can be an identifiable person, an unidentifiable person (a "typical" homemaker), a company or organization, or an inanimate figure such as a cartoon character. Many firms use celebrities as the source of their marketing communications.

Celebrity sources may enhance attitude change for a variety of reasons.[14] They may attract more attention to the advertisement than would noncelebrities. Or, in many cases, they may be viewed as more credible than noncelebrities. Third, consumers may identify with or desire to emulate the celebrity. Finally, consumers may associate known characteristics of the celebrity with attributes of the product which coincide with their own needs or desires.

The effectiveness of using a celebrity to endorse a firm's product can generally be improved by matching the image of the celebrity with the personality of the product and the actual or desired self-concept of the target market. For example, Linda Evans ("Dynasty") scored higher than average in brand awareness and attitude shift with her

FIGURE 13–6 Matching Endorser with Product and Target Audience

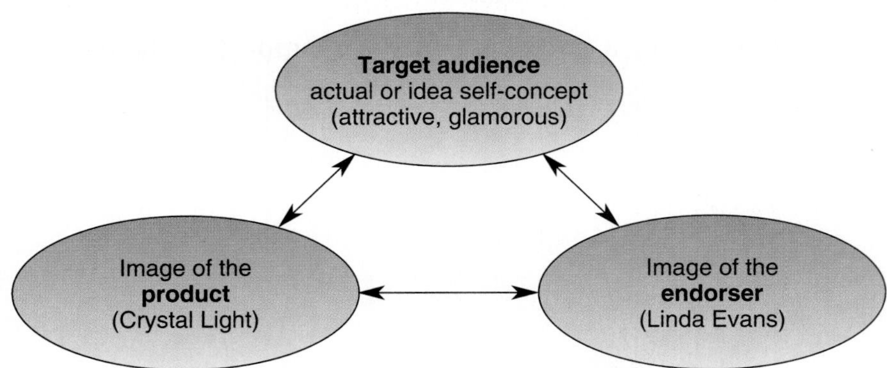

endorsement of Crystal Light. Her image of mature, sophisticated, sexy glamour matched the ideal self-concept of many members of the target audience as well as the benefits and product positioning of Crystal Light (a powdered, diet soft drink). It is unlikely that John Madden would have had the same impact. When the three components shown in Figure 13–6 are well matched, effective attitude formation or change can result.[15] For example, celebrity endorsements by Jimmy Connors and Joe Montana are credited with increasing Nuprin's sales almost 25 percent. Managerial Application 13–4 shows ads using celebrity endorsers who are effective with their target markets.

Using a celebrity as a company spokesperson creates special risks for the sponsoring organization. Few well-known personalities are admired by everyone. Thus, it is important to be certain that most of the members of the relevant target markets will respond favorably to the spokesperson. An additional risk is that some behavior involving the spokesperson will affect the individual's credibility after he/she is associated with the firm. For example, while serving as spokespersons for the Beef Industry Council, Cybill Shepherd admitted in a magazine interview that she avoided red meat and James Garner had heart surgery. The Florida Citrus Commission and Quaker State motor oil quit using Burt Reynolds after his highly publicized divorce from Loni Anderson. PepsiCo has had problems with commercials featuring Madonna (after a controversial video), Mike Tyson (after his conviction for rape), Magic Johnson (after acquiring AIDS through an admittedly extensive series of affairs), and Michael Jackson (after child molestation charges).

Appeal Characteristics

Fear Appeals make use *of the threat of negative* (*unpleasant*) *consequences if attitudes or behaviors are not altered.* While fear appeals have been studied primarily in terms of physical fear (physical harm from smoking, unsafe driving, and so forth), social fears (disapproval of one's peers for incorrect clothing, bad breath, or inadequate coffee) are also frequently used in advertising. For fear appeals to be successful, the level of fear induced must not be so high as to cause the consumer to distort or reject the message. In addition, it is critical that the source of the fear-arousing message be viewed as highly credible. Using a fear appeal as a way to gain attention and stress the dangers of cocaine use, the Partnership for a Drug-Free America sponsors the ad shown in Managerial

MANAGERIAL APPLICATION 13–4

Ads Using Celebrity Endorsers

Application 13–5. While they may not always be appropriate and are often difficult to utilize, fear appeals can influence attitudes.[16]

Humorous Appeals At almost the opposite end of the spectrum from fear appeals are message appeals built around humor.[17] Humor in an ad appears to have the following impacts:

- Attracts attention.
- Does not generally affect comprehension.
- Does not generally increase persuasion.
- Does not increase source credibility.
- Increases liking of the ad.
- Humor related to the product or in a usage situation is more effective than unrelated humor.
- What is humorous varies sharply across market segments.
- The nature of the product affects the appropriateness of using humor.

MANAGERIAL APPLICATION

13–5

A Strong Fear Appeal and an Effective Humorous Appeal

Cocaine can make you blind.

Cocaine fools your brain.

When you first use it, you may feel more alert, more confident, more sociable, more in control of your life.

In reality, of course, nothing has changed. But to your brain, the feeling seems real.

From euphoria...

You want to experience it again. So you do some more coke.

Once more, you like the effects. It's a very clean high. It doesn't really feel like you're drugged. Only this time, you notice you don't feel so good when you come down. You're confused, edgy, anxious, even depressed.

Fortunately, that's easy to fix. At least for the next 20 minutes or so. All it takes is another few lines, or a few more hits on the pipe.

You're discovering one of the things that makes cocaine so dangerous.

It compels you to keep on using it. (Given unlimited access, laboratory monkeys take cocaine until they have seizures and die.)

If you keep experimenting with cocaine, quite soon you may feel you need it just to function well. To perform better at work, to cope with stress, to escape depression, just to have a good time at a party or a concert.

Like speed, cocaine makes you talk a lot and sleep a little. You can't sit still. You have difficulty concentrating and remembering. You feel aggressive and suspicious towards people. You don't want to eat very much. You become uninterested in sex.

To paranoia...

Compulsion is now definitely addiction. And there's worse to come.

You stop caring how you look or how you feel. You become paranoid. You may feel people are persecuting you, and you may have an intense fear that the police are waiting to arrest you. (Not surprising, since cocaine is illegal.)

You may have hallucinations. Because coke heightens your senses, they may seem terrifyingly real.

As one woman overdosed, she heard laughter nearby and a voice that said, "I've got you now." So many people have been totally convinced that bugs were crawling on or out of their skin, that the hallucination has a nickname: the coke bugs.

Especially if you've been smoking cocaine, you may become violent, or feel suicidal.

When coke gets you really strung out, you may turn to other drugs to slow down. Particularly downers like alcohol, tranquilizers, marijuana and heroin. (A speedball—heroin and cocaine—is what killed John Belushi.)

If you saw your doctor now and he didn't know you were using coke, he'd probably diagnose you as a manic-depressive.

To psychosis...

Literally, you're crazy.

But you know what's truly frightening? Despite everything that's happening to you, even now, you may still feel totally in control.

That's the drug talking.

Cocaine really does make you blind to reality. And with what's known about it today, you probably have to be something else to start using coke in the first place.

Dumb.

Partnership for a Drug-Free America

A Strong Fear Appeal

An Effective Humorous Appeal

Managerial Application 13–5 contains an ad making effective use of humor.

Comparative Ads In an effort to stimulate comparative shopping, the FTC has encouraged companies to use comparisons of their products against competitors in their advertisements. The FTC's reasoning is that the consumer benefits when competition is strongest, and comparative advertising is intended to promote competition as companies strive to improve their products relative to competing products.

Comparative ads often produce no additional gain to the image of the sponsoring brand, and sometimes unfavorable impressions result. However, in other instances comparative ads produce positive results for advertisers as well as consumers. Available evidence suggests that comparative ads should follow these guidelines:

- Comparative advertising may be particularly effective for promoting *new* brands with strong product attributes.
- Comparative advertising is likely to be more effective if its claims are *substantiated* by *credible* sources.

- Comparative advertising may be used effectively to establish a brand's *position* or to upgrade its *image* by association.
- *Audience characteristics*, especially the extent of *brand loyalty* associated with the sponsoring brand, are important. Users or owners of the named competitor brands appear to be resistant to comparative claims.
- Since people consider comparative advertisements to be more *interesting* than noncomparative advertisements (as well as being more ''offensive''), these commercials may be effective if the product category is relatively static and noncomparative advertising has ceased to be effective.
- Appropriate *theme* construction can significantly increase the overall effectiveness of comparative advertising.
- It is important to ascertain how many product *attributes to mention* in a comparative advertisement.
- *Print media* appear to be better vehicles for comparative advertisements since print lends itself to more thorough comparisons.[18]

Emotional Appeals Emotional or feeling ads are being used with increasing frequency. **Emotional ads** *are designed primarily to elicit a positive affective response rather than provide information or arguments.* As we saw in Chapter 11 (pages 315–18), emotional ads such as those that arouse feelings of warmth trigger a physiological reaction. They are also liked more than neutral ads and produce more positive attitudes toward the product. Emotional advertisements may enhance attitude formation or change by increasing:

- The ad's ability to attract and maintain attention.
- The level of mental processing given the ad.
- Ad memorability.
- Liking of the ad.
- Product liking through classical conditioning.
- Product liking through high-involvement processes.[19]

Value-Expressive versus Utilitarian Appeals **Value-expressive appeals** *attempt to build a personality for the product or create an image of the product user.* **Utilitarian appeals** *involve informing the consumer of one or more functional benefits that are important to the target market.* Which is best under what conditions?

Both theory and some empirical evidence indicate that utilitarian appeals are most effective for utilitarian products and value-expressive appeals are most effective for value-expressive products.[20] That is, one should not do image advertising for lawn mowers or factual advertising for perfumes. However, many products such as automobiles, some cosmetics, and clothes serve both utilitarian and functional purposes. Which approach is best for these products? There is no simple answer. Some marketers opt to present both types of appeals, others focus on one or the other, and others vary their approach across market segments. Managerial Application 13–6 contains an example of each approach.

Message Structure Characteristics

One-Sided versus Two-Sided Messages In advertisements and sales presentations, marketers generally present only the benefits of their product without mentioning any negative characteristics it might possess or any advantages a competitor might have. These are **one-sided messages** since only one point of view is expressed. The idea of a **two-sided message**, presenting both good and bad points, is counterintuitive, and most marketers are reluctant to try such an approach. However, two-sided messages are generally more

MANAGERIAL APPLICATION

13–6

A Value-Expressive Appeal and a Utilitarian Appeal

A Value-Expressive Appeal

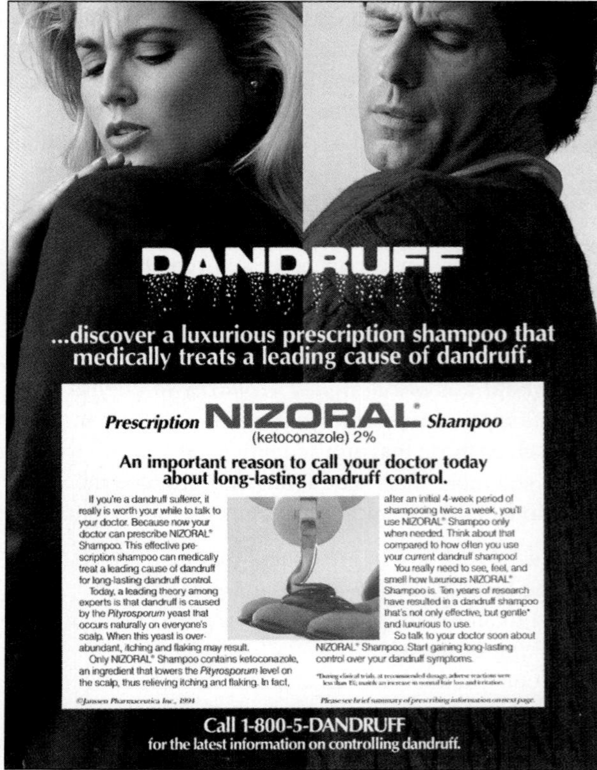

A Utilitarian Appeal

effective than one-sided messages in terms of changing a strongly held attitude. In addition, they are particularly effective with highly educated consumers. One-sided messages are most effective at reinforcing existing attitudes. However, product type, situational variables, and advertisement format influence the relative effectiveness of the two approaches.[21]

Nonverbal Components In Chapter 10 (pages 282–83), we discussed how pictures enhance imagery and facilitate learning. Pictures,[22] music,[23] surrealism,[24] and other nonverbal cues[25] are also effective in attitude change. Emotional ads, described earlier, often rely primarily or exclusively on nonverbal content to arouse an emotional response. Nonverbal ad content can also affect cognitions about a product. For example, an ad showing a person drinking a new beverage after exercise provides information about appropriate usage situations without stating "good after exercise."

While the impact of nonverbal ad elements is not yet completely understood, it is clear that they can have significant influence, both positive and negative.[26] Therefore, the nonverbal portion of advertising messages should be designed and tested with as much care as the verbal portion.

MARKET SEGMENTATION AND PRODUCT DEVELOPMENT STRATEGIES BASED ON ATTITUDES

Market Segmentation

The identification of market segments is a key aspect of marketing. Properly designed marketing programs should be built around the unique needs of each market segment. The importance of various attributes is one way of defining customer needs for a given product. Segmenting consumers on the basis of their most important attribute or attributes is called **benefit segmentation**.[27]

To define benefit segments, a marketer needs to know the importance attached to the respective attributes of a particular product or service. Then benefit segments can be formed by grouping consumers with similar attribute importance ratings into segments, such that within a segment consumers are seeking the same benefit(s).

Additional information about consumers within each segment is obtained to develop a more complete picture of each segment. Then, knowing the primary benefit sought by each segment and the descriptive characteristics of each segment, separate marketing programs can be developed for each of the segments to be served by a particular organization. Exhibit 13–2 shows benefit segments of relevance to the arts market.[28]

EXHIBIT 13–2

Benefit Segments for the Arts Market

	Current Users		
	Cultural Aspirants	**Temporary Diversion**	**Peak Aesthetic Experience**
Benefits sought	Enlightenment; cultural exposure. Intellectual expansion. Identification with the "cognoscenti."	Passive entertainment; relaxation. Noncognitive diversion. A social medium. An evening out.	Emotional and intellectual involvement/stimulation. Professional excellence; creativity and beauty.
Category beliefs	Arts attendance helps provide the intellectual sophistication of the "cognoscenti" with whom I identify.	Arts performances should offer entertainment and diversion; a relaxing atmosphere while enjoying the company of friends and family.	Arts performances should offer a high level of artistic excellence, and permit complete emotional and intellectual involvement.
Preferred leisure activities	Reading, crafts, antiquing. "Serious" arts performances.	Dining out, movies, skiing, biking, sightseeing. Lighter art performances.	Crafts, sailing, reading, skiing, etc. "Professional" arts performances of particular merit.

(continued)

EXHIBIT 13–2 Benefit Segments for the Arts Market (*continued*)

	Current Users		
	Cultural Aspirants	**Temporary Diversion**	**Peak Aesthetic Experience**
Participation	Frequent.	Infrequent to moderate.	Moderate to frequent.
Occasions of participation	Evening, weekends—whenever programs offered.	Predominantly weekends.	Evenings, weekends—performances and activities of special interest.
Media habits	Local/national newspapers. Posters, mailers, handbills.	Local newspapers, posters, and handbills. Moderate TV and radio.	Local/national newspapers. Posters, mailers, handbills. Light TV and radio.
Personality/ lifestyle	Other-directed. Impressionable.	Other-oriented and socially active.	Sophisticated and well educated; inner-directed. Socially active.
Demographics	Age: Younger, 21–35. College education. Beginning professional career.	Age: 25–49. High school or some college education. Income: $10,000–$15,000.	Sophisticates of all ages. College educated; professional. Income: $15,000 and over.

	Nonusers			
	Security Seekers	**Hedonists**	**Pragmatists**	**Children-Oriented**
Benefits sought	Relaxation, security of family and friends. Peer approval. To feel at ease.	Entertainment. Excitement. Action.	Convenience. Diversion. Feeling of productivity and involvement.	Upward mobility for children; well-rounded education for children.
Category beliefs	Arts are designed for more sophisticated group. Would feel insecure, uncomfortable, and out of place.	Arts are too formal, serious, and passive.	Arts are for snobbish, nonactive people. Don't understand or relate to arts. Find them boring, uninteresting.	Children should have the educational and social opportunities needed for a successful life.

(*continued*)

EXHIBIT 13-2

Benefit Segments for the Arts Market (*concluded*)

	Nonusers			
	Security Seekers	**Hedonists**	**Pragmatists**	**Children-Oriented**
Preferred leisure activities	Television, dining out, family outings. Peer and family-oriented activities.	Hunting, fishing, boating, sports, etc. Action-oriented activities.	Gardening, hunting, woodworking, sewing. Productive activities.	Family activities; outings, camping, sports, etc. Scouting, school, clubs encouraged.
Participation	Low to moderate.	High.	Moderate to high.	Moderate to high.
Occasions of participation	Weekends, holidays, vacations.	Evenings, weekends, whenever possible.	Evenings, weekends, vacations.	Encouraged to become involved frequently.
Media habits	Local newspapers. Heavy radio and TV.	Local/national newspapers. Moderate radio and TV. Special-interest magazines; posters.	Local newspapers. Low to moderate TV. Special-interest magazines, posters, mailers.	Local newspapers. Mailers. Moderate radio and TV.
Personality/ lifestyle	Reticent, insecure, conforming. Oriented toward family and friends.	Outgoing, active, fast-paced lifestyle.	Practical, organized. Family- and work-oriented.	Conservative, practical, hard-working. Family-oriented.
Demographics	Age: 25–64; unskilled or semiskilled. Education: High school or less. Income: Below average.	Age: 25–49; technician, white collar. Education: High school/ college. Income: Above average.	Age: 35–64; tradesman. Education: High school or technical school. Income: Above average.	Age: 35–49; semiskilled or clerical. Education: High school. Income: Average.

Product Development

While the importance consumers attach to key attributes provides a meaningful way to understand needs and form benefit segments, the ideal levels of performance indicate their desired level of performance in satisfying those needs. Thus, these ideal levels of performance can provide valuable guidelines in developing a new product or reformulating an existing one.

To illustrate how ideal levels can be used in product development, Exhibit 13–3 describes how Coca-Cola used this approach in developing a new soft drink.[29] The first step is to *construct a profile of a segment of consumers' ideal level of performance* with respect to key attributes of a soft drink. For a particular type of soft drink, four attributes were identified and the average ideal level of performance was obtained from consumer ratings. If there is a wide range of ideal ratings for a particular attribute, further segmentation may be required.

A second step involves *creation of a product concept that closely matches the ideal profile*. The concept could be a written description, picture, or actual prototype of the product to be developed. As section B shows in Exhibit 13–3, consumers evaluated the product concept developed by Coca-Cola as being fairly close to their ideal level of performance on each of the four attributes. It appears that only their concept of color was off target by being a little too dark.

The next step is to *translate the concept into an actual product*. When this was done by Coca-Cola and presented to the consumers, consumers did not perceive it to be similar to either the product concept or their ideal levels of performance (see section C of Exhibit 13–3). While the actual product achieved a reasonable attitude rating, the product concept scored higher (section D, Exhibit 13–3). Thus, the product could benefit from further improvement.

Based on this information, management would attempt to further improve the actual product to better align it with ideal levels of performance prior to market introduction. This same type of procedure can be used to help design appealing ads, packages, or retail outlets.

SUMMARY

Attitudes can be defined as the way we think, feel, and act toward some aspect of our environment. A result of all the influences discussed so far in the text, attitudes influence, as well as reflect, the lifestyle individuals pursue. Attitudes, therefore, are the focal point of a great deal of marketing strategy.

The understanding and use of attitudes is clearer when they are perceived as having three component parts: cognitive, affective, and behavioral. The *cognitive component* consists of the individual's beliefs or knowledge about the object. The cognitive component is generally assessed by using a version of the *multiattribute attitude model*. Feelings or emotional reactions to an object represent the *affective component* of the attitude. The *behavioral component* reflects overt actions and statements of behavioral intentions with respect to specific attributes of the object or the overall object. In general, all three components of an attitude tend to be consistent with each other. Thus, if marketing managers can influence one component, the other components may also be influenced.

Attitude change strategies can focus on affect, behavior, cognition, or some combination. Attempts to change affect generally rely on classical conditioning. Change strategies focusing on behavior rely more on operant conditioning. Changing cognitions usually involves information processing and cognitive learning.

EXHIBIT 13-3

Using the Multiattribute Attitude Model in the Product Development Process

A. Ideal soft drink*

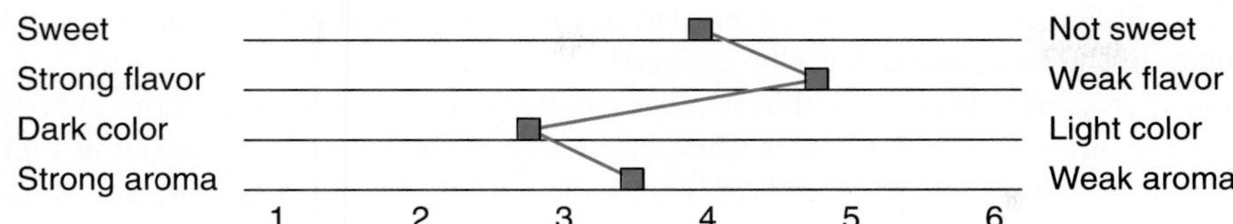

B. Product concept*

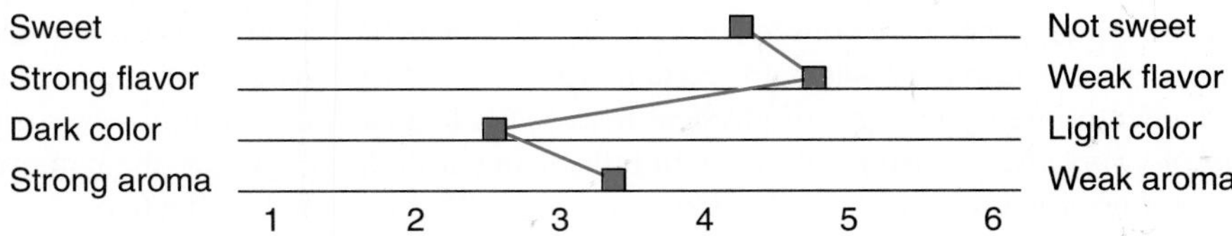

C. Actual product*

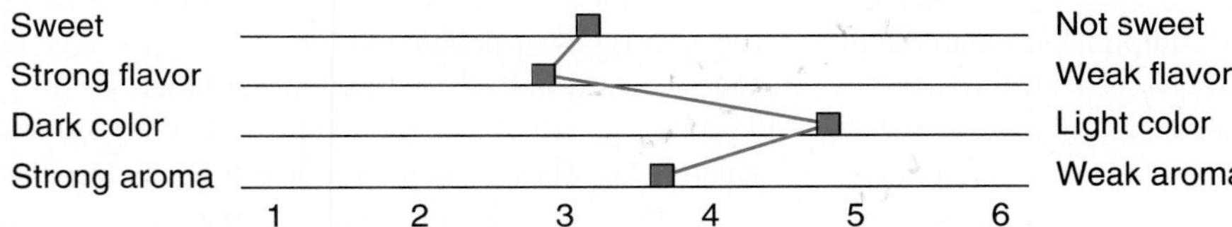

D. Attitude toward concept and product

$$
\begin{aligned}
A_{\text{concept}} &= 25\,|4.17 - 4.43| + 25\,|4.63 - 4.90| + 25\,|3.16 - 2.60| + 25\,|3.64 - 3.62| \\
&= 25(.15) + 25(.27) + 25(.56) + 25(.02) \\
&= 25
\end{aligned}
$$

$$
\begin{aligned}
A_{\text{product}} &= 25\,|4.17 - 3.25| + 25\,|4.63 - 3.17| + 25\,|3.16 - 4.64| + 25\,|3.64 - 3.68| \\
&= 25(.92) + 25(1.46) + 25(1.48) + 25(.04) \\
&= 97.5
\end{aligned}
$$

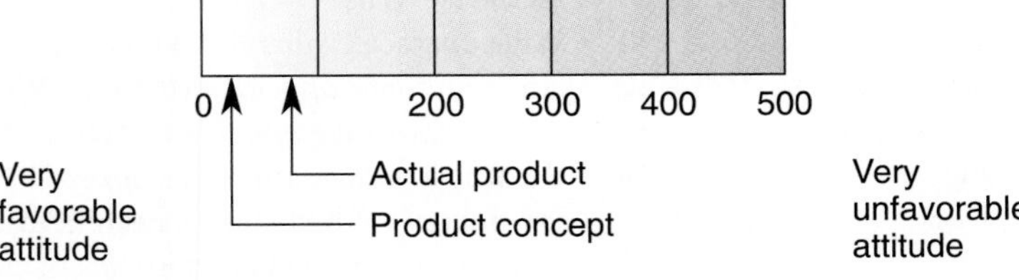

* Measured on a six-point schematic differential scale.

There are four basic strategies for influencing attitudes by altering the cognitive structure of a consumer's attitude: First, it is possible to change the beliefs about the attributes of the brand. Second, one might change the relative importance of these beliefs. Third, new beliefs could be added to the present attitude. And finally, the beliefs about the attributes of the ideal brand could be changed.

Source credibility is composed of two basic dimensions: *trustworthiness* and *expertise*. Influencing attitudes is much easier when the source of the message is viewed as highly credible by the target market. *Celebrities* are widely used as product or company spokespersons. They are most effective when their image matches the personality of the product and the actual or desired self-concept of the target market.

The appeals used to change attitudes are important and are varied. *Fear appeals* make use of the threat of negative consequences if attitudes or behaviors are not altered. They are useful in persuasive messages for certain types of products. While fear appeals have been studied primarily in terms of physical fear, social fears are also used in advertising. *Humorous appeals* can also be effective in influencing attitudes. However, the humorous message must remain focused on the brand or main selling point to be effective.

Comparative ads produce mixed results. They are most effective for unknown brands having a strong functional advantage. The decision to use a *value-expressive* or *utilitarian* appeal depends on whether the brand fills value-expressive or utilitarian needs. However, this is complicated when the brand fills both types of needs. *Emotional appeals* have been found to have a strong effect on attitudes toward both the ad and the product.

Two aspects of the structure of the message affect its effectiveness. The effectiveness of *one- versus two-sided messages* depends largely on the situation and characteristics of the target audience. *Nonverbal aspects* of the ad, such as pictures, surrealism, and music also affect attitudes.

Attitudes, particularly the cognitive component, are the basis for market segmentation strategies, such as *benefit segmentation*, and for new-product development strategies.

REVIEW QUESTIONS

1. What is an *attitude*?
2. What are the *components* of an attitude?
3. Are the components of an attitude consistent? What factors reduce the apparent consistency between attitude components?
4. What is a *multiattribute attitude model*?
5. What strategies can be used to change the ________ component of an attitude?
   a. Affective.
   b. Behavioral.
   c. Cognitive.
6. What are the two characteristics of the source of a message that influences its ability to change attitudes? Describe each.
7. What is *source credibility*? What causes it?
8. Why are *celebrity sources* sometimes effective? What risks are associated with using a celebrity source?
9. Name five possible characteristics of an appeal that would influence or change attitudes? Describe each.
10. Are *fear appeals* always effective in changing attitudes? Why?
11. What characteristics should *humorous ads* have?
12. Are *emotional appeals* effective? Why?
13. Are *comparative appeals* effective? Why?
14. What is a *value-expressive appeal*? A *utilitarian appeal*? When should each be used?
15. What are the two characteristics of the message structure that influence its ability to change attitudes? Describe each.
16. What are the *nonverbal* components of an ad? What impact do they have on attitudes?
17. When is a *two-sided message* likely to be more effective than a *one-sided message*?
18. How can attitudes guide new-product development?
19. What is a *benefit segment*?

DISCUSSION QUESTIONS

20. Which version of the multiattribute attitude model and which attributes would you use to assess student attitudes toward _______? Justify your answer.
    a. This class.
    b. Toothpaste.
    c. In-line skates.
    d. A stereo system.
    e. Soft drinks.
    f. Salt.
21. Assume you wanted to improve or create favorable attitudes among college students toward _______. Would you focus primarily on the affective, cognitive, or behavioral component? Why?
    a. Sierra Club.
    b. Clausthaler (nonalcoholic beer).
    c. IBM PCs.
    d. Your state's senators.
    e. Sexual abstinence before marriage.
    f. Folgers coffee.
    g. Beef.
    h. Butter.
22. How would you use the multiattribute attitude model to develop a _______?
    a. Campus bookstore.
    b. Nonalcoholic beer.
    c. Perfume for teenagers.
    d. Soft drink for consumers over age 65.
23. Suppose you used the multiattribute attitude model and developed a nonalcoholic beer that was successful in the United States. Could you use the same model in _______? If not, how would it change?
    a. Japan.
    b. China.
    c. Germany.
    d. Brazil.
24. Suppose you wanted to form highly negative attitudes toward drug consumption among college students.
    a. Which attitude component would you focus on? Why?
    b. Which message characteristic would you use? Why?
    c. What type of appeal would you use? Why?
25. What communications characteristics would you use in an attempt to improve college students' attitudes toward _______?
    a. Schwinn bicycles.
    b. Buick automobiles.
    c. Church attendance.
    d. Broccoli.
    e. Aqua Velva after-shave lotion.
    f. Wendy's.
26. Name two good and two inappropriate celebrity spokespersons for each of the products in Question 25.
27. Using the benefit segments shown in Exhibit 13–2, develop a marketing strategy to increase patronage among _______.
    a. Current users.
    b. Nonusers.
28. What benefit segments do you think exist for stadium attendance at professional football?

APPLICATION EXERCISES

29. Find and copy two magazine or newspaper advertisements, one based on the affective component and the other on the cognitive component. Discuss the approach of each ad in terms of its copy and illustration and what effect it creates in terms of attitude. Also, discuss why the marketer might have taken that approach in each advertisement.
30. Repeat Question 29 for utilitarian and value-expressive appeals.
31. Identify a television commercial that uses a humorous appeal and then interview five other individuals not enrolled in your class and measure their:
    a. Awareness of this commercial.
    b. Recall of the brand advertised.
    c. Recall of relevant information.
    d. Liking of the commercial.
    e. Preference for the brand advertised.

    Then evaluate your results and assess the level of communication that has taken place in terms of these five consumers' exposure, attention, interpretation, and preferences for this product and commercial.

32. Describe a magazine or television advertisement using ______. Evaluate the effectiveness of the ad.
    a. Source credibility.
    b. Celebrity source.
    c. Fear appeal.
    d. Humorous appeal.
    e. Emotional appeal.
    f. Comparative approach.
    g. Extensive nonverbal elements.
    h. A two-sided appeal.
33. Measure another student's ideal beliefs and belief importance for ______. Examine these ideal beliefs and importance weights and then develop a verbal description (i.e., concept) of a new brand of ______ that would satisfy this student's needs. Next, measure that student's attitude toward the concept you have developed in your verbal description.
    a. Soft drink.
    b. Restaurant.
    c. Bicycle.
    d. Toothpaste.
    e. Perfume.
    f. Senator.
34. Use the multiattribute attitude model to assess 10 students' attitudes toward various ______. Measure their behavior with respect to these objects. Are they consistent? Explain any inconsistencies.
    a. Magazines.
    b. Soft drinks.
    c. Toothpaste.
    d. Cars.
    e. Computers.
    f. Pizza restaurants.
35. Develop two advertisements for ______. One ad should focus on the cognitive component and the other on the affective component.
    a. Crest toothpaste.
    b. Sierra Club.
    c. Diet Pepsi.
    d. Reducing drug abuse.
    e. Increasing church attendance.
    f. Ford pickups.
36. Repeat Question 35, using utilitarian and value-expressive appeals.
37. Describe three instances when your purchase behavior was inconsistent with your attitude toward the brand you purchased. Explain why.

REFERENCES

[1]J. Gardner, ''Plastics Seek $18M Image Boost,'' *Advertising Age*, November 9, 1992, p. 12; and B. Garfield, ''Plastics Industry Molds Wrong approach in Ads,'' *Advertising Age*, November 23, 1992, p. 38.

[2]M. Fishbein and I. Aizen, *Belief, Attitude, Intention and Behavoir: An Introduction to Theory and Research* (Reading, Mass.: Addison Wesley Publishing, 1975), p. 6.

[3]See L. R. Kahle et al., ''Social Values in the Eighties: A Special Issue,'' *Psychology & Marketing*, Winter 1985, pp. 231–306.

[4]R. B. Zajonc, ''Feeling and Thinking: Preferences Need No Inferences,'' *American Psychologist*, February 1980, pp. 151–75. See also Y. Tsal, ''On the Relationship between Cognitive and Affective Processes,'' and R. B. Zajonc and H. Markus, ''Must All Affect Be Mediated by Cognition,'' both in *Journal of Consumer Research*. December 1985, pp. 358–62, 363–64; and J. A. Muncy, ''Affect and Cognition,'' in *Advances in Consumer Research XIII*, ed. R. J. Lutz (Provo, Utah: Association for Consumer Research, 1986), pp. 226–30.

[5]S. E. Beatty and L. R. Kahle, ''Alternative Hierarchies of the Attitude-Behavior Relationship,'' *Journal of the Academy of Marketing Science*, Summer 1988, pp. 1–10; I. E. Berger and A. A. Mitchell, ''The Effect of Advertising on Attitude Accessibility, Attitude Confidence, and Attitude-Behavior Relationship'' and R. H. Fazio, M. C. Powell, and C. J. Williams, ''The Role of Attitude Accessibility in the Attitude-to-Behavior Process,'' both in *Journal of Consumer Research*, December 1989, pp. 269–79 and 280–88; and M. G. Millar and A. Tesser, ''Attitudes and Behavior,'' in *Advances in Consumer Research XVII*, ed. M. E. Goldberg, G. Gorn, and R. W. Pollay (Provo, Utah: Association for Consumer Research, 1990), pp. 86–90.

[6]J. A. Cote, J. McCullough, and M. Reilly, ''Effects of Unexpected Situations on Behavior-Intention Differences,'' *Journal of Consumer Research*, September 1985, pp. 188–94.

[7]See footnote 5, Chapter 10.

[8]See footnote 23 in Chapter 11; and P. M. Homer, ''The Mediating Role of Attitude toward the Ad,'' *Journal of Marketing Research*, February 1990, pp. 78–88; and B. Mittal, ''The Relative Roles of Brand Beliefs and Attitude,'' *Journal of Marketing Research*, May 1990, pp. 209–19.

[9]C. Obermiller, ''Varieties of Mere Exposure,'' *Journal of Consumer Research*, June 1985, pp. 17–30; C. Janiszewski, ''Preconscious Processing Effects,'' *Journal of Consumer Research*, September 1988, pp. 199–209; R. F. Bornstein, ''Exposure and Affect,'' *Psychological Bulletin*, September 1989, pp. 265–84; P. Anand, M. B. Holbrook, and D. Stephens, ''The Formation of Affective Judgments,'' *Journal of Consumer Research*, December 1988, pp. 386–391; T. B. Heath, ''The Logic of Mere Exposure'' and P. Anand and M. B. Holbrook, ''Reinterpretation of Mere

Exposure or Exposure of Mere Reinterpretation,'' both in *Journal of Consumer Research*, September 1990, pp. 237–41 and 242–44; and S. A. Hawkins and S. J. Hoch, ''Low-Involvement Learning,'' *Journal of Consumer Research*, September 1992, pp. 212–25.

[10]L. J. Marks and M. A. Kamins, ''The Use of Product Sampling and Advertising,'' *Journal of Marketing Research*, August 1988, pp. 266–81.

[11]R. E. Smith and W. R. Swinyard, ''Cognitive Response to Advertising and Trial,'' *Journal of Advertising*, no. 3, 1988, pp. 3–14; M. J. Manfredo, ''A Test of Assumptions Inherent in Attribute-Specific Advertising,'' *Journal of Travel Research*, Winter 1989, pp. 8–13; Y. Yi, ''The Indirect Effects of Advertisements Designed to Change Product Attribute Beliefs,'' *Psychology & Marketing*, Spring 1990, pp. 47–63; and Mittal, ''The Relative Roles,'' (see footnote 8).

[12]D. W. Stewart and D. H. Furse, *Effective Television Advertising* (Lexington, Mass.: Lexington Books, 1986); and D. W. Stewart and S. Koslow, ''Executional Factors and Advertising Effectiveness,'' *Journal of Advertising*, no. 3, 1989, pp. 21–32.

[13]P. M. Homer and L. R. Kahle, ''Source Expertise, Time of Source Identification, and Involvement in Persuasion,'' *Journal of Advertising*, no. 1, 1990, pp. 30–39; D. R. Lichtenstein, S. Burton, and B. S. O'Hara, ''Marketplace Attributions and Consumer Evaluations of Discount Claims,'' *Psychology & Marketing*, Fall 1989, pp. 163–80; and M. E. Goldberg and J. Hartwick, ''The Effects of Advertiser Reputation and Extremity of Advertising Claim on Advertising Effectiveness,'' *Journal of Consumer Research*, September 1990, pp. 172–79.

[14]L. Kahle and P. Homer, ''Physical Attractiveness of the Celebrity Endorser,'' *Journal of Consumer Research*, March 1985, pp. 954–61; K. Debevec and E. Iyer, ''The Influence of Spokespersons in Altering a Product's Gender Image,'' *Journal of Advertising*, no. 4, 1986, pp. 12–20; M. A. Kamins, ''Celebrity and Noncelebrity Advertising in a Two-Sided Context,'' *Journal of Advertising Research*, July 1989, pp. 34–41; R. Ohanian, ''Construction and Validation to Measure Celebrity Endorsers' Perceived Expertise, Trustworthiness, and Attractiveness,'' *Journal of Advertising*, no. 3, 1990, pp. 39–52; and R. Ohanian, ''The Impact of Celebrity Spokespersons' Perceived Image,'' *Journal of Advertising Research*, February/March 1991, pp. 46–54. For a different perspective, see G. McCracken, ''Who Is the Celebrity Endorser?'' *Journal of Consumer Research*, December 1989, pp. 310–21.

[15]M. A. Kamins, ''An Investigation into the 'Match-up' Hypothesis in Celebrity Advertising,'' *Journal of Advertising*, no. 1, 1990, pp. 4–13; and S. Misra and S. E. Beatty, ''Celebrity Spokesperson and Brand Congruence,'' *Journal of Business Research*, September 1990, pp. 159–73.

[16]S. W. McDaniel and V. A. Zeithaml, ''The Effect of Fear on Purchase Intentions,'' *Psychology & Marketing*, Fall/Winter 1984, pp. 73–82; and M. S. LaTour and S. A. Zahra, ''Fear Appeals as Advertising Strategy,'' *Journal of Consumer Marketing*, Spring 1989, pp. 61–70.

[17]C. Scott, D. M. Klein, and J. Bryant, ''Consumer Response to Humor in Advertising,'' *Journal of Consumer Research*, March 1990, pp. 498–501; A. Chattopadhyay and K. Basu, ''Humor in Advertising,'' *Journal of Marketing Research*, November 1990, pp. 466–76; M. G. Weinberger and L. Campbell, ''The Use and Impact of Humor in Radio Advertising,'' *Journal of Advertising Research*, January 1991, pp. 44–52; and M. G. Weinberger and C. S. Gulas, ''The Impact of Humor on Advertising,'' *Journal of Advertising*, December 1992, pp. 35–59.

[18]See C. Pechmann and D. W. Stewart, ''The Effects of Comparative Advertising on Attention, Memory, and Purchase Intentions,'' *Journal of Consumer Research*, September 1990, pp. 180–91; J. B. Gotlieb and D. Sarel, ''Comparative Advertising Effectiveness'' *Journal of Advertising*, no. 1, 1991, pp. 38–45; C. Pechmann and S. Ratneshwar, ''The Use of Comparative Advertising for Brand Positioning,'' *Journal of Consumer Research*, September 1991, pp. 145–60; C. Pechmann and D. W. Stewart, ''How Direct Comparative Ads and Market Share Affect Brand Choice,'' *Journal of Advertising Research*, December 1991, pp. 47–55; T. E. Barry, ''Comparative Advertising,'' *Journal of Advertising Research*, March/April 1993, pp. 19–29; and R. L. Rose et al., ''When Persuasion Goes Undetected,'' *Journal of Marketing Research*, August 1993, pp. 315–30.

[19]See footnote 8.

[20]J. S. Johar and M. J. Sirgy, ''Value-Expressive versus Utilitarian Advertising Appeals,'' *Journal of Advertising*, September 1991, pp. 23–33; and S. Sharitt, ''Evidence for Predicting the Effectiveness of Value-Expressive versus Utilitarian Appeals,'' *Journal of Advertising*, June 1992, pp. 47–51.

[21]J. M. Hunt and M. F. Smith, ''The Persuasive Impact of Two-Sided Selling Appeals for an Unknown Brand Name,'' *Journal of the Academy of Marketing Science*, Spring 1987, pp. 11–17; L. L. Golden and M. I. Alpert, ''Comparative Analysis of the Relative Effectiveness of One- and Two-Sided Communication for Contrasting Products,'' *Journal of Advertising*, no. 1, 1987, pp. 18–25; M. A. Kamins and H. Assael, ''Two-Sided versus One-Sided Appeals,'' *Journal of Marketing Research*, February 1987, pp. 29–39; M. A. Kamins and L. J. Marks, ''Advertising Puffery,'' *Journal of Advertising*, no. 4, 1987, pp. 6–15. M. A. Kamins et al., ''Two-Sided versus One-Sided Celebrity Endorsement,'' *Journal of Advertising*, no. 2, 1989, pp. 4–10.

[22]E. C. Hirschman, ''The Effect of Verbal and Pictorial Advertising Stimuli,'' *Journal of Advertising*, no. 2, 1986, pp. 27–34; and M. P. Gardner and M. J. Houston, ''The Effects of Verbal and Visual Components of Retail Communications,'' *Journal of Retailing*, Spring 1986, pp. 64–78.

[23]G. Tom, ''Marketing with Music,'' *Journal of Consumer Marketing*, Spring 1990, pp. 49–53; J. I. Alpert and M. I. Alpert, ''Music Influences on Mood and Purchase Intention,'' *Psychology & Marketing*, Summer 1990, pp. 109–33; and G. L. Sullivan, ''Music Format Effects in Radio Advertising,'' *Psychology & Marketing*, Summer 1990, pp. 97–108.

[24]P. N. Homer and L. R. Kahle, ''A Social Adaptation Explanation of the Effects of Surrealism on Advertising,'' *Journal of Advertising*, no. 2, 1986, pp. 50–54.

[25]See J. Kisielius and B. Sternthal, ''Examining the Vividness Controversy,'' *Journal of Consumer Research*, March 1986, pp. 418–31; C. A. Kelley, ''A Study of Selected Issues in Vividness Research,'' in *Advances in Consumer Research XVI*, ed. T. K. Srull (Provo, Utah: Association for Consumer Research, 1989), pp. 574–80;

[26]See P. W. Miniard, D. Sirdeshmukh, and D. E. Innis, ''Peripheral Persuasion and Brand Choice,'' *Journal of Consumer Research*, September 1992, pp. 226–39.

[27]R. I. Haley and P. J. Weingarden, ''Running Reliable Attitude Segmentation Studies,'' *Journal of Advertising Research*, January 1987, pp. 51–55; M. Greenberg and S. S. McDonald, ''Successful Needs/Benefits Segmentation,'' *Journal of Consumer Marketing*, Summer 1989, pp. 29–33; and R. H. Wicks, ''Product Matching in Television News Using Benefit Segmentation,'' *Journal of Advertising Research*, November 1989, pp. 64–71.

[28]M. Steinberg, G. Miaoulis, and D. Lloyd, ''Benefit Segmentation Strategies for the Performing Arts,'' in *Educators Conference Proceedings*, ed. B. J. Walker (Chicago: American Marketing Association, 1982), pp. 289–93. See also J. W. Harvey, ''Benefit Segmentation for Fund Raisers,'' *Journal of the Academy of Marketing Science*, Winter 1990, pp. 77–86.

[29]H. E. Bloom, ''Match the Concept and the Product,'' *Journal of Advertising Research*, October 1977, pp. 25–27.

SECTION 3 CASES

Bayer Aspirin's Line Extension* Case 3–1

For many years, aspirin dominated the market for nonprescription pain relief and Bayer aspirin dominated the aspirin market. However, in recent years, acetaminophen- and ibuprofen-based pain relievers have taken over much of the market. By 1989, aspirin-based products held only 40 percent of the total analgesics market. This dropped to 35 percent by 1992. Bayer has about a 6.6 percent share of the total analgesic market and 19 percent of the aspirin market.

Competition in the analgesics market is intense. There are three main types of analgesics—aspirin, acetaminophen, and ibuprofen. There are several advertised brands within each type of analgesic as well as private label and store brands. Product differences within analgesic categories are limited.

The intense competition has given rise to product proliferation and niche strategies. All the private label and store brands compete on price. They may sell for half the price of the national brands. Advil is the leader in the ibuprofen category with a 50 percent share. Motrin with a 15 percent share has used three different commercials to target backache, arthritis, and headache pain. It attempts to ''maintain the brand's appeal as a general analgesic while reaching out to specific groups of pain sufferers through advertising.'' The strategy appears to be working as its share is growing. Nuprin (13 percent share) has attempted to compete with a focus on muscle aches, using celebrities such as Jimmy Connors, Michael Chang, and Joe Montana.

Similar niche strategies are appearing in the acetaminophen and aspirin categories. Acetaminophen-based Midol is attempting to position itself as ''the menstrual relief specialist.'' It further focuses with such line extensions as Midol PM Nighttime Formula and Midol IB Cramp Relief Formula. Tylenol is increasingly positioned in terms of arthritis pain relief though it is also widely used for headache relief.

Recent medical findings indicate that the regular use of aspirin helps certain heart and colon conditions. Bayer introduced Therapy Bayer for this application, but aspirin sales in general and Bayer aspirin sales both continue their relative decline.

Excedrin was historically behind Bayer in the aspirin category. However, it now has a greater total market share in the overall analgesics market (7.1 versus 6.6). It has managed to grow its market share by aggressively adding line extensions: ibuprofen-based Excedrin IB and acetaminophen-based Excedrin AF and Excedrin PM.

Bayer management is considering introducing non-aspirin-based analgesics using the Bayer name.

Discussion Questions

1. What is Bayer aspirin's current product position?
2. What are the benefits and risks of introducing an acetaminophen- and/or ibuprofen-based analgesic with the Bayer name? Should they do this?
3. If they proceed, what would they want consumers to learn about the new brands? What learning principles should they use?
4. Develop an ad or series of ads to introduce a Bayer acetaminophen- and/or ibuprofen-based analgesic.
   a. Explain the perception principles that you used to design the ad(s).
   b. Explain the learning principles you used to design the ad(s).
   c. Explain the attitude influence principles you used to design the ad(s).
5. Develop an ad or series of ads to introduce a Bayer acetaminophen- and/or ibuprofen-based analgesic using a:

*Source: Adapted from P. Sloan, ''Bayer to Offer Non-Aspirin Pain Reliever,'' *Advertising Age*, July 13, 1992, p. 12.

   a. Lifestyle-based theme.
   b. Self-concept-based theme.
   c. Personality-based theme.
5. Develop an ad or series of ads to introduce a Bayer acetaminophen- and/or ibuprofen-based analgesic focusing on the:
   a. Cognitive component of an attitude.
   b. Affective component of an attitude.
   c. Behavioral component of an attitude.

Case 3–2 Calgene Inc. versus the Pure Food Campaign*

Over the past decade, Calgene Inc. has invested $20 million in research to develop a rot-resistant tomato. Tomatoes make an enzyme called polygalacturonase (PG) that causes them to soften as they ripen. To avoid damage to tomatoes during shipping to, and handling in, supermarkets and to extend their shelf life, growers pick tomatoes when they are green and hard, then treat them with ethylene. Ethylene is the chemical that normally causes ripening on the vine. This process will eventually turn the green tomatoes red but they remain relatively pale, mushy, and tasteless.

The technique that Calgene used to solve this problem is called gene-splicing. Calgene researchers developed a procedure to prevent the tomato from producing PG. They make an *antisense*, or mirror image, of the gene that carries instructions for the enzyme. They then insert the antisense gene into the tomato's DNA. This blocks production of PG and allows growers to wait until the tomato is turning red before harvesting. The result is a redder, firmer, more flavorful tomato.

Calgene intends to market the tomatoes as MacGregor's Tomatoes and the seeds as FLAVR SAVR™ (see Exhibit A). Given better texture, color, and taste, the product should be a major success with few problems, right? Unfortunately for Calgene, it is not that simple.

The smallest problem Calgene faces is cost. The process costs significantly more than standard tomato production and will require a 30 to 100 percent premium at retail. However, given the product's advantages, this should not unduly restrict sales.

A much more serious problem is the general environment in which the product is being launched. Many consumers are skeptical of modern science and are convinced that artificial products are inherently inferior and/or dangerous. There is a seemingly endless series of discoveries that products which were once considered safe can cause cancer or other problems. The tremendous success of *Jurassic Park* reveals the public's fascination with science and DNA experiments gone amuck.

Both consumers and farmers are concerned and are conservative. As one farmer stated: *My family has been in this business for 65 years, and I'm not about to crawl in a test tube with scientists.* Businesses are also conservative. Campbell Soup Co. funded much of Calgene's research on the new tomato. However, Campbell's will not use them until after they are popular with consumers: *We are not jeopardizing this business. We clearly have to show ourselves and the consumer what the benefits are to justify moving ahead.*

Calgene's position is made more difficult by a genetically engineered bovine growth hormone (BGH) developed by Monsanto. When injected into cows, BGH can increase milk production by 15 percent. The potential health risk associated with BGH, though small or nonexistent, have made it very controversial. Many of the concerns associated with BGH are being generalized to all products that involve genetic engineering.

The final major hurdle facing Calgene is the Pure Food Campaign headed by Jeremy Rifkin, who has vowed to ''pursue this product until it is dead in the water.'' Rifkin opposes biotech in agriculture on philosophical, religious, and scientific grounds. He attacks such activities by using lawsuits, by lobbying for tight

*Adapted from J. Hamilton, ''A Storm Is Breaking Down on the Farm,'' *Business Week*, December 14, 1992, pp. 98–101; B. Johnson, ''Biotech-Created Tomatoes Ripe for Controversy,'' *Advertising Age*, October 19, 1992, p. 12; and C. Miller, ''Food Fight Rages,'' *Marketing News*, September 14, 1992, p. 1.

FLAVR SAVR's Product Label

EXHIBIT A

regulations or prohibitions, and by generating negative publicity and boycotts.

Rifkin has created concerns about Flavr Savr that are not justified. He has responded to questions about Flavr Savr with warnings that splicing animal genes into plants (which some firms, though not Calgene, have attempted) violates natural law, could offend vegetarians and Jews who eat kosher, and could transfer lethal allergens into new foods.

Rifkin's Pure Food Campaign is urging farmers, retailers, shippers, and restaurants to boycott the product. The theme for this campaign is simple: *Americans have an ample supply of good natural products, so why take chances?* Over 1,500 chefs from prestigious restaurants have joined the boycott.

Calgene is countering by providing as much information as possible to retailers, restaurants, the public, and others, given its limited budget. It discloses the true nature of its product on labels and P-O-P displays (see Exhibit A), and in detailed brochures at vegetable counters. It is providing an 800 number that consumers can call with questions. It also voluntarily submitted the Flavr Savr tomato to the Food and Drug Administration for extended safety testing and approval. Once this is granted, Calgene plans to go national on a region-by-region basis as rapidly as possible.

Discussion Questions

1. Conduct an innovation analysis (Exhibit 7–2) and recommend specific diffusion enhancement strategies for Flavr Savr.
2. What product position would you try to establish for Flavr Savr tomatoes? Why?
3. What learning approach and principles would you use to "teach" consumers about Flavr Savr tomatoes?
4. How would you establish a favorable attitude for Flavr Savr tomatoes?
5. If you were Rifkin, how would you establish a negative attitude about Flavr Savr tomatoes?
6. What name and logo or tag line would you use for the product? Why?
7. Develop an ad or marketing approach to develop a positive attitude toward Flavr Savr tomatoes, focusing on the ______ component.
   a. Cognitive.
   b. Affective.
   c. Behavioral.
8. Develop an ad or marketing approach to develop a positive attitude toward Flavr Savr tomatoes, using ______.
   a. Humor.
   b. Emotion.
   c. Utilitarian appeal.
   d. Value-expressive appeal.
   e. Celebrity endorser.
   f. Self-concept.
9. Develop an ad or marketing approach to develop a negative attitude toward Flavr Savr tomatoes, using ______.
   a. Humor.
   b. Emotion.
   c. Utilitarian appeal.

d. Value-expressive appeal.
e. Celebrity endorser.
f. Self-concept.
g. Fear.

10. Evaluate Calgene's brand name and label (Exhibit A).
11. What ______ lifestyle segment(s) would be the best target markets for Flavr Savr tomatoes? Why?
    a. VALS 2.
    b. PRIZM.
    c. GLOBAL SCAN.

Case 3–3 Texaco's CleanSystem3

Many consumers believe that most brands of gasoline are identical. They make purchase decisions based on price or nonproduct characteristics of the company or individual service station. Gasoline manufacturers have responded by developing programs to ensure quality service and facilities at service stations that carry their brand. In addition, corporate image advertising, advertising focused on special features of the brand's service stations, and promotions (games with prizes and free or discounted gifts) have been common.

Currently, Amoco has 7.31 percent of the 116-billion-gallon U.S. market. Shell is second with 7.27 percent and Texaco is third with 6.98 percent.

Texaco recently developed a new additive which it is putting in all three grades of Texaco gasoline. According to Texaco, the new gasoline, CleanSystem3, will improve engine performance, lower emissions, and increase gas mileage. Other detergent gasolines can deliver on one or two of these claims but not all three. For example, Shell Oil's *FormulaShell* and Mobil Oil's *Super Plus Detergent Gasoline* advertise the ability to clean the automobile's engine with continued use. Analysts indicate that Texaco does indeed have a functional advantage though they expect other gasoline producers to be able to duplicate Texaco's CleanSystem3 in the near future.

Texaco is replacing all their current gasoline (System3) with CleanSystem3. It will continue to sell at the same price as the existing gasoline. Texaco's major objective for the improved product is to increase market share.

Texaco began its marketing program for CleanSystem3 with a brief teaser campaign starring race-car driver Mario Andretti. This was followed by a corporate campaign with the theme "Look for the next generation of clean gasoline." Product-specific advertising will begin on the Grammy Awards in March. It will run on network and spot TV, spot radio, and in magazines. Drivers will be invited to: *Give us 60 days and watch what can happen.* The umbrella theme for the campaign will be: *Changing what gasoline can do.* A 30-minute infomercial, *The Freedom to Move*, will run in eight key markets. James Earl Jones does voice-over in both the TV and radio ads.

Texaco will run newspaper ads in 51 markets with coupons for a dollar off on a fill-up. It will also sponsor a "frequent-fueler" program with rebates of $5 after nine fill-ups. Texaco will be the official petroleum advertiser on ABC and NBC telecasts of Major League Baseball starting in July. Texaco stations will be the first retail outlet for all-star balloting.

The initial advertising and promotional campaign will cost approximately $20 million.

Discussion Questions

1. How would you change consumers' attitude that most gasolines are the same?
2. Conduct an innovation analysis (Exhibit 7–2) and recommend specific diffusion-enhancement strategies for CleanSystem3.
3. What product position would you try to establish for CleanSystem3? Why?
4. What learning approach and principles would you use to "teach" consumers about CleanSystem3?

*Adapted from L. Rickard and G. Levin, "Texaco Tanks UP on Marketing Tactics for New Detergent Gas," *Advertising Age*, February 28, 1994, p. 3+.

5. How would you establish a favorable attitude for CleanSystem3?
6. What name and logo or tag line would you use for the product? Why? Evaluate the CleanSystem3 name.
7. Develop an ad or marketing approach to create a positive attitude toward CleanSystem3, focusing on the ________ component.
   a. Cognitive.
   b. Affective.
   c. Behavioral.
8. Develop an ad or marketing approach to create a positive attitude toward CleanSystem3, using ________.
   a. Humor.
   b. Emotion.
   c. Utilitarian appeal.
   d. Value-expressive appeal.
   e. Celebrity endorser.
   f. Self-concept.
9. What ________ lifestyle segment(s) would be the best target markets for CleanSystem3? Why?
   a. VALS 2.
   b. PRIZM.
   c. GLOBAL SCAN.
10. To what motive(s) would you appeal to induce consumers to try CleanSystem3?
11. Develop an ad for CleanSystem3 that would attract the attention of consumers who are not interested in gasoline or automobiles. Explain how your ad will attract attention and why it will also convey the desired message or image.

Made in Mexico*

Case 3–4

The passage of NAFTA greatly lowered the trade barriers between Canada, the United States, and Mexico. Many manufacturers in each country are actively preparing for opportunities to export to the other two countries as well as for increased competition from imports from those countries.

Productos Superior, Inc., is a leading manufacturer of appliances in Mexico. The firm is considering a major effort to market its brand in the United States. Product testing indicates that its appliances are slightly above average in terms of quality, design, and reliability compared to the brands currently sold in America. Productos Superior's cost structure is such that its products will cost 10 to 20 percent less than products with similar quality currently selling in the United States.

Productos Superior's management is very concerned about the image that products made in Mexico have in America. Since Productos Superior is virtually unknown in the United States, management is concerned that consumers will generalize any image they have of products made in Mexico onto Productos Superior's products. While it has yet to conduct research on the image that appliances made in Mexico have in the United States, it did find a study on the general image U.S. consumers had of products made in other countries.

Exhibit A contains the results of this study. Respondents were asked to rate "the typical product made in '________' on a 1 to 10 scale, with 1 being 'very poor' and 10 being 'excellent.' "

Discussion Questions

1. Should Productos Superior's management be concerned that the relatively weak image of products made in Mexico will be attached to their line of products? Why?
2. How can Productos Superior introduce its appliances and avoid consumers attaching the negative aspects of "Made in Mexico" to their brand?
3. Develop a marketing strategy including specific ads to introduce Productos Superior appliances into the U.S. market.
4. What product position would you try to establish for Productos Superior appliances? Why?
5. What learning approach and principles would

*The company name and data in this case are fictitious.

EXHIBIT A

U.S. Consumer Perceptions of Products Made in Other Countries

	Country				
Attribute	**United States**	**Japan**	**Germany**	**Taiwan**	**Mexico**
Quality	7.3	8.7	9.1	6.9	5.2
Style	8.2	8.5	8.7	7.1	6.7
Reliability	7.8	8.2	8.9	7.4	5.4
Price	8.3	7.9	6.2	9.1	9.0
Design	8.5	8.2	9.3	7.6	6.2
Prestige	7.4	7.3	8.2	6.9	4.3

you use to ''teach'' consumers about Productos Superior appliances?

6. How would you establish a favorable attitude for Productos Superior appliances?
7. What name and logo or tag line would you use for Productos Superior's appliance line in the United States? Why?
8. Develop an ad or marketing approach to create a positive attitude toward Productos Superior appliances, focusing on the ______ component.
   a. Cognitive.
   b. Affective.
   c. Behavioral.
9. Develop an ad or marketing approach to create a positive attitude toward Productos Superior appliances, using ______.
   a. Humor.
   b. Emotion.
   c. Utilitarian appeal.
   d. Value-expressive appeal.
   e. Celebrity endorser.
   f. Self-concept.
10. What ______ lifestyle segment(s) would be the best target markets for Productos Superior appliances? Why?
    a. VALS 2.
    b. PRIZM.
    c. GLOBAL SCAN.
11. To what motive(s) would you appeal to induce consumers to purchase Productos Superior appliances?
12. Develop an ad for Productos Superior appliances that would attract the attention of consumers who are not interested in appliances. Explain how your ad will attract attention and why it will also convey the desired message or image.

Case 3–5 Nature's Way Homeopathic Drugs*

Homeopathic drugs treat ailments with small doses of natural substances that cause symptoms similar to those the patient wants to cure. For example, one homeopathic allergy remedy contains a tiny amount of *allium cepa*, an onion extract. Onions cause tearing and runny noses as do allergies. The theory is that the body's response to these naturally triggered symptoms will relieve the more serious symptoms such as the allergy as well.

*Adapted from M. Magiera, ''Homeopathic Drugs Naturally Want Spot in Mainstream Market,'' *Advertising Age*, August 31, 1992, pp. 3+.

Because of their minute dosages, most homeopathic remedies are exempt for the Food & Drug Administration's safety and effectiveness reviews. This gives the marketers of these products considerable freedom to make effectiveness claims for homeopathic remedies. While homeopathic medicines are widely used in Europe, they have been ignored by physicians, retailers (except natural food stores), and consumers in America. Recently, consumer interest in homeopathic medicines has increased and some drug and supermarket chains are beginning to carry the product. Sales have increased from about $75 million in 1988 to $200 million in 1992.

Increased publicity about the benefits of natural medicines in general and homepathic medicines in particular will enhance interest and sales in the future. For example, *Reader's Digest* is publishing "The Family Guide to Natural Medicine," which contains a chapter favorable to homeopathic medicine.

Nature's Way is a leading marketer of herbal products. It recently decided to launch a line of 18 homeopathic remedies, including insomnia, allergy, and headache formulas called *Medicine from Nature*. Each remedy will cost about seven dollars. A number of other marketers are beginning to advertise specific homeopathic remedies regionally and nationally.

Despite increased publicity and acceptance, few American physicians recommend homeopathic medicines and few retail outlets carry them. While many people are reluctant to go to their doctors for every ailment, most Americans are unaware of homeopathic medicines which can be purchased without a doctor's prescription. Of those who have some degree of awareness, only a small percent know very much about them.

Discussion Questions

1. What product position would you try to establish for *Medicine from Nature*? Why?
2. What learning approach and principles would you use to "teach" consumers about *Medicine from Nature*?
3. How would you establish a favorable attitude for *Medicine from Nature*?
4. What name and logo or tag line would you use for *Medicine from Nature*? Why? Evaluate the *Medicine from Nature* name.
5. Develop an ad or marketing approach to create a positive attitude toward *Medicine from Nature*, focusing on the ________ component.
   a. Cognitive.
   b. Affective.
   c. Behavioral.
6. Develop an ad or marketing approach to create a positive attitude toward *Medicine frm Nature*, using ________.
   a. Humor.
   b. Emotion.
   c. Utilitarian appeal.
   d. Value-expressive appeal.
   e. Celebrity endorser.
   f. Self-concept.
7. What ________ lifestyle segment(s) would be the best target markets for *Medicine from Nature*? Why?
   a. VALS 2.
   b. PRIZM.
   c. GLOBAL SCAN.
8. To what motive(s) would you appeal to induce consumers to use *Medicine from Nature*?
9. Develop an ad for *Medicine from Nature* that would attract the attention of consumers who are not interested in medicine. Explain how your ad will attract attention and why it will also convey the desired message or image.
10. What values are associated with the use of this product category? Are they shifting in a favorable or unfavorable direction?

Grinstead Inns*

Case 3–6

Columbia Corporation owns and manages a diverse set of lodging establishments with a strong market position in upper- and middle-price/quality segments of the lodging market. However, a number of market research studies demonstrated a growing market opportunity in the economy segment where Columbia did not have a lodging

*Source: T. Leigh, "Competitive Assessment in Services Industries," *Planning Review*, January/February 1989, pp. 10–19.

FIGURE A

Market Demand and Price Segments of the Lodging Market

Price Segment	Number of Rooms	Revenue (billions)
Over $80 per night	139,000 (6%)	$ 5.4 (14%)
$60–$80	381,000 (16%)	12.1 (32%)
$45–$60	474,000 (21%)	9.1 (24%)
$20–$45	1,180,000 (51%)	10.1 (27%)
Under $20	164,000 (6%)	.7 (3%)
	2,338,000	$37.4

alternative. Columbia needed to evaluate this opportunity and decide if and how to effectively enter the economy segment.

Market Demand and Segmentation

The total market demand for lodging in the United States is over $37 billion a year. This demand is served with 2.3 million beds that are available at a variety of price points, as shown in Figure A. The lodging market can be segmented by need, which is easily translated into price. Those wanting top of the line in accommodations and service can find lodging in the higher-priced segment. At the other extreme, low price provides the bare necessities. Other combinations of price and quality are positioned based on need.

At the top end of the market, 6 percent of the rooms are available at over $80 per night. While accounting for only 6 percent of the rooms, the upper end of this market represents 14 percent of the dollars spent on lodging each year. Though the $20-to-$45 segment of the lodging market has the largest supply of rooms (51 percent of the market), the $60-to-$80 segment represents the largest revenue potential (32 percent of the market).

Customer Analysis

Consumer research is a core element of Columbia's marketing strategy. Columbia routinely conducts studies of the travel habits of both business and pleasure travelers. These studies offer insights into the economy segment with respect to customer demographics and lifestyle, usage rates and patterns, primary and secondary benefits sought, price preferences, chain loyalty, location preferences, and customer satisfaction. To supplement this data, several additional studies were specifically focused on the economy-segment market. These studies are briefly summarized below:

- *Telephone surveys* were performed on each competitor. Direct calls to customers staying in competitors' rooms provided information on customer profiles, frequency of visits, performance on primary and secondary benefits sought, and overall satisfaction.
- *In-lobby surveys* were performed in the lobbies of competing motel chains. The focus of this research was on customer satisfaction and customer profiles.
- *Day-night observation surveys* were conducted to determine competitor occupancy levels and license plate states of origin.
- *Consumer studies* included focus groups with economy-segment customers and two large sample surveys of business travelers who frequently stayed at economy motels. One survey interviewed 800 such business travelers to verify demographic information, attitudes, interests, opinions, and benefits sought. The second survey (600 business travelers staying at economy lodging) solicited customer response to Columbia's product concept relative to competitor offerings.

These efforts enabled Columbia to discover the benefits desired by the economy-segment market (outlined in Figure B).

Competitor Analysis

Columbia's competitor analysis revealed the emergence of many regional economy-class chain motels, as shown in Figure C. While the six major nationwide chains had 304,000 beds, new economy-class chains

FIGURE B

Economy-Segment Business Traveler Benefits

Primary Benefit Sought	Attributes of Primary Benefit
Quality rooms	Large work desk Chair and ottoman Remote-control free cable TV Climate-control system Two-compartment bath Exterior and interior entry doors
Efficient and friendly staff	Friendly service Extra help Room service when food available
Superior amenities and services	Complementary coffee and tea Outdoor pool Small meeting room Free local telephone calls Thick towels
Convenient location	Easy to find Easy access Plenty of parking
Pricing	Good value for money Credit cards Excellent prices

FIGURE C

Competitive Structure of the Economy Segment

Type	Competitors	National	Rooms
New economy-class chains	49	1	185,000
Traditional chains	6	4	304,000
Consortia	1	1	168,000
Independents	Many	None	474,000

offered 185,000 beds and independents, another 405,000 beds. With many competitors focusing on the economy-class segment, Columbia felt it had to achieve a value-added position in this segment that would differentiate Grinstead from other competitors.

This led to a more detailed competitor analysis, which is summarized in Figure D. From this analysis, Columbia judged Competitor D (in Figure D) to occupy the position it would like to command.

Product Positioning

Columbia's strategy was to introduce a differential product so as to not confuse the image and positioning of other Columbia lodging products. To accomplish this objective, Columbia created a new lodging alternative called Grinstead Inns. As shown in Figure E, the objective of this product concept was to uniquely position Grinstead in the lower-price/quality segment while preserving the image and unique positioning of other Columbia lodging alternatives.

The positioning of Grinstead was critical. Grinstead Inns had to differentiate itself from other Columbia lodging alternatives while also differentiating itself from competing economy lodging competitors. This would require understanding target customer needs and competitor strengths and weaknesses in this segment.

FIGURE D Key Competitors in the New Economy-Class Group

Competitor	Strengths	Weaknesses
Competitor A	Physical product Low price Product consistency	Limited locations No management system Building exterior
Competitor B	Product consistency Low price First-floor entry	Product quality Decor Site requirements
Competitor C	National reputation Physical product National advertising	Confused image Poor site selection
Competitor D	Consistent product Good value Superior locations Tightly positioned	Decor Amenities package

FIGURE E Columbia's Product Line Strategy

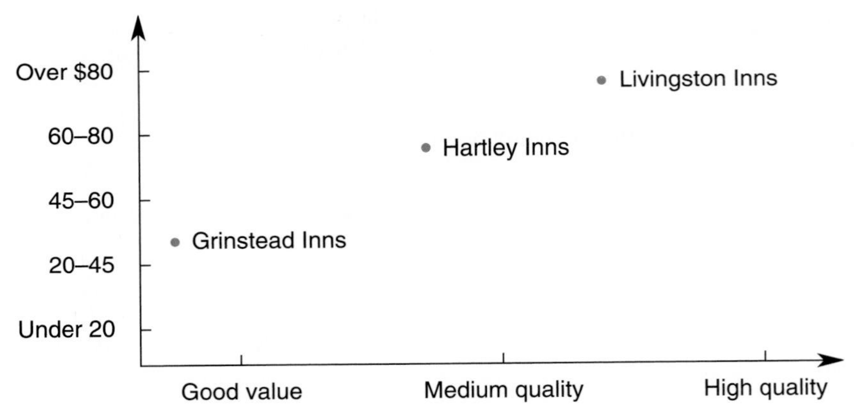

Grinstead Strategy

Based on studies of customers and competitors, Columbia's Grinstead strategy was to position itself a few dollars per night above Competitor D while outperforming Competitor D on its key weaknesses (decor and amenities package).

Discussion Questions

1. Is it necessary to completely differentiate Grinstead Inns from other inns owned and managed by Columbia? What are the benefits of this approach? What are the costs?
2. To what degree did Columbia benefit from customer and competitor analysis in developing a position strategy for Grinstead Inns?
3. Describe Grinstead's positioning in the economy-class segment.
4. Which consumers in the economy-class segment are most likely to respond to Grinstead Inns' product positioning?

Levi Strauss

Case 3–7

By the early 80s, Levi Strauss had grown to a $2.8-billion-a-year company. Over half this revenue was derived from the sale of jeans, which grew at the rate of 23 percent per year in the 70s. However, by the mid-80s, this market was becoming saturated. To continue to grow, Levi Strauss had to develop new products and penetrate new markets.

To better understand the clothing market, the company invested in a large-scale consumer behavior study that examined the clothing preferences, buying habits, demographics, and lifestyles of some 2,000 males. From this very large base of information, the company hoped to discover new market opportunities. It uncovered five distinct market segments for men's clothing, depicted in Figure A. Each segment has unique lifestyles and clothing preferences.

The Utilitarian

This segment of the men's apparel market represents about 26 percent of male consumers. These consumers wear jeans as a way of life, for work and play. Jeans are an important part of their lifestyle and communicate the casualness they desire to portray. This segment represents a very important part of Levi's present sales in the jeans market.

The Trendy Casual

This segment is more contemporary and conscious of the latest fashion trends. In the study they were characterized as your ''John Travolta type.'' They represent 19 percent of the men's apparel market. These consumers like to be noticed, and having the right clothes is important to them. They are very active socially and are a large part of the urban night-life scene.

Price Shopper

These men shop for the lowest price. They represent 15 percent of the men's apparel market. Because they are price shoppers, they are more inclined to shop discount stores and lower-priced department stores and to respond to price-off sales.

The Traditionalist

A hard-core department store shopper, the traditionalist is very conservative. This conservatism is reflected in his political preferences as well as his clothing preferences. Traditionalists are the largest consumers of polyester clothing and are generally slow to adopt new clothing changes. They make up 19 percent of the market. They prefer to shop for clothes with their wives or girlfriends, whose opinions they value in making clothing purchase decisions.

The Classic Independent

Clearly the most significant thing to come out of the men's apparel consumer research study was uncovering the Q-2 segment, the ''Classic Independent.'' This segment makes up 21 percent of male shoppers, but it

FIGURE A

Segmentation of the Men's Apparel Market

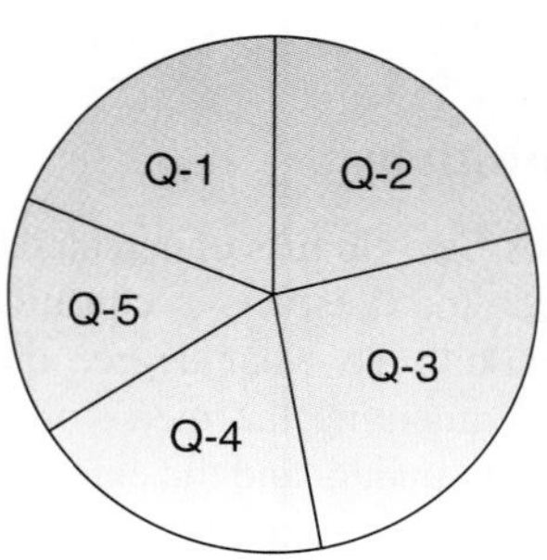

Segment	Size	Segment Name
Q-1	19%	Traditionalist
Q-2	21	Classic independent
Q-3	26	Utilitarian
Q-4	19	Trendy casual
Q-5	15	Price shopper

FIGURE B Sample Lifestyle Characteristics of the Classic Independent

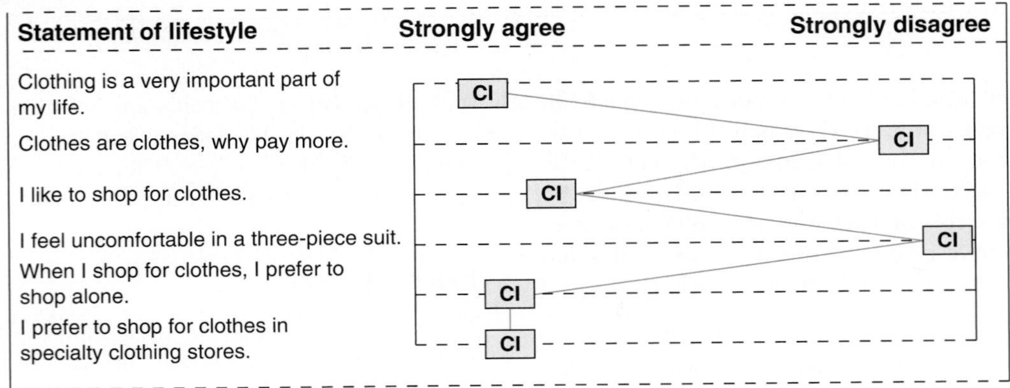

TABLE A Levi's Marketing Mix Strategy for the Classic Independent

Marketing Mix	Description
Product	Tailored suits (that can be purchased as separates eliminating the need for alterations), pants, and sports coats
Price	\$160 suits, \$85–\$100 coats, \$30–\$45 pants
Brand name	Levi's Tailored Classic
Distribution	Major department stores
Advertising	Heavy television advertising

consumes 46 percent of men's natural fiber clothing. These men take a great deal of pride in how they look, and their clothes have to be right. Price is not a major consideration, and they prefer to shop at specialty stores. They purchase the best clothing and prestigious brands. They want the best fit, which they believe requires tailoring, and they are willing to pay for it. They prefer to shop alone and enjoy the process of picking out their clothing. The Levi Strauss team felt that this segment represented a significant opportunity. Figure B profiles the lifestyle of the typical consumer in this segment of the menswear market.

Proposed Market Strategy

To attract the Classic Independent, Levi Strauss developed a line of tailored clothing including men's three-piece suits, slacks, and sports coats. The new line was called Levi's Tailored Classics. The clothing required no tailoring. The consumer could select individual pants, vest, and jacket to assure a desired fit.

The pants could retail for \$30 to \$45, coats for \$85 to \$100, and three-piece suits for \$160 (1982 prices). These prices were consistent with this segment's standard expenditures. Levi's Tailored Classics were sold through department stores. A heavily television and print advertising campaign was planned to launch and properly position the Levi's Tailored Classic. Considerable effort was made to inform and convince the Classic Independent that the Levi's line of suits fits their needs. Summarized in Table A is the marketing mix strategy Levi Strauss implemented in going after the Classic Independent.

Discussion Questions

1. How well does Levi Strauss understand the clothing preferences and lifestyles of consumers in the menswear market? To what degree did it do a good job of segmenting the men's apparel market? Does it fully understand the emotional aspect of clothing purchase and use?

2. Construct a list of demographics, use behaviors, clothing preferences, general attitudes toward life, and specific attitudes toward clothes that would need to be measured to produce the market segmentation it obtained.
3. How would consumers from each of the other four menswear segments respond to the lifestyle statements in Figure B?
4. What problems do you see with the proposed target-market strategy? Describe the information processing that a Classic Independent would go through in reacting to the Levi's market offering.
5. What changes would you recommend in Levi's strategy? Describe these changes with respect to how they would better fit the clothing preferences and lifestyle of the target buyer.

The Sugar Association, Inc. Case 3–8

Answer the following true/false questions:

1. **A teaspoon of sugar contains less than 20 calories.**
2. **The Academy of General Dentistry recommends a low-sugar diet to minimize risks of tooth decay.**
3. **The American Dietetic Association does not recommend a reduced-sugar diet for Americans.**
4. **The Food and Drug Administration (FDA) places sugar on its list of foods that are Generally Recognized as Safe (GRAS).**
5. **No artificial sweetener is on the FDA's GRAS list.**

The answers are true (16 calories), false, true, true, and true. While evidence on the nutritional as well as taste benefits of sugar has been accumulating rapidly, many Americans remain unaware of these facts. To correct any misperceptions concerning sugar, as well as to counter aggressive marketing activities for artificial sweeteners, the Sugar Association recently decided to launch an advertising campaign.

Prior to designing the campaign, the association conducted a major consumer survey to determine demographics, attitudes, and values associated with sugar consumption. Some of the key findings are:

- Eighty-six percent "like" or "love" sweets.
- Sugar and sugar-sweetened foods are associated with the happy, pleasurable moments in life.
- Users of artificial sweeteners like sugar and sugar-sweetened foods to the same extent as nonusers and they use about as much sugar.
- Heavy-user households (40+ pounds per year) constitute 30 percent of sugar users but represent 77 percent of household sugar consumption. They bake more often and are more likely to eat sugar-sweetened snacks, desserts, and breakfasts. Seventy-five percent have children at home compared to 48 percent of light users (10 pounds or less per year). Heavy users say they "love" sweets, while light and moderate users "like" sweets.
- Over two-thirds of the respondents agreed with these statements:

  "I feel I can enjoy snacks/desserts because my eating habits are generally healthy."
  "Enjoying sweets is a natural and normal part of a child's life."

- Over half the respondents felt they should limit their families' consumption of both sugar and artificial sweeteners.

While the results of the survey are generally very positive, officials of the Sugar Association are worried about the continued existence of concern over the quantity of sugar consumed. They are also concerned that the continued extensive promotion of sugar-free products will cause consumers to presume that sugar is somehow bad.

Discussion Questions

1. Explain how consumers might "learn" that sugar is bad, based on frequently seen promotions for sugar-free products.
2. What values are involved in the consumption of sugar versus artificial sweeteners?
3. The attitude survey produced strong positive attitudes toward sugar, and yet over half the

respondents felt they should limit their families' intake of sugar. How do you account for this?

4. What product position would you try to establish for sugar? Why?
5. What learning approach and principles would you use to "teach" consumers about sugar?
6. How would you establish a favorable attitude for sugar?
7. Develop an ad or marketing approach to create a positive attitude toward sugar, focusing on the ________ component.
   a. Cognitive.
   b. Affective.
   c. Behavioral.
8. Develop an ad or marketing approach to create a positive attitude toward sugar, using ________.
   a. Humor.
   b. Emotion.
   c. Utilitarian appeal.
   d. Value-expressive appeal.
   e. Celebrity endorser.
   f. Self-concept.
   g. Fear.
9. What ________ lifestyle segment(s) would be the best target markets for sugar? Why?
   a. VALS 2
   b. PRIZM
   c. GLOBAL SCAN
10. To what motive(s) would you appeal to induce consumers to use sugar?
11. Develop an ad for sugar that would attract the attention of consumers who are not interested in sugar or cooking. Explain how your ad will attract attention and why it will also convey the desired message or image.
12. What values are associated with the use of this product category? Are they shifting in a favorable or unfavorable direction?

Case 3–9 Weyerhaeuser and Branded Lumber

Bill Wachtler recently found himself once again reviewing Weyerhaeuser's tentative plans to utilize a branding strategy for most of its lumber and building materials products (including dimension lumber such as 2 × 4s and plywood). The need for such an approach seemed obvious.

The repair and remodel (R&R) market accounted for 20 percent of lumber consumption and over $90 billion in expenditures (lumber and nonlumber) in 1987. Unlike housing, R&R consumption did not fluctuate widely with economic shifts. Further, this market is projected to continue growing in importance. R&R lumber consumption is divided approximately equally between do-it-yourselfers (DIYers) and contractors. Most of the contractors are relatively small.

Home centers and similar large chains and buying units have grown rapidly in importance and will soon dominate distribution to DIYers and many smaller contractors. These chains have sophisticated buying units and push hard to minimize prices paid to the lumber producers. With lumber viewed as a commodity, they can play one producer against another for price concessions. The target-market DIY consumer has distinctive characteristics and behavior, as summarized in Figure A.

Bill felt that the above facts indicated both the need and opportunity to introduce branded lumber. He was also mindful of the price premium obtained by firms that had successfully branded "commodity" products, such as "Perdue" in chickens and "Sunkist" in oranges.

Despite what appeared to be obvious advantages to a branding strategy, several factors caused Bill to worry. First, if it was such an obvious strategy, why was no other lumber company pursuing it? Second, there was a widespread belief that, within lumber grades, "a 2 × 4 is a 2 × 4." Finally, there were the results of yet another company study indicating that brand name was not important to lumber buyers (see

Demographic and Behavioral Profile and Do-It-Yourself Consumers

FIGURE A

- 35–44-year-olds are most active.
- 85 percent of projects involve homes over 10 years of age.
- 60 percent have lived in the home 10 years or more.
- 53 percent have incomes between $20,000 and $50,000.
- 43 percent are two-income families.
- Major projects generally involve both DIY and contractor activities.
- Renters do about one-third of the projects.
- Store location is a key factor in outlet selection, though a third will drive 16–30 minutes to reach a preferred store.
- 90 percent of all purchases are planned in advance.
- 52 percent of all projects are initiated by females.
- A sense of accomplishment is a major motivation for DIY projects (both male and female).
- Financial necessity is also an important motivation, but cost-conscious shoppers are after value rather than lowest cost.
- 70 percent of DIYers say brand names are an important factor in buying nonlumber home-improvement products.
- Leading causes, in order, for brand switching between nonlumber home-improvement brands: quality/warranty, special prices, salesperson, brand availability, and package information.

Do-It-Yourselfers' Ratings of the Importance of Attributes of Boards

FIGURE B

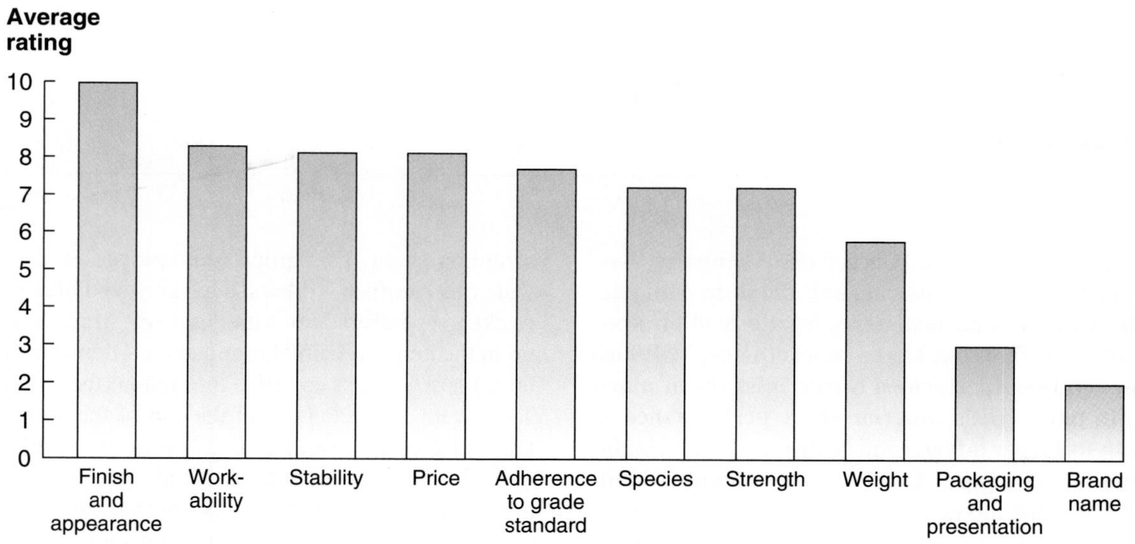

Source: C. Casson, "The Many Faces of Home Modernization," *Building Supply Home Center*, May 1986, pp. 52–64; and Weyerhaeuser internal reports.

Figure B). Bill wondered how he could convince a very customer-oriented management that branding was a good strategy when customers consistently said they did not consider brand name in their purchase decisions.

Discussion Questions

1. Why does brand name rate as unimportant in this market?
2. Can consumers learn (be taught) that brand name is an important product attribute?
3. If it decides to brand lumber, how should Weyerhaeuser position its brand?
4. Would lifestyle segmentation be an appropriate way to segment this market?
5. Develop a presentation for Wachtler to present to top management arguing for an aggressive branding strategy.
6. What learning approach and principles would you use to "teach" consumers about Weyerhaeuser branded lumber?
7. How would you establish a favorable attitude for Weyerhaeuser branded lumber?
8. Develop an ad or marketing approach to create a positive attitude toward Weyerhaeuser branded lumber, focusing on the ______ component.
   a. Cognitive.
   b. Affective.
   c. Behavioral.
9. Develop an ad or marketing approach to create a positive attitude toward Weyerhaeuser branded lumber, using ______.
   a. Humor.
   b. Emotion.
   c. Utilitarian appeal.
   d. Value-expressive appeal.
   e. Celebrity endorser.
   f. Self-concept.
   g. Fear.
10. What ______ lifestyle segment(s) would be the best target markets for Weyerhaeuser branded lumber? Why?
    a. VALS 2.
    b. PRIZM.
    c. GLOBAL SCAN
11. To what motive(s) would you appeal to induce consumers to use Weyerhaeuser branded lumber?

Case 3–10 Sprite Billboard Advertising Test

For many years the Coca-Cola Company has sought to develop a noncola soft drink to compete with 7UP. In blind taste tests, Sprite is often preferred over 7UP, but in the marketplace, 7UP has consistently outperformed Sprite in share of market. In part, 7UP's superior share performance is due to its larger advertising budget and well-established brand image. To better understand if and how billboard advertising could attract consumers to Sprite, a small-scale consumer study was conducted.

The Consumption Study

Eighty employees from a large commercial organization were recruited to participate in a soft-drink consumption study. This group of employees included a wide mix of office workers, managers, and blue-collar workers. A refrigerator with eight soft drinks was set up in the employee lunchroom, and participants could take a soft drink at any time throughout the workday. They were instructed to put the cap of the soft drink they selected in a slotted bin adjacent to the refrigerator. Each participant was assigned a slot with his or her name below it. In this way, an individual history of brand choice could be recorded each day. Participants consumed an average of two soft drinks per day. The soft drinks used in the study are shown in Table A.

A one-week warm-up period enabled the participants to adjust to the novelty of the situation. Following this, their individual choice behavior was tracked

TABLE A

Soft Drinks Used in the Consumption Study

	Cola	Noncola
Sugared	Coca-Cola Pepsi-Cola	7UP Sprite
Nonsugared	Tab Diet Pepsi	Fresca Diet 7UP

FIGURE A

Perceptual Map of Competing Brands and Ideal Brands

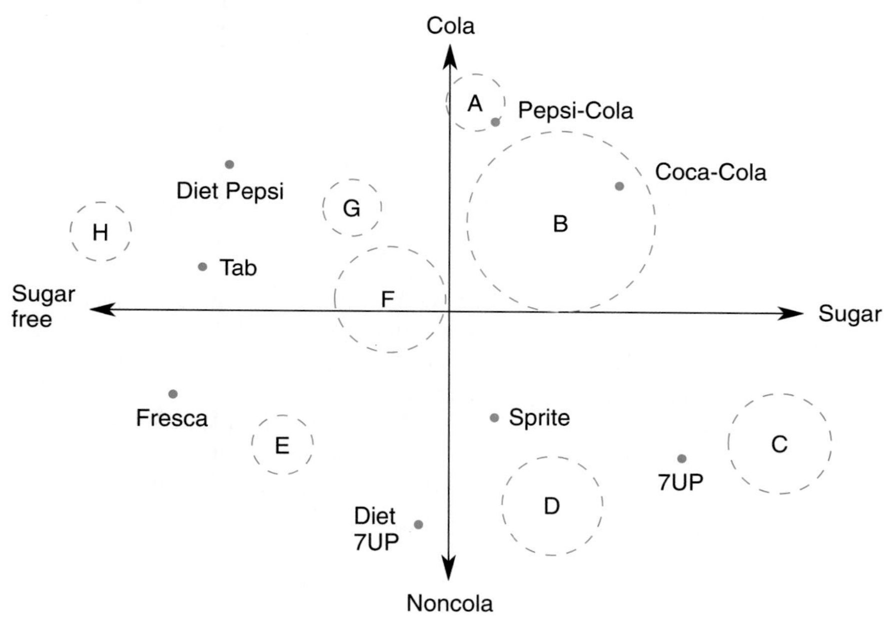

for 10 weeks. After the fourth week, a Sprite advertisement occupied the space on a large billboard that could be seen easily by all employees entering and exiting this commercial establishment. The Sprite billboard looked very much like Sprite magazine print ads. In this manner, the study was able to track consumption of the eight soft drinks for a four-week period prior to exposure to the billboard ad, and then measure how that behavior changed with the presence of a Sprite billboard advertisement.

The Results

The perceptual map shown in Figure A was created using consumer perceptions and brand preferences. It indicates the perceived similarity of competing brands and the location of ideal brands for different groups of consumers (indicated by the circles with the size of the circle representing the number of consumers with that ideal brand). The letters shown indicate the ideal soft drink based on consumer preferences. The larger the circle, the larger the proportion of consumers preferring that ideal brand. As can be seen, Sprite is perceived to be more similar to 7UP than to other soft drinks, and consumers with ideal brands near 7UP should be more attracted to Sprite if the Sprite advertisement has the desired effect.

As shown in Table B, Sprite's share in this study was very close to 2 percent through the four weeks leading up to the introduction of the Sprite billboard advertisement. Immediately following the introduction, Sprite's share more than doubled and stayed over

TABLE B

Sprite's Weekly Market Share

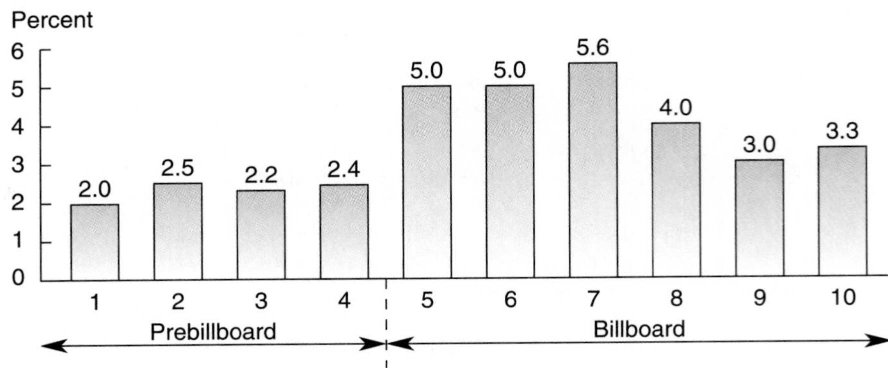

5 percent for three weeks. Sprite's share then dropped to 4 percent in week four of the billboard ad (week eight overall) and stabilized around 3 percent for the remainder of the study.

Analysis of competing brand shares showed that after introduction of the Sprite billboard, 7UP, Diet 7UP, and Fresca lost market share. By the end of the 10 weeks (six weeks of billboard advertising), Fresca had recovered its lost share, but 7UP and Diet 7UP were still down in share although some of their lost share was gained back.

Discussion Questions

1. What factors would cause Sprite's market share to go up after introduction of a billboard advertisement? Be specific as to the perceptual and learning processes that had to take place.
2. What factors contributed to Sprite's share decline after three weeks of billboard exposure?
3. Describe the results of this experiment with respect to low-involvement learning.
4. What are the marketing strategy implications of this billboard advertising experiment?

SECTION FOUR

CONSUMER DECISION PROCESS

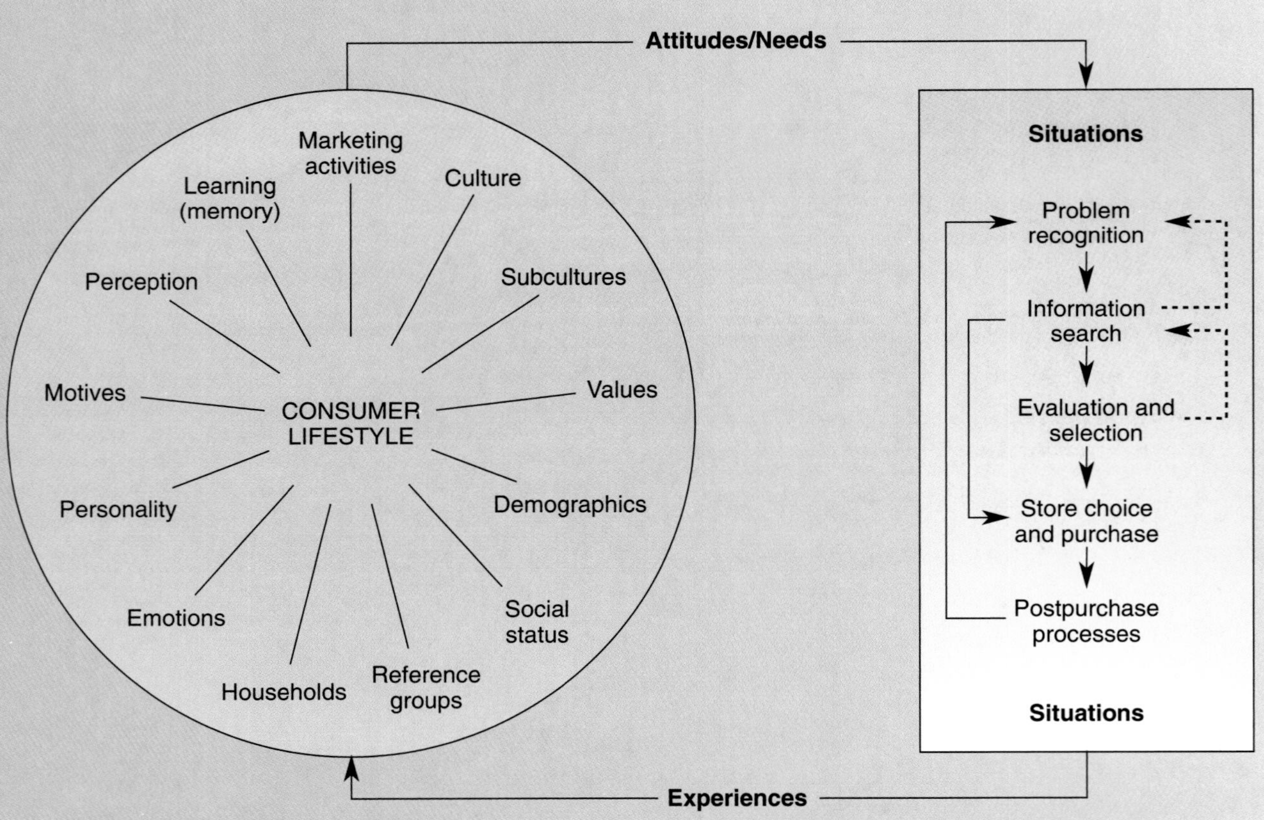

Up to now we have focused on various sociological and psychological factors that contribute to different patterns of consumer behavior. Though these various influences play a significant role in behavior, all behavior takes place within the context of a situation. Therefore, behavior may vary among consumers as well as for the same consumer from one situation to another. Chapter 14 provides a discussion of the impact situational variables have on consumer behavior.

Of particular importance to marketers is how situations and internal and external sources of influence affect the consumer purchase decision process. The extended consumer decision process, as shown in the figure at left, is composed of a sequential process: problem recognition; information search; brand evaluation; store choice and purchase; and use, satisfaction, disposition, and repurchase motivation. However, extended decision making occurs only in those relatively rare situations when the consumer is highly involved in the purchase. Lower levels of purchase involvement produce limited or habitual decision making. Chapter 15 describes those various types of decisions and their relationship to involvement. It also analyzes the first stage of the process—problem recognition.

Information search constitutes the second stage in the consumer decision process, and it is discussed in Chapter 16. The nature of consumer information search and those factors that influence different levels of prepurchase information search are considered. Chapter 17 examines the brand evaluation and selection process. Chapter 18 deals with outlet selection and the in-store influences that often contribute to brand switching. The final stage of the consumer decision process, presented in Chapter 19, involves behavior after purchase, including postpurchase feelings, use behavior, satisfaction, disposition, and repurchase motivation. Throughout these six chapters we attempt to present what consumers do at different stages of the consumer decision process, what factors contribute to their behavior, and what actions can be taken by marketers to affect their behavior.

CHAPTER 14

SITUATIONAL INFLUENCES

Information Professionals, Inc., offers a service called ''advertiming.'' The service relies on an extensive computer database that compares consumption patterns with the current weather. Based on observed relationships between weather and product category sales, the firm uses weather forecasts to advise its clients on spot advertising buys, sales, point-of-purchase displays, and related issues.

A number of firms have used simpler versions of this approach for some time. For example, Blistex, Inc., and Campbell Soup have based spot radio advertising on weather forecasts for several years. However, Information Professionals provides data on less obvious relationships and products. For example, does hot cocoa sell better on a warm but dark winter day or on a frigid but bright day? The answer is dark and warm. Therefore, cocoa advertisers would be better off timing spot buys and special promotions to coincide with dark, cloudy days as opposed to average days, or cold, clear days.[1]

As the model we have used to organize this text stresses, the purchase decision and consumption process always occur in the context of a specific situation. Therefore, before examining the decision process, we must first develop an understanding of situations.

As marketers we need to understand which situations affect the purchase of our products and how we might best serve target market buyers when these situations arise. We should view the consumer and the marketing activities designed to influence that consumer in light of the situations the consumer faces.

TYPES OF SITUATIONS

The consumption process occurs within three broad categories of situations: the communications situation, the purchase situation, and the usage situation. Each is described below.

The Communications Situation

The situation in which consumers receive information has an impact on their behavior. Whether we are alone or in a group, in a good mood or bad, in a hurry or not, influences the degree to which we see and listen to marketing communications. Is it better to advertise on a happy or sad television program? A calm or exciting program? These are some of the questions managers must answer with respect to the communications situation.

If we are interested in the product and are in a receptive communications situation, a marketer is able to deliver an effective message to us. However, finding high-interest potential buyers in receptive communications situations is a difficult challenge. For example, consider the difficulty a marketer would have in communicating to you in the following communications situations:

- Your favorite team just lost the most important game of the year.
- Final exams begin tomorrow.
- Your roommates only watch news programs.
- You have the flu.
- You are driving home on a cold night, and your car heater doesn't work.

The Purchase Situation

Situations can also affect product selection in a purchase situation. Mothers shopping with children are more apt to be influenced by the product preferences of their children than when shopping without them. A shortage of time, such as trying to make a purchase between classes, can affect the store chosen, the number of brands considered, and the price you are willing to pay.

Marketers must understand *how* purchase situations influence consumers in order to develop marketing strategies that enhance the purchase of their products. For example, how would you alter your decision to purchase a beverage in the following purchase situations?

- You are in a very bad mood.
- A good friend says, "That stuff is bad for you."
- You have an upset stomach.
- There is a long line at the checkout counter as you enter the store.
- You are with someone you want to impress.

The Usage Situation

A consumer may use a different brand of wine to serve dinner guests than for personal use in a nonsocial situation. A family may choose a different vacation depending on who is going.

Marketers need to understand the usage situations for which their products are, or may become, appropriate. Based on this knowledge, marketers can communicate how their products can create consumer satisfaction in each relevant usage situation. For example, Managerial Application 14–1 shows one of a series of ads designed to position *Baileys* as appropriate for casual, romantic situations.

What beverage would you prefer to consume in each of the following usage situations?

- Friday afternoon after your last final exam.
- With your parents for lunch.
- After dinner on a cold, stormy evening.
- At a dinner with a friend you have not seen in several years.
- After working in the yard on a hot day.

CHARACTERISTICS OF SITUATIONAL INFLUENCE

We define **situational influence** as:

> All those factors particular to a time and place of observation which do not follow from a knowledge of personal (intra-individual) and stimulus (choice alternative) attributes and which have a demonstrable and systematic effect on current behavior.[2]

A situation is a set of factors outside of and removed from the individual consumer as well as removed from the characteristics of the primary stimulus object (e.g., a product, a

MANAGERIAL APPLICATION 14–1

Positioning Baileys as Appropriate for Casual, Romantic Situations

FIGURE 14–1

The Role of the Situation in Consumer Behavior

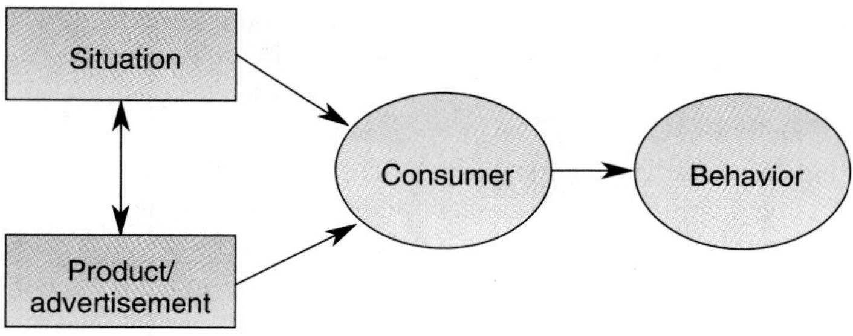

television advertisement) to which the consumer is reacting (e.g., purchasing a product, viewing a commercial). As indicated in Figure 14–1, consumers do not respond to stimuli such as advertisements and products presented by marketers in isolation. Instead, they respond to marketing influences and the situation simultaneously.

While marketers have traditionally studied the effect an object such as a product or advertisement has on the consumer's behavior, they have often ignored the influence of the situation. Thus, marketers stand to gain a great deal by studying the roles their products play in different situations. For example, a wine marketer should be able to develop better strategy from knowing that wine is often given as a house gift, but seldom as a birthday gift.

In order to utilize situational influences, a marketer must understand three important aspects of this influence:

- When a particular situation affects consumer behavior.
- How strong the effect is likely to be.
- The way in which the situation influences behavior.

To integrate the influence of situation into marketing strategy, we must first give careful attention to the degree that the situation *interacts* with a given product and a given set of target consumers. Then we must evaluate the situation more systematically in terms of *when it occurs*, the *strength of its influence*, and the *nature of its influence on behavior*. For example, time spent doing leisure activities is influenced by physical surroundings (e.g., temperature and weather), social influences, and a person's mood. To be effective in marketing a particular leisure activity (e.g., sports event, movies), a marketer must understand how and when these situational influences will impact a consumer's decision to spend time on that activity.

SITUATIONAL CLASSIFICATION

A number of different approaches to classifying situations have been proposed. The most widely accepted scheme includes five types of situational influences: physical surrounding, social surrounding, time perspectives, task objectives, and antecedent states.[3]

Physical Surroundings

Physical surroundings include geographical and institutional location, decor, sounds, aromas, lighting, weather, and visible configurations of merchandise or other material surrounding the stimulus object. Physical surroundings are a widely recognized type of situational influence. For example, store interiors are often designed to create specific feelings in shoppers that can have an important cuing or reinforcing effect on purchase. A retail clothing store specializing in extremely stylish, modern clothing would want to reflect this to customers in the physical characteristics of the purchase situation. The fixtures, furnishings, and colors should all reflect an overall mood of style, flair, and newness. In addition, the store personnel should appear to carry this theme in terms of their own appearance and apparel. These influences generate appropriate perceptions of the retail environment, which in turn influence the purchase decision.[4]

Evidence indicates that customers are more satisfied with services acquired in an organized, professional-appearing environment than with those acquired in a disorganized environment.[5]

The color *red* is effective at attracting consumers' attention and interest. However, while physically arousing, red is also perceived as tense and negative. Softer colors such as *blue* are less attention-attracting and arousing. They are perceived as calm, cool, and positive. Which color would be best for store interiors? Research indicates that blue is superior to red in terms of generating positive outcomes for both the retailer (sales) and the consumer (satisfaction).[6]

Music influences consumers' moods, which influence a variety of consumption behaviors.[7] Is slow-tempo or fast-tempo background music better for a restaurant? Table 14–1 indicates that slow music increased gross margin for one restaurant by almost 15 percent per customer group compared to fast music! However, before concluding that all restaurants should play slow music, examine the table carefully. Slow music appears to have relaxed and slowed down the customers, resulting in more time in the restaurant and substantially more purchases from the bar. Restaurants without bars that rely on rapid customer turnover may be better off with fast-tempo music.

Figure 14–2 illustrates how crowding produces negative outcomes for both the retail outlet and the consumer.[8] In many instances, marketers have limited control over the physical situation. For example, there are many forms of retailing, such as mail order,

TABLE 14–1

The Impact of Background Music on Restaurant Patrons

Variables	Slow Music	Fast Music
Service time	29 min.	27 min.
Customer time at table	56 min.	45 min.
Customer groups leaving before seated	10.5%	12.0%
Amount of food purchased	$55.81	$55.12
Amount of bar purchases	$30.47	$21.62
Estimated gross margin	$55.82	$48.62

Source: R. E. Milliman, "The Influence of Background Music on the Behavior of Restaurant Patrons," *Journal of Consumer Research*, September 1986, p. 289.

FIGURE 14–2

The Impact of Physical Density on Shopper Perceptions, Shopping Strategies, and Postpurchase Processes

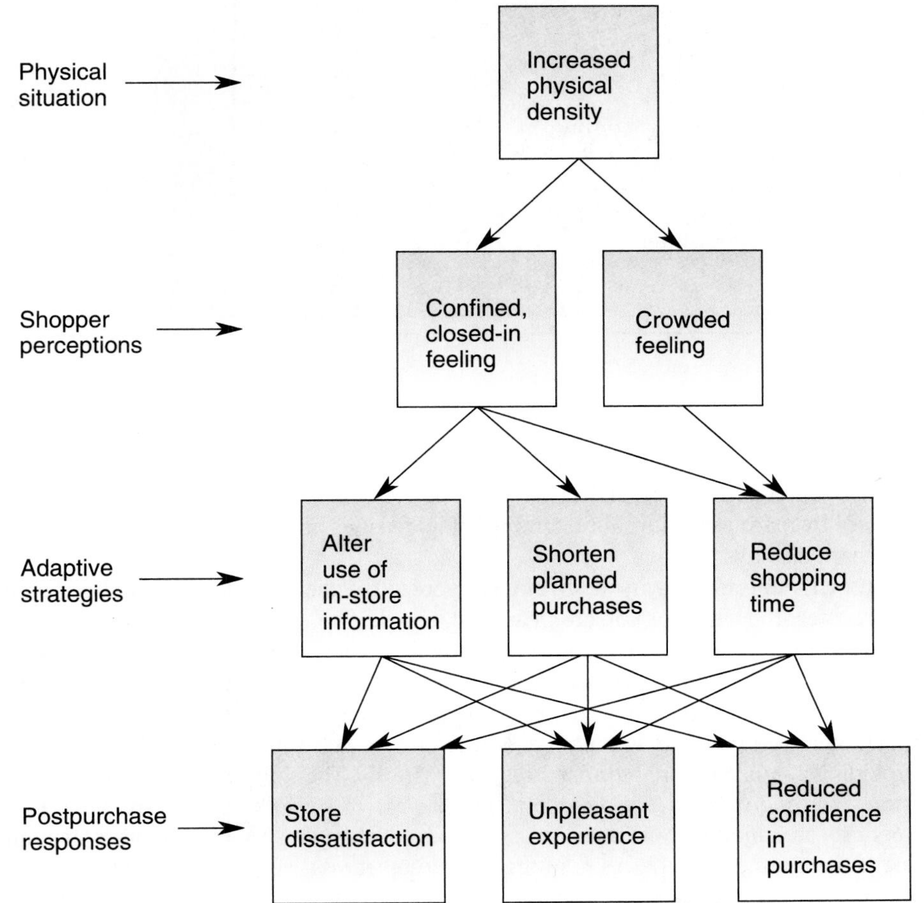

Source: Adapted from G. Harrell, M. Hutt, and J. Anderson, "Path Analysis of Buyer Behavior under Conditions of Crowding," *Journal of Marketing Research*, February 1980, pp. 45–51.

MANAGERIAL APPLICATION

14–2 Positioning Beefeater as an Appropriate Hot Weather Drink

door-to-door, and vending machines, where control is minimal. Still, the marketer tries to account for the physical situation by carefully selecting appropriate outlets and product mixes for vending machines, and instructing door-to-door sales personnel to "control the situation" by rearranging furniture, turning off televisions or radios, and bringing in point-of-purchase displays.

As a marketing manager you should ask yourself if the physical surroundings could possibly affect the behavior you are interested in and, if so, in what ways. Note that there are many possible behaviors that a marketer could be interested in: actual purchase, shopping (looking), receiving information (such as watching TV advertisements), and so forth. An analysis of nonpurchase motivations for shopping found physical activity and sensory stimulation to be two important motives.[9] Enclosed shopping malls offer clear advantages in providing a safe, comfortable area for leisurely strolls. The sights and sounds of a variety of stores and individuals also provide a high degree of sensory stimulation. Both these factors play an important role in the overall success of shopping centers and other shopping areas. If there are physical aspects of the situation that you can influence and/or control, then you should do so in a manner that will make the physical situation compatible with the lifestyle of your target market.

Often you can neither control nor influence the physical situation the consumer will encounter, such as winter versus summer for beverage consumption. In these cases, it is appropriate to alter the various elements of the marketing mix to match the needs and expectations of the target market. Both Dr Pepper and Lipton's tea have varied their advertising between summer and winter based on physical changes in the environment and consumers' reactions to these changes. Managerial Application 14–2 shows an ad positioning *Beefeater* as an appropriate summer drink.

Social Surroundings

Social surroundings are the other individuals present during the consumption process. Our actions are frequently influenced, if not altogether determined, by those around us. For example, Chinese-, Mexican-, and Anglo-Americans prefer different types of food in situations where business associates are present versus those where parents are present.[10]

Figure 14–3 illustrates the impact of the social situation on the attributes desired in a dessert. Notice that economy and taste are critical for personal and family consumption, while general acceptance is the key for the party situation. What does this suggest in terms of advertising strategy?

Social influence is a significant force acting on our behavior since individuals tend to comply with group expectations, particularly when the behavior is visible. Thus shopping, a highly visible activity, and the use of many publicly consumed brands are subject to social influences. Shopping with others has been found to influence the purchase of such standard products as meat, chicken, and cereal, while beer consumption changes with the presence of guests, at parties, and during holidays.[11]

Shopping can provide a social experience outside the home for making new acquaintances, meeting existing friends, or just being near other people. Some people seek status

Impact of Social Situations on Desired Dessert Attributes

FIGURE 14–3

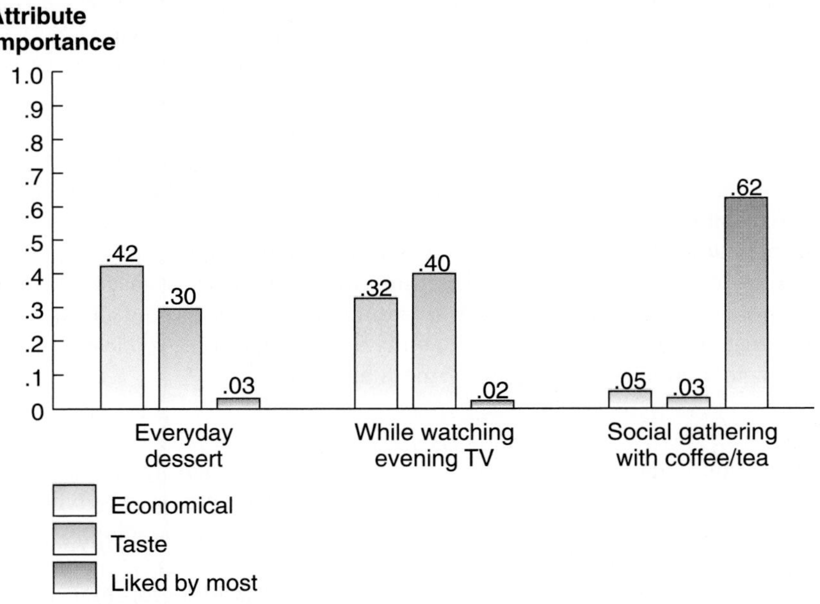

Source: J. B. Palmer and R. H. Cropnick, "New Dimension Added to Conjoint Analysis," *Marketing News*, January 3, 1986, p. 62.

and authority in shopping since the salesperson's job is to wait on the customer. This allows these individuals a measure of respect or prestige that may otherwise be lacking in their lives. Thus, consumers, on occasion, shop *for* social situations rather than, or in addition to, products.

Frequently, as a marketing manager, you will not have any control over social characteristics of a situation. For example, when a television advertisement is sent into the home, the advertising manager cannot control who the viewer is with at the time of the reception. However, the manager can utilize the knowledge that some programs are generally viewed alone (weekday, daytime programs), some are viewed by the entire family (Walt Disney), and others by groups of friends (Super Bowl). The message presented can be structured to these viewing situations. Managerial Application 6–1 (page 146) shows an attempt to position *Bud Light* as appropriate for a certain type social situation.

There are a number of occasions where marketing managers can influence the social aspects of a situation. For instance, the advertiser can encourage you to ''ask a friend'' or, better yet, ''bring a friend along.'' Some firms, such as Tupperware, have been ingenious in structuring social situations that encourage sales. Salespersons know that frequently they can use the shopper's companion as an effective sales aid by soliciting his or her opinion and advice.

Temporal Perspectives

Temporal perspectives are situational characteristics that deal with the effect of time on consumer behavior. Time as a situational factor can manifest itself in a number of different ways. The amount of time available for the purchase has a substantial impact on the consumer decision process. As a generalization, we can say that the less time there is available (i.e., increased time pressure), the shorter will be the information search, the less available information will be used, and the more suboptimal purchases will be made.[12]

Time as a situational influence affects our choice of stores. A number of retail firms have taken advantage of the temporal perspective factor. Perhaps the most successful of these is the 7-Eleven chain, which caters almost exclusively to individuals who either are in a hurry or who want to make a purchase after regular shopping hours.

Limited purchase time can also result in a smaller number of product alternatives being considered. The increased time pressure experienced by many dual-career couples and single parents tends to increase the incidence of brand loyalty, particularly for nationally branded products. The obvious implication is that these consumers feel safer with nationally branded or ''known'' products, particularly when they do not have the time to engage in extensive comparison shopping.

Time pressures and technology have combined to produce rapid growth in high-quality, easy-to-prepare foods, as well as other time-saving products. Managerial Application 14–3 shows how a computer marketer is positioning one of its products as a means to take advantage of unexpected time availability. (See Managerial Application 10–6, page 291, for another product targeting this same situation.)

Task Definition

Task definition is the reason the consumption activity is occurring. The major task dichotomy used by marketers is between purchases for self-use versus gift-giving. Consumers use different shopping strategies and purchase criteria when shopping for gifts versus shopping for the same item for self-use.[13]

One study found that wedding gifts tend to be *utilitarian* (the top four attributes are durability, usefulness, receiver's need, and high performance), while birthday gifts tend to be *fun* (the top four attributes are enjoyability, uniqueness, durability, and high perform-

MANAGERIAL APPLICATION 14–3

A Temporal Situation Product-Positioning Strategy

ance). Thus, both the general task definition (gift giving) and the specific task definition (gift-giving occasion) influence purchase behavior. Managerial Application 14–4 is an ad focused on a traditional gift-giving situation.

Antecedent States

Antecedent states are features of the individual person that are not lasting characteristics. Rather, they are momentary moods or conditions. For example, we all experience states of depression or high excitement from time to time that are not normally part of our individual makeup.

Moods are transient feeling states that are generally not tied to a specific event or object.[14] They tend to be less intense than emotions and may operate without the individual's awareness. While moods may affect all aspects of a person's behavior, they generally do not completely interrupt ongoing behavior as an emotion might. Individuals use such terms as happy, cheerful, peaceful, sad, blue, and depressed to describe their moods.

Moods both affect and are affected by the consumption process.[15] For example, television, radio, and magazine program content can influence our mood and arousal level, which, in turn, influences our information-processing activities.[16] Moods also influence our decision processes and the purchase and consumption of various products. For example, one study found that positive moods were associated with increased browsing and "impulse" purchasing. Negative moods also increased impulse purchasing in some consumers.[17]

In addition to responding to consumer needs induced by moods, marketers attempt to influence moods and to time marketing activities with positive mood-inducing events. Restaurants, bars, shopping malls, and many other retail outlets are designed to induce positive moods in patrons. Music is often played for this reason.[18] Many companies prefer

MANAGERIAL APPLICATION

14–4

A Gift-Giving Positioning Strategy

to advertise during "light" television programs because viewers tend to be in a good mood while watching these shows.

Momentary conditions differ somewhat from moods. Whereas moods reflect states of mind, **momentary conditions** reflect states of being such as being tired, being ill, having a great deal of money, being broke, and so forth. However, for conditions, as for moods, to fit under the definition of antecedent states, they must be momentary and not constantly with the individual. Hence, an individual who is short of cash only momentarily will probably act differently than someone who is always short of cash.

SITUATIONAL INFLUENCES AND MARKETING STRATEGY

Individuals do not encounter situations randomly. Instead, most people "create" many of the situations they face. Thus, individuals who choose to engage in physically demanding sports such as jogging, tennis, or racquetball are indirectly choosing to expose themselves to the situation of "being tired" or "being thirsty." This allows marketers to consider advertising and segmentation strategies based on the situations that individuals selecting given lifestyles are likely to encounter.

After determining the influence of different situations on purchase behavior for a product category, a marketer must determine which products or brands are most likely to be purchased when that situation arises. One method of dealing with this question is to jointly scale situations and products. An example is shown in Figure 14–4. Here, *use situations* that ranged from "private consumption at home" to "consumption away from home where there is a concern for other people's reaction to you" were scaled in terms of their similarity and relationship to products appropriate for that situation. For a use situation described as "to clean my mouth upon rising in the morning," toothpastes and

Use Situations and Product Positioning

FIGURE 14–4

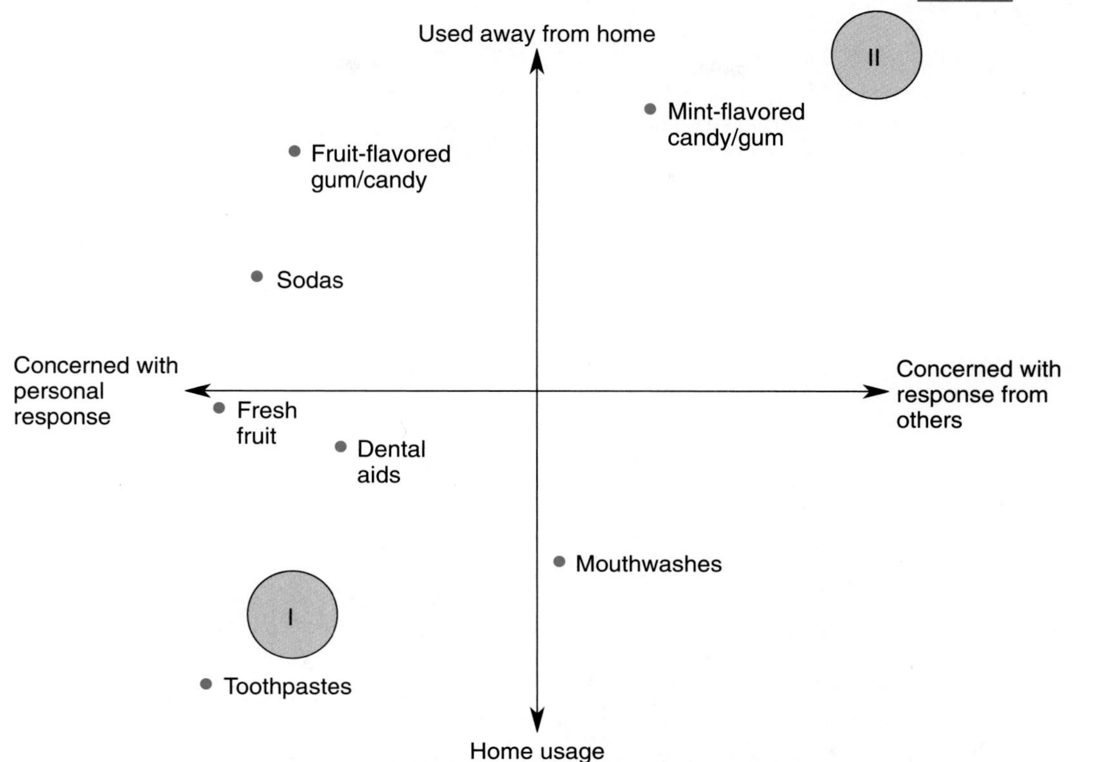

mouthwashes are viewed as most appropriate. However, a use situation described as ''before an important business meeting late in the afternoon,'' involves both consumption away from home and a concern for the response others have to you. As a result, mint-flavored gums or candies would best serve this use situation.

Exhibit 14–1 outlines the steps a firm can take in studying the use situation to better segment markets, position products, and create advertisements designed to communicate this positioning. Exhibit 14–2 applies this methodology to suntan lotion.[19]

SUMMARY

Marketing managers should view the consumer and marketing activities designed to affect and influence that consumer in light of the situations that the consumer faces. A *consumer situation* is a set of factors outside of and removed from the individual consumer, as well as removed from the characteristics or attributes of the product.

Situations, for the purpose of helping to explain consumer behavior, have been classified into a scheme of five objectively measured variables. *Physical surroundings* include geographical and institutional location, decor, sound, aromas, lighting, weather, and displays of merchandise or other material surrounding the product. Retailers are particularly concerned with the effects of physical surroundings.

Person–Situation Segmentation Procedure

EXHIBIT 14–1

Segmentation Procedure

Step 1: Use observational studies, focus group discussions, and secondary data to discover whether different usage situations exist and whether they are determinant, in the sense that they appear to affect the importance of various product characteristics.

Step 2: If step 1 produces promising results, survey consumers to better understand benefits, product perceptions, and product use. Measure benefits and perceptions by usage situation, as well as by individual difference characteristics. Assess situation-usage frequency by recall estimates or usage situation diaries.

Step 3: Construct a person–situation segmentation matrix. The rows are the major usage situations and the columns are groups of users identified by a single characteristic or combination of characteristics.

Step 4: Rank the cells in the matrix in terms of their submarket sales volume. The situation–person combination that results in the greatest consumption of the product would be ranked first.

Step 5: State the major benefits sought, important product dimensions, and unique market behavior for each nonempty cell of the matrix.

Step 6: Position your competitor's offerings within the matrix. The person–situation segments they currently serve can be determined by the product features they promote and other marketing strategies.

Step 7: Position your offering within the matrix on the same criteria.

Step 8: Assess how well your current offering and marketing strategy meet the needs of the supermarkets compared to the competition.

Step 9: Identify market opportunities based on submarket size, needs, and competitive advantage in each person–situation segment.

Adapted from P. Dickson, ''Person–Situation: Segmentation's Missing Link,'' *Journal of Marketing*, Fall 1982, pp. 56–64.

Social surroundings deal with other persons present who could have an impact on the individual consumer's behavior. The characteristics of the other persons present, their roles, and interpersonal interactions are potentially important social situational influences.

Temporal perspectives deals with the effect of time on consumer behavior. It includes such concepts as time of day, time since last purchase, time since or until meals or payday, and time constraints imposed by commitments. Convenience stores have evolved and been successful by taking advantage of the temporal perspective factor.

Task definition reflects the purpose or reason for engaging in the consumption behavior. The task may reflect different buyer and user roles anticipated by the individual. For example, a person shopping for dishes to be given as a wedding present is in a different situation than if the dishes were for personal use.

Antecedent states are features of the individual person that are not lasting or relatively enduring characteristics. They are momentary moods or conditions. *Momentary moods* are such things as temporary states of depression or high excitement, which all people expe-

EXHIBIT 14–2

Person/Situation Segments for Suntan Lotions

Suntan Lotion Use Situation	Potential Users of Suntan Lotion				
	Young Children	Teenagers	Adult Women	Adult Men	Situation Benefits
Beach/boat activities	Prevent sunburn/ skin damage	Prevent sunburn while tanning	Prevent sunburn/ skin change/ dry skin	Prevent sunburn	Container floats
Home/pools sunbathing	Prevent sunburn/ skin damage	Tanning without sunburn	Tanning without skin damage or dry skin	Tanning without sunburn/ skin damage	Lotion won't stain clothes or furniture
Tanning booth		Tanning	Tanning with moistur-izer	Tanning	Designed for sunlamps
Snow skiing		Prevent sunburn	Prevent sunburn/ skin damage/ dry skin	Prevent sunburn	Antifreeze formula
Person benefits	Protection	Tanning	Protection and tan-ning with soft skin	Protection and tanning	

rience. *Momentary conditions* are such things as being tired, ill, having a great deal of money (or none at all), and so forth.

Situational influences may have very direct influences, but they also interact with product and individual characteristics to influence behavior. In some cases, the situation will have no influence whatsoever, because the individual's characteristics or choices are so intense that they override everything else. But the situation is always potentially important and therefore is of concern to marketing managers.

REVIEW QUESTIONS

1. What is meant by the term *situation*? Why is it important for a marketing manager to understand situation influences on purchasing behavior?
2. What are *physical surroundings* (as a situational variable)? Give an example of how they can influence the consumption process.
3. What are *social surroundings* (as a situational

variable)? Give an example of how they can influence the consumption process.

4. What is *temporal perspective* (as a situational variable)? Give an example of how it can influence the consumption process.
5. What is *task definition* (as a situational variable)? Give an example of how it can influence the consumption process.
6. What are *antecedent conditions* (as a situational variable)? Give an example of how they can influence the consumption process.
7. What is a *mood*? How does it differ from an *emotion*? How do moods influence behavior?
8. What is meant by the statement, ''Situational variables may interact with object or personal characteristics''?
9. Are individuals randomly exposed to situational influences? Why?
10. How can consumption situations be used in market segmentation?
11. How does crowding affect shopping behavior?

DISCUSSION QUESTIONS

12. Discuss the potential importance of each situational influence in developing a marketing strategy to promote the purchase of (or gifts to):
    a. Christian Children's Fund.
    b. Domino's Pizza.
    c. Fondue pot.
    d. Bud Light.
    e. Cut flowers.
    f. Life insurance.
13. What product categories seem most susceptible to situational influences? Why?
14. In those instances where marketers have little control over the consumption situation, why is it important for them to understand how the situation relates to the consumption of their product?
15. How would you change the situational classification scheme presented in the chapter?
16. Flowers are ''appropriate'' gifts for women over many situations but seem to be appropriate for men only when they are ill. Why is this so? Could FTD change this?
17. Speculate on what a matrix like the one shown in Exhibit 14–2 would look like for ______.
    a. Wine.
    b. Magazines.
    c. Frozen foods.
    d. Restaurants.
    e. Bicycles.
    f. Canned vegetables.
18. Does Table 14–1 have implications for outlets other than restaurants? If yes, which ones and why?
19. Does your shopping behavior and purchase criteria differ between purchases made for yourself and purchases made as gifts?
20. Describe a situation in which a mood (good or bad) caused you to make an unusual purchase.

PROJECT QUESTIONS

21. Interview 5 people who have recently purchased ______. Determine the role, if any, played by situational factors.
    a. A movie ticket.
    b. A pet.
    c. Flowers.
    d. Take-out or delivered food.
    e. Wine.
    f. Shoes.
22. Interview a ______ salesperson. Determine the role, if any, this individual feels situational variables play in his/her sales.
    a. Clothing.
    b. Automobile.
    c. Insurance.
    d. Jewelry.
23. Conduct a study using a small (10 or so) sample of your friends in which you attempt to isolate the situational factors that influence the type, brand, or amount of ______ purchased or used.
    a. Novels.
    b. Perfume.
    c. Movies.
    d. Fresh vegetables.
    e. Church attendance.
    f. Popcorn or similar snacks.
24. Create a list of 10 to 20 use situations relevant to campus area restaurants. Then interview 10 students and have them indicate which of these

situations they have encountered and ask them to rank order these situations in terms of how likely they are to occur. Discuss how a restaurant could use this information in trying to appeal to the student market.

25. Select a product and develop three distinct marketing strategies based on situational influences that affect the consumption of that product.
26. Copy three advertisements that are clearly based on a situational appeal. For each advertisement, indicate:
    a. Which situational variable is involved.
    b. Why the company would use this variable.
    c. Your evaluation of the effectiveness of this approach.
27. Create a ''wedding gift,'' ''birthday gift,'' and ''self-use'' ad for ______. Explain the differences across the ads.
    a. Fondue set.
    b. Tool kit.
    c. Portable grill.
    d. Set of kitchen knives.
    e. Food processer.
    f. Clock/radio/alarms.
28. Interview 10 students and determine instances where their mood affected their purchases. What do you conclude?

REFERENCES

[1]D. A. Michals, ''Pitching Products by the Barometer,'' *Business Week*, July 8, 1985, p. 45.

[2]R. W. Belk, ''Situational Variables and Consumer Behavior,'' *Journal of Consumer Research*, December 1975, p. 158.

[3]Ibid.

[4]See S. Grossbart, R. Hampton, B. Rammohan, and R. S. Lapidus, ''Environmental Dispositions and Customer Response to Store Atmospheres,'' *Journal of Business Research*, November 1990, pp. 225–41.

[5]M. J. Bitner, ''Evaluating Service Encounters,'' *Journal of Marketing*, April 1990, pp. 69–82.

[6]See J. A. Bellizzi and R. E. Hite, ''Environmental Color, Consumer Feelings, and Purchase Likelihood,'' *Psychology & Marketing*, September 1992, pp. 347–63.

[7]G. C. Bruner II, ''Music, Mood, and Marketing,'' *Journal of Marketing*, October 1990, pp. 94–104.

[8]See S. Eroglu and G. D. Harrell, ''Retail Crowding,'' *Journal of Retailing*, Winter 1986, pp. 346–63; M. K. M. Hui and J. E. G. Bateson, ''Testing a Theory of Crowding in the Service Environment,'' in *Advances in Consumer Research XVII*, eds. M. E. Goldberg, G. Gorn, and R. W. Pollay (Provo, Utah: Association for Consumer Research, 1990), pp. 866–73; S. A. Eroglu and K. A. Machleit, ''An Empirical Study of Retail Crowding,'' *Journal of Retailing*, Summer 1990, pp. 201–21.

[9]E. M. Tauber, ''Why Do People Shop?'' *Journal of Marketing*, October 1972, p. 47. See also R. A. Westbrook and W. C. Black, ''A Motivation-Based Shopper Typology,'' *Journal of Retailing*, Spring 1985, pp. 78–103.

[10]D. M. Stayman and R. Deshpande, ''Situational Ethnicity and Consumer Behavior,'' *Journal of Consumer Research*, December 1989, pp. 361–71.

[11]J. A. Cote, J. McCullough, and M. Reilly, ''Effects of Unexpected Situations on Behavior-Intention Differences,'' *Journal of Consumer Research*, September 1985, p. 193. See also S. Chow, R. L. Celsi, and R. Abel, ''The Effects of Situational and Intrinsic Sources of Personal Relevance on Brand Choice Decisions,'' in *Advances in Consumer Research XVI*, eds. M. E. Goldberg, G. Gorn, and R. W. Pollay (Provo, Utah: Association for Consumer Research, 1990), pp. 755–60.

[12]B. E. Mattson and A. J. Dobinsky, ''Shopping Patterns,'' *Psychology & Marketing*, Spring 1987, pp. 42–62; C. W. Park and E. S. Iyer, ''The Effects of Situational Factors on In-Store Grocery Shopping Behavior,'' *Journal of Consumer Research*, March 1989, pp. 422–33; and M. Hahn, R. Lawson, and Y. G. Lee, ''The Effects of Time Pressure and Information Load on Decision Quality,'' *Psychology & Marketing*, September 1992, pp. 365–78.

[13]See D. M. Andrus, E. Silver, and D. E. Johnson, ''Status Brand Management and Gift Purchase,'' *Journal of Consumer Marketing*, Winter 1986, pp. 5–13; and C. Goodwin, K. L. Smith, and S. Spiggle, ''Gift Giving,'' in *Advances XVII*, see footnote 7, pp. 690–98; E. Fisher and S. J. Arnold, ''More than a Labor of Love,'' and M. DeMoss and D. Mick, ''Self-Gifts,'' both in *Journal of Consumer Research*, December 1990, pp. 322–32; and T. I. Garner and J. Wagner, ''Economic Dimensions of Household Gift-Giving,'' *Journal of Consumer Research*, December 1991, pp. 368–79.

[14]M. P. Gardner, ''Mood States and Consumer Behavior,'' *Journal of Consumer Research*, December 1985, pp. 281–300.

[15]M. P. Gardner and R. P. Hill, ''Consumers' Mood States,'' *Psychology & Marketing*, Summer 1988, pp. 169–82, D. Kuykendall, ''Mood and Persuasion,'' *Psychology & Marketing*, Spring 1990, pp. 1–9; P. A. Knowles, S. J. Grove, and W. J. Burroughs, ''An Experimental Examination of Mood Effects,'' *Journal of the Academy of Marketing Science*, Spring 1993, pp. 135–42; and J. Hornik, ''The Role of Affect in Consumers' Temporal Judgments'' *Psychology & Marketing*, May 1993, pp. 239–55.

[16]M. E. Goldberg and G. J. Gorn, ''Happy and Sad TV Programs,'' *Journal of Consumer Research*, December 1987, pp. 387–403; D. M. Sanbonmatsu and F. R. Kardes, ''The Effects of Physiological Arousal on Information Processing and Persuasion,'' *Journal of Consumer Research*, December 1988, pp. 379–85; S. N. Singh and J. C. Hitchon, ''The Intensifying Effects of Exciting Television Programs on the Reception of Subsequent Behavior,'' *Psychology & Marketing*, Spring 1989, pp. 1–31; R. Batra and

D. M. Stayman, ''The Role of Mood in Advertising Effectiveness,'' *Journal of Consumer Research*, September 1990, pp. 203–14; D. Kuykendall and J. P. Keating, ''Mood and Persuasion,'' *Psychology & Marketing*, Spring 1990, pp. 1–9; and M. A. Kamins, L. J. Marks, and D. Skinner ''Television Commercial Evaluation in the Context of Program Induced Mood,'' *Journal of Advertising*, June 1991, pp. 1–14.

[17]J. Jeon, *An Empirical Investigation of the Relationship between Affective States, In-Store Browsing, and Impulse Buying* (Tuscaloosa: The University of Alabama, unpublished dissertation, 1990).

[18]See J. I. Alpert and M. I. Alpert, ''Music Influences on Mood and Purchase Intentions,'' *Psychology & Marketing*, Summer 1990, pp. 109–33.

[19]For a similar approach, see D. Ball, C. Lamb, and R. Brodie, ''Segmentation and Market Structure When Both Consumer and Situational Characteristics Are Explanatory,'' *Psychology & Marketing*, September 1992, pp. 395–408.

CONSUMER DECISION PROCESS AND PROBLEM RECOGNITION

Consumer groups and some government officials have been concerned that many consumers are not aware of health and other problems associated with alcohol use. As a result of these concerns, since November 1989 all alcoholic beverage containers must carry the following warning:

GOVERNMENT WARNING: (1) ACCORDING TO THE SURGEON GENERAL, WOMEN SHOULD NOT DRINK ALCOHOLIC BEVERAGES DURING PREGNANCY BECAUSE OF THE RISK OF BIRTH DEFECTS, (2) CONSUMPTION OF ALCOHOLIC BEVERAGES IMPAIRS YOUR ABILITY TO DRIVE A CAR OR OPERATE MACHINERY, AND MAY CAUSE HEALTH PROBLEMS.

In addition to the label warnings, some groups want all advertising of alcoholic beverages to carry warnings. In April 1990, Senators Gore and Kennedy introduced legislation that would require every print and broadcast ad to carry one of five rotated health warnings. Two of the five warnings are:

SURGEON GENERAL'S WARNING: DRINKING DURING PREGNANCY MAY CAUSE MENTAL RETARDATION AND OTHER BIRTH DEFECTS. AVOID ALCOHOL DURING PREGNANCY.

WARNING: ALCOHOL MAY BE HAZARDOUS IF YOU ARE USING ANY OTHER DRUGS, SUCH AS OVER-THE-COUNTER, PRESCRIPTION, OR ILLICIT DRUGS.

Television ads would include voice-overs as well as visual warnings.

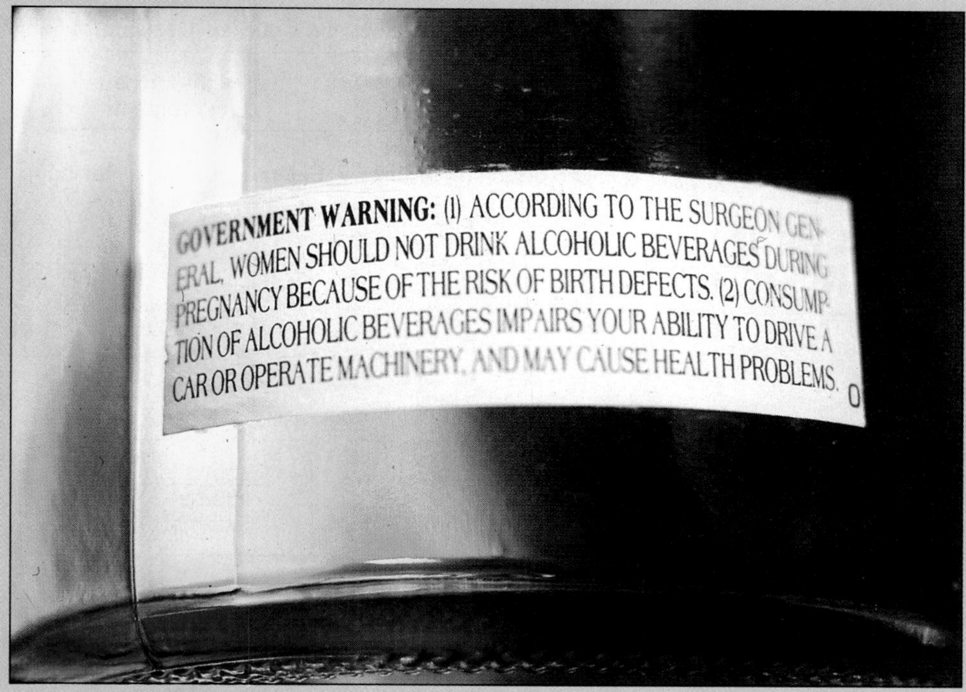

Problem recognition is the first stage of the consumer decision process. In the example, Senators Gore and Kennedy hope to cause problem recognition among some consumers of alcoholic beverages. It is their hope that problem recognition will lead to decisions to avoid alcohol while pregnant, taking other medications, driving a car, or operating machinery.

This chapter examines the nature of the consumer decision process and analyzes the first step in that process, problem recognition, in some detail. Within problem recognition, we focus on: (1) the process of problem recognition, (2) the uncontrollable determinants of problem recognition, and (3) marketing strategies based on the problem recognition process.

TYPES OF CONSUMER DECISIONS

The term *consumer decision* produces an image of an individual carefully evaluating the attributes of a set of products, brands, or services and rationally selecting the one that solves a clearly recognized need for the least cost. It has a rational, functional connotation. While consumers do make many decisions in this manner, many others involve little conscious effort. Further, many consumer decisions focus not on brand attributes but rather on the feelings or emotions associated with acquiring or using the brand or with the environment in which the product is purchased or used.[1] Thus, a brand may be selected not because of an attribute (price, style, functional characteristics) but because ''It makes me feel good'' or ''My friends will like it.''

While purchases and related consumption behavior driven by emotional or environmental needs have characteristics distinct from the traditional attribute-based model, we believe the decision process model provides useful insights into all types of consumer purchases. As we describe consumer decision making in this and the next four chapters,

FIGURE 15–1

Low-purchase involvement → High-purchase involvement

Habitual decision making
- Problem recognition: Selective
- Information search: Limited internal
- Purchase
- Postpurchase: No dissonance; Very limited evaluation

Limited decision making
- Problem recognition: Generic
- Information search: Internal; Limited external
- Alternative evaluation: Few attributes; Simple decision rules; Few alternatives
- Purchase
- Postpurchase: No dissonance; Limited evaluation

Extended decision making
- Problem recognition: Generic
- Information search: Internal; External
- Alternative evaluation: Many attributes; Complex decision rules; Many alternatives
- Purchase
- Postpurchase: Dissonance; Complex evaluation

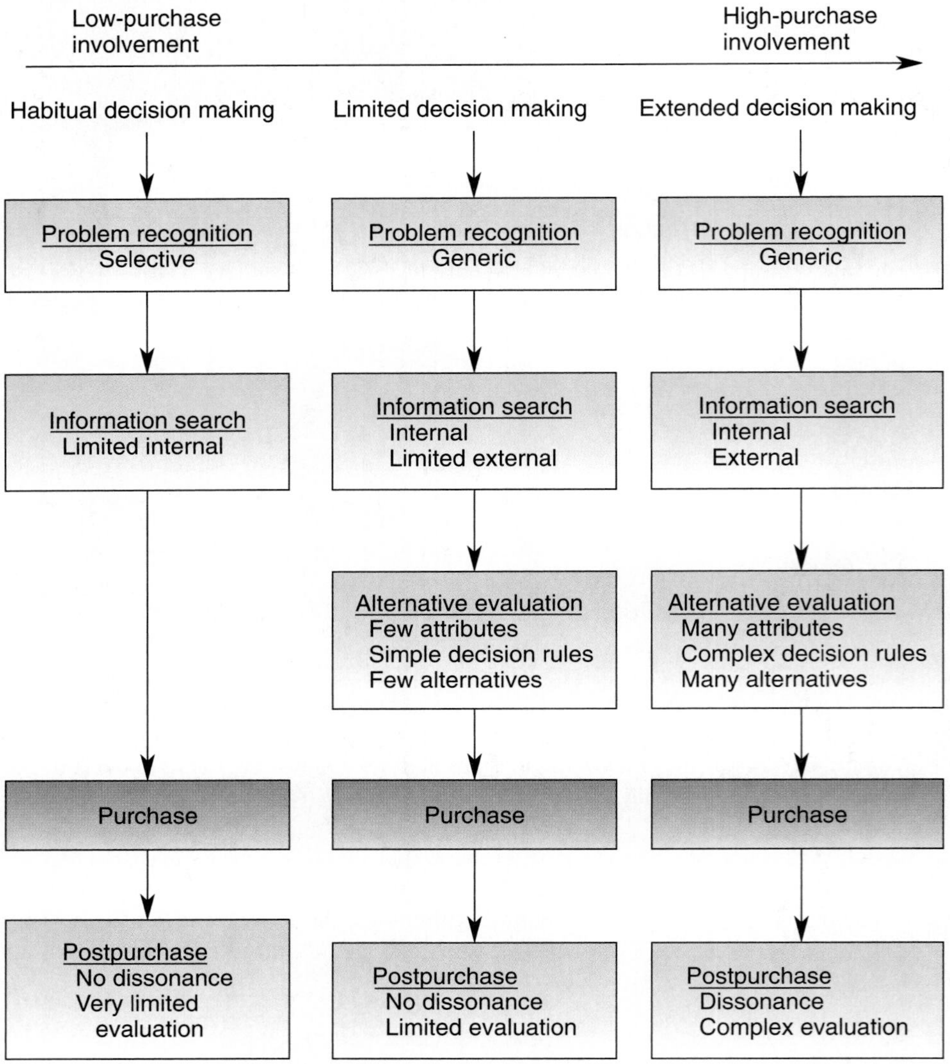

we will indicate how it helps us understand emotion-, environment-, and attribute-based decisions.

As Figure 15–1 indicates, there are various types of consumer decision processes. As the consumer moves from a very low level of involvement *with the purchase situation* to a high level of involvement, decision making becomes increasingly complex. While purchase involvement is a continuum, it is useful to consider habitual, limited, and extended decision making as general descriptions of the types of processes that occur along various points on the continuum. You should keep in mind that the types of decision processes are not distinct but blend into each other.

Before describing each type of decision process, the concept of purchase involvement must be clarified. We define **purchase involvement** as the *level of concern for, or interest in, the purchase process triggered by the need to consider a particular purchase.*[2] Thus, purchase involvement is a temporary state of an individual, family, or household unit. It is influenced by the interaction of individual, product, and situational characteristics.[3]

Note that purchase involvement is *not* the same as product involvement. You may be very involved with a brand (Budweiser or Crest or Volvo) or a product category (beer or toothpaste or cars) and yet have a very low level of involvement with the purchase process because of brand loyalty. Or, you may have a rather low level of involvement with a product (school supplies or automobile tires) but have high level of purchase involvement because you desire to set an example for a child, impress a friend who is on the shopping trip, or save money. Of course, there are individual differences in general involvement level and in the involvement response to particular situations.

The following sections provide a brief description of how the purchasing process changes as purchase involvement increases.

Habitual Decision Making

Habitual decision making in effect involves *no* decision per se. As Figure 15–1 indicates, a problem is recognized, internal search (long-term memory) provides a single preferred solution (brand), that brand is purchased, and an evaluation occurs only if the brand fails to perform as expected. Habitual decisions occur when there is very low involvement with the purchase and result in repeat purchasing behavior.

A completely habitual decision does not even include consideration of the ''do not purchase'' alternative. For example, you might notice that you are nearly out of Aim toothpaste and resolve to purchase some the next time you are at the store. You don't even consider not replacing the toothpaste or purchasing another brand. At the store, you scan the shelf for Aim and pick it up without considering alternative brands, its price, or other potentially relevant factors.

Habitual decisions can be broken into two distinct categories: brand loyal decisions and repeat purchase decisions. These two categories are described briefly below and examined in detail in Chapter 19.

Brand Loyalty At one time you may have been highly involved in selecting a toothpaste and, in response, used an extensive decision-making process. Having selected Aim as a result of this process, you may now purchase it without further consideration, even though using the best available toothpaste is still important to you. Thus, you are committed to Aim because you believe it best meets your overall needs and you have formed an emotional attachment to it (you like it). You are brand loyal. It will be very difficult for a competitor to gain your patronage.

Repeat Purchases In contrast, you may believe that all catsups are about the same and you may not attach much importance to the product category or purchase. Having tried Del Monte and found it satisfactory, you now purchase it using habitual decision making. Thus, you are a repeat purchaser of Del Monte catsup, but you are not committed to it. A competitor could gain your patronage rather easily.

Both brand loyalty and repeat purchasing can have a strong situational component. For example, many consumers are either brand loyal to or generally purchase a ''price'' brand beverage, snack, or food for personal consumption and a different brand for use with guests.

Limited Decision Making

Limited decision making covers the middle ground between habitual decision making and extensive decision making. In its simplest form (lowest level of purchase involvement), limited decision making is very similar to habitual decision making.[4] For example, while in a store you may notice a point-of-purchase display for Jell-O and pick up two boxes without seeking information beyond your memory that ''Jell-O tastes good,'' or ''Gee, I haven't had Jell-O in a long time.'' In addition, you may have considered no other alternative except possibly a very limited examination of a ''do not buy'' option. Or, you may have a decision rule that you buy the cheapest brand of instant coffee available. When you run low on coffee (problem recognition), you simply examine coffee prices the next time you are in the store and select the cheapest brand.

Limited decision making also occurs in response to some emotional or environmental needs. For example, you may decide to purchase a new brand or product because you are ''bored'' with the current, otherwise satisfactory, brand. This decision might involve evaluating only the newness or novelty of the available alternatives. Or, you might evaluate a purchase in terms of the actual or anticipated behavior of others. For example, you might order or refrain from ordering wine with a meal depending on the observed or expected orders of your dinner companions.[5]

Extended Decision Making

As Figure 15–1 indicates, **extended decision making** is the response to a very high level of purchase involvement. Extensive internal and external information search is followed by a complex evaluation of multiple alternatives. After the purchase, doubt about its correctness is likely and a thorough evaluation of the purchase takes place. Relatively few consumer decisions reach this extreme level of complexity. However, products such as homes, personal computers, and complex recreational items such as backpacks and tents are frequently purchased via extended decision making.

Even decisions that are heavily emotional may involve substantial cognitive efforts. For example, we may agonize over a decision to take a cruise even though the need being met and the criteria being evaluated are emotions or feelings rather than attributes per se, and are therefore typically fewer in number with less external information available.

Marketing Strategy and Types of Consumer Decisions

The brief descriptions of the various types of consumer decisions provided above should be ample to indicate that marketing strategies appropriate for extended decision making would be less than optimal for limited or habitual decisions. As Figure 15–1 illustrates, most stages of the consumption process are affected by purchase involvement. We devote a chapter to each of these stages.

THE PROCESS OF PROBLEM RECOGNITION

A day rarely passes in which we do not face several consumption problems. Routine problems of depletion, such as the need to get gasoline as the gauge approaches empty, or the need to replace a frequently used food item, are readily recognized, defined, and resolved. The unexpected breakdown of a major appliance such as a refrigerator or stove creates an unplanned problem which is also easily recognized but is often more difficult to resolve. Recognition of other problems, such as the need for a personal computer, may take longer as they may be subtle and evolve slowly over time.

Feelings, such as boredom, anxiety, or the ''blues,'' may arise quickly or slowly over time. Such feelings are often recognized as problems subject to solution by purchasing

FIGURE 15–2

The Process of Problem Recognition

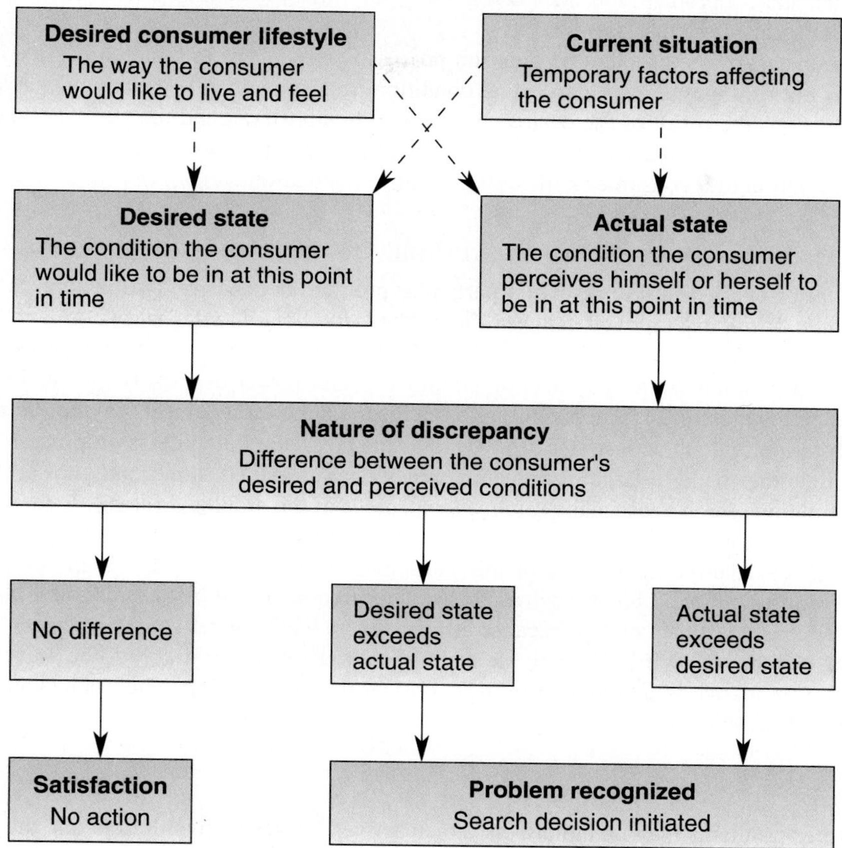

behavior (I'm sad, I think I'll go shopping/to a movie/to a restaurant). At other times, such feelings may trigger consumption behaviors without deliberate decision making. A person feeling "restless" may eat snack food without really thinking about it. In this case, the "problem" remains unrecognized (at the conscious level) and the solutions tried are often inappropriate (eating may not reduce restlessness).[6]

The Nature of Problem Recognition

Problem recognition is the first stage in the consumer decision process. In each of the situations described above, **problem recognition** *is the result of a discrepancy between a desired state and an actual state that is sufficient to arouse and activate the decision process.* The kind of action taken by consumers in response to recognized problems relates directly to the situation, its importance to the consumer, and the dissatisfaction or inconvenience created by the problem.

Without recognition of a problem, there is no need for a consumer decision. This condition is illustrated in Figure 15–2 when there is no discrepancy between the consumer's desired state (what the consumer would like) and the actual state (what the consumer perceives as already existing). On the other hand, when there is a discrepancy between a consumer desire and the perceived actual state, recognition of a problem occurs.[7] Figure

15–2 shows that any time the desired state is perceived as being greater than or less than the actual state, a problem has been recognized. Any time the desired state is equal to the actual state, no problem exists.

At the heart of the problem recognition process is the *degree* to which a desired condition is out of alignment with an actual condition. In Figure 15–2, consumer desires are represented as the result of the desired lifestyle of the consumer and the current situation (time pressures, physical surroundings, and so forth). Perceptions of the actual state also vary in relation to a consumer's lifestyle and current situation.

The Desire to Resolve Recognized Problems

The level of one's desire to resolve a particular problem depends on two factors: (1) *the magnitude of the discrepancy between the desired and actual states* and (2) *the relative importance of the problem.* An individual could desire to have a car that averages at least 25 miles per gallon while still meeting certain size and power desires. If the current car obtains an average of 24.5 miles per gallon, a discrepancy exists, but it may not be large enough to motivate the consumer to proceed to the next step in the decision process.

On the other hand, a large discrepancy may exist and the consumer may not proceed to information search because the *relative importance* of the problem is small. A consumer may desire a new Ford Mustang and own a 10-year-old Toyota. The discrepancy is large. However, the relative importance of this particular discrepancy may be small compared to other consumption problems such as those related to housing, utilities, and food. Relative importance is a critical concept because all consumers have budget constraints, time constraints, or both. Only the relatively more important problems are likely to be solved. In general, importance is determined by how critical the problem is to the maintenance of the desired lifestyle.

Types of Consumer Problems

Consumer problems may be either active or inactive. An **active problem** is one the consumer is aware of or will become aware of in the normal course of events. An **inactive problem** is one of which the consumer is not yet aware. This concept is very similar to the concept of felt need discussed in the Diffusion of Innovations section of Chapter 7. The following example should clarify the distinction between active and inactive problems.

> Timberlane Lumber Co. acquired a source of supply of Honduran pitch pine. This natural product lights at the touch of a match, even when damp, and burns for 15 to 20 minutes. It will not flare up and is therefore relatively safe. It can be procured in sticks 15 to 18 inches long and 1 inch in diameter. These sticks can be used to ignite fireplace fires, or they can be shredded and used to ignite charcoal grills.
>
> Prior to marketing the product, Timberlane commissioned a marketing study to estimate demand and guide in developing marketing strategy. Two large samples of potential consumers were interviewed. The first sample was asked how they lit their fireplace fires and what problems they had with this procedure. Almost all of the respondents used newspaper, kindling, or both, and almost none experienced any problems. The new product was then described, and the respondents were asked to express the likelihood that they would purchase such a product. Only a small percentage expressed any interest. However, a sample of consumers that actually used the new product for several weeks felt it was a substantial improvement over existing methods and expressed a desire to continue using the product. Thus, the problem was there

Nonmarketing Factors Affecting Problem Recognition

FIGURE 15–3

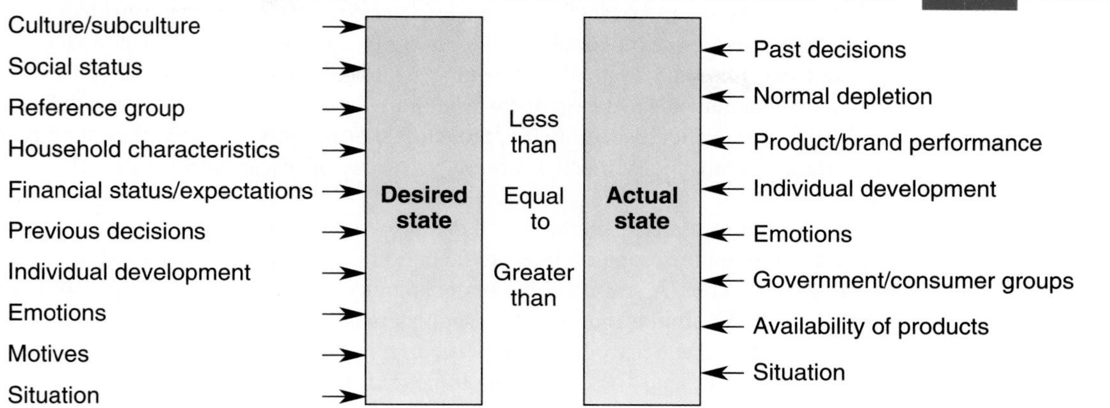

(because the new product was strongly preferred over the old by those who tried it), but most consumers were not aware of it. This is an *inactive problem.* Before the product can be successfully sold, the firm must activate problem recognition.

In contrast, a substantial percentage of those interviewed about lighting charcoal fires expressed a strong concern about the safety of liquid charcoal lighter. These individuals expressed great interest in purchasing a safer product. This is an *active problem.* Timberlane need not worry about problem recognition in this case. Instead, it can concentrate on illustrating how its product solves the problem that the consumers already know exists.

As this example indicates, active and inactive problems require vastly different marketing strategies. The problem addressed by the Gore/Kennedy legislation described at the beginning of this chapter appears to be inactive for many consumers.

UNCONTROLLABLE DETERMINANTS OF PROBLEM RECOGNITION

A discrepancy between what is desired by a consumer and what the consumer has is the necessary condition for problem recognition. A discrepancy can be the result of a variety of factors that influence consumer desires, perceptions of the existing state, or both. These factors are often beyond the direct influence of the marketing manager—for example, a change in family composition. Figure 15–3 summarizes the major nonmarketing factors that influence problem recognition. The marketing factors influencing problem recognition are discussed in the next section of this chapter.

MARKETING STRATEGY AND PROBLEM RECOGNITION

Marketing managers have four concerns related to problem recognition. First, they need to know what problems consumers are facing. Second, managers must know how to develop the marketing mix to solve consumer problems. Third, they occasionally want to cause consumers to recognize problems. Finally, there are times when managers desire to suppress problem recognition among consumers. The remainder of this chapter discusses these issues.

Measuring Consumer Problems

A wide variety of approaches are used to determine the problems consumers face. The most common approach undoubtedly is *intuition*. That is, a manager can analyze a given product category and logically determine where improvements could be made. Thus, soundless vacuum cleaners or dishwashers are logical solutions to potential consumer problems. The difficulty with this approach is that the problem identified may be of low importance to most consumers. Therefore, a variety of research techniques are commonly employed.

A common research technique is the *survey*, which asks relatively large numbers of individuals about the problems they are facing. This was the technique used by Timberlane, as described earlier. A second common technique is *focus groups*. Focus groups are composed of 8 to 12 similar individuals—such as male college students, lawyers, or teenage girls—brought together to discuss a particular topic. A moderator is present to keep the discussion moving and focused on the topic, but otherwise the sessions are free flowing. Both surveys and focus groups tend to take one of three approaches to problem identification: *activity analysis*, *product analysis*, or *problem analysis*. A third technique, *human factors research*, does not rely on surveys or focus groups. *Emotion research*, a fourth effort, attempts to discover the role emotions play in problem recognition.

Activity Analysis Activity analysis focuses on a particular activity such as preparing dinner, maintaining the lawn, or lighting the fireplace fire. The survey or focus group attempts to determine what problems the consumers feel occur during the performance of the activity. For example, Johnson Wax had a national panel of women report on how they cared for their hair and the problems they encountered. Their responses revealed a perceived problem with oiliness that existing brands could not resolve. As a result, Johnson Wax developed Agree Shampoo and Agree Creme Rinse, both of which became very successful.

Product Analysis Product analysis is similar to activity analysis, but examines the purchase and/or use of a particular product or brand. Thus, consumers may be asked about problems associated with using their lawn mower or their popcorn popper. Curlee Clothing used focus groups to analyze the purchase and use of men's clothing. The results indicated a high level of insecurity in purchasing men's clothing. This insecurity was combined with a distrust of both the motivations and competence of retail sales personnel. As a result, Curlee initiated a major effort to train retail sales personnel through specially prepared films and training sessions.

Problem Analysis Problem analysis takes the opposite approach from the previous techniques. It starts with a list of problems and asks the respondent to indicate which activities, products, or brands are associated with those problems. Such a study dealing with packaging could include questions such as:

- ________ packages are hard to open.
- Packages of ________ are hard to reseal.
- ________ doesn't pour well.
- Packages of ________ don't fit on the shelf.
- Packages of ________ waste too many resources.

Human Factors Research Human factors research attempts to determine human capabilities in areas such as vision, strength, response time, flexibility, and fatigue and the effect on these capabilities of lighting, temperature, and sound. While many methods can be employed in human factors research, observational techniques such as slow-motion and time-lapse photography, video recording, and event recorders are particularly useful to marketers.

This type of research can be particularly useful in identifying functional problems that consumers are unaware of. For example, it can be used in the design of such products as vacuum cleaners, lawn mowers, and computers to minimize user fatigue.

Emotion Research Marketers are just beginning to conduct research on the role of emotions in the decision process. One approach is focus group research and one-on-one personal interviews that focus on either (1) the emotions associated with a certain product or (2) the products associated with reducing or arousing certain emotions. For more subtle or sensitive emotions or products, projective techniques (see Exhibit 11–2, page 308) can provide useful insights.[8]

Reacting to Problem Recognition

Once a consumer problem is identified, the manager may structure the marketing mix to solve the problem. This can involve product development or alteration, modifying channels of distribution, changing pricing policy, or revising advertising strategy. For example, many people want to reduce their fat and salt intake for health and/or weight control reasons. They also want to continue to enjoy their meals and snacks. Frito-Lay has developed *Rold Gold®* fat-free, reduced-sodium pretzels in response to this consumer problem (see Managerial Application 15–1).

As you approach graduation, you will be presented with opportunities to purchase insurance, acquire credit cards, and solve other problems associated with the onset of financial independence and a major change in lifestyle. These opportunities, which will be presented through both personal sales contact and advertising media, reflect various firms' knowledge that many individuals in your situation face problems that their products will help solve.

Weekend and night store hours are a response of retailers to the consumer problem of limited weekday shopping opportunities. Solving this problem has become particularly important to families with both spouses employed.

The examples described above represent only a small sample of the ways in which marketers react to consumer problem recognition. Basically, each firm must be aware of the consumer problems it can solve, which consumers have these problems, and the situations in which the problems arise.

Activating Problem Recognition

There are occasions when the manager will want to influence problem recognition rather than react to it. In the earlier example involving the fire starters, Timberlane faced having to activate problem recognition in order to sell its product as a fireplace starter. Toy marketers are attempting to reduce their dependence on the Christmas season by activating problem recognition at other times of the year. For example, Fisher-Price has had "rainy day" and "sunny day" promotions in the spring and summer months.

Generic versus Selective Problem Recognition Two basic approaches to causing problem recognition are *generic problem recognition* and *selective problem recognition*. These are analogous to the economic concepts of generic and selective demand.

Generic problem recognition involves a *discrepancy that a variety of brands within a product category can reduce*. Generally, a firm will attempt to influence generic problem recognition when the problem is latent or of low importance and:

MANAGERIAL APPLICATION

15–1

A Product Designed to Solve an Emerging Consumer Problem

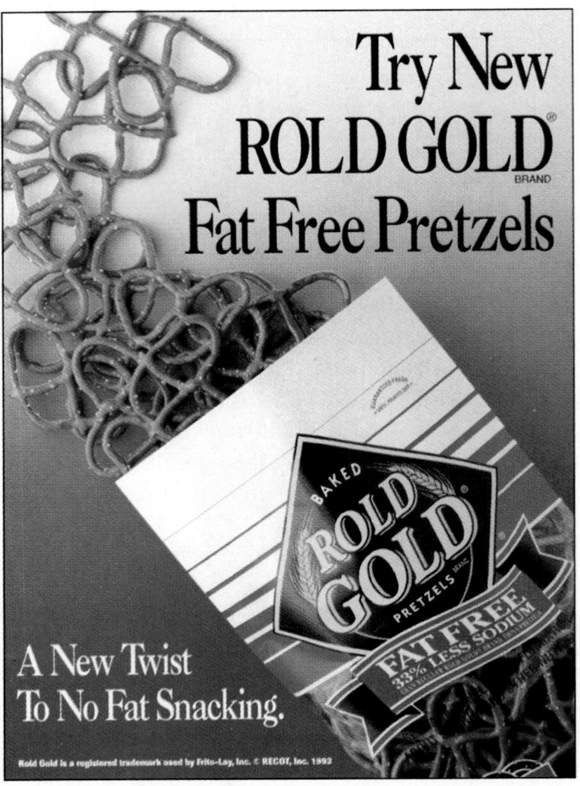

1. It is early in the product life cycle.
2. The firm has a very high percentage of the market.
3. External search after problem recognition is apt to be limited.
4. It is an industrywide cooperative effort.

Door-to-door sales for such products as encyclopedias and vacuum cleaners attempt to arouse problem recognition, in part because the salesperson can then limit external search to one brand. Cooperative advertising frequently focuses on generic problem recognition. Likewise, virtual monopolies such as U.S. Tobacco in the moist snuff industry (Skoal, Copenhagen, Happy Days) can focus on generic problem recognition since any sales increase will probably come to their brands. However, a smaller firm that generates generic problem recognition for its product category may be generating more sales for its competitors than for itself.

The advertisement for *ACES* shown in Managerial Application 15–2 is heavily focused on generic demand. Note that the headline and the top half of the copy attempts to make individuals aware of the health harm caused by free radicals and the ability of certain vitamins (antioxidants) to minimize this harm. The balance of the ad does focus on the

MANAGERIAL APPLICATION 15–2

An Advertisement That Will Generate Generic Demand

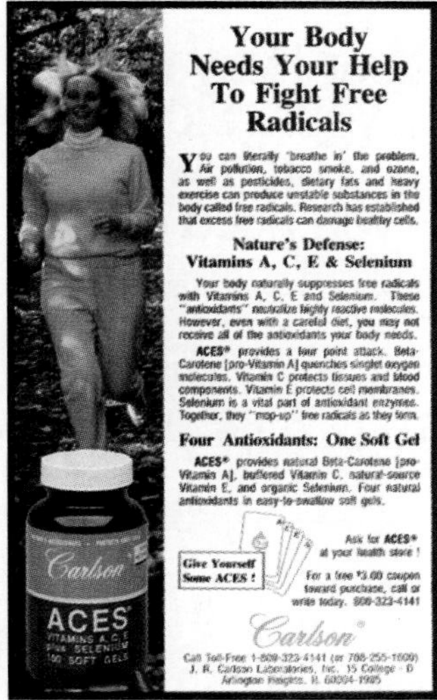

ACES brand to build selective demand. Since antioxidant vitamin supplements (as a single supplement) are new, as is the knowledge of the role of free radicals in health, such generic advertising is appropriate.

Contrast the *ACES* ad shown in Managerial Application 15–2 with the *Tums®* ad shown in Managerial Application 15–3. While both attempt to trigger a health-related problem recognition, the *Tums®* ad is much more *focused on creating selective demand.* The Tums package is the visual center of the ad and the copy stresses the unique advantages of *Tums®*. Firms attempt to cause selective problem recognition to gain or maintain market share, while increasing generic problem recognition generally results in an expansion of the total market.

Approaches to Activating Problem Recognition How can a firm influence problem recognition? Recall that problem recognition is a function of the (1) *importance* and (2) *magnitude* of a discrepancy between the desired state and an existing state. Thus, the firm can attempt to influence the size of the discrepancy by altering the desired state or the perceptions of the existing state. Or, the firm can attempt to influence the perception of the importance of an existing discrepancy.

There is evidence that individuals and product categories both differ in their responsiveness to attempts to change desired or perceived existing states.[9] Thus, marketers must be sure that the selected approach is appropriate for their product category and target market.

Influence Desired State Many marketing efforts attempt to influence the desired state. That is, marketers often advertise the benefits their products will provide, hoping that these benefits will become desired by consumers. The BMW ad shown in Managerial

MANAGERIAL APPLICATION

15–3

An Advertisement That Will Generate Selective Demand

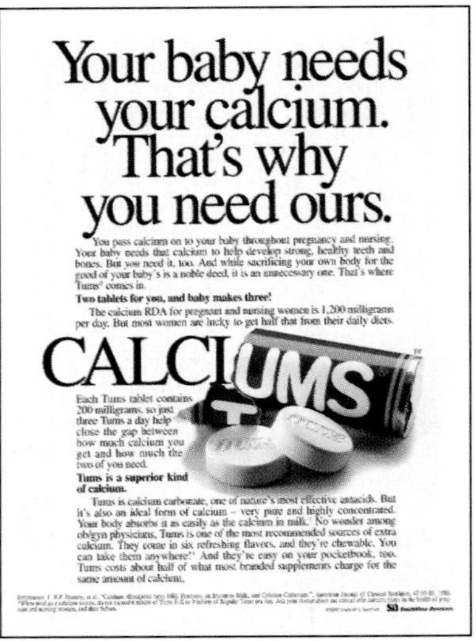

Application 15–4 promotes a state of excitement and personal freedom. It is attempting to influence the desired state of its target market with respect to commuting and pleasure riding.

Influence Perceptions of Existing State It is also possible to influence perceptions of the existing state through advertisements. Many personal care and social products take this approach. ''Even your best friend won't tell you . . .'' or ''Mary is a great worker but her coffee . . .'' are examples of messages designed to generate concern about an existing state. The desired state is assumed to be fresh breath and good coffee. These messages are designed to cause individuals to question if their existing state coincides with this desired state.

The ad for Baby Orajel® in Managerial Application 15–5 on page 436 attempts to make parents aware that the actual state of their children's teeth may not be as healthy as they had thought. This would trigger problem recognition that could be solved with the Baby Orajel® product.

The Timing of Problem Recognition Consumers often recognize problems at times when purchasing a solution is difficult or impossible:

- We decide we need snow chains when caught in a blizzard.
- We become aware of a need for insurance *after* an accident.
- We desire a flower bed full of tulips in the spring but forgot to plant bulbs in the fall.
- We want cold medicine when we are sick and don't feel like driving to the store.

In some instances, marketers attempt to help consumers solve such problems after they arise. For example, some pharmacies will make home deliveries. However, the more

MANAGERIAL APPLICATION 15–4

An Advertisement Designed to Influence the Desired State

common strategy is to trigger problem recognition in advance of the actual problem. That is, it is often to the consumer's and marketer's advantage for the consumer to recognize and solve potential problems *before* they become actual problems.

While some companies, particularly insurance companies, attempt to initiate potential problem recognition through mass media advertising, others rely more on point-of-purchase displays and other in-store influences (see Chapter 18). Retailers, as well as manufacturers, are involved in this activity. For example, prior to snow season, the following sign was placed on a large rack of snow shovels in the main aisle of a large hardware store:

> REMEMBER LAST WINTER
> WHEN YOU *NEEDED*
> A SNOW SHOVEL?
> THIS YEAR
> BE PREPARED!

MANAGERIAL APPLICATION

15-5

An Advertisement Focusing on the Actual State

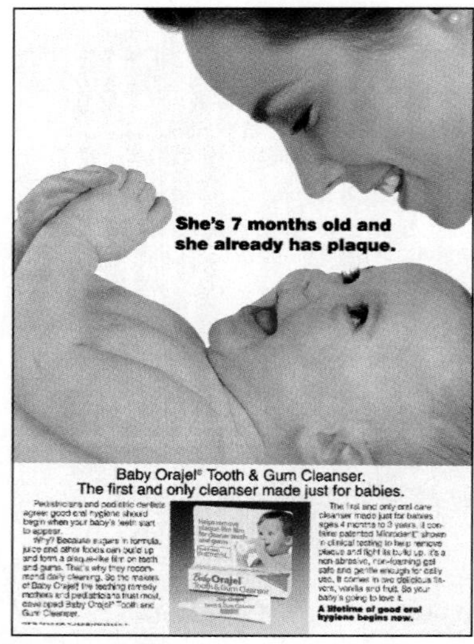

Suppressing Problem Recognition

As we have seen, competition, consumer organizations, and governmental agencies occasionally introduce information in the marketplace that triggers problem recognition that particular marketers would prefer to avoid. The American tobacco industry has made strenuous attempts to minimize consumer recognition of the health problems associated with cigarette smoking. For example, a Newport cigarette advertisement showed a happy, laughing couple under the headline, ''Alive with pleasure.'' This could easily be interpreted as an attempt to minimize any problem recognition caused by the mandatory warning at the bottom of the advertisement, ''Warning: The Surgeon General has determined that cigarette smoking is dangerous to your health.''

Makers of brands with substantial habitual or limited decision purchases do not want their current customers to recognize problems with their brands. Effective quality control and distribution (limited out-of-stock situations) are important in these circumstances. Packages and package inserts that assure the consumer of the wisdom of the purchase are also common.

SUMMARY

Consumer decision making becomes more extensive and complex as *purchase involvement* increases. The lowest level of purchase involvement is represented by *habitual decisions*: a problem is recognized, long-term memory provides a single preferred brand, that brand is purchased, and only limited postpurchase evaluation occurs. As one moves from *limited decision making* toward *extended decision making*, information search increases, alternative evaluation becomes more extensive and complex, and postpurchase evaluation becomes more thorough.

Problem recognition involves the existence of a discrepancy between the consumer's desired state (what the consumer would like) and the actual state (what the consumer perceives as already existing). Both the desired state and the actual state are influenced by the consumer's lifestyle and current situation. If the discrepancy between these two states is sufficiently large and important, the consumer will begin to search for a solution to the problem.

A number of factors beyond the control of the marketing manager can affect problem recognition. The desired state is commonly influenced by:

1. Culture/subculture.
2. Social status.
3. Reference groups.
4. Household characteristics.
5. Financial status/expectations.
6. Previous decisions.
7. Individual development.
8. Motives.
9. Emotions.
10. Current situation.

The actual state is influenced by:

1. Past decisions.
2. Normal depletion.
3. Product/brand performance.
4. Individual development.
5. Emotions.
6. Government/consumer groups.
7. Availability of products.
8. Current situation.

Before marketing managers can respond to problem recognition generated by outside factors, they must be able to *measure* consumer problems. Surveys and focus groups using *activity*, *product*, or *problem analysis* are commonly used to measure problem recognition. *Human factors research* approaches the same task from an observational perspective. *Emotion research* focuses on the emotional causes of and responses to product purchase and use.

Once managers are aware of problem recognition patterns among their target market, they can react by designing the marketing mix to solve the recognized problem. This may involve product development or repositioning, a change in store hours, a different price, or a host of other marketing strategies.

Marketing managers often want to influence problem recognition rather than react to it. They may desire to generate *generic problem recognition*, a discrepancy which a variety of brands within a product category can reduce; or to induce *selective problem recognition*, a discrepancy which only one brand in the product category can solve.

Attempts to *activate problem recognition* generally do so by focusing on the desired state. However, attempts to make consumers aware of negative aspects of the existing state are also common. In addition, marketers attempt to influence the timing of problem recognition by making consumers aware of potential problems before they arise.

Finally, managers attempt to minimize or suppress problem recognition by current users of their brands.

REVIEW QUESTIONS

1. What is meant by *purchase involvement*? How does it differ from product involvement?
2. What factors influence purchase involvement?
3. How does consumer decision making change as purchase involvement increases?
4. What is the role of *emotion* in the consumer decision process?
5. How do *habitual*, *limited*, and *extended decision making* differ? How do the two types of habitual decision making differ?

6. What is *problem recognition*?
7. What influences the motivation to resolve a recognized problem?
8. What is the difference between an *active* and an *inactive problem*? Why is this distinction important?
9. How does lifestyle relate to problem recognition?
10. What are the main uncontrollable factors that influence the *desired* state?
11. What are the main uncontrollable factors that influence the *existing* state?
12. How can you measure problem recognition?
13. In what ways can marketers react to problem recognition? Give several examples.
14. How does *generic problem recognition* differ from *selective problem recognition*? Under what conditions would a firm attempt to influence generic problem recognition? Why?
15. How can a firm influence problem recognition? Give examples.
16. How can a firm suppress problem recognition?

DISCUSSION QUESTIONS

17. What products do you think *generally* are associated with habitual, limited, and extended decision making? Under what conditions, if any, would these products be associated with a different form of decision making?
18. What products do you think *generally* are purchased or used for emotional reasons? How would the decision process differ for an emotion-driven purchase compared to a more functional purchase?
19. What products do you think *generally* are associated with brand loyal habitual decision making, and which with repeat purchase habitual decision making? Justify your response.
20. Describe two purchases you have made using habitual decision making, two using limited decision making, and two using extended decision making. What caused you to use each type of decision process?
21. Describe five recent purchases you have made. What uncontrollable factors, if any, triggered problem recognition? Did they affect the desired state, the actual state, or both?
22. How would you measure consumer problems among:
    a. College students.
    b. Pre-teens.
    c. Snow boarders.
    d. New homeowners.
    e. Vegetarians.
    f. Newly retired individuals.
23. How would you determine the existance of consumer problems of relevance to a marketer of _______.
    a. Camping equipment.
    b. Personal computers.
    c. Beauty aids.
    d. Children's clothing.
    e. Pet products.
    f. Fast foods.
24. What factors will contribute to problem recognition for you following graduation? How might each of these factors affect your lifestyle and cause changes in your desired state for products and services? Which products and services might you now view as less satisfactory, causing you to seek better solutions in the form of more personally satisfying products and services?
25. Discuss the types of products that resolve specific problems which occur for most consumers at different stages of their household life cycle.
26. How would you activate problem recognition for:
    a. United Way.
    b. Clausthaler (a nonalcoholic beer).
    c. Eddie Bauer men's cologne.
    d. Hush Puppy shoes.
    e. AIDS prevention.
    f. Vegetarian fast-food chain.
27. Name several products, brands, or companies that could reasonably encourage generic problem recognition. Justify your selection.
28. How would you influence the time of problem recognition for:
    a. Life insurance.
    b. Toys as gifts.
    c. Health checkups.
    d. Car tires.
    e. Swimsuits.
    f. Sunscreen.

APPLICATION EXERCISES

29. Interview five other students and identify three consumer problems they have recognized. For each problem, determine:
    a. The relative importance of the problem.
    b. How the problem occurred.
    c. What caused the problem (i.e., change in desired or actual states).
    d. What action they have taken.
    e. What action is planned to resolve each problem.
30. Find and describe an advertisement that is attempting to activate problem recognition. Analyze the advertisement in terms of the type of problem and the action the ad is suggesting. Also, discuss any changes you would recommend to improve the effectiveness of the ad in terms of activating problem recognition.
31. Interview five other students and identify three recent instances when they engaged in habitual, limited, and extended decision making (a total of nine decisions). What specific factors appear to be associated with each type of decision?
32. Interview five other students and identify six products that each buys using a habitual decision process. Also, identify those that are based on brand loyalty and those that are merely repeat purchases. What characteristics, if any, distinguish the brand loyal products from the repeat products?
33. Find and describe two advertisements or point-of-purchase displays that attempt to influence the timing of problem recognition. Evaluate their likely effectiveness.
34. Using a sample from a relevant market segment, conduct an activity analysis for an activity that interests you. Prepare a report on the marketing opportunities suggested by your analysis.
35. Using a sample from a relevant market segment, conduct a product analysis for a product that interests you. Prepare a report on the marketing opportunities suggested by your analysis.
36. Conduct a problem analysis, using a sample of college freshmen. Prepare a report on the marketing opportunities suggested by your analysis.
37. Conduct an emotion research analysis, using college students. Prepare a report on the marketing opportunities suggested by your analysis.
38. Interview five smokers and ascertain what problems they see associated with smoking.
39. Interview someone from the local office of the American Cancer Society concerning their attempts to generate problem recognition among smokers.

REFERENCES

[1]J. C. Mowen, ''Beyond Consumer Decision Making,'' *Journal of Consumer Marketing*, Winter 1988, pp. 15–25.

[2]Based on A. A. Mitchell, ''Involvement: A Potentially Important Mediator of Consumer Behavior,'' in *Advances in Consumer Research VI*, ed. W. L. Wilkie (Chicago: Association for Consumer Research, 1979), pp. 191–96. See also D. R. Rahtz and D. L. Moore, ''Product Class Involvement and Purchase Intent,'' *Psychology & Marketing*, Summer 1989, pp. 113–27; B. Mittal, ''Measuring Purchase-Decision Involvement,'' *Psychology & Marketing*, Summer 1989, pp. 147–62; M. P. Venkatraman, ''Involvement and Risk,'' *Psychology & Marketing*, Fall 1989, pp. 229–47; T. Otker, ''The Highly Involved Consumer'' and B. von Keitz, ''Consumer Involvement,'' both in *Marketing and Research Today*, February 1990, pp. 30–36 and 37–45.

[3]Based on H. H. Kassarjian, ''Low Involvement: A Second Look,'' in *Advances in Consumer Research VIII*, ed. K. B. Monroe (Chicago: Association for Consumer Research, 1981), pp. 31–33; and M. E. Slama and A. Tashchian, ''Selected Socioeconomic and Demographic Characteristics Associated with Purchasing Involvement,'' *Journal of Marketing*, Winter 1985, pp. 72–82.

[4]W. D. Hoyer, ''An Examination of Consumer Decision Making for a Common Repeat Purchase Product,'' *Journal of Consumer Research*, December 1984, pp. 822–29; and A. d'Astous, I. Bensouda, and J. Guindon, ''A Re-examination of Consumer Decision Making for a Repeat Purchase Product,'' in *Advances in Consumer Research XVI*, ed. T. K. Srull (Provo, Utah: Association for Consumer Research, 1989), pp. 433–38.

[5]See B. Mittal, ''Must Consumer Involvement Always Imply More Information Search?'' in *Advances XVI*, ed. Srull.

[6]See M. DeMoss and Mick D.G., ''Self-Gifts,'' *Journal of Consumer Research*, December 1990, pp. 322–32; and R. Belk, ''Materialism,'' *Journal of Consumer Research*, December 1985, pp. 265–80.

[7]For a more thorough treatment, see G. C. Bruner II, ''Recent Contributions to the Theory of Problem Recognition,'' in *1985 AMA*

Educator's Proceedings, ed. R. F. Lusch et al. (Chicago: American Marketing Association, 1985), pp. 11–15; and G. C. Bruner II and R. J. Pomazal, "Problem Recognition: The Crucial First Stage of the Consumer Decision Process," *Journal of Consumer Marketing*, Winter 1988, pp. 53–63.

[8]See E. Day, "Share of Heart," *Journal of Consumer Research*, Winter 1989, pp. 5–12.

[9]Bruner and Pomazal, "Problem Recognition"; G. C. Bruner II, "The Effect of Problem Recognition Style on Information Seeking," *Journal of the Academy of Marketing Science*, Winter 1987, pp. 33–41; G. C. Bruner II, "Profiling Desired State Type Problem Recognizers," *Journal of Business and Psychology*, no. 2, 1989, pp. 167–87; and G. C. Bruner II, "Problem Recognition Style," *Journal of Consumer Studies and Home Economics*, no. 14, 1990, pp. 29–40.

CHAPTER

16

INFORMATION SEARCH

The computer game puts the player in the Big Bend National Park in Texas. The objective is to maneuver through the rugged country to photograph wildlife and beat a time deadline. The player has a camera, a map, a cellular phone, and a Jeep Grand Cherokee. The game diskette provides more than the game, however. It is, in effect, a high-tech sales brochure. It allows users to review all the vehicles in the Jeep/Eagle line. The viewer can obtain specifications, change options and colors, compare various models with those of competitors, and calculate monthly payment schedules.

Jeep runs ads in weekly news magazines, business publications, and lifestyle magazines, with an 800 number consumers can use to order the game for $6.95. Jeep, like other marketers using computer diskettes to communicate with potential customers, is trying to reach younger, affluent, technologically oriented males. According to a Jeep executive: *Our buyers tend to be very educated, and they're intensive researchers. A lot of them are looking for alternative forms of information.*

In addition to Jeep, Cadillac, Buick, Ford, BMW, Volvo, and Nissan have used interactive software to promote their automobiles. Buick pioneered this approach in 1987 and has distributed more than a million diskettes since then. Buick executives credit the program with helping them capture sales from import owners who tend to be interested in high-tech innovations. Not only is this approach to communicating with customers innovative, Buick's current diskette contains a trivia game on U.S. innovation, including references to Buick accomplishments. Its prior diskette included a golf game. Ford's Diskette contains a driving simulation.

According to Dennis Snyder, president of the firm that developed a number of these diskettes: *Interaction is becoming the name of the game. People want to participate, not just passively watch advertising.*[1]

Reaching today's consumer is an extremely challenging task. While many consumers are active searchers and want to be able to interact with the advertisement, other purchasers of the same product are willing to spend little or no effort to obtain product or brand information before making a purchase.

Consumers continually recognize problems and opportunities, so internal and external searches for information to solve these problems are ongoing processes. Searching for information is not free. Information search involves mental as well as physical activities that consumers must perform. It takes time, energy, money, and can often require giving up more desirable activities.

The benefits of information search, however, often outweigh the cost of search. For example, search may produce a lower price, a preferred style of merchandise, a higher quality product, a reduction in perceived risk, or greater confidence in the choice. In addition, the physical and mental processes involved in information search are, on occasion, rewarding in themselves. Finally, we must keep in mind that consumers acquire a substantial amount of relevant information without deliberate search—through low-involvement learning (Chapter 10).

This chapter examines six questions related to information search:

1. What is the nature of information search?
2. What types of information are sought?
3. What sources of information are used?
4. How extensive is external information search?

5. Why do consumers engage in external search?
6. What marketing strategies can be developed based on patterns of search behavior?

NATURE OF INFORMATION SEARCH

Once a problem is recognized, relevant information from long-term memory is used to determine if a satisfactory solution is known, what the characteristics of potential solutions are, what are appropriate ways to compare solutions, and so forth. This is **internal search.** If a resolution is not reached through internal search, then the search process is focused on external stimuli relevant to solving the problem. This is **external search.**

A great many problems are resolved by the consumer using only previously stored information. If, in response to a problem, a consumer recalls a single, satisfactory solution (brand or store), no further information search or evaluation may occur. The consumer purchases the recalled brand and *habitual decision making* has occurred. For example, a consumer who catches a cold may recall that Dristan nasal spray provided relief in the past. Dristan then is purchased at the nearest store without further information search or evaluation.

Likewise, a consumer may notice a new product in a store because of the attention-attracting power of a point-of-purchase display. He or she reads about the attributes of the product and recalls an unresolved problem that these attributes would resolve. The purchase is made without seeking additional information. This represents *limited decision making* involving mainly internal information.

Had the consumer in the example above looked for other brands that would perform the same task or looked at another store for a lower price, we would have an example of limited decision making using both internal and external information. As we move into *extended decision making*, the relative importance of external information search tends to increase. However, even in extended decision making, internal information often provides some or all of the appropriate alternatives, evaluative criteria, and characteristics of various alternatives.

External information can include:

- The opinions, attitudes, behaviors, and feelings of friends, neighbors, and relatives.
- Professional information that is provided in pamphlets, articles, books, and personal contacts.
- Direct experiences with the product through inspection or trial.
- Marketer-generated information presented in advertisements and displays and by sales personnel.

Deliberate external search (as well as low-involvement learning) also occurs in the absence of problem recognition.[2] Ongoing or exploratory search is done both to acquire information for later use and because the process itself is pleasurable. For example, individuals highly involved with an activity such as tennis are apt to seek information about tennis-related products on an ongoing basis without a recognized problem with their existing tennis equipment. This search could involve reading ads in tennis magazines, visiting tennis equipment shops, observing professionals on television, and/or talking with and observing fellow players and local professionals. These activities would provide the individual both pleasure and information for future use.

Like search triggered by problem recognition, ongoing search is a function of individual, product, market, and situational factors. The outcome of search includes increased

FIGURE 16–1

Information Search in Consumer Decisions

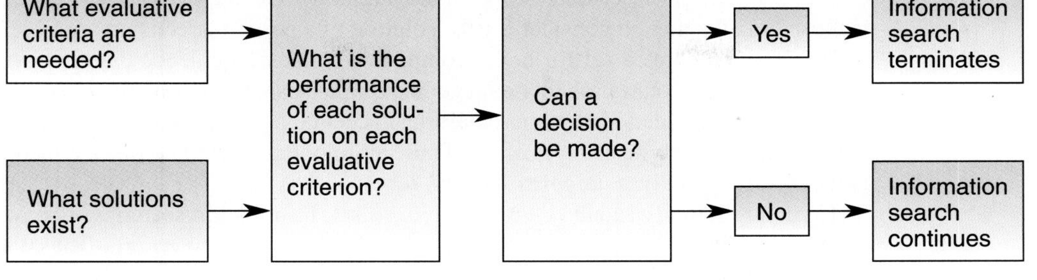

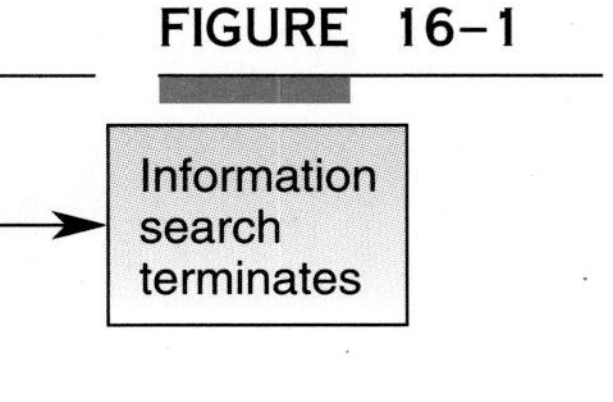

product and market knowledge leading to future buying efficiencies and enhanced personal influence, increased unplanned purchases, and personal satisfaction or pleasure.[3]

TYPES OF INFORMATION SOUGHT

A consumer decision requires information on the following:

- The appropriate evaluative criteria for the solution of a problem.
- The existence of various alternative solutions.
- The performance level or characteristic of each alternative solution on each evaluative criterion.

Information search, then, seeks each of these three types of information, as shown in Figure 16–1.

Evaluative Criteria

Suppose you are provided with money to purchase a personal computer, perhaps as a graduation present. Assuming you have not been in the market for a computer recently, your first thought would probably be: "What features do I want in a computer?" You would then engage in internal search to determine the features or characteristics required to meet your needs. These desired characteristics are your *evaluative criteria.* If you have had limited experience with computers, you might also engage in external search to learn which characteristics a good computer should have. You could check with friends, read *Consumer Reports,* talk with sales personnel, or personally inspect several computers. Thus, one potential objective of both internal and external search is *the determination of appropriate evaluative criteria.* A detailed discussion of evaluative criteria appears in Chapter 17.

Appropriate Alternatives

After (and while) searching for appropriate evaluative criteria, you would probably seek *appropriate alternatives*—in this case brands or, possibly, stores. Again, you would start with an internal search. You might say to yourself:

> IBM, Compaq, Toshiba, Apple, Epson, Radio Shack, AST, and HP all make personal computers. After my brother's experience, I'd never buy Radio Shack, I've heard good things about IBM, Apple, and Compaq. I think I'll check them out.

The eight brands that you thought of are known as the **awareness set**. The awareness set is composed of three subcategories of considerable importance to marketers.[4] The three brands that you have decided to investigate are known as the **evoked set**. An evoked set is those brands one will consider for the solution of a particular consumer problem. If you do not have an evoked set for home computers, or lack confidence that your evoked set is adequate, you would probably engage in external search to learn about additional alternatives. You may also learn about additional acceptable brands as an incidental aspect of moving through the decision process. Thus, an important outcome of information search is the development of a complete evoked set.

If you are initially satisfied with the evoked set, information search will be focused on the performance of the brands in the evoked set on the evaluative criteria. Thus, the evoked set is of particular importance in structuring subsequent information search and purchase.

The brand you found completely unworthy of further consideration is a member of what is called the **inept set**. Brands in the inept set are actively disliked by the consumer. Positive information about these brands is not likely to be processed even if it is readily available.

In our example, AST, Toshiba, Epson, and HP were brands of which you were aware but were basically indifferent toward. They compose what is known as an **inert set**. Consumers will generally accept favorable information about brands in the inert set, although they do not seek out such information. Brands in this set are generally acceptable when preferred brands are not available. Thus, the eight brands in the initial awareness set can be subdivided as follows:

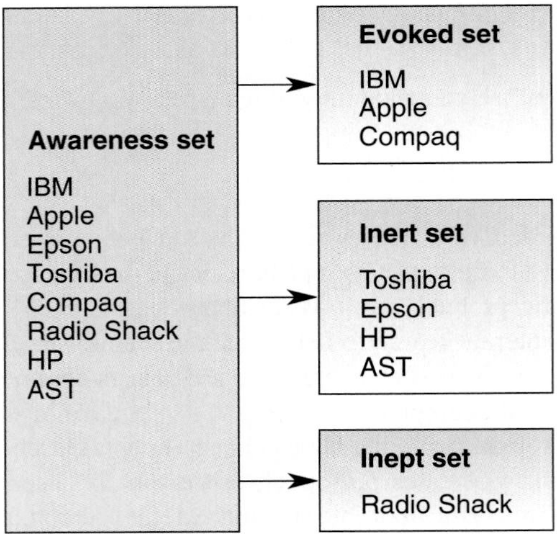

Figure 16–2 illustrates the general relationships among these classes of alternatives.

Figure 16–3 illustrates the results of several studies comparing the size of the awareness and evoked sets for a variety of products. Notice that in all cases the evoked set is substantially smaller than the awareness set. Since the evoked set generally is the one from which consumers make final evaluations and decisions, *marketing strategy that focuses only on creating awareness may be inadequate.*

Alternative Characteristics

To choose among the brands in the evoked set, the consumer compares them on the relevant evaluative criteria. This process requires the consumer to gather information about *each brand on each pertinent evaluative criterion.* In our example of a computer purchase, you

Categories of Decision Alternatives

FIGURE 16–2

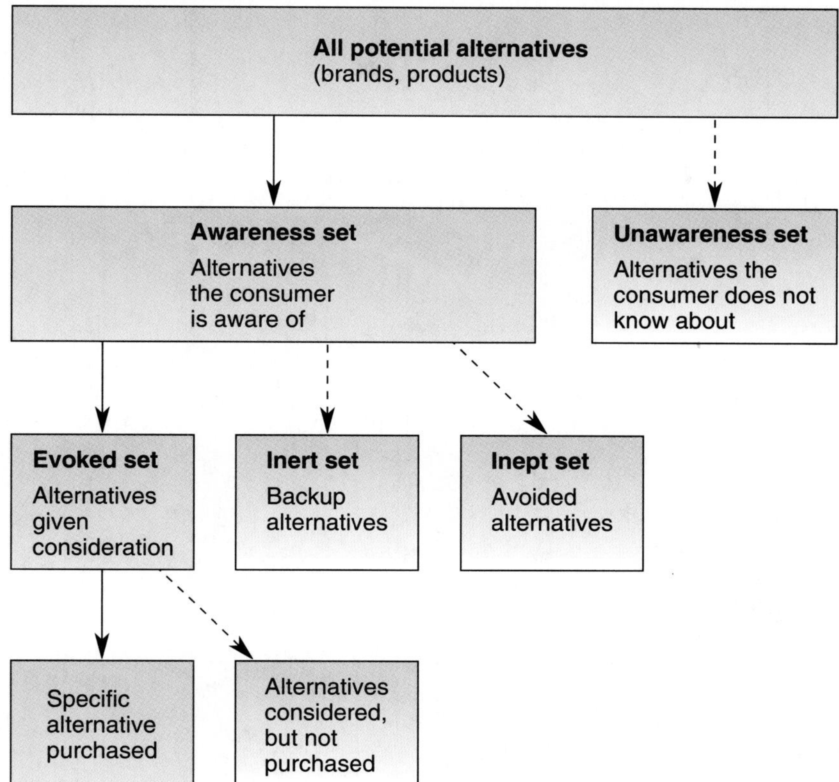

might collect information on the price, memory, speed, weight, screen clarity, and ability to expand memory for each brand you are considering.

In summary, consumers engage in internal and external search for (1) appropriate evaluative criteria, (2) the existence of potential solutions, and (3) the characteristics of potential solutions. However, extensive search generally occurs for only a few comsumption decisions. Habitual and limited decision making which involve little or no active external search are the rule. In addition, consumers acquire substantial information without deliberate search through low-involvement learning.

SOURCES OF INFORMATION

Refer again to our rather pleasant example of receiving cash with which to purchase a personal computer. We suggested that you might recall what you know about computers, check with friends, consult *Consumer Reports*, talk with sales personnel, or personally inspect several computers to collect relevant information. These represent the five primary sources of information available to consumers:

1. *Memory* of past searches, personal experiences, and low-involvement learning.
2. *Personal sources*, such as friends and family.
3. *Independent sources*, such as consumer groups and government agencies.

FIGURE 16–3 Awareness and Evoked Sets for Various Products

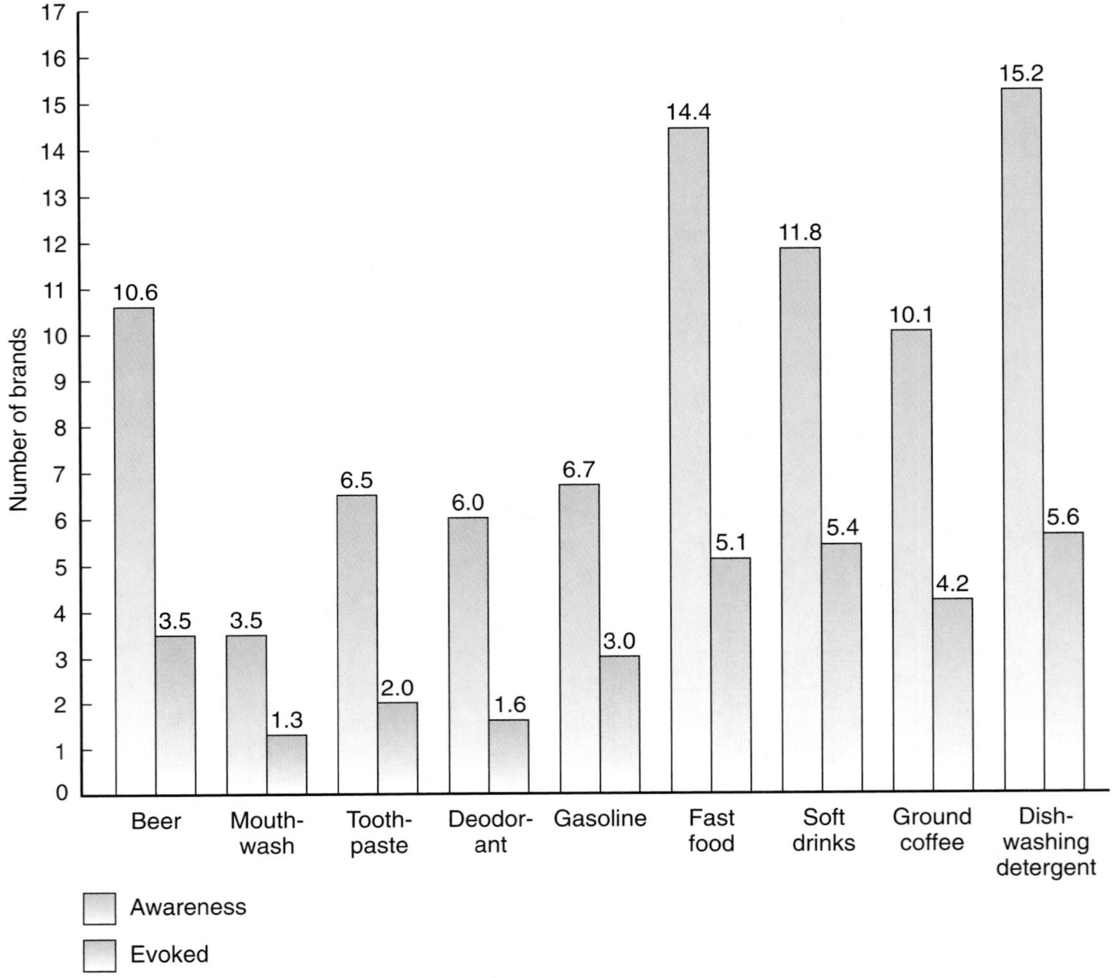

Source: J. Roberts, ''A Grounded Model of Consideration Set Size and Composition,'' in *Advances in Consumer Research XVI,* ed. T. K. Srull (Provo, Utah: Association for Consumer Research, 1989), p. 750.

4. *Marketing sources*, such as sales personnel and advertising.
5. *Experiential sources*, such as inspection or product trial.

These sources are shown in Figure 16–4.

Internal information is the primary source used by most consumers most of the time (habitual and limited decision making). However, note that information in long-term memory was *initially* obtained from external sources. That is, you may resolve a consumption problem using only or mainly stored information. At some point, however, you acquired that information from an external source, such as direct product experience, friends, or low-involvement learning.

Information Sources for a Purchase Decision

FIGURE 16–4

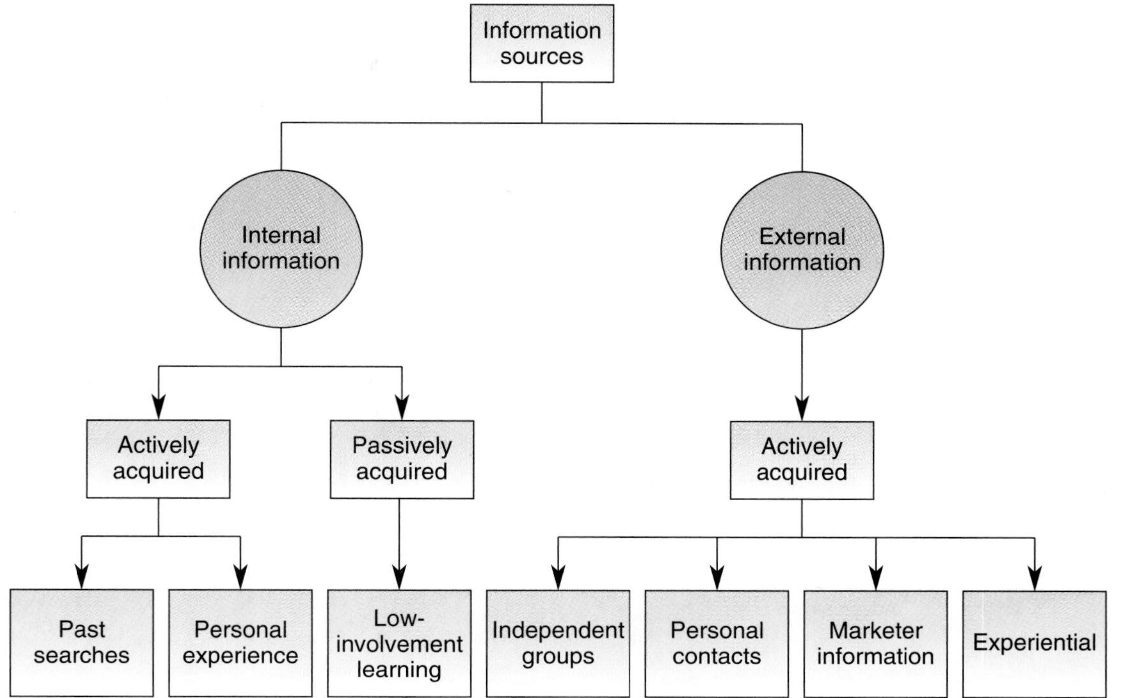

Source: Adapted from H. Beales, M. B. Jagis, S. C. Salop, and R. Staelin, "Consumer Search and Public Policy," *Journal Consumer Research,* June 1981, p. 12.

Marketing-originated messages are only one of five potential information sources, and they are frequently found to be of limited direct value in consumer decisions. Figure 16–5 illustrates the dominant role of personal sources for new residents seeking a professional service (Figure 7–1 illustrates the same phenomenon for a product).[5]

However, marketing activities influence all five sources. Thus, the characteristics of the product, the distribution of the product, and the promotional messages about the product provide the underlying or basic information available in the market. An independent source such as *Consumer Reports* bases its report on the functional characteristics of the product. Personal sources such as friends also must base their information on experience with the product or its promotion (or on other sources that have had contact with the product or its promotion).

A substantial amount of marketing activity is designed to influence the information that consumers will receive from nonmarketing sources. For example, when Johnson & Johnson introduced a new-formula baby bath:

> Product information, demonstrations, monographs, journal ads, and direct-mail programs were targeted at pediatricians and nurses to capitalize on health-care professionals' direct contact with new mothers. Print ads and coupons appeared in baby care publications, and a film exploring the parent-infant bonding process was distributed to teaching centers, hospitals, and medical schools.

FIGURE 16–5

Prepurchase Information Search for Services after a Move

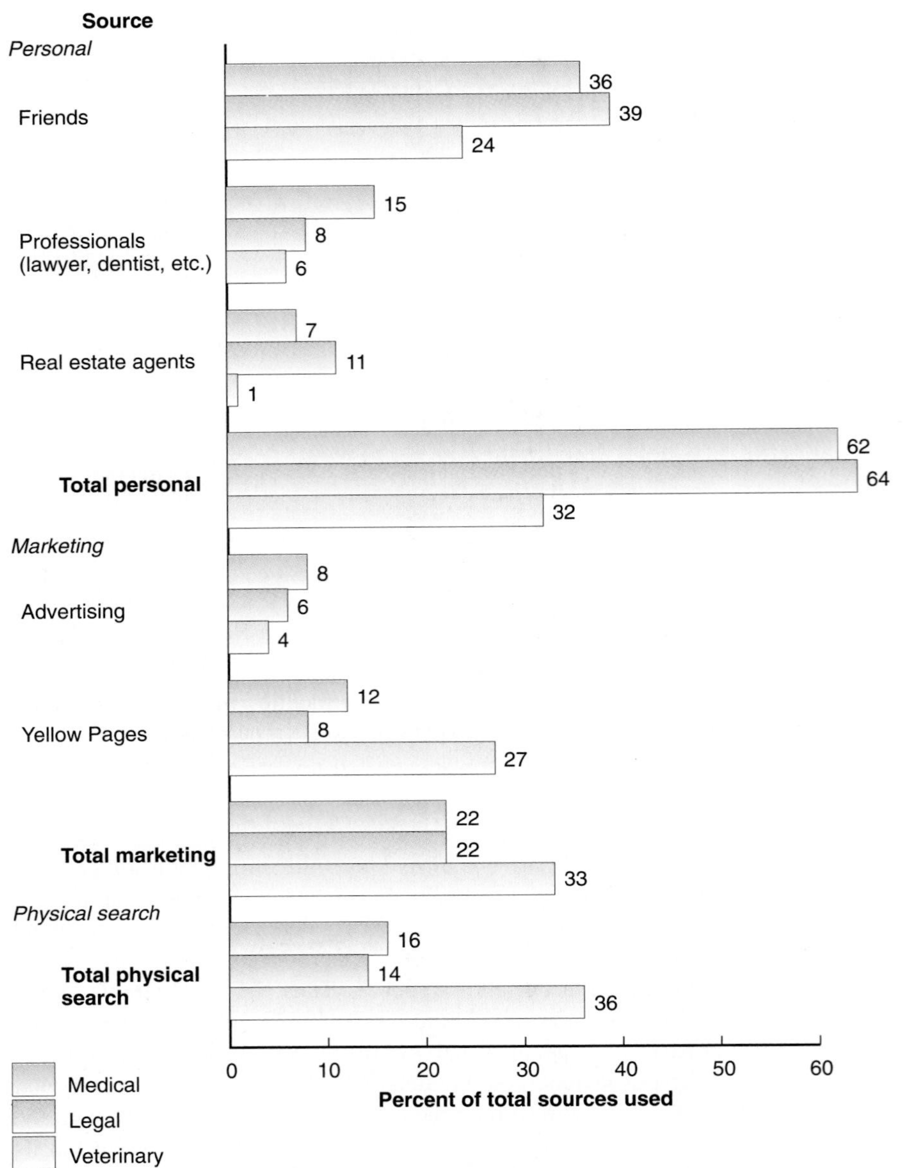

Source: J. B. Freiden and R. E. Goldsmith, ''Prepurchase Information Seeking for Professional Services,'' *Journal of Services Marketing,* Winter 1989, p. 49.

AMOUNT OF EXTERNAL INFORMATION SEARCH

Marketing managers are particularly interested in external information search, as this provides them with direct access to the consumer. How much external information search do consumers actually undertake? Most purchases are a result of habitual or limited decision making and therefore involve little or no external search immediately prior to purchase.

Percent of Purchasers Who Compare Brands or Models before Buying

FIGURE 16–6

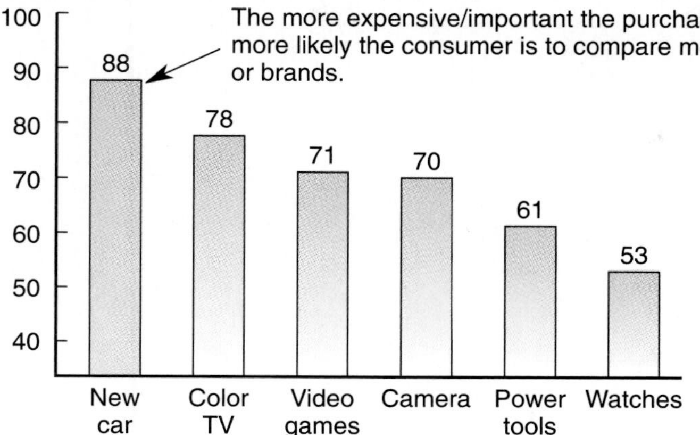

Source: *Warranties Rule Consumer Follow-Up* (Washington, D.C.: Federal Trade Commission, 1984), p. 26.

This is particularly true for relatively low-priced convenience goods such as soft drinks, canned foods, and detergents. Therefore, the discussion in this section focuses on major purchases such as appliances, professional services, and automobiles. Intuitively, we would expect substantial amounts of direct external search prior to such purchases.

Different measures of external information search have been used: (1) number of stores visited; (2) number of alternatives considered; (3) number of personal sources used; and (4) overall or combination measures. Each of these measures of search effort assesses a different aspect of behavior, yet each measure supports one observation: *external information search is skewed toward limited search, with the greatest proportion of consumers performing little external search immediately prior to purchase.*

Surveys of *shopping behavior* have shown a significant percent of all durable purchases are made after visiting only one store.[6] The *number of alternatives* considered also shows a limited amount of prepurchase search. Figure 16–6 indicates that for some product categories, such as watches, almost half of the purchasers considered only one brand *and* one model. Another study found that 27 percent of the purchasers of major appliances considered only one brand.[7]

Measures of the use of *personal* and other *nonmarket* sources also show somewhat limited levels of search. Approximately 40 percent of the purchasers of a new appliance consulted others, and one-fourth consulted *Consumer Reports*.[8]

Based on six separate studies that span more than 30 years, two product categories, four services, and two countries, we can classify consumers in terms of their total external information search as (1) nonsearchers, (2) limited information searchers, and (3) extended information searchers.[9] This classification system is shown in Table 16–1. Approximately half of the purchases are preceded by virtually no external information search; about one-third are associated with limited information search; and only 12 percent involve extensive information seeking prior to the purchase.

A given individual might exhibit extended search for one purchase, limited for one, and be a nonsearcher for yet another. However, extended information seeking has been found to be characteristic of some individuals.[10]

TABLE 16–1 Total Information-Seeking Behavior

Search Behavior	Katona and Mueller (1955)*	Newman and Staelin (1972)*	Claxton, Fry, and Portis (1974)*	Kiel and Layton (1981)†	Urbany, Dickson, and Wilkie (1989)*	Freiden and Goldsmith (1989)‡
Nonsearchers	65%	49%	65%	24%	24%	55%
Limited Information Seekers	25	38	27	58	45	38
Extended Information Seekers	10	13	8	18	11	7

*American consumers, major appliance.

†Australian consumers, automobiles.

‡American consumers, professional services.

Conclusions on Degree of External Information Search Most consumers engage in minimal external information search *immediately* prior to the purchase of consumer durables. The level of search for less important items is even lower. As you will see in the next section, limited information search does not necessarily mean that the consumer is not following a sound purchasing strategy. Nor does it mean that substantial amounts of internal information are not being used.[11]

COSTS VERSUS BENEFITS OF EXTERNAL SEARCH

Why do 50 percent of the buyers of major appliances described above do little or no external search, while 12 percent engage in extensive external search? Part of the answer lies in the differences between the buyers in terms of their perceptions of the benefits and costs of search associated with a particular purchase situation as shown in Figure 16–7.[12]

The benefits of external information search can be tangible, such as a lower price, a preferred style, or higher quality product. Or the benefits can be intangible in terms of reduced risk, greater confidence in the purchase, or even providing enjoyment.[13] Perceptions of these benefits are likely to vary with the consumer's experience in the market, media habits, and the extent to which the consumer interacts with others or belongs to differing reference groups. Therefore, one reason 50 percent of major appliance buyers do little or no external search is that they do not perceive discernible benefits resulting from such an effort.

Furthermore, acquisition of external information is not free, and consumers may engage in limited search because the costs of search exceed the perceived benefits. The costs of search can be both monetary and nonmonetary. Monetary costs include out-of-pocket expenses related to the search effort, such as the cost of transportation, parking, and time-related costs which include lost wages, lost opportunities, charges for child care, and so forth. Nonmonetary costs of search are less obvious but may have an even greater impact than monetary costs. Almost every external search effort involves some physical and psychological strain. Frustration and conflict between the search task and other more desirable activities, as well as fatigue, may shorten the search effort.

Perceived Costs and Benefits of Consumer Search Guide Search Effort

FIGURE 16–7

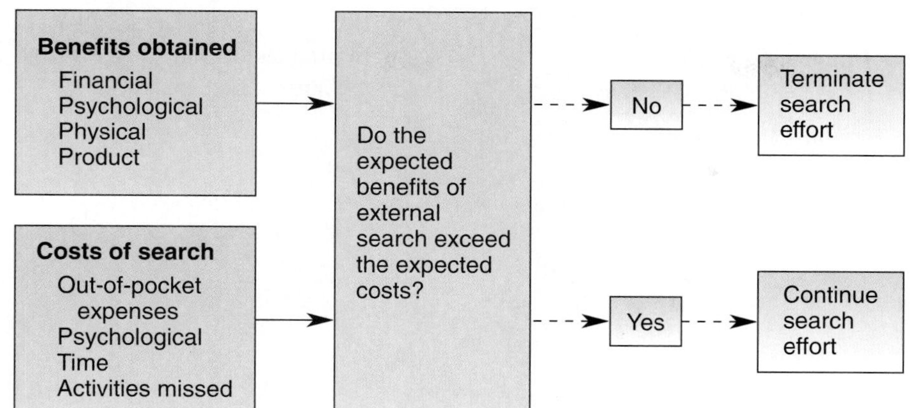

In this section, we are going to examine four basic types of factors that influence the expected benefits and perceived costs of search: *market characteristics, product characteristics, consumer characteristics*, and *situation characteristics*. These four factors and their components are shown in Exhibit 16–1.

Market Characteristics

Market characteristics include the number of alternatives, price range, store distribution, and information availability. It is important to keep in mind that it is the consumer's perception of, or beliefs about, the market characteristics that influence shopping behavior, *not* the actual characteristics.[14] While beliefs and reality are usually related, they often are not identical.

Obviously, the greater the *number of alternatives* (products, stores, brands) available to resolve a particular problem, the more external search there is likely to be. At the extreme, there is no need to search for information in the face of a complete monopoly such as utilities or driver's licenses. Likewise, the *range of prices* among equivalent brands in a product class is a major factor in stimulating external search. For example, shopping 36 retail stores in Tucson for five popular branded toys produced a total low cost of $51.27 and a total high cost of $105.95. Clearly, efficient shopping for these products in this market would provide a significant financial gain.

Store distribution—the number, location, and distances between retail stores in the market—affects the number of store visits a consumer will make before purchase. Because store visits take time, energy, and in many cases money, a close proximity of stores will increase this aspect of external search.

In general, *information availability* is directly related to information use. However, too much information can cause information overload (Chapter 9, page 245) and the use of less information. In addition, readily available information tends to produce learning over time, which may reduce the need for additional external information immediately prior to a purchase. *Advertising, point-of-purchase displays, sales personnel, packages, other consumers*, and *independent sources* such as *Consumer Reports* are major sources of consumer information.

EXHIBIT 16–1

Factors Affecting External Search

Influencing Factor	Increasing the Influencing Factor Causes the Search to:
I. Market characteristics	
A. Number of alternatives	Increase
B. Price range	Increase
C. Store concentration	Increase
D. Information availability	Increase
1. Advertising	
2. Point-of-purchase	
3. Sales personnel	
4. Packaging	
5. Experienced consumers	
6. Independent sources	
II. Product characteristics	
A. Price	Increase
B. Differentiation	Increase
C. Positive products	Increase
III. Consumer characteristics	
A. Learning and experience	Decrease
B. Shopping orientation	Mixed
C. Social status	Increase
D. Age and household life cycle	Mixed
E. Perceived risk	Increase
IV. Situation characteristics	
A. Time availability	Increase
B. Purchase for self	Decrease
C. Pleasant surroundings	Increase
D. Social surroundings	Mixed
E. Physical/mental energy	Increase

Product Characteristics

Product characteristics such as *price level* and *differentiation* tend to influence external search with higher prices and greater differentiation associated with increased external search.

Consumers appear to enjoy shopping for *positive products*—those whose acquisition results in positive reinforcement. Thus, shopping for flowers and plants, dress clothing, sports equipment, and cameras is viewed as a positive experience by most consumers. In contrast, shopping for *negative products*—those whose primary benefit is negative reinforcement (removal of an unpleasant condition)—is viewed as less pleasant. Shopping for groceries, extermination services, and auto repairs is not enjoyed by most individuals. Other things being equal, consumers are more likely to engage in external search for positive products.[15]

Consumer Characteristics

A variety of consumer characteristics affect perceptions of expected benefits, search costs, and the need to carry out a particular level of external information search.[16] A satisfying *experience* with a particular brand is a positively reinforcing process. It increases the probability of a repeat purchase of that brand and decreases the likelihood of external search. As a result, external search is greater for consumers having a limited purchase experience with brands in a particular product category.

However, there is evidence that at least some familiarity with a product class is necessary for external search to occur.[17] For example, external search prior to purchasing a new automobile is high for consumers who have a high level of *general knowledge about cars*, and low for consumers who have a substantial level of *knowledge about existing brands*.[18] Thus, consumers facing a completely unfamiliar product category may feel threatened by the amount of new information or may simply lack sufficient knowledge to conduct an external search.

External search tends to increase with various measures of *social status* (education, occupation, and income), though middle-income individuals search more than those at higher or lower levels.[19] *Age* of the shopper is inversely related to information search. That is, external search appears to decrease as the age of the shopper increases.[20] This may be explained in part by increased learning and product familiarity gained with age. New households and individuals moving into new stages of the *household life cycle* have a greater need for external information than established households.[21]

The *perceived risk* associated with unsatisfactory product performance, either instrumental or symbolic, increases information search prior to purchase.[22] Higher perceived risk is associated with increased search and greater reliance on personal sources of information and personal experiences.

However, perceived risk is unique to the individual. It varies from one consumer to another and for the same consumer from one situation to another. For example, the purchase of a bottle of wine may not involve much perceived risk when buying for one's own consumption. However, the choice of wine may involve considerable perceived risk when buying wine for a dinner party for one's boss. While perceived risk varies across consumers and situations, some products are generally seen as riskier than others (see Exhibit 18–3, page 495). For example, services are generally perceived as riskier than physical products.[23]

Consumers tend to form general approaches or patterns of external search. These general approaches are termed *shopping orientations*.[24] While individuals will exhibit substantial variation from the general pattern across situations and product categories, many do take a stable shopping approach to most products across a wide range of situations (see Exhibit 18–4, page 496).

Situation Characteristics

As was indicated in Chapter 14, situational variables can have a major impact on search behavior. For example, recall that one of the primary reactions of consumers to crowded store conditions is to minimize external information search. *Temporal perspective* is probably the most important situational variable with respect to search behavior. As the time available to solve a particular consumer problem decreases, so does the amount of external information search.[25] Gift-giving situations (*task definition*) tend to increase perceived risk, which, as we have seen, increases external search.[26] Shoppers with limited physical or emotional energy (*antecedent state*) will search for less information than others. Pleasant *physical surroundings* increase the tendency to search for information (at least *within* that outlet). *Social surroundings* can increase or decrease search depending on the nature of the social setting.

EXHIBIT 16–2

Marketing Strategies Based on Information Search Patterns

Brand Position	Target Market Decision-Making Pattern: Habitual Decision Making (no search)	Limited Decision Making (limited search)	Extended Decision Making (extensive search)
Brand in evoked set	Maintenance strategy	Capture strategy	Preference strategy
Brand not in evoked set	Disrupt strategy	Intercept strategy	Acceptance strategy

MARKETING STRATEGIES BASED ON INFORMATION SEARCH PATTERNS

Sound marketing strategies take into account the nature of information search engaged in by the target market prior to purchase. Two dimensions of search are particularly appropriate: the type of decision influences the level of search, and the nature of the evoked set influences the direction of the search. Exhibit 16–2 illustrates a strategy matrix based on these two dimensions. This matrix suggests the six distinct marketing strategies discussed in the following sections.

Maintenance Strategy

If our brand is purchased habitually by the target market, our strategy is to maintain that behavior. This requires consistent attention to product quality, distribution (avoiding out-of-stock situations), and a reinforcement advertising strategy. In addition, we must defend against the disruptive tactics of competitors. Thus, we need to maintain product development and improvements and to counter short-term competitive strategies such as coupons, point-of-purchase displays, or rebates.

Morton salt and Del Monte canned vegetables have large habitual repeat purchaser segments which they have successfully maintained. Budweiser, Marlboro, and Crest have large brand-loyal habitual purchaser segments. They have successfully defended their market positions against assaults by major competitors in recent years. In contrast, Liggett & Myers lost 80 percent of its market share when it failed to engage in maintenance advertising.[27] Quality control problems caused Schlitz to lose substantial market share. Managerial Application 16–1 shows part of Crest's and Tide's maintenance strategies against the challenge of multiple competitors.

Disrupt Strategy

If our brand is not part of the evoked set and our target market engages in habitual decision making, our first task is to *disrupt* the existing decision pattern. This is a difficult task since the consumer does not seek external information or even consider alternative brands before a purchase. Low-involvement learning over time could generate a positive product position for our brand, but this alone would be unlikely to shift behavior.

MANAGERIAL APPLICATION 16–1

Two Maintenance Strategy Ads

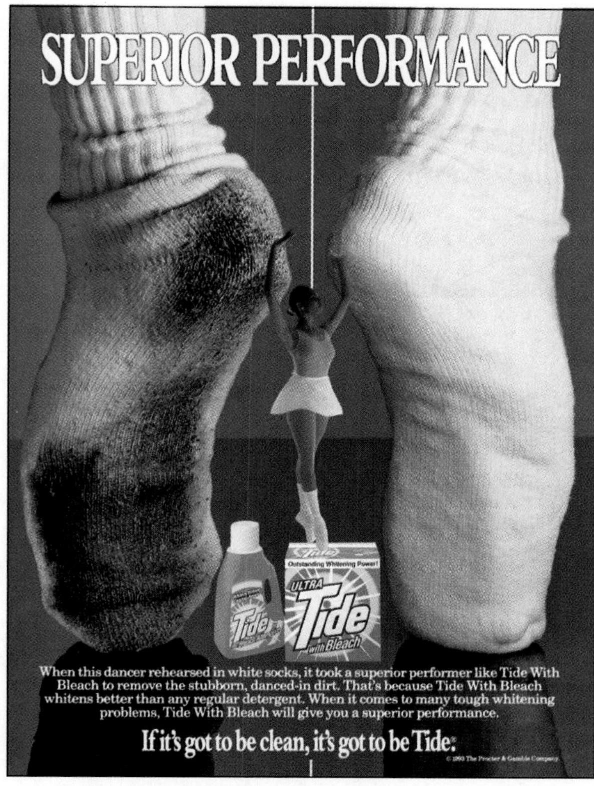

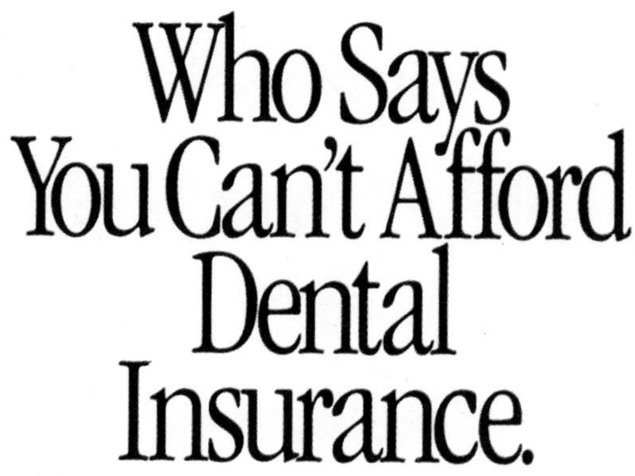

In the long run, a major product improvement accompanied by attention-attracting advertising could shift the target market into a more extensive form of decision making. In the short run, attention-attracting advertising aimed specifically at breaking habitual decision making can be successful. Free samples, coupons, rebates, and tie-in sales are common approaches to disrupting habitual decision making.

Managerial Application 16–2 is an example of a disrupt-based strategy. Notice that the product contains a unique feature and is positioned as benefitting both teeth and gums. Strong benefit claims such as those made in the Oral-B *Tooth and Gum Care* ad are necessary to disrupt the habitual decision making common in this product category.

Capture Strategy

Limited decision making generally involves a few brands that are evaluated on only a few criteria such as price or availability. Much of the information search occurs at the point-of-purchase or in readily available media prior to purchase. If our brand is one of the brands given this type of consideration by our target market, our objective is to capture as large a share of their purchases as practical.

MANAGERIAL APPLICATION

16–2

A Disrupt Strategy Ad

Since these consumers engage in limited search, we need to know where they search and what information they are looking for. In general, we will want to supply information, often on price and availability, in local media through cooperative advertising and at the point-of-purchase through displays and adequate shelf space. We will also be concerned with maintaining consistent product quality and adequate distribution.

Intercept Strategy

If our target market engages in limited decision making and our brand is not part of their evoked set, our objective will be to intercept the consumer during the search for information on the brands in the evoked set. Again, our emphasis will be on local media with cooperative advertising and at the point-of-purchase with displays, shelf space, package design, and so forth. Coupons can also be effective. We will have to place considerable emphasis on attracting the consumers' attention as they will not be seeking information on our brand. The Domino's Pizza promotion shown in Managerial Application 16–3 was distributed in the newspaper. It would be effective as part of a capture and/or intercept strategy.

MANAGERIAL APPLICATION 16-3

An Effective Capture or Intercept Strategy

In addition to the strategies mentioned above, low-involvement learning, product improvements, and free samples can be used to move the brand into the target market's evoked set.

Preference Strategy

Extended decision making with our brand in the evoked set requires a preference strategy. Since extended decision making generally involves several brands, many attributes, and a number of information sources, a simple capture strategy may not be adequate. Instead we need to structure an information campaign that will result in our brand being preferred by members of the target market.

The first step is a strong position on those attributes important to the target market. This is discussed in considerable detail in Chapter 17. Next, information must be provided in all the appropriate sources. This may require extensive advertising to groups that do not purchase the item but recommend it to others (e.g., druggists for over-the-counter drugs, veterinarians and county agents for agricultural products). Independent groups should be encouraged to test the brand, and sales personnel should be provided detailed information on the brand's attributes. In addition, it may be wise to provide the sales personnel with

MANAGERIAL APPLICATION 16–4

Part of a Preference Strategy

extra motivation (e.g., extra commissions paid by the manufacturer) to recommend the product. Point-of-purchase displays and pamphlets should also be available.

The Andersen windows ad shown in Managerial Application 16–4 is part of an effective preference strategy.

Acceptance Strategy

Acceptance strategy is very similar to preference strategy. However, it is complicated by the fact that the target market is not seeking information about our brand. Therefore, in addition to the activities involved in the preference strategy described above, we must attract their attention or otherwise motivate them to learn about our brand.

Consider the following quote by Lee Iaccoca while head of Chrysler:

> Our biggest long-term job is to get people in [the showroom] to see how great these cars are—to get some traffic—and let them compare, so we're going head to head on price and value.[28]

Because of this situation, Chrysler implemented an acceptance strategy. In addition to product improvements and heavy advertising, Chrysler literally paid consumers to seek information about their cars! They did this by offering cash to individuals who would test drive a Chrysler product prior to purchasing a new car.

Long-term advertising designed to enhance low-involvement learning is another useful technique for gaining acceptance. Extensive advertising with strong emphasis on attracting attention can also be effective. The primary objective of these two approaches is not to "sell" the brand. Rather they seek to move the brand into the evoked set. Then, when a purchase situation arises, the consumer will seek additional information on this brand.

SUMMARY

Following problem recognition, consumers may engage in extensive internal and external search, limited internal and external search, or only internal search. Information may be sought on (1) the appropriate *evaluative criteria* for the solution of the problem, (2) the existence of various *alternative solutions*, and (3) the *performance* of each alternative solution on each evaluative criterion.

Most consumers, when faced with a problem, can recall a limited number of brands that they feel are probably acceptable solutions. These acceptable brands, the *evoked set*, are the initial ones that the consumer seeks additional information on during the remaining internal and external search process. Therefore, marketers are very concerned that their brands fall within the evoked set of most members of their target market. A substantial amount of advertising has this as its primary objective.

Consumer internal information (information stored in memory) may have been actively acquired in previous searches and personal experiences or it may have been passively acquired through low-involvement learning. In addition to their own *memory*, consumers can seek information from four major types of external sources: (1) *personal sources*, such as friends and family; (2) *independent sources*, such as consumer groups, paid professionals, and government agencies; (3) *marketing sources*, such as sales personnel and advertising; and (4) *experiential sources*, such as direct product inspection or trial. The fact that only one of these four information sources is under the direct control of the firm suggests the need to pay close attention to product performance and customer satisfaction after the purchase.

Explicit external information search *after* problem recognition is limited. This emphasizes the need to communicate effectively with consumers prior to problem recognition. Characteristics of the market, the product, the consumer, and the situation interact to influence the level of search.

It is often suggested that consumers generally should engage in relatively extensive external search prior to purchasing an item. However, this view ignores the fact that information search is not free. It takes time, energy, money, and can often require giving up more desirable activities. Therefore, consumers should engage in external search only to the extent that the expected benefits such as a lower price or a more satisfactory purchase outweigh the expected costs.

Sound marketing strategy takes into account the nature of information search engaged in by the target market. The level of search and the brand's position in or out of the evoked set are two key dimensions. Based on these two dimensions, six potential information strategies are suggested: (1) *maintenance*, (2) *disrupt*, (3) *capture*, (4) *intercept*, (5) *preference*, and (6) *acceptance*.

REVIEW QUESTIONS

1. When does *information search* occur? What is the difference between internal and external information search?
2. What kind of information is sought in an external search for information?
3. What are *evaluative criteria* and how do they relate to information search?
4. How does a consumer's *awareness set* influence information search?
5. What roles do the *evoked set, inert set,* and *inept set* play in a consumer's information search? Why are some brands in a consumer's evoked set and others in the inert or inept sets?
6. What are the primary sources of information available to consumers, and what effect does each have on information search?
7. How do *nonsearchers, information searchers,* and *extended information searchers* differ in their search for information? Which category of consumers appears most rational to you and why?
8. What factors might influence the search effort of consumers who are essentially one-stop shoppers? How do these factors differ in terms of how they influence information searchers and extended information searchers?
9. What factors have to be considered in the total cost of the information search? How might these factors be different for different consumers?
10. Explain how different *market characteristics* affect information search.
11. How do different *consumer characteristics* influence a consumer's information search effort?
12. How do *product characteristics* influence a consumer's information search effort?
13. How do *situational characteristics* influence a consumer's information search effort?
14. How do individuals with differing shopping orientations differ in (a) shopping patterns, and (b) demographics (see Chapter 18)?
15. Describe the information search characteristics that should lead to each of the following strategies:
    a. Maintenance.
    b. Disrupt.
    c. Capture.
    d. Intercept.
    e. Preference.
    f. Acceptance.
16. Describe each of the strategies listed in Question 15.

DISCUSSION QUESTIONS

17. Pick a product that you believe would require each strategy in Exhibit 16–2 (six products in total). Justify your selection. Develop a specific marketing strategy for each (six strategies in total).
18. How would you utilize Figure 16–5 to develop a marketing communications strategy for a provider of the services listed?
19. Of the products shown in Figure 16–3, which product class is most likely to exhibit the most brand switching? Explain your answer in terms of the information provided in Figure 16–3.
20. Using the information presented in Figure 16–6, discuss the differences in comparison between product categories. What factors might contribute to these differences?
21. What information sources do students on your campus use when purchasing:
    a. Textbooks?
    b. Dress clothes?
    c. Sports equipment?
    d. Cold remedies?
    e. Weekend entertainment.
    f. A pet?
    g. Jewelry?
    h. Mother's Day gifts?

    Consider the various sources listed in Figure 16–4 (p. 449) in developing your answer. Do you think there will be individual differences? Why?
22. What factors contribute to the size of an awareness set, evoked set, inert set, and inept set?
23. Discuss factors that may contribute to external information search and factors that act to reduce external search for information before purchase of ________.

a. Automobile repairs.
b. Life insurance.
c. Medical care.
d. Wine.
e. Soft drinks.
f. Vitamins.

24. Is it ever in the best interest of a marketer to encourage potential customers to carry out an extended prepurchase search? Why or why not?
25. What implications for marketing strategy does Figure 16–2 suggest?
26. What role, if any, should the government play in ensuring that consumers have easy access to relevant product information? How should it accomplish this?
27. Describe a recent purchase in which you engaged in extensive search and one in which you did little prepurchase search. What factors caused the difference?
28. What is your awareness set, evoked set, inert set, and inept set for ______? In what ways, if any, do you think your sets will differ from the average member of your class? Why?
    a. Wine.
    b. Toothpaste.
    c. Mountain bikes.
    d. Deodorant.
    e. Perfume.
    f. Lawyers.
    g. Restaurants.
    h. Detergents.

APPLICATION EXERCISES

29. Complete Question 21 using a questionnaire and information from 10 students not in your class. Prepare a report discussing the marketing implications of your findings.
30. For the same products listed in Question 28, ask 10 students to list all the brands they are aware of in each product category. Then have them indicate which ones they might buy (evoked set), which ones they are indifferent toward (inert set), and which brands of those they listed they strongly dislike and would not purchase (inept set). What are the marketing implications of your results?
31. Develop a short questionnaire designed to measure the information search consumers engage in prior to (1) purchasing a mountain bike or (2) renting an apartment. Your questionnaire should include measures of types of information sought, as well as sources that provide this information. Also include measures of the relevant consumer characteristics that might influence information search, as well as some measure of past experience with the products. Then interview two recent purchasers of each product, using the questionnaire you have developed. Analyze each consumer's response and classify each consumer in terms of information search. What are the marketing implications of your results?
32. For each strategy in Exhibit 16–2, find one brand that appears to be following that strategy. Describe in detail how it is implementing the strategy.
33. Develop a questionnaire to measure shopping orientations among college students. Arrange for 50 students to complete the questionnaire. Classify the students into relevant orientations. Why do these differing orientations exist?
34. Develop a questionnaire to determine which products college students view as positive and which they view as negative. Measure the shopping effort associated with each type. Explain your overall results and any individual differences you find.

REFERENCES

[1]R. Serafin, ''Cars Find Ad Power in Computers,'' *Advertising Age*, June 14, 1993, p. 12.

[2]J. A. Lesser and S. Jain, ''A Preliminary Investigation of the Relationship between Exploratory and Epistemic Shopping Behavior,'' in *1985 AMA Educators' Proceedings*, ed. R. F. Lusch et al. (Chicago: American Marketing Association, 1985), pp. 75–81; J. A. Lesser and S. S. Marine, ''An Exploratory Investigation of the Relationship between Consumer Arousal and Shopping Behavior,'' in *Advances in Consumer Research XIII*, ed. R. J. Lutz (Provo, Utah: Association for Consumer Research, 1986), pp. 17–21; P. H. Bloch, D. L. Sherrell, and N. M. Ridgway, ''Consumer Search,'' *Journal of Consumer Research*, June 1986, pp. 119–26; and P. H. Bloch, N. M. Ridgway, and D. L. Sherrell, ''Extending the Concept of Shopping,'' *Journal of the Academy of Marketing Science*, Winter 1989, pp. 13–22.

[3]Ibid., Bloch, Sherrell, and Ridgway; and L. F. Feick and L. L. Price, ''The Market Maven,'' *Journal of Marketing*, January 1987, pp. 83–97.

[4]See J. W. Alba and A. Chattopadhyay, ''Salience Effects in Brand Recall,'' *Journal of Marketing Research*, November 1986,

pp. 363–69; N. H. Abougomaah, J. L. Schlacter, and W. Gaidis, "Elimination and Choice Phases in Evoked Set Formation," *Journal of Consumer Marketing*, Fall 1987, pp. 67–73; J. G. Lynch, Jr., H. Marmorstein, and M. F. Weigold, "Choices from Sets Including Remembered Brands," *Journal of Consumer Research*, September 1988, pp. 169–84; G. Punj and N. Srinivasan, "Influence of Expertise and Purchase Experience on the Formation of Evoked Sets," T. S. Gruca, "Determinants of Choice Set Size," and J. Roberts, "A Grounded Model of Consideration Set Size and Composition," all in *Advances in Consumer Research XVI*, ed. T. K. Srull (Provo, Utah: Association for Consumer Research, 1989), pp. 507–14, 515–21, 749–57, and P. Nedungadi, "Recall and Consumer Consideration Sets," *Journal of Consumer Research*, December 1990, pp. 263–76; and Jill Roberts and J. M. Lattin, "Development and Testing of a Model of Consideration Set Composition," *Journal of Marketing Research*, November 1991, pp. 429–40. For the role of evoked sets in store selection, see footnote 5, Chapter 18.

[5]D. H. Furse, G. N. Punj, and D. W. Stewart, "A Typology of Individual Search Strategies among Purchasers of New Automobiles," *Journal of Consumer Research*, March 1984, pp. 417–31; and L. L. Price and L. F. Feick, "The Role of Interpersonal Sources in External Search," in *Advances in Consumer Research XI*, ed. T. C. Kinnear (Chicago: Association for Consumer Research, 1984), pp. 250–55; and footnote 2, Chapter 7.

[6]R. A. Westbrook and C. Farnell, "Patterns of Information Source Usage among Durable Goods Buyers," *Journal of Marketing Research*, August 1979, pp. 303–12; and J. E. Urbany, P. R. Dickson, and W. L. Wilkie, "Buyer Uncertainty and Information Search," *Journal of Consumer Research*, September 1989, pp. 208–215.

[7]Ibid., Urbany, Dickson, and Wilkie.

[8]Ibid.

[9]G. Katona and E. Mueller, "A Study of Purchase Decisions," in *Consumer Behavior: The Dynamics of Consumer Reaction*, ed. L. Clark (University Press, 1955), pp. 30–87; and J. Newman and R. Staelin, "Prepurchase Information Seeking for New Cars and Major Household Appliances," *Journal of Marketing Research*, August 1972, pp. 249–57; J. Claxton, J. Fry, and B. Portis, "A Taxonomy of Prepurchase Information Gathering Patterns," *Journal of Consumer Research*, December 1974, pp. 35–42; G. C. Kiel and R. A. Layton, "Dimensions of Consumer Information Seeking Behavior," *Journal of Marketing Research*, May 1981, pp. 233–39; J. B. Freiden and R. E. Goldsmith, "Prepurchase Information-Seeking for Professional Services," *Journal of Services Marketing*, Winter 1989, pp. 45–55; and footnote 6, Urbany, Dickson, and Wilkie. See also B. L. Bagus, "The Consumer Durable Replacement Buyer," *Journal of Marketing*, January 1991, pp. 42–51.

[10]H. B. Thorelli and J. L. Engledow, "Information Seekers and Information Systems: A Policy Perspective," *Journal of Marketing*, Spring 1980, pp. 9–27. See also footnote 3, Feick and Price.

[11]G. Punj, "Presearch Decision Making in Consumer Durable Purchases," *Journal of Consumer Marketing*, Winter 1987, pp. 71–82.

[12]For a more elaborate model, see N. Srinivasan and B. T. Ratchford, "An Empirical Test of a Model of External Search for Automobiles," *Journal of Consumer Research*, September 1991, pp. 233–42. See also H. Marmorstein, D. Grewal, and R. P. H. Fishe, "The Value of Time Spent in Price-Comparison Shopping," *Journal of Consumer Research*, June 1992, pp. 52–61; and S. Forsythe, S. Butler, and R. Schaeffer, "Surrogate Usage in the Acquisition of Women's Business Apparel," *Journal of Retailing*, Winter 1990, pp. 446–69.

[13]R. A. Westbrook and W. C. Black, "A Motivation-Based Shopper Typology," *Journal of Retailing*, Spring 1985, pp. 78–103; T. Williams, M. Slama, and J. Rogers, "Behavioral Characteristics of the Recreational Shopper," *Journal of the Academy of Marketing Science*, Summer 1985, pp. 307–16; and B. Morris, "As a Favored Pastime, Shopping Ranks High," *The Wall Street Journal*, July 30, 1987, p. 1.

[14]C. P. Duncan and R. W. Olshavsky, "External Search: The Role of Consumer Beliefs," *Journal of Marketing Research*, February 1982, pp. 32–43; see also D. R. Lichtenstein, N. M. Ridgway, and R. G. Netemeyer, "Price Perceptions and Consumer Shopping Behavior," *Journal of Marketing Research*, May 1993, pp. 234–45.

[15]S. Widrick and E. Fram, "Identifying Negative Products," *Journal of Consumer Marketing*, no. 2, 1983, pp. 59–66.

[16]See M. E. Slama and A. Taschian, "Selected Socioeconomic and Demographic Characteristics Associated with Purchasing Involvement," *Journal of Marketing*, Winter 1985, pp. 72–82; and see footnote 9, Bagus.

[17]M. Brucks, "The Effects of Product Class Knowledge on Information Search Behavior," *Journal of Consumer Research*, June 1985, pp. 1–16; and S. E. Beatty and S. M. Smith, "External Search Effort," *Journal of Consumer Research*, June 1987, pp. 83–95.

[18]G. N. Punj and R. Staelin, "A Model of Consumer Information Search Behavior for New Automobiles," *Journal of Consumer Research*, March 1983, pp. 368–80.

[19]See footnotes 6 and 16.

[20]C. M. Schaninger and D. Sciglimipaglia, "The Influence of Cognitive Personality Traits and Demographics on Consumer Information Acquisition," *Journal of Consumer Research*, September 1981, pp. 208–16.

[21]See J. Rudd and F. J. Kohout, "Individual and Group Consumer Information Acquisitions in Brand Choice Situations," *Journal of Consumer Research*, December 1983, pp. 303–9.

[22]See footnote 12, Srinivasan and Ratchford.

[23]K. B. Murray, "A Test of Services Marketing Theory," *Journal of Marketing*, January 1991, pp. 10–25.

[24]See footnote 13, Westbrook and Black; J. R. Lumpkin, "Shopping Orientation Segmentation of the Elderly Consumer," *Journal of the Academy of Marketing Science*, Spring 1985, pp. 271–89; T. Williams, M. Slama, and J. Rogers, "Behavioral Characteristics of the Recreational Shopper," *Journal of Academy of Marketing Science*, Summer 1985, pp. 307–16; and J. R. Lumpkin, J. M. Hawes, and W. R. Darden, "Shopping Patterns of the Rural Consumer," *Journal of Business Research*, February 1986, pp. 63–81.

[25]See footnote 17, Beatty and Smith; and B. E. Mattson and A. J. Dobinsky, "Shopping Patterns," *Psychology & Marketing*, Spring 1987, pp. 47–62.

[26]C. J. Cobb and W. D. Hoyer, "Direct Observation of Search Behavior," *Psychology & Marketing*, Fall 1985, pp. 161–79.

[27]"L&M Lights Up Again," *Marketing and Media Decisions*, February 1984, p. 69.

[28]R. Gray, "Chrysler Hinges Price on Popularity," *Advertising Age*, October 5, 1981, p. 7.

CHAPTER

17

ALTERNATIVE EVALUATION AND SELECTION

7

Sunbeam Appliance Company recently completed a very successful redesign of its many lines of small kitchen appliances. The redesign of their food processor line illustrates the four-stage process used:

1. A *Consumer Usage and Attitude Survey* to determine how and for what purpose products in the product category are used, frequency of use, brand ownership, brand awareness, and attitudes toward the product.
2. A *Consumer Attribute and Benefit Survey* to provide importance ratings of product attributes and benefits desired from the product category, along with perceptions of the degree to which each brand provides the various attributes and benefits.
3. A *Conjoint Analysis Study* (a technique described in this chapter) to provide data on the structure of consumers' preferences for product features and their willingness to trade one feature for more of another feature. Conjoint analysis provides the relative importance *each* consumer attaches to various levels of each potential product feature. This allows individuals with similar preference structures to be grouped into market segments.
4. *Product Line Sales and Market Share Simulations* to determine the best set of food processors to bring to the market. Based on the preference structures and sizes of the market segments discovered in step 3 above and the perceived characteristics of competing brands, the market share of various Sunbeam product sets was estimated using computer simulations.[1]

The above process involved interviewing hundreds of product category users. Twelve different product attributes were tested and four distinct market segments were uncovered. The existing product line was replaced with four new models (down from six) targeted at three of the four segments. The results were increased market share, reduced costs, and increased profitability.

The opening example describes Sunbeam's successful analysis of consumers' desired product benefits (evaluative criteria) and the manner in which they choose between products with differing combinations of benefits. The process by which consumers evaluate and choose among alternatives is illustrated in Figure 17–1, and is the focus of this chapter.

We concentrate on three main areas. First, the nature and characteristics of evaluative criteria (the features the product should have) will be described. Evaluative criteria are particularly important since consumers select alternatives based on relative performance on the appropriate evaluative criteria.

After examining evaluative criteria, we focus on the ability of consumers to judge the performance of products. Finally, we examine the decision rules that consumers use in selecting one alternative from those considered.

Before delving into the evaluation and selection of alternatives, you should remember that many purchases involve little or no evaluation of alternatives. Habitual decisions do not require the evaluation of any alternatives. The last purchase is repeated without considering other information. Limited decisions may involve comparing a few brands (small evoked set) on one or two dimensions (I'll buy Heinz or Del Monte catsup, depending on which is cheaper at Safeway).

Alternative Evaluation and Selection Process

FIGURE 17–1

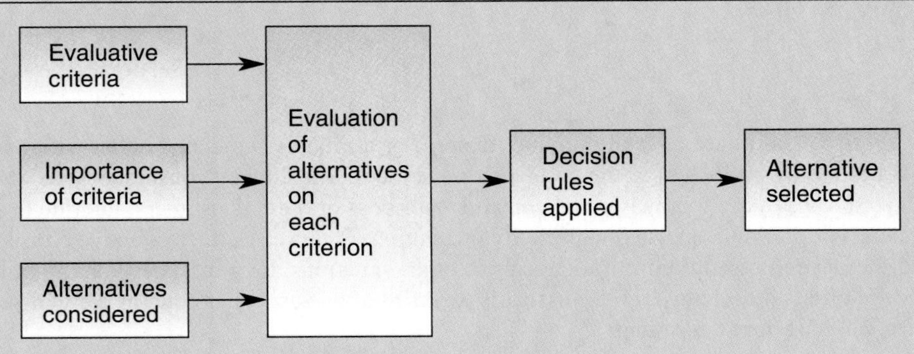

MANAGERIAL APPLICATION

17–1

A Product Positioned on the Feelings It Provides Rather than on Physical Attributes

Products purchased primarily for emotional reasons may involve anticipating the effect of purchase or use on feelings rather than on analysis of product attributes per se. Managerial Application 17–1 positions *Laser* strictly in terms of the feelings its use will provide. Likewise, a product purchased primarily in response to a social situation often involves anticipation of the reaction of others to the product instead of an analysis of its attributes.

EVALUATIVE CRITERIA

Evaluative criteria are *the various features a consumer looks for in response to a particular type of problem.* Before purchasing a calculator, you might be concerned with cost, size, power source, capabilities, display, and warranty. These would be your evaluative criteria. Someone else could approach the same purchase with an entirely different set of evaluative criteria.

Nature of Evaluative Criteria

Evaluative criteria are typically product features or attributes associated either with benefits desired by customers or the costs they must incur. Thus, many consumers who want to avoid cavities use toothpaste that contains fluoride. For these consumers, fluoride is an evaluative criterion associated with cavity prevention. In this case, the evaluative criterion and the desired benefit are not identical. In other situations, they may be. For example, price is often an evaluative criterion that is identical to one aspect of cost (as we will see, price can have many meanings).

MANAGERIAL APPLICATION

17–2

Ads Stressing Different Types of Evaluative Criteria for Similar Products

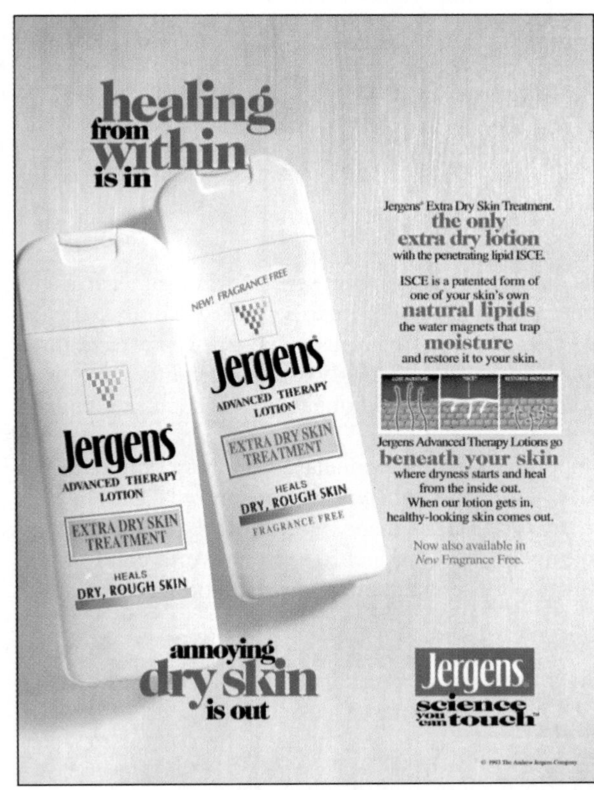

Evaluative criteria can differ in type, number, and importance. The *type of evaluative criteria* a consumer uses in a decision varies from *tangible* cost and performance features to *intangible* factors such as style, taste, prestige, and brand image. Equally important in many purchase decisions is the way we *feel* about a brand. Feelings or emotions surrounding a brand are difficult for consumers to articulate and for marketing managers to measure or manipulate. Yet feelings play a critical role in the purchase of products ranging from soft drinks to automobiles.

Managerial Application 17–2 shows how two similar products are stressing very different types of evaluative criteria. The *Jergens* ad stresses tangible attributes and technical performance. The *Nivea* ad focuses on intangible attributes and feelings.

The number of evaluative criteria used depends on the product, the consumer, and the situation.[2] Naturally, for fairly simple products such as toothpaste, soap, or facial tissue, the number of evaluative criteria used are few.[3] On the other hand, the purchase of an automobile, stereo system, or house may involve numerous criteria.[4] Characteristics of the individual (such as product familiarity and age) and characteristics of the purchase situation (such as time pressure) also influence the number of evaluative criteria considered.[5]

The importance that consumers assign to each evaluative criterion is of great interest to marketers. Three consumers could use the six evaluative criteria shown below when considering a laptop computer. However, if the importance they assigned each criterion varied as shown below, they would likely purchase different brands.

	Importance Rank for		
Criteria	**Consumer A**	**Consumer B**	**Consumer C**
Price	**1**	6	3
Processor	5	**1**	4
Display quality	3	3	**1**
Memory	6	**2**	5
Weight	4	4	**2**
After-sale support	**2**	5	6

Consumer A is concerned primarily with cost and support services. Consumer B wants computing speed and power. Consumer C is concerned primarily with ease of use. If each of these three consumers represented a larger group of consumers, we would have three distinct market segments based on the importance assigned the same criteria. Of course, we could have other segments that consider other or additional criteria such as a built-in modem or battery life.

The evaluative criteria, and the importance that individuals assign them, influence not only the brands selected but if and when a problem will be recognized. This in turn influences if and when a purchase of any type will be made. For example, consumers who attach more importance to automobile styling and product image relative to comfort and cost buy new cars more frequently than do those with the opposite importance rankings.[6]

Measurement of Evaluative Criteria

Before a marketing manager or a public policy decision maker can develop a sound strategy to affect consumer decisions, he or she must determine:

- Which evaluative criteria are used by the consumer.
- How the consumer perceives the various alternatives on each criterion.
- The relative importance of each criterion.

Consumers sometimes will not or cannot verbalize their evaluative criteria for a product. Therefore, it is often difficult to determine which criteria they are using in a particular brand-choice decision, particularly if emotions or feelings are involved. This is even more of a problem when trying to determine the relative importance they attach to each evaluative criterion.

Determination of Which Evaluative Criteria Are Used To determine which criteria are used by consumers in a specific product decision, the marketing researcher can utilize either *direct* or *indirect* methods of measurement. *Direct* methods include asking consumers what information they use in a particular purchase or, in a focus group setting, observing what consumers say about products and their attributes. Of course, direct measurement techniques assume that consumers can and will provide data on the desired attributes.

In the research that led to the development of Sunbeam's new food processor line, consumers readily described their desired product features and benefits. However, direct questioning is not always as successful. For example, Hanes Corporation suffered substantial losses ($30 million) on its *L'erin* cosmetics line when, *in response to consumer interviews*, it positioned it as a functional rather than a romantic or emotional product.

Perceptual Mapping of Beer Brand Perceptions

FIGURE 17–2

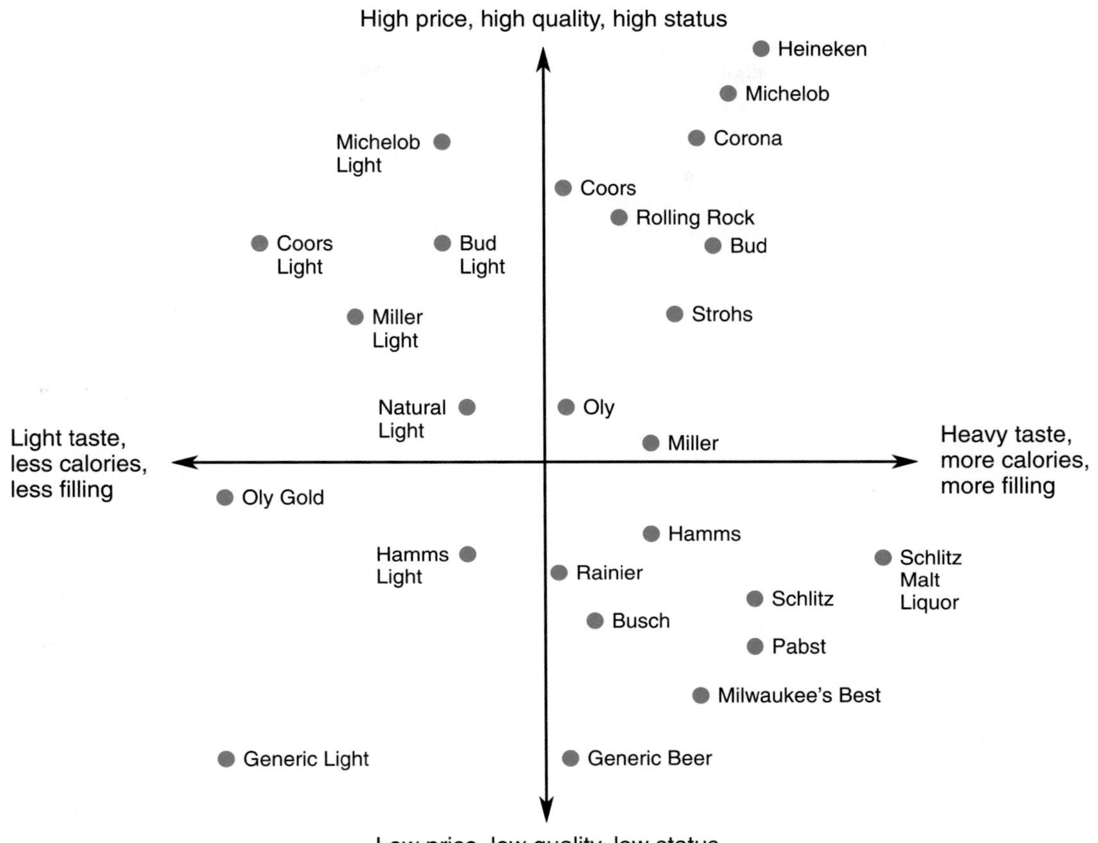

Eventually the brand was successfully repositioned as glamorous and exotic, although consumers did not *express* these as desired attributes.[7]

Indirect measurement techniques differ from direct in that they assume consumers will not or cannot state their evaluative criteria. Hence, frequent use is made of indirect methods such as **projective techniques** (see Exhibit 11–2), which allow the person to indicate what criteria someone else might use. The ''someone else'' is very probably the person being asked, of course, and we have indirectly determined the evaluative criteria used. This approach is particularly useful for discovering emotional-type criteria.

Perceptual mapping is another useful indirect technique for determining evaluative criteria. Consumers judge the similarity of alternative brands, then these judgments are processed via a computer to derive a spatial configuration or perceptual map of the brands. No evaluative criteria are specified. The consumer simply ranks the similarity between all pairs of alternatives, and a perceptual configuration is derived in which the consumer's evaluative criteria are the dimensions of the configuration.[8]

For example, consider the perceptual map of beers shown in Figure 17–2. This configuration was derived from a consumer's evaluation of the relative similarity of these brands of beer. Examining this perceptual map, we can identify the horizontal axis on the basis of physical characteristics such as taste, calories, and fullness. The vertical axis is characterized by price, quality, and status. This procedure allows us to understand consumer perceptions and the evaluative criteria they use to differentiate brands.

Determination of Consumers' Judgments of Brand Performance on Specific Evaluative Criteria A variety of methods are available for measuring consumers' judgments of brand performance on specific attributes. These include *rank ordering scales*, *semantic differential scales*, and *Likert scales* (see Appendix A). The semantic differential scale is probably the most widely used technique.

The **semantic differential scale** lists each evaluative criterion in terms of opposite levels of performance, such as fast-slow, expensive-inexpensive, and so forth. These opposites are separated by five to seven intervals and placed below the brand being considered, as shown below.

IBM ThinkPad 500

Expensive	___	X	___	___	___	___	___	Inexpensive
High quality	X	___	___	___	___	___	___	Low quality
Heavy	___	___	___	___	X	___	___	Light
Easy to read display	___	___	___	X	___	___	___	Hard to read display

Consumers are asked to indicate their judgments of the performance of the brand by marking the blank that best indicates how accurately one or the other term describes or fits the brand. The end positions indicate *extremely*, the next pair *very*, the middle-most pair, *somewhat*, and the middle position *neither-nor*. Thus, the respondent in the example above evaluated the IBM ThinkPad as very expensive, extremely high quality, somewhat light, with a display that is neither easy nor hard to read.

None of these techniques are very effective at measuring emotional responses to products or brands. Projective techniques can provide some insights. BBDO's Emotional Measurement System for ads (page 317) could easily be adapted to measure responses to products as well. This area clearly needs further development.

Determination of the Relative Importance of Evaluative Criteria The importance assigned to evaluative criteria can be measured either by direct or by indirect methods. The **constant sum scale** is the most common method of direct measurement. This method requires the consumer to allocate 100 points to his or her evaluative criteria, depending on the importance of each criterion. For example, in evaluating the importance of laptop computer criteria, a 100-point constant sum scale might produce the following results:

Evaluative Criteria	Importance (in points)
Price	5
Processor	35
Display quality	20
Memory	25
After-sale support	5
Weight	10
Total	100

This consumer rated the processor as much more important than other attributes, with memory and display quality also important. Weight, after-sale support, and price were not as important. Other evaluative criteria that could have been considered, such as battery

EXHIBIT 17–1

Using Conjoint Analysis to Determine the Importance of Evaluative Criteria

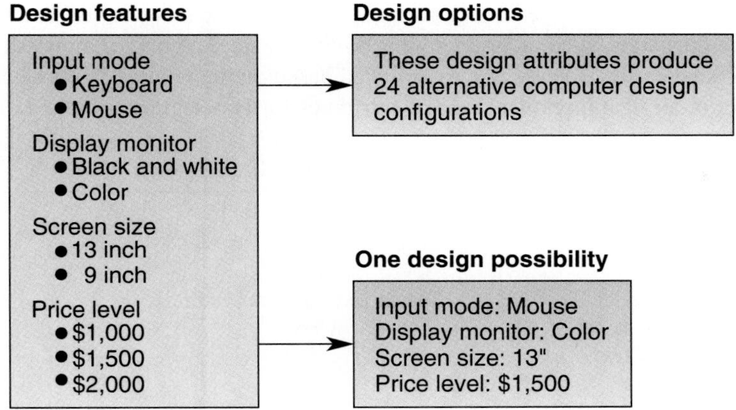

Consumer preferences

Price
Preference
3
2
1
0
$1,000 $1,500 $2,000

Screen size
Preference
3
2
1
0
9" 13"

Display monitor
Preference
3
2
1
0
Black and white Color

Input mode
Preference
3
2
1
0
Keyboard Mouse

Relative importance

Evaluative criteria	Importance
Input mode	45%
Display monitor	5
Screen size	25
Price level	25

- Input mode is the most important feature in this example, and the mouse is the preferred option.
- While price and screen size are also important, price becomes a factor between $1,500 and $2,000.

life, presumably are not important to this consumer and therefore have implicit importance weights of zero.

The most popular indirect measurement approach is **conjoint analysis**. In conjoint analysis, the consumer is presented with a set of products or product descriptions in which the potential evaluative criteria vary.[9] For example, in Exhibit 17–1, a consumer was asked to rank in terms of overall preference 24 different computer designs featuring different levels of four key evaluative criteria. The preferences were then analyzed in light of the variations in the attributes. The result is a preference curve for each evaluative criterion which reflects the importance of that attribute. For example, input mode and screen size are shown to be particularly important evaluative criteria for this consumer.

Conjoint analysis was used in the Sunbeam example that opened this chapter. Sunbeam tested 12 different attributes, such as price, motor power, number of blades, bowl shape, and so forth. As stated earlier, four segments emerged based on the relative importance of these attributes. In order of importance, the key attributes for two segments were:

Cheap/Large Segment	Multispeed/Multiuse Segment
$49.99 price	$99.99 price
4-quart bowl	2-quart bowl
Two speeds	Seven speeds
Seven blades	Functions as blender and mixer
Heavy-duty motor	Cylindrical bowl
Cylindrical bowl	
Pouring spout	

It should be noted that conjoint analysis is limited to the attributes listed by the researcher. Thus, a conjoint analysis of soft-drink attributes would not indicate anything about calorie content unless the researcher listed it as a feature. The Sunbeam study did not test such attributes as brand name, color, weight, or safety features. If an important attribute is omitted, incorrect market share predictions are likely to result. In addition, conjoint analysis is not well suited for measuring the importance of emotional responses.

INDIVIDUAL JUDGMENT AND EVALUATIVE CRITERIA

If you were buying a laptop computer, you would probably make direct comparisons across brands of features such as price, weight, and display clarity. These comparative judgments may not be completely accurate. For example, the display that is the easiest to read in a five-minute trial may not be the easiest to read over a two-hour work session. For other attributes, such as quality, you might not be able to make direct comparisons. Instead, you might rely on brand name or price to indicate quality. The accuracy of direct judgments and the use of one attribute to indicate performance on another (surrogate indicators) are critical issues for marketers.

Accuracy of Individual Judgments

The average consumer is not adequately trained to judge the performance of competing brands on complex evaluative criteria such as quality or durability. For more straightforward criteria, however, most consumers can and do make such judgments. Prices generally can be judged and compared directly. However, even this can be complex. Is a liter of Coca-Cola selling for 95 cents a better buy than a quart selling for 89 cents? Consumer groups have pushed for unit pricing to make such comparisons simpler. The federal truth-in-lending law was passed to facilitate direct price comparisons among alternative lenders.

The ability of an individual to distinguish between similar stimuli is called **sensory discrimination**. This involves such variables as the sound of stereo systems, the taste of food products, or the clarity of display screens. The minimum amount that one brand can differ from another with the difference still being noticed is referred to as the **just noticeable difference (j.n.d.)**. Marketers seeking to find a promotable difference between their brand and a competitor's must surpass the j.n.d. in order for the improvement or change to be noticed by consumers. On the other hand, a marketer sometimes may want to change a product feature but not have the consumer perceive any change and hence not surpass the j.n.d.

The higher the initial level of the attribute, the greater the amount that attribute must be changed before the change will be noticed. Thus, a small addition of salt to a pretzel would not distinguish the product from a competitor's unless the competitor's pretzel contained only a very limited amount of salt. This relationship is expressed formally as:

$$\text{j.n.d.} = \frac{\Delta I}{I} = K$$

where

$$\begin{aligned} \text{j.n.d.} &= \text{Just noticeable difference.} \\ I &= \text{Initial level of the attribute.} \\ \Delta I &= \text{Change in the attribute.} \\ K &= \text{Constant that varies with each sense mode.} \end{aligned}$$

Example: Lifting weights

$$\begin{aligned} I &= 100 \text{ lbs.} \\ K &= .02 \text{ for weight} \\ \text{j.n.d.} &= \frac{\Delta I}{100} = .02 \\ \Delta I &= 100 \text{ lbs.} \times .02 \\ \Delta I &= 2 \text{ lbs. for j.n.d.} \end{aligned}$$

For one to detect a weight change, more than 2 pounds would have to be added or taken away from the original 100 pounds. This formula is known as **Weber's law**. Values for K have been established for several senses and can be utilized in the development of functional aspects of products.[10] More useful than the formula itself is the general principle behind it—*individuals typically do not notice relatively small differences between brands or changes in brand attributes.* Makers of candy bars have utilized this principle for years. Since the price of cocoa fluctuates widely, they simply make small adjustments in the size of the candy bar rather than altering price. Marketers want some product changes, such as reductions in the size of the candy bars, to go unnoticed. These changes must be below the j.n.d. Positive changes, such as going from a quart to a liter, must be above the j.n.d. or it may not be worthwhile to make them, unless advertising can convince people that meaningful differences exist.

Use of Surrogate Indicators

Consumers frequently use an observable attribute of a product to indicate the performance of the product on a less observable attribute. For example, most of us use price as a guide to the quality of at least some products. As stated earlier, an attribute used to stand for or indicate another attribute is known as a **surrogate indicator**.

Consumers' reliance on an attribute as a surrogate indicator of another attribute is a function of its predictive value and confidence value.[11] *Predictive value* refers to the consumer's perception that one attribute is an accurate predictor of the other. *Confidence value* refers to the consumer's ability to distinguish between brands on the surrogate indicator. Thus, a consumer might believe that ingredients accurately (high predictive value) indicate the nutritional value of foods but not use them as indicators, due to an inability to make the complex between-brand comparisons.

MANAGERIAL APPLICATION

17–3

Use of a Surrogate Indicator

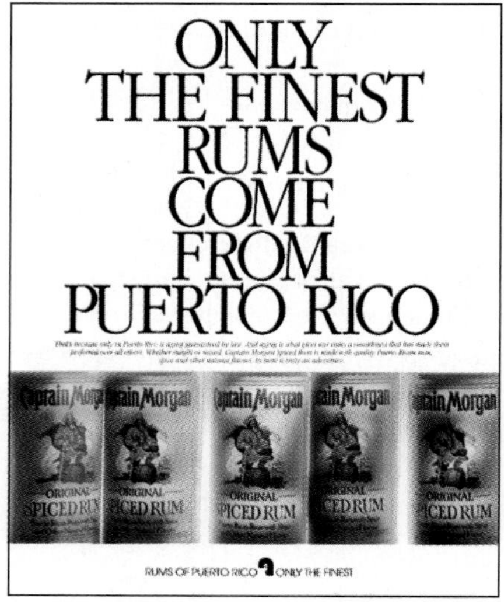

Perhaps the most widely used surrogate indicator, due in part to its high confidence value, is price. Price has been found to influence the perceived quality of shirts, radios, and after-shave lotion, appliances, carpeting, automobiles, and numerous other product categories.[12] These influences have been large, but, as might be expected, they decline with increases in visible product differences, prior product use, and additional product information. Unfortunately, for many products the relationship between price and functional measures of quality is low.[13] Thus, consumers using price as a surrogate for quality frequently make suboptimal purchases.

Brand name often is used as a surrogate indicator of quality. It has been found to be very important when it is the only information the consumer has available and to interact with or, on occasion, replace the impact of relative price.[14] Store image, packaging, color, country of manufacture, and warranties have also been found to affect perceptions of quality.[15] Managerial Application 17–3 illustrates a very direct use of country of manufacture as an indicator of quality.

Surrogate indicators are based on consumers' beliefs that two features such as price level and quality level generally ''go together.'' Consumers also form beliefs that certain variables do not go together—such as *light weight* and *strong*, *rich taste* and *low calories*, and *high fiber* and *high protein*.[16] Marketers attempting to promote the presence of two or more variables that many consumers believe to be mutually exclusive have a high risk of failure unless very convincing messages are used. Thus, it is important for marketers to fully understand consumers' beliefs about the feasible relationships of attributes related to their products.

Evaluative Criteria, Individual Judgments, and Marketing Strategy

Marketers recognize and react to the ability of individuals to judge evaluative criteria, as well as to their tendency to use surrogate indicators. For example, most new consumer products are initially tested against competitors in **blind tests**. A blind test is one in which the consumer is not aware of the product's brand name. Such tests enable the marketer to evaluate the functional characteristics of the product and to determine if a j.n.d. over a particular competitor has been obtained without the contaminating or "halo" effects of the brand name or the firm's reputation.

Marketers also make direct use of surrogate indicators. For example, Andecker is advertised as "the most expensive taste in beer." This is an obvious attempt to utilize the price–quality relationship that many consumers believe exists for beer. On occasion, prices are raised to increase sales because of the presumed price–quality relationship. For example, a new mustard packaged in a crockery jar did not achieve significant sales priced at 49 cents, but it did at one dollar.[17]

Marketers frequently use brand names as an indicator of quality.[18] *Elmer's* glue stressed the well-established reputation of its brand in promoting a new super glue (ads for Elmer's Wonder Bond said: *Stick with a name you can trust.*) Other firms stress *Made In America*, *Italian Styling*, or *German Engineering*.

Other types of surrogate indicators are also used. A marketer stressing the rich taste of a milk product, for example, would want to make it cream colored rather than white, and a hot, spicy sauce would be colored red. GE guarantees absolute satisfaction with their major appliances for 90 days. This strategy not only greatly reduces any perceived risk associated with purchasing a GE major appliance, it serves as a strong surrogate indicator of product quality.

How can a lesser-known brand convince a target market that it is equal or superior to a more prestigious competitor? Carnation has sought to convince consumers that its Coffee-Mate nondairy creamer tastes as good in coffee as cream does by advertising the results of a well-controlled blind taste test that confirmed this. Sylvania has followed a similar strategy by advertising the results of blind tests involving one of its models of television sets and similar models of well-known competitors.

DECISION RULES

Suppose you have evaluated a particular model of each of the six laptop computer brands in your evoked set on six evaluative criteria: price, weight, processor, battery life, display quality, and after-sale support. Further, suppose that each brand excels on one attribute but falls short of one or more of the remaining attributes, as shown below:

	Consumer Perceptions*					
Evaluative Criteria	**NEC**	**Compaq**	**Hewlett-Packard**	**Macintosh**	**IBM**	**Toshiba**
Price	5	3	3	4	2	1
Weight	3	4	5	4	3	4
Processor	5	5	5	2	5	5
Battery life	1	3	1	3	1	5
After-sale support	3	3	4	3	5	3
Display quality	3	3	3	5	3	3

*Rated from 1 (very poor) to 5 (very good).

Which brand would you select? The answer would depend upon the decision rule you utilize. Consumers frequently use five decision rules, either singularly or in combination: conjunctive, disjunctive, lexicographic, elimination-by-aspects, and compensatory. The conjunctive and disjunctive decision rules may produce a set of acceptable alternatives, while the remaining rules generally produce a single "best" alternative.

Conjunctive Decision Rule

The **conjunctive decision rule** establishes minimum required performance standards for each evaluative criterion and selects all brands that surpass these minimum standards. In essence, you would say: "I'll consider all (or I'll buy the first) brands that are all right on the attributes I think are important." For example, assume that the following represent your minimum standards:

Price	3
Weight	4
Processor	3
Battery life	1
After-sale support	2
Display quality	3

Any brand of computer falling below *any* of these minimum standards (cutoff points) would be eliminated from further consideration. In this example, four computers are eliminated—IBM, NEC, Macintosh, and Toshiba. These are the computers that failed to meet *all* the minimum standards. Under these circumstances, the remaining brands may be equally satisfying. Or, the consumer may use another decision rule to select a single brand from these two alternatives.

Because individuals have limited ability to process information, the conjunctive rule is very useful in reducing the size of the information processing task to some manageable level. It first eliminates those alternatives which do not meet minimum standards. This is often done in the purchase of such products as homes or in the rental of apartments. A conjunctive rule is used to eliminate alternatives that are out of a consumer's price range, outside the location preferred, or that do not offer other desired features. Once alternatives not providing these features are eliminated, another choice rule may be used to make a brand choice among those alternatives that satisfy these minimum standards.

The conjunctive decision rule is commonly used in many low-involvement purchases as well. In such a purchase, the consumer evaluates a set of brands one at a time and selects the first brand that meets all the minimum requirements.

Disjunctive Decision Rule

The **disjunctive decision rule** establishes a minimum level of performance for each important attribute (often a fairly high level). All brands that surpass the performance level for *any* key attribute are considered acceptable. Using this rule, you would say: "I'll consider all (or buy the first) brands that perform really well on any attribute I consider to be important." Assume that you are using a disjunctive decision rule and the attribute cutoff points shown below:

Price	5
Weight	5
Processor	Not critical
Battery life	Not critical
After-sale support	Not critical
Display quality	5

You would find NEC (price), Hewlett-Packard (weight), and Macintosh (display quality) to warrant further consideration. As with the conjunctive decision rule, you might purchase the first brand you find acceptable, use another decision rule to choose among the three, or add additional criteria to your list.

Elimination-by-Aspects Decision Rule

The **elimination-by-aspects rule** requires the consumer to rank the evaluative criteria in terms of their importance and to establish a cutoff point for each criterion. All brands are first considered on the most important criterion. Those that do not surpass the cutoff point are dropped from consideration. If more than one brand passes the cutoff point, the process is repeated on those brands for the second most important criterion. This continues until only one brand remains. Thus, the consumer's logic is: ''I want to buy the brand that has an important attribute that other brands do not have.''

Consider the rank-order and cutoff points shown below. What would you choose using the elimination-by-aspects rule?

	Rank	**Cutoff Point**
Price	1	3
Weight	2	4
Display quality	3	4
Processor	4	3
After-sale support	5	3
Battery life	6	3

Price would eliminate IBM and Toshiba. Of those remaining, Compaq, Hewlett-Packard, and Macintosh surpass the weight hurdle. Notice that Toshiba also exceeded the minimum weight requirement but was not considered because it had been eliminated in the initial consideration of price. Only Macintosh exceeds the third requirement, display quality.

Using the elimination-by-aspects rule, we end up with a choice that has all the desired features of all the other alternatives, plus one more. In this case, Macintosh would be selected.

Lexicographic Decision Rule

The **lexicographic decision rule** requires the consumer to rank the criteria in order of importance. The consumer then selects the brand that performs *best* on the most important attribute. If two or more brands tie on this attribute, they are evaluated on the second most important attribute. This continues through the attributes until one brand outperforms the others. The consumer's thinking is something like this: ''I want to get the brand that does best on the attribute of most importance to me. If there is a tie, I'll break it by choosing the one that does best on my second most important criterion.''

The lexicographic decision rule is very similar to the elimination-by-aspects rule. The difference is that the lexicographic rule seeks maximum performance at each stage while the elimination-by-aspects seeks satisfactory performance at each stage. Thus, using the lexicographic rule and the data from the elimination-by-aspects example above would result in the selection of NEC, because it has the best performance on the most important attribute. Had NEC been rated a 4 on price, it would be tied with Macintosh. Then, Macintosh would be chosen based on its superior weight rating.

When this rule is being used by a target market, it is essential that your product equal or exceed the performance of all other competitors on the most important criteria. Outstanding performance on lesser criteria will not matter if we are not competitive on the most important ones.

Compensatory Decision Rule

The four previous rules are *noncompensatory* decision rules, since very good performance on one evaluative criterion cannot compensate for poor performance on another evaluative criterion. On occasion, consumers may wish to average out some very good features with some less attractive features of a product in determining overall brand preference. Therefore, the **compensatory decision rule** states that the brand that rates highest on the sum of the consumer's judgments of the relevant evaluative criteria will be chosen. This can be illustrated as:

$$R_b = \sum_{i=1}^{n} W_i B_{ib}$$

where

R_b = Overall rating of brand *b*.
W_i = Importance or weight attached to evaluative criterion *i*.
B_{ib} = Evaluation of brand *b* on evaluative criterion *i*.
n = Number of evaluative criteria considered relevant.

If you used the relative importance scores shown below, which brand would you choose?

	Importance Score
Price	30
Weight	25
Processor	10
Battery life	05
After-sale support	10
Display quality	20
	100

Using this rule, Macintosh has the highest preference. The calculations for Macintosh are as follows:

$$\begin{aligned} R_{\text{Macintosh}} &= 30(4) + 25(4) + 10(2) + 5(3) + 10(3) + 20(5) \\ &= 120 + 100 + 20 + 15 + 30 + 100 \\ &= 385 \end{aligned}$$

As shown below, each decision rule yields a somewhat different choice. Therefore, you must understand which decision rules are being used by target buyers in order to position a product within this decision framework.

Decision Rule	Brand Choice
Conjunctive	Hewlett-Packard, Compaq
Disjunctive	Macintosh, Hewlett-Packard, NEC
Elimination-by-aspects	Macintosh
Lexicographic	NEC
Compensatory	Macintosh

MANAGERIAL APPLICATION 17–4

Ads Assuming Different Decision Rules

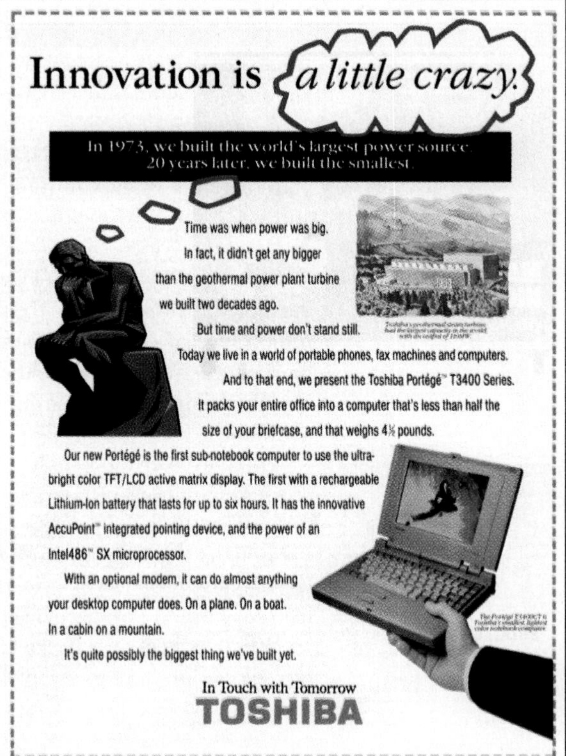

Marketing Applications of Decision Rules

Consumers do not assign explicit numerical weights to the importance of attributes, nor do they assign numerical scores to the performance levels of various brands. These choice models are merely representations of the vague decision rules commonly used by consumers in brand selections.

To date, we cannot answer the question as to which rules are used by consumers in which situations. However, research done in specific situations indicates that people do *use* the rules.[19] Low-involvement purchases probably involve relatively simple decision rules (conjunctive, disjunctive, elimination-by-aspects, or lexicographic), since consumers will attempt to minimize the mental ''cost'' of such decisions.[20] High-involvement decisions often may involve not only more complex rules (compensatory) but may involve stages of decision making with different attributes being evaluated using different rules at each stage.[21] Of course, individual and situational characteristics also influence the type of decision rule used.[22]

A marketing manager must determine, for the market segment under consideration, which is the most likely rule or combination of rules and then develop appropriate marketing strategy. In Managerial Application 17–4, the HP *DeskJet* color printer assumes that consumers assign price a critical role in their decision process for this product. In contrast, Toshiba assumes that, in combination, consumers in its target market for the *Portégé* T3400 evaluate seven criteria.

SUMMARY

During and after the time that consumers gather information about various alternative solutions to a recognized problem, they evaluate the alternatives and select the course of action that seems most likely to solve the problem.

Evaluative criteria are the various features a consumer looks for in response to a particular problem. They are the performance levels or characteristics consumers use to compare different brands in light of their particular consumption problem. The number, type, and importance of evaluative criteria used differ from consumer to consumer and across product categories.

The measurement of (1) which evaluative criteria are used by the consumer, (2) how the consumer perceives the various alternatives on each criterion, and (3) the relative importance of each criterion is a critical first step in utilizing evaluative criteria to develop marketing strategy. While the measurement task is not easy, a number of techniques ranging from direct questioning to projective techniques and multidimensional scaling are available.

Evaluative criteria such as price, size, and color can be judged easily and accurately by consumers. Other criteria, such as quality, durability, and health benefits, are much more difficult to judge. In such cases, consumers often use price, brand name, or some other variable as a *surrogate indicator* of quality. To overcome such surrogate indicators, many lesser-known or lower-priced brands advertise the results of (or encourage participation in) *blind* brand comparisons.

When consumers judge alternative brands on several evaluative criteria, they must have some method to select one brand from the various choices. Decision rules serve this function. A decision rule specifies how a consumer compares two or more brands. Five commonly used decision rules are *disjunctive*, *conjunctive*, *lexicographic*, *elimination-by-aspects*, and *compensatory*. Marketing managers must be aware of the decision rule(s) used by the target market, since different decision rules require different marketing strategies.

REVIEW QUESTIONS

1. What are *evaluative criteria* and on what characteristics can they vary?
2. How can you determine which evaluative criteria consumers use?
3. What methods are available for measuring consumers' judgments of brand performance on specific attributes?
4. How can the importance assigned to evaluative criteria be assessed?
5. What is *sensory discrimination*, and what role does it play in the evaluation of products? What is meant by a *just noticeable difference*? How have marketers used this concept in marketing products?
6. What are *surrogate indicators*? How are they used in the consumer evaluation process? How have marketers used surrogate indicators in positioning various products?
7. What is the *disjunctive decision rule*?
8. What is the *conjunctive decision rule*?
9. What is the *lexicographic decision rule*?
10. What is the *elimination-by-aspects decision rule*?
11. What is the *compensatory decision rule*?

12. How can knowledge of consumers' evaluative criteria and criteria importance be used in developing marketing strategy?

13. How can knowledge of the decision rule consumers might use in a certain purchase assist a firm in developing marketing strategy?

DISCUSSION QUESTIONS

14. List the evaluative criteria and the importance of each that you would use in purchasing (or renting or giving to) ______. Would situational factors change the criteria? The importance weights? Why?
    a. A vacation.
    b. A charity.
    c. An apartment.
    d. An everyday watch.
    e. A fast-food meal.
    f. A Mother's Day present.
    g. An automobile.
    h. Sunglasses.
15. Repeat Question 14, but speculate on how your instructor would answer. In what ways might his or her answer differ from yours? Why?
16. Identify five products for which surrogate indicators may be used as evaluative criteria in a brand choice decision. Why are the indictors used, and how might a firm enhance their use (i.e., strengthen their importance)?
17. The table below represents a particular consumer's evaluative criteria, criteria importance, acceptable level of performance, and judgments of performance with respect to several brands of mopeds. Discuss the brand choice this consumer would make when using the lexicographic, compensatory, and conjunctive decision rules.
18. Describe the decision rule(s) you used or would use in the following:
    a. Choosing a doctor.
    b. Selecting a nice restaurant.
    c. Selecting a novel.
    d. Donating to a charity.
    e. Selecting a TV show.
    f. Buying a soft drink.
    g. Buying a bicycle.
    h. Buying a computer.

    Would you use different rules in different situations? Which ones? Why?
19. Describe your last two ''major'' and your last two ''minor'' purchases. What evaluative criteria and decision rules did you use for each? How did they differ? Why?
20. Discuss surrogate indicators that could be used to evaluate the perceived quality of a ______.
    a. University.
    b. Wine.
    c. Sports equipment.
    d. Perfume.
    e. Frozen vegetable line.
    f. Automobile.
    g. Insurance policy.
    h. Jewelry store.
21. For what products would emotion or a feeling response be an important attribute? Why?

Evaluative Criteria	Criteria Importance	Minimum Acceptable Performance	Alternative Brands: Motron	Vespa	Cimatti	Garelli	Puch	Moto-becane
Price	30	4	2	4	2	4	2	4
Horsepower	15	3	4	2	5	5	4	5
Weight	5	2	3	3	3	3	3	3
Gas economy	35	3	4	4	3	2	4	5
Color selection	10	3	4	4	3	2	5	2
Frame	5	2	4	2	3	3	3	3

Note: 1 = Very poor; 2 = Poor; 3 = Fair; 4 = Good; and 5 = Very good.

APPLICATION EXERCISES

22. Develop a list of evaluative criteria that students might use in evaluating alternative apartments they might rent. After listing these criteria, go to the local newspaper or student newspaper, select several apartments, and list them in a table similar to the one in Question 17. Then have five other students evaluate this information and have each indicate the apartment they would rent if given only those alternatives. Next, ask them to express the importance they attach to each evaluative criterion, using a 100-point constant-sum scale. Finally, provide them with a series of statements which describe different decision rules and ask them to indicate the one that best describes the way they made their choice. Calculate the choice they should have made given their importance ratings and stated decision rules. Have them explain any inconsistent choices.
23. Develop a short questionnaire to elicit the evaluative criteria consumers might use in selecting a ______. Also, have each respondent indicate the relative importance he/she attaches to each of the evaluative criteria. Then, working with several other students, combine your information and develop a segmentation strategy based on consumer evaluative criteria and criteria importance. Finally, develop an advertisement for each market segment to indicate that their needs would be served by your brand.
    a. Toothpaste.
    b. Pefume.
    c. Everyday shoes.
    e. Casual restaurant.
    f. Automobile.
    g. Charity.
    h. Pet.
    i. Exercise club.
24. Set up a taste-test experiment to determine if volunteer taste testers can perceive a just noticeable difference between three different brands of ______. To set up the experiment, store each test brand in a separate but identical container and label the containers *L*, *M*, and *N*. Provide volunteer taste testers with an adequate opportunity to evaluate each brand before asking them to state their identification of the actual brands represented as *L*, *M*, and *N*. Evaluate the results and discuss the marketing implications of these results.
    a. Cola.
    b. Diet cola.
    c. Lemon-lime drink.
    d. Carbonated water.
    e. Chips.
    f. Juice.
25. For a product considered high in social status, develop a questionnaire that measures the evaluative criteria of that product, using both a *direct* and an *indirect* method of measurement. Compare the results and discuss their similarities and differences and which evaluative criteria are most likely to be utilized in brand choice.
26. Find and copy two ads that encourage consumers to use a surrogate indicator.
27. Find and copy two ads that attempt to change the importance consumers assign to product class evaluative criteria.
28. Interview two ______ salespersons. Ascertain the evaluative criteria, importance weights, decision rules, and surrogate indicators that they believe consumers use when purchasing their product. What marketing implications are suggested if their beliefs are accurate for large segments?
    a. Automobile.
    b. Furniture.
    c. Insurance.
    d. Bicycle.
    e. Dress shoes.
    f. Jewelry.

REFERENCES

[1]A. L. Page and H. F. Rosenbaum, "Redesigning Product Lines with Conjoint Analysis," *Journal of Product Innovation Management*, no. 4, 1987, pp. 120–37.

[2]See also R. W. Belk, M. Wallendorf, and J. F. Sherry, Jr., "The Sacred and Profane in Consumer Behavior," *Journal of Consumer Behavior*, June 1989, pp. 1–38.

[3]R. Wahlers, "Number of Choice Alternatives and Number of Product Characteristics as Determinants of the Consumer's Choice of an Evaluation Process Strategy," in *Advances in Consumer Research*, ed. A. Mitchell (Chicago: Association for Consumer Research, 1982), pp. 544–49.

[4]J. Freidenard and D. Bible, "The Home Purchase Process: Measurement of Evaluative Criteria through Purchase Measures," *Journal of the Academy of Marketing Science*, Fall 1982, pp. 359–76.

[5]D. Schellinch, "Cue Choice as a Function of Time Pressure

and Perceived Risk,'' in *Advances in Consumer Research*, ed. R. Bagozzi and A. Tybout (Chicago: Association for Consumer Research, 1983), pp. 470–75.

[6]B. L. Bagus, ''The Consumer Durable Replacement Buyer,'' *Journal of Marketing*, January 1991, pp. 42–51.

[7]B. Abrams, ''Hanes Finds L'eggs Methods Don't Work with Cosmetics,'' *The Wall Street Journal*, February 3, 1983, p. 33.

[8]For details, see D. S. Tull and D. I. Hawkins, *Marketing Research* (New York: Macmillan, 1993), pp. 420–34.

[9]Ibid., pp. 405–19.

[10]R. L. Miller, ''Dr. Weber and the Consumer,'' *Journal of Marketing*, January 1962, pp. 57–61; and J. J. Wheatley, J. S. Y. Chiu, and A. Goldman, ''Physical Quality, Price, and Perceptions of Product Quality: Implications for Retailers,'' *Journal of Retailing*, Summer 1981, pp. 100–116.

[11]G. L. Sullivan and K. J. Burger, ''An Investigation of the Determinants of Cue Utilization,'' *Psychology & Marketing*, Spring 1987, pp. 63–74.

[12]A. R. Rao and K. B. Monroe, ''The Effect of Price, Brand Name, and Store Name on Buyers' Perceptions of Product Quality,'' *Journal of Marketing Research*, August 1989, pp. 351–57; D. J. Moore and R. W. Olshavsky, ''Brand Choice and Deep Price Discounts,'' *Psychology & Marketing*, Fall 1989, pp. 181–96; P. Chao, ''The Impact of Country Affiliation on the Credibility of Product Attribute Claims,'' *Journal of Advertising Research*, May 1989, pp. 35–41; G. J. Tellis and G. J. Gaeth, ''Best Value, Price-Seeking, and Prize Aversion,'' *Journal of Marketing*, April 1990, pp. 35–45; J. Gotlieb and D. Sarel, ''The Influence of Type of Advertisement, Price, and Source Credibility on Perceived Quality,'' *Journal of the Academy of Marketing Science*, Summer 1992, pp. 253–60; J. B. Gotlieb and D. Sarel, ''Effects of Price Advertisements,'' *Journal of Business Research*, May 1991, pp. 195–210; and D. R. Lichtenstein, N. M. Ridgway, and R. G. Netemeyer, ''Price Perceptions and Consumer Shopping Behavior,'' *Journal of Marketing Research*, May 1993, pp. 234–45.

[13]D. J. Curry and P. C. Riesz, ''Prices and Price/Quality Relationships,'' *Journal of Marketing*, January 1988, pp. 36–52; D. R. Lichtenstein and S. Burton, ''The Relationship between Perceived and Objective Price-Quality,'' *Journal of Marketing Research*, November 1989, pp. 429–43; and S. Burton and D. R. Lichtenstein, ''Assessing the Relationship between Perceived and Objective Price-Quality,'' in *Advances in Consumer Research XVII*, eds. M. E. Goldberg, G. Gorn, and R. W. Pollay (Provo, Utah: Association for Consumer Research, 1990), pp. 715–22.

[14]See footnote 12, Rao and Monroe.

[15]See C. A. Kelley, ''An Investigation of Consumer Product Warranties as Market Signals,'' *Journal of the Academy of Marketing Science*, Summer 1988, pp. 72–78; S.-T. Hong and R. S. Wyer, Jr., ''Effects of Country-of-Origin and Product-Attribute Information on Product Evaluation,'' *Journal of Consumer Research*, September 1989, pp. 175–87; M. Wall, J. Liefeld, and L. A. Heslop, ''Impact of Country-of-Origin Cues,'' and V. V. Cordell, ''Competitive Context and Price as Moderators of Country-of-Origin Preferences,'' both in *Journal of the Academy of Marketing Science*, Spring 1991, pp. 105–14, and 123–28; M. Hastak and S.-T. Hong, ''Country-of-Origin Effects,'' *Psychology & Marketing*, Summer 1991, pp. 129–43; and T. A. Shimp, S. Samiee, and T. J. Madden, ''Countries and Their Products,'' *Journal of the Academy of Marketing Science*, Fall 1993, pp. 323–30.

[16]K. M. Elliott and D. W. Roach, ''Are Consumers Evaluating Your Products the Way You Think and Hope They Are,'' *Journal of Consumer Marketing*, Spring 1991, pp. 5–14.

[17]K. B. Monroe, *Pricing* (New York: McGraw-Hill, 1979), p. 38.

[18]C. F. Hite, R. E. Hite, and T. Minor, ''Quality Uncertainty, Brand Reliance, and Dissipative Advertising,'' *Journal of the Academy of Marketing Science*, Spring 1991, pp. 115–22; and P. Sellers, ''Brands,'' *Fortune*, August 23, 1993, pp. 52–56.

[19]C. W. Park and D. C. Smith, ''Product-Level Choice,'' *Journal of Consumer Research*, December 1989, pp. 289–99; and M. L. Ursic and J. G. Helgeson ''The Impact of Choice and Task Complexity on Consumer Decision Making,'' *Journal of Business Research*, August 1990, pp. 69–86.

[20]See S. M. Shugan, ''The Cost of Thinking,'' *Journal of Consumer Research*, September 1980, pp. 99–111; and W. D. Hoyer, ''An Examination of Consumer Decision Making for a Common Repeat Purchase Product,'' *Journal of Consumer Research*, December 1984, pp. 822–29.

[21]See N. K. Malhotra, ''Multi-Stage Information Processing Behavior,'' *Journal of the Academy of Marketing Science*, Winter 1982, pp. 54–71; and C. W. Park and R. J. Lutz, ''Decision Plans and Consumer Chores Dynamics,'' *Journal of Marketing Research*, February 1982, pp. 180–215.

[22]See J. G. Helgeson and M. L. Ursic, ''Information Load, Cost/Benefit Assessment and Decision Strategy Variability,'' *Journal of the Academy of Marketing Science*, Winter 1993, pp. 13–20.

CHAPTER 18

OUTLET SELECTION AND PURCHASE

Kmart is America's second-largest retail chain. It achieved this position through aggressively positioning itself as a no-frills discount store offering mid- and lower-quality brands at rock-bottom prices. Martha Stewart is a syndicated columnist, author, and authority on food and entertaining. Her books on entertaining retail for around $50 and attract affluent, professional audiences. Kmart and Ms. Stewart appear to have very little in common.

Kmart signed Ms. Stewart as consultant and ad spokeswoman for its home fashions division. Ms. Stewart will make personal appearances in Kmart stores and help create new kitchen, bed, and bath products, some of which will bear her name. She will also prepare a series of "Kitchen Kornerstone" brochures offering tips on cooking, decor, and entertaining which will be distributed by the Kitchen Korner boutiques located in Kmart stores. Finally, she will represent Kmart in both television and print media ads. Why is a discount image store using such an upscale strategy?

The answer is quite simple. Ms. Stewart represents a continuation of an attempt begun several years ago to give Kmart an enhanced image. The Jaclyn Smith Signature collection, the use of Jaclyn Smith in ads, inclusion of more top national brands, a new logo, and store redesigns began the process. The Jaclyn Smith strategy, bringing relatively upscale fashions into Kmart, was seen as very risky when initiated in 1985 but has proven very successful.

Kmart has examined the changes occurring in America's demographics and values and has concluded that the major growth opportunities are in the quality, style, and service areas, not the low-quality, low-price area. It is attempting to serve the mass market that increasingly values quality and style but retains a need for value as well.

To the extent Kmart succeeds, top line manufacturers will face competition from Kmart's private labels, as well as a need to secure distribution through its over 2,000 outlets.[1]

Selecting a retail outlet involves the same process as selecting a brand,[2] as described in the previous chapters. That is, the consumer recognizes a problem which requires an outlet to be selected, engages in internal and possibly external search, evaluates the relevant alternatives, and applies a decision rule to make a selection. We are not going to repeat our discussion of these steps. However, we will describe the evaluative criteria that consumers frequently use in choosing retail outlets, consumer characteristics that influence the criteria used, and in-store characteristics that affect the amounts and brands purchased.

Before turning to the above topics, we need to clarify the meaning of the term *retail outlet*. It refers to any source of products or services for consumers. In earlier editions of this text we used the term *store*. However, increasingly consumers see or hear descriptions of products in catalogs, direct-mail pieces, various print media, or on television or radio and acquire them through mail or telephone orders. Generally referred to as in-home shopping, it represents a small but rapidly growing percent of total retail sales.[3]

In addition to in-home shopping, a substantial volume of retail trade occurs in other nonstore settings, such as garage sales, flea markets, farmer's markets, swap meets, and consumer-to-consumer (through classified ads and computer bulletin boards). Thus, the retail shopping environment is increasingly complex, challenging, and exciting for both consumers and marketers.

OUTLET CHOICE VERSUS PRODUCT CHOICE

Outlet selection is obviously important to managers of retail firms such as Kmart and L. L. Bean. However, it is equally important to consumer goods marketers. There are three basic sequences a consumer can follow when making a purchase decision: (1) brand (or item) first, outlet second; (2) outlet first, brand second; or (3) brand and outlet simultaneously.[4]

Our model and discussion in the previous two chapters suggests that brands are selected first and outlets second. This situation may arise frequently. For example, in our computer example in the previous chapter, you may read about computers in relevant consumer publications and talk with knowledgeable individuals. Based on this information you select a brand and purchase it from the store with the lowest price (or best location, image, service, or other relevant attributes).

For many individuals and product categories, stores rather than brands form the evoked set.[5] In our computer example, you might be familiar with one store—Campus Computers—that sells personal computers. You decide to visit that store and select a computer from the brands available there.

A third strategy is to compare the brands in your evoked set at the stores in your evoked set. The decision would involve a simultaneous evaluation of both store and product attributes. Thus, you might choose between your second preferred computer at a store with friendly personnel and excellent service facilities versus your favorite computer at an impersonal outlet with no service facilities.

The appropriate marketing strategies for both retailers and manufacturers differ depending on the decision sequence generally used by the target market. Exhibit 18–1 highlights some of the key strategic implications. The *Trends* ad in Managerial Application 18–1 uses national advertising to trigger a desire for the product and provides an 800 number to direct consumers to the appropriate outlets.

ATTRIBUTES AFFECTING RETAIL OUTLET SELECTION

The selection of a specific retail outlet, whether before or after a brand decision, involves a comparison of the alternative outlets on the consumer's evaluative criteria. As was the case with products, retail outlets are generally selected from among those in the consumer's evoked set.[6] This section considers a number of evaluative criteria commonly used by consumers to select retail outlets.

Outlet Image

A story on Sears in *Advertising Age* explained:

> The task facing Sears is very, very difficult. Sears has to set completely new strategies that are responsive to the new realities. For one thing, it has to make its stores attractive. Consumers have a myriad of retailing choices, and they are also conservative and frugal. Retailers first must make them want to spend and second induce them to spend at their store. Sears is not good at that; it doesn't stand out, and *it doesn't stand for anything* (italics added). Do you know any woman who wants a Sears cocktail dress? Its hard goods get in the way of its soft goods and vice versa.[7]

The retailing expert quoted above is describing Sears' image. A given consumer's or target market's perception of all of the attributes associated with a retail outlet is generally referred to as the outlet's **image**.[8] Exhibit 18–2 lists nine dimensions and some 23

MANAGERIAL APPLICATION 18–1

Advertising Based on Product Selection before Outlet Selection

EXHIBIT 18–1

Marketing Strategy Based on the Consumer Decision Sequence

Decision Sequence	Level in the Channel	
	Retailer	**Manufacturer**
(1) Outlet first, Brand second	Image advertising Margin management on shelf space, displays Location analysis Appropriate pricing	Distribution in key outlets Point-of-purchase, shelf space, and position Programs to strengthen existing outlets
(2) Brand first, Outlet second	Many brands and/or key brands Co-op ads featuring brands Price specials on brands Yellow Pages listings under brands	More exclusive distribution Brand availability advertising (Yellow Pages) Brand image management
(3) Simultaneous	Margin training for sales personnel Multiple brands/key brands High-service or low-price structure	Programs targeted at retail sales personnel Distribution in key outlets Co-op advertising

EXHIBIT 18–2

Dimensions and Components of Store Image

Dimension	Component(s)
Merchandise	Quality, selection, style, and price
Service	Layaway plan, sales personnel, easy return, credit, and delivery
Clientele	Customers
Physical facilities	Cleanliness, store layout, shopping ease, and attractiveness
Convenience	Location and parking
Promotion	Advertising
Store atmosphere	Congeniality, fun, excitement, comfort
Institutional	Store reputation
Post-transaction	Satisfaction

components of these nine dimensions of store image.[9] The merchandise dimension, for example, takes into account such components as quality, selection, style, and price, while the service dimension includes components related to credit, financing, delivery, and sales personnel. Notice that the store atmosphere component is primarily emotional or feeling in nature.

Since the components in Exhibit 18–2 were developed for stores, they require some adjustments for use with other types of retail outlets. For example, 800 numbers, 24-hour operations, and ample in-bound phone lines (no busy signals) are more relevant to the convenience of a catalog merchant such as L. L. Bean than are location and parking, as listed in the table.

Marketers make extensive use of image data in formulating retail strategies.[10] First, marketers control most of the elements that determine an outlet's image. Second, differing groups of consumers desire different things from various types of retail outlets.[11] Thus, a focused, managed image that matches the target market's desires is essential for most retailers.

Department stores traditionally attempted to "be all things to all people." As a result, they suffered serious losses to more specialized competitors as markets became increasingly segmented during the 1980s. Their images were too diffuse to attract customers. In response, many have sought to evolve into collections of distinctive specialty stores or stores-within-stores, each with a sharply focused image keyed to a well-defined target market. Managerial Application 18–2 shows how Sears is now positioning its junior department.

Other outlets concentrate on one or more attributes that are important to a segment of consumers or that are important to most consumers in certain situations. Catalog showroom merchants have successfully followed the first approach. They appeal to a segment that wants low prices on well-known brands but does not care about in-store sales help or pleasant decor. 7-Eleven Food Stores have followed the second approach, which is to provide customers "what they want, when they want it, where they want it." Thus, they focus on providing convenience for consumers in those situations where convenience is an important attribute.

MANAGERIAL APPLICATION 18-2

Positioning for a Component of a Department Store

Not only individual stores but also shopping areas (downtown, malls, neighborhoods) have images. Thus, retailers should be concerned not only with their own image but also with the image of their shopping area. The ability to aggressively portray a consistent, integrated image is a significant advantage for shopping malls.

Retail Advertising

Retailers use advertising to communicate their attributes, particularly sale prices, to consumers. A major study on the impact of retail grocery advertising concluded:

> In summary, a substantial number of consumers rely on newspaper grocery store advertising in making their choices about where to shop, what to buy, and when to do their shopping. They are apparently willing to modify their choice of products and stores or to shop at one time rather than another in the expectation of increasing their overall satisfaction.[12]

Of particular importance is the role of price advertising. It is clear that price advertising can attract people to stores. Revealing results were obtained in a major study involving newspaper ads in seven cities for a range of product categories (motor oil, sheets, digital watches, pants, suits, coffee makers, dresses, and mattresses). The impact of the retail

FIGURE 18–1

Expenditures of Individuals Drawn to a Store by an Advertised Item

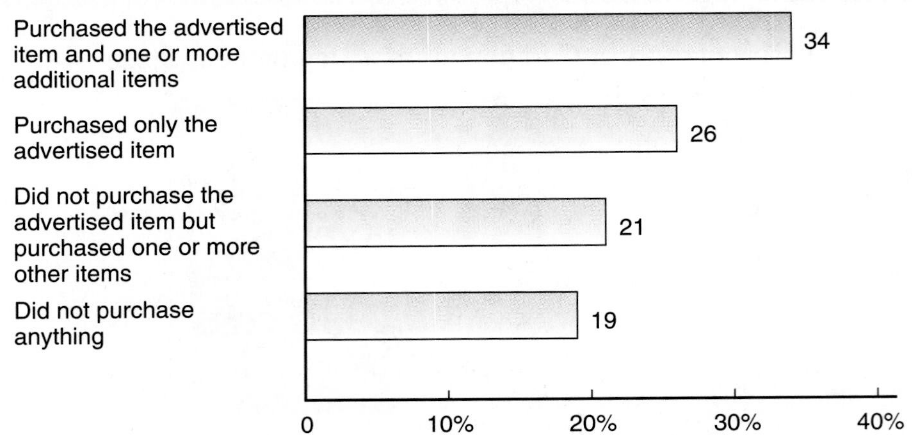

advertisements varied widely by product category. For example, 88 percent of those who came to the store in response to the advertisement for motor oil purchased the advertised item, compared to only 16 percent of those responding to the dress ad. Approximately 50 percent of the shoppers overall purchased the advertised item that attracted them to the store.

As Figure 18–1 illustrates, purchases of the advertised item understate the total impact of the ad. Sales of additional items to customers who came to purchase an advertised item are referred to as **spillover sales**. Spillover sales in this study equaled sales of the advertised items. That is, for every $1 spent on the sale item by people who came to the store in response to the advertising, another $1 was spent on some other item(s) in the store.[13] The nature of these unplanned additional purchases is explored in the section of this chapter dealing with in-store influences.

Price Advertising Decisions Retailers face three decisions when they consider using price advertising:

1. How large a price discount should be used?
2. Should comparison or reference prices be used?
3. What verbal statements should accompany the price information?

Unfortunately, only limited information is available to guide the manager in these decisions.

Consumers tend to assume that any advertised price represents a price reduction or sale price. Showing a comparison price increases the perceived savings significantly. However, the strength of the perception varies with the manner in which the comparison or **reference price** is presented. The best approach seems to be to present the sale price, the regular price, and the dollar amount saved. Most consumers understand reference prices and are influenced by them but do not completely believe them. Since price and sale advertising have a strong impact on consumer purchases, the FTC and many states have special guidelines and regulations controlling their use.

Such words or phrases as "now only," "compare at," or "special" appear to enhance the perceived value of a sale. Unfortunately, the findings we have been discussing vary

MANAGERIAL APPLICATION 18–3

Sale Price Advertising

by product category, brand, initial price level, consumer group, and retail outlet.[14] Thus, a retail manager must confirm these generalizations for his or her store and product line.

In the Sears ad in Managerial Application 18–3, the sale price and the dollar savings are emphasized. In contrast, the Target ad presents only the sale price.

Outlet Location and Size

The location of a retail outlet plays an important role in consumer store choice. If all other things are approximately equal, the consumer generally will select the closest store. Likewise, the size of an outlet is an important factor in store choice. Unless a customer is particularly interested in fast service or convenience, larger outlets are preferred over smaller outlets, all other things being equal.

Several methods for calculating the level of store attraction based on store size and distance have been developed. One such model is called the **retail attraction model** (also called the **retail gravitation model**). A popular version of this model is

$$MS_i = \frac{\dfrac{S_i}{T_i^{\lambda}}}{\displaystyle\sum_{i=1}^{n} \frac{S_i}{T_i^{\lambda}}}$$

where:

MS_i = Market share of store i.
S_i = Size of store i.
T_i = Travel time to store i.
λ = Attraction factor for a particular product category.

In the retail gravitation model, store size generally is measured in square footage and assumed to be a measure of breadth of merchandise. Likewise, the distance or travel time to a store is assumed to be a measure of the effort, both physical and psychological, to reach a given retail area. Because willingness to travel to shop varies by product class, the travel time is raised to the λ power. This allows the effect of distance or travel time to vary by product.[15]

For a convenience item or minor shopping good, the attraction coefficient is quite large since shoppers are unwilling to travel very far for such items. However, major high-involvement purchases such as automobiles or specialty items such as wedding dresses generate greater willingness to travel to distant trading areas. When this is the case, the attraction coefficient is small and the effect of travel time as a deterrent is reduced.

CONSUMER CHARACTERISTICS AND OUTLET CHOICE

The preceding discussion by and large has focused on store attributes independently of the specific characteristics of the consumers in the target market. However, different consumers have vastly differing desires and reasons for shopping.

This section of the chapter examines two consumer characteristics that are particularly relevant to store choice: perceived risk and shopper orientation.

Perceived Risk

The purchase of products involves a certain amount of risk that may include both economic and social consequences. Certain products, because of their expense or technical complexity, represent high levels of *economic risk.* Products closely related to a consumer's public image present high levels of *social risk.* Exhibit 18–3 shows that socks and gasoline are low in economic and social risk, while hairstyles and gifts are low in economic risk but high in social risk. Other products, such as personal computers and auto repairs, are low in social risk but high in economic risk. Finally, automobiles and living room furniture are high in both economic and social risk.[16] Exhibit 18–3 also indicates the role of the situation in perceived risk. Wine is shown as low in both social and economic risk when consumed at home but high in social risk when served while entertaining.

The perception of these risks *differs* among consumers, based in part on their past experiences and lifestyles. For this reason, **perceived risk** is considered a consumer characteristic as well as a product characteristic. For example, while many individuals would feel no social risk associated with the brand of jeans owned, others would.

Like product categories, retail outlets are perceived as having varying degrees of risk. Traditional outlets are perceived as low in risk, while more innovative outlets such as direct mail and television shopping programs are viewed as higher risk.[17]

The above findings lead to a number of insights into retailing strategy including:

- Nontraditional outlets need to minimize the perceived risk of shopping if they sell items with either high economic or social risk. Managerial Application 18–4 shows how Lands' End attempts to reduce perceived risk by stressing toll-free ordering,

MANAGERIAL APPLICATION 18–4

Reducing Perceived Risk

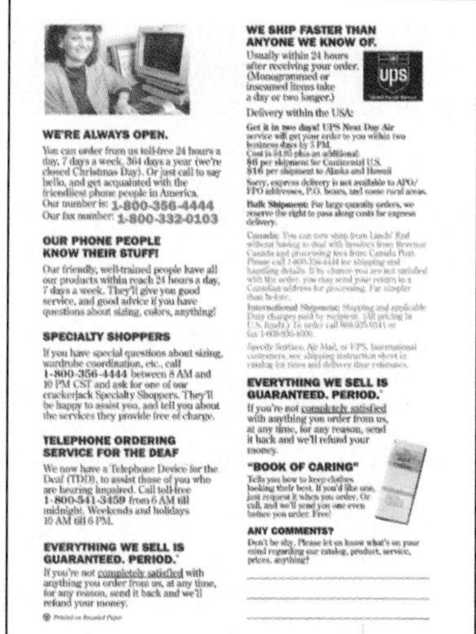

EXHIBIT 18–3

The Economic and Social Risk of Various Types of Products

Social Risk	Economic Risk	
	Low	**High**
Low	Wine (home use) Socks Kitchen supplies Pens/pencils Gasoline	Personal computer Auto repairs Clothes washer Insurance Doctor/lawyer
High	Fashion accessories Hairstyles Gifts (inexpensive) Wine (entertaining) Aerobics suits	Business suits Living room furniture Automobile Snow board Ski suit

24-hour toll-free customer service telephones with trained assistants, and a 100 percent satisfaction guarantee. Word-of-mouth from satisfied customers reinforces these advertised policies.

- Nontraditional outlets, particularly discount stores, need brand-name merchandise in those product categories with high perceived risk. Kmart is pursuing this strategy as well as trying to upgrade its overall image.
- Traditional outlets have a major advantage with high-perceived-risk product lines. These lines should generally be their primary strategy focus. Low-risk items can be

EXHIBIT 18–4

Seven Basic Shopper Orientations

Inactive Shoppers (15%* of all shoppers) have extremely restricted lifestyles and shopping interests. Best characterized by their inactivity, Inactive Shoppers do not engage in outdoor or do-it-yourself activities except for working in the yard or garden. They do not express strong enjoyment or interest in shopping, nor are they particularly concerned about such shopping attributes as price, employee service, or product selection.

Active Shoppers (12.8%) have demanding lifestyles and are ''tough'' shoppers. They engage in all forms of outdoor activities and are usually do-it-yourselfers. Actives enjoy ''shopping around,'' and price is a major consideration in their search. However, given their full range of interests outside of shopping, Actives appear to shop more as an expression of their intense lifestyles rather than being interested in finding bargains. Therefore, these shoppers balance price with quality, fashion, and selection in their search for value.

Service Shoppers (10%) demand a high level of in-store service when shopping. They usually seek convenient stores with friendly, helpful employees. Conversely, they quickly become impatient if they have to wait for a clerk to help them.

Traditional Shoppers (14.1%) share Active Shoppers' preoccupation with outdoor activities, but not their enthusiasm for shopping. They actively hike, camp, hunt, and fish, and are do-it-yourselfers who often work on their cars. In general, though, Traditional Shoppers are not price sensitive nor do they have other strong shopper requirements.

(*continued on following page*)

used to round out the overall assortment. They can be promoted through point-of-purchase materials and price discounts.

- Economic risks can be reduced through warranties and similar policies. Social risk is harder to reduce. A skilled sales force and known brands can help reduce this type of risk.

Shopping Orientation

Individuals go shopping for more complex reasons than simply acquiring a product or set of products. Diversion from routine activities, exercise, sensory stimulation, social interactions, learning about new trends, and even acquiring interpersonal power (''bossing'' clerks) have been reported as nonpurchase reasons for shopping.[18] Of course, the relative importance of these motives varies both across individuals and within individuals over time as the situation changes. A shopping style that puts particular emphasis on certain activities is called a **shopping orientation**.

Shopping orientations are closely related to general lifestyle and are subject to similar influences. For example, one study found that retail work experience, stage in the household life cycle, and income help to predict shopping orientation.[19]

Seven Basic Shopper Orientations (*continued*)

EXHIBIT 18–4

Dedicated Fringe Shoppers (8.8%) present clear motives for being heavy catalog shoppers. They are do-it-yourselfers and are more likely than average to try new products. They have almost a compulsion for being different. Dedicated Fringe Shoppers are disinterested in extreme socializing. They have little interest in television and radio advertisements and exhibit limited brand and store loyalty. Therefore, the catalog presents a medium for obtaining an expanded selection of do-it-yourself and other products, and this reflects their individualism.

Price Shoppers (10.4%), as the name implies, are most identifiable by their extreme price consciousness. Price Shoppers are willing to undertake an extended search to meet their price requirements, and they rely heavily on all forms of advertising to find the lowest prices.

Transitional Shoppers (6.9%) seem to be consumers in earlier stages of the family life cycle who have not yet formalized their lifestyle patterns and shopping values. They take an active interest in repairing and personalizing cars. Most participate in a variety of outdoor activities. They are more likely than average to try new products. Transitional Shoppers exhibit little interest in shopping around for low prices. They are probably ''eclectic shoppers'' because they appear to make up their minds quickly to buy products once they become interested.

*Note that the percents add to only 78, as 22 percent of the respondents did not fit into any of these seven categories.

Source: J. A. Lesser and M. A. Hughes, ''The Generalizability of Psychographic Market Segments across Geographic Locations,'' *Journal of Marketing*, January 1986, p. 23.

Exhibit 18–4 and Table 18–1 describe seven commonly held shopping orientations. The opportunities for developing segment-specific marketing strategies are clearly evident. Likewise, the difficulty one outlet would encounter in appealing to all segments should be obvious.

Shopping orientation influences both the specific retail outlet selected and the general type of outlet. For example, shoppers who derived little or no pleasure from the shopping process itself are prime markets for convenience stores, in-home shopping (catalogs, telephone), and minimum in-store service outlets, such as catalog showroom merchants. Given the valuable strategic insights provided by thorough shopping orientation studies, this tool will play an increasingly important role in retail management.

IN-STORE INFLUENCES THAT ALTER BRAND CHOICES

As Figure 18–2 on page 499 indicates, it is not uncommon to enter a retail outlet with the intention of purchasing a particular brand and to leave with a different brand or additional items. Influences operating within the store induce additional information processing and

TABLE 18–1 Selected Demographic Characteristics of Shopper Types

Characteristics	Shopper Types: Inactive	Active	Service	Traditional	Dedicated Fringe	Price	Transitional
Age							
18–34	35.5%	54.6%	40.9%	52.3%	46.3%	36.9%	63.8%
35–44	20.4	21.3	23.7	21.3	21.7	22.4	12.6
45–64	31.5	19.7	28.3	22.9	25.2	29.0	19.1
65 or older	12.6	4.4	7.1	3.5	6.7	11.7	4.5
Sex							
Male	36.1	46.6	48.6	62.3	50.0	25.6	45.0
Female	63.9	53.4	51.4	37.7	50.0	74.4	55.0
Social class							
Lower	49.9	51.5	43.4	43.7	48.8	45.4	55.9
Middle	46.3	46.0	52.6	53.2	47.5	50.0	40.5
Upper	3.8	2.5	4.0	3.1	3.7	4.6	3.6
Stage of family life cycle (condensed)							
Young singles not living at home	7.7	5.0	6.8	8.0	5.9	2.5	8.5
Young married couples	21.4	38.6	26.4	34.7	33.9	26.5	46.9
Older married couples with dependent children	32.5	34.8	38.8	37.2	29.6	33.5	23.8
Older married couples without dependent children	27.9	20.0	23.1	18.8	27.2	29.3	17.8
Solitary survivors	10.6	1.6	4.9	1.3	3.4	8.2	3.0

Source: J. A. Lesser and M. A. Hughes, ''The Generalizability of Psychographic Market Segments across Geographic Locations,'' *Journal of Marketing*, January 1986, p. 24.

subsequently affect the final purchase decision. This portion of the chapter examines five variables that singularly and in combination influence brand decisions inside a retail store: *point-of-purchase displays*, *price reductions*, *store layout*, *stockout situations*, and *sales personnel*. As illustrated in Figure 18–3, each of these influences has the potential of altering a consumer's evaluation and purchase behavior.

The Nature of Unplanned Purchases

The fact that consumers often purchase brands different from or in addition to those planned has led to an interest in *impulse purchases*. Impulse purchases are defined generally as *purchases made in a store that are different from those the consumer planned to make prior to entering the store*. Unfortunately, the term *impulse purchase*, and even its more accurate substitute, *unplanned purchase*, implies a lack of rationality or alternative evaluation. However, this is not necessarily true.[20] The decision to purchase Del Monte rather than Green Giant peas because Del Monte is on sale is certainly not illogical. Nor is an unplanned decision to take advantage of the unexpected availability of fresh strawberries.

Supermarket Decisions: Two Thirds Are Made In-Store

FIGURE 18–2

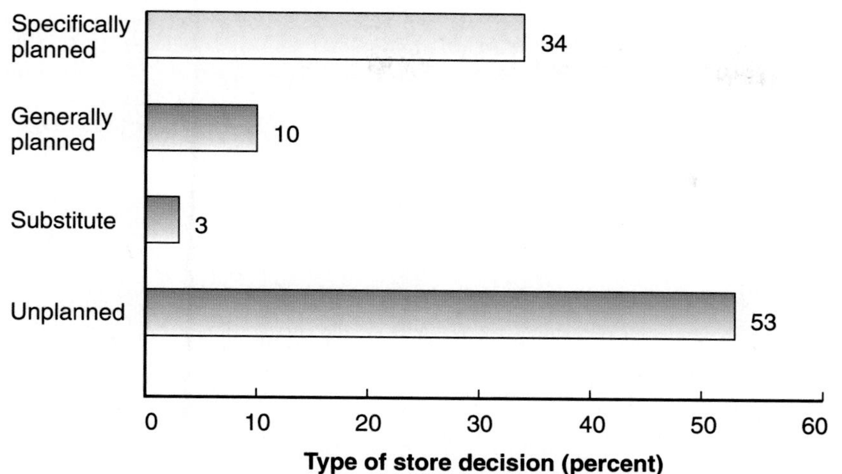

In-Store Influences that Impact Alternative Evaluation and Purchase

FIGURE 18–3

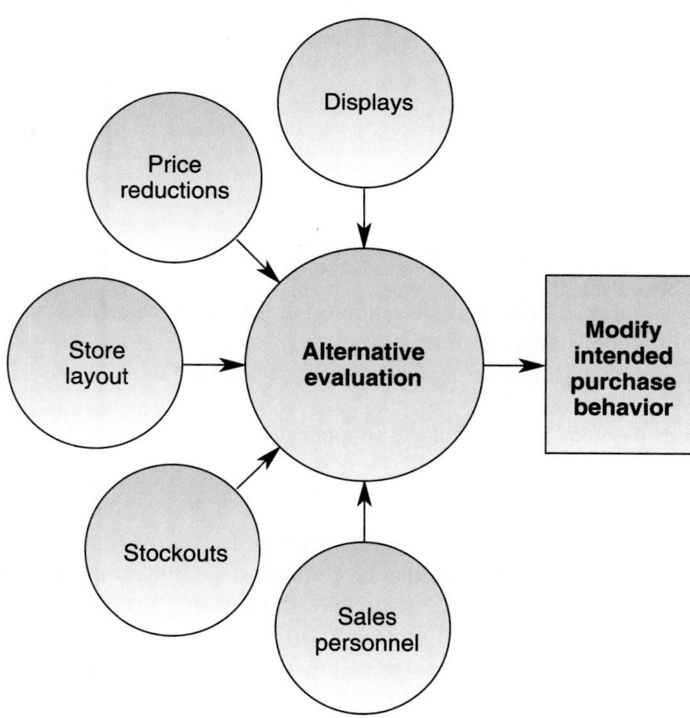

Considering in-store purchase decisions as the result of additional information processing within the store leads to much more useful marketing strategies than considering these purchases to be random or illogical.[21] This approach allows the marketer to utilize knowledge of the target market, its motives, and the perception process to increase sales of specific items. The Point-of-Purchase Advertising Institute uses the following definitions:

TABLE 18–2

Shopper Purchase Behavior

Product	Specifically Planned	Generally Planned	+	Substituted	+	Unplanned	=	In-Store Decisions
Total study average*	34%	10%		3%		53%		66%
Grooming*	26	9		—		65		74
Magazines/newspapers*	12	3		1		84		88
Oral hygiene products*	26	4		3		57		75
Snack foods*	17	10		5		68		83
Tobacco products*	42	3		1		54		58
Baby foods*	51	11		—		37		49
Detergents*	38	6		6		50		62
Apparel*	23	3		4		71		76
Cereal*	32	9		4		55		68
Soft drinks*	41	9		4		45		59
Alcoholic beverages, mixers*	42	11		3		44		58
Fruits, vegetables*	46	8		—		46		54
Dairy products*	43	10		2		45		57
Cold remedies**	28	35		19		18		72
Toothpaste/toothbrushes**	38	31		16		15		62
Antacids/laxatives**	39	37		12		12		61
Facial cosmetics**	40	34		11		15		60

Sources: **1987 POPAI Consumer Buying Habits Study* (Englewood, N.J.: Point-of-Purchase Advertising Institute, 1987); **1992 POPAI/Horner Canadian Drug Store Study (Englewood, N.J.: Point-of-Purchase Advertising Institute, 1992).

- **Specifically planned.** A specific brand or item decided on before visiting the store and purchased as planned.
- **Generally planned.** A pre-store decision to purchase a product category such as vegetables but not the specific item.
- **Substitute.** A change from a specifically or generally planned item to a functional substitute.
- **Unplanned.** An item bought that the shopper did not have in mind upon entering the store.
- **In-store decisions.** The sum of generally planned, substitute, and unplanned purchases.

Table 18–2 illustrates the extent of purchasing (in the United States and Canada) that is not specifically planned. It reveals that consumers make a great many brand decisions *after* entering the store. Thus, marketing managers not only must strive to position their brand in the target market's evoked set, they also must attempt to influence the in-store decisions of their potential consumers. Retailers must not only attract consumers to their outlets, they should structure the purchasing environment in a manner that provides maximum encouragement for unplanned purchases.

In-store marketing strategies are particularly important for product categories characterized by very high rates of in-store purchase decisions. For example, grooming supplies (88 percent in-store decisions) and snack foods (83 percent in-store decisions) represent major opportunities. In contrast, soft drinks, alcoholic beverages, and baby food represent less opportunity for in-store marketing strategies.

We now turn our attention to some of the variables that manufacturers and retailers can alter to influence in-store decisions.

Impact of Advertising and Point-of-Purchase Displays on Sales of Juice and Cereal

FIGURE 18–4

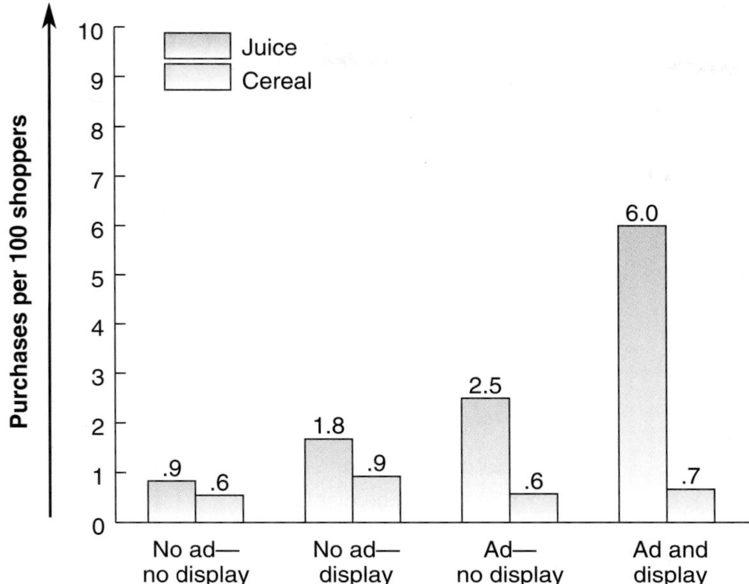

Source: *1987 POPAI Consumer Buying Habits Study* (Englewood, N.J.: Point-of-Purchase Advertising Institute, 1987).

Point-of-Purchase Displays

Point-of-purchase (P-O-P) displays are common in the retailing of many products, and the impact these displays have on brand sales is often tremendous. Figure 18–4 provides a visual representation of this impact for juice and cereal. Notice the impact that product type has on the effectiveness of P-O-P material. Figure 18–5 illustrates the importance of the location of the P-O-P display. Although the sales impact of displays (and ads) varies widely with the type and location of the display and between product classes and between brands within a product category, there is generally a strong increase in sales.[22]

When effective in-store display is combined with advertising, the results can be greater than the sum of the two individually. For example, in Figure 18–6, all four brands of peanut butter experienced percentage sales gains that were far greater when both the display and advertisements were utilized.

Price Reductions and Promotional Deals

Price reductions and promotional deals (coupons, multiple-item discounts, and gifts) are frequently accompanied by the use of some point-of-purchase materials. Therefore, the relative impact of each is sometimes not clear. Nonetheless, there is ample evidence that in-store price reductions affect brand decisions. The general pattern is a sharp increase in sales when the price is first reduced, followed by a return to near-normal sales over time or after the price reduction ends.

Sales increases in response to price reductions come from four motivations.[23] First, current brand users may buy ahead of their anticipated needs (stockpiling). Stockpiling often leads to increased consumption of the brand since it is readily available. Second, users of competing brands may switch to the reduced price brand. These new brand buyers may or may not become repeat buyers of the brand. Third, nonproduct category buyers

FIGURE 18–5

The Effect of P–O–P Display Location on Sales of Listerine Mouthwash

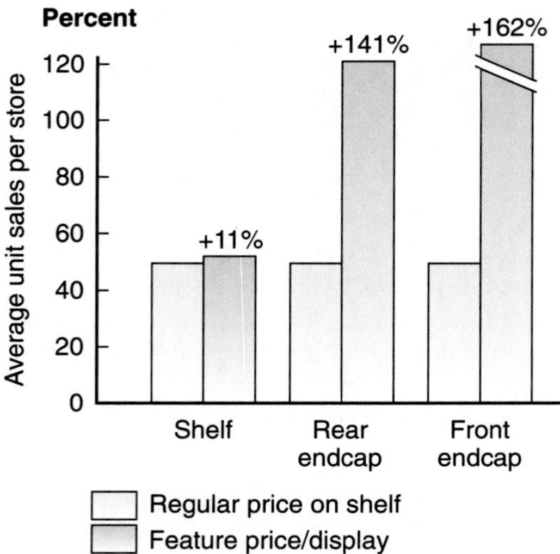

Source: *POPAI/Warner-Lambert Canada P–O–P Effectiveness Study* (Englewood Cliffs, N.J.: Point-of-Purchase Advertising Institute, 1992).

FIGURE 18–6

Impact of Display and Advertising on Peanut Butter Sales (percent sales gains)

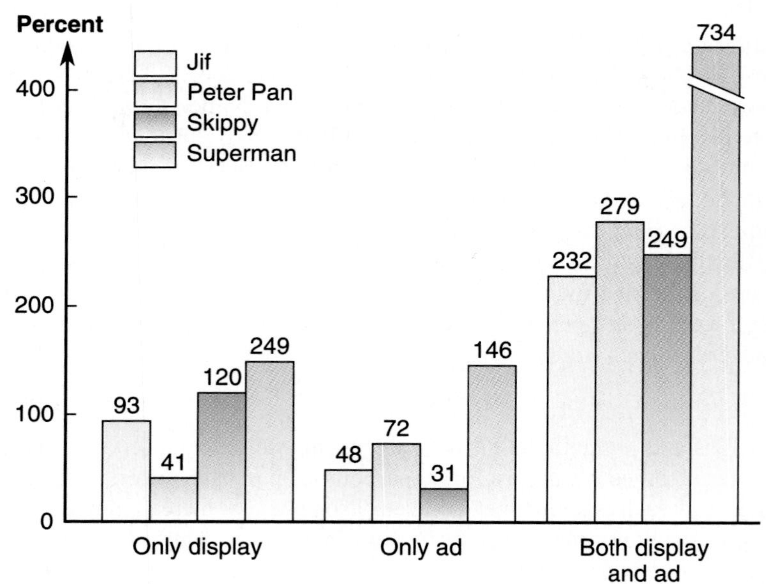

Source: "Display Effectiveness: An Evaluation, Part II," *The Nielsen Researcher*, 1983, p. 7.

may buy the brand because it is now a superior value to the substitute product or to ''doing without.'' Finally, consumers who do not normally shop at the store may come to the store to buy the brand.

Not all households respond to price reductions and deals similarly. Available evidence suggests that households with ample resources (a strong financial base rather than a high income) are more likely to take advantage of deals than are other households. Thus, stores oriented toward financially established consumers can anticipate a strong response to price reductions and other promotional deals. Similarly, products subject to stockpiling by consumers (nonperishables) exhibit more price elasticity than do perishable products.[24]

Price reductions offer differing advantages to the manufacturer and the retailer. As suggested above, the reduced-price brand generates much of its increased sales volume from other brands or substitute products. Thus, the retailer's sales seldom increase as much as the manufacturer's sales. Further, if the reduced-price brand offers the retailer a lower margin, the retailer's profits may decline. Of course, most retailers need some items ''on sale'' to generate and maintain consumer interest.

Store Layout

The location of items within a store has an important influence on the purchase of both product categories and brands. Typically, the more visibility a product receives, the greater the chance it will be purchased. ShopRite grocery stores were forced to alter their standard store layout format when they acquired an odd-shaped lot. The major change involved moving the appetizer-deli section normally located adjacent to the meat section in the rear of the store to a heavy traffic area near the front of the store. The impact was unexpected:

- The appetizer-deli section accounts for 7 percent of this store's sales rather than the normal 2 percent.
- This increased profits, as these items average 35 percent gross margin compared to 10 percent gross margin for most items.[25]

Most modern stores are, like ShopRite, designed to route consumers past high-margin items likely to be purchased on an unplanned basis.

Store Atmosphere

While a store's layout has an influence on the traffic flow through the store, the store's *atmosphere* or environment affects the shopper's mood and willingness to visit and linger. **Store atmosphere** is influenced by such attributes as lighting, layout, presentation of merchandise, fixtures, floor coverings, colors, sounds, odors, dress and behavior of sales personnel, and the number, characteristics, and behavior of other customers. Atmosphere is referred to as *servicescape* when describing a service business such as a hospital, bank, or restaurant.[26]

An example of the impact of store atmosphere was presented in Chapter 14 (see Table 14–1). There we described how fast-tempo music decreased, and slow-tempo music increased, the amount of time restaurant patrons spent in the restaurant, the per-table consumption of bar beverages, and the gross margin of the restaurant.[27]

Montgomery Ward obtained a 30 percent increase in apparel sales by improving its store's atmosphere as follows:

> Carpeting surrounds the redone apparel sections, and merchandise is individually highlighted with small, freestanding racks holding only a few items. The walls also are used for display, giving visual interest as well as squeezing more

FIGURE 18–7 Store Atmosphere and Shopper Behavior

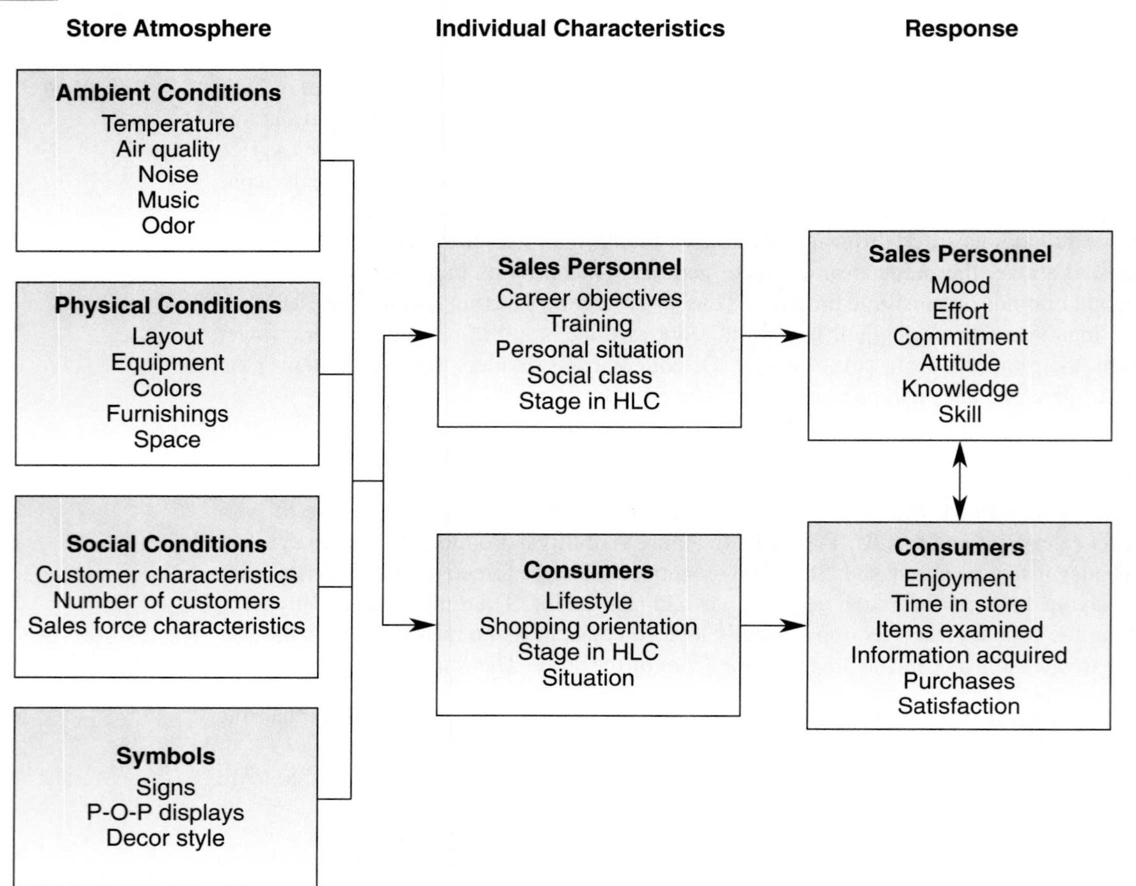

Source: Adapted from M. J. Bitner, "Servicescapes," *Journal of Marketing*, April 1, 1992, pp. 57–71.

offerings into the same space. "The thrust of remodeling is to improve traffic patterns and attract more attention to the merchandise."[28]

Figure 18–7 illustrates the way store atmosphere influences shopper behavior. Several things in this figure are noteworthy. First, the physical environment interacts with the characteristics of individuals to determine response. Thus, an atmosphere that would produce a favorable response in teenagers might produce a negative response in older shoppers. Second, the store atmosphere influences *both* the sales personnel and the customers, whose interactions then influence each other.

Stockouts

Stockouts, the store being temporarily out of a particular brand, obviously affect a consumer purchase decision. He or she then must decide whether to buy the same brand but at another store, switch brands, delay the purchase and buy the desired brand later at the same store, or forgo the purchase altogether. In addition, the consumer's verbal behaviors and attitudes may change. Exhibit 18–5 summarizes the impacts that a stockout situation

EXHIBIT 18–5

Impact of a Stockout Situation

I. Purchase behavior
- A. Purchase a substitute brand or product at the original store. The substitute brand/product may or may not replace the regular brand in future purchases.
- B. Delay the purchase until the brand is available at the original store.
- C. Forgo the purchase entirely.
- D. Purchase the desired brand at a second store. All of the items initially desired may be purchased at the second store or only the stockout items. The second store may or may not replace the original store on future shopping trips.

II. Verbal behavior
- A. The consumer may make negative comments to peers about the original store.
- B. The consumer may make positive comments to peers about the substitute store.
- C. The consumer may make positive comments to peers about the substitute brand/product.

III. Attitude shifts
- A. The consumer may develop a less favorable attitude toward the original store.
- B. The consumer may develop a more favorable attitude toward the substitute store.
- C. The consumer may develop a more favorable attitude toward the substitute brand/product.

may have.[29] None of the likely outcomes is particularly favorable for the original store or brand. Thus, effective distribution and inventory management are critical for both manufacturers and retailers.

Sales Personnel

Sales personnel can have a major impact on consumer purchases. In fact, many department stores are placing increased emphasis on effectively training their sales force. However, high cost and turnover are causing other outlets to move as close to total self-service as possible.

For most low-involvement decisions, self-service is predominant. As purchase involvement increases, the likelihood of interaction with a salesperson also increases. Thus, most studies of effectiveness in sales interactions have focused on high-involvement purchases such as insurance, automobiles, or industrial products. There is no simple explanation for effective sales interactions. Instead, the effectiveness of sales efforts is influenced by the interactions of:

- The salesperson's knowledge, skill, and authority.
- The nature of the customer's buying task.
- The customer–salesperson relationship.[30]

MANAGERIAL APPLICATION

18–5

Competing for Purchase Financing

INTRODUCING THE CARD THAT LETS YOU EARN FREE GASOLINE. WHAT'S THE CATCH? YOU HAVE TO BUY STUFF. Which should not be all that hard to do, since no card on the planet is more accepted than MasterCard and no gasoline on the planet is used more than Shell.

To apply, call us: 1-800-FREE GAS.

Thus, specific research is required for each target market and product category to determine the optimal personnel selling strategy.

PURCHASE

Once the brand and store have been selected, the consumer must complete the transaction. This involves what is normally called "purchasing" the product. Traditionally, this involved giving cash to acquire the rights to the product. However, credit plays a major role in consumer purchases in today's society. Without credit, a great many purchases simply could not be made.

The use of bank credit cards such as Visa, MasterCard, Diners Club, and American Express, and store charge cards such as Sears, Ward's, and Penney's provides an increasingly popular way of financing a purchase decision.

Of course, credit not only is a means to purchase a product; it is a product itself. Thus, the decision to purchase a relatively expensive item may trigger problem recognition for credit. Since a variety of forms of credit are available, the decision process then may be repeated for this problem. Managerial Application 18–5 shows how one company is competing for this business.

SUMMARY

Most consumer products are acquired through some form of a retail outlet. Thus consumers must select outlets as well as products. There are three general ways these decisions can be made: (1) *simultaneously*; (2) *item first, outlet second*; or (3) *outlet first, item second.* Both the manufacturer and the retailer must be aware of the decision sequence used by their target market. It will have a major impact on their marketing strategy.

The decision process used by consumers to select a retail outlet is the same as the process described in Chapters 15 through 17 for selecting a brand. The only difference is in the nature of the evaluative criteria used. The store's *image* and the type and amount of *retail advertising* exert important influences as evaluative criteria. The major dimensions of store image are merchandise, service, clientele, physical facilities, convenience, promotion, store atmosphere, institutional, and posttransaction factors. *Outlet location* is an important attribute for many consumers, with closer outlets being preferred over more distant ones. Larger outlets generally are preferred over smaller outlets. These variables have been used to develop *retail gravitation models.* These models can predict the market share of competing shopping areas with reasonable accuracy.

Shopping orientation refers to the general approach one takes to acquiring both brands and nonpurchase satisfactions from various types of retail outlets. A knowledge of a target market's shopping orientations for a product category is extremely useful in structuring retailing strategy.

While in a store, consumers often purchase a brand or product that differs from their plans before entering the store. Such purchases are referred to as *impulse* or *unplanned purchases.* Unfortunately, both of these terms imply a lack of rationality or decision processes. It is more useful to consider such decisions as being the result of additional information processing induced by in-store stimuli. Such variables as point-of-purchase displays, price reductions, store layout, sales personnel, and brand or product stockouts can have a major impact on sales patterns.

Once the outlet and brand have been selected, the consumer must acquire the rights to the item. Increasingly this involves the use of credit—particularly the use of credit cards. However, major purchases often require the consumer to make a second purchase decision: ''What type of credit shall I buy to finance this purchase?'' Financial institutions increasingly recognize the opportunities in the consumer credit field and are beginning to utilize standard consumer goods marketing techniques.

REVIEW QUESTIONS

1. The consumer faces both the problem of what to buy and where to buy it. How do these two types of decisions differ?
2. How does the sequence in which the brand/outlet decision is made affect the brand strategy? The retailer strategy?
3. What is a *store image* and what are its dimensions and components?
4. Describe the impact of retail advertising on retail sales.
5. What is meant by the term *spillover sales*? Why is it important?
6. What are the primary price advertising decisions confronting a retailer?
7. How does the size and distance to a retail outlet affect store selection and purchase behavior?
8. Describe the model of *retail gravitation* presented in the chapter.
9. How is store choice affected by the *perceived risk* of a purchase?
10. What is meant by *social risk*? How does it differ from *economic risk*?
11. What is a *shopping orientation*?
12. Describe several shopping orientations.
13. What is meant by *in-store purchase decision*? Why is it important?
14. Once in a particular store, what in-store characteristics can influence brand choice? Give an example of each.
15. What can happen in response to a *stockout*?
16. What factors determine the effectiveness of a salesperson?
17. What is meant by *store atmosphere*?
18. What role does the method of payment play in the final implementation of a purchase decision?

DISCUSSION QUESTIONS

19. How would you measure the image of a retail outlet?
20. Does the image of a retail outlet affect the image of the brands it carries?
21. How are social and economic risks likely to affect different prospective buyers of _______? Will either type of risk affect store choice? If so, in what way?
    a. Tie.
    b. Men's underwear.
    c. Perfume (as a gift).
    d. Life insurance.
    e. In-line skates.
    f. Wine (to serve guests).
    g. Dishwasher.
    h. Diaper service.
22. What in-store characteristics could retailers use to enhance the probability of purchase among individuals who visit a store? Describe each factor in terms of how it should be used, and describe its intended effect on the consumer for the following products:
    a. Mouthwash.
    b. Software.
    c. Coffee after a meal.
    d. Flowers from a supermarket.
    e. New car.
    f. Lamps.
23. What type of store atmosphere is most appropriate for each of the following store types. Why?
    a. Outdoor sports equipment.
    b. Garden supplies.
    c. Computer software.
    d. Personal computers.
    e. Automobiles.
    f. Expensive furniture.
    g. Inexpensive furniture.
    h. Ice cream.
24. How would a retailer's and a manufacturer's interest differ in a price reduction on a brand?
25. Retailers often engage in "loss leader" advertising, in which a popular item is advertised at or below cost. Does this make sense? Why?
26. How do you respond to a stockout of your preferred brand of _______? What factors other than product category influence your response?
    a. Toothpaste.
    b. Frozen pizza.
    c. Underwear.
    d. Laptop computer.
    e. Catsup.
    f. Gasoline.
27. What percent of your purchases are "unplanned"? Do you consider your unplanned purchases to be "irrational"?
28. What are the marketing strategy implications of:
    a. Exhibit 18–5.
    b. Figure 18–7.
    c. Figure 18–6.
    d. Figure 18–5.
    e. Figure 18–4.
    f. Table 18–2.
    g. Figure 18–2.
    h. Exhibit 18–4/Table 18–1.
    i. Exhibit 18–2.
    j. Figure 18–1.

APPLICATION EXERCISES

29. Pick a residential area in your town and develop a gravitational model for (a) nearby supermarkets and (b) shopping malls. Conduct telephone surveys to test the accuracy of your model.
30. Develop a questionnaire to measure the image of _______. Have other students complete these questionnaires for three or four competing outlets. Discuss the marketing implications of your results.
    a. Men's clothing stores.
    b. Women's clothing stores.
    c. Discount stores.
    d. Bookstores.
    e. Pizza restaurants.
    f. Catalogs.
    g. Convenience stores.
    h. Sporting goods stores.
    i. Nice restaurants.
    j. Sears, Wards, Penneys, Kmart.

31. For several of the products listed in Table 18–2 interview several students not enrolled in your class and ask them to classify their last purchase as specially planned, generally planned, substitute, or unplanned. Then combine your results with your classmates' to obtain an estimate of student behavior. Compare student behavior with the behavior shown in Table 18–2 and discuss any similarities or differences.
32. Arrange with a local retailer (convenience store, drugstore, and so on) to temporarily install a point-of-purchase display. Then set up a procedure to unobtrusively observe the frequency of evaluation and selection at the display.
33. Visit three retail stores selling the same type of merchandise and prepare a report on their use of P-O-P displays.
34. Interview the manager of a drug, department, or grocery store on their views of P-O-P displays and price advertising.
35. Answer Question 26 using a sample of 20 students. What are the marketing implications of your results?
36. Develop an appropriate questionnaire and construct a new version of Exhibit 18–3, using products relevant to college students. What are the marketing implications of this table?
37. Determine through interviews the general shopping orientations of students on your campus. What are the marketing implications of your findings?

REFERENCES

[1]P. Strnad, ''Kmart Dangles Lure for Affluent Shoppers,'' *Advertising Age*, August 24, 1987, p. 12; and P. Strnad, ''Kmart's Antonini Moves Far beyond Retail 'Junk' Image,'' *Advertising Age*, July 25, 1988, p. 1.

[2]For differing views, see W. R. Darden and M.-J. Dorsch, ''An Action Strategy Approach to Examining Shopping Behavior,'' *Journal of Business Research*, November 1990, pp. 289–308; and J. A. Lesser and P. Kamal, ''An Inductively Derived Model of the Motivation to Shop,'' *Psychology & Marketing*, Fall 1991, pp. 177–96.

[3]See J. K. Frenzen and H. L. Davis, ''Purchasing Behavior in Embedded Markets,'' *Journal of Consumer Research*, June 1990, pp. 1–12; J. F. Sherry, Jr., ''A Sociocultural Analysis of a Midwestern American Flea Market,'' *Journal of Consumer Research*, June 1990, pp. 13–30; J. F. Sherry, Jr., ''Dealers and Dealing in a Periodic Market,'' *Journal of Retailing*, Summer 1990, pp. 174–200; and R. W. Belk, J. F. Sherry, Jr., and M. Wallendorf, ''A Naturalistic Inquiry into Buyer and Seller Behavior at a Swap Meet,'' *Journal of Consumer Research*, March 1988, pp. 449–70.

[4]See J. J. Stoltman, J. W. Gentry, K. A. Anglin, and A. C. Burns, ''Situational Influences on the Consumer Decision Sequence,'' *Journal of Business Research*, November 1990, pp. 195–207.

[5]S. Spiggle and M. A. Sewall, ''A Choice Sets Model of Retail Selection,'' *Journal of Marketing*, April 1987, pp. 97–111; A. Finn and J. Louviere, ''Shopping-Center Patronage Models,'' *Journal of Business Research*, November 1990, pp. 259–75; E. J. Wilson and A. G. Woodside, ''A Comment on Patterns of Store Choice and Customer Gain/Loss Analysis,'' *Journal of the Academy of Marketing Science*, Fall 1991, pp. 377–82; and A. G. Woodside and R. J. Trappey III, ''Finding Out Why Customers Shop Your Store and Buy Your Brand,'' *Journal of Advertising Research*, November 1992, pp. 59–78. For the role of evoked sets in product selection, see footnote 4, Chapter 16.

[6]Ibid.

[7]S. Hume, ''Sears' Next Struggle,'' *Advertising Age*, October 5, 1992, p. 4.

[8]S. M. Keaveney and K. A. Hunt, ''Conceptualization and Operationalization of Retail Store Image,'' *Journal of the Academy of Marketing Science*, Spring 1992, pp. 165–176.

[9]J. D. Lindquist, ''Meaning of Image,'' *Journal of Retailing*, Winter 1974, pp. 29–38; see also R. Hansen and T. Deutscher, ''An Empirical Investigation of Attribute Importance in Retail Store Selection,'' *Journal of Retailing*, Winter 1977–1978, pp. 59–73, and M. R. Zimmer and L. L. Golden, ''Impressions of Retail Stores,'' *Journal of Retailing*, Fall 1988, pp. 265–93.

[10]See J. E. M. Steenkamp and M. Wedel, ''Segmenting Retail Markets on Store Image,'' *Journal of Retailing*, Fall 1991, pp. 300–320.

[11]See D. Mazursky and J. Jacoby, ''Exploring the Development of Store Images,'' *Journal of Retailing*, Summer 1986, pp. 145–65; S. W. McDaniel and J. J. Burnett, ''Consumer Religiosity and Retail Store Evaluative Criteria,'' *Journal of the Academy of Marketing Science*, Spring 1990, pp. 101–12; and W. K. Darley and J.-S. Linn, ''Store-Choice Behavior for Pre-Owned Merchandise,'' *Journal of Business Research*, May 1993, pp. 17–31.

[12]*A Study of Consumer Response to the Availability of Advertised Specials*, National Technical Information Service, U.S. Department of Commerce (PB80-128507).

[13]*The Double Dividend* (New York: Newspaper Advertising Bureau Inc., February 1977).

[14]See A. D. Cox and D. Cox, ''Competing on Price,'' *Journal of Retailing*, Winter 1990, pp. 428–45; R. G. Walters, ''Assessing the Impact of Retail Price Promotions,'' *Journal of Marketing*, April 1991, pp. 17–28; A. Biswas and E. A. Blair, ''Contextual Effects of Reference Prices,'' *Journal of Marketing*, July 1991, pp. 1–12; D. R. Lichtenstein, S. Burton, and E.-J. Karson, ''The Effect of Semantic Cues on Consumer Perceptions of Reference Price Ads,''

Journal of Consumer Research, December 1991, pp. 380–91; G. E. Mayhew and R. S. Winer, "An Empirical Analysis of Internal and External Reference Prices," *Journal of Consumer Research*, June 1992, pp. 62–70; A. Biswas, "The Moderating Role of Brand Familiarity in Reference Price Perceptions," *Journal of Business Research*, November 1992, pp. 251–62; A. Biswas and S. Burton, "Consumer Perceptions of Tensile Price Claims in Advertisements," *Journal of the Academy of Marketing Science*, Summer 1993, pp. 217–30; and K. N. Rajendran and G.-J. Tellis, "Contextual and Temporal Components of Reference Price," *Journal of Marketing*, January 1994, pp. 22–39.

[15]C. S. Craig, A. Ghosh, and S. McLafferty, "Models of the Retail Location Process: A Review," *Journal of Retailing*, Spring 1984, pp. 5–33.

[16]Based on V. Prasad, "Socioeconomic Product Risk and Patronage Preferences of Retail Shoppers," *Journal of Marketing*, July 1975, p. 44.

[17]J. M. Hawes and J. R. Lumpkin, "Perceived Risk and the Selection of a Retail Patronage Mode," *Journal of Academy of Marketing Science*, Winter 1986, pp. 37–42; Lumpkin and Hawes, "Retailing without Stores, *Journal of Business Research*, April 1985, pp. 139–51; T. A. Festervand, D. R. Snyder, and J. D. Tsalikis, "Influence of Catalog vs. Store Shopping and Prior Satisfaction on Perceived Risk," *Journal of the Academy of Marketing Science*, Winter 1986, pp. 28–36.

[18]See R. A. Westbrook and W. C. Black, "A Motivation-Based Shopper Typology," *Journal of Retailing*, Spring 1985, pp. 78–103.

[19]W. R. Darden and R. D. Howell, "Socialization Effects of Retail Work Experience on Shopping Orientations," *Journal of the Academy of Marketing Science*, Fall 1987, pp. 52–63.

[20]See S. Spiggle, "Grocery Shopping Lists," in *Advances in Consumer Research XIV*, ed. M. Wallendorf and P. Anderson (Provo, Utah: Association for Consumer Research, 1987), pp. 241–45; E. S. Iyer, "Unplanned Purchasing," *Journal of Retailing*, Spring 1989, pp. 40–57; and C. W. Park, E. S. Iyer, and D. C. Smith, "The Effects of Situational Factors on In-Store Grocery Shopping Behavior," *Journal of Consumer Research*, March 1989, pp. 422–33.

[21]See C. J. Cobb and W. D. Hoger, "Planned versus Impulse Purchase Behavior," *Journal of Retailing*, Winter 1986, pp. 384–409; and K. Bawa, J. T. Lanwehr, and A. Krishna, "Consumer Response to Retailers' Marketing Environments," *Journal of Retailing*, Winter 1989, pp. 471–95.

[22]See J. P. Gagnon and J. T. Osterhaus, "Effectiveness of Floor Displays on the Sales of Retail Products," *Journal of Retailing*, Spring 1985, pp. 104–17; *POPAI/DuPont Consumer Buying Habits Study* (Englewood, N.J.: Point-of-Purchase Advertising Institute, 1987); *POPAI/Horner Drug Store Study* (Englewood, N.J.: Point-of-Purchase Advertising Institute, 1992); A. J. Greco and L. E. Swayne, "Sales Response of Elderly Consumers to P-O-P Advertising," *Journal of Advertising Research*, September 1992, pp. 43–53; and *POPAI/Kmart/Procter & Gamble Study of P-O-P Effectiveness* (Englewood, N.J.: Point-of-Purchase Advertising Institute, 1993); D. D. Archabal et al., "The Effect of Nutrition P-O-P Signs on Consumer Attitudes and Behavior," *Journal of Retailing*, Spring 1987, pp. 9–24, presents contrasting results. See also D. W. Schumann et al., "The Effectiveness of Shopping Cart Signage," *Journal of Advertising Research*, February 1991, pp. 17–22.

[23]M. M. Moriarity, "Retail Promotional Effects on Intra- and Interbrand Sales Performance," *Journal of Retailing*, Fall 1985, pp. 27–47. See also B. E. Kahn and D. C. Schmittlein, "The Relationship Between Purchase Made on Promotion and Shopping Trip Behavior," *Journal of Retailing*, Fall 1992, pp. 294–315; and K. Helsen and D. C. Schmittlein, "How Does a Product Market's Typical Price–Promotion Pattern Affect the Timing of Households' Purchases?" *Journal of Retailing*, Fall 1992, pp. 316–38.

[24]D. S. Litvack, R. J. Calantone, and P. R. Warshaw, "An Examination of Short-Term Retail Grocery Price Effects," *Journal of Retailing*, Fall 1985, pp. 9–25. See also G. Ortmeyer, J. M. Lattin, and D. B. Montgomery, "Individual Differences in Response to Consumer Promotions," *International Journal of Research in Marketing*, no. 8, 1991, pp. 169–86.

[25]"Store of the Month," *Progressive Grocer*, October 1976, pp. 104–10.

[26]M. J. Bitner, "Servicescapes," *Journal of Marketing*, April 1992, pp. 57–71. See also J. C. Ward, M. J. Bitner, and J. Barnes, "Measuring the Prototypicality and Meaning of Retail Environments," *Journal of Retailing*, Summer 1992, pp. 194–220; R. A. Kerin, A. Jain, and P. J. Howard, "Store Shopping Experience and Consumer Price–Quality-Value Perceptions," *Journal of Retailing*, Winter 1992, pp. 376–98; and J. Baker, D. Grewal, and M. Levy, "An Experimental Approach to Making Retail Store Environmental Decisions," *Journal of Retailing*, Winter 1992, pp. 445–60.

[27]See also R. Yalch and E. Spangenberg, "Effects of Store Music on Shopping Behavior," *Journal of Consumer Marketing*, Spring 1990, pp. 55–63.

[28]"Ward's Remodeling Its Image," *Advertising Age*, July 28, 1980, p. 40.

[29]W. H. Motes and S. B. Castleberry, "A Longitudinal Field Test of Stockout Effects on Multi-Brand Inventories," *Journal of the Academy of Marketing Science*, Fall 1985, pp. 54–68; and M. A. Emmelhainz, J. R. Stock, and L. W. Emmelhainz, "Consumer Responses to Retail Stock-outs," *Journal of Retailing*, Summer 1991, pp. 138–47.

[30]See G. A. Churchill, Jr., et al., "The Determinants of Salesperson Performance," *Journal of Marketing Research*, May 1985, pp. 103–18; B. A. Weitz, H. Sujan, and M. Sujan, "Knowledge, Motivation, and Adaptive Behavior," *Journal of Marketing*, October 1986, pp. 174–91; N. M. Ford et al., "Psychological Tests and the Selection of Successful Salespeople," *Review of Marketing 1987*, ed. M. Houston (Chicago: American Marketing Association, 1987); and D. M. Szymanski, "Determinants of Selling Effectiveness," *Journal of Marketing*, January 1988, pp. 64–77.

POSTPURCHASE PROCESSES, CUSTOMER SATISFACTION, AND CUSTOMER COMMITMENT

LifeScan, a Johnson & Johnson company, makes meters that diabetics use to monitor their blood sugar levels. Several years ago, a single meter was found to be defective. In response, the company notified 600,000 customers virtually overnight and recalled the entire product line. Customers responded positively to this show of concern by LifeScan. Its market share has increased by 7 percent since the recall, according to Holly Kulp, director of customer services.

LifeScan attempts to make customer satisfaction the top priority of every employee for the following reasons:

- Generating a new customer costs three to five times more than retaining an existing one.
- "Highly satisfied" customers are six times more likely to repurchase than "just satisfied" customers are.
- Customers who have had problems that were resolved to their satisfaction become significantly more loyal than customers who had never experienced a problem.
- Only 14 percent of customers abandon a firm due to a product performance problem, whereas 66 percent defect because they find service people indifferent or inaccessible.
- Studies have shown that a 5 percent increase in customer retention can raise profitability by 25 to 85 percent.

To create "highly satisfied" customers, LifeScan has a full-time manager of customer loyalty who works closely with the marketing and customer service departments to measure and improve customer satisfaction and retention. Customer service representatives field 1.3 million calls per year and are trained and empowered to make decisions to satisfy each caller. These service reps also play a key role in new-product development activities.

LifeScan offers its customers a 24-hour toll-free hot line, telecommunications capability for the deaf (diabetes contributes to hearing impairment), 24-hour meter replacement (meters are

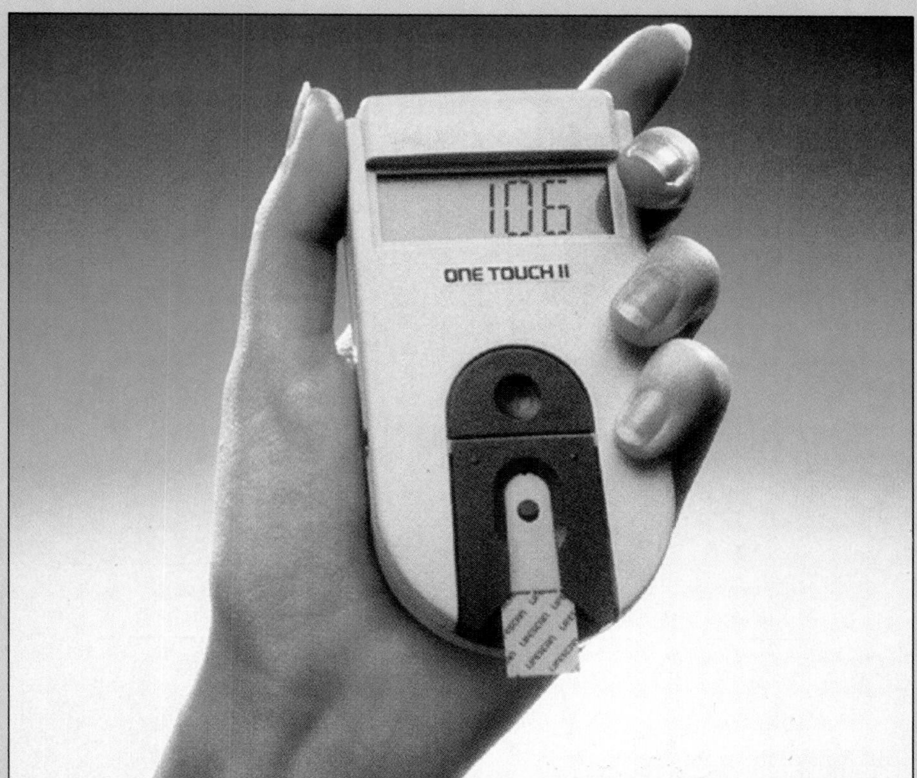

stored at Federal Express in Memphis to make this possible), educational information, a newsletter, and a five-year product warranty. Additional services are provided to distributors and health care professionals.

To ensure that these activities are effective, LifeScan maintains daily phone statistics, conducts quarterly satisfaction surveys to supplement the annual satisfaction survey, and stays in touch with its customers in other ways as well.[1]

While LifeScan is more advanced than most firms, it is not unique in its focus on producing not satisfied customers but committed customers. In this chapter we will examine the postpurchase processes that produce customer satisfaction and commitment and the marketing strategies these processes suggest. Figure 19–1 illustrates the relationship among these processes.

POSTPURCHASE DISSONANCE

Try to recall the last time you made an important purchase in which you had to consider a variety of alternatives that differed in terms of the attributes they offered. Perhaps it was a decision such as selecting a college close to home where you would have many friends or one further away but better academically. Immediately after you committed yourself to one alternative or the other, you likely wondered:

FIGURE 19–1

Postpurchase Consumer Behavior

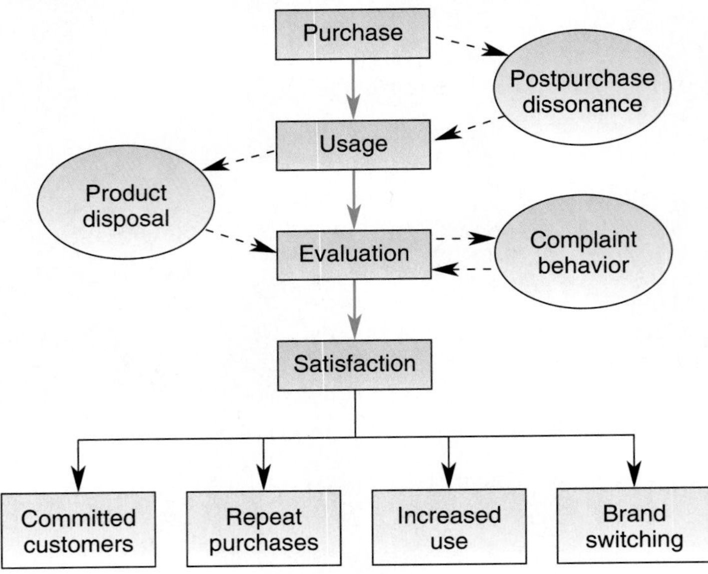

- Did I make the right decision?
- Should I have done something else?

This is a very common reaction after making a difficult, relatively permanent decision. Doubt or anxiety of this type is referred to as **postpurchase dissonance**.[2]

Figure 19–1 indicates that some, but not all, consumer purchase decisions are followed by postpurchase dissonance. The probability of a consumer experiencing postpurchase dissonance, as well as the magnitude of such dissonance, is a function of:

- *The degree of commitment or irrevocability of the decision.* The easier it is to alter the decision, the less likely the consumer is to experience dissonance.
- *The importance of the decision to the consumer.* The more important the decision, the more likely dissonance will result.
- *The difficulty of choosing among the alternatives.* The more difficult it is to select from among the alternatives, the more likely the experience and magnitude of dissonance. Decision difficulty is a function of the number of alternatives considered, the number of relevant attributes associated with each alternative, and the extent to which each alternative offers attributes not available with the other alternatives.
- *The individual's tendency to experience anxiety.* Some individuals have a higher tendency to experience anxiety than do others. The higher the tendency to experience anxiety, the more likely the individual will experience postpurchase dissonance.

Dissonance occurs because making a relatively permanent commitment to a chosen alternative requires one to give up the attractive features of the unchosen alternatives. This is inconsistent with the desire for those features. Thus, habitual and most limited decision making will not produce postpurchase dissonance, since one does not consider any attractive features in an unchosen brand that do not also exist in the chosen brand. For example, a consumer who has an evoked set of four brands of coffee could consider them to be equivalent on all relevant attributes except price and, therefore, always purchases the least expensive brand. Such a purchase would not produce postpurchase dissonance.

Because most high-involvement purchase decisions involve one or more of the factors which lead to postpurchase dissonance, these decisions often are accompanied by dissonance. And, since dissonance is unpleasant, consumers generally attempt to reduce it.

The consumer may utilize one or more of the following approaches to reduce dissonance:

- Increase the desirability of the brand purchased.
- Decrease the desirability of rejected alternatives.
- Decrease the importance of the purchase decision.

While postpurchase dissonance may be reduced by internal reevaluations, searching for additional external information that serves to confirm the wisdom of a particular choice is also a common strategy. Naturally, information that supports the consumer's choice acts to bolster confidence in the correctness of the purchase decision.

The consumer's search for information *after* the purchase greatly enhances the role that advertising and follow-up sales efforts can have. To build customer confidence in choosing their brand, many manufacturers design advertisements for recent purchasers, in hopes of helping reduce postpurchase dissonance.

PRODUCT USE

Most consumer purchases involve habitual or limited decision making and therefore arouse little or no postpurchase dissonance. Instead, the purchaser or some other member of the purchasing unit uses the product without first worrying about the wisdom of the purchase. And, as Figure 19–1 shows, even when postpurchase dissonance occurs, it is still generally followed by product use.

Observing consumers as they utilize products can be an important source of new-product ideas. For example, observations of consumer modifications of existing bicycles led to the commercial development of the immensely popular "stingray" style of children's bicycle. However, almost all consumer-observation research is conducted in an artificial setting or is conducted with the consumer's permission. As a result, few non-standard product uses are observed.

Many firms attempt to obtain relevant information on product usage via surveys using standard questionnaires or focus groups. Such surveys can lead to new-product development, indicate new uses or markets for existing products, or indicate appropriate communications themes. For example, what product feature and communications themes are suggested by Figure 19–2?

Understanding how products are used also can lead to more effective packaging. For example, Table 19–1 on page 517 summarizes the level of dissatisfaction with the packaging of various products. Because this type of dissatisfaction occurs at the time of use, it is difficult for marketers to monitor. To solve such problems, the marketer has to understand how the product and package are used.

Use behavior can vary regionally. For example, there are major regional variations in how coffee is consumed—with or without cream, with or without sugar, in a mug or a cup, and so forth. Thus, a coffee marketer may find it worthwhile to prepare regional versions of the major advertising theme to reflect regional usage patterns.

Retailers can frequently take advantage of the fact that the use of one product may require or suggest the use of other products. Consider the following product "sets": houseplants and fertilizer, canoes and life vests, cameras and carrying cases, sport coats and

FIGURE 19–2 Product Usage Index for VCRs, Microwaves, and Personal Computers

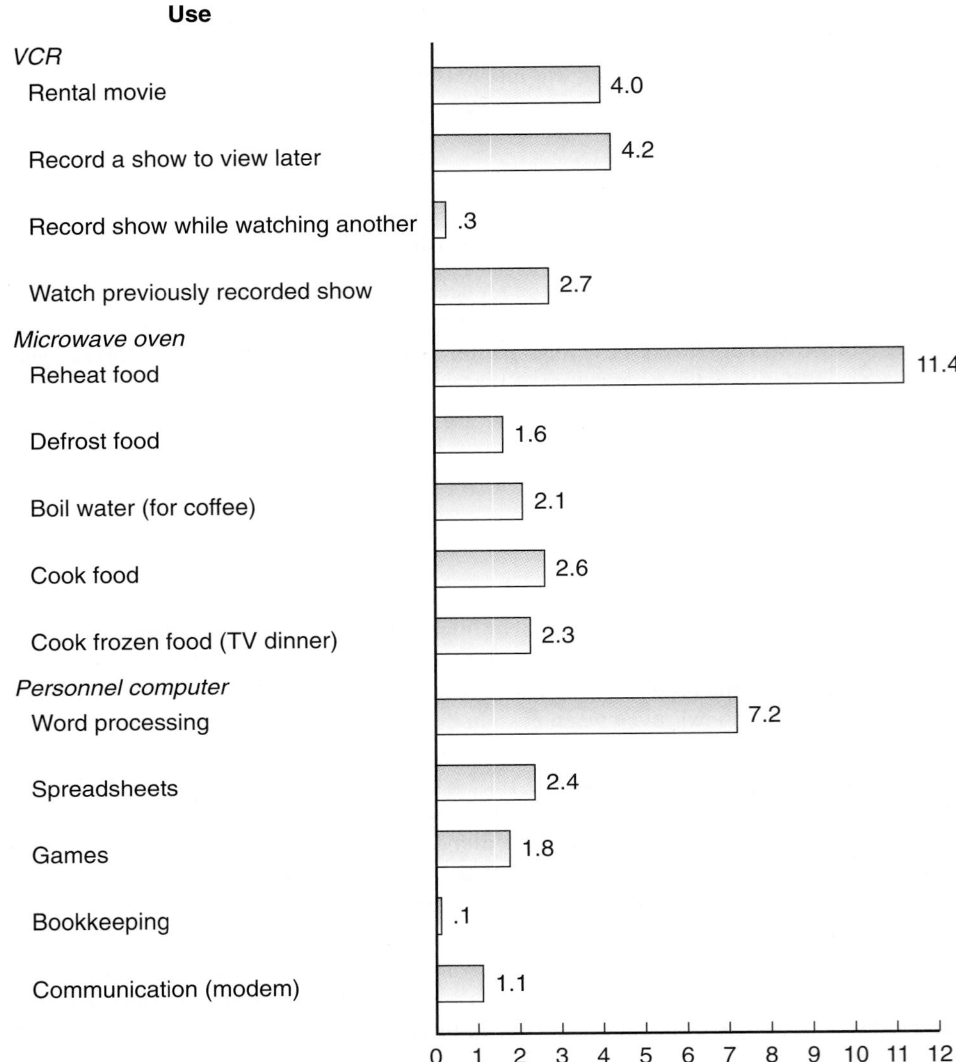

Note: Figures refer to the average number of days per month a product is used for that specific purpose.
Source: Adapted from S. Ram and H. J. Jung, "The Conceptualization and Measurement of Product Usage," *Journal of the Academy of Marketing Science*, Winter 1990, pp. 67–76.

ties, and dresses and shoes. In each case, the use of the first product is made easier, more enjoyable, or safer by the use of the related product. Retailers can promote such items jointly or train their sales personnel to make relevant complementary sales. However, to do so requires a sound knowledge of how the products actually are utilized.

Increasingly stringent product liability laws are forcing marketing managers to examine how consumers use their products. These laws have made firms responsible for harm caused by product failure *not only when the product is used as specified by the manufacturer but in any reasonably foreseeable use of the product.* For example, Parker Brothers voluntarily recalled its very successful plastic riveting tool, Riviton, at a cost approaching

TABLE 19–1

Product Use Problems Due to Packaging*

Product	Percent Dissatisfied	Product	Percent Dissatisfied
Lunch meat	77%	Noodles	49%
Bacon	76	Lipstick	47
Flour	65	Nail polish	46
Sugar	63	Honey	44
Ice cream	57	Crackers	44
Snack chips	53	Frozen seafood	40
Cookies	51	Nuts	39
Detergents	50	Cooking oil	37
Fresh meat	50	Ketchup	34

*Percentage of respondents who indicated dissatisfaction with the packaging of these products.

Source: Bill Abrahms, "Packaging Often Irks Buyers, but Firms Are Slow to Change," *The Wall Street Journal*, January 29, 1982, p. 23.

$10 million. The reason was the deaths of two children who choked after swallowing one of the tool's rubber rivets. Both Wham-O Manufacturing and Mattel have been involved in similar recalls. Thus, the manufacturer must design products with both the primary purpose *and* other potential uses in mind. This requires substantial research into how consumers actually use the products.

When marketers discover confusion about the proper way to use a product, it is often to their advantage to teach consumers how to use it. Managerial Application 19–1 shows part of a four-page insert that Gillette ran in *Teen* magazine. This insert both promoted the Gillette *Sensor for Women* and instructed young women on the optimal way to shave their legs.

DISPOSITION

Disposition of the product or the product's container may occur before, during, or after product use. Or, for products that are completely consumed, such as an ice cream cone, no disposition may be involved.

The United States produced 200 million tons of household and commercial refuse in 1987, over 1,500 pounds per person, and this figure does not include industrial waste. Landfills are rapidly being filled. New Jersey must truck half its household waste to out-of-state landfills up to 500 miles away. Collection and dumping costs for a household in suburban Union County near New York City increased to over $400 per year in 1987. Environmental concerns involving dioxins, lead, and mercury are growing. Clearly, disposition is a major concern for marketers.[3]

Millions of pounds of product packages are disposed of every day. These containers are thrown away as garbage or litter, used in some capacity by the consumer, or recycled. Creating packages that utilize a minimal amount of resources is important for economic reasons as well as being a matter of social responsibility. Producing containers that are easily recyclable or that can be reused also has important consequences beyond social responsibility. Certain market segments consider the recyclable nature of the product

MANAGERIAL APPLICATION

19–1

Product Use Advertising

container to be an important product attribute. These consumers anticipate disposition of the package as an attribute of the brand during the alternative evaluation stage. Thus, ease of disposition can be used as a marketing mix variable in an attempt to capture certain market segments.

Marketers are beginning to respond to consumers' concerns with recyclable packaging, as the examples below illustrate:

- Rubbermaid is repositioning its trash barrel line to a Recycling Container line. The new line has four models designed to store newspapers, cans, bottles, and yard waste.
- Procter & Gamble uses recycled paper in 80 percent of its product packaging and is packaging liquid Spic and Span, Tide, Cheer, and Downy in containers made from recycled packages.
- Mobil Chemical Co. recently introduced Hefty degradable trash bags. Poly-Tech Inc. sells Ruggies and Sure-Sac degradable bags (however, the bags require exposure to sunlight to degrade).
- The plastics industry has introduced a coding system that identifies a container's plastic resin composition and indicates whether it can be recycled.

Product Disposition Alternatives

FIGURE 19–3

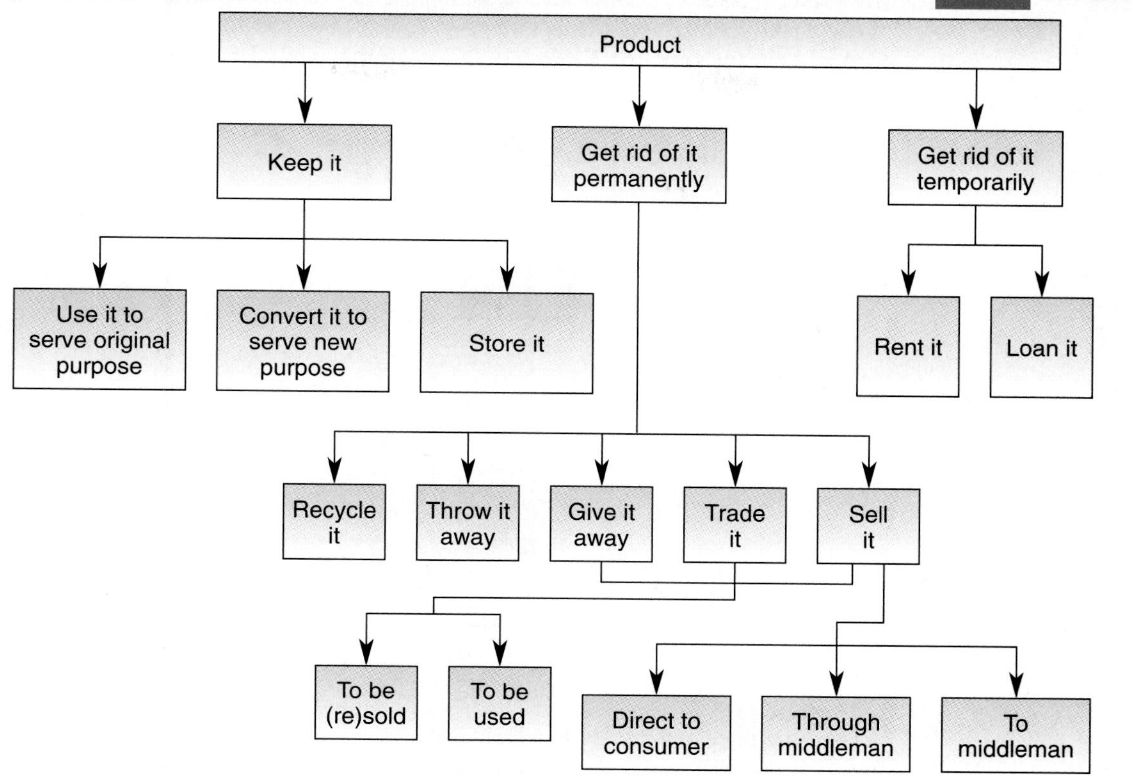

Source: Adapted from J. Jacoby, C. K. Berning, and T. F. Dietvorst, "What about Disposition?" *Journal of Marketing*, April 1977, p. 23.

For many product categories, a physical product continues to exist even though it may no longer meet a consumer's needs. A product may no longer function physically (instrumental function) in a manner desired by a consumer. Or, it may no longer provide the symbolic meaning desired by the consumer. An automobile that no longer runs is an example of a product ceasing to function instrumentally. An automobile whose owner decides it is out of style no longer functions symbolically (for that particular consumer). In either case, once a replacement purchase is made (or even before the purchase), a disposition decision must be made.

Figure 19–3 illustrates the various alternatives for disposing of a product. Unfortunately, very little is known about the demographic or psychological characteristics of individuals who tend to select particular disposal methods. It appears that situational variables such as the availability of storage space, the current needs of friends, the availability of recycling or charitable organizations, and so forth *may* be the primary determinants of disposition behavior.

Product Disposition and Marketing Strategy

Why should a marketing manager be concerned about the disposition of a used product? The primary reason is that disposition decisions affect the purchase decisions of both the individual making the disposition and other individuals in the market for that product category.

MANAGERIAL APPLICATION

19–2

An Advertisement Based on Concerns with Product Disposition

There are three major ways in which disposition decisions can affect a firm's marketing strategy. *First*, disposition sometimes must occur before acquisition of a replacement because of physical space or financial limitations. For example, because of a lack of storage space, a family living in an apartment may find it necessary to dispose of an existing bedroom set before acquiring a new one. Or, someone may need to sell his current bicycle to raise supplemental funds to pay for a new bicycle. If consumers experience difficulty in disposing of the existing product, they may become discouraged and withdraw from the purchasing process. Thus, it is to the manufacturer's and retailer's advantage to assist the consumer in the disposition process.

Second, frequent decisions by consumers to sell, trade, or give away used products may result in a large used product market which can reduce the market for new products. A manufacturer may want to enter such a market by buying used products or taking trade-ins and repairing them for the rebuilt market. This is common for automobile parts such as generators and, to a lesser extent, for vacuum cleaners.

A *third* reason for concern with product disposition is the fact that the United States is not completely a throwaway society. Many Americans continue to be very concerned with waste and how their purchase decisions affect waste. Such individuals might be willing to purchase, for example, a new vacuum cleaner if they were confident that the old one would be rebuilt and resold. However, they might be reluctant to throw their old vacuums away or to go to the effort of reselling the machines themselves. Thus, manufacturers and retailers could take steps to ensure that products are reused. Such steps could increase the demand for new products, while meeting the needs of consumers for less-expensive versions of the product.

Managerial Application 19–2 contains a newspaper ad for Pit Stop that is designed to appeal to consumers concerned about the disposition of used oil and oil filters.

PURCHASE EVALUATION

As we saw in Figure 19–1, a consumer's evaluation of a purchase is influenced by postpurchase dissonance, product use, and product disposition. Not all purchase evaluations are influenced by each of these three processes. Rather, these processes are potential influencing factors that may affect the evaluation of a particular purchase. You should also note that the outlet or the product or both may be involved in the evaluation.[4] Finally, keep in mind that habitual decisions and many limited decisions are actively evaluated only if some factor, such as an obvious product malfunction, directs attention to the purchase.

The Evaluation Process

A particular alternative such as a product, brand, or retail outlet is selected because it is thought to be a better overall choice than other alternatives that were considered in the purchase process. Whether that particular item was selected because of its presumed superior functional performance or because of some other reason, such as a generalized liking of the item, consumers have some level of expected performance that it should provide. The expected level of performance can range from quite low (this brand isn't very good but it's the only one available and I'm in a hurry) to quite high.[5] As you might suspect, expectations and perceived performance are not independent. In general, we tend to perceive performance to be in line with our expectations (up to a point).[6]

After (or while) using the product or outlet, the consumer will perceive some level of performance. This perceived performance level can be noticeably above the expected level, noticeably below the expected level, or at the expected level. As Exhibit 19–1 indicates, satisfaction with the purchase is primarily a function of the initial performance expectations and perceived performance relative to those expectations.[7] In addition, individuals differ somewhat in their tendency to be satisfied or dissatisfied with purchases. As stated earlier, habitual and many limited decisions are actively evaluated *only* if there is a noticeable product failure.

In Exhibit 19–1, you can see that a store or brand whose performance confirms a low-performance expectation generally will result in neither satisfaction nor dissatisfaction but rather with what can be termed *nonsatisfaction.* That is, you are not likely to feel disappointment or engage in complaint behavior. However, the use of the product will not reduce the likelihood of a search for a better alternative the next time the problem arises.

EXHIBIT 19–1

Expectations, Performance, and Satisfaction

Perceived Performance Relative to Expectation	Expectation Level: Below Minimum Desired Performance	Expectation Level: Above Minimum Desired Performance
Better	Satisfaction*	Satisfaction/Commitment
Same	Nonsatisfaction	Satisfaction
Worse	Dissatisfaction	Dissatisfaction

*Assuming the perceived performance surpasses the minimum desired level.

A brand whose perceived performance fails to confirm expectations generally produces dissatisfaction. If the discrepancy between performance and expectation is sufficiently large or if initial expectations were low, the consumer may restart the entire decision process. The item causing the problem recognition most likely will be placed in the inept set (see Chapter 16) and no longer be considered. In addition, complaint behavior and negative word-of-mouth communications may be initiated.

When perceptions of product performance match expectations that are at or above the minimum desired performance level, satisfaction generally results. Likewise, performance above the minimum desired level that exceeds a lower expectation tends to produce satisfaction. Satisfaction reduces the level of decision making the next time the problem is recognized. That is, a satisfactory purchase is rewarding and encourages one to repeat the same behavior in the future (habitual decision making). Satisfied customers are also likely to engage in positive word-of-mouth communications about the brand.

Product performance that exceeds expected performance will generally result in satisfaction and sometimes in commitment. Commitment, discussed in depth in the next section means that the consumer feels loyal to a particular brand and is somewhat immune to actions by competitors.

The need to produce satisfied consumers has important implications in terms of positioning the level of promotional claims. Since dissatisfaction is, in part, a function of the disparity between expectations and perceived product performance, unrealistic consumer expectations created by promotional exaggeration can contribute to consumer dissatisfaction.

The need to develop realistic consumer expectations poses a difficult problem for the marketing manager. For a brand or store to be selected by a consumer, it must be viewed as superior on the relevant combination of attributes. Therefore, the marketing manager naturally wants to emphasize the positive aspects of the brand or outlet. If such an emphasis creates expectations in the consumer that the product cannot fulfill, a negative evaluation may occur. Negative evaluations can produce brand switching, unfavorable word-of-mouth communications, and complaint behavior. Thus, the marketing manager must balance enthusiasm for the product with a realistic view of the product's attributes.

Dimensions of Performance Since performance expectations and actual performance are major factors in the evaluation process, we need to understand the dimensions of product performance.[8] For many products, there are two dimensions to performance: instrumental, and expressive or symbolic. **Instrumental performance** relates to the physical functioning of the product. That the product operates properly is vital to the evaluation of a dishwasher, sewing machine, or other major appliance. **Symbolic performance** relates to aesthetic or image-enhancement performance. For example, the durability of a sport coat is an aspect of instrumental performance, while styling represents symbolic performance.

Is symbolic or instrumental performance more important to consumers as they evaluate product performance? The answer to this question undoubtedly varies by product category and across consumer groups. However, a number of studies focusing on clothing provide some insights into how these two types of performance are related.

Clothing appears to perform five major functions: protection from the environment, enhancement of sexual attraction, aesthetic and sensuous satisfaction, an indicator of status, and an extension of self-image. Except for protection from the environment, these functions are all dimensions of symbolic performance. Yet studies of clothing returns, complaints about clothing purchases, and discarded clothing indicate that physical product failures are the primary cause of dissatisfaction. One study on the relationship between performance expectations, actual performance, and satisfaction with clothing purchases reached the following general conclusion:

> Dissatisfaction is caused by a failure of instrumental performance, while complete satisfaction also requires the symbolic functions to perform at or above the expected levels.[9]

These findings certainly cannot be generalized to other product categories without additional research. However, they suggest that the marketing manager should maintain performance at the minimum expected level on those attributes that lead to dissatisfaction, while attempting to maximize performance on those attributes that lead to increased satisfaction.

DISSATISFACTION RESPONSES

Figure 19–4 illustrates the major options available to a dissatisfied consumer.[10] The first decision is whether or not to take any external action. By taking no action, the consumer decides to ''live with'' the unsatisfactory situation. This decision is a function of the importance of the purchase to the consumer, the ease of taking action, and the characteristics of the consumer involved. It is very important to note that even when no external action is taken, the consumer is likely to have a less favorable attitude toward the store or brand.

Consumers who take action in response to dissatisfaction, generally pursue one or more of five alternatives. As Figure 19–4 indicates, most of these alternatives are damaging to the firm involved both directly in terms of lost sales and indirectly in terms of a customer with a less favorable attitude. Therefore, marketers should strive to minimize dissatisfaction *and* to effectively resolve dissatisfaction when it occurs.

In general, consumers are satisfied with the vast majority of their purchases. Still, because of the large number of purchases that individuals make each year, most individuals

Dissatisfaction Responses

FIGURE 19–4

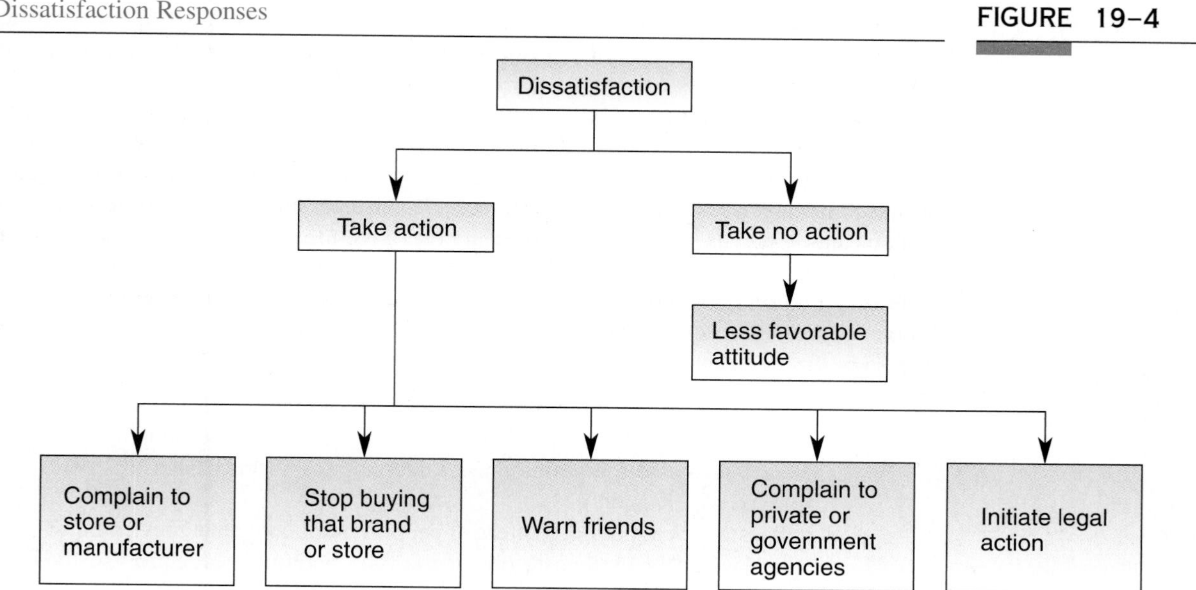

experience dissatisfaction with some of their purchases.[11] For example, one study asked 540 consumers if they could recall a case in which one or more of the grocery products they normally purchase were defective. They recalled 1,307 separate unsatisfactory purchases. These purchases produced the following actions (the study did not measure negative word-of-mouth actions, i.e., warning friends):

- 25 percent of these unsatisfactory purchases resulted in brand switching.
- 19 percent caused the shopper to stop buying the products.
- 13 percent led to an in-store inspection of future purchases.
- 3 percent produced complaints to the manufacturer.
- 5 percent produced complaints to the retailer.
- 35 percent resulted in the item being returned.

In a similar study of durable goods, 54 percent of the dissatisfied customers said they would not purchase the brand again, and 45 percent warned their friends about the product.[12]

Marketing Strategy and Dissatisfied Consumers Marketers need to satisfy consumer expectations by (1) creating reasonable expectations through promotional efforts and (2) maintaining consistent quality so the reasonable expectations are fulfilled. Since dissatisfied consumers tend to express their dissatisfaction to their friends, dissatisfaction may cause the firm to lose future sales to the unhappy consumer's friends as well as to the unhappy consumer.[13]

The evidence presented in this chapter suggests that it is virtually impossible to ''please all the people all the time.'' When a consumer is dissatisfied, the most favorable consequence is for the consumer to communicate this dissatisfaction to the firm but to no one else. This alerts the firm to problems, enables it to make amends where necessary, and minimizes negative word-of-mouth communications. In addition, complaints generally work to the consumer's advantage. Evidence indicates that about two-thirds of all expressed complaints are resolved to the consumer's satisfaction.[14]

Unfortunately, many individuals do not communicate their dissatisfaction to the firm involved. Those who do complain tend to have more education, income, self-confidence, and independence, and are more confident in the business system than those who do not complain.[15] Thus, a firm that relies on complaints for feedback on problems will miss the concerns of key market segments.

Complaints about products frequently go to retailers and are not passed on to manufacturers. One study found that more than 80 percent of the complaints were presented to retailers, while less than 10 percent went directly to the manufacturer.[16] Many firms attempt to overcome this by establishing and promoting ''consumer hot lines''—toll-free numbers that consumers can use to contact a representative of the firm when they have a complaint. General Electric spends $10 million a year on its 800-number ''Answer Center,'' which handles 3 million calls annually. GE feels that the payback is ''multiple times'' that.[17] Procter & Gamble provides the following examples of benefits received from their hot line:

- Duncan Hines brownie mix: ''We learned that people in high-altitude areas need special instructions for baking, and these soon were added to the packages. We also found that one of the recipes on a box label was confusing, so we changed it.''
- Toothpaste: ''We spotted a pattern of people complaining that they couldn't get the last bit of toothpaste out of the tube without it breaking, so the tubes were strengthened.''

- A sudden group of calls indicated that the plastic tops on Downy fabric softener bottles were splintering when twisted on and off, creating the danger of cut fingers. P&G identified the supplier of the fragile caps and learned that it had recently changed its formula. The new-formula caps were becoming brittle as they aged. Most of the bad caps had not left the factory, and P&G simply replaced them. Thus, a costly (financially and image-wise) product recall was avoided.
- P&G often receives calls with positive testimonials. These are forwarded to the appropriate advertising agency, where they are analyzed for insights into why people like the product. Several P&G campaigns have been based on these unsolicited consumer comments.[18]

While hot lines and other procedures increase the ease with which consumers can express a complaint, they are not sufficient. Most consumers who complain want a *tangible* result. Failure to deal effectively with this expectation can produce increased dissatisfaction.[19] Therefore, firms need to solve the cause of consumer complaints, not just allow them the opportunity to complain.

Burger King, which receives up to 4,000 calls a day on its 24-hour hot line (65 percent are complaints), resolves 95 percent of the problems on the initial call. To be certain the customers are truly satisfied, 25 percent are called back within a month.

Unfortunately, many corporations are not organized to effectively resolve and learn from consumer complaints, although individual managers strive to respond positively to complaints.[20] This area represents a major opportunity for many businesses.[21] In fact, for many firms, retaining once-dissatisfied customers by encouraging and responding effectively to complaints is more economical than attracting new customers through advertising or other promotional activities.[22] It has been estimated that it costs only one-fifth as much to retain an old customer as to obtain a new one.[23] The FTC has prepared a guideline to assist firms with this activity.[24]

CUSTOMER SATISFACTION, REPEAT PURCHASES, AND CUSTOMER COMMITMENT

Ford Motor Company did not begin to systematically monitor customer satisfaction until 1986. Fortunately, customer-satisfaction measures are now a key part of Ford's performance-measurement system. The logic is simple: satisfied customers are twice as likely as unhappy ones to stick with their current make, and three times as likely to return to the same dealer.

Ford now spends over $10 million annually to survey all its customers, first about a month after purchase and again a year later. Each dealership receives a monthly QCP (quality, commitment, performance) report covering sales, vehicle preparation, service, and overall performance. Customers also rate the automobile itself. These QCP ratings not only provide dealers feedback but also serve as the basis for contests, bonuses, new franchise awards, and so forth.

Many dealerships are adopting customer-satisfaction measures locally to monitor and reward their own sales and service personnel. For example, Tasca Lincoln-Mercury in Massachusetts has divided its service department into six teams, each of which wears a different-colored uniform. The teams compete for monthly bonuses of $500 to $800 based on customer-satisfaction measures.[25]

Ford is typical of the many American firms that were forced by increased international and domestic competition to focus their efforts on producing satisfied customers rather

FIGURE 19–5 Committed Customers

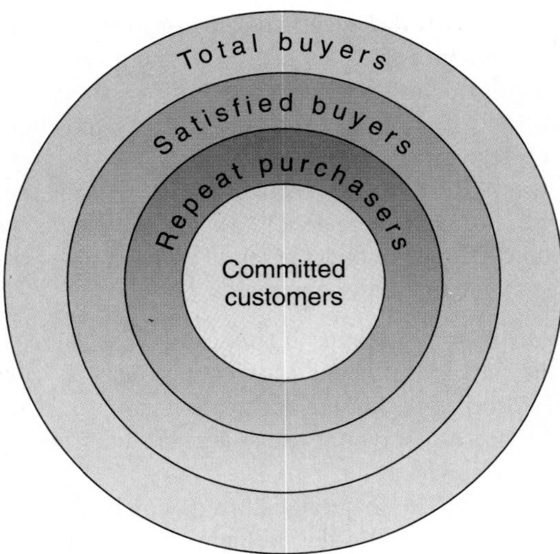

than on producing short-term sales. As we just saw, customers who are not satisfied are unlikely to continue using a brand and they are likely to communicate to friends and associates the causes of their dissatisfaction. In contrast, satisfied customers are likely to repurchase the brand the next time a need arises.[26]

However, given increasingly sophisticated and value-conscious consumers and multiple brands that perform at satisfactory levels, producing satisfied customers is necessary but not sufficient for many marketers. Instead, the objective is to produce committed or brand-loyal customers.

Figure 19–5 illustrates the composition of the buyers of a particular brand at any point in time. Of the total buyers, a certain percentage will be satisfied with the purchase. As we have seen, marketers are spending considerable effort to make this percentage as high as possible. The reason for these efforts is that a percentage of these satisfied customers will become or remain repeat purchasers. **Repeat purchasers** are often more profitable than new customers.

As we saw earlier, some dissatisfied customers will also become or remain repeat purchasers. These individuals will not perceive any available satisfactory alternatives or will believe that the expected benefits of renewed search are not worth the expected costs. However, they may engage in negative word-of-mouth and are very vulnerable to competitors' actions.

While repeat purchasers are desirable, *mere* repeat purchasers are very vulnerable to competitor actions. That is, they are buying the brand due to habit or because it is readily available where they shop, or because it has the lowest price, or for similar superficial reasons. These customers have no commitment to the brand. That is, they are not brand loyal. **Brand loyalty** is defined as:

1. A biased (i.e., nonrandom),
2. Behavioral response (i.e., purchase),
3. Expressed over time,
4. By some decision-making unit,
5. With respect to one or more alternative brands out of a set of such brands, and
6. Is a function of psychological (decision-making, evaluative) processes.[27]

A brand-loyal, or **committed customer**, has an emotional attachment to the brand or firm. The customer likes the brand in a manner somewhat similar to friendship. Consumers use expressions such as—*I trust this brand* and *I believe in this firm*—to describe their commitment.

Brand loyalty can arise through identification, where a consumer believes the brand reflects and reinforces some aspect of the consumer's self-concept. This type of commitment is most common for symbolic products such as beer and automobiles. Brand loyalty may also arise through performance well above the level the consumer expects (and believes that other brands could deliver). Such superior performance can be related to the product or the firm itself or, as mentioned earlier, to the manner in which the firm responds to a complaint or a customer problem.

Committed customers are unlikely to consider additional information when making a purchase. They are also resistant to competitors' marketing efforts such as coupons. Even when loyal customers do buy a different brand to take advantage of a promotional deal, they generally return to their original brand for their next purchase.[28] Committed customers are more receptive to line extensions and other new products offered by the same firm. Finally, committed customers are likely to be a source of positive word-of-mouth communications. It is for these reasons that many marketers have attempted to create committed customers as well as satisfied customers.

Repeat Purchasers, Committed Customers, and Marketing Strategy

An important step in developing a marketing strategy for a particular segment is to specify the objectives being pursued. Several distinct possibilities exist:

1. Attract new users to the product category.
2. Capture competitors' current customers.
3. Encourage current customers to use more.
4. Encourage current customers to become repeat purchasers.
5. Encourage current customers to become committed customers.

Each of the objectives listed above will require different strategies and marketing mixes.[29] The first two objectives require the marketer to convince potential customers that the marketer's brand will provide superior value to not using the product or to using another brand. This is shown in the first four stages of Figure 19–6. Advertisements promising

Customer Satisfaction Outcomes

FIGURE 19–6

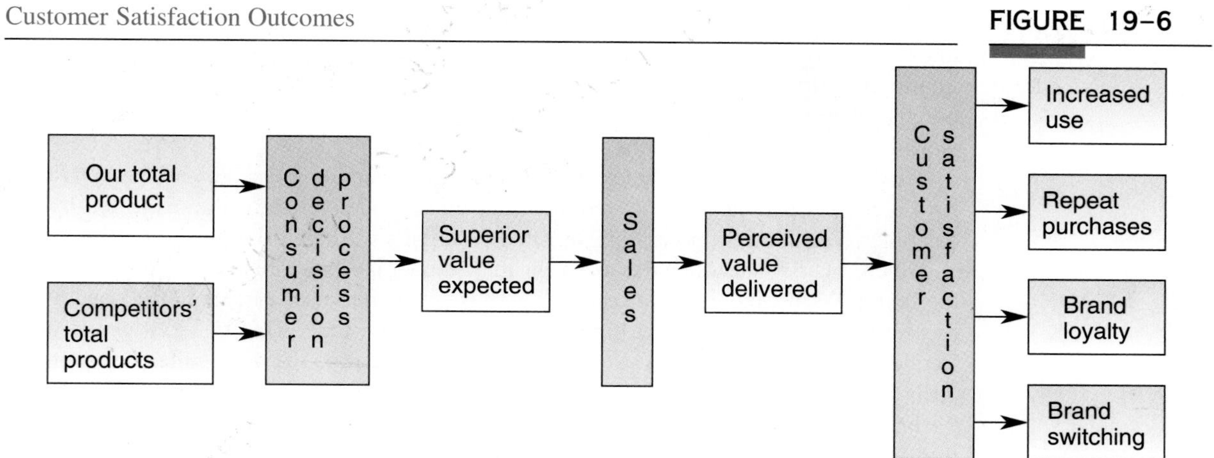

MANAGERIAL APPLICATION

19–3 Advertisements Designed to Increase Product/Brand Use

superior benefits, coupons, free trials, and similar strategies are common approaches. While many firms are content to consider the sale the last step, most firms now realize the critical importance of retaining customers after the initial sale. This is true even for infrequently purchased items (rather than repeat sales, the marketer wants positive, or at least neutral, word-of-mouth communications).

The next three objectives all require customer satisfaction as a necessary precondition. As Figure 19–6 indicates, this requires that the firm deliver the value expected by the customer. Techniques for creating satisfied customers were described earlier.

Given satisfied customers, a marketer may encourage those customers to use more of the brand.[30] This may involve convincing those customers who use more than one brand to use the marketer's brand a higher percentage of the time. This is a key objective of frequent-flier programs that award higher "points" per mile the more miles flown on the airline in a year. Another approach to increasing consumption is to show new ways to use the brand or new situations for which it is appropriate. Managerial Application 19–3 shows two ads designed to increase the consumption of a product and brand.

A substantial amount of effort is currently being focused on the fourth objective—encouraging repeat purchases. While these programs are generally called customer loyalty programs, many are designed to generate repeat purchases rather than committed customers.[31] In addition to frequent-flier programs offered by most major airlines, programs designed to generate repeat purchases include:

- Saks-Fifth Avenue (Saks First) and Sears (Best Customer) identify frequent shoppers and make them members of their store "clubs." As members, they receive extra services, preshopping at sales, fashion newsletters, and so forth.
- Arby's Restaurants has Club Arby's, which electronically tracks purchases and offers food prizes to repeat customers.
- Waldenbooks' Preferred Customer Program offers discounts and rebates to repeat purchasers. It also segments its membership, based on the types of books each customer buys. This allows it to deliver customized direct-mail ads to its frequent shoppers.

While programs such as those described above are often very effective at generating repeat purchases, they do not necessarily create committed customers. Committed customers have a reasonably strong emotional attachment to the product or firm. Generating committed customers requires that the firm consistently meet or exceed customer expectations. Further, customers must believe that the firm is treating them fairly and is, to some extent at least, concerned about their well-being. Thus, generating committed customers requires a customer-focused attitude in the firm. It also requires that this attitude be translated into actions that meet customers' needs.[32] The following example illustrates this attitude:

> Great Plains Software shipped a program that contained several bugs. As soon as this was discovered, the firm spent $250,000 to mail a new version to every buyer. It also wrote to all 2,700 of its dealers, described the problem and the replacement program, and offered to compensate any dealer whose business was harmed by the mistake.

SUMMARY

Following some purchases, consumers experience doubts or anxiety about the wisdom of the purchase. This is known as *postpurchase dissonance.* It is most likely to occur (1) among individuals with a tendency to experience anxiety, (2) after an irrevocable purchase, (3) when the purchase was important to the consumer, and (4) when it involved a difficult choice between two or more alternatives. Postpurchase dissonance is important to the marketing manager because, if not resolved, it can result in a returned product or a negative evaluation of the purchase.

Whether or not the consumer experiences dissonance, most purchases are followed by *product use.* This use may be by the purchaser or by some other member of the purchasing unit. Marketing managers are interested in product use for a variety of reasons. The major reason is that consumers use a product to fulfill certain needs. If the product does not fulfill these needs, a negative evaluation may result. Therefore, managers must be aware of how products perform in use. Monitoring product usage can indicate new uses for existing products, needed product modifications, appropriate advertising themes, and opportunities for new products. Product liability laws have made it increasingly important for marketing managers to be aware of all potential uses of their products.

Disposition of the product or its package may occur before, during, or after product use. Understanding disposition behavior has become increasingly important to marketing managers because of the ecological concerns of many consumers, the costs and scarcity of raw materials, and the activities of federal and state legislatures and regulatory agencies. The ease of recycling or reusing a product's container is a key product attribute for many consumers. Product disposition is a major consideration in marketing strategy because: (1) disposition sometimes must precede the purchase due to financial or space limitations; (2) certain disposition strategies may give rise to a used or rebuilt market; and (3) difficult or unsatisfactory disposition alternatives may cause some consumers to withdraw from the market for a particular item.

Postpurchase dissonance, product usage, and disposition are potential influences on the *purchase evaluation process.* Consumers develop certain expectations about the ability of the product to fulfill instrumental and symbolic needs. To the extent that the product meets these needs, satisfaction is likely to result. When expectations are not met, dissatisfaction is the likely result.

Taking no action; switching brands, products, or stores; and warning friends are all common reactions to a negative purchase evaluation. A marketing manager generally should encourage dissatisfied consumers to complain directly to the firm and to no one else. This alerts the firm to problems and provides it with an opportunity to make amends. Unfortunately, only a fairly small, unique set of consumers tends to complain. Developing such strategies as consumer hot lines can increase the percentage of dissatisfied consumers who complain to the firm.

After the evaluation process and, where applicable the complaint process, consumers have some degree of repurchase motivation. There may be a strong motive to avoid the brand, a willingness to repurchase it some of the time, a willingness to repurchase it all of the time, or some level of *brand loyalty*, which is a willingness to repurchase coupled with a psychological commitment to the brand.

Marketing strategy does not always have the creation of brand loyalty as its objective. Rather, the manager must examine the makeup of the brand's current and potential consumers and select the specific objectives most likely to maximize the overall organizational goals.

REVIEW QUESTIONS

1. What are the major *postpurchase processes* engaged in by consumers?
2. How does the *type of decision process* affect the postpurchase processes?
3. What is *postpurchase dissonance*? What characteristics of a purchase situation are likely to contribute to postpurchase dissonance?
4. In what ways can a consumer reduce postpurchase dissonance?
5. In what ways can a marketer help reduce postpurchase dissonance?
6. What is meant by the *disposition of products and product packaging*, and why does it interest governmental regulatory agencies?
7. Why are marketers interested in disposition?
8. What factors influence *consumer satisfaction*? In what way do they influence consumer satisfaction?
9. What is the difference between *instrumental* and *symbolic performance*, and how does each contribute to consumer satisfaction?
10. What courses of action can a consumer take in response to dissatisfaction?
11. How do consumers typically respond when dissatisfied?
12. What would marketers like consumers to do when dissatisfied? How can marketers encourage this?
13. What is the relationship between customer satisfaction, repeat purchases, and committed customers?

14. What is the difference between repeat purchasers and brand-loyal customers?
15. Why are marketers interested in having brand-loyal customers?
16. What are five objectives that a marketing strategy for a particular segment might have?
17. How will marketing strategy differ across the five objectives that a firm might have for a particular segment?

DISCUSSION QUESTIONS

18. How should *retailers* deal with consumers immediately after purchase to reduce postpurchase dissonance? What specific action would you recommend, and what effect would you intend it to have on the recent purchaser of:
    a. A laptop computer.
    b. On-line skates.
    c. Mouthwash.
    d. Life insurance.
    e. An automobile.
    f. A large-screen TV.
19. Answer Question 18 from a manufacturer's perspective.
20. Discuss how you could determine how consumers actually use their ________. How could this information be used to develop marketing strategy?
    a. Microwave.
    b. Camcorder.
    c. Laptop computer.
    d. Mouthwash.
    e. Bleach.
    f. Radios.
21. How would you go about measuring consumer satisfaction among purchasers of ________? What questions would you ask, and what additional information would you collect and why? How could this information be used for evaluating and planning marketing programs?
    a. Legal services.
    b. Personal computers.
    c. Fast-food restaurant.
    d. Frozen pizza.
    e. Grocery store.
    f. In-line skates.
22. An A. C. Nielsen study found that 61 percent of the unsatisfactory purchases of health and beauty aids, such as deodorants, shampoos, or vitamins, were followed by continued purchase of the brand. Only 27 percent of the unsatisfactory purchases of paper products were followed by repeat purchases of the same brand. Why is there such a large difference?
23. Based on those characteristics that contribute to postpurchase dissonance, discuss several product purchases that are most likely to result in dissonance and several that will not create this effect.
24. What level of product dissatisfaction should a marketer be content with in attempting to serve a particular target market? What characteristics contribute to dissatisfaction, regardless of the marketer's efforts?
25. Describe the last time you were dissatisfied with a purchase. What action did you take? Why?
26. What are the marketing implications of:
    a. Figure 19–1
    b. Figure 19–2
    c. Table 19–1
    d. Figure 19–3
    e. Exhibit 19–1
    f. Figure 19–4.
    g. Figure 19–5.
    h. Figure 19–6.

APPLICATION EXERCISES

27. Develop a questionnaire designed to measure consumer satisfaction of a clothing purchase of $25 or more. Include in your questionnaire items that measure the product's instrumental and expressive dimensions of performance, as well as what the consumer wanted in terms of instrumental and expressive performance. Then, interview several consumers to obtain information on actual performance, expected performance, and satisfaction. Using this

information, determine if the consumer received (i.e., evaluation of performance) what they expected and relate any difference to consumer expressions of satisfaction. What are the marketing implications of your results?

28. Develop a survey to measure student dissatisfaction with service purchases. For purchases they were dissatisfied with, determine what action they took to resolve this dissatisfaction and what was the end result of their efforts.
29. Develop a questionnaire to measure repeat purchase behavior and brand loyalty. Measure the repeat purchase behavior and brand loyalty of 10 students with respect to ______. Determine *why* the brand-loyal students are brand loyal.
    a. Fast-food restaurants.
    b. Toothpaste.
    c. Deodorant.
    d. Soft drinks
    e. Gum.
    f. Clothing stores.
30. With the cooperation of a major durables retailer, assist the retailer in sending a postpurchase letter of thanks to every other customer immediately after purchase. Then, approximately two weeks after purchase, contact the same customers (both those who received the letter and those who did not) and measure their purchase satisfaction. Evaluate the results.
31. Interview a grocery store manager and a department store manager. Determine the types of products their customers are most likely to complain about and the nature of those complaints.
32. Measure 10 students' disposition behaviors with respect to ______. Determine *why* they use the alternatives they do.
    a. Soft-drink containers.
    b. Magazines.
    c. Food cans.
    d. Newspapers.
    e. Plastic items.
    f. Large items.
33. Implement Question 20 with a sample of students.
34. Implement Question 21 with a sample of students.

REFERENCES

[1]T. Tripett, "Product Recall Spurs Company to Improve Customer Satisfaction," *Marketing News*, April 11, 1994, p. 6.

[2]The basic theory of cognitive dissonance of which postpurchase dissonance is a subset is present in L. Festinger, *A Theory of Cognitive Dissonance* (Stanford, Calif.: Stanford University Press, 1957). An overview is available in W. H. Cummings and M. Venkatesan, "Cognitive Dissonance and Consumer Behavior: A Review of the Evidence," *Journal of Marketing Research*, August 1976, pp. 303–8.

[3]F. Rice, "Where Will We Put All That Garbage?" *Fortune*, April 11, 1988, pp. 96–100.

[4]See J. M. Carman, "Consumer Perceptions of Service Quality," *Journal of Retailing*, Spring 1990, pp. 33–55; D. K. Tse, F. M. Nicosia, and P. C. Wilton, "Consumer Satisfaction as a Process," *Psychology and Marketing*, Fall 1990, pp. 177–93; and D. Halstead, D. Hartman, and S. L. Schmidt, "Multisource Effects on the Satisfaction Process," *Journal of the Academy of Marketing Science*, Spring 1994, pp. 114–29.

[5]See V. A. Zeithaml, L. L. Berry, and A. Parasuraman, "The Nature and Determination of Customer Expectations of Service," *Journal of the Academy of Marketing Science*, Winter 1993, pp. 1–12.

[6]S. J. Hoch and Y. W. Ha, "Consumer Learning," *Journal of Consumer Research*, September 1986, pp. 221–33; and J. Deighton and R. M. Schindler, "Can Advertising Influence Experience?" *Psychology & Marketing*, Summer 1988, pp. 103–15.

[7]R. L. Oliver and J. E. Swan, "Consumer Perceptions of Interpersonal Equity and Satisfaction in Transactions," *Journal of Marketing*, April 1989, pp. 21–35; and R. L. Oliver and J. E. Swan, "Equity and Disconfirmation Perceptions as Influences on Merchant and Product Satisfaction," *Journal of Consumer Research*, December 1989, pp. 372–83. For discussions of both conceptual measurement issues, see J. J. Cronin, Jr., and S. A. Taylor, "Measuring Service Quality," and T. A. Oliva, R. L. Oliver, and I. C. MacMillan, "A Castastrophe Model for Developing Service Strategies," both in *Journal of Marketing*, July 1992, pp. 55–69 and 83–96; R. A. Peterson and W. R. Wilson, "Measuring Customer Satisfaction," *Journal of the Academy of Marketing Science*, Winter 1992, pp. 61–72; R. K. Teas, "Expectations, Performance Evaluation, and Customers' Perceptions of Quality," *Journal of Marketing*, October 1993, pp. 18–34; and A. Parasuraman, V. A. Zeithaml, and L. L. Berry, "Reassessment of Expectations as a Comparison Standard," J. J. Cronin, Jr., and S. A. Taylor, SERVPERF versus SERVQUAL," and R. K. Teas, "Expectations as a Comparison Standard," all in *Journal of Marketing*, January 1994, pp. 111–24, 125–31, and 132–39.

[8]R. N. Maddox, "The Structure of Consumers' Satisfaction: Cross-Product Comparisons," *Journal of the Academy of Marketing Science*, Winter 1982, pp. 37–53.

[9]I. E. Swan and L. J. Combs, "Product Performance and Consumer Satisfaction: A New Concept," *Journal of Marketing*, April 1976, pp. 25–33; see also B. D. Gelb, "How Marketers of Intangibles Can Raise the Odds for Consumer Satisfaction," *Journal of Consumer Marketing*, Spring 1985, pp. 55–61; and R. A. Westbrook, "Product/Consumption-Based Affective Responses and Postpurchase Processes," *Journal of Marketing Research*, August 1987, pp. 258–70.

[10]J. Singh, "A Typology of Consumer Dissatisfaction Response Styles," *Journal of Retailing*, Spring 1990, pp. 57–97; J. Singh, "Voice, Exit, and Negative Word-of-Mouth Behaviors," *Journal of the Academy of Marketing Science*, Winter 1990, pp. 1–15; K. Gronhaug and O. Kvitastein, "Purchases and Complaints," *Psychology & Marketing*, Spring 1991, pp. 21–35; and S. W. Kelley and M. A. Davis, "Antecedents to Customer Expectations for Service Recovery," *Journal of the Academy of Marketing Science*, Winter 1994, pp. 52–61.

[11]F. K. Shuptrine and G. Wenglorz, "Comprehensive Identification of Consumers' Marketplace Problems and What They Do about Them," in *Advances in Consumer Research VIII*, ed. K. B. Monroe (Chicago: Association for Consumer Research, 1981), pp. 687–92.

[12]See also S. P. Brown and R. F. Beltramini, "Consumer Complaining and Word-of-Mouth Activities," in *Advances in Consumer Research XVI*, ed. T. K. Srull (Provo, Utah: Association for Consumer Research, 1989), pp. 9–11; and J. E. Swan and R. L. Oliver, "Postpurchase Communications by Consumers," *Journal of Retailing*, Winter 1989, pp. 516–533.

[13]M. L. Richins, "Negative Word-of-Mouth by Dissatisfied Consumers," *Journal of Marketing*, Winter 1983, pp. 68–78; M. L. Richens, "Word-of-Mouth as Negative Information," in *Advances in Consumer Research XI*, ed. T. C. Kinnear (Provo, Utah: Association for Consumer Research, 1984), pp. 687–702; and M. T. Curren and V. S. Folkes, "Attributional Influences on Consumers' Desires to Communicate about Products," *Psychology & Marketing*, Spring 1987, pp. 31–45.

[14]*Better Business Bureau's Inquiries and Complaints, 1979 Statistical Summary* (New York: Council of Better Business Bureaus, Inc., undated), p. 7; and see footnote 11, Shuptrine and Wenglorz.

[15]K. L. Bernhardt, "Consumer Problems and Complaint Actions of Older Americans: A National View," *Journal of Retailing*, Fall 1981, pp. 107–23; W. O. Bearden and J. E. Teel, "An Investigation of Personal Influences on Consumer Complaining," *Journal of Retailing*, Fall 1981, pp. 2–20; M. S. Moyer, "Characteristics of Consumer Complaints," *Journal of Public Policy & Marketing,* vol. 3, 1984, pp. 67–84; and M. A. Morganosky and H. M. Buckley, "Complaint Behavior," in *Advances in Consumer Research XIV*, ed. M. Wallendorf and P. Anderson (Provo, Utah: Association for Consumer Research, 1987), pp. 223–26.

[16]See footnote 11, Shuptrine and Wenglorz.

[17]B. Bowers, "For Firms, 800 Is a Hot Number," *The Wall Street Journal*, November 9, 1989, p. B-1.

[18]J. A. Prestbo, "At Procter & Gamble, Success Is Largely Due to Heeding Consumer," *The Wall Street Journal*, April 29, 1980, p. 23.

[19]C. Goodwin and I. Ross, "Consumer Evaluations of Response to Complaints," *Journal of Consumer Marketing*, Spring 1990, pp. 39–47.

[20]A. J. Resnik and R. R. Harmon, "Consumer Complaints and Managerial Response," *Journal of Marketing*, Winter 1983, pp. 86–97; C. J. Cobb, G. C. Walgren, and M. Hollowed, "Differences in Organizational Responses to Consumer Letters of Satisfaction and Dissatisfaction," in *Advances in Consumer Research*, ed. M. Wallendorf and P. Anderson (Provo, Utah: Association for Consumer Research, 1987), pp. 227–31; and C. Fornell and R. Westbrook, "The Vicious Circle of Consumer Complaints," *Journal of Marketing*, Summer 1984, p. 68.

[21]M. J. Etzel and B. I. Silverman, "A Managerial Perspective on Directions for Retail Customer Dissatisfaction Research," *Journal of Retailing*, Fall 1981, 124–31; and M. C. Gilly and R. W. Hansen, "Consumer Complaint Handling as a Strategic Marketing Tool," *Journal of Consumer Marketing*, Fall 1985, pp. 5–16.

[22]C. Fornell and B. Wernerfelt, "Defensive Marketing Strategy by Customer Complaint Management," *Journal of Marketing Research*, November 1987, pp. 337–46.

[23]P. Sellers, "What Customers Really Want," *Fortune*, June 4, 1990, pp. 58–62.

[24]*Handling Consumer Complaints: In-House and Third-Party Strategies, no. 018–000–00284–1* (Washington, D.C.: U.S. Government Printing Office), p. 19. See also C. Cina, "Creating an Effective Customer Satisfaction Program," *Journal of Consumer Research*, Fall 1989, pp. 27–33.

[25]T. Moore, "Would You Buy a Car from This Man?" *Fortune*, April 11, 1988, pp. 72–74. See also R. Serafin, "Auto Makers Stress Consumer Satisfaction," *Advertising Age*, February 23, 1987, p. S-12.

[26]See S. B. Knouse, "Brand Loyalty and Sequential Learning Theory," *Psychology & Marketing*, Summer 1986, pp. 87–98.

[27]J. Jacoby and D. B. Kyner, "Brand Loyalty versus Repeat Purchasing Behavior," *Journal of Marketing Research*, February 1973, pp. 1–9. For an excellent technical discussion see A .S. Dick and K. Basu, "Customer Loyalty," *Journal of the Academy of Marketing Science*, Spring 1994, pp. 99–113.

[28]D. Mazursky, P. LaBarbera, and A. Aiello, "When Consumers Switch Brands," *Psychology & Marketing*, Spring 1987, pp. 17–30; see also G. J. Tellis, "Advertising Exposure, Loyalty, and Brand Choice," *Journal of Marketing Research*, May 1988, pp. 134–44; and J. Deighton, C. M. Henderson, and S. A. Neslin, "The Effects of Advertising on Brand Switching and Repeat Purchasing," *Journal of Marketing Research*, February 1994, pp. 28–43.

[29]See S. P. Raj, "Striking a Balance between Brand 'Popularity' and Brand Loyalty," *Journal of Marketing*, Winter 1985, pp. 53–59.

[30]B. Wansink and M. L. Ray, "Estimating an Advertisement's Impact on One's Consumption of a Brand," *Journal of Advertising Research*, May 1992, pp. 9–16.

[31]See G. Levin, "Marketers Flock to Loyalty Offers," *Advertising Age*, May 24, 1993, p. 13; and C. Miller, "Rewards for the Best Customers," *Marketing News*, July 5, 1993, pp. 1 ff.

[32]See F. Rice, "The New Rules of Superlative Services," and P. Sellers "Keeping the Buyers," both in *Fortune*, Autumn/Winter 1993, pp. 50–53 and 56–58.

SECTION 4 CASES

Case 4–1 Fisherman's Friend®

Fisherman's Friend has been described in a variety of ways:

> **They taste terrible, they look ugly, and their packaging is dull and boring.**
>
> **A cough lozenge with a funny name, a horrible taste, and a minuscule ad budget.**
>
> **(The) product tastes horrible, it is packaged wrong by contemporary standards, and it has a funny-sounding name.**
>
> **(They) look like flattened doggie treats, and the powerful taste of menthol, eucalyptus, licorice, and pepper can leave you rolling your eyes and gasping for breath.**

In 1982, Greg Blazic, a former accountant at Beatrice Cos., obtained U.S. distribution rights to Fisherman's Friend® from England-based Lofthouse of Fleetwood. Lofthouse has been marketing the product for 125 years. It was initially developed to help North Atlantic cod fishermen cope with colds, hence the name.

The two previous U.S. distributors had failed in their attempts to market the product. For a while, it appeared that Blazic would also fail. ''I was thrown out of so many places in the early years, it was incredible.''

Part of the problem was the name:

> When you go in to sell a product called Fisherman's Friend, people look at you very strangely. People think its some kind of bait, or a brand of worm or something.

Asking a healthy store manager or buyer to try the product didn't help. According to Blazic, the product tastes ''absolutely wretched. It's like eating Vicks VapoRub.'' The packaging is rather plain white paper with red and black letters. Each package contains 19 lozenges. It sells for $.99 to $1.09 a package, compared to Sucrets at $2.39 per box.

Eight years after taking over distribution, Blazic has moved Fisherman's Friend into the number one position in unit sales (21 percent compared to number two Sucrets' 19 percent) in drugstores (about 37 percent of total cough lozenge sales are in drugstores). On a dollar basis, the product is in fourth place (12 percent) due to its lower price. Its unit share in supermarkets (40 percent of total cough lozenge sales) is only 2 percent (compared to Sucrets' 45 percent). Supermarket penetration is the next objective for Blazic.

How did Blazic succeed where his two predecessors had failed? First, rather than downplaying the product's strong taste, he used it as an asset:

> When you were growing up, wasn't it a belief of your grandmother that no medicine works unless it tastes bad? I think there is a psychology about that. For something to really work you have to pay your dues.

The firm's morning drive-time radio spots (its media budget is only $500,000) take advantage of both the unusual name and the taste. The morning disc jockeys are not provided scripts. They are instructed to have fun with the spots but not to make fun of the product's effectiveness. Thus, they make jokes about the product's name and have lines like ''with the taste that's not for wimps.'' However, they do indicate that it works. The firm will air approximately 335,000 individual radio commercials during the 1990–91 cough-and-cold season (November through February).

The creative breakthrough that allowed Blazic to get his first drug-chain distribution was the plastic boat point-of-purchase display that is still used. The orange-and-black boat is 15 inches long and 7 inches wide. Mounted on a 10-inch pedestal, it holds 25 packets, and the two display cartons on the pedestal hold another 50 packets. Thus, the counter display is very attention attracting, holds 75 packets, and takes very little counter space. Initially, "people bought because of the boat, not because of the product." The boat was cute. The copy with the display emphasizes "extra strong" and "effective in England for 125 years." Of course, the fishing boat is associated with and reinforces the product's unusual name.

Fisherman's Friend has been a remarkable success story so far. However, new challenges await Blazic. How long can he continue to gain market share in the drugstore channel? How can he increase his minuscule share in the supermarket channel?

Discussion Questions

1. What behavior principles account for the current success of Fisherman's Friend?
2. What impact has the product's relatively low price had on its success? What would happen if prices were increased 25 percent? 50 percent? 100 percent?
3. Do people who buy cough lozenges at supermarkets differ from those who buy them at drugstores? If so, how? What implications do these differences have for Blazic's plans to gain share in supermarkets?
4. Describe the decision process a consumer might go through to select a cough lozenge. What aspects of this process would lead some consumers to purchase Fisherman's Friend and others to purchase other brands?

South Hills Mall Kids' Club* — Case 4–2

South Hills Mall is an 11-year-old enclosed center located in the hub of a concentrated retail area along U.S. Route 9 in Poughkeepsie, New York. The mall has 90 stores and is anchored by Sears, Hess's, and Kmart. South Hills attracts all demographic groups, but older shoppers (over 45 years of age) are responsible for nearly half of the center's sales. The mall is positioned to appeal to Middle America's desire for value and service.

A two-level, superregional, upscale center with 5 anchors and 167 stores recently opened on the parcel adjacent to South Hills. The competing center has strong appeal for young and middle-aged shoppers (under 45 years of age) and also attracts a larger percentage of shoppers with incomes exceeding $50,000.

Since the opening of the new center, South Hills Mall began to lose its share of the young family shoppers (ages 20 to 45). The erosion of this key shopper group negatively impacted traffic and sales.

To counter the increased competition, Jill Hofstra, marketing director for South Hills Mall, developed the South Hills Mall Kids' Club, with these objectives in mind.:

1. Reinforce the South Hills Mall's position as a provider of genuine value and extra services to shoppers.
2. Develop a program that will give South Hills Mall the competitive edge in building loyalty and frequency of visits from the young-family shopper group.
3. Strengthen sales and traffic from this key shopper group.

The Kids' Club

To attract the young-family shopper group, Hofstra decided to target children with a consistent message, using a monthly direct-mail program. The message was to deliver an incentive or promise of value to

*This case was prepared by, and is used with permission of, Jill A. Hofstra, Certified Marketing Director, South Hills Mall.

stimulate shopping visits to the mall. Thus, the Kids' Club was born.

The club was launched in January 1990, with a day of festivities, including clowns, jugglers, music, marionette shows, and face painters. In addition, the local police department conducted child fingerprinting sessions, the traffic safety commission provided children's safety sessions, and the mall merchants sponsored in-store activities and giveaways.

To recruit members, invitations were sent to 550 prospective Kids' Club members, and the event was also promoted in print and radio advertising. Over 1,600 children turned out and received their free membership kit, free button, balloon, and T-shirt.

Kids' Club is geared for children 12 and under. Membership is free and very easy. Kids or their parents fill out an application at the Customer Service Center. Then, every month, members receive a postcard outlining special surprises and promotions geared toward them and their families. In addition to the excitement of receiving their own personal mail, kids enjoy the fun of solving a different riddle each month and discovering what their surprise gift will be.

In February, the Kids' Club sponsored a local circus performance and gave away tickets to the show. Redeeming the Kids' Club postcards for free Valentine's Day stickers created a 20.6 percent response rate. In March, 27.6 percent of Kids' Club members took advantage of a free photo with the Easter Bunny.

April's special promotion included free inflatable kites and a chance to win a pair of tickets to a play (29 percent response). In May, kids created a mug for Mother's Day, and in June, they picked up a free gift for Dad. The July beach-ball giveaway attracted hundreds of children.

TABLE A First-Year Budget

Initial expenses	
Postcards	$ 474.16
Mailing list	
Setup	243.34
Postage	137.50
T-shirts	6,659.91
Balloons	350.00
Buttons (year's supply)	2,415.48
Button cards (year's supply)	471.60
Signage	483.00
Baby mailer (year's supply)	380.70
Entertainment (clowns, jugglers, face painters, puppets, music)	1,225.00
Decorations	400.00
Print advertising	1,589.92
Radio advertising	1,584.00
Production (postcard, print, radio advertising, and all collateral materials)	3,258.00
	$19,672.61
Additional monthly expenses	
Postcards	$ 474.16
Production	300.00
Giveaways*	1,000.00
Postage	410.00

*If no sponsorship.

New babies are invited to join the club. New parents receive a packet that includes Kids' Club registration, a bib, and shoelaces with the Kids' Club logo. They also are informed of the mall's free stroller policy and receive coupons from the mall merchants. Recruitment of new members is done through mall signage, periodic print and radio advertising, and through customer service personnel. Mall merchants also have the chance to get involved by signing up new members, sponsoring a particular month's giveaway, or coordinating merchandising activities.

Kids' Club is designed so that everyone wins. Kids love the free surprises. Parents enjoy receiving special messages about mall events. The mall hopes to gain increased traffic and shopper loyalty when Kids' Club members and their families visit the Customer Service Center to redeem their postcards each month. The first-year budget for the program is shown in Table A.

Discussion Questions

1. What view of the household decision process is reflected in this program?
2. This program will have the most appeal to children of what age?
3. To which social class(es) will this program have the most appeal?
4. In what ways could this program be improved?
5. What ethical issues are associated with this program?

Federated Stores

Case 4–3

A large, well-known department store (a member of Federated Stores, Inc.) wanted to better understand the effectiveness of its retail promotions. The store, which had above-average quality and competitive prices, typically ran newspaper and radio advertisements during a retail promotion. Its television advertising was primarily institutional and did not address specific retail promotions. While the management team knew that they had to advertise their retail promotions, they never felt comfortable with the effectiveness of their advertising efforts. What they really wanted to know was how they could improve their advertising efforts in order to get a bigger response per dollar spent.

Advertising Study

Prepromotion Survey To better understand the effectiveness of their advertising, a study of advertising exposure, interpretation, and purchases was conducted. A well-defined target market of 50,000 potential buyers was identified, and 50 in-depth interviews were conducted to determine the appropriate merchandise, price, ad copy, and media for the test. In addition, the store's image and that of three competing stores were measured.

Based on this information, a line of merchandise that would appeal to consumers in this target market was selected. The merchandise was attractively priced, and ad copy was carefully created to communicate and appeal to the demographics and lifestyles of the target consumers. The retail promotion was run for one week, and full-page newspaper ads promoting the retail merchandise were run each day in the two local newspapers. Radio advertisements also ran on two radio stations whose listener demographics matched the target market. Eight radio advertisements were aired each day of the promotion, two in each of four time slots: early morning, mid-day, early evening (7–10 P.M.), and late evening (after 10 P.M.).

In-Promotion Survey Each evening, a sample of 100 target market consumers was interviewed by telephone as follows:

1. Target consumers were asked if they had read the newspaper or listened to the radio that day. If so, how extensively? This would determine their exposure to the advertisement.
2. After a general description of the merchandise, they were asked to recall any related retail advertisements they had seen or heard.
3. If they recalled the ad, they were asked to describe the ad, the merchandise promoted, sale prices, and the sponsoring store.
4. If they were accurate in their ad interpretation, they were asked to express their intentions to purchase.

FIGURE A Advertising Awareness over Five Days of Advertising

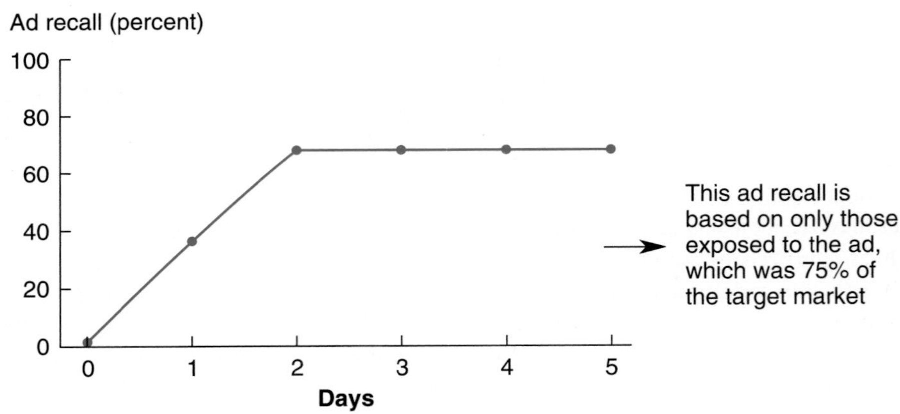

FIGURE B Overall Ad Effectiveness and Market Penetration

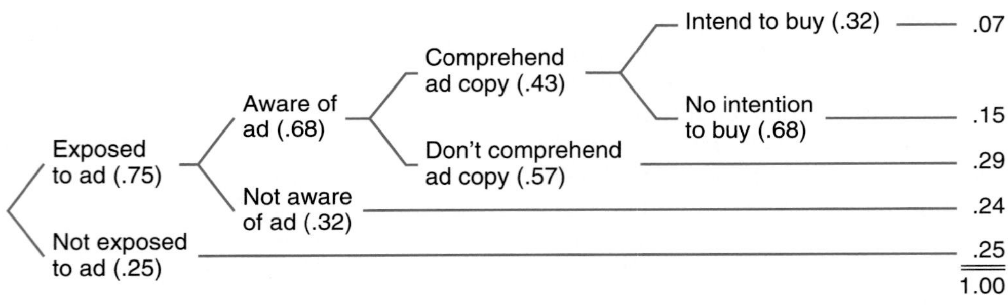

5. Additional questions that could be useful in future promotions targeted at this consumer segment were also asked.

Postpromotion Survey Immediately following the retail promotion, 500 target market consumers were surveyed to determine what percentage of the target market actually purchased the promoted merchandise. It was also important to determine which sources of information influenced them in their decision to purchase and the amount of their purchase.

Results of Study

The combination of targeted daily newspaper and radio advertising produced a cumulative recall of the advertisement among those exposed to the ad by either newspaper, radio, or both. As shown in Figure A, the largest gains in recall (awareness) were made in the first two days of advertising effort. After day two, only marginal gains in awareness occurred.

After two days of ad exposure, ad awareness reached a maximum of 68 percent. However, effectiveness of the advertising effort cannot be judged only on awareness of the promotion. Information collected on ad interpretation and intention to buy is also important in evaluating the effectiveness of advertising. Using the information collected during the promotion, Figure B was constructed.

While ad exposure (75 percent) and ad awareness (68 percent) were high, correct interpretation of the ad was low. In this case only 43 percent of those exposed to *and* aware of the ad copy could accurately recall important details, such as which store was promoting the retail sale. Of those who did comprehend the ad copy, 33 percent intended to respond by purchasing the advertised merchandise. This yields an overall intention to buy, based on the ad, of 7 percent. As shown in Figure B, the biggest area of lost opportunity was due to those who did not accurately interpret the ad copy.

The post-promotion survey estimated that only 4.2 percent of the target market consumers made purchases of the promotional merchandise during the promotion period. However, the average total amount of purchase was $45, roughly double the average price of the promotion merchandise. In terms of how these buyers learned of the promotion, 46 percent mentioned *newspaper A*, 23 percent mentioned *newspaper B*, 15 percent learned of the sale through word-of-mouth communication, and 10 percent mentioned the radio.

Overall, the retail promotion yielded almost $100,000 in sales and was judged a success in many ways. However, management was concerned over the results presented in Figure B, since a significant sales opportunity was missed by not achieving a higher level of ad comprehension. They believe that a more effective ad would have at least 75 percent correct interpretation among those aware of the ad. This in turn would almost double sales with no additional cost.

Discussion Questions

1. Discuss the learning and retention of information in this case within the context of high- and low-involvement learning. Why might some target consumers have higher levels of involvement in learning of this retail promotion than others?
2. Discuss Figure B and why the overall estimated market penetration (7 percent) was higher than actual market penetration (4.2 percent). How might this model be improved to achieve a more accurate estimate of market penetration?
3. With respect to future retail advertising promotions, what recommendations would you make to improve the overall profitability of the advertising effort? Recall that management's ultimate concern was to achieve a ''bigger response per dollar spent.''
4. Is management realistic in desiring 75 percent correct interpretation among those aware of the ad? What could be done to improve interpretation?

Condoms

Case 4–4

With the government promoting condoms as the safest way outside of abstinence to avoid the AIDS disease, with several manufacturers engaged in aggressive marketing, and with increased educational efforts, their sales should be growing rapidly. However, in early 1994, sales were flat. According to one industry executive: *The perception is that more and more people are using condoms, but the reality is that usage has leveled off. The onus is really on us manufacturers to educate consumers.*

Condom sales grew at a double-digit rate in the late 1980s. This growth was spurred by former Surgeon General Everett Koop's report strongly advocating the use of condoms to stem the spread of AIDS. The CDC (Center for Disease Control and Prevention) followed up by mailing to every U.S. household a pamphlet explicitly discussing condoms. This effort, coupled with Rock Hudson's highly publicized death from AIDS, caused the product category sales to increase by 40 to 50 percent. However, when sales growth stalled, even the announcement that Magic Johnson was HIV-positive caused only a small increase in condom use.

Surveys conducted for the CDC indicate that slightly less than half of the sexually active teenagers use condoms. Many experts believe this figure to be overstated. According to an expert on marketing to youth:

> It's very P.C. [politically correct] to say you use them, but I think it's less than that. It's such a hard sell. There's a lot of cultural baggage to overcome. Guys feel there's less enjoyment and its not macho, and I just don't know how many girls would force the issue. They have to be taught how to do this with grace and panache. Marketers really have to take a bottoms-up approach, going in depth over all the issues relative to sex and how condom usage fits in, and that's going to take a lot of insight into the consumer.

EXHIBIT A

Other experts believe that the tendency for young adults to believe that nothing really bad can happen to them is a major factor in the limited use of condoms among one of the most-at-risk groups.

The U.S. government has recently begun encouraging the use of condoms through a series of public service announcements (PSAs). One ad shows a frisky little condom in its package as it springs from a dresser drawer and skitters across the bedroom floor awaking a sleeping cat as it passes. Then it jumps onto a bed and dives under the sheets where a couple appear to be in passionate embrace. A voice-over says: *It would be nice if latex condoms were automatic, but since they're not, using them should be.*

Another PSA, prepared in both English and Spanish, shows two Latin lovers. She unbuttons his shirt. He pulls off her earring. She kicks off a shoe. Then she asks: *Did you bring it?* He replies: *I forgot it.* She concludes the evening by turning on the light and saying: *Then forget it.*

While all three major networks have agreed to run the PSAs, none of them will show commercials for condoms. Fox began accepting such commercials in 1992 but is stringent in what it will allow for content. For example, it turned down a commercial for Lifestyles condoms that featured a close-up of a woman saying: *I'll do a lot for love, but I'm not ready to die for it.* In contrast, many cable program channels, such as MTV, accept condom advertising.

There are four major condom marketers. Carter-Wallace markets the Trojan brand with an estimated 60 percent market share. It is currently running a series of full-page print ads that ridicule common excuses for not using a condom. The ads are mostly blank with the excuse at the top of the page, the words GET REAL in large, bold type in the middle of the page, with a put-down of the excuse directly underneath, and a picture of the Trojan package at the bottom of the page. A recent ad looked like this:

> "I didn't use one because I didn't have one with me."
>
> **GET REAL**
>
> If you don't have a parachute, don't jump, genius.
>
> TROJAN

Safetex, the smallest of the four major firms, has concentrated on developing niche products geared to a young, hip audience and to securing trade support. One of its successful products is its Gold Circle brand which is discreetly wrapped in a round foil package so that it does not look like a condom package.

Ansell, which markets Lifestyles condoms, uses print ads in magazines and cable television, especially MTV. It also advertises in college newspapers with ad headlines that state—*More thoughtful than a box of chocolates*—and an offer of a $1.00 sample kit and coupons. While 70 percent of its sales are to males, Ansell also targets females (see Exhibit A). One television ad shows a group of women stating that they: *never would with a guy that calls you Oooo baby, never would with guys who high-five,* and finally, never *with a guy who thinks he can get away not wearing a condom.* The ad closes with a picture of a Lifestyles box and a voice-over saying: *Not with me. Not in this day and age.*

Discussion Questions

1. What type of decision process is typically used in the decision to purchase and use condoms?
2. Why is condom use limited among sexually active young people?
3. What actions should the government take to promote either abstinence or the use of condoms, given the dangers of AIDS?
4. Should the networks accept condom advertising? Why?
5. Assume you are the marketing manager for one of the major condom marketers. Develop a marketing program to increase the percentage of sexually active young people using condoms. Describe how each stage of the decision process is considered in your strategy.
6. Assume you are the national manager for a regional or national chain of ______. How would you attempt to increase sales of condoms in your outlets? What risks, if any, would your program have?
   a. Grocery stores
   b. Convenience stores.
   c. Pharmacies (selling primarily prescription drugs and over-the-counter medicines and beauty aids).
   d. Drugstores.

Source: C. Miller, "Condom Sales Cool Off," *Marketing News*, February 28, 1994, p. 14.

RCA and GE Televisions

Case 4–5

"I've got 18 months," says Joseph Clayton, referring to the length of time he believes he has to make major gains in sales and profits in the competitive U.S. television market. In 1988, French conglomerate Thomson gave General Electric $800 million plus its medical equipment business for General Electric's GE and RCA television brands. Since then, it has spent another $300 million modernizing the American plants.

Unfortunately, the brands' market shares continued to decline under the leadership of Thomson's first manager (see Figure A). (This individual focused heavily on image building through such activities as sponsoring the America's Cup race.) Attempts to increase prices in 1991 also hurt sales and share of both brands.

Clayton has taken a much more aggressive approach. Rather than hiking prices, he is cutting prices on some models. Clayton's strategy is to hold share in the smaller sets where price competition is intense, and to grow share in the more lucrative big-screen TVs. Though big-screen TVs represent only 5 percent of the units sold, at prices of $2,000 and more they make up 22 percent of retail dollar sales (nearly $2 billion). They have a gross margin of about 35 percent compared to a 20 percent margin for a 20-inch set.

To grow share in the big-screen market, Clayton is using competitive pricing and introducing new styles. In the RCA line, rounded edges have replaced sharp corners and blacks and grays have replaced the *faux*-wood look. GE's redesigned models are due out soon. The advertising budget has been doubled to $30

FIGURE A Market Shares (*in units*)

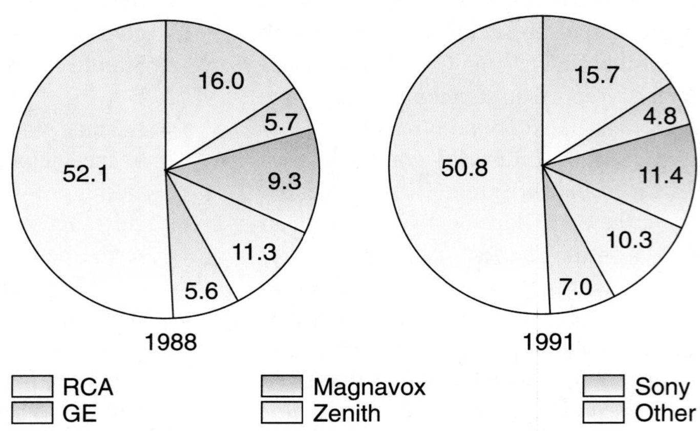

million. The ads stress product features and performance. They are also testing an in-store display of a "home theater" with RCA large-screen TVs, VCRs, and speakers.

These efforts have already borne fruit. GE and RCA's combined market share of big-screen sets has increased from 5 percent to 20 percent since 1990. However, Clayton's next move is generating considerable controversy. He plans to roll out the first wide-screen TV. The new rectangular screen would provide more spectacular viewing than the standard square screen.

The problem with the wide-screen TV is the fact that there are no programs being broadcast in the wide-screen format. The advent of high-definition TV may result in wide-screen broadcasts. Until then, the sets will show broadcasts with black bands on the sides. A zoom can fill the screen but it cuts off the top and bottom of the picture.

Clayton justifies the wide-screen introduction as an announcement of RCA's technological leadership. He feels that it should be considered an advertisement that will help sales of current products and become profitable itself in the future.

Discussion Questions

1. What is the decision process used by customers to purchase a normal-sized TV? Does this process differ for a big-screen TV?
2. Describe the decision process that would result in the purchase of a wide-screen TV.
3. Do the evaluative criteria used in the choice of a normal TV differ from those involved in the purchase of a big-screen TV?
4. Do individuals purchasing a normal TV have different causes of problem recognition from those purchasing a big-screen TV?
5. How could Clayton increase the sales of his normal-sized TVs?
6. If you managed a chain of stores that sold TVs and other appliances, how would you select and use P-O-P (point-of-purchase) displays and co-op advertising allowances?
7. Evaluate Clayton's decision to be the first to develop and introduce a wide-screen TV.

Source: Adapted from L. Therrien, "Thomson Needs A Hit," *Business Week*, July 6, 1992, p. 80; and T. Lefton, "Trade Baited with New Message", *Brandweek*, November 9, 1992, p. 3.

A Product Failure at Saturn

Case 4–6

Saturn, a division of General Motors, advertises around the theme:

> **A different kind of company.**
> **A different kind of car.**

Though Saturn cars cost only $10,000 to $16,000, the firm attempts to provide its customers the same level of service and consideration typically associated with expensive luxury cars. Its stated objective is to be "the friendliest, best-liked car company in America." The manager of two dealerships in Maryland states:

> **We're going to do more than what the customer expects, and in the long run, I think it will enhance our image.**

Saturn's attempt to build an image of a high-quality car built by skilled, caring workers and sold in helpful, nonpressure dealerships, had received two small tests in its first two years. In one, it had to recall and replace 1,836 cars that had received improper coolant. In another, it had to repair 1,480 cars with faulty seat-back recliners. In the second case, the firm made a TV commercial showing a Saturn representative flying to Alaska to fix the car of a resident who had purchased it in the lower 48.

However, in 1993 Saturn began receiving reports of a wire short-circuiting and causing a fire. Thirty-four fires (no injuries) were reported. Saturn faced a dilemma. A recall would involve 350,000 cars and a direct expense of as much as $35 million dollars. Any negative publicity associated with the recall could seriously depress sales. Saturn had yet to break even and General Motors was under serious financial pressure.

Saturn managers decided to deal with the problem in a manner consistent with its company objective described early. It quickly notified all purchasers of the affected cars and asked them to contact their dealers to have the defective wire replaced at no charge. The dealerships extended their operating hours, hired extra personnel, arranged door-to-door pickup and delivery, provided free car washes, and often provided barbecues or other festivities. All the repaired cars had a courtesy card placed inside that said:

> We'd like to thank you for allowing us to make this correction today. We know an event like this will test our relationship, so we want to repeat to you our basic promise—that everyone at Saturn is fully committed to making you as happy a Saturn owner as we can.

According to Steve Shannon, Saturn's director of consumer marketing, the decision to handle the recall in this manner was simple:

> The measure of whether we are a different kind of company is how we handle the bad times as well as the good. We're trying to minimize the inconvenience and show that we stand behind the cars, so that our owners don't lose faith in us or the cars.

How have consumers responded to the recall? Kim Timbers learned of the recall from friends who had heard of it on news reports before she received her letter from Saturn. She took her car to the dealer who served her coffee and doughnuts during the 25-minute repair. Her response:

> I expected this would be my first bad experience with Saturn. But it was so positive, I trust them even more than when I purchased the car.

Discussion Questions

1. Describe the evaluative process and outcome that Ms. Timbers went through.
2. Saturn is attempting to create committed customers. Do you think it is succeeding? Why?
3. Evaluate the manner by which Saturn handled the recall. What options did it have?
4. How will publicity about the recall affect Saturn's image among non-owners?
5. How can Saturn determine if the direct cost of the recall is justified in terms of consumer response?
6. What should Saturn do after the recall is over?

Source: Adapted from R. Serafin, "Saturn Recall a Plus," *Advertising Age*, August 16, 1993, p. 4.

Case 4–7 Supermarket Positioning Strategies

Each chain has to stand for something. No retailer can be all things to all people. If you don't have a clearly defined niche in the marketplace, and you don't generate top-of-mind awareness at least among that segment of the market that wants what you say you stand for, you are lost.

Being known for *something* is extremely important. Whether we call it positioning or whether we call it something else, there is an incredible need for more of it.

Over time, all retailers—in fact, all businesses—move toward the middle, and that's the source of their decline over the long term.

The above quotes reflect the thinking of experts on the supermarket industry. Supermarkets face competition from a myriad of sources today. At one extreme are convenience chains, such as 7-Eleven, and small specialty stores that carry gourmet items, ethnic foods, or health foods, and even neighborhood delis. At the other extreme are price competitors such as warehouse clubs (Price Club, Costco), discounters (Wal-Mart), deep-discount drugstores (Drug Emporium), and specialty chains (Petco).

In response, many supermarkets advertise price reductions *and* provide extensive services and offerings. Many analysts doubt that this approach is likely to succeed in the long run. The cost structure associated with a pleasant shopping environment, wide selection, and extensive services is generally too high to sustain continued deep-discount prices.

Bill Bishop, president of a consulting firm focusing on supermarkets, believes that, with many store locations to choose from and less time to shop, consumers will increasingly select supermarkets on the basis of image rather than location or weekly specials. According to Bishop:

> There's probably a greater opportunity for traditional advertising in the advancement and promotion of stores. Advertising, in the image-building sense, is becoming much more important. Customer service is also enormously powerful at building loyalty and difficult to copy in the short-term.

Discussion Questions

1. Do you agree with the quotes at the beginning of this case? Justify your response.
2. What image dimensions do consumers use to evaluate supermarkets?
3. Develop several possible images a supermarket could strive for.
4. Describe the images of the major supermarkets in your area.
5. Pick a supermarket in your area and describe the optimal image for it. Then describe what it must do to achieve that image. Develop an advertisement to promote the image you are recommending.

Source: Adapted from B. Johnson, ''Supermarkets Take 'Position,' '' *Advertising Age*, May 10, 1993, p. S-1.

Case 4–8 Starbucks Gourmet Coffee

Starbucks was founded in 1971 by three academics. In Berkeley, the three friends met a Dutchman, Alfred Peet, who ran a coffee shop that was the focal point for the emerging food scene in the area. The three academics moved to Seattle and opened a coffee shop in Pike's Market featuring the fresh, high-quality beans used by Peet. They named the shop Starbucks after the coffee-loving first mate in Herman Melville's *Moby Dick*. According to one of the founders,

Coffee Sales in the United States (in billions)

FIGURE A

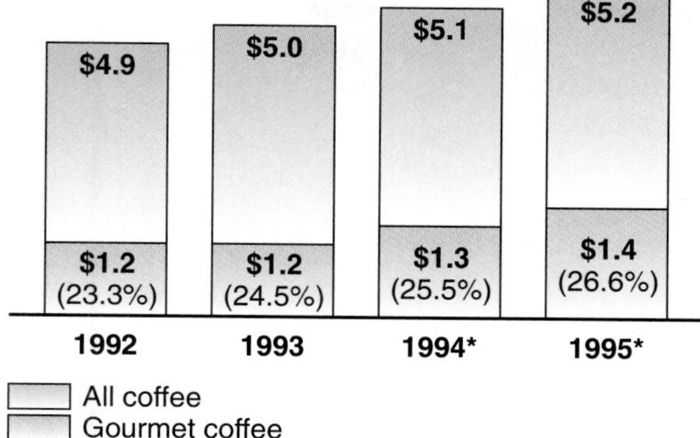

We didn't set out to build a business. We were enthusiastic and energetic, but not very focused.

In 1982, Howard Schultz joined Starbucks as director of marketing and retail sales. In 1983, while visiting in Italy, he was struck by the enormous number of coffee shops where Italians started the day and later gathered to chat. "As soon as I saw it, I knew we should be doing this."

This revelation started the transformation of Starbucks. As Figure A indicates, sales of gourmet coffee in the United States have risen more rapidly than sales of regular coffee, and Starbucks sales have grown even more rapidly.

Schultz bought Starbucks from the three original owners in 1987. The firm lost money for three straight years while Schultz attempted to encourage consumption of darker, richer coffees. With a very limited budget, the firm began with billboards and transit ads with the headline "Familiarity breeds contempt" to encourage consumers to try the new product.

Schultz targeted 35- to 45-year-olds with higher-than-average incomes and educations. Women received slightly more emphasis than men. A manager described the basic strategy thusly: "We were trying to appeal to the top and have the market move to us."

Positive word-of-mouth communications, limited but effective advertising, a decision to provide brewing equipment and beans to restaurants, and consistent product quality led to eventual success in Seattle. Distributing the beans through mail-order with ads in magazines such as the *New Yorker* began to develop national awareness.

Soon Washington state was saturated with Starbucks coffee shops (which sell coffee for on-premise consumption as well as to go, and also the coffee beans). California was targeted next, and outlets were opened in Washington, D.C.; Denver; and Chicago. In 1994, there were 280 Starbucks outlets (1993 sales were $163.5 million). The firm plans to open 260 new stores by 1996. Schultz wants to have 6,000 outlets by the turn of the century.

Starbucks is considering launching a major television campaign but is concerned that its educational message doesn't translate well into a 30-second commercial. Therefore, it is considering an infomercial. Management is also concerned that standard advertising might destroy the unique mystique that surrounds Starbucks coffee.

Starbucks is facing challenges from numerous coffee bars that have appeared everywhere. Many of these are in portable stands and are set up in mall parking lots, gas station driveways, and virtually anywhere there is a high traffic flow. Also, machines now produce higher quality coffee than in the past. Virtually all grocery stores now sell "gourmet" coffee beans, which can be ground in the store or taken home whole.

Discussion Questions

1. What caused the major growth in the sales of gourmet coffee in the United States?
2. What caused Starbucks' success?

3. Should Starbucks conduct a major television advertising campaign? Justify your answer.
4. Should Starbucks prepare and use an infomercial? Justify your answer.
5. Is a goal of 6,000 outlets in the next 5 to 10 years reasonable? What must Starbucks do to accomplish this objective?
6. What types of situational factors could Starbucks use in its marketing strategy?
7. What is the decision process a potential customer would use to decide to purchase (or not purchase) Starbucks coffee? How can Starbucks use this knowledge to develop marketing strategy and tactics?

Source: Adapted from A. Z. Cuneo, ''Starbucks' Word-Of-Mouth Wonder,'' *Advertising Age*, (March 7, 1994), p. 12.

SECTION FIVE

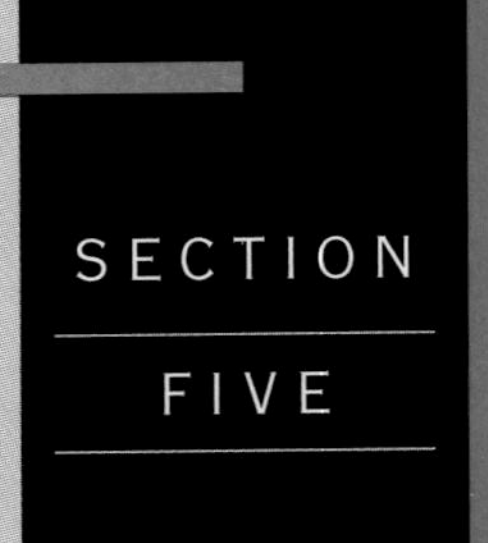

ORGANIZATIONS AS CONSUMERS

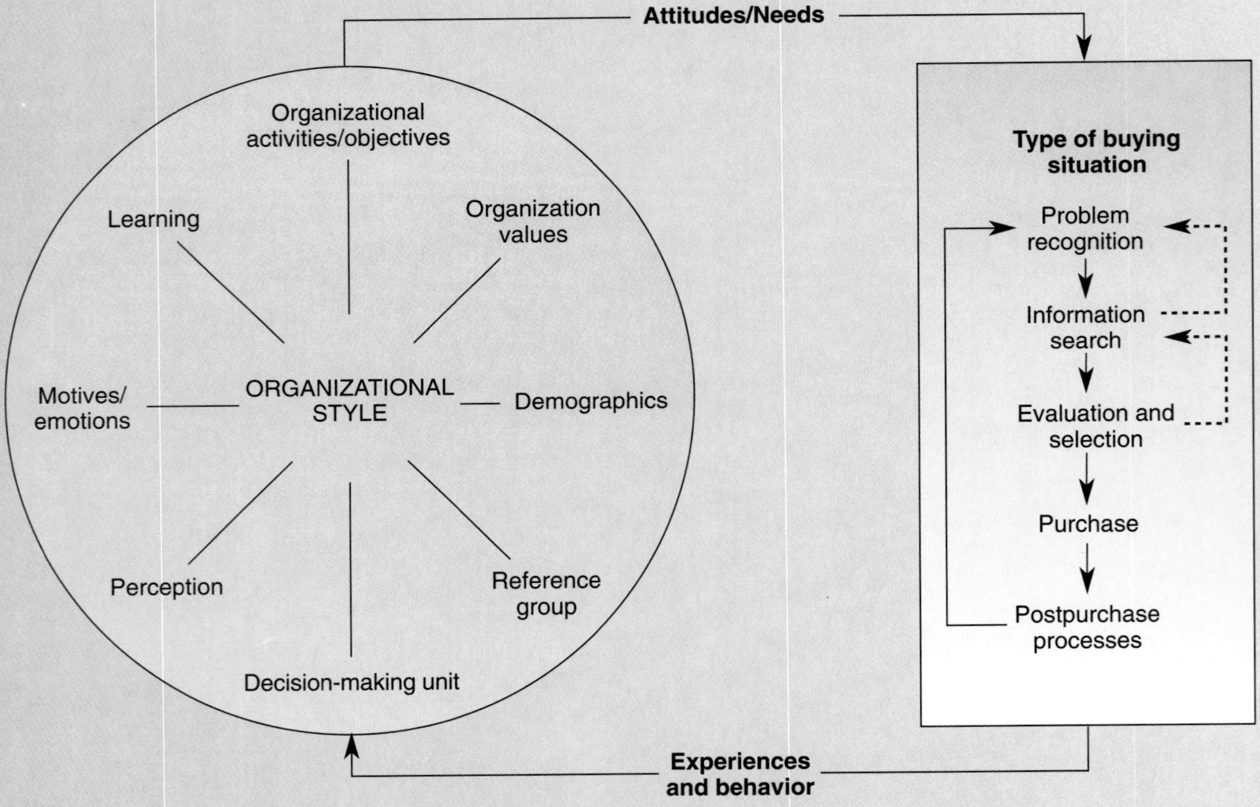

Attitudes/Needs
Organizational activities/objectives
Organization values
Learning
Motives/ emotions
ORGANIZATIONAL STYLE
Demographics
Perception
Reference group
Decision-making unit
Type of buying situation
Problem recognition
Information search
Evaluation and selection
Purchase
Postpurchase processes
Experiences and behavior

The stereotype of organizational buying behavior is one of a cold, efficient, economically rational process. Computers rather than humans could easily, and perhaps preferably, fulfill this function. Fortunately, nothing could be further from the truth. In fact, organizational buying behavior is at least as "human" as individual or household buying behavior.

Organizations pay price premiums for well-known brands and for prestige brands. They avoid risk and fail to properly evaluate products and brands both before and after purchase. Individual members of organizations use the purchasing process as a political arena and attempt to increase their personal, departmental, or functional power through purchasing. Marketing communications are perceived and misperceived by individual organization members. Likewise, organizations and individual members of organizations learn correct and incorrect information about the world in which they operate.

Organizational decisions take place in situations with varying degrees of time pressure, importance, and newness. They typically involve more people and criteria than do individual or household decisions. Thus, the study of organizational buying behavior is a rich and fun-filled activity.

On the facing page, we present our model of consumer buying behavior as modified for organizational buying. This section of the text explains the required modifications.

CHAPTER 20

ORGANIZATIONAL BUYER BEHAVIOR

The selection of an information systems vendor in Fortune 1000 companies is based on a complex process. While the main decision maker is usually the director of information systems, there are numerous other ''influencers,'' notably the chief executive officers and lower-level information systems managers.

Harris is well known in the field of information and telecommunications technology but needed to boost its recognition in the office automation marketplace since its acquisition of Lanier Business Products, Inc.

The strategy, ''Make Another Great Decision,'' involved advertising and unusual and dramatic direct-mail materials (audio- and videotapes) with multiple mailings to different decision makers in each Fortune 1000 company.

The campaign was implemented in four stages:

1. In February, a full-page teaser ad was placed in *The Wall Street Journal* listing the names of 500 firms that would be receiving the Harris mailings. The ad also encouraged other interested firms to request the material via a toll-free phone number.
2. Three packages of materials were mailed to the target companies. Package No. 1 went to corporate CEOs and included a letter from Harris chairman Joseph A. Boyd introducing Concept III, a brochure, and a 3-minute microtape presentation enclosed in a complimentary Harris/Lanier *Portable Caddy* portable dictation machine. MIS directors received a letter, a brochure, a 12-minute videocassette on the Concept III, and a gift flier describing the available incentives. Information systems managers received a letter, a brochure, an 8-minute audiocassette, a gift flier, and a business-reply card for requesting a visit from a Harris rep.
3. A Harris national accounts sales rep followed up with each MIS director a few days later to make appointments for product demonstrations.
4. Incentives, offered to MIS directors and information systems managers who agreed to a demonstration of

Concept III, included Light Tech binoculars or a set of ''The Excellence Challenge'' tapes for the former, and a ''Beep 'n Keep'' key ring or a Braun voice control clock for the latter.[1]

Understanding the needs of organizations, large or small, profit or nonprofit, governmental or commercial, requires many of the same skills and concepts used to understand individual consumer or household needs. While larger and often more complex, organizations—like consumers—develop preferences, attitudes, and behaviors through perceptions, information processing, and experience. Likewise, organizations have an organizational style that creates a relatively stable pattern of organizational behavior.

Like households, organizations make many buying decisions. In some instances these buying decisions are routine replacement decisions for a frequently purchased, commodity-like product or service. At the other end of the continuum, organizations face new, complex purchase decisions that require careful problem definition, extensive information search, a long and often very technical evaluation process, perhaps a negotiated purchase, and a long period of use and postpurchase evaluation. In many instances, each stage of this decision process is very formal, and prescribed guidelines are followed.

Because there are so many similarities between analyzing consumer behavior and analyzing organizational buyer behavior, our basic conceptual model of buyer behavior still holds. Of course, some aspects of the model, such as social status, do not apply, but most

FIGURE 20–1 Overall Model of Organizational Buyer Behavior

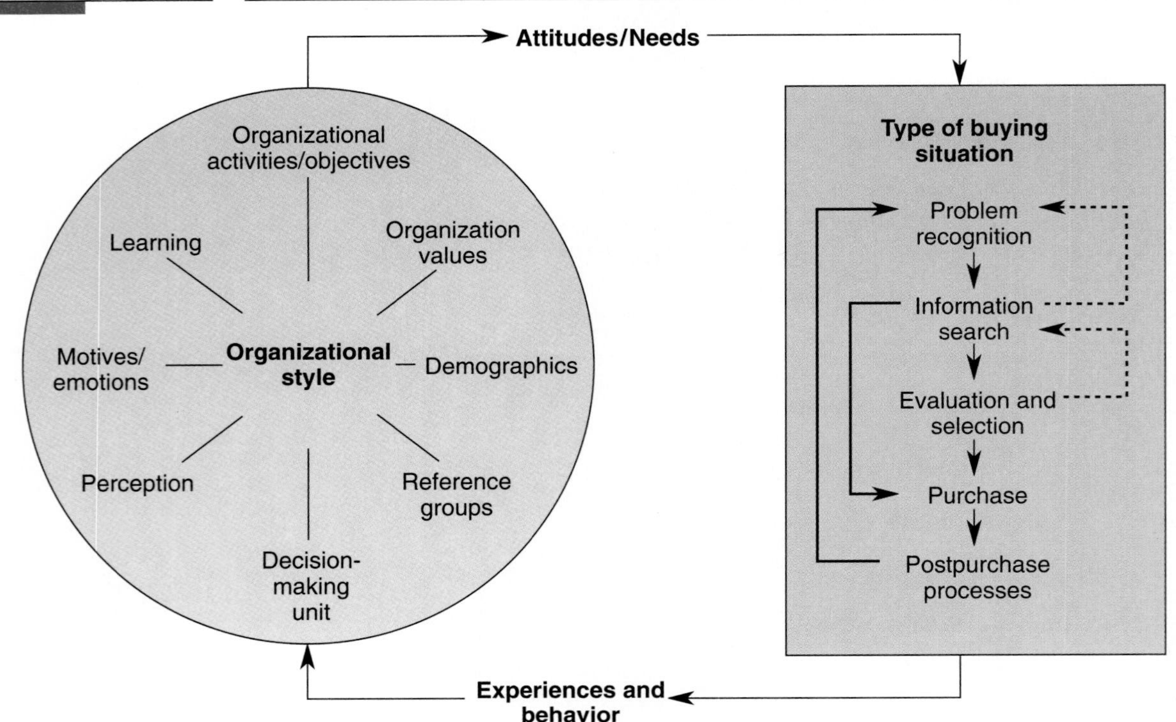

others apply with some modification. The purpose of this chapter is to discuss how this model of consumer behavior should be modified for application to organizational buying behavior, and how the concepts of this model operate when marketing to organizations rather than to individual consumers or households.

OVERALL MODEL OF ORGANIZATIONAL BUYER BEHAVIOR

At the hub of our consumer model of buyer behavior is consumer lifestyle. Organizations also have a style or manner of operating that we characterize as organizational style (see Figure 20–1). Organizational style is much like lifestyle in that organizations vary dramatically in terms of how they make decisions and how they approach problems involving risk, innovation, and change.

Organizational Style

Organizational style reflects and shapes organizational needs and attitudes, which in turn influence how organizations make decisions. For example, the Environmental Protection Agency, the Red Cross, and IBM are three large organizations. Each has a different organizational style with respect to how they gather information, process information, and make decisions. Because they each have different needs, objectives, and styles, they in turn have different experiences and attitudes. These differences influence how each organization solves purchase problems.

Organizations occasionally seek to change their organizational style. Jack Welch, the CEO of the General Electric Company, has sought to make GE more aggressive and entrepreneurial. To accomplish this, he has changed many values and organizational behaviors with respect to taking risk and challenging conventional thinking. It is his hope that this change in organizational style will create a more responsive, faster-growing General Electric Company.

Another example is Apple Computer. Imagine how they have changed from a garage-type operation to a small, innovative company to a worldwide supplier of computers and computer software. At each stage of organizational evolution, the style of the Apple organization changed, as did its needs and attitudes which, in turn, altered how it purchased products and services. Xerox markets to both General Electric and Apple Computer. These are two very different kinds of organizations, and both are undergoing change. As a result, Xerox and others must analyze and understand the buyer behavior of each organization in order to develop marketing strategies that best serve the needs of each organizational customer.

FACTORS INFLUENCING ORGANIZATIONAL STYLE

While we can imagine that the organizational style of the IRS and of IBM would be quite different, we should also recognize that the behavior and style of IBM and DEC, or Honda and Toyota, could also be quite different, even though they compete for many of the same customers. As shown earlier in Figure 20–1, an organization's style is at the hub of our organizational buyer behavior model. The remainder of the chapter is devoted to how various factors help shape organizational style and influence purchase decision making.

Organizational Activities/Objectives

The activities and objectives of organizations influence their style and behavior. For example, the Navy, in procuring an avionics system for a new fighter plane, operates differently than Boeing does in purchasing a very similar system for a commercial aircraft. The Navy is a government organization carrying out a public objective, while Boeing seeks a commercial objective at a profit. The objectives of the two organizations differ, as do their organizational style and buyer behavior.

However, we cannot assume two organizations have the same organizational style just because they share common objectives or activities. Scandinavian Airlines and Singapore Airlines are both government owned and operated, and both are noted internationally for offering the highest-quality service. Few private airlines can match their excellence in service, yet several other government-run airlines are renowned for poor service. Thus, an assumption that government organizations provide less (or more) service is not accurate. The activities an organization engages in and the objectives it pursues are only two of the many influences that shape organizational style and behavior.

Exhibit 20–1 is a matrix that provides examples of the interface between broad organizational types and activities. Organizational types are categorized as commercial, governmental, nonprofit, and cooperative. The general nature of organizational activity is described as routine, complex, or technical. For example, a government organization purchasing highway maintenance services would operate differently from a government organization procuring missiles. Likewise, a cooperative wholesale organization set up as a buying cooperative for several retailers would have a different organizational style from

EXHIBIT 20–1

Organizational Activities Based upon Type of Organization and Nature of Activity

Type of Organization	Nature of Organizational Activity		
	Routine	**Complex**	**Technical**
Commercial	Office management	Human resource management	New product development
Governmental	Highway maintenance	Tax collection	Space exploration
Nonprofit	Fund raising	Increase number of national parks	Organ donor program
Cooperative	Compile industry statistics	Establish industry standards	Applied research

a cooperative research institute set up by firms in the semiconductor industry. And a nonprofit organization involved in organ donations is likely to differ from one organized to gather industry statistics.

Organizational Values

IBM and Apple Computer both manufacture and market computers. However, each organization has a distinct organizational style. IBM is corporate, formal, and takes itself seriously. Apple is less formal, creative, and promotes a more open organizational style. Both are successful, though each has a unique set of values that creates vastly different corporate cultures. Marketing managers must understand these differences in order to best serve the respective organizational needs.[2]

As you examine the eight values listed in Exhibit 20–2, think of how IBM might differ from Apple or how Federal Express might differ from the United States Post Office. Each is a large organization, but each brings to mind a different set of values that underlies its organizational style. To the degree that organizations differ on these values, a firm marketing to them will have to adapt its marketing approach.

The values as presented in Exhibit 20–2 are representative of an innovative organization that seeks change, views problems as opportunities, and rewards individual efforts. It is hard to imagine the U.S. Post Office or many other bureaucratic organizations encouraging such values. On the other hand, these values underlie many high-technology start-up organizations.

Shared Values and Value Conflicts Individuals and organizations both have values. Unfortunately, these value sets are not always consistent. As a result, two different value systems can be operating within an organization. To the degree that these value systems are consistent, decision making and implementation of decisions will move smoothly.[3]

For example, Figure 20–2 lists the personal values for a software engineer in a small hi-tech firm along with the organization's values. The similarity between the individual's values and the organization's values creates a limited degree of shared values. The greater the number of positive linkages between personal and organizational values, the less

EXHIBIT 20–2

Organizational Values that Influence Organizational Style

1. Risk taking is admired and rewarded.
2. Competition is more important than cooperation.
3. Hard work comes first, leisure second.
4. Individual efforts take precedence over collective efforts.
5. Any problem can be solved.
6. Active decision making; passive decision makers will not survive.
7. Change is encouraged and actively sought.
8. Performance is more important than rank or status.

FIGURE 20–2

Personal, Organizational, and Shared Values

Personal Values	Shared Value Linkages	Organizational Values
Individual	⟷	Individualistic
Youth oriented		Mature in orientation
Cooperative		Competitive
Performance driven	⟷	Performance driven
Likes change	⟷	Change is good
Risk taking	⟷	Risk taking is rewarded
Problem solver	⟷	Problem solving is good
Passive decision maker		Active decision making
Nonmaterialistic		Materialistic
Hard worker	⟷	Hard work is rewarded
Security oriented		Profit focused

⟷ Positive linkages (shared values)

conflict and the easier it will be for this individual to make decisions that are consistent with his and the organization's values.

The distinction between individual values/objectives and organizational values/objectives is critical. Marketers must recognize that individuals may make purchasing decisions on behalf of the organization that are based solely on the values/objectives of the organization, solely on the values/objectives of the individual, or on a compromise between the two. Thus, marketers must recognize situations where conflict between individual and organizational values/objectives exists and how it is likely to be resolved. Then they must design products and communications based on this knowledge.[4]

Consider the two ads in Managerial Application 20–1. The ad for the Postal Service focuses on the appropriate level of performance at a very low relative price. This assumes that the objective is profit maximizing (cost control), which is the stated objective of many organizations. The UPS ad recognizes the risk to the *individual* involved in shipping important documents. Thus, it puts primary emphasis on reducing career risk with secondary emphasis on cost savings.

MANAGERIAL APPLICATION

20–1

Ads Appealing to Distinct Values

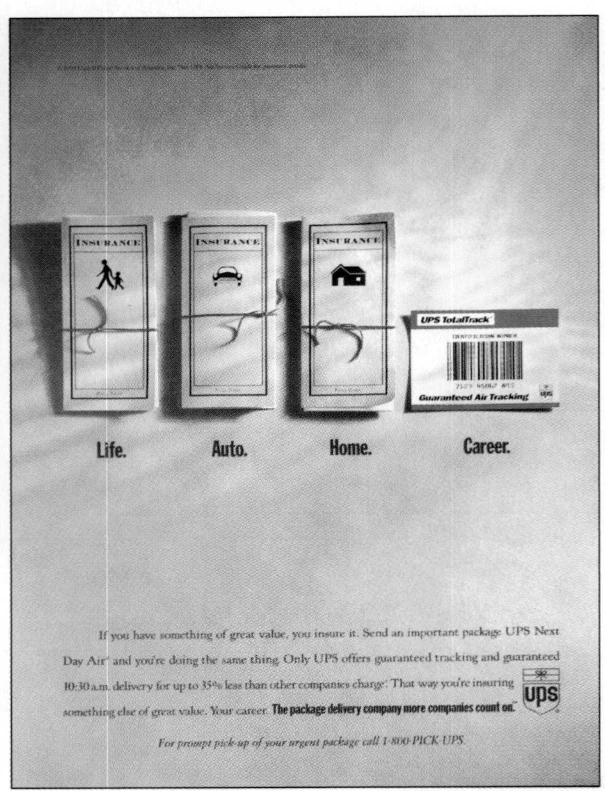

Organizational Demographics

We discussed earlier the important role of consumer demographics in understanding consumer behavior. Organizational demographics are equally important. Organizational demographics involve both organization characteristics—such as size, location, industry category, and type of ownership—and characteristics of the composition of the organization, such as the gender, age, education, and income distribution of employees.[5]

Large organizations are more likely to have a variety of specialists who attend to purchasing, finance, marketing, and general management, while in smaller organizations one or two individuals may have these same responsibilities. Larger organizations are generally more complex, since more individuals participate in managing the organization's operations. This creates a different style of organization and often requires a different marketing approach.

Macrosegmentation Organizations with distinguishing demographics can be grouped into market segments. These segments, based on differences in needs due to organizational demographics, are called **macrosegments.** As we will discuss shortly, this is quite different from microsegmentation of the decision-making unit. Thus, organizational markets can have a two-tiered segmentation scheme referred to as macro- and microsegmentation.[6] In Exhibit 20–3, electricity-producing utilities were first grouped into 12 macrosegments based

Organizational Segmentation Strategy Based on Organizational Demographics

EXHIBIT 20–3

Served Market Several thousand firms that purchase electrical equipment for conversion and regulation of electricity.

Demographics These electric utilities differ on the basis of:

Size: Large, medium, and small.
Location: Four geographical regions.
Organization: Public utilities, rural electric co-ops, investor-owned utilities, and industrial firms.

Customer Needs Based on these organizational demographics, meaningful differences were found for 12 distinct segments on the basis of the following purchase criteria:

1. Price.
2. Quality.
3. Warranty.
4. Availability of spare parts.
5. Reliability.
6. Ease of installation.
7. Maintenance requirements.
8. Energy losses.
9. Appearance of product.

Customer Loyalty Each of the 7,000 potential customers were classified on the basis of customer loyalty as:

Firm loyal: Very loyal and not likely to switch.
Competitive: Preferred vendor, but number two is very close.
Switchable: A competitor is the preferred vendor, but we are a close second.
Competitor loyal: Very loyal to a competitor.

Marketing Strategy

1. For each segment, focus on specific needs important to that segment.
2. Increase customer-need-specific market communications to *each* of the 12 segments.
3. Increase sales coverage to customers classified as "competitive" and "switchable," while decreasing coverage of those classified as "firm loyal" and "competitor loyal."

Results The year the marketing strategy was implemented, total market demand *decreased* by 15 percent. In addition, one of the three sales regions did not implement the strategy. Shown below are the percent changes in sales by sales region and customer loyalty. Which sales region do you think did not participate in the needs-based organizational marketing strategy? You're right!

Customer Loyalty	Sales Region 1	2	3
Loyal	+2%	+3%	+3%
Competitive	+26	+18	−9
Switchable	+16	+8	−18
Competitor-loyal	−4	−3	−4
Total	+18%	+12%	−10%

Source: Adapted from Dennis Gensch, "Targeting the Switchable Industrial Customer," *Marketing Science*, Winter 1984, pp. 41–54.

on size, location, and type of ownership. Differences in customer loyalty, a microsegmentation variable, were used to further segment each of the 12 groups.

Reference Groups

As in consumer behavior, organizational behavior and purchasing decisions are influenced by reference groups. Reference group members may perceive products differently than users do. This, in turn, will influence users' perceptions and decisions.[7]

Perhaps the most powerful type of reference group in industrial markets is that of lead users. **Lead users** are innovative organizations that derive a great deal of their success from leading change. As a result, their adoption of a new product, service, technology, or manufacturing process is watched and often emulated by the majority.[8]

Other reference groups such as trade associations, financial analysts, and dealer organizations also influence an organization's decision to buy or not buy a given product, or to buy or not buy from a given supplier. To manage the influence of reference groups in the hi-tech industry, Regis McKenna developed the concept of the **reference group infrastructure.** The success of a high-technology firm depends on how they influence the reference groups located along the continuum separating the supplier from its consumer market. The more the firm gains positive written and word-of-mouth communication and endorsement throughout this infrastructure, the greater its chances of customers treating it as a preferred source of supply. Figure 20–3 provides two illustrations of this concept.

If we combine the concept of lead users with the reference-group infrastructure as shown in Figure 20–4, we have a more comprehensive picture of organizational reference-group systems. Since the lead users play such a critical role, their adoption of a product, technology, or vendor can influence the overall infrastructure in two powerful ways. First, a lead-user decision to adopt a given supplier's innovative product adds credibility to the product and supplier. This in turn has a strong positive impact on the infrastructure that stands between the firm and its remaining target customers. Second, a lead-user decision to purchase will have a direct impact on firms inclined to follow market trends.

Decision-Making Unit

Because of the nature, size, and consequences of some organizational decisions, decision-making units within organizations can become large and complex. Large, highly structured organizations ordinarily involve more individuals in a purchase decision than do smaller, less formal organizations. Important decisions are likely to draw into the decision process individuals from a wider variety of functional areas and organizational levels than are less-important purchase decisions.[9]

The decision-making unit can be partitioned by area of functional responsibility and type of influence. Functional responsibility can include specific functions such as manufacturing, engineering, transportation, research and development, and purchasing, as well as general management. Each function views the needs of the organization differently and as a result uses different importance weights or evaluative criteria.

In Table 20–1, we see that attribute importance differs sharply between buyers and operations personnel in retail and wholesale firms. Each member of the decision-making unit has somewhat different needs. For a positive purchase decision to result, these needs have to be collectively met in some fashion.

How the final purchase decision is made is in part determined by individual power,[10] expertise,[11] the degree of influence each functional area possesses in this organizational decision, how the organization resolves group decision conflicts,[12] and the nature of the decision.[13]

Reference Group Infrastructure for Personal Computers and Microprocessors

FIGURE 20–3

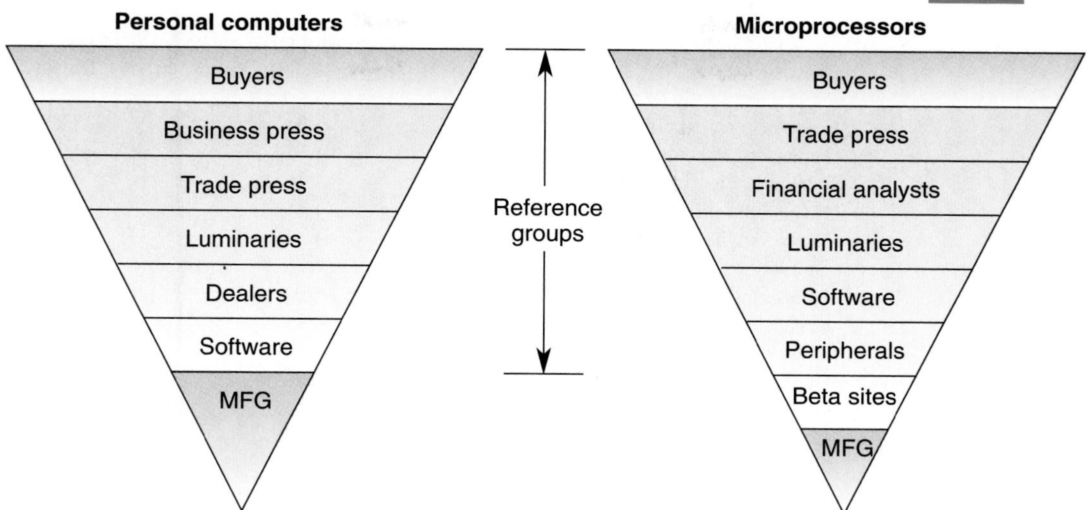

Source: Adapted from Regis McKenna, *The Regis Touch: The New Marketing Strategies for Uncertain Times* (Menlo Park, Calif.: Addison-Wesley, 1985).

Combining Lead-User and Infrastructure Reference Groups

FIGURE 20–4

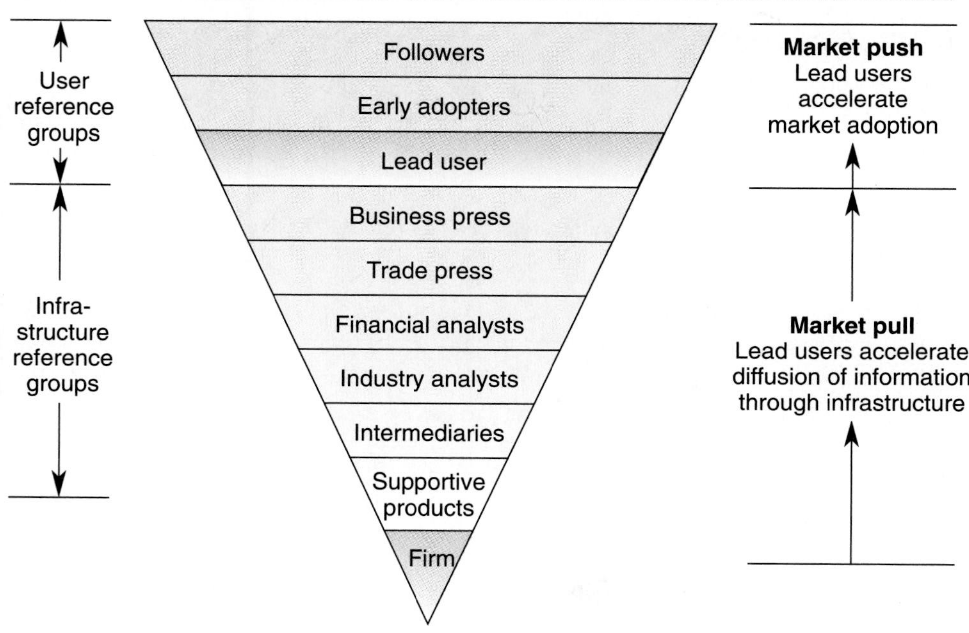

Source: Roger Best and Reinhard Angelhard, ''Strategies for Leveraging a Technology Advantage,'' *Handbook of Business Strategy,* 1988.

TABLE 20–1 Service Attribute Importance for Retail and Wholesale Buyers and Operations Personnel

Attribute*	Buyer Rating	Operations Rating
Ease of placing orders	**4.01**	3.71
Line-item availability	**4.55**	4.31
Packages clearly identified	4.46	**4.82**
Meets appointments	4.46	**4.73**
Delivers when requested	**4.87**	4.70
Delivered sorted and segregated	4.36	**4.75**
Palletizing/unitizing capability	3.72	**4.37**
Master carton packaging quality	3.81	**4.48**
Shelf unit packaging quality	3.97	**4.29**
Complete/accurate documentation	4.54	**4.81**
Well-documented deal/style codes	4.36	**4.60**
Length of order cycle	**4.14**	3.61
Consistency of order cycle	**4.38**	3.88

*All are significantly different at the .05 level

Adapted from M. B. Cooper, C. Droge, and P. J. Daugherty, "How Buyers and Operations Personnel Evaluate Service," *Industrial Marketing Management,* no. 20 (1991), p. 83.

TABLE 20–2 Management Involvement and Decision Importance

Amount of Purchase Decision	CEO	Div. Pres.	General Mgr.	Dir. Mfg.	Plant Mgr.	MIS Mgr.	Dept. Mgr.	Shift Mgr.
	Management Involvement in 47 Purchase Decisions							
$1–$5K	0%	14%	100%	100%	100%	100%	86%	43%
$5K–$10K	7	36	100	100	100	100	86	36
Over $10K	33	58	100	100	100	100	83	17
	Number of Communications in 47 Purchase Decisions							
$1–$5K	0	3	28	40	54	70	36	14
$5–$10K	1	6	24	32	47	54	32	9
Over $10K	6	17	37	43	83	110	86	3
Total (835)	7	26	89	115	184	234	154	26

Source: M. C. LaForge and L. Stone, "An Analysis of the Industrial Buying Process by Means of Buying Center Communications," *The Journal of Business and Industrial Marketing,* Winter/Spring, 1989, pp. 31–32.

Members of the decision-making unit play various roles, such as information gatherer, key influencer, decision maker, purchaser, and/or user.[14] A plant manager could play all five roles, while corporate engineers may simply be sources of information. The role a function plays in an organizational decision varies by type of decision and organizational style. Table 20–2 illustrates how management involvement in decision making in a textile firm varied as a function of the dollar amount of the decision.

Microsegmentation Macrosegmentation allows a marketer to group customers with like needs and organizational demographics into market segments. **Microsegmentation** is the grouping of organizational customers on the basis of similar decision-making units or styles. Customer organizations that are heavily dominated by technical people might be segmented from those dominated by purchasing agents and finance managers. Recognizing these key differences in the structure of a decision-making unit allows the firm to customize its strategies.

Decision-making units and microsegmentation strategies based on differences in their structure are likely to vary over the product life cycle. Consider the changes in the decision-making unit that took place in the purchase of microprocessors by an original equipment manufacturer over the stages of the microprocessor's product life cycle. Early stages in the life of a new product presented a judgmental new task decision, and the size and structure of the decision-making unit (DMU) resulted in a complex decision process. As the product grew in its utilization, a simple modified rebuy decision evolved, as did a change in the functional structure of the decision-making unit. Finally, as the microprocessor moved into a mature stage, it became a routine low-priority decision involving primarily the purchasing function. These changes are illustrated below:

Stage of Product Life Cycle	Type of Purchase Situation	Size of DMU	Key Functions Influencing the Purchase Decision
Introduction	Judgmental new task	Large	Engineering and R&D
Growth	Simple modified rebuy	Medium	Production and top management
Maturity	Routine low priority	Small	Purchasing

Perception

To build a position with organizational customers, a firm must go through the same sequential stages of exposure, attention, and interpretation as required with consumers. A customer develops certain images of seller organizations from their products, people, and organizational activities. Like people, organizations have memories and base their decisions on images or memories they have developed. Once an image is formed by an organization, it is very difficult to change. Therefore, it is important for an organization to develop a sound communications strategy to build and reinforce a desired image or brand position.

Business-to-business advertising is one way to communicate information and imagery to buyers. Because electronic media such as television and radio are less effective in reaching organizational customers, print ads, direct mail, and personal presentations are common.

Compared to consumer advertising, organizational advertising is generally longer and more detailed. Longer advertising copy is more effective than shorter copy in business-to-business communications. Ads with fewer than 150 words are less likely to stimulate ad readership than ads with longer copy. However, this relationship is not linear, as ads with very long ad copy (greater than 200 words) are also less effective in stimulating ad readership. Thus, ad copy between 150 and 200 words seems to be most effective in stimulating readership.[15]

Managerial Application 20–2 contains two ads targeted at industrial buyers. Both ads have extensive copy. However, both also use color and other attention-attracting devices as described in Chapter 9.

Ad size and repetition have a positive effect on awareness and action. As shown in Figure 20–5, a 20 percent gain in awareness is achieved when two or more ads are placed in the same issue of a specialized business magazine. The size of the advertisement also affects action in the form of inquiries generated by the advertisement. Based on a study

MANAGERIAL APPLICATION

20–2

Ads Aimed at Organizational Buyers

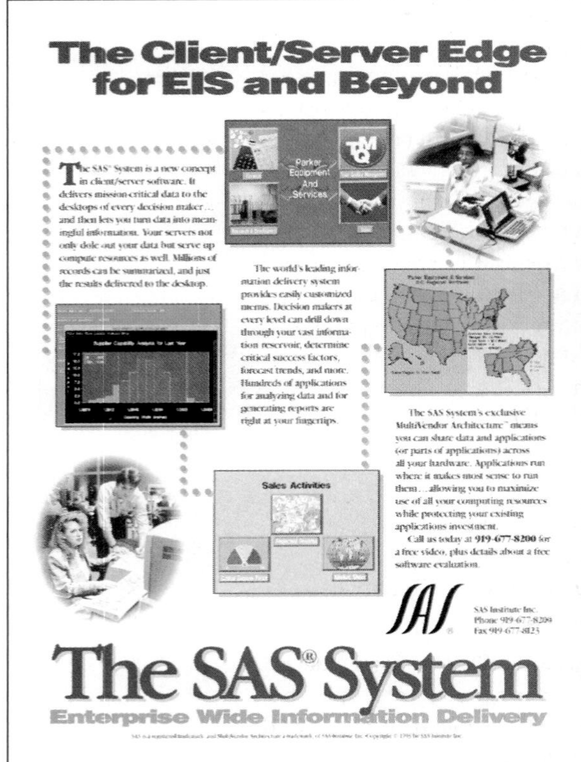

FIGURE 20–5 Impact of Ad Repetition and Ad Size

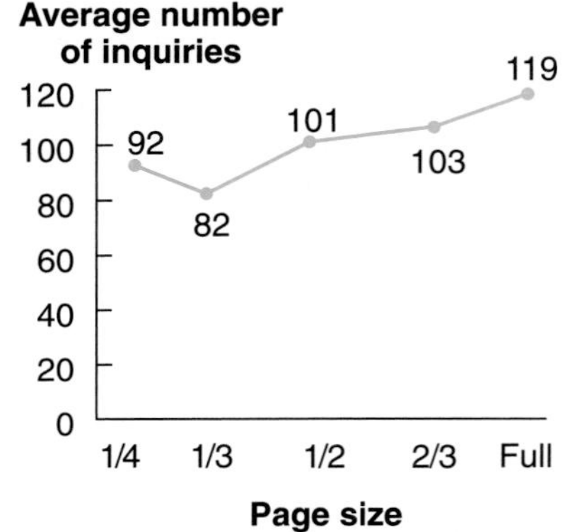

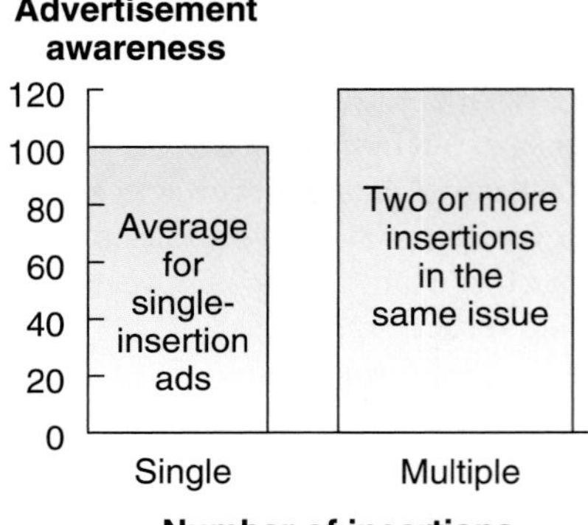

Source: Cahners Advertising Research Report, nos. 250.1 and 120.3.

of 500,000 inquiries to ads run in *Plastic World, Electronics Design News,* and *Design News,* one can see in Figure 20–5 that the average number of inquiries increased with ad size.

The potential power of industrial advertising can be seen in its impact on a safety product sold to industrial organizations. A precampaign period was used to determine base sales without trade advertising. The first-year sales increased almost fourfold with advertising in one trade publication using an eight-page advertising schedule: six black-and-white ads and two color ads. When three color spreads were added to the schedule, sales continued to climb. When ad frequency was again increased, this time to 6 black-and-white single-page ads and 11 color spreads, product sales rose to 6.7 times precampaign sales.[16]

Motives and Emotions

Organizational decisions tend to be less emotional than many consumer purchase decisions. However, because humans with psychological needs and emotions influence these decisions, this aspect of marketing to an organizational customer cannot be overlooked or underestimated. Most organizations have as an objective to either improve their performance or lower their cost as a result of the purchases they make. Recognizing these fundamental organizational motives, Ball Corporation's Container Group utilizes the following sales strategy:

> In the glass container business it costs more to make a tall, slender jar than one that is short and squat. If an account is using a tall jar, the salesperson points out the economies in changing to a squat jar. If a prospective customer already has a shorter jar, the salesperson promotes the addition of a taller, more slender jar to appeal to today's weight-conscious consumer.

However, the Ball Corporation sales strategy doesn't stop there. Developing a rational organizational benefit is the first step; the second is appealing to the emotions of individuals making the decision. With careful study of the personal motives, psychological needs, and emotions of decision makers and influencers, Ball Corporation gears its presentations to ''excite'' its buyers to take action in ways not possible with normal means of communication. Clifton Reichard, vice president of sales of Ball Corporation's Glass Container Group, points out:

> Businesspeople are human and social as well as interested in economics and investments, and salespeople need to appeal to both sides. Purchasers may claim to be motivated by intellect alone, but the professional salesperson knows they run on both reason and emotion.[17]

Quite often there is considerable personal or career risk in organizational purchase decisions. The risk of making a bad purchase decision can elicit feelings of self-doubt or psychological discomfort. These are personal emotions that will influence a new-task purchase decision. Federal Express appeals to risk avoidance with ads that ask, in essence:

> How do you explain to your boss that the important papers didn't arrive but you saved the company $5 by using a less expensive overnight mail service?

LEARNING

Like individuals, organizations learn through their experiences and perceptions.[18] Positive experiences with vendors are rewarding and tend to be repeated. Purchasing processes and procedures that prove effective tend to be institutionalized in rules and policies. Likewise,

EXHIBIT 20–4 Organizational Purchase Situations and Buying Responses

Variables	1 Casual	2 Routine Low Priority	3 Simple Modified Rebuy	4 Judgmental New Task	5 Complex Modified Rebuy	6 Strategic New Task
Situational Characteristics						
Purchase importance	Of minor importance	Somewhat important	Quite important	Quite important	Quite important	Extremely important
Task uncertainty	Little uncertainty	Moderately uncertain	Little uncertainty	Great amount of uncertainty	Little uncertainty	Moderately uncertain
Extensiveness of choice set	Much choice	Much choice	Narrow set of choices	Narrow set of choices	Much choice	Narrow set of choices
Buyer power	Little or no power	Moderate power	Moderate power	Moderate power	Strong power position	Strong power position
Buying Activities						
Search for information	No search made	Little effort at searching	Moderate amount of search	Moderate amount of search	High level of search	High level of search
Use of analysis techniques	No analysis performed	Moderate level of analysis	Moderate level of analysis	Moderate level of analysis	Great deal of analysis	Great deal of analysis
Proactive focus	No attention to proactive issues	Superficial consideration of proactive focus	High level of proactive focus	Moderate proactive focus	High level of proactive focus	Proactive issues dominate purchase
Procedural control	Simply transmit the order	Follow standard procedures	Follow standard procedures	Little reliance on established procedures	Follow standard procedures	Little reliance on established procedures

Source: M. D. Bunn, "Taxonomy of Buying Decision Approaches," *Journal of Marketing,* January 1993, p. 47.

negative experiences with vendors produce learning and avoidance behavior, and purchasing procedures that don't work are generally discarded.

Direct experience is not necessary for organizational learning to occur. Organizations learn through the cognitive information processing of their members. The same general principles described in Chapter 10 for individual learning operate in an industrial setting.

PURCHASE SITUATION

While the style of each organization may differ in unique ways, the buying process is also influenced by the complexity and difficulty of the decision task. Less complex, low-risk, routine decisions are generally made by an individual or a small group without extensive effort. At the other extreme are organizational decisions that are complex and have major organizational implications. A continuum of purchase situations lies between these two extremes. A useful categorization of organizational purchase situations is: casual, routine low priority, simple modified rebuy, judgmental new task, complex modified rebuy, and strategic new task.[19] These six purchase situations are profiled in Exhibit 20–4 and described in the following paragraphs.

Casual Purchase This situation occurs when the purchase is of minor importance, there is little uncertainty surrounding the purchase, there are multiple vendors, and the buyer has limited purchasing power. The typical purchase response involves no effort to search for information, no analysis is performed, no consideration is given to proactive issues (strategic and long-term considerations), and substantial procedure control is exercised.

Routine Low-Priority Purchase This process tends to occur for repetitive purchases that are somewhat important, with a moderate level of uncertainty, a substantial number of choices available, and a moderate amount of buyer power. It involves limited search effort, a moderate amount of analysis, superficial consideration of proactive issues, and standard rules and procedures.

Simple Modified Rebuy This strategy is used when the purchase is quite important to the firm, there is little uncertainty, a narrow set of choices, and moderate buyer power. It requires a moderate amount of search and analysis, a high level of proactive focus, and a tendency to follow standard procedures.

Judgmental New Task This approach tends to occur when the buying decision is quite important, there is substantial uncertainty, a narrow set of choices, and the firm has moderate buyer power. The firm engages in moderate search, analysis, and proactive focusing but with little reliance on established procedures (since there is no precedent to follow, the firm must ''decide as it goes'').

Complex Modified Rebuy This process is used when the decision is quite important, with little uncertainty, many choices, and strong buyer power. It is characterized by extensive search, sophisticated analysis, a strong proactive focus, and adherence to established procedures.

Strategic New Task This task occurs when the decision is extremely important to the firm, there is a moderate level of uncertainty, a narrow set of choices, and the firm has strong buyer power. It involves a high level of search, extensive analysis, an intense focus on proactive issues, but little reliance on established procedures.

Clearly, the marketing strategy and tactics for one particular type of purchase situation would be inappropriate for others. Thus, marketers must understand the purchase task confronting their organizational consumers and develop appropriate marketing strategies.

ORGANIZATIONAL DECISION PROCESS

Because organizational decisions typically involve more individuals in more complex decision tasks than do individual or household decisions, marketing efforts to affect this process are much more complex.[20] Shown in Exhibit 20–5 are stages in the decision process and sources of influence at each stage in a large insurance company's decision to add microcomputers to its office management function. At each stage, sources of influence both within and outside the decision-making unit were important. Altogether, there were 12 separate sources of influence, each with different levels of influence and affecting different stages of the purchase decision process.

To have a chance to win this large office systems microcomputer contract, a selling firm must provide relevant information to each source of influence. This is not a simple task, given that each source of influence has different motives and different criteria for evaluating alternative products, as well as different media habits. To the degree a

EXHIBIT 20–5 Decision Process in Purchasing Microcomputers for a Large Insurance Company

Stages of the Purchase Decision Process	Key Influences Within Decision-Making Unit	Influences Outside the Decision-Making Unit
Problem recognition	Office manager Sales manager	Field sales agents Administrative clerks Accounting manager Microcomputer sales representative
Information search	Data processing manager Office manager Purchasing manager	Operations personnel Microcomputer sales representative Other corporate users Office systems consultant
Alternative evaluation	General management Data processing manager Office manager Sales manager Purchasing manager	Office systems consultant Microcomputer sales representative
Purchase decision	General management Office manager Purchasing manager	
Product usage	Office manager Sales manager	Field sales agents Administrative clerks Accounting personnel Microcomputer sales representative
Evaluation	Office manager Sales manager General management	Field sales agents Administrative clerks Accounting personnel

microcomputer company satisfies the information needs of each, it will improve its chances of winning this large contract.

Problem Recognition

In Exhibit 20–5, the sales manager and office manager were the first key influencers within the decision-making unit to recognize the need to add microcomputers to their organization. Recognition of this problem, however, could have come about in several ways. In this instance, a continuing problem between field sales agents and internal administrative

Group Involvement in the Decision Process in Hi-Tech Organizations

TABLE 20–3

Stages of Decision Process	Percent Involved in Each Stage of Decision Process					
	Board of Directors	Top Management	Head of Department	Lab Technician or Operator	Purchasing Manager or Buyer	Finance Manager Accountant
Recognizing the need to purchase	7%	26%	70%	30%	0%	3%
Determining product specifications	0	33	74	33	3	0
Deciding which suppliers to consider	3	33	56	14	19	0
Obtaining quotations and proposals	0	26	52	19	14	3
Evaluating quotations and proposals	7	63	63	3	11	7
Final product or supplier selection	21	48	48	7	11	0

Source: R. Abratt, ''Industrial Buying in Hi-Tech Markets,'' *Industrial Marketing Management* 15 (1986), p. 295.

clerks led the office manager and sales manager to recognize the problem. Aiding their recognition of the problem were accounting personnel and microcomputer sales representatives who called on the office manager. The combination of these sources of influence eventually led to an increased level of importance and the subsequent stage of information search.

Table 20–3 demonstrates that in hi-tech markets, the head of a department is most likely to recognize a problem or need to purchase. Perhaps more important is that purchasing managers are not a source of problem recognition. This points out the danger of salespeople only calling on purchasing people. As shown in Table 20–3, problem recognition and determining specifications often occur without much involvement of purchasing personnel.

A business marketing to another business has to understand how their products or services will impact the client's cost of operations and performance. While the client's business is always seeking ways to economically improve its operations, it may not recognize problems that prevent them from improving. Thus, the task of the selling organization is to understand the needs of the client organization so that they can point out problems and solutions that the client organization has not yet recognized.

For example, a computer manufacturer pointed out to a large bank that their entire statewide banking system could be shut down if a fire or other disaster occurred in a given building. The bank literally could not function if the information were lost. This unrecognized problem led the bank to purchase a backup system and locate it in a building in another part of the state. While the need had gone unnoticed for years without loss to the

TABLE 20–4 Marketing Communications for Different Classes of Industrial Products

Type of Marketing Communication	Type of Industrial Product: Major Capital	Minor Capital	Component Parts	Raw Materials	Industrial Supplies
Trade advertising	9.7%	9.3%	6.4%	8.3%	10.1%
Technical literature	19.7	21.2	15.3	22.5	19.1
Direct mail	5.2	5.9	3.7	2.6	6.3
Sales promotions	5.4	7.6	11.8	8.3	11.6
Trade shows	12.5	7.8	6.2	4.8	4.4
Salespeople	47.5	48.4	56.6	53.2	48.5

Source: D. W. Jackson, J. E. Keith, and R. K. Burdick, "The Relative Importance of Various Promotional Elements in Different Industrial Purchase Situations," *Journal of Advertising,* 16 (1987), p. 30.

bank, shortly after the back-up system was installed, six floors of the bank building caught fire and destroyed the original system. The next day, the bank operated as normal from its remote backup building.

Information Search

Information search can be both formal and informal.[21] Site visits to evaluate a potential vendor, laboratory tests of a new product or prototype, and investigation of possible product specifications are part of formal information search. Informal information search can occur during discussions with sales representatives, while attending trade shows, or reading industry-specific journals.

Table 20–4 summarizes the information sources used by purchasing agents across a variety of purchase situations. In all cases, the input provided by salespeople had the largest impact. However, the role of other types of information varied by type of purchase.

Evaluation and Selection

The evaluation of possible vendors and selection of a given vendor often follows a **two-stage decision process.**[22] The first stage is making the buyer's approved vendor list. A conjunctive decision process is very common. In this manner, the organization can screen out potential vendors that do not meet all their minimum criteria. In a government missile purchase, 41 potential manufacturers of a given missile electronics system were first identified. After site visits to inspect manufacturing capability, and resources, this list of 41 was pared down to 11. The remaining 11 all met the government's minimum criteria, and from this group the government would eventually contract with two.

A second stage of organizational decision making could involve other decision rules such as disjunctive, lexicographic, compensatory, or elimination-by-aspects. For the government purchase discussed above, a lexicographic decision process was next used with the most important criterion being price. Using this decision rule, two vendors were selected.

The process of evaluation and selection is further complicated by the fact that different members of the decision-making unit have differing evaluative criteria. In Table 20–5 we see that purchasing's set of performance criteria differs from that of general management or engineering. In addition, each of these members of the decision-making unit has a

Evaluative Criteria and Organizational Role

TABLE 20-5

Evaluative Criteria Used in Purchase Decisions	Functional Role in Organization			
	Purchasing	Management	Engineering	Operations
Vendor offers broad line	X	X		
Many product options available	X	X		
Ease of maintenance of equipment			X	X
Competence of service technician		X	X	X
Overall quality of service		X	X	
Product warranty	X	X	X	X
Delivery (lead time)				X
Time needed to install equipment	X			X
Construction costs	X		X	X
Vendor has the lowest price	X	X	X	
Financial stability of vendor	X		X	X
Vendor willing to negotiate price	X			
Vendor reputation for quality	X	X	X	
Salesperson competence		X	X	X
Compatibility with equipment	X	X		
Available computer interface	X			

Source: Adapted from D. H. McQuiston and R. G. Walters, ''The Evaluative Criteria of Industrial Buyers: Implications for Sales Training,'' *The Journal of Business and Industrial Marketing,* Summer/Fall 1989, p. 74.

different preference for information and, therefore, salesperson competencies. For example, purchasing is more concerned with pricing policies, terms and conditions, and order status; engineers are more concerned with product knowledge, product operations, and applications knowledge.

Purchase and Decision Implementation

Once the decision to buy from a particular organization has been made, the method of purchase must be determined. From the seller's point of view this means how and when they will get paid. In many government purchases, payment is not made until delivery. Other government purchase agreements could involve progress payments. When a firm is working on the construction of a military aircraft that will take several years, the method of payment is critical. Many businesses offer a price discount for payment within 10 days. Others may extend credit and encourage extended payment over time.

On an international basis, purchase implementation and method of payment are even more critical. One electronics firm with limited experience in international business found it very easy to sell its electronic system in Nigeria. However, they couldn't get paid. They later found out that this is very normal and one needs to use letters of credit to get paid with any degree of certainty. Some countries prohibit the removal of capital from their country without an offsetting purchase. This led Caterpillar Tractor Company to sell earth-moving equipment in South America in exchange for raw materials, such as copper, which they could sell or use in their manufacturing operations. Another company signed a long-term contract at a very low price when the exchange rate favored the seller. This ensured the seller a good price when the exchange rate fluctuated, and provided the buyer a lower-than-average price.

TABLE 20–6 Customer and Management Perceptions of the Importance of After-Sale Services

After-Sales Service Item	Importance of Service Item			Ratings of Service		
	Customers	Managers	Gap	Customers	Managers	Gap
Attitude and behavior of technician	11.5	8.4	3.1	7.04	7.56	−.52
Availability of technical service staff	16.1	12.9	3.2	7.64	8.12	−.48
Repair time when service needed	15.4	17.4	−2.0	6.36	7.71	−1.35
Dispatch of breakdown call	15.5	9.8	5.7	6.92	7.57	−.65
Availability of spare parts during call	10.0	10.1	−.1	7.16	7.49	−.33
Service contract options	5.2	6.8	−1.6	6.88	7.48	−.60
Price-performance ratio for services rendered	8.1	14.5	−6.4	6.12	7.30	−1.18
Response time when service needed	18.2	20.1	−1.9	5.92	7.09	−1.17

Source: H. Kasper and J. Lemmink, ''After-Sales Service Quality: Views between Industrial Customers and Service Managers'' *Industrial Marketing Management,* 18 (1989), p. 203.

Terms and conditions—payments, warranties, delivery dates, and so forth—are both complex and critical in business-to-business markets. One U.S. manufacturer of steam turbines lost a large order to a foreign manufacturer because their warranty was written too much to the advantage of the seller.

Usage and Postpurchase Evaluation

After-purchase evaluation of products is typically more formal for organizational purchases than are household evaluations of purchases. In mining applications, for example, a product's life is broken down into different components such that total life-cycle cost can be assessed. Many mines will operate different brands of equipment side-by-side to determine the life-cycle costs of each before repurchasing one in larger quantities.

A major component of postpurchase evaluation is the service the seller provides after the sale. Table 20–6 indicates the importance that one group of customers and managers assigned to different aspects of after-sales service. Notice that the managers did not have a very good understanding of what was important to their customers. The table indicates that they also viewed their service performance more favorably than their customers did. Clearly, this firm is unlikely to produce satisfied customers.

SUMMARY

Like households, organizations make many buying decisions. In some instances these buying decisions are routine replacement decisions and at other times new, complex purchase decisions. Six purchase situations are common to organizational buying: casual, routine low priority, simple modified rebuy, judgmental new task, complex modified rebuy, and strategic new task. Each of these purchase situations will elicit different organizational behaviors, since the decision-making unit increases in size and complexity as the importance of the purchase decision increases.

Organizations have a style or manner of operating that we characterize as *organizational style.* The type of organization (commercial, governmental, nonprofit, or cooperative) and the nature of their activity (routine, complex, or technical) helps shape an organization's style.

Organizations hold *values* that influence the organization's style. These values are also held in varying degrees by individuals in the organization. When there is a high degree of shared values between the individuals and the organization, decision making occurs smoothly. *Demorgraphics* also influence organizational style. Differences in location, industry, type of ownership, and composition of workforce each play a role in determining how an organization approaches purchase decisions. The process of grouping buyer organizations into market segments on the basis of similar needs and demographics is called *macrosegmentation.*

Reference groups play a key role in business-to-business markets. *Reference-group infrastructures* exist in most organizational markets. These reference groups often include third-party suppliers, distributors, industry experts, trade publications, financial analysts, and key customers. *Lead users* have been shown to be a key reference group that influences both the reference group infrastructure and other potential users.

Organizations also develop images, have motives, and learn. Seller organizations can affect how they are perceived through a variety of communication alternatives. Print advertising, direct mail, and sales calls are the most common. Whereas organizations have ''rational'' motives, their decisions are influenced and made by people with emotions. A seller organization has to understand and satisfy both to be successful. Organizations learn through their experiences and information-processing activities.

The organizational decision process involves problem recognition, information search, evaluation and selection, purchase implementation, and postpurchase evaluation. Seller organizations can help buyer organizations discover unrecognized problems and aid them in their information search. Quite often, a seller organization can influence the information search such that they establish the choice criteria to be used in evaluation and selection. A conjunctive process is typical in establishing an evoked set, and other decision rules are used for selecting a specific vendor.

Purchase implementation is more complex and the terms and conditions more important than in household decisions. How payment is made is of major importance. Finally, use and postpurchase evaluation are often quite formal. Many organizations will conduct detailed in-use tests to determine the life-cycle costs of competing products or spend considerable time evaluating a new product before placing large orders. Satisfaction is dependent on a variety of criteria and on the opinions of many different people. To achieve customer satisfaction, each of these individuals has to be satisfied with the criteria important to him or her.

REVIEW QUESTIONS

1. How can an organization have a *style*? What factors contribute to different organizational styles?
2. How would different organizational activities and objectives affect organizational style?
3. What are *organizational values*? How do they differ from *personal values*?
4. What is meant by *shared values*?
5. What are *organization demographics*, and how do they influence organizational style?
6. Define *macrosegmentation*, and describe the variables used to create a macrosegmentation of an organizational market.
7. Define *microsegmentation*, and describe the variables used to create microsegments.
8. What types of *reference groups* exist in organizational markets?
9. What are *lead users*, and how do they influence word-of-mouth communication and the sales of a new product?
10. What is a *decision-making unit*? How does it vary by purchase situation?
11. How are purchase decisions made when there is disagreement within the DMU?
12. How can a seller organization influence *perceptions* of a buyer organization?

13. What are *organizational motives*, and how do personal motives interact with organizational motives in an organizational buying decision?
14. How do organizations learn?
15. How can a seller organization influence problem recognition?
16. What are the best means of influencing an organization's information search? How does each influence awareness/interest and evaluation/selection?
17. What is a *two-stage decision process*?
18. Why can purchase implementation be a critical part of the organizational decision process?
19. How do usage and postpurchase evaluation differ between households and organizations?
20. What are the six purchase situations commonly encountered by organizations? How do organizations typically respond to each situation?

DISCUSSION QUESTIONS

21. Describe three organizations with distinctly different organizational styles. Explain why they have different organizational styles and the factors that have helped shape the style of each.
22. Describe how Federal Express might vary in its organizational style from _______. Justify your response.
    a. U.S. Postal Service.
    b. UPS.
    c. Airborne Express.
23. Discuss how _______ differs from _______ in terms of organizational activities and objectives. Discuss how these differences influence organizational styles.
    a. Your University, a regional retail chain.
    b. The Navy, General Motors.
    c. Nike, DuPont.
    d. Toyota, Ford.
24. How could an organization's values interact with an individual's values such that a purchase decision would be biased by the individual's personal values?
25. Discuss how the organizational demographics of _______ might differ from _______. How do these demographic distinctions influence organizational style and buyer behavior?
    a. Apple Computer, Air Force.
    b. IBM, the United Way.
    c. Coca-Cola, the FBI.
26. Discuss how IBM might use a macrosegmentation strategy to sell microcomputers to businesses.
27. Discuss how IBM might use a microsegmentation strategy to sell microcomputers to businesses.
28. Discuss how a small hi-tech firm could influence the reference group infrastructure and the lead users to accelerate adoption of its products in the market.
29. Discuss the marketing implications of the decision-making structure shown in Exhibit 20–5. Then, using the information shown in Exhibit 20–5, discuss how you would develop your marketing strategy for this purchase situation.
30. "Industrial purchases, unlike consumer purchases, do not have an emotional component." Comment.
31. Describe a situation in which both organizational motives and personal emotions could play a role in the outcome of a purchase decision. What marketing efforts are needed to satisfy both types of needs?
32. Will your personal values influence the type of organization you will work for? In what ways?
33. Review Exhibit 20–3. For what other industries would this be a sound approach?
34. For *each* of the six purchase situations described in the chapter, describe a typical purchase for _______:
    a. A large manufacturer.
    b. A large law firm.
    c. The IRS.
    d. Your University.
    e. A small retailer.
35. What are the marketing strategy implications of Table 20–1?
36. What are the marketing strategy implications of Table 20–3?
37. What are the marketing strategy implications of Table 20–4?
38. What are the marketing strategy implications of Table 20–6?

APPLICATION EXERCISES

39. Interview an appropriate person at a large and at a small organization and ask each to identify purchase situations that could be described as casual, routine low priority, simple modified rebuy, judgmental new task, complex modified rebuy, and strategic new task. For each organization and purchase situation determine the following:
    a. Size and functional representation of the decision-making unit.
    b. The number of choice criteria considered.
    c. Length of the decision process.
    d. Number of vendors or suppliers considered.
40. For a given industrial organization arrange to review the trade publications they subscribe to. Identify three industrial ads in these publications which vary in copy length, one very short (under 100 words), one with approximately 150 words, and one very long (over 250 words). Arrange to have these ads read by three or four people in the organization. Have each reader rank the ads in terms of preference (independent of product or manufacturer preference). Then ask each to describe what they like or dislike about each ad. Discern the role that copy length played in their evaluation.
41. Interview a representative from a commercial, governmental, nonprofit, and cooperative organization. For each determine their organizational demographics, activities, and objectives. Then relate these differences to differences in their organizational styles.
42. For a given organization, identify reference groups that influence the flow of information in their industry. Create a hierarchical diagram as shown in Figure 20–3 and 20–4, and discuss how this organization could influence groups that would in turn create favorable communication concerning this organization.
43. For a large organization of interest to you, replicate Exhibit 20–5 and Table 20–3 for an important purchase.

REFERENCES

[1]"Corporate Purchase Influencers Target of Direct-Mail Campaign," *Marketing News*, April 25, 1986.

[2]D. Conner, B. Finnan, and E. Clements, "Corporate Culture and Its Impact on Strategic Change in Banking," *Journal of Retail Banking*, Summer 1987, pp. 16–24.

[3]G. Badovick and S. Beatty, "Shared Organizational Values: Measurement and Impact upon Strategic Marketing Implementation," *Journal of the Academy of Marketing Science*, Spring 1987, pp. 19–26.

[4]J. F. Tanner, Jr., "Predicting Organizational Buyer Behavior," *Journal of Business and Industrial Marketing*, Fall 1990, pp. 57–64.

[5]H. Hlavacek and B. C. Ames, "Segmenting Industrial and Hi-Tech Markets," *Journal of Business Strategy*, Fall 1986, pp. 39–50.

[6]J. Choffray and G. Lilien, "Industrial Market Segmentation by the Structure of the Purchasing Decision Process," *Industrial Marketing Management*, no. 9 (1980), pp. 337–42.

[7]Adapted from J. H. Martin, J. M. Daley, and H. B. Burdg, "Buying Influences and Perceptions of Transportation Services," *Industrial Marketing Management* 17 (1988), pp. 311–12.

[8]A. N. Link and J. Neufeld, "Innovation vs. Imitation: Investigating Alternative R&D Strategies," *Applied Economics*, no. 18 (1986), pp. 1359–63.

[9]H. Brown and R. Brucker, "Charting the Industrial Buying Stream," *Industrial Marketing Management* 19 (1990), pp. 55–61.

[10]A. Kohli, "Determinants of Influence in Organizational Buying: A Contingency Approach," *Journal of Marketing*, July 1989, pp. 50–65.

[11]R. Thomas, "Bases of Power in Organizational Buying Decisions," *Industrial Marketing Management* 13 (1984), pp. 209–17.

[12]D. R. Lambert, P. D. Boughton, and G. R. Banville, "Conflict Resolution in Organizational Buying Centers," *Journal of the Academy of Marketing Science*, no. 14 (1986), pp. 57–62.

[13]E. J. Wilson, G. L. Lilien, and D. T. Wilson, "Developing and Testing a Contingency Paradigm of Group Choice in Organizational Buying," *Journal of Marketing Research*, November 1991, pp. 452–66.

[14]M. Berkowitz, "New Product Adoption by the Buying Organization: Who Are the Real Influencers?" *Industrial Marketing Management*, no. 15 (1986), pp. 33–43.

[15]L. Soley, "Copy Length and Industrial Advertising Readership," *Industrial Marketing Management*, no. 15 (1986), pp. 245–51.

[16]"Study: Increase Business Ads to Increase Sales," *Marketing News*, March 14, 1988, p. 13.

[17]C. Reichard, "Industrial Selling: Beyond Price and Resistance," *Harvard Business Review*, March–April, 1985, p. 132.

[18]See J. M. Sinkula, "Market Information Processing and Organizational Learning," *Journal of Marketing*, January 1994, pp. 35–45.

[19]M. D. Bunn, ''Taxonomy of Buying Decision Approaches,'' *Journal of Marketing*, January 1993, pp. 38–56. See also R. R. Dholakia, J. L. Johnson, A. J. Della Bitta, and N. Dholakia, ''Decision-making Time in Organizational Buying Behavior,'' *Journal of the Academy of Marketing Science*, Fall 1993, pp. 281–92; and M. D. Bunn, ''Key Aspects of Organizational Buying,'' *Journal of the Academy of Marketing Science*, Spring 1994, pp. 160–69.

[20]R. Abratt, ''Industrial Buying in Hi-Tech Markets,'' *Industrial Marketing Management*, no. 15 (1986), pp. 293–98.

[21]See A. M. Weiss and J. B. Heide, ''The Nature of Organizational Search in High-Technology Markets,'' *Journal of Marketing Research*, May 1993, pp. 220–33.

[22]R. LeBlanc, ''Insights into Organizational Buying,'' *Journal of Business and Industrial Marketing*, Spring 1987, pp. 5–10; G. Gordon, R. Calantone, and C. A. diBenedetto, ''How Electrical Contractors Choose Distributors,'' *Industrial Marketing Management*, no. 20 (1991), pp. 29–42; E. Day and H. C. Barksdale, Jr., ''How Firms Select Professional Services,'' *Industrial Marketing Management*, no. 21 (1992), pp. 85–91; and A. G. Lockett and P. Naude, ''Winning a Large Order,'' *Industrial Marketing Management* no. 20 (1991), pp. 169–75.

SECTION 5 CASES

Rydco, Inc.

Case 5–1

Rydco, Inc., specializes in the manufacture and marketing of steel products with unique durability, resistance to breakage, and long life. Over the course of five years, Rydco has developed an expertise in steel that goes far beyond commodity steel products. In fact, most of Rydco's products command a 15 to 25 percent price premium because of their unique performance capabilities.

Products and Customer Needs

Rydco product development has focused on applications in mining, construction, and forestry. In all cases, Rydco products are geared for tough applications in which the wear life (how long the product lasts) and problems with breakage are important factors in buying decisions. In many hard-rock mining and construction applications, an ordinary steel product coming in contact with the earth could wear out in less than a week. In addition, problems with breakage can be serious in mining applications, since broken steel parts can get mixed with ore and do considerable damage to manufacturing equipment during processing.

Rydco recently surveyed its customers' needs. Shown in Table A are customer-importance ratings of purchase criteria and customer perceptions of Rydco relative to competitors. On the top three most important purchase criteria, Rydco is rated ahead of its competition. While Rydco's prices are higher, customers are willing to buy its products because of its superior performance on the top three purchase criteria. For the three least important purchase criteria, Rydco is rated behind its competitors.

Noncustomer Survey

The customer needs and perceptions shown in Table A are those of existing customers served by Rydco. While this information is important, Rydco had not made any attempt to understand the needs and perceptions of noncustomers. Since Rydco already had a large share of its existing customers' purchases, growth meant adding new products and finding new customers. Because the noncustomer base was nine times larger than its current customer base, Rydco decided to conduct a noncustomer survey to find out more about noncustomer needs and perceptions of Rydco.

A portion of the noncustomer survey results are shown in Table B. While noncustomer perceptions of Rydco relative to competition are similar to those of existing customers, their needs are very different.

Purchase Criteria, Importance Weights, and Competitive Position of Rydco Customers **TABLE A**

Purchase Criteria	Importance	Competitive Position
Wear life of product	25%	Very good
Breakage	20	Very good
After-sale support	15	Very good
Price of product	14	Poor
Availability	10	Very poor
Delivery	10	Poor
Design productivity	6	Poor

TABLE B Noncustomer Needs and Perceptions of Rydco

Purchase Criteria	Importance	Competitive Position
Availability	30%	Very poor
Design productivity	25	Poor
Price	20	Poor
Delivery	15	Poor
Wear life	5	Very good
After-sale support	3	Very good
Breakage	2	Very good

FIGURE A Customer Decision Process

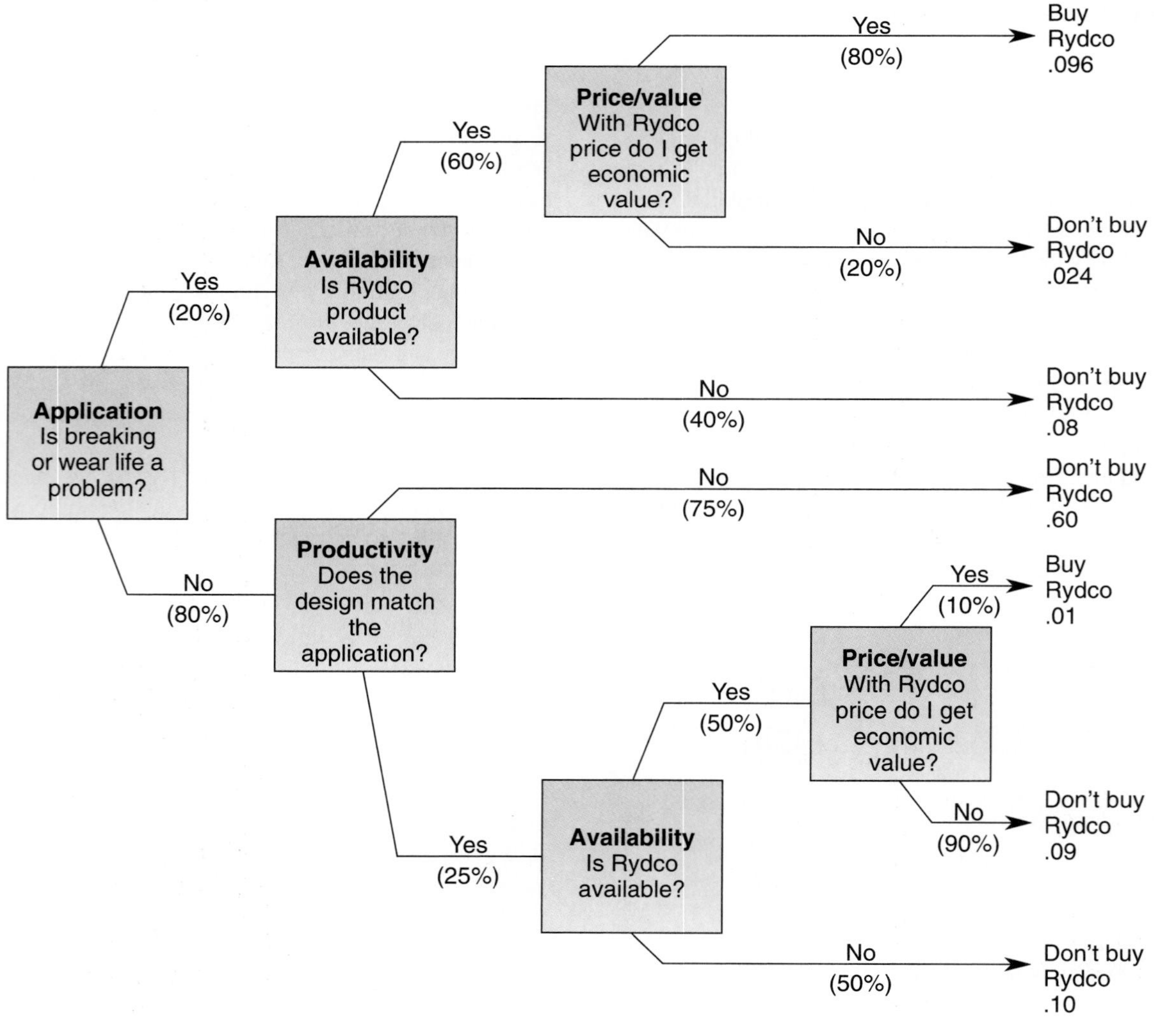

Noncustomers rated availability, price, and design productivity as their three most important purchase criteria. These are among the bottom four purchase criteria for existing customers.

Customer Decision Process

The wide difference in customer and noncustomer needs led to a recognition that the company did not adequately know how purchase decisions were made for either existing customers or noncustomers. While Tables A and B demonstrate differences in purchase criteria, these results do not provide sufficient insight into how these purchase criteria were used in a purchase decision. To find out, a purchase decision study was conducted, using a random sample of both customers and noncustomers.

The results of the purchase decision survey are shown in Figure A.

In making a decision to buy, customers first ask whether wear life or breakage is a problem. In 80 percent of user applications, this is not an issue. Thus, Rydco's key benefits are not relevant for 80 percent of the applications encountered in mining, construction, and forestry.

If the application does warrant concern for wear life and/or breakage, availability is the next key concern. Rydco products are not available when needed 40 percent of the time. If they are available, decision makers look at price in relationship to the product's economic value—the overall cost of the product including price, savings from increased wear life and potential damage from breakage, and added value derived from after-sale support. In 80 percent of the applications where wear life and/or breakage are a problem, Rydco wins the business. However, this occurs in only roughly 10 percent of all user applications.

In applications where wear life or breakage is not a concern, the decision process focused on design productivity, where Rydco was weak. Because of poor performance in this area, the company was not considered in 75 percent of these user applications. When the Rydco product did fit the application, it was only available 50 percent of the time. And because higher price was not offset with savings due to wear life, breakage, or after-sales support, Rydco only obtained 10 percent of these purchases. The net impact is less than 1 percent of these applications.

Figure A demonstrates where and why Rydco obtains its market share, but more importantly, it reveals where and why it loses market share. While its overall market share is around 10 percent, it has almost a 50 percent market share when wear life and breakage are important. Outside this area of application, the company is barely able to obtain a 1 percent market share.

Discussion Questions

1. What are the limitations to looking at just customer or noncustomer ratings of purchase criteria?
2. What additional benefits can be obtained by understanding how purchase decisions are made?
3. Where should Rydco focus its efforts, and what would be the impact of these efforts?
4. Explain how Rydco's high price could cost less in applications where wear life, breakage, and after-sale support are important. Also, explain why the economic value of the product is less attractive in applications where wear life and breakage are not a concern.

Loctite Corporation

Case 5–2

Loctite Corporation is a world leader in the manufacture and marketing of glues and adhesives. The company is well known among customers for products such as Super-Glue. However, a large portion of Loctite's annual sales is derived from industrial glues and adhesives used in a wide variety of industrial and electronic applications.

RC-601

One of Loctite's exciting new products was a nonmigrating thiotropic anaerobic gel that could be used to repair worn machine parts with a minimum of manufacturing downtime. Loctite branded the new product RC-601 and priced it slightly under $10 per tube. RC-

TABLE A Industrial Decision Influencer Research Findings

Decision Influencer	Needs and Behavioral Characteristics
Design engineers	Prefer lots of technical data. They have to be convinced that it works based on calculations. They are "risk avoiders" and less likely to try new products until technically proven to work and work under a variety of industrial conditions.
Production personnel	Prefer reliable, time-proven solutions. They want to know where new products have been used successfully. Production personnel are "today-oriented" with a tremendous concern for "reliable solutions." They are less likely to try new products until they have a proven and credible performance record.
Maintenance workers	These are the fixers; they keep things running around the plant. They typically have less formal technical education and are more likely to have worked their way up from a lesser job in the factory. They prefer pictures of how things work and should be used, and are uncomfortable with technical charts and graphs. Maintenance workers are more likely to try new products and typically do not need purchase authorization for purchases under $25.

601 was sold through industrial distributors, along with other Loctite products targeted for industrial applications.

This pricing allowed Loctite's industrial distributors to make a desirable margin, while enabling Loctite to make an 85 percent profit margin. At a price less than $10 per 50 ml (1.69 fl oz) tube, management felt that industrial buyers would readily try the product. Advertisements describing the technical characteristics of RC-601 and how it could be used were placed in a wide variety of industrial trade magazines.

Anatomy of a New-Product Failure

It took less than one year for Loctite to realize that RC-601 was not achieving the sales success expected. The product was pulled from the market and shelved for several months. While the product worked well, Loctite's failure to convince industrial users of RC-601's strength and reliability lead to the product's initial failure. To learn more about perceptions of this product and the needs of different industrial decision makers, Loctite engaged in industrial buyer behavior research.

The market research focused on three types of industrial purchase decision makers—design engineers, production personnel, and maintenance workers. While purchasing agents would logically be the industrial purchaser, Loctite felt that the actual users would make the decision to use or not use an industrial adhesive such as RC-601. The results of the industrial buyer research are summarized in Table A.

Building a Target Customer Marketing Strategy

Based on these research results, it became clear that Loctite's initial effort to market its new product had *no target customer.* The results also suggested that maintenance workers would be the most logical starting point, and that Loctite needed a marketing strategy that targeted the maintenance worker. This raised several marketing strategy questions:

- Is the brand name RC-601 the right name to communicate target customer benefits?
- How should the new product be communicated to maintenance workers?
- Is the price slightly under $10 too low?

- How should we promote trial usage of this new product?

Recognizing the maintenance worker as the target customer, management realized that the name RC-601 had little meaning. A new name, Quick Metal, was thought to be much better because it communicated both the time (quick) and strength (metal) benefits of the product. To further reinforce the application, the "Q" in Quick Metal was made to look like a gear shaft, the major area of industrial maintenance application. A silver box was also designed to reinforce the association with metal.

An ad was developed that used pictures to demonstrate "how to use," not technical data or graphs. Also the ad reinforced key customer benefits:

- Salvages worn parts.
- Prevents costly downtime—keeps machinery running until the new part arrives.
- Adds reliability to repairs—use with new parts to prevent future breakdowns.

This ad was also used as a piece of direct-mail literature. Overall, the new brand name, logo, packaging, and targeted advertisement were geared to appeal to the target customer, the industrial maintenance worker.

Based on the economic savings Quick Metal offered and the fact that purchases under $25 could be made without authorization, Loctite elected to price Quick Metal at $17.75 for a 50 ml (1.69 fl oz) tube. Six-milliliter tubes were also made available and used extensively in sales promotions to stimulate trial usage.

With a target customer and a marketing strategy designed around the needs of this target customer, Loctite relaunched its new product and achieved a level of success that far exceeded sales expectations.

Discussion Questions

1. Why did the RC-601 marketing strategy fail and the Quick Metal marketing strategy succeed?
2. What role did the brand name and package design have on perceptions of the product and on the ability of target customers to remember key product benefits?
3. Would the strategy have been as successful with the Quick Metal name and package but no target industrial customer? Explain your position.
4. What changes would Loctite have to make to be successful in marketing Quick Metal to production personnel?

American Vinyl Siding, Inc.* — Case 5-3

Many companies in mature, old-line manufacturing industries such as steel, forest products, and metal mining see their markets moving from basic commodities to high-margin, "value-added" products. For commodity-type products, success requires technological skill, economies of scale, and production know-how. But in "value-added" products, success depends on various product and service benefits that are tailored for specific customer segments.

Demand for siding for commercial and residential buildings, like many industrial goods, is a derived demand, because demand for siding depends on the demand for housing and remodeling. Siding products include wood products, aluminum, brick, and vinyl materials.

American Vinyl Siding is a manufacturer and marketer of vinyl siding for residential and commercial buildings. Siding for residential housing accounts for 4.7 billion square feet of siding per year. Wood products account for 51 percent of this demand. Wood products include cedar/redwood, hardwood, plywood, and spruce/pine. Nonwoods include brick, aluminum, and vinyl.

Market Structure

While wood products hold a small lead over nonwood products in the demand for siding for residential homes, the market is shifting. Over the past several years, the demand for hardwoods and aluminum siding has declined, while demand for plywood and vinyl has

*Source: S. Sinclair and E. Stalling, "Perceptual Mapping: A Tool for Industrial Marketing: A Case Study," *The Journal of Business and Industrial Marketing*, Winter/Spring 1990, pp. 55–66.

FIGURE A

Market Shares of Competing Siding Materials

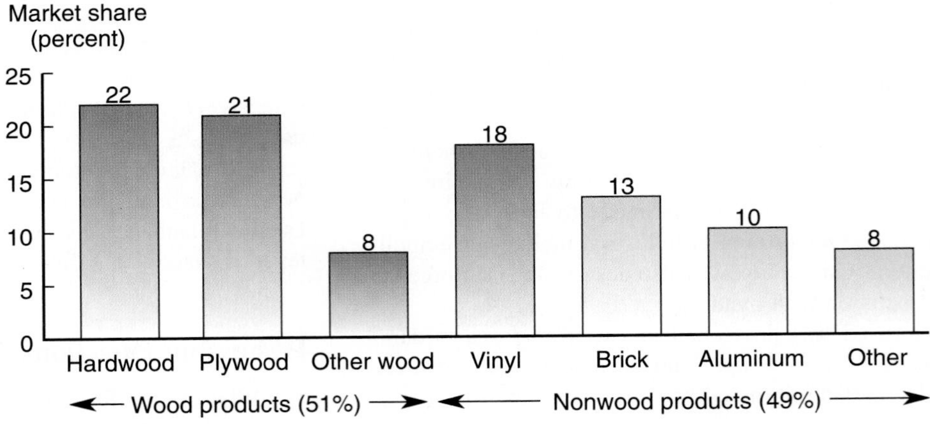

FIGURE B

Product Attributes Considered on a Siding Purchase Decision

Price	Dent resistance
Fade resistance	Weather resistance/long life
High status/quality image	Texture/variety
Fast/easy application	Dimensional/shape stability
Low/easy maintenance	Wide color selection
Appearance	

increased. The demand for brick and other wood siding has not changed. Shown in Figure A are the market shares for each of the competing types of siding.

Customer Needs and Perceptions

A survey of customer needs revealed the 11 performance criteria shown in Figure B. While all these criteria were thought to be important considerations in selecting one type of siding over another, an additional study of consumer perceptions was conducted to reveal more precisely which of these criteria differentiate competing siding alternatives. Figure C illustrates part of the results of this study.

The vinyl customer perception study revealed that 4 of the 11 dimensions listed in Figure B were used to differentiate competing siding products. Two of the dimensions were Maintenance/Weathering (Dimension I) and Appearance/Status (Dimension II). A second set of dimensions included Dent Resistance (Dimension III) and Application/Economy (Dimension IV). Also shown in Figure C is the ideal product for four different home-price segments.

Based upon the perceptions shown in Figure C, vinyl siding is strongest on the dimensions of Maintenance/Weathering and Application/Economy. Vinyl was perceived to be less attractive (Appearance/Status) and neutral on Dent Resistance. In all cases, consumers in Segment 1 (homes under $70,000) prefer vinyl siding. Even with respect to Appearance/Status, customers in Segment 1 prefer vinyl siding. Segment 2 is the second most attractive segment among customers, while Segment 4 (expensive homes) is the least likely to prefer vinyl siding.

Discussion Questions

1. Why would consumers list 11 performance attributes in evaluating alternative siding materials and

Customer Perceptions of Siding Alternatives

FIGURE C

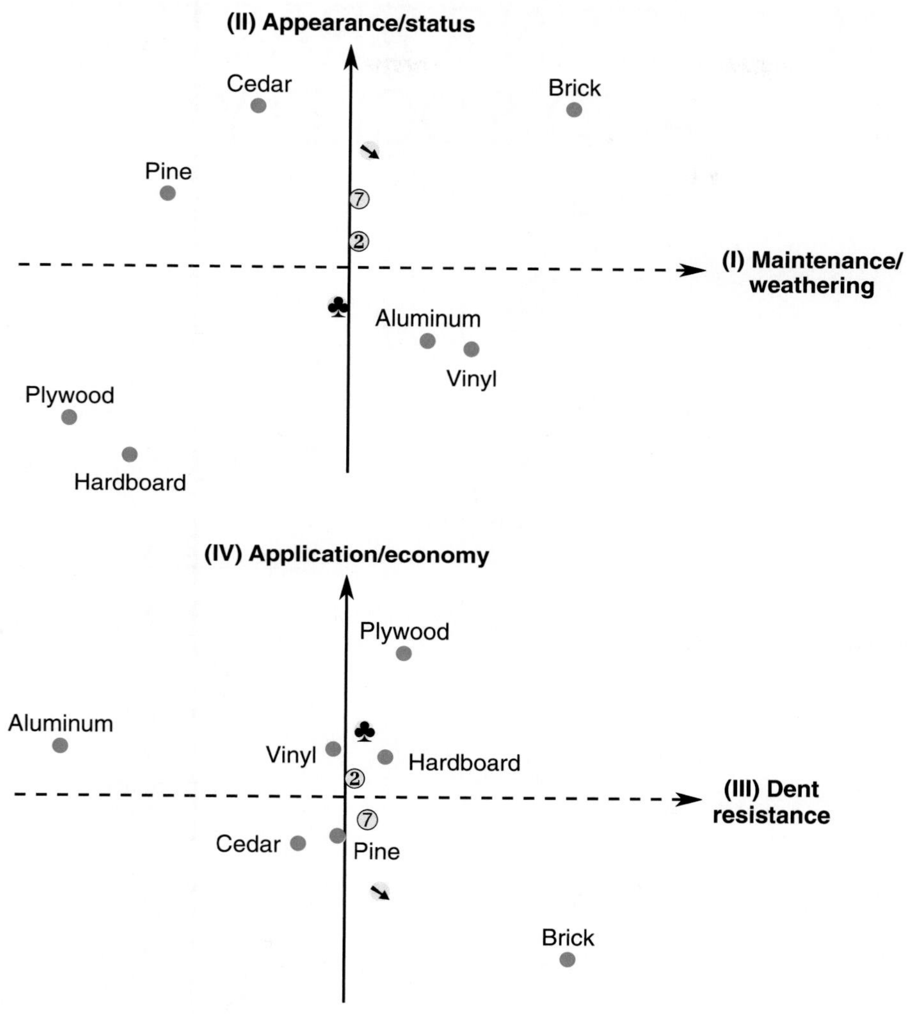

then use only 4 of the 11 in differentiating alternative siding materials?

2. Which siding materials pose the biggest competitive threat to vinyl siding? Why?
3. How should American Vinyl Siding promote its product and to whom?
4. What could American Vinyl Siding do to improve its perception on appearance and status?
5. Who do you think plays which role(s) in the decision of type and brand of siding for a new home? Does this vary as the price of the home increases?

SECTION SIX

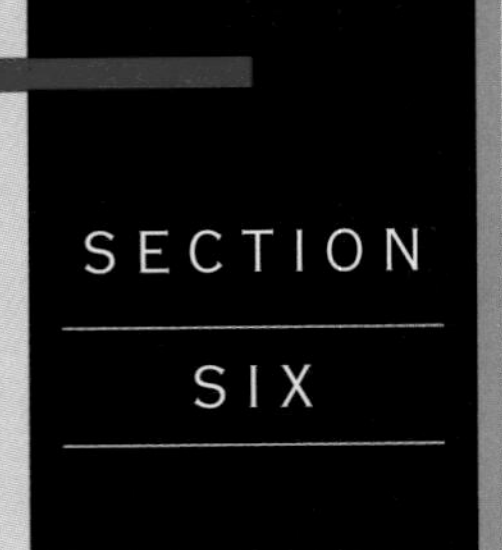

CONSUMER BEHAVIOR, MARKETING PRACTICE, AND SOCIETY

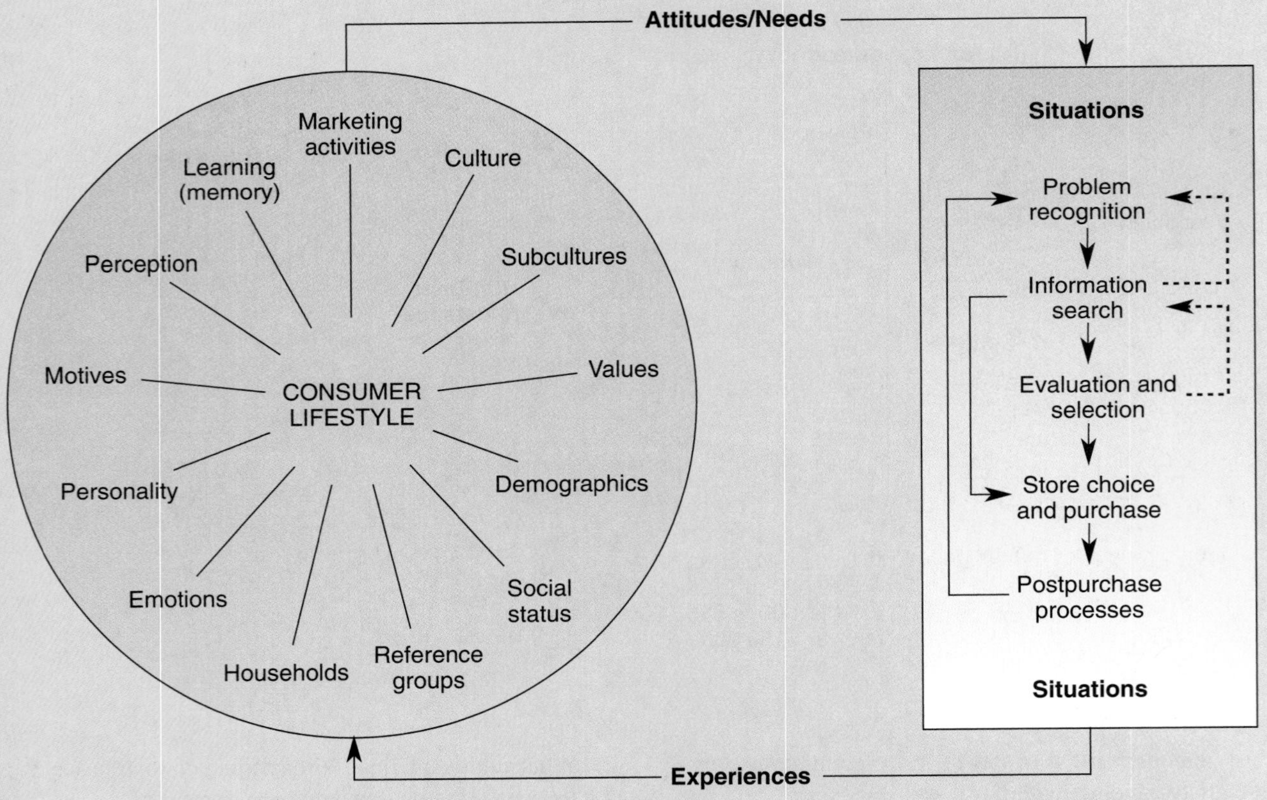

Attitudes/Needs
Marketing activities
Culture
Subcultures
Values
Demographics
Social status
Reference groups
Households
Emotions
Personality
Motives
Perception
Learning (memory)
CONSUMER LIFESTYLE
Situations
Problem recognition
Information search
Evaluation and selection
Store choice and purchase
Postpurchase processes
Situations
Experiences

Throughout the text we have emphasized that a knowledge of consumer behavior is as important to those who regulate consumer behavior as it is to those who engage in direct marketing activities. Likewise, a knowledge of consumer behavior is absolutely essential to those who attempt to market causes rather than products or services. Perhaps less obvious, but equally true, a knowledge of consumer behavior is important for informed citizenship. After all, it is individual citizens who through their purchases and political choices determine what type of marketplace and society we will have.

In this section, we will briefly analyze the current consumerism movement. This movement arose in the 1960s as a result of general dissatisfaction with the marketing system and specific marketing practices. For the past thirty years it has had varying degrees of influence on regulatory policy and the sales of individual firms.

A common objective of the consumerism movement is the regulation of marketing activities. There is particular concern focused on marketing aimed at children. This concern arises because of the tremendous amount of time children watch commercial television and their limited ability to fully comprehend commercial messages. Regulators also focus on advertising, product, and pricing practices aimed at adults.

Cause marketing attempts to sell ideals and causes rather than products or services. While complicated, cause marketing is also exciting and fulfilling.

In this section of the text, we will consider all of these issues and their relation to consumer behavior.

CONSUMERISM, REGULATORY ISSUES, AND CAUSE MARKETING

In 1988, Roper and other public opinion polls began to indicate that a substantial number of consumers would choose a brand based on its positive (lack of negative) impact on the environment. Many others stated that they would pay a premium for products and brands that were superior in terms of their impact on the environment (see Chapter 3, pp. 70–71). As a result, many firms began to improve the performance of their products relative to the environment and to advertise these improvements. This activity became known as *green marketing*. It included activities ranging from changing to a less environmentally harmful manufacturing process, to using recycled and/or recyclable materials, to using less packaging materials.

Unfortunately, different marketers used the same claims, such as *environmentally friendly* or *environmentally safe*, to refer to vastly differing performance levels. Further, some firms made *green claims* that were misleading if not completely false. For example, some firms made claims such as ''Now completely phosphorous free!'' when they had contained only a trace amount of phosphorous before. While the claim is true, the elimination of trace amounts of phosphorous from the product in question had no beneficial environmental impact.

Such contradictory and misleading claims produced cynicism among many consumers for all green claims and a variety of conflicting state and federal government regulations concerning green claims. This, in turn, caused reputable firms to drop environment claims and may well have reduced the impetus to produce environmentally sound products. The primary problem from the marketers' standpoint was the impossibility (or high cost) of complying with a multitude of complex and conflicting state and federal regulations. For example, Procter & Gamble, Kraft General Foods, Mary Kay Cosmetics, and other firms that had been active in developing and promoting recycled and recyclable products and packages sharply reduced their use of such claims.

To enable consumers to receive the information they need to make environmentally sound choices and to allow marketers to benefit from their efforts to develop environmentally sound products, the Federal Trade Commission (FTC) recently issued a set of voluntary guidelines for green claims. While neither the states nor the firms have to follow the guidelines, it appears that state and federal agencies will not prosecute firms within the guidelines and will prosecute those who fall outside them. The general guidelines include dozens of examples of acceptable and unacceptable practices to guide marketers, including the following:

- A ''recycled'' label on a soft-drink bottle made from recycled material wouldn't be considered misleading even if the cap isn't made from recycled material.
- An ad touting a package as ''50% more recycled content than before'' could be misleading if the recycled content had increased from 2% to 3%.
- An ad calling a trash bag ''recyclable'' without qualification would be deemed misleading because bags aren't ordinarily separated from other trash at landfills or incinerators.
- An ad touting a shampoo bottle as containing ''20% more recycled content'' would be considered misleading if it didn't say whether the product is being compared with a rival or the product's previous container.
- Labels promoting products as ''environmentally safe'' or ''environmentally friendly'' must specify what portion of the product is being referred to; otherwise, they would be deceptive.

- A trash bag marked ''degradable'' without qualification likely would be deceptive because trash bags are customarily disposed of in incineration facilities or landfills that minimize exposure to the elements.
- A shampoo advertised as ''biodegradable'' without qualification wouldn't be deceptive if the marketer has competent and reliable scientific support showing it will decompose in a short time.[1]

As the opening example indicates, marketing practices such as green marketing sometimes produce actions that consumers find inappropriate. If enough consumers become sufficiently upset with specific actions, they or consumer groups that represent them will demand regulatory action at the local, state, or federal level. However, to be effective, such action must be based on a sound understanding of consumer behavior.

In this chapter we will examine the nature of *consumerism*—a social movement with the purpose of enhancing the power of buyers relative to that of sellers. A common objective of consumerism is the *regulation of marketing activities.* We will examine this type of regulation in light of the consumer behavior principles upon which sound regulation must be based. Finally, we will briefly consider *cause marketing*—marketing activities undertaken to support an idea or social cause, such as gun control or blood donations.

CONSUMERISM

There have been several consumerism movements in the history of the United States (similar patterns have occurred in most countries). By **consumerism movement** we mean *a sustained period of political activity by consumers who are dissatisfied with various aspects of the marketing system.* Such movements generally produce boycotts of some firms or products and legislation designed to remedy at least some of the problems concerning consumers.

The current consumerism movement began in the early 1960s. Many suggest that it was crystallized in 1962 when President John F. Kennedy presented his famous Consumers' Bill of Rights in a speech to Congress:

1. The *right to safety*: to be protected against the marketing of goods which are hazardous to health or life.
2. The *right to be informed*: to be protected against fraudulent, deceitful, or grossly misleading information, advertising, labeling, or other practices, and to be given the facts needed to make an informed choice.
3. The *right to choose*: to be assured, wherever possible, access to a variety of products and services at competitive prices; and in those industries in which competition is not workable and government regulation is substituted, an assurance of satisfactory quality and service at fair prices.
4. The *right to be heard*: to be assured that consumer interest will receive full and sympathetic consideration in the formulation of government policy, and fair and expeditious treatment in its administrative tribunals.[2]

The consumerism movement is not a well-organized political group or set of groups with a precise, long-term agenda. Rather it refers more to a state-of-mind in many consumers that inclines them to support the boycott or regulatory actions suggested by more active consumer groups. While some consumers are concerned about marketing activities aimed at children, others are concerned about environmental or social issues. Many belong to no direct consumerism groups. However, by responding in a pro-consumerism manner to polls, by voting for pro-consumer candidates and legislation, and by buying certain brands rather than others, they give strength to the movement.

Large numbers of consumers do not become disenchanted with the marketing system without cause. A high level of consumer dissatisfaction or distrust suggests that marketers either do not understand consumer behavior sufficiently to effectively meet consumer needs or they do understand consumer behavior and choose to misuse this understanding to take advantage of consumers. Both of these factors are undoubtedly true to an extent. Many other factors also contribute to general consumer dissatisfaction. Some of these include:

- The marketplace is much more impersonal. With the disappearance of the small local store, consumers must generally deal with strangers in an impersonal environment. (Note that consumers voted for this impersonal environment with their shopping choices.)
- Product complexity has increased dramatically. Until the late 1950s many consumers understood how most of the products they purchased functioned and could repair them if necessary. However, the advent of the transistor, the computer chip, and sophisticated engine designs left most consumers technologically illiterate. Consumers can no longer directly evaluate a product or many services.
- Advertising has become more intrusive. With global competition increasing the number of firms in each product category and technology increasing the number of product categories and media, the number of advertisements has grown almost exponentially.
- The increase in two-earner families and single-parent families and a decline in real wages has placed time and financial constraints on many individuals. These individuals need to make sound purchases but often lack the information and time to do so.
- The mass media are quick to publicize unethical or questionable practices by marketers. Thus, evening news shows give prime coverage to the actions of a few firms. However, this coverage gives some the impression that fraud and dangerous products are more widespread than they are.
- Many individuals would like the United States to be less materialistic and more concerned with other values. They would like to restrict marketing activities in an attempt to limit Americans' focus on ''things.''

As the list above suggests, marketing activities are a vital part of our society and they are affected by many of the same forces that affect other parts of our lives. In this chapter, we will focus on those issues raised by the consumerism movement that are under the control of marketing managers and which a knowledge of consumer behavior can influence.

REGULATORY ISSUES

The consumerism movement's interests evolve over time as the legal structure and marketing practices change. We will examine four areas that have been of enduring concern to the movement and for which consumer behavior theory and knowledge are particularly relevant: marketing to children, consumer information, pricing issues, and product issues.

Marketing to Children

A consistent concern of the consumerism movement over the years has been advertising and other marketing efforts aimed at children. As a result, there are a variety of state, federal, and voluntary guidelines and rules governing marketing to children. Despite these rules, many feel that some marketers continue to take advantage of children and that the overall marketing system, particularly advertising, is socializing children to value things (products) rather than intangibles such as relationships and integrity.

One basis for the concern over marketing to children is based on Piaget's **stages of cognitive development** which indicate that children lack the ability to fully process and understand information (including marketing messages) until around 12 years of age:

1. *The period of sensorimotor intelligence (0 to 2 years).* During this period, behavior is primarily motor. The child does not yet "think" conceptually, though "cognitive" development is seen.
2. *The period of preoperational thought (3 to 7 years).* This period is characterized by the development of language and rapid conceptual development.
3. *The period of concrete operations (8 to 11 years).* During these years the child develops the ability to apply logical thought to concrete problems.
4. *The period of formal operations (12 to 15 years).* During this period the child's cognitive structures reach their greatest level of development and the child becomes able to apply logic to all classes of problems.[3]

This theory and the research that supports it is the basis for most regulation of advertising aimed at children and, according to critics, for some marketing programs that deliberately exploit children.

The Ability of Children to Comprehend Commercial Messages Quebec's Consumer Protection Act prohibits commercial advertising to persons under 13 years of age. The United States Federal Trade Commission has considered proposals to eliminate all advertisements to young children and advertisements for sugared food products aimed at older children. The American advertising industry's primary self-regulatory body, the National Advertising Division of the Council of Better Business Bureaus, maintains a special unit to review advertising aimed at children—the Children's Advertising Review Unit (CARU). Some of the guidelines relating to information processing which guide CARU's policing of children's advertising are shown in Exhibit 21–1. CARU and others are interested in the impact that the *content* of children's advertising has, as well as the ability of children to process advertising messages. However, our current focus is limited to children's abilities to *comprehend* advertising messages.[4] There are two components to this concern: (1) Can children discern the differences between program and commercial? and, (2) Can children understand specific aspects of commercials, such as comparisons?

Most research indicates that younger children (under seven) have at least some difficulty in distinguishing commercials from programs (either not noticing the change or thinking of commercials as another program). It also appears that younger children are less able to determine the selling intent of commercials. However, there is some evidence that young children are aware of the selling intent but cannot verbalize this intent.[5] Currently, the advertising industry strives to separate children's commercials from the programs by prohibiting overlapping characters and by using *separators* such as: "We will return after these messages." This problem is growing in intensity as children's products are increasingly the "stars" of animated children's television programs.[6]

The second aspect of comprehension involves specific words or types of commercials that children might misunderstand. For example, research indicates that disclaimers such as "Part of a nutritious breakfast," "Each sold separately," and "Batteries not included," are ineffective with preschool children.[7] Thus, the CARU has special rules for comparison advertising, and prohibits price minimizations such as "only," and "just." It also suggests specific phrasing for certain situations such as "your mom or dad must say it's OK before

EXHIBIT 21-1

Information-Processing-Related Guidelines of the Children's Advertising Review Unit

1. Care should be taken not to exploit a child's imagination. Fantasy, including animation, is appropriate for younger as well as older children. However, it should not create unattainable performance expectations nor exploit the younger child's difficulty in distinguishing between the real and the fanciful.
2. The performance and use of a product should be demonstrated in a way that can be duplicated by the child for whom the product is intended.
3. All price representations should be clearly and concisely set forth. Price minimizations such as "only" or "just" should not be used.
4. Program personalities or characters, live or animated, should not promote products, premiums, or services in or adjacent to programs primarily directed to children in which the same personality appears.
5. Children have difficulty distinguishing product from premium. If product advertising contains a premium message, care should be taken that the child's attention is focused primarily on the product. The premium message should be clearly secondary.

Source: *Self-Regulation Guidelines for Children's Advertising* (Council of Better Business Bureaus, Inc. Children's Advertising Review Unit, 1993).

you call," rather than "ask your parents' permission." Several cases involving CARU and the information-processing skills of children are:

> **LJN Toys.** A television commercial for its Photon electronic target game showed the guns appearing to shoot red laser beams. The commercial included a visual disclaimer: "Red beam for illustration only." Because the commercial ran during children's programming, the CARU challenged the adequacy of the disclaimer.
>
> **Mattel Toys.** A TV commercial showed Monstroid, a figure in its Masters of the Universe line, apparently grabbing other figures automatically. Copy said, "Now, a raging terror grabs hold of the universe. . . . When Monstroid gets wound up, it grabs. . . ." CARU challenged the ad on the basis that children would not understand that Monstroid's grip is manually operated.[8]
>
> **Hasbro.** A TV commercial directed to children promoted a "My Little Pony" movie for "only" $1.00. CARU challenged the use of price minimizations such as *only* or *just* "because children aren't sophisticated enough to comprehend the relative value of money.[9]

Likewise, the Federal Trade Commission (FTC) applied sanctions to Lewis Galoob Toys and its ad agency. The ads cited showed a doll dancing and a toy airplane flying, both of which require human assistance to do so. The ads also failed to disclose that assembly was required for certain toy sets. Finally, the firm failed to "clearly and conspicuously" disclose that two toys shown together had to be purchased separately. An FTC spokesperson noted that the ads never appeared on network stations and speculated that the networks' internal review processes for children's ads would have precluded their being shown.[10]

Concerns about the Impact of the Content of Commercial Messages on Children Even if children accurately comprehend television ads, there are serious concerns about the effects the content of these messages has on children. These concerns stem in part from the substantial amount of time American children spend viewing television. Children between 2 and 11 years of age spend more than 25 hours per week watching television and are thus exposed to almost 25,000 television commercials per year.[11] This viewing is spread throughout the week, though prime time (Monday–Sunday, 7:30–11:00 P.M.) is most popular, except for younger viewers who watch Saturday morning programs extensively.

The large amount of time children devote to watching television, including commercials, gives rise to three major areas of concern:

- The potential for commercial messages to generate intrafamily conflict.
- The impact of commercial messages on children's values.
- The impact of commercial messages on children's health and safety.

The CARU is deeply concerned about these issues. Four of the six basic "principles" that underline the CARU's guidelines for advertising directed at children focus on these concerns (the other two are concerned with children's information-processing capabilities). They are:

- Recognizing that advertising may play an important role in educating the child, advertisers should communicate information in a truthful and accurate manner with full recognition that the child may learn practices from advertising which can affect his or her health and well-being.
- Advertisers are urged to capitalize on the potential of advertising to influence behavior by developing advertising that, wherever possible, addresses itself to positive and beneficial social behavior such as friendship, kindness, honesty, justice, generosity, and respect for others.
- Care should be taken to incorporate minority and other groups in advertisements in order to present positive and prosocial roles and role models wherever possible. Social stereotyping and appeals to prejudice should be avoided.
- Although many influences affect a child's personal and social development, it remains the prime responsibility of the parents to provide guidance for children. Advertisers should contribute to this parent-child relationship in a constructive manner.

Several of the specific guidelines derived from these principles are provided in Exhibit 21–2.

Family Conflict Advertising can generate family conflict by encouraging children to want products their parents do not want them to have or cannot afford to buy. One study of family conflict found that:

- A majority of children were stimulated by television commercials to ask for toys and cereals.
- Nearly half of these children argued with their parents over denials of their requests.
- More than half became angry with their mothers when the request was denied.[12]

Such conflict is natural and is not necessarily bad. It can, in fact, lead to useful learning experiences. But the concern is that the level of conflict induced by consistent viewing of advertising is unhealthy.[13]

EXHIBIT 21–2

Content Related Guidelines of the Children's Advertising Review Unit

1. Representation of food products should be made so as to encourage sound use of the product with a view toward healthy development of the child and development of good nutritional practices. Advertisements representing mealtime should clearly and adequately depict the role of the product within the framework of a balanced diet. Snack foods should be clearly represented as such, and not as substitutes for meals.
2. Children should not be encouraged to ask parents or others to buy products. Advertisements should not suggest that a parent or adult who purchases a product or service for a child is better, more intelligent or more generous than one who does not. Advertising directed toward children should not create a sense of urgency or exclusivity, for example, by using words like "now" and "only."
3. Benefits attributed to the product or service should be inherent in its use. Advertisements should not convey the impression that possession of a product will result in more acceptance of a child by his or her peers. Conversely, it should not be implied that lack of a product will cause a child to be less accepted by his or her peers. Advertisements should not imply that purchase and use of a product will confer upon the user the prestige, skills, or other special qualities of characters appearing in advertising.
4. Advertisements for children's products should show them being used by children in the appropriate age range. For instance, young children should not be shown playing with toys safe only for older children.
5. Advertisements should not portray adults or children in unsafe situations, or in acts harmful to themselves or others. For example, when athletic activities (such as bicycle riding or skateboarding) are shown, proper precautions and safety equipment should be depicted.

Source: *Self-Regulatory Guidelines for Children's Advertising* (Council of Better Business Bureaus, Inc. Children's Advertising Review Unit, 1993).

Health and Safety Concern also has risen that advertising may promote unsafe or dangerous behavior. In many instances, advertising directed at adults is viewed by children and the consequences are potentially harmful, as described below:

> A television commercial for Calgonite automatic dishwasher detergent showed a woman inside an automatic dishwasher. The commercial was withdrawn voluntarily after CARU received a complaint that a three-year-old child had climbed into a dishwasher shortly after viewing the commercial.[14]

The problem caused by the Calgonite commercial illustrates the difficulty of complying with the safety guideline. This commercial was not aimed at children nor shown during a children's program. The fact that children watch prime time television extensively places an additional responsibility on marketers. You must ensure that all of your commercials are appropriate for children from a safety standpoint.

Ensuring that advertisements portray only safe uses of products is sometimes difficult, but it is not a controversial area. Advertising of health-related products, particularly snack foods and cereals, is much more controversial.[15] The bulk of the controversy focuses on the heavy advertising emphasis placed on sugared products. Advertising sugared products does increase their consumption. However, this same advertising may also increase the consumption of related products, such as milk. What is not known (and probably cannot be determined) are the eating patterns that would exist in the absence of such advertising. That is, if children did not know about cereals such as Cap'n Crunch, would they eat a more nutritious breakfast, a less nutritious breakfast, or perhaps no breakfast at all? However, extensive viewing of child-oriented advertising has been found to correlate with low nutritional awareness.[16]

Unfortunately, some marketers have not been very responsible in this area. For example, children's diets are higher in overall fat and saturated fat than health guidelines call for and obesity among children is increasing. From 1989 to 1993, the percentage of high-fat foods advertised during Saturday morning children's TV programs increased from 16 percent of all food advertising to 41 percent. Most of the ads are for fast food, particularly hamburgers and pizzas. Such advertising undoubtedly influences children's food choices and subsequent health. It should be noted that other successful marketers of products consumed by children, such as Coca-Cola and PepsiCo, do not advertise on children's shows.[17]

Values Advertising is frequently criticized as fostering overly materialistic, self-focused, and short-term values in children. It has also been charged with portraying undesirable stereotypes of women and minority groups. Unfortunately, we do not have sound evidence on the impact of advertising on children's values. However, CARU principles and guidelines strongly encourage advertisers to portray positive values in advertisements aimed at children. About 10 percent of CARU's cases involve the area of values.

Most ads aimed at children meet all CARU guidelines. However, some would claim that thousands of similar ads, all promoting the acquisition of products, have the cumulative effect of distorting children's values. These individuals want regulations that sharply limit the amount of advertising that can be directed at children.

Summary on Advertising to Children The CARU recently examined 604 hours of children's programming on ABC, NBC, CBS, USA Network, Nickelodeon, and two independent broadcasters. There were 10,329 commercials aired during the 604 hours. Of these 10,329 commercials, 385 were in violation of one of CARU's guidelines. Fast-food ads accounted for 109 of the violations, with Burger King having 83. The most common offense was to devote most of the commercial to describing a premium rather than the primary product. CARU guidelines require that ads aimed at children emphasize the product.

Advertiser compliance was highest on the three networks (which have their own review processes) with a 2 percent violation rate, independent stations were next at 3.7 percent, while 5 percent of the ads on cable violated the CARU guidelines.[18] Thus, the vast majority of ads meet CARU guidelines. However, given the enormous amount of time children spend watching television, most will see many ads that are in violation of these guidelines. In addition, these guidelines do not address such issues as advertising high-fat foods. Nor do they (nor could they) oppose generating desires for products that many families cannot afford. Nonetheless, CARU has greatly enhanced the level of responsibility in advertising aimed at children. Many consumer advocates would like it to expand the areas it covers and increase the stringency of its rules.

Controversial Marketing Activities Aimed at Children There are a number of marketing activities targeted at children in addition to television advertising that are controversial.[19] We will describe two in this section.

Kids' Clubs Kids' clubs are one of the fastest growing ways to market to children.[20] Firms such as Fox, Chuck E. Cheese, Toys "R" Us, Burger King, Disney, Hyatt, and Delta Airlines sponsor kids' clubs. The clubs typically provide membership certificates, a magazine, the chance to win prizes, and discounts or coupons for products offered by the sponsor. Kids' clubs vary widely in what they offer the members and how ethically they are run. Here is how Consumers Union characterized the majority of them:

> In a real club, kids are likely to find friends, shared interests and activities, and opportunities for fun and growth. In the promotional clubs common years ago, kids were likely to get membership cards, decoder rings, or other symbols that reinforced loyalty to the sponsoring radio or TV program, comic, or other product. In one of the new kids' clubs, kids are likely to get hard sell from many advertisers, a monthly magazine cum sales catalog, discount coupons, and other powerful incentives to buy.
>
> Clubs disguise commercial messages. Kids are invited to join something that promises to be "theirs," but turns out to be a way of manipulating them to buy things. The ad messages come disguised as "advice from *your* club," making them more difficult to resist.[21]

Exhibit 21–3 describes the Nickelodeon Club and an advertisement that Nickelodeon used to attract advertisers to its club magazine. The selling intent of this club seems apparent.

Consumers Union has the following recommendation for regulating kids' clubs:

> The Federal Trade Commission should recognize that kids' clubs, whose purpose is to sell products, may mislead children, even if the commercial nature of the clubs is obvious to adults. The FTC should require kids' clubs to provide a substantial non-merchandising service or activity for kids. Clubs intending to sell members' names in mailing lists should disclose that fact and give kids the opportunity to keep their names off the list.

Would the Burger King Kids Club described below meet the requirements recommended by Consumers Union?

> Kids (or their parents) can pick up a membership form at any Burger King for free. After it is sent in, they receive a kit containing a membership certificate, stickers, a membership card and iron-on transfers for T-shirts. On their birthdays, they receive a card good for a free meal at their local Burger King. Bimonthly Kids Club newsletters are distributed through the restaurants. A quarterly 32-page, full-color magazine is sent to the members' homes. There are three different versions of the magazine geared to the age of the member. Each issue has six pages of outside advertising. Burger King does not sell its membership list.[22]

Advertising in the Classroom In 1989, Whittle Communications created a substantial controversy when it launched a closed-circuit television network (Channel One) that would provide 12 minutes of news to participating schools. If the schools' teachers agree to have their students watch the program most days, they receive the TV equipment free. However,

EXHIBIT 21-3 The Nickelodeon Club

The Characteristics of the Club

A one-year membership (which includes a subscription to Nichelodeon Magazine) costs $9.95 (but a special $7.95 introductory offer is advertised in the premiere issue). The magazine, with an insert promoting club membership, was launched in May 1990 through Pizza Hut. That insert promised special "kids-only" prices on club merchandise and "special offers or discounts" at Pizza Hut, Universal Studios in Florida, and TCBY yogurt. In addition to eight pages of ads, Nickelodeon magazine devoted nine pages to the "Nick Store," where club merchandise is offered at two prices, a kid's price and a higher adult's price. One-third (17 of 52) of its pages sells things to kids. Other popular kid's magazines with no club affiliation tend to devote a smaller percent of their pages to advertising: One-fourth (22 of 80) pages of Sports Illustrated for Kids is ads, as is about one-sixth to one-tenth of 3-2-1 Contact. Club members will also be sent product samples and coupons from Nick Club advertisers.

What the Nickelodeon Club Promises Advertisers

"You (the advertiser) can capture *all* the excitement of the Nickelodeon name, the on-air attitude, and the off-air environment, by delivering your product message or coupon to the young consumers of today and the brand-loyal customers of tomorrow. With the Nick Nack Pack (product samples and coupons mailed to kids) and the Nickelodeon Magazine, Nick offers you home delivery of an entire generation—the Nickelodeon generation."

The preceding quote is from the packet Nickelodeon sends to prospective advertisers. It also quotes the Nickelodeon/Yankelovich Youth Monitor: "All kids tend to influence their parents across a number of categories—clothing, food, entertainment, nontraditional and larger ticket items," it says. Among the data given: "60% of kids buy products because they have coupons for them." No wonder coupons are being offered by several kids clubs, and even in the classroom.

While the kids are joining a fun club, Nickelodeon is building a large database of names. Along with the Sassy and MTV clubs, Nickelodeon offers to sell its kids' club membership list to direct-mail advertisers.

Source: *Selling America's Kids* (Yonkers, N.Y.: Consumers Union Educational Services, 1990), pp. 15–16.

the news program contains two minutes of commercials. Unlike home viewing, watching this news program is not voluntary and students cannot skip to other channels when the commercials are aired.

While Channel One generated substantial publicity, numerous corporations place direct and indirect ads in schools every day:

- Many first-grade teachers use the AT&T Adventure Club, which includes student newsletters, classroom posters, and teaching guides. It is designed to develop an understanding of communications and to build AT&T brand awareness. Scholastic Inc., one of the nation's largest publishers of books and magazines for children, sends out single-sponsor educational magazines and other teaching tools for 40 companies. Procter & Gamble offers laundry tips and Tide for classroom demonstrations. Kentucky Fried Chicken and *Good Housekeeping* sponsor a classroom contest for Mother's Day cards. McDonald's provides educational materials on such topics as nutrition.

- Scholastic Inc. developed a program for Minute Maid to encourage 3.7 million elementary school kids to read a book a week over their summer vacation. Kids who sent away for a chart to keep track of their progress also received coupons for Minute Maid products. For each coupon redeemed, Minute Maid donated 10 cents to a nonprofit organization that promotes reading.

Exhibit 21–4 describes a number of other "educational materials" programs offered by marketers for use in schools and Consumers Union's evaluation of the promotional content of these materials. Consumers Union and other groups want schools to be "ad-free" zones. They feel that all material provided to schools by organizations should be:

Accurate: Be consistent with established facts, appropriately referenced, and current.
Objective: Present all relevant points of view, and clearly state the sponsor's bias.
Complete: Not mislead by omission.
Nondiscriminatory: Avoid ethnic, age, race, and gender stereotypes.
Noncommercial: Not contain any of the sponsor's brand names, trademarks, related trade names, or corporate identification in the text or illustrations; avoid implied or explicit sales messages.
Evaluative: Encourage cognitive evaluation of the subject taught.

While many firms would agree with most of the above requirements, complete compliance with the noncommercial standard would greatly reduce the motivation of firms to provide valuable (sometimes) material to the schools.

As mentioned earlier, there are many other controversial activities involving marketing to children. One is the magnitude of advertising focused on kids. During a recent May, Nike ran 90 commercials for its shoes on MTV and only 21 on sports programs.[23] Many persons are concerned that this consistent pressure to buy and own things is producing negative values in children. Another concern is using celebrities such as Nintendo, Michael Jordan, David Robinson, André Agassi, and Paula Abdul to promote products to kids. Ads that appear to be entertainment (television shows), puzzles, comics, and games are also controversial. Managerial Application 21–1 on page 598 is an example of such an ad.

Consumer Information

There are three major concerns focused on the information that marketers provide to consumers, generally in the form of advertisements—the accuracy of the information provided, the adequacy of the information provided, and the cumulative impact of marketing information on society's values. We will briefly look at advertising's impact on our values before focusing on the accuracy and adequacy of consumer information.

We discussed the impact of advertising on values in the previous section on advertising to children. The concern is the same for advertising directed at adults—the long-term effect of a constant flow of messages stressing ownership and/or narcissistic values may be negative both for individuals and society.

EXHIBIT 21–4

''Educational'' Materials Supplied to Schools

Corporate Sponsor	Teaching Material	Promotional Content
Polaroid	*Polaroid Education Program* (lesson book, camera—''A visual approach to teaching basic skills.'')	*High.* Mentions ''Polaroid'' in every lesson and assignment, and requires 10 proofs of film purchase for the camera.
Kodak	*Corkers* (bulletin board ideas) & *Teaching Tips from Kodak* (tips from teachers on using photography to teach)	*Low.* Encourages taking photos but never mentions ''Kodak.''
Chef Boyardee	*Teach . . . Good Nutrition* (Sets of reproducible masters)	*High.* Has its name and logo on every master; names its products in all recipes; and just encourages kids to eat pizza (no nutrition education).
McDonald's	*Nutrient Pursuit* (poster and activity to teach the four basic food groups)	*Low.* Its name isn't on the materials, but its logo is on the masters. Nutrition education is weak.
Tampax	*Mysteries of Me* (lesson plans and masters for three activities)	*High.* Pushes using Tampax by name, gives girls a coupon to order a $3 starter kit or a free sample, and has its name on the poster.

(*continued on following page*)

Consider the ad in Managerial Application 21–2 on page 599. In itself it is a seemingly harmless ad. However, critics would charge that it stresses a narcissistic view of the world by focusing on exercise primarily to enhance a woman's looks rather than her health. When people see such themes repeated thousands of times for hundreds of products, they learn to consider a person's looks to be more important than other attributes. Further, those who cannot afford such products or who are not ''good-looking'' suffer. Others would argue that individuals have been concerned with their looks and possessions in virtually all cultures and times. They argue that advertising does not cause a society's values, it merely reflects them.

EXHIBIT 21–4

Corporate Sponsor	Teaching Material	Promotional Content
Procter & Gamble	*Perspectives* (case studies of P&G's past to teach economics and history)	*Moderate.* Builds P&G's image and talks about its products, but doesn't ''sell.''
	Food Preparation (booklet and worksheets)	*Moderate.* Uses P&G brand-name products in recipes, and includes coupons for free P&G products ''for demonstrations/discussions.''
Reynolds Wrap	*''Preserve Freshness and Flavor with The Best Wrap Around''* poster with teaching guide on back	*High.* Shows more than 30 foods wrapped in aluminum foil; says ''Freeze in it! Cook in it! Store in it!'' All information pushes using foil.
Almond Board of California	*''Everybody's Nuts About Almonds''* poster with teaching guide on back	*High.* Shows only almonds and package; ''Nutrition'' teaching guide shows why almonds are nutritionally superior to other nuts, including peanuts, and why they're so healthy—one-sided and misleading.

Source: *Selling America's Kids* (Yonkers, N.Y.: Consumers Union Educational Services, 1990), pp. 9–10.

Consumer Information Accuracy Consider the package shown in Exhibit 21–5 on page 600. The front panel and side headline strongly imply that the product is ''fat free.'' Yet the ingredients list shows that it contains one gram of fat per serving. Since a serving is 90 calories and a gram of fat is 9 calories, this ''nonfat'' product derives 10 percent of its calories from fat. This could cause problems for individuals on restricted fat diets.

Suppose you saw a snorkel or swim fins with the National Association of Scuba Diving Schools' ''Seal of Approval'' on the package. What would this mean to you? Many of us would interpret it to mean that the product had been tested by the association or was manufactured to conform to a set of standards established by the association. However,

MANAGERIAL APPLICATION

21–1

An Entertainment-Focused Ad

the FTC charged that the seal was *sold* for use on diving products *without tests or standards.*[24]

Because of such problems, various consumer groups and regulatory agencies are deeply concerned with the interpretation of marketing messages.[25] However, determining the exact meaning of a marketing message is not a simple process.[26] Exhibit 21–6 on page 601 illustrates some of the areas where controversy over the interpretation of various marketing messages has existed.

Obtaining accurate assignments of meaning is made even more difficult by the variation in information-processing skills and motivations among differing population groups.[27] For example, this warning was ruled inadequate in a product liability case:

> Always inflate tire in safety cage or use a portable lock ring guard. Use a clip-on type air chuck with remote valve so that operator can stand clear during tire inflation.

MANAGERIAL APPLICATION 21-2

An Ad Emphasizing Beauty

The court held that (1) ''There is a duty to warn *foreseeable* users of all hidden dangers'' and (2) ''in view of the unskilled or semiskilled nature of the work and the existence of many in the workforce who do not read English, warnings *in the form of symbols* might have been appropriate since the employee's ability to take care of himself was limited.''[28] Thus, marketers must often go to considerable lengths to provide messages that the relevant audience will interpret correctly. Fortunately, we are developing considerable knowledge on effectively presenting such difficult messages as product risks, nutrition, and affirmative disclosures, as well as standard messages.[29] Nonetheless, thorough pretesting of messages to consumers is recommended.

The examples above indicate the difficulty of regulating the explicit verbal content of ads. Regulating the more subtle meanings implied by the visual content of ads is much more difficult. For example, some are critical of beer advertisements that portray active young adults in groups having fun and consuming beer. These critics contend that the visual message of these ads is that alcohol consumption is the appropriate way for young adults to be popular and have fun. To date, both government and business self-regulatory

EXHIBIT 21–5 Misleading Packaging?*

GREEN SPRING
LITE TIME
Premium Nonfat Skim
MILK

GREEN SPRING
LITE TIME
Premium Nonfat Skim
MILK

NUTRITION INFORMATION
PER SERVING

SERVING SIZE	ONE CUP
SERVINGS PER CONTAINER	8
CALORIES	90
PROTEIN	9 GRAMS
CARBOHYDRATE	12 GRAMS
FAT	1 GRAM
SODIUM	130mg

PERCENTAGE OF U.S.
RECOMMENDED DAILY
ALLOWANCES (U.S. RDA)

PROTEIN	20	VITAMIN D	25
VITAMIN A	10	VITAMIN B_6	4
VITAMIN C	4	VITAMIN B_{12}	15
THIAMINE	8	PHOSPHORUS	25
RIBOFLAVIN	30	MAGNESIUM	10
NIACIN	0	ZINC	6
CALCIUM	30	PANTOTHENIC ACID	6
IRON	0		

SKIM MILK, WITH VITAMIN D_3
AND VITAMIN A PALMITATE ADDED.

GREEN SPRING DAIRY

*The name of the dairy is fictitious.

groups have avoided attempting to regulate all but the most blatant visual communications. The most controversial current case is the use by R. J. Reynolds of the ''Old Joe the Camel'' character in cigarette ads and packages. Since Old Joe is very popular with children and teenagers, critics contend that R. J. Reynolds in using this symbol to encourage young people to smoke (see Case 6–4).

Generally, advertisers agree to stop running ads that either the government or the Better Business Bureau finds to be misleading. Blatantly misleading ads may result in fines to the firms involved. In addition, the FTC has the right to require corrective advertising. **Corrective advertising** *is advertising run by a firm to cause consumers to ''unlearn'' inaccurate information they acquired as a result of the firm's earlier advertising.*[30] Three examples of corrective advertising messages are:

- ''Do you recall some of our past messages saying that Domino sugar gives you strength, energy, and stamina? Actually, Domino is not a special or unique source of strength, energy, and stamina. No sugar is, because what you need is a balanced diet and plenty of rest and exercise.''

  (To be run in one of every four ads for one year.)

EXHIBIT 21-6

Regulation and the Interpretation of Marketing Messages

- The 4th U.S. Circuit Court of Appeals ruled that meat from a turkey thigh can be called a ''turkey ham'' even if it contains no pork. A lower court had reached the opposite conclusion. The ruling appeared to rely heavily on a technical definition of the term *ham*.
- Maximum Strength Anacin's claim that it is ''the maximum strength allowed'' was ruled illegal because it ''implies that an appropriate authority has authorized the sale of products like Maximum Strength Anacin.'' No such authorization exists.
- The Association of Petroleum Re-Refiners petitioned the FTC to reconsider its Trade Regulation Rule which requires all re-refined oil products to ''clearly and conspicuously'' label the origin of the product. This has meant that ''made from used oil'' appears on all labels. The association feels that this disparages the quality of such lubricants, and they want to use the phrase ''recycled oil product'' instead.
- The National Advertising Division (NAD) of the Council of Better Business Bureaus stated that ads which contained statements like ''savings up to *X* percent'' should have at least 10 percent of the total sale items reduced by the maximum shown in the ad.
- The Florida Citrus Commission is challenging the right of Procter & Gamble's Citrus Hill Plus Calcium and Coca-Cola Foods' Minute Maid Calcium Fortified orange juices to use the label ''100% juice'' or ''100% pure'' or ''juice.'' If *anything* is added to the natural product, the Florida commission requires that it be labeled a beverage or drink, not a juice. The FDA has a more liberal regulation.
- Keebler Company's claim of ''Baked not fried'' for Wheatables and Munch'ems snack crackers was challenged before the NAD. While the crackers are baked, they are sprayed with vegetable oil after baking and have a fat content similar to fried products.
- The National Advertising Review Board is considering an appeal by Stone Container Corp. of NAD rulings against its claims of ''environmentally safe,'' ''all-natural paper bags,'' and ''biodegradable and recyclable paper'' for its Yard Master lawn bags. The NAD ruled that ''environmentally safe'' is too general, since consumers might not realize the claim doesn't apply to the source materials, the manufacturing process or all uses of the product. Although the bags are made from wood products, the NAD ruled they are not ''all natural'' since intensive chemical and physical treatments are used during manufacturing. And, although the bags are biodegradable when composted, the NAD felt that the necessity for composting should be clearly described in the claims.

- ''If you've wondered what some of our earlier advertising meant when we said Ocean Spray cranberry juice cocktail has more food energy than orange juice or tomato juice, let us make it clear: we didn't mean vitamins and minerals. Food energy means calories. Nothing more.

  ''Food energy is important at breakfast since many of us may not get enough calories, or food energy, to get off to a good start. Ocean Spray cranberry juice cocktail helps because it contains more food energy than most other breakfast drinks.

  ''And Ocean Spray cranberry juice cocktail gives you and your family vitamin C plus a great wake-up taste. It's . . . the other breakfast drink.''

  (To be run in one of every four ads for one year.)
- Sugar Information, Inc.: ''Do you recall the messages we brought you in the past about sugar? How something with sugar in it before meals could help you curb your appetite? We hope you didn't get the idea that our little diet tip was any magic formula for losing weight. Because there are no tricks or shortcuts; the whole diet subject is very complicated. Research hasn't established that consuming sugar before meals will contribute to weight reduction or even keep you from gaining weight.''

  (To be run for one insertion in each of seven magazines.)[31]

Adequacy of Consumer Information It is important that consumers have not only accurate information, but adequate information as well. To ensure information adequacy, a number of laws have been passed, such as the federal truth-in-lending legislation. This law requires full disclosure of finance charges and other aspects of credit transactions.

Nutritional labeling has been required for years and was significantly revised in 1994. While research findings on the impact of such labels is mixed, it does provide valuable information to many consumers. Many experts feel that the 1994 revisions will increase its usefulness. Unfortunately, as with many such programs, those who are relatively disadvantaged in terms of education and income are least able to use this type of information.[32]

Marketers, consumer groups, and public officials would like consumers to have all the information they need to make sound choices. One approach is to provide all potentially relevant information. This approach is frequently recommended by regulatory agencies and is required for some product categories such as drugs. Problems with this approach can arise, however. For example, a relatively simple, one-page advertisement for ModiCon oral contraceptive required a second full page of small type telling of dosage, precautions, and warnings in order to comply with federal full-disclosure regulations (See Case 6–3).

The assumption behind the full-disclosure approach is that each consumer will utilize those specific information items required for the particular decision. Unfortunately, consumers frequently do not react in this manner, particularly for low-involvement purchases. Instead, they may experience *information overload* (see Chapter 9, page 245) and ignore all or most of the available data. For example:

> A federal act required banks belonging to the Federal Reserve to explain to their customers the detailed protections built into money transfer systems available in electronic banking. Thus, Northwestern National Bank of Minneapolis was forced to create and mail a pamphlet explaining Amended Regulation E to its 120,000 customers. At a cost of $69,000 the bank created and mailed the 4,500-word pamphlet.

In 100 of the pamphlets, the bank placed a special paragraph that offered the reader $10 just for finding that paragraph. The pamphlets were mailed in May and June. As of August, not one person had claimed the money![33]

Product Issues

Consumer groups have two major concerns with products—*Is it safe?* and *Is it environmentally sound?* A variety of federal and state agencies are involved in assuring that products are safe to use. The most important are the Food and Drug Administration and the Consumer Product Safety Commission. Product safety is generally not a controversial issue. However, it is impossible to remove all risk from products.

Should tricycles be banned? Accidents involving tricycles are a major cause of injury to young children. Manufacturers, consumer groups, and individuals differ on where the line should be drawn and who should draw it. Some feel that tricycles should indeed be banned. Others feel that parents should decide if their children should ride tricycles. However, both would agree that information on both the risks of tricycle riding and ways of reducing the risk should be made available to purchasers (though there is disagreement on who should make the data available and how it should be made available). Of course, tricycles represent only one of many products subject to such a debate.

We examined consumers' desires for environmentally sound products in some detail in Chapter 3 (pages 70–71). As indicated there, many consumers want products whose production, use, and disposition produce minimal environmental harm. Many marketers are striving to produce such products. Nonetheless, many consumer groups want regulations requiring faster movement in this area and required rather than voluntary compliance with environmental standards.

Pricing Issues

Consumer groups want prices that are fair (generally defined as competitively determined) and accurately stated (contain no hidden charges). The Federal Trade Commission is the primary federal agency involved in regulating pricing activities.

Unit pricing is the presentation of price information on a common basis such as per ounce across brands. Such information, when properly displayed, can greatly facilitate price comparisons.

Perhaps the most controversial pricing area today is the use of reference prices. A **reference price** is a price provided by the manufacturer or retailer in addition to the actual current price of the product. Such terms as *Compare at $X, Usually $X, Suggested retail price $Y—Our price only $X* are common ways of presenting reference prices. The concern arises when the reference price is one at which no or few sales actually occur. While most states and the federal government have regulations concerning the use of reference prices, they are difficult to enforce and many consumers are skeptical of them.[34]

CAUSE MARKETING

Cause marketing is the application of marketing principles and tactics to advance a cause, such as a charity (United Way), an ideology (environmental protection), or an activity (exercise). It differs from traditional marketing (including services and not-for-profit marketing) in the completely intangible and abstract nature of the "product." At one extreme, such as a health-related campaign, there are potential direct benefits to the individual. However, in general, the benefits to the individual are very indirect (a better society in which to live). Often, the benefit is purely or primarily emotional.[35] Individuals are

MANAGERIAL APPLICATION

21–3

Ads that Market Causes

requested to change beliefs or behaviors, or provide funds because it is "the right thing to do" and you will "feel good" or "be a better person" because of it.

Examine the two ads in Managerial Application 21–3. What are the benefits being promised to those who respond? Why would an individual "buy" one of these "products"? Why do most individuals fail to "purchase" the "products" advertised in these ads?

Cause marketing is an exciting area because there are many worthwhile causes and the challenge of marketing ideas is unique. However, the approach should be exactly the same as marketing a product. That is, the marketer is trying to "sell" the cause and the potential donor or believer is the same as a potential customer.

The process is the same as described in Figure 1–2 (page 6). Individuals engaged in cause marketing need to engage in the same types of analyses and market segmentation procedures as do product marketers. They also need to manipulate those aspects of the marketing mix they can control in light of the anticipated decision processes of their target markets.

SUMMARY

Consumerism is a loose, unstructured social movement with the purpose of enhancing the power of buyers relative to the power of sellers. The current consumerism movement began in the 1960s as large numbers of consumers became increasingly dissatisfied with marketing practices. However, such nonmarketing forces as the increasing technological sophistication of products, increased time and financial pressures on many families, and consumer choices which produced an impersonal marketplace have also contributed to the consumerism movement.

Consumer groups often attempt to change the marketing practices of individual firms or industries through discussion, publicity, or boycotts. However, the solution preferred by many groups is governmental regulation. Four major areas of continuing concern to consumer groups and regulators are: marketing to children, consumer information, pricing issues, and product issues.

Marketing to children is a source of increasing concern to the consumerism movement. A major reason for this concern is evidence based on Piaget's *theory of cognitive development* that children are not able to fully comprehend commercial messages. This had led to rules issued by both the Federal Trade Commission (FTC) and the Children's Advertising Review Unit (CARU) of the National Advertising Division of the Council of Better Business Bureaus. These rules focus mainly on being sure that commercials are clearly separated from the program content and that the words and pictures in the commercials do not mislead children having limited cognitive skills.

In addition to concerns about children's comprehension of advertisements, there is concern about the effect of the content of commercials on children. Will commercials cause children to want items that their parents do not want them to have or cannot afford? Denying children's requests might lead to an unhealthy level of family conflict.

The extensive advertising of high-fat and high-sugar products raises a concern about its effect on the health of children. Since children watch a substantial amount of prime-time television, there is also a danger that ads aimed at adults will inspire children to take inappropriate actions.

Finally, there is concern that the enormous amount of advertising that children view will lead to values that are overly materialistic.

There are a number of marketing activities aimed at children other than advertising that cause concerns. *Kids' clubs* with a strong emphasis on sales to children have been strongly criticized. Corporate programs that place strong sales messages in "educational" materials supplied to schools have also come under attack.

The consumerism movement is also concerned that adults receive accurate and adequate information about products. The impact of numerous ads that focus on narcissistic values and product ownership on society's values is a controversial issue.

The consumerism movement, regulators, and responsible marketers want consumers to have sufficient, adequate information to make sound purchase decisions. Attempts to regulate the amount of information provided sometimes overlooks *information overload* and are not effective.

The focus of the consumerism movement on products is twofold: *Is it safe?* and *Is it environmentally sound?*

Concern with pricing is that prices be *fair* and *accurately presented* in a manner that allows comparison across brands.

Cause marketing is the application of marketing principles and tactics to advance a cause, such as a charity, an ideology, or proper nutrition. It should be based on the same behavioral principles and marketing practices as products marketing.

REVIEW QUESTIONS

1. What is the *consumerism movement*? What are its objectives?
2. What is the *Consumers' Bill of Rights*?
3. What caused the consumerism movement to come into existence?
4. What are the major concerns in marketing to children?
5. What is a major reason for particular concern about marketing to children?
6. Describe Piaget's stages of cognitive development.
7. What are the two main issues concerning children's ability to comprehend advertising messages?
8. What is *CARU*? What does it do? What are some of its rules?
9. What are the major concerns about the content of commercial messages on children?
10. How can advertisements to children create family conflict?
11. What are the issues concerning the impact of advertising on children's health and safety?
12. What are the issues concerning the impact of advertising on children's values?
13. What are the concerns associated with kids' clubs sponsored by commercial firms?
14. How do firms advertise in the classroom? What issues does this raise?
15. What is Consumers Union's recommendation concerning advertising in the classroom?
16. What are the issues concerning the impact of advertising on adults' values?
17. What are the concerns with consumer information accuracy?
18. What are the concerns with consumer information adequacy?
19. What is *information overload*?
20. What is *corrective advertising*?
21. What are the major consumerism issues with respect to products?
22. What are the major consumerism issues with respect to prices?
23. What is *unit pricing*?
24. What is a *reference price*? What is the concern with reference prices?
25. What is *cause marketing*?
26. What special techniques are required for cause marketing?

DISCUSSION QUESTIONS

27. A television advertisement for General Mills's Total cereal made the following claim: ''It would take 16 ounces of the leading natural cereal to equal the vitamins in 1 ounce of fortified Total.'' The Center for Science in the Public Interest filed a petition against General Mills claiming that the advertisement is deceptive. It was the center's position that the claim overstated Total's nutritional benefits because the cereal is not 16 times higher in other factors important to nutrition.
    a. Is the claim misleading? Justify your answer.
    b. How should the FTC proceed in cases such as this?
    c. What are the implications of cases such as this for marketing management?
28. In recent years, manufacturers of meat products have introduced a product labeled as ''turkey ham.'' The product looks like ham and tastes like ham but it contains no pork; it is all turkey. A nationwide survey of consumers showed that most believed that the meat product contained both turkey and ham. The USDA approved this label based on a dictionary definition for the technical term *ham*: the thigh cut of meat from the hind leg of any animal. Discuss how consumers processed information concerning this product and used this information in purchasing this product. (One court ruled the label to be misleading but was overruled by a higher court.)
    a. Is the label misleading?
    b. How should the FTC proceed in such cases?
29. The FTC has required manufacturers to produce corrective advertisements in cases in which the manufacturer deceived the public

with a particular claim or implied claim that was not true. The purpose of the corrective ad is to properly inform the public so they are not deceived in their perceptions of a particular brand. When this is accomplished, the firm may remove the corrective ad. This is based on the assumption that new learning has occurred. Some feel that after the corrective ad is removed, it is only a matter of time before consumer perceptions of the falsely advertised product will return to their prior level. Do you agree? Why?

30. Do you consider yourself to be a consumerist? Why, or why not?
31. What, if anything, would you add to the *Consumers' Bill of Rights*?
32. What factors, in addition to those discussed in the chapter, helped cause the consumerism movement?
33. How strong is the consumerism movement?
34. How much, if any, advertising should be allowed on television programs aimed at children?
35. What do you think of the rules in Exhibit 21–1?
36. Can television commercials cause unhealthy levels of family conflict? What should CARU or the FTC do to limit this danger?
37. Should there be special rules governing the advertising of food and snack products to children?
38. Does advertising influence children's values? What can the FTC and/or CARU do to ensure that positive values are promoted? Be precise in your response.
39. What rules, if any, should govern kids' clubs?
40. Does the Burger King Kids Club meet the requirements recommended by Consumers Union?
41. Does the Nickelodeon Club meet the requirements recommended by Consumers Union?
42. What rules, if any, should govern advertising and promotional messages presented in the classroom?
43. Do you agree that the ad in Managerial Application 21–2 promotes a narcissistic value set?
44. Does advertising influence or reflect a society's values?
45. What is your opinion of the package shown in Exhibit 21–5?
46. What is your opinion on each of the cases described in Exhibit 21–6?
47. Do you agree that beer advertisements portraying groups of active young adults having fun while consuming beer teach people that the way to be popular and have fun is to consume alcohol?
48. Do you think corrective advertising works? Evaluate the three corrective messages described in the text.
49. Since riding tricycles is a major cause of accidental injury to young children, the product should be banned. State and defend your position on this issue.
50. To what extent, if at all, do you use nutrition labels? Why?
51. To what extent, is at all, do you use unit prices?
52. Describe any cause marketing activities that you recall. Did any of these cause you to do anything (including change an attitude)? Why? Why did the others have no impact?
53. Do you believe reference prices generally reflect prices at which substantial amounts of the product are normally sold?

APPLICATION EXERCISES

54. Interview 10 students and determine their degree of concern and activities with respect to consumerism issues. What do you conclude?
55. Watch two hours of Saturday morning children's programming on a commercial channel. Note how many commercials are run. What products are involved? What are the major themes? Would hundreds of hours of viewing these commercials over the course of several years have any impact on children's values?
56. Interview a child 2 to 4 years of age, one between 5 and 7, and one between 8 and 10. Determine their understanding of the selling intent and techniques of television commercials.
57. Interview two children who belong to one or more kids' clubs. Describe the club and the

child's reactions to it. Determine the extent to which the club is successful in selling things to the child.

58. Interview two grade school teachers and get their responses to material provided by corporations and Consumers Union's proposed rules for such materials.

59. Repeat question 55 for prime time television and adults.

60. Find and copy or describe two ads that you feel are misleading. Justify your selection.

61. Visit a large supermarket. Identify the best and worst breakfast cereal considering both cost and nutrition. What do you conclude?

REFERENCES

[1]S. W. Colford, "FTC Green Guidelines May Spark Ad Efforts," *Advertising Age*, August 3, 1992, pp. 1+.

[2]*Message from the President of the United States Relative to Consumers' Protection and Interest Program*, Document No. 364, House of Representatives, 87th Congress, 2d session, March 15, 1962.

[3]See Chapter 9, footnote 53.

[4]For detailed coverage of this area see G. M. Armstrong and M. Brucks, "Dealing with Children's Advertising," *Journal of Public Policy & Marketing* 7 (1988), pp. 98–113.

[5]See M. G. Hoy, C. E. Young, and J. C. Mowen, "Animated Host-Selling Advertisements," *Journal of Public Policy and Marketing* 5 (1986), 171–84; M. C. Macklin, "Preschoolers' Understanding of the Information Function of Television Advertising," *Journal of Consumer Research*, September 1987, pp. 229–39; and M. Brucks, G. M. Armstrong, and M. E. Goldberg, "Children's Use of Cognitive Defenses against Television Advertising," *Journal of Consumer Research*, March 1988, pp. 471–82.

[6]"NAD Slams Spot from Mattel," *Advertising Age*, October 19, 1987, p. 6; and S. Weinstein, "Fight Heats up against Kids' TV 'Commershows'," *Marketing News*, October 9, 1989, p. 2.

[7]M. A. Stutts and G. G. Hunnicutt, "Can Young Children Understand Disclaimers?" *Journal of Advertising*, no. 1 (1987), pp. 41–46.

[8]"VLI Is Challenged," *Advertising Age*, February 16, 1987, p. 12.

[9]"NAD Ruling Gives Total Victory," *Advertising Age*, July 17, 1989, p. 41.

[10]S. W. Colford, "FTC Hits Galoob, Agency for Ads," *Advertising Age*, December 10, 1990, p. 62.

[11]R. Weisskoff, "Current Trends in Children's Advertising," *Journal of Advertising Research*, March 1985, pp. 12–14.

[12]C. K. Atkin, *The Effects of Television Advertising on Children*, report submitted to Office of Child Development, 1975. See also L. Isler, E. T. Popper, and S. Ward, "Children's Purchase Requests and Parental Responses," *Journal of Advertising Research*, November 1987, pp. 28–39.

[13]J. Dagnoli, "Consumers Union Hits Kids Advertising," *Advertising Age*, July 23, 1990, p. 4.

[14]"B-M Drops Spots after Query by NAD," *Advertising Age*, April 20, 1981, p. 10.

[15]See D. L. Scammon and C. L. Christopher, "Nutrition Education with Children via Television: A Review," *Journal of Advertising*, Second Quarter 1981, pp. 26–36.

[16]A. R. Wiman and L. M. Newman, "Television Advertising and Children's Nutritional Awareness," *Journal of the Academy of Marketing Science*, Spring 1989, pp. 179–88.

[17]E. DeNitto, "Fast-Food Ads Come under Fire," *Advertising Age*, February 14, 1994, p. S-14.

[18]S. W. Colford, "Top Kid TV Offender: Premiums," *Advertising Age*, April 29, 1991, p. 52.

[19]See *Selling America's Kids* (Yonkers, N.Y.: Consumers Union Educational Services, 1990).

[20]C. Miller, "Marketers Hoping Kids Will Join Club," *Marketing News*, January 31, 1994, pp. 1–2.

[21]See footnote 19, p. 15.

[22]See footnote 20, p. 2.

[23]See footnote 19, p. 14.

[24]"Diving Association May Not Use 'Seal of Approval' Unless Based on Tests," *FTC New Summary*, May 21, 1982, p. 1.

[25]G. T. Ford and J. E. Calfee, "Recent Developments in FTC Policy on Deception," *Journal of Marketing*, July 1986, pp. 82–103; G. E. Miracle and T. R. Nevett, "Improving NAD/NARB Self-Regulation of Advertising," *Journal of Public Policy and Marketing* 7 (1988), pp. 114–26.

[26]K. G. Grunert and K. Dedler, "Misleading Advertising," *Journal of Public Policy and Marketing* 4 (1985), pp. 153–65; and P. N. Bloom, "A Decision Model for Prioritizing and Addressing Consumer Information Problems," *Journal of Public Policy and Marketing* 8 (1989), pp. 161–80.

[27]G. J. Gaeth and T. B. Heath, "The Cognitive Processing of Misleading Advertising," *Journal of Consumer Research*, June 1987, pp. 43–54; C. A. Cole and G. J. Gaeth, "Cognitive and Age-Related Differences in the Ability to Use Nutritional Information in a Complex Environment," *Journal of Marketing Research*, May 1990, pp. 175–84; and W. Mueller, "Who Reads the Label?" *American Demographics*, January 1991, pp. 36–40.

[28]B. Reid, "Adequacy of Symbolic Warnings," *Marketing News*, October 25, 1985, p. 3.

[29]J. R. Bettman, J. W. Payne, and R. Staelin, "Cognitive Considerations in Designing Effective Labels for Presenting Risk Information"; M. Venkatesan, W. Lancaster, and K. W. Kendall, "An Empirical Study of Alternate Formats for Nutritional Information Disclosure," both in *Journal of Public Policy & Marketing* 5

(1986), pp. 1–28, and pp. 29–43; R. Snyder, ''Misleading Characteristics of Implied-Superiority Claims,'' *Journal of Advertising*, no. 4 (1989), pp. 54–61; and C. Moorman, ''The Effects of Stimulus and Consumer Characteristics on the Utilization of Nutrition Information,'' *Journal of Consumer Research*, December 1990, pp. 362–74.

[30]See W. L. Wilkie, D. L. McNeill, and M. B. Mazis, ''Marketing's 'Scarlet Letter',*'' Journal of Marketing*, Spring 1984, pp. 11–31.

[31]J. P. Peter and J. C. Olson, *Understanding Consumer Behavior* (Burr Ridge, Ill.: Richard D. Irwin, 1994), pp. 413–14.

[32]See footnote 29.

[33]''$10 Sure Thing,'' *Time*, August 4, 1980, p. 51.

[34]See Chapter 18, footnote 14.

[35]See R. P. Bagozzi and D. J. Moore, ''Public Service Advertisements,'' *Journal of Marketing*, January 1994, pp. 56–70.

SECTION 6 CASES

Case 6–1 Code of Comparative Price Advertising of the Better Business Bureaus, Inc.

In the fall of 1988, the Council of Better Business Bureaus began to develop voluntary guidelines for comparative price advertising. The goal was to promote truthful and helpful advertising that is productive for retailers, acceptable to consumer protection officials, and informative for consumers. In September 1989, an initial *draft* of the *proposed* guidelines was distributed for comments to a wide range of firms, individuals, and organizations. A portion of the *draft* is contained below.

Draft Guidelines

1. Comparative Price, Value, and Savings Claims

Advertisers may offer a price reduction or savings by comparing their selling price with:

1. Their own former price.
2. The current price of identical merchandise offered by others in the market area.
3. The current price of comparable merchandise offered by others in the market area.
4. A manufacturer's list price.

When any one of these comparisons is made in advertising, the claim should be based on, and substantiated in accordance with, the criteria set forth below. Savings claims should be substantiated on the basis of evidence existing when the claim is made, or, if the advertising must be submitted in advance of publication, a reasonable time prior to when the claim is made.

Most consumers reasonably expect that claims of price reductions expressed in terms of a percent "off" or a specific dollar "saving" are reductions or savings from an advertiser's own former price. Accordingly, unless the savings claimed is in fact based on the advertiser's own former price, the basis for the reduction (item 2, 3, or 4 above) should be affirmatively disclosed, such as, "Buy from us and save $50. Sold elsewhere at $199. Our price $149." For example, it would be misleading for an advertiser, without explanation, to claim a savings from a "ticketed price" if the advertiser could not establish that the "ticketed price" was a genuine former price.

* * *

b. Comparison with Current Price of Identical Merchandise Sold by Others

(1) General In retail advertisements, external price comparisons are utilized with frequency. Such a marketing technique, if done fairly and nondeceptively, can enhance competition in the marketplace to the benefit of consumers.

The comparative price should represent a prevailing price, offered in representative principal retail outlets in the market area, and not merely an isolated and unrepresentative price. The comparative price should be such that the consumer would consider the advertiser's lower price to be a saving. An advertiser should not rely on competitors' prices as comparisons to its own price in situations where the advertiser has substantial reason to doubt whether the competitors' prices are genuine and bona fide.

(2) Representative Principal Retail Outlets Principal retail outlets will generally be those outlets that offer the merchandise being advertised and individually or collectively represent a significant share of the market for the merchandise.

A representative sample must at least include a reasonable cross section of principal retail outlets. Factors such as location, size, and pricing methodologies are some examples of relevant considerations in selecting the cross section of outlets. Relying on representative outlets will help advertisers avoid the implication that consumers may not be able to find prices lower than the advertiser's, when that is not the case.

Unless the advertiser compares its own usual or regular price to usual or regular prices of the representative principal retail outlets, the advertiser should disclose the basis for all prices used in the comparison, that is, whether the advertiser's and the competitor prices are regular or sale prices.

For example, the following would be considered a deceptive price comparison. ''Offered elsewhere at $25, Our price $15.'' In this case, only a few, smaller outlying stores offer the product at $25. All of the larger stores located near the advertiser's store offer that product for less than $25. Thus, $25 is not a prevailing price in the market area and the consumer may not be getting a genuine bargain.

(3) Market or Trade Area A market or trade area is the area in which the advertiser does business. The responsibilities of the advertiser may vary with the breadth of the advertiser's trade area and the scope of the comparative price claim, i.e., whether the comparative claim is unqualified or limited in scope.

For instance, if the advertiser does not define the trade areas in the advertisement (Offered elsewhere at $9.99. Our price $7.99), the advertiser should be prepared to substantiate that the competition's price is the prevailing price charged by representative principal retail outlets in each area in which the advertising was principally disseminated.

If, on the other hand, the advertiser specifically circumscribes the scope of its claim in a clear and conspicuous manner (''Offered in major department stores in the ten largest cities in America for $189 to $199, our price $149.99''), the advertiser should be prepared to substantiate the prevailing prices in representative principal outlets in the specific trade areas referenced. Care should also be taken with this type of claim to assure that markets selected within the trade area are representative. The advertiser should also disclose clearly and conspicuously that prices in the community where the ad is disseminated may vary from those found in the areas described in the claim.

(4) Descriptive Terminology Descriptive terminology used by advertisers includes: ''Sold elsewhere at $_______.'' ''Offered by _______ for $49.99, Our price $41.99.'' ''Our price 20% below prices elsewhere.''

* * *

g. Sale

(1) An advertiser may use terms implying a reduction in price from a price in effect before the advertisement (such as, but not limited to, ''sale,'' ''sale prices'' or ''now only $'') if there is a significant reduction from the advertiser's bona fide former price in effect before the advertisement and the sale opportunity is for a limited period of time.

However, notwithstanding the previous sentence, an advertiser may use terms offering a sale regardless of the size of the reduction offered so long as the actual percentage or dollar amount of the reduction is clearly and conspicuously disclosed.

If the sale exceeds thirty days the advertiser should be prepared to substantiate that the offering is indeed a valid reduction and has not become the regular price.

Substantiation of the implied former price should meet the tests described in Section 1.a with respect to comparisons to a stated former price.

(2) The term ''sale'' or similar terms may be used where not all items appearing in the advertisement are reduced in price from the advertiser's own price if the advertisement clearly distinguishes the items which are reduced in price from those which are not, and a significant percentage of items in the advertisement are reduced from the advertiser's own price.

(3) The day after the ''sale'' ends the advertiser shall increase the price of the items reduced in price to the price charged by the advertiser before the ''sale'' or to a price which is higher than the ''sale'' price. Time limits advertised in sales with specified durations (for example, ''one day only,'' ''three-day sale,'') should be strictly observed. The requirement to increase the price after the ''sale'' shall not apply however to clearance (when the retailer is liquidating inventory from its own stock and does not replenish inventory), closeout or permanent markdown items which the advertiser expects not to have available for sale for a reasonable period of time after the sale ends, provided the advertiser either (a) discloses that the items are clearance, closeout, or permanent

markdown, or (b) does not subsequently advertise the price reduction as a ''sale.''

(4) An advertiser may use the terms ''introductory sale,'' ''will be'' or terms of similar meaning to refer to savings from a higher price at which an item will be offered in the future, provided that the item is increased in price the day after the sale ends, and the sale is for a limited period of time.

(5) Price predictions—advertisers may currently advertise future increases in their own prices on a subsequent date provided that they do, in fact, increase the price to the stated amount on that date and maintain it for a reasonably substantial period of time thereafter.

* * *

i. ''Up to'' Savings Claims

Savings or price reduction claims covering a group of items with a range of savings should state both the minimum and maximum savings without undue or misleading display of the maximum. The number of items available at the maximum savings should comprise a significant percentage, typically 10%, of all the items in the offering, unless local or state law requires otherwise.

j. Price Matching and Lowest Price Claims

(1) Definitions and General Standards A price-matching claim is an offer to consumers stating that if they find a competitor's price that is lower than the advertiser's price for any product covered by the claim, the advertiser will reduce its price for that product to that consumer so that the competitor's price will be matched or beaten. Price-matching claims should satisfy the criteria in paragraph (2).

A lowest-price claim is one in which a factual representation is made, explicitly or implicitly, that the advertiser has the lowest prices in the market area for every product covered by the claim. Lowest-price claims are difficult, if not impossible, to substantiate and advertisers should use great caution before making such a claim. Lowest-price claims should satisfy the criteria in paragraph (3).

It is very important that clear and understandable language be used to describe a price-matching or lowest-price claim in order to avoid communicating an offer that is not really intended by the advertiser. For example, when an advertiser intends to make a price-matching claim and does not intend to represent that it has determined that no competitors sell any of the covered products for less, it should be careful not to use language with superlatives such as ''lowest'' or ''best'' to describe its prices.

Some claims can reasonably be interpreted either as price-matching or lowest-price claims even if superlatives are not used, depending on the context and layout of the advertising. Examples of such a claim are ''We will not be undersold'' or ''Lower price guarantee.'' If such claims are not qualified in any way the advertiser should be prepared to substantiate them as lowest-price claims, since without explanation they are likely to be interpreted as such by consumers. However, if a clear and conspicuous disclosure of a price-matching policy, including its terms and conditions, accompanies this type of claim, and is stated in close conjunction with the claim, it may be used to promote a price-matching pledge so long as the criteria in paragraph (2) are satisfied.

Some claims are not reasonably susceptible to any interpretation other than as lowest-price claims (such as ''lowest prices guaranteed''), and no inconsistent accompanying language should be used to promote matching programs unless the advertiser is prepared to substantiate the lowest-price claim.

(2) Price Matching An advertiser using a price-matching pledge in its advertising must disclose all material terms and conditions in a clear and conspicuous manner in any print advertisement in which there is a reference to the pledge. Included in the disclosure of the terms and conditions should be any evidence the consumer will be required to provide. Subsequent references in multipage advertisements should, in a clear and conspicuous manner, refer the consumer to the appropriate location of the full disclosure. Any advertisements on the radio or television that refer to the price-matching pledge should disclose that an explanation of the program is available at a specific location, i.e., retail stores. Any advertiser that offers products to the public at a retail location should conspicuously disclose the full-price matching pledge at that retail location through signing or otherwise communicating the material terms and conditions to the public.

The evidence required of a competitor's price should not place an unealistic or unreasonable burden on the consumer. An advertiser may require a consumer to present verifiable evidence of a competitor's selling price such as a competitor's current advertisement. An example of an unrealistic burden is requiring completed sales contracts or actual purchases at a competitor's store prior to matching that price.

When a price-matching claim is made, the manufacturer's model number or model name should be disclosed in the advertising or made avilable upon request in the retail store in order to allow consumers to be able to take advantage of the pledge.

A price-matching pledge should accurately state the scope of the pledge so that consumers will reasonably be placed on notice if any items carried and/or advertised by the advertiser are not covered by the pledge. The advertiser should make information about the scope of the pledge readily available to consumers on request at the retail location.

Examples of language that convey a price-matching pledge are as follows:

> ''We'll match any store's advertised price on name brand products''; ''We'll meet the competition's current advertised price on the identical item''; and ''We guarantee we'll match your best price.''

(3) Lowest-Price Claims A factual claim that an advertiser's prices are the lowest in a market area requires systematic, timely, and ongoing monitoring of all competitors and all products covered by the claim. Unverifiable claims should not be used.

Despite an advertiser's best efforts to ascertain competitive prices, the rapidity with which prices fluctuate and the difficulty of determining prices of all sellers at all times preclude an absolute knowledge of the truth of generalized lowest-price claims. Thus, if the claim purports to cover a large number of competitors or a large number of items, it is not likely that any monitoring program could be fashioned to assure the accuracy of the claim.

Narrow claims covering few items and few competitors, while still difficult to substantiate, may be more susceptible to substantiation than generalized claims. Even in the case of narrower claims the advertiser should be prepared to adjust its prices immediately if a competitor lowers its price during the period in which the advertiser's claim is applicable. Examples of representations that convey a lowest-price claim are as follows:

> ''We undersell everyone''; ''Our prices beat the competition''; ''Our prices are the best''; ''Lowest prices''; ''Guaranteed lowest prices''; ''We guarantee our prices are the lowest''; ''Nobody sells for less.''

Discussion Question

1. Evaluate the *proposed* guidelines in light of your knowledge of consumer information processing.

People for the Ethical Treatment of Animals

Case 6–2

PETA, People for the Ethical Treatment of Animals, conducts a strong anti-fur campaign as part of its overall mission. Kim Stallwood, PETA's executive director, describes their program as follows:

> As part of PETA's mission to end all abuse and exploitation of animals, the objective of PETA's anti-fur campaign is to take the profit out of trapping animals and raising them on fur ''farms'' (sometimes called ''ranches'') by dissuading people from buying or wearing fur coats and accessories.
>
> One of our most effective efforts to prevent people from buying fur has been the placing of print advertisements in *Interview* and *Details* magazines. These highly visible publications related to fashion reach many potential fur buyers.
>
> Another important activity has been the Rock Against Fur (RAF) concerts of 1989 and 1990. This year's RAF was organized by PETA and Ron Delsener Enterprises and was held in New York's Palladium. For this event, several rock stars and bands donated their talents to raise funds for PETA's anti-fur campaign. Thousands

EXHIBIT A

> attended, and many newspaper articles resulted from the concerts.
>
> We also have organized many anti-fur demonstrations, including a recent one at the Seattle Fur Exchange. A few months ago, we held a champagne celebration outside the premises of a prominent Washington, D.C., area fur store that had just announced it was going out of business.

PETA's current campaign involves top fashion photographer Steven Klein and supermodel Christy Turlington. This campaign, which features Ms. Turlington shown nude in a billboard above Hollywood's Sunset Strip (see Exhibit A), has generated tremendous publicity for PETA and the anti-fur movement. Both Turlington and Klein donated their time and talents. Ms. Turlington modeled fur until four years ago when she learned more about the nature of the industry. Now she not only refuses to wear fur, she refuses to appear in photos where others are wearing it.

Discussion Questions

1. Evaluate PETA's marketing strategy.
2. Evaluate the strategy of using Ms. Turlington in the billboard.
3. Develop a strategy for PETA to reduce fur use.
4. If you were the fur industry, how would you counter PETA's actions?

Case 6–3 Consumer Advertising of ORTHO-NOVUM® 7/7/7 Birth Control Pills

In late 1992, Ortho Pharmaceutical launched the first broad-scale national advertising campaign to feature a branded oral contraceptive (and one of the first for any prescription drug). The three-page ad appeared in such magazines as *Glamour, Mademoiselle, Self, Vogue, Health,* and *People.* Since then a number of other prescription drugs have been advertised directly to consumers. However, the number thus advertised is smaller than one would expect, given the volume of prescription drug sales and consumers' desires for information.

Marketers place part of the blame for their limited advertising in this area on the Food and Drug

EXHIBIT A

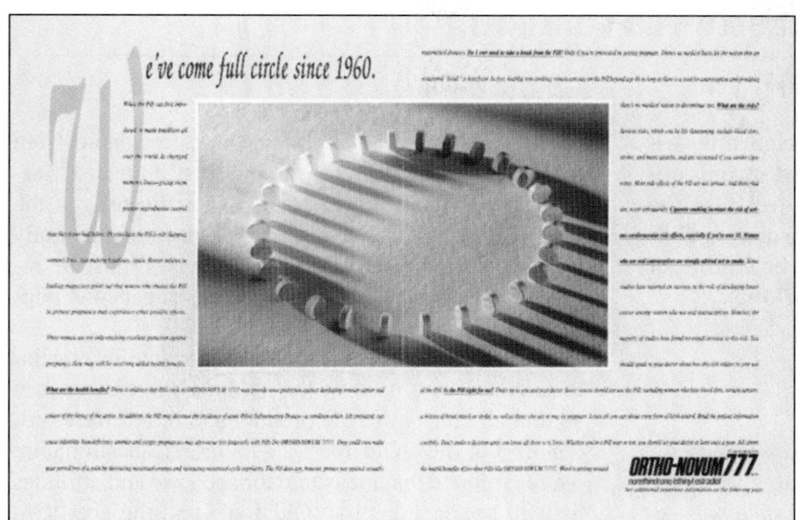

Administration's (FDA) rules. Advertising critics are also critical of the FDA rules in this area. Both marketers and consumer activists object to the amount of information the FDA requires marketers to provide and the way it is provided.

The FDA rules were developed for advertisements directed at medical doctors. When pharmaceutical firms began considering advertising to consumers, the same rules were applied. The basic requirements are:

- If the drug and its use are identified, the marketer must provide a "brief summary" of product data. In addition, the ad copy itself must clearly indicate potential hazards and limits.
- Ads that discuss a disease but that do not name a specific product do not have to include the "brief summary."

Thus, an ad that stated "There is now a cure for baldness, see your doctor" without naming a product would not have to present the "brief summary" or discuss potential hazards in the copy of the ad. This requirement is not controversial. Likewise, the requirement that the ad copy be fair and balanced in terms of presenting risks as well as benefits is not controversial in principle though disagreements arise in particular cases. It is the "brief summary" that both marketers and consumer activists object to.

Exhibit A contains Ortho's ad for ORTHO-NOVUM® 7/7/7. The ad was a two-page spread with an additional page immediately following. The following page is the "brief summary"! Virtually any prescription drug ad would require a brief summary with similar details. Presenting such summaries clearly increases the cost of the ad. In fact, it would almost double the cost of a full-page ad. This clearly reduces the amount of such advertising available to consumers.

Dr. Sidney Wolfe, director of Public Citizen's Health Research Group (a consumerist group) also objects to the "brief summary" requirement. However, he objects because a marketer could place vital information about the dangers of a drug in the brief summary and few consumers would ever read it. (No one has made such claims about the Ortho ad in this case. In fact it has been praised as a model ad.)

Discussion Questions

1. Evaluate Ortho's ad.
2. What percent of the people who read the first two pages of the Ortho ad will read the "brief summary"?
3. Evaluate the FDA's rules. Develop a superior set of rules to govern prescription drug advertising aimed at consumers.

Source: J. Weber and J. Carey, "Drug Ads," *Business Week*, January 18, 1993, pp. 58–59; and material supplied by Ortho Pharmaceutical Corporation.

Case 6–4 "Old Joe the Camel" Cigarette Advertising

R. J. Reynolds' advertising of Camel cigarettes using "Old Joe the Camel" has aroused strong opposition from numerous groups who feel that the cartoon character encourages smoking among children and teenagers. The results of three studies of Old Joe and children are described below.

Study A

High school students from Georgia, Massachusetts, Nebraska, New Mexico, and Washington were the teenage subjects. One school from each state was selected, based on its administration's willingness to participate. A target of 60 students in each grade, 9 through 12, was set. Classes were selected to provide a sample of students at all levels of academic ability. The students were told that the study involved advertising and that their participation would be anonymous. The obtained sample size was 1,055.

Since adult brand preferences are available from national studies, the adult sample was limited to Massachusetts. All drivers renewing their licenses at the Registry of Motor Vehicles on the days of the study were asked to participate. Since licenses must be renewed in person, this provided a heterogeneous population. This produced a sample of 345.

Seven "Old Joe" ads that had appeared in popular magazines were used in the study. One was masked so that all clues as to the product and brand were hidden except the "Old Joe" character. A questionnaire was developed that measured tobacco use and attitudes as well as reactions to "Old Joe" and the six "Old Joe" ads.

Subjects were first shown the masked ad and asked if they had seen the "Old Joe" character before and the product and brand he represents. They then were shown the six ads, one at a time, and asked to indicate how the ad and the "Old Joe" character appeal to them. The key results are shown in Table A.

TABLE A Comparison of Student and Adult Responses to Camel's "Old Joe" Cartoon Character Advertisements

	Massachusetts Students	Total Students*	Total Adults†
Number of subjects‡	224	1055	345
Have seen Old Joe, %	99.6	97.7§	72.2§
Know product, %	100	97.5§	67.0§
Know brand, %	97.3	93.6§	57.7§
Think ads look cool, %	54.1	58.0§	39.9§
Ads are interesting, %	73.9	73.6§	55.1§
Like Joe as friend, %	31.1	35.0§	14.4§
Think Joe is cool, %	38.6	43.0§	25.7§
Smoke Camel, %¶	21.8	33.0§	8.7§

*Age range, 12 to 19 years.

†Age range, 21 to 87 years.

‡This is the total number of subjects in each category; due to incomplete questionnaires, respondents for some questions may be fewer.

§$P<.0001$.

¶Percentage of smokers who identify Camel as their favorite brand.

Study B

Two hundred twenty-nine children aged three to six were recruited from 10 preschools in Augusta and Atlanta. The preschools were selected judgmentally to produce a balanced sample in terms of socioeconomic variables. The sample had these characteristics: age—3 (35 percent), 4 (29 percent), 5 (26 percent), 6 (10 percent); gender—male (54 percent), female (46 percent); race—black (27 percent), white (73 percent); parents' education—less than 12 years (29 percent), 12–16 years (54 percent), over 16 years (17 percent); and parent(s) smokes (34 percent).

Each child was tested separately in a quiet part of the classroom. The child was told that he or she would play a game matching cards (which had pictures of company logos on them) with pictures of products. The 12 products (see Table B) pictured on the game board were then named and a sample matching was done. The child was then given a test logo to match. After the card was placed on the board, the child was told, ''That's good.'' No other instructions were

TABLE B

Logos Tested,* Correct Product Response, and Recognition Rates for 229 Subjects Aged 3 to 6 Years

Product Category	Logo	Correct Product Response	Recognition Rate (%)
Children's brands	Disney Channel	Mickey Mouse	91.7
	''McDonald's''	Hamburger	81.7
	''Burger King''	Hamburger	79.9
	''Domino's Pizza''	Pizza	78.2
	''Coca Cola''	Glass of cola	76.0
	''Pepsi''	Glass of cola	68.6
	''Nike''	Athletic shoe	56.8
	''Walt Disney''	Mickey Mouse	48.9
	''Kellogg's''	Bowl of cereal	38.0
	''Cheerios''	Bowl of cereal	25.3
Cigarette brands	Old Joe	Cigarette	51.1
	''Marlboro'' and red roof	Cigarette	32.8
	Marlboro man	Cigarette	27.9
	Camel and pyramids	Cigarette	27.1
	''Camel''	Cigarette	18.0
Adult brands	''Chevrolet''	Automobile	54.1
	''Ford''	Automobile	52.8
	Apple	Computer	29.3
	''CBS''	Television	23.1
	''NBC''	Television	21.0
	''Kodak''	Camera	17.9
	''IBM''	Computer	16.2
Surgeon General's warning		Cigarette	10.0

*(Quotation marks on the logo indicate that the brand name is part of the test item.

TABLE C The Affective Response of Children Aged 6 to 11 to Old Joe Advertising

Character	Familiarity	+Q	−Q
Tony the Tiger	91%	41	16
Energizer Bunny	83	47	21
Joe Camel	58	22	59
Average product character	79	36	23
Average cartoon character	64	39	22

given. Following each match, the card was removed from the board and the child was given the next card. Each child matched 22 logos.

The ''Old Joe'' logo was a picture of the head and shoulders of the ''Old Joe'' cartoon-type character used in the Camel advertising campaign.

The results are provided in Table B. Of the various sociodemographic variables, only age affected recognition of the picture of ''Old Joe'' as a cigarette logo (from 30 percent of the three-year-olds to 91 percent of the six-year-olds). Thus, although cigarettes are not advertised on television, ''Old Joe'' is as widely recognized by six-year-olds as is Mickey Mouse.

Study C

A mail questionnaire was sent to 1,800 children, teens, and adults in November 1992. It measured familiarity and liking of a number of cartoon-type product ''spokespersons.'' In contrast to a number of other surveys, this survey found a relatively low level of awareness of ''Old Joe'' among children aged 6–11 as shown below:

Age	Percent Aware
6–11	58
12–17	79
>17	76
Total	74

Liking was measured in this study as either a positive Q score or a negative Q score. A positive Q score is the number of respondents who rated a spokesperson as ''one of my favorites'' divided by the number familiar with the brand. A negative Q score is the number of respondents who rated a spokesperson as ''fair'' or ''poor'' divided by the number familiar with the brand. Old Joe received a positive Q score of only 14 among the entire sample and a negative of 59. Old Joe was least disliked among 6- to 8-year-old boys who still gave a negative Q of 48. He received a positive Q of 22 from both the 6 to 11 and the 12 to 17 groups. More detailed results for the 6- to 11-year-old group are in Table C.

Discussion Questions

1. Evaluate the methodology of the three studies.
2. How do you explain the differences in the findings of the three studies?
3. How would you determine the impact that Old Joe advertising has on children's attitudes toward smoking?
4. What regulations, if any, should be placed on cigarette advertising that uses characters such as Old Joe?

Sources: J. R. DiFranza, ''RJR Nabisco's Cartoon Camel Promotes Camel Cigarettes to Children,'' *JAMA* (December 11, 1991), pp. 3149–53; P. M. Fischer, et al., ''Brand Logo Recognition by Children Aged 3 to 6 Years,'' *JAMA* (December 11, 1991), pp. 3145–48; G. Levin, ''Joe Camel Can't Light Up Children in 'Q' Ratings,'' *Advertising Age*, March 1, 1993, p. 8.

CONSUMER RESEARCH METHODS

In this appendix, we want to provide you with some general guidelines for conducting research on consumer behavior. While these guidelines will help you get started, a good marketing research text is indispensable if you need to conduct a consumer research project or evaluate a consumer research proposal.* Figure A–1 summarizes the various methods of obtaining consumer information that we will discuss in this section.

SECONDARY DATA

Any research project should begin with a thorough search for existing information relevant to the project at hand. *Internal* data such as past studies, sales reports, and accounting records should be consulted. *External* data including reports, magazines, government organizations, trade associations, marketing research firms, advertising agencies, academic journals, trade journals, and books should be thoroughly researched.

Computer searches are fast, economical means of conducting such searches. Most university and large public libraries have computer search capabilities, as do most large firms. However, computer searches will often miss reports by trade assocations and magazines. Therefore, magazines that deal with the product category or that are read by members of the relevant market should be contacted. The same is true for associations (for names and addresses see *Encyclopedia of Associations*, Gale Research Inc.).

SAMPLING

If the specific information required is not available from secondary sources, we must gather primary data. This generally involves talking to or observing consumers. However, it could involve asking knowledgeable others, such as sales personnel, about the consumers. In either case, time and cost contraints generally preclude us from contacting every single potential consumer. Therefore, most consumer research projects require a *sample*—a deliberately selected portion of the larger group. This requires a number of critical decisions as outlined in Figure A–2. Mistakes made at this point are difficult to correct later in the study. The key decisions are briefly described below.

*This appendix is based on D. S. Tull and D. I. Hawkins, *Marketing Research* (New York: Macmillan, 1993).

Methods of Obtaining Consumer Information

FIGURE A–1

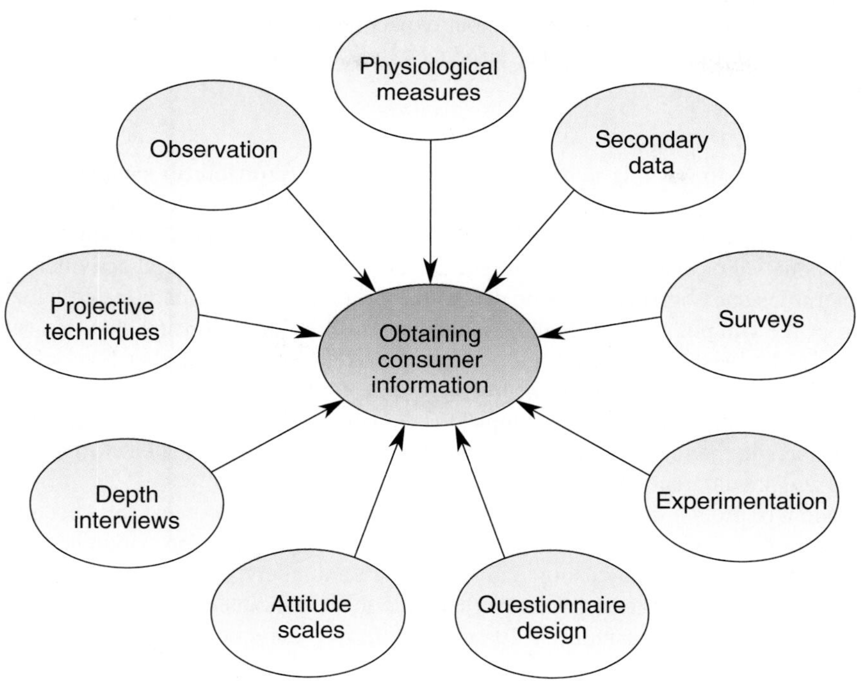

The Consumer Sampling Process

FIGURE A–2

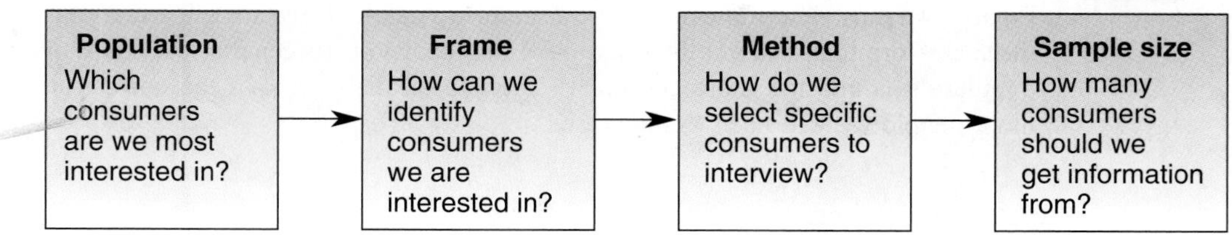

Define the Population

The first step is to define the consumers in which we are interested. Do we want to talk to current brand users, current product-category users, or potential product-category users? Do we want to talk with the purchasers, the users, or everyone involved in the purchase process? The population as we define it must reflect the behavior on which our marketing decision will be based.

Specify the Sampling Frame

A sampling frame is a ''list'' or grouping of individuals or households that reflects the population of interest. A phone book and shoppers at a given shopping mall can each serve as a sampling frame. Perfect sampling frames contain every member of the population one time. Phone books do not have households with unlisted numbers, and many people do not visit shopping malls while others visit them frequently. This is an area in which we generally must do the best we can without expecting a perfect frame. However, we must be very alert for biases that may be introduced by imperfections in our sampling frame.

Select a Sampling Method

The major decision at this point is between a random (probability) sample and a nonrandom sample. Nonrandom samples, particularly judgment samples, can provide good results. A judgment sample involves the *deliberate* selection of knowledgeable consumers or individuals. For example, a firm might decide to interview the social activities officers of fraternities and sororities to estimate campus attitudes toward a carbonated wine drink aimed at the campus market. Such a sample might provide useful insights. However, it might also be biased, since such individuals are likely to have a higher level of income and be more socially active than the average student.

The most common nonrandom sample, the convenience sample, involves selecting sample members in the manner most convenient for the researcher. It is subject to many types of bias and should generally be avoided.

Random or probability samples allow some form of a random process to select members from a sample frame. It may be every third person who passes a point-of-purchase display, house addresses selected by using a table of random numbers, or telephone numbers generated randomly by a computer. Random samples do not guarantee a *representative* sample. For example, a random sample of 20 students, from a class containing 50 male and 50 female students *could* produce a sample of 20 males. However, this would be unlikely. More important, if random procedures are used, we can calculate the likelihood that our sample is not representative within specified limits.

Determine Sample Size

Finally, we must determine how large a sample to talk to. If we are using random sampling, there are formulas that can help us make this decision. In general, the more diverse our population is and the more certain we want to be that we have the correct answer, the more people we will need to interview.

SURVEYS

Surveys are systematic ways of gathering information from a large number of people. They generally involve the use of a structured or semistructured questionnaire. Surveys can be administered by mail, telephone, or in person. Personal interviews generally take place in shopping malls and are referred to as *mall intercept* interviews.

Each approach has advantages and disadvantages. Personal interviews allow the use of complex questionnaires, product demonstrations, and the collection of large amounts of data. They can be completed in a relatively short period of time. However, they are very expensive and are subject to interviewer bias. Telephone surveys can be completed rapidly, provide good sample control (who answers the questions), and are relatively inexpensive. Substantial amounts of data can be collected, but it must be relatively simple. Interviewer bias is possible. Mail surveys take the longest to complete and must generally be rather short. They can be used to collect modestly complex data, and they are very economical. Interviewer bias is not a problem.

Using an Experiment to Evaluate the Impact of an Independent Variable on a Dependent Variable

FIGURE A–3

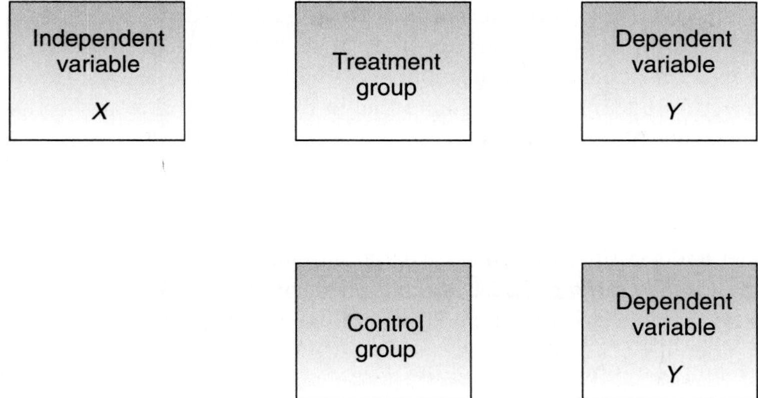

A major concern in survey research is nonresponse bias. In most surveys, fewer than 50 percent of those selected to participate in the study actually do participate. In telephone and personal interviews, many people are not at home or refuse to cooperate. In mail surveys, many people refuse or forget to respond.

We can increase the response rate by callbacks in telephone and home personal surveys. The callbacks should be made at different times and on different days. Monetary inducements (enclosing 25 cents or $1.00) increase the response rate to mail surveys, as do prenotification (a card saying that a questionnaire is coming) and reminder postcards.

If less than a 100 percent response rate is obtained, we must be concerned that those who did not respond differ from those who did. A variety of techniques are available to help us estimate the likelihood and nature of nonresponse error.

EXPERIMENTATION

Experimentation involves changing one or more variables (product features, package color, advertising theme) and observing the effect this change has on another variable (consumer attitude, repeat purchase behavior, learning). The variable(s) that is changed is called an *independent* variable. The variable(s) that may be affected is called a *dependent* variable. The objective in experimental design is to structure the situation so that any change in the dependent variable is very likely to have been caused by a change in the independent variable.

The basic tool in designing experimental studies is the use of control and treatment groups. A *treatment group* is one in which an independent variable is changed (or introduced) and the change (or lack of) in the dependent variable is noted. A *control group* is a group similar to the treatment group except that the independent variable is not altered. There are a variety of ways in which treatment and control groups can be combined to produce differing experimental designs. One such design is illustrated in Figure A–3.

In addition to selecting an appropriate experimental design, we must also develop an experimental environment. In a laboratory experiment, we carefully control for all outside influences. This generally means that we will get similar results every time we repeat a study. Thus, if we have people taste several versions of a salad dressing in our laboratory, we will probably get similar preference ratings each time the study is repeated with similar consumers (internal validity). However, this does not necessarily mean that consumers will prefer the same version at home or in a restaurant (external validity).

In a field experiment, we conduct our study in the most relevant environment possible. This often means that unusual outside influences will distort our results. However, if our results are not distorted, they should hold true in the actual market application. Thus, if we have consumers use several versions of our salad dressing in their homes, competitor actions, unusual weather, or product availability might influence their response (internal validity). However, absent such unusual effects, the preferred version should be preferred if actually sold on the market.

QUESTIONNAIRE DESIGN

All surveys and many experiments use questionnaires as data collection devices. A questionnaire is simply a formalized set of questions for eliciting information. It can measure (1) *behavior*—past, present, or intended; (2) *demographic characteristics*—age, gender, income, education, occupation; (3) *level of knowledge*; and (4) *attitudes and opinions*. The process of questionnaire design is outlined in Figure A–4.

FIGURE A–4 Questionnaire Design Process

1. *Preliminary decisions*
   Exactly what information is required?
   Exactly who are the target respondents?
   What method of communication will be used to reach these respondents?
2. *Decisions about question content*
   Is this question really needed?
   Is this question sufficient to generate the needed information?
   Can the respondent answer the question correctly?
   Will the respondent answer the question correctly?
   Are there any external events that might bias the response to the question?
3. *Decisions about the response format*
   Can this question best be asked as an open-ended, multiple-choice, or dichotomous question?
4. *Decisions concerning question phrasing*
   Do the words used have but one meaning to all the respondents?
   Are any of the words or phrases loaded or leading in any way?
   Are there any implied alternatives in the question?
   Are there any unstated assumptions related to the question?
   Will the respondents approach the question from the frame of reference desired by the researcher?
5. *Decisions concerning the question sequence*
   Are the questions organized in a logical manner that avoids introducing errors?
6. *Decisions on the layout of the questionnaire*
   Is the questionnaire designed in a manner to avoid confusion and minimize recording errors?
7. *Pretest and revise*
   Has the final questionnaire been subjected to a thorough pretest, using respondents similar to those who will be included in the final survey?

ATTITUDE SCALES

Attitudes are frequently measured on specialized scales.

Noncomparative rating scales require the consumer to evaluate an object or an attribute of the object without directly comparing it to another object. *Comparative rating scales* provide a direct comparison point (a named competitor, ''your favorite brand,'' ''the ideal brand''). An example of each follows:

How do you like the taste of California Cooler?

Like it very much	Like it	Dislike it	Strongly dislike it
_____	_____	_____	_____

How do you like the taste of Gleem compared to Ultra Bright?

Like it much more	Like it more	Like it about the same	Like it less	Like it much less
_____	_____	_____	_____	_____

Paired comparisons involve presenting the consumer two objects (brands, packages) at a time and requiring the selection of one of the two according to some criterion such as overall preference, taste, or color. *Rank order scales* require the consumer to rank a set of brands, advertisements, or features in terms of overall preference, taste, or importance. The *constant sum* scale is similar except it also requires the respondent to allocate 100 points among the objects. The allocation is to be done in a manner that reflects the relative preference or importance assigned each object. The *semantic differential scale* requires the consumer to rate an item on a number of scales bounded at each end by one of two bipolar adjectives. For example:

Honda Accord

Fast	X	__	__	__	__	__	__	Slow
Bad	__	__	__	__	__	X	__	Good
Large	__	__	__	X	__	__	__	Small
Inexpensive	__	__	__	__	X	__	__	Expensive

The instructions indicate that the consumer is to mark the blank that best indicates how accurately one or the other term describes or fits the attitude object. The end positions indicate ''extremely,'' the next pair indicate ''very,'' the middle-most pair indicate ''somewhat,'' and the middle position indicates ''neither-nor.'' Thus, the consumer in the example rates the Honda Accord as extremely fast, very good, somewhat expensive, and neither large nor small. *Likert scales* ask consumers to indicate a degree of agreement or disagreement with each of a series of statements related to the attitude object such as:

1. Macy's is one of the most attractive stores in town.

Strongly agree	Agree	Neither agree nor disagree	Disagree	Strongly disagree
_____	_____	_____	_____	_____

2. *The service at Macy's is* not *satisfactory.*

Strongly agree	Agree	Neither agree nor disagree	Disagree	Strongly disagree
_____	_____	_____	_____	_____

3. *The service at a retail store is very important to me.*

Strongly agree	Agree	Neither agree nor disagree	Disagree	Strongly disagree
_____	_____	_____	_____	_____

To analyze responses to a Likert scale, each response category is assigned a numerical value. These examples could be assigned values, such as *strongly agree* = 1 through *strongly disagree* = 5, or the scoring could be reversed, or a −2 through +2 system could be used.

DEPTH INTERVIEWS

Depth interviews can involve one respondent and one interviewer, or they may involve a small group (8 to 15 respondents) and an interviewer. The latter are called *focus group interviews*, and the former are termed *individual depth interviews* or *one-on-ones*. Groups of four or five are often referred to as *mini-group interviews*. Depth interviews in general are commonly referred to as *qualitative research*.

Individual depth interviews involve a one-to-one relationship between the interviewer and the respondent. The interviewer does not have a specific set of prespecified questions that must be asked according to the order imposed by a questionnaire. Instead, there is freedom to create questions, to probe those responses that appear relevant, and generally to try to develop the best set of data in any way practical. However, the interviewer must follow one rule: he or she must not consciously try to affect the content of the answers given by the respondent. The respondent must feel free to reply to the various questions, probes, and other, more subtle ways of encouraging responses in the manner deemed most appropriate.

Individual depth interviews are appropriate in six situations:

1. Detailed probing of an individual's behavior, attitudes, or needs is required.
2. The subject matter under discussion is likely to be of a highly confidential nature (e.g., personal investments).
3. The subject matter is of an emotionally charged or embarrassing nature.
4. Certain strong, socially acceptable norms exist (e.g., baby feeding) and the need to conform in a group discussion may influence responses.
5. A highly detailed (step-by-step) understanding of complicated behavior or decision-making patterns (e.g., planning the family holiday) is required.
6. The interviews are with professional people or with people on the subject of their jobs (e.g., finance directors).

Focus group interviews can be applied to (1) basic need studies for product ideas creation, (2) new-product idea or concept exploration, (3) product-positioning studies, (4) advertising and communications research, (5) background studies on consumers' frames of reference, (6) establishment of consumer vocabulary as a preliminary step in questionnaire development, and (7) determination of attitudes and behaviors.

The standard focus group interview involves 8 to 12 individuals. Normally, the group is designed to reflect the characteristics of a particular market segment. The respondents are selected according to the relevant sampling plan and meet at a central location that generally has facilities for taping or filming the interviews. The discussion itself is ''led'' by a moderator. The competent moderator attempts to develop three clear stages in the one- to three-hour interview: (1) establish rapport with the group, structure the rules of group interaction, and set objectives; (2) attempt to provoke intense discussion in the relevant areas; and (3) attempt to summarize the groups' responses to determine the extent of agreement. In general, either the moderator or a second person prepares a summary of each session, after analyzing the session's transcript.

PROJECTIVE TECHNIQUES

Projective techniques are designed to measure feelings, attitudes, and motivations that consumers are unable or unwilling to reveal otherwise. They are based on the theory that the description of vague objects requires interpretation, and this interpretation can only be based on the individual's own attitudes, values, and motives.

Exhibit 11–2 provides descriptions and examples of the more common projective techniques.

OBSERVATION

Observation can be used when: (1) the behaviors of interest are public, (2) they are repetitive, frequent, or predictable, and (3) they cover a relatively brief time span. An observational study requires five decisions:

1. *Natural versus contrived situation:* Do we wait for a behavior to occur in its natural environment or do we create an artificial situation in which it will occur?
2. *Open versus disguised observation:* To what extent are the consumers aware that we are observing their behavior?
3. *Structured versus unstructured observation:* Will we limit our observations to predetermined behaviors or will we note whatever occurs?
4. *Direct or indirect observations:* Will we observe the behaviors themselves or merely the outcomes of the behaviors?
5. *Human or mechanical observations:* Will the observations be made mechanically or by people?

PHYSIOLOGICAL MEASURES

Physiological measures are direct observations of physical responses to a stimulus such as an advertisement. These responses may be controllable, such as eye movements, or uncontrollable, such as the galvanic skin response. The major physiological measures are described in Exhibit 9–3.

APPENDIX B

CONSUMER BEHAVIOR AUDIT*

In this section we provide a list of key questions to guide you in developing marketing strategy from a consumer behavior perspective. This audit is no more than a checklist to minimize the chance of overlooking a critical behavioral dimension. It does not guarantee a successful strategy. However, thorough and insightful answers to these questions should greatly enhance the likelihood of a successful marketing program.

Our audit is organized around the key decisions that marketing managers must make. The first key decision is the selection of the target market(s) to be served. This is followed by the determination of a viable product position for each target market. Finally, the marketing mix elements—product, place, price, and promotion—must be structured in a manner consistent with the desired product position. This process is illustrated in Figure B–1.

MARKET SEGMENTATION

Market segmentation is the process of dividing all possible users of a product into groups that have similar needs the products might satisfy. Market segmentation should be done prior to the final development of a new product. In addition, a complete market segmentation analysis should be performed periodically for existing products. The reason for continuing segmentation analyses is the dynamic nature of consumer needs.

A. External influences
   1. Are there cultures or subcultures whose value system is particularly consistent (or inconsistent) with the consumption of our product?
   2. Is our product appropriate for male or female consumption? Will ongoing gender-role changes affect who consumes our product or how it is consumed?
   3. Do ethnic, social, regional, or religious subcultures have different consumption patterns relevant to our product?
   4. Do various demographic or social-strata groups (age, gender, urban/suburban/rural, occupation, income, education) differ in their consumption of our product?
   5. Is our product particularly appropriate for consumers with relatively high (or low) incomes compared to others in their occupational group (ROCI)?
   6. Can our product be particularly appropriate for specific roles, such as students or professional women?
   7. Would it be useful to focus on specific adopter categories?

*Revised by Richard Pomazal of Wheeling Jesuit College.

Consumer Influences Drive Marketing Decisions

FIGURE B–1

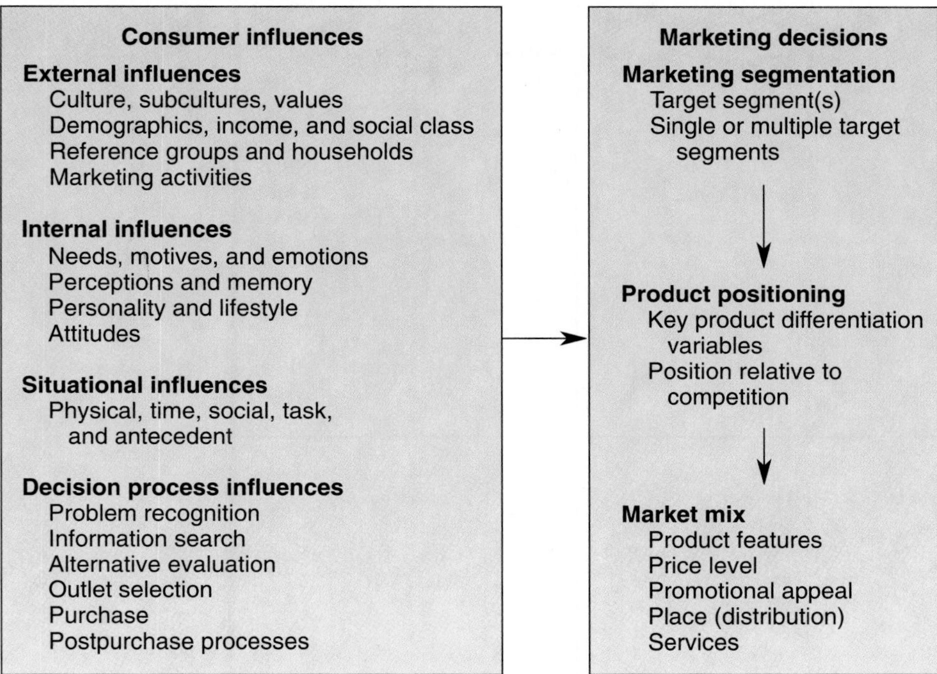

8. Do groups in different stages of the household life cycle have different consumption patterns for our product? Who in the household is involved in the purchase process?

B. Internal influences
   1. Can our product satisfy different needs or motives in different people? What needs are involved? What characterizes individuals with differing motives?
   2. Is our product uniquely suited for particular personality types? Self-concepts?
   3. What emotions, if any, are affected by the purchase and/or consumption of this product?
   4. Is our product appropriate for one or more distinct lifestyles?
   5. Do different groups have different attitudes about an ideal version of our product?

C. Situational influences
   1. Can our product be appropriate for specific types of situations instead of (or in addition to) specific types of people?

D. Decision-process influences
   1. Do different individuals use different evaluative criteria in selecting the product?
   2. Do potential customers differ in their loyalty to existing products/brands?

PRODUCT POSITION

A product position is the way the consumer thinks of a given product/brand relative to competing products/brands. A manager must determine what a desirable product position would be for *each* market segment of interest. This determination is generally based on the answers to the same questions used to segment a market, with the addition of the

FIGURE B–2 Kmart Positioning and Desired Repositioning

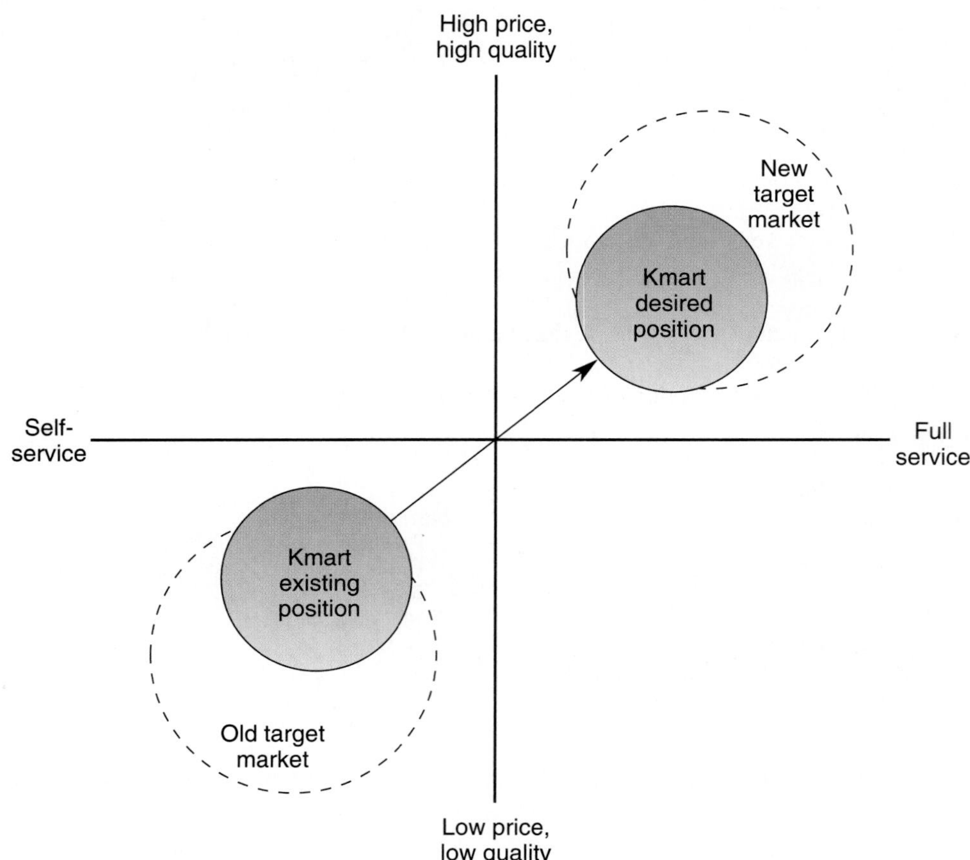

*Dashed circles are various market segments.

consumer's perceptions of competing products/brands. Of course, the capabilities and motivations of existing and potential competitors must also be considered. Illustrated in Figure B–2 is how Kmart is currently positioned and the market segment it currently serves, along with its desired positioning and new target market.

A. Internal influences
   1. What is the general semantic memory structure for this product category in each market segment?
   2. What is the ideal version of this product in each market segment for the situations the firm wants to serve?

B. Decision-process influences
   1. Which evaluative criteria are used in the purchase decision? Which decision rules and importance weights are used?

PRICING

The manager must set a pricing policy that is consistent with the desired product position. Price must be broadly conceived as everything a consumer must surrender to obtain a product. This includes time and psychological costs as well as monetary costs.

A. External influences
   1. Does the segment hold any values relating to any aspect of pricing, such as the use of credit or "conspicuous consumption"?
   2. Does the segment have sufficient income, after covering living expenses, to afford the product?
   3. Is it necessary to lower price to obtain a sufficient relative advantage to ensure diffusion? Will temporary price reductions induce product trial?
   4. Who in the household evaluates the price of the product?
B. Internal influences
   1. Will price be perceived as an indicator of status?
   2. Is economy in purchasing this type of product relevant to the lifestyle(s) of the segment?
   3. Is price an important aspect of the segment's attitude toward the brands in the product category?
   4. What is the segment's perception of a fair or reasonable price for this product?
C. Situational influences
   1. Does the role of price vary with the type of situation?
D. Decision-process factors
   1. Can a low price be used to trigger problem recognition?
   2. Is price an important evaluative criterion? What decision rule is applied to the evaluative criteria used? Is price likely to serve as a surrogate indicator of quality?
   3. Are consumers likely to respond to in-store price reductions?

DISTRIBUTION STRATEGY

The manager must develop a distribution strategy that is consistent with the selected product position. This involves the selection of outlets if the item is a physical product, or the location of the outlets if the product is a service.

A. External influences
   1. What values do the segments have that relate to distribution?
   2. Do the male and female members of the segments have differing requirements of the distribution system? Do working couples, single individuals, or single parents within the segment have unique needs relating to product distribution?
   3. Can the distribution system capitalize on reference groups by serving as a means for individuals with common interests to get together?
   4. Is the product complex such that a high service channel is required to ensure its diffusion?
B. Internal influences
   1. Will the selected outlets be perceived in a manner that enhances the desired product position?
   2. What type of distribution system is consistent with the lifestyle(s) of each segment?
   3. What attitudes does each segment hold with respect to the various distribution alternatives?
C. Situational influences
   1. Do the desired features of the distribution system vary with the situation?
D. Decision-process factors
   1. What outlets are in the segment's evoked set? Will consumers in this segment seek information in this type of outlet?
   2. Which evaluative criteria does this segment use to evaluate outlets? Which decision rule?

3. Is the outlet selected before, after, or simultaneously with the product/brand? To what extent are product decisions made in the retail outlet?

PROMOTION STRATEGY

The manager must develop a promotion strategy, including advertising, nonfunctional package-design features, publicity, promotions, and sales-force activities that are consistent with the product position.

A. External factors
   1. What values does the segment hold that can be used in our communications? Which should be avoided?
   2. How can we communicate to our chosen segments in a manner consistent with the emerging gender-role perceptions of each segment?
   3. What is the nonverbal communication system of each segment?
   4. How, if at all, can we use reference groups in our advertisements?
   5. Can our advertisements help make the product part of one or more role-related product clusters?
   6. Can we reach and influence opinion leaders?
   7. If our product is an innovation, are there diffusion inhibitors that can be overcome by promotion?
   8. Who in the household should receive what types of information concerning our product?

B. Internal factors
   1. Have we structured our promotional campaign such that each segment will be exposed to it, attend to it, and interpret it in the manner we desire?
   2. Have we made use of the appropriate learning principles so that our meaning will be remembered?
   3. Do our messages relate to the purchase motives held by the segment? Do they help reduce motivational conflict if necessary?
   4. Are we considering the emotional implications of the ad and/or the use of our product?
   5. Is the lifestyle portrayed in our advertisements consistent with the desired lifestyle of the selected segments?
   6. If we need to change attitudes via our promotion mix, have we selected and properly used the most appropriate attitude-change techniques?

C. Situational influences
   1. Does our campaign illustrate the full range of appropriate usage situations for the product?

D. Decision-process influences
   1. Will problem recognition occur naturally, or must it be activated by advertising? Should generic or selective problem recognition be generated?
   2. Will the segment seek out or attend to information on the product prior to problem recognition, or must we reach them when they are not seeking our information? Can we use low-involvement learning processes effectively? What information sources are used?
   3. After problem recognition, will the segment seek out information on the product/brand, or will we need to intervene in the purchase-decision process? If they do seek information, what sources do they use?
   4. What types of information are used to make a decision?
   5. How much and what types of information are acquired at the point of purchase?

6. Is postpurchase dissonance likely? Can we reduce it through our promotional campaign?
7. Have we given sufficient information to ensure proper product use?
8. Are the expectations generated by our promotional campaign consistent with the product's performance?
9. Are our messages designed to encourage repeat purchases, brand-loyal purchases, or neither?

PRODUCT

The marketing manager must be certain that the physical product, service, or idea has the characteristics required to achieve the desired product position in each market segment.

A. External influences
   1. Is the product designed appropriately for all members of the segment under consideration, including males, females, and various age groups?
   2. If the product is an innovation, does it have the required relative advantage and lack of complexity to diffuse rapidly?
   3. Is the product designed to meet the varying needs of different household members?

B. Internal influences
   1. Will the product be perceived in a manner consistent with the desired image?
   2. Will the product satisfy the key purchase motives of the segment?
   3. Is the product consistent with the segment's attitude toward an ideal product?

C. Situational influences
   1. Is the product appropriate for the various potential usage situations?

D. Decision-process influences
   1. Does the product/brand perform better than the alternatives on the key set of evaluative criteria used by this segment?
   2. Will the product perform effectively in the foreseeable uses to which this segment may subject it?
   3. Will the product perform as well or better than expected by this segment?

CUSTOMER SATISFACTION AND COMMITMENT

Marketers must produce satisfied customers to be successful in the long run. It is often to a firm's advantage to go beyond satisfaction and create committed or loyal customers.

1. What factors lead to satisfaction with our product?
2. What factors could cause customer commitment to our brand or firm?

NAME INDEX

CASE INDEX

SUBJECT INDEX

R

S

PHOTO CREDITS

CHAPTER 1

p. 5, ©Caroline Parsons, Aria Pictures; p. 10, *left:* Courtesy Tiger's Milk, *right:* Courtesy PowerFood, Inc.; p. 12, Courtesy Lost Arrow Corp; p. 13, *left:* Courtesy General Motors Corp., *right:* Courtesy Hyundai Motor America; p. 14, Reprinted by permission of Radio Shack; p. 16, Courtesy North American Philips Corporation.

CHAPTER 2

p. 31, Courtesy Globo TV Network-Brazil; p. 38, Courtesy The Coca-Cola Company. Coca-Cola is a registered trademark of the Coca-Cola Company; p. 45, Courtesy Chrysler International Corporation; p. 56, Courtesy Hanes Hosiery; p. 59, Courtesy "Toys 'R' Us."

CHAPTER 3

p. 67, Courtesy The Gillette Company; p. 71, Courtesy The Martin Agency; p. 72, Courtesy Church & Dwight Company, Inc.; p. 74, Courtesy General Motors Corp.; p. 75, Courtesy Fisher-Price; p. 84, Courtesy Maybelline, Inc.; p. 87, Courtesy MCI.

CHAPTER 4

p. 95, ©Tony Stone Images; p. 101; *top,* Courtesy Maybelline, Inc., *bottom,* Courtesy Tyco Toys, Inc.; p. 102, *left:* Courtesy State Farm Insurance Companies, *right:* Chrysler Corporation; p. 103, Stove Top is a registered trademark of Kraft General Foods, Inc. Used with permission.

CHAPTER 5

p. 119, ©Brent Weinbrenner: MGA/Photri; p. 124, Courtesy McGuire Company; p. 125, Courtesy Rosewood Hotels & Resorts, Inc.; p. 126, Courtesy Hiram Walker & Sons, Inc.; p. 127, Courtesy Lane Furniture; p. 128, Courtesy International Correspondence Schools.

CHAPTER 6

p. 143, Courtesy Reebok International; p. 146, Courtesy Fleishman-Hillard Agency; p. 148, Courtesy Saturn Corporation; p. 153, Courtesy Eagle Creek; p. 155, Courtesy Pentax Corporation; p. 156, Courtesy Trek Fitness; p. 157, Copyright ©1993 Mazda Motor of America Inc. Used with permission.

CHAPTER 7

p. 163, ©New Products Showcase; p. 170, Courtesy PowerFood, Inc.; p. 172, Courtesy Timex Corporation; p. 173, Courtesy Panasonic.

CHAPTER 8

p. 187, Courtesy Burger King; p. 192, *left:* Courtesy J.C. Penney Company, Inc., *right:* Courtesy Steel Jeans; p. 193, *left:* Courtesy Kemper Mutual, *right:* Courtesy Wailea; p. 195, Courtesy Pharmavite; p. 199, ©Johnson & Johnson Consumer Products, Inc., 1993; p. 203, Courtesy American Home Food Products, Inc.

SECTION TWO CASES

p. 211, Courtesy The Copper Cricket; p. 227, Courtesy The Procter & Gamble Company; p. 229, Courtesy Nabisco Foods Group.

CHAPTER 9

p. 237, Courtesy Reef Brazil Global; p. 244, Courtesy Peugeot; p. 245, Courtesy Van Munching & Company, Inc.; p. 248, Courtesy Oxford Industries; p. 258, Courtesy Schiefflin & Somerset Company; p. 259, Courtesy Carillon Importers, Ltd.

CHAPTER 10

p. 269, Courtesy The Peninsula Gateway; p. 271, *left:* Courtesy Nabisco Foods Group, *right:* Courtesy Citibank (South Dakota) N.A.; p. 275, Courtesy Skippers, Inc.; p. 277, Courtesy Hoffman-LaRoche, Inc.; p. 279, Courtesy Whitehall Laboratories; p. 285, Courtesy Eddie Bauer, Inc.; p. 291, ©1994 Nintendo. Used courtesy of Nintendo.

CHAPTER 11

p. 299, Photo by Sharon Hoogstraten; p. 302, Courtesy TBWA Advertising; p. 305, Reprinted with permission from Carter-Wallace, Inc. ©Carter-Wallace, Inc. All Rights Reserved. p. 306, Courtesy CJC Holdings-Artcarver; p. 316, *left:* Courtesy Cía

Nestlé, S.A. de C.V., Mexico, *right:* Courtesy Oshkosh B'gosh, Inc.; p. 320, *left:* Courtesy Asics Tiger Corporation, *right:* Reprinted with permission of Joseph E. Seagram & Sons, Inc.

CHAPTER 12

p. 329, Courtesy Canon USA, Inc.; p. 331, Courtesy Club Med Sales, Inc.; p. 341, *left:* Courtesy B&B, *right:* Courtesy Helene Curtis, Inc.

CHAPTER 13

p. 357, Courtesy American Plastics Council; p. 365, *left:* Courtesy Rumple Minz, *right:* Courtesy Coty, Inc.; p. 368, *left:* Courtesy Kellogg Company, *right:* Courtesy Digital Equipment Corporation; p. 369, Courtesy General Mills, Inc.; p. 341, *left:* Courtesy Club Sportswear, *right:* Courtesy Medalist Apparel, Inc.; p. 372, *left:* Courtesy Partnership for a Drug Free America, *right:* Courtesy Shimano; p. 374, *left:* Janssen Pharmaceutica, Inc. ©1994, *right:* Courtesy Campari.

CHAPTER 14

p. 405, Courtesy Schering-Plough HealthCare Products, Inc.; p. 407, Courtesy The Paddington Corporation; p. 410, Courtesy Hiram Walker & Sons, Inc.; p. 413, Courtesy NEC USA, Inc.; p. 414, Courtesy Gerber Products Company and FTD.

CHAPTER 15

p. 423, ©Nicholas Communications, Inc.; p. 434, Courtesy Frito-Lay, Inc.; p. 435, Courtesy J.R. Carlson Laboratories, Inc.; p. 436, Courtesy SmithKline Beecham International Co.; p. 437, Courtesy BMW of North America; p. 438, Courtesy Del Laboratories, Inc.

CHAPTER 16

p. 443, Courtesy Chrysler Corporation; p. 457, ©The Procter & Gamble Company; p. 458, Courtesy Oral-B Laboratories; p. 459, Courtesy Domino's; p. 460, Courtesy Andersen Windows, Inc.

CHAPTER 17

p. 468, Courtesy Laser; p. 469, *left:* Courtesy The Andrew Jergens Company, *right:* Courtesy Beiersdorf, Inc.; p. 476, Reprinted with permission of Joseph E. Seagram & Sons, Inc.; p. 481, *left:* Courtesy Hewlett-Packard Company, *right:* Courtesy Toshiba America, Inc.

CHAPTER 18

p. 489, Courtesy Trends Clothing Corp.; p. 491, Courtesy Sears, Roebuck and Company; p. 493, *left:* Courtesy Dayton Hudson Stores, Inc., *right:* Courtesy Sears, Roebuck and Company; p. 495, Courtesy Lands' End; p. 506, Courtesy Shell Oil Co.

CHAPTER 19

p. 513, Courtesy Lifescan, Inc., a Johnson & Johnson company; p. 518, Courtesy The Gillette Company; p. 520, Courtesy Pit Stop U.S.A.; p. 528, *left:* Courtesy National Pork Producers Council, *right:* Courtesy Del Monte Foods.

SECTION FOUR CASES

p. 540, Courtesy Ansell, Inc.

CHAPTER 20

p. 551, Advertisement ©1994 Canon U.S.A., Inc. Photography ©Scott Morgan; p. 556, *left:* Courtesy United States Postal Service, *right:* Courtesy United Parcel Service; p. 562, *left:* Courtesy Software Media Consultants, *right:* Advertisement ©1994 Canon U.S.A., Inc. Photography ©Scott Morgan.

CHAPTER 21

p. 585, Courtesy Chemical Manufacturer's Association; p. 598, Courtesy Viacom International and Suntory Water Corporation; p. 604, *left:* Courtesy Jansport Inc. and The Breast Cancer Fund, *right:* Courtesy Christian Children's Fund.

SECTION FIVE CASES

p. 614, Courtesy People for the Ethical Treatment of Animals; p. 615, Courtesy Ortho Pharmaceutical Corporation.